LEMNITZER

LEMNITZER

★ ★ ★ ★

A Soldier for His Time

L. James Binder

Brassey's

WASHINGTON • LONDON

Editorial Offices: Order Department:
  22883 Quicksilver Drive   P.O. Box 960
  Dulles, Va. 20166   Herndon, Va. 20172

Brassey's books are available at special discounts for bulk
purchases for sales promotions, premiums, fund-raising, or
educational use.

Library of Congress Cataloging-in-Publication Data
Binder, L. James.
Lemnitzer : a soldier for his time / L. James Binder. — 1st ed.
p. cm.
Includes bibliographical references and index.
ISBN 1-57488-107-8
1. Lemnitzer, Lyman L. (Lyman Louis), 1899– . 2. Generals—
United States—Biography. 3. United States. Army—Officers—
Biography. 4. Supreme Commander for the Allied Powers. 5. United
States. Office of the Chairman of the Joint Chiefs of Staff.
I. Title.
U53.L46B56 1997
355′.0092—dc21
[B]   97-19134
CIP

Designed by Pen & Palette Unlimited
Coast Artillery collar insignia courtesy of
The Casemate Museum, Fort Monroe, Virginia

First Edition
10 9 8 7 6 5 4 3 2 1
Printed in the United States of America

DEDICATION

To my dear Margie, who is always there.

 **An AUSA Institute of Land Warfare Book**

The Association of the United States Army, or AUSA, was founded in 1950 as a nonprofit organization dedicated to education concerning the role of the U.S. Army, to providing material for military professional development, and to the promotion of proper recognition and appreciation of the profession of arms. Its constituencies include those who serve in the Army today, including Army National Guard, Army Reserve, and Army civilians, the retirees and veterans who have served in the past, and all their families. A large number of public-minded citizens and business leaders are also an important constituency. The Association seeks to educate the public, elected and appointed officials, and leaders of the defense industry on crucial issues involving the adequacy of our national defense, particularly those issues affecting land warfare.

In 1988, AUSA established within its existing organization a new entity known as the Institute of Land Warfare. ILW's mission is to extend the educational work of AUSA by sponsoring a wide range of publications, to include books, monographs, and essays on key defense issues, as well as workshops, symposia, and since 1992, a television series. Among the volumes chosen as "An AUSA Institute of Land Warfare Book" are both new texts and reprints of titles of enduring value. Topics include history, policy issues, strategy, and tactics. Publication as an AUSA Book does not indicate that the Association of the United States Army and the publisher agree with everything in the book but does suggest that AUSA and the publisher believe the book will stimulate the thinking of AUSA members and others concerned about important defense-related issues.

CONTENTS

(Photos follow page 204.)

$$\star \quad \star \quad \star \quad \star$$

FOREWORD

This is the story of one of the most respected U.S. Army officers of the twentieth century, a man of unusual accomplishments and service to his country, but one whose story has heretofore remained largely untold. Lyman Louis Lemnitzer was a man who sprang from modest beginnings in northeastern Pennsylvania, whose lifetime spanned the horse-and-buggydays to the election of George Bush as president, whose military service extended from the days of the mule-pack artillery to the landing on the moon in 1969. During that long period, Lemnitzer occupied a series of difficult positions. His responsibilities were heavy, sometimes physically dangerous. Yet this is the story of a completely unpretentious man, who never wore his accomplishments on his sleeve, who never talked down to an associate or subordinate, and who retired to the modest hometown of Honesdale, from which he had entered West Point.

Lyman (Lem) Lemnitzer's early career in the Army followed a fairly routine pattern. Commissioned in the West Point Class of 1920 as a second lieutenant of coast artillery, his first twenty years of service were unremarkable. In June of 1942, six months after Pearl Harbor, he was a colonel in Army Ground Forces headquarters, then located in Washington, D.C. He was promoted to brigadier general, given command of an antiaircraft artillery brigade, and sent to join the American buildup in the United Kingdom. His abilities as a planner had long since been noticed, however, and Gen. Mark W. Clark, deputy to Gen. Dwight D. Eisenhower, brought him into the planning section of Allied Force Headquarters in London. Lemnitzer was now doing the work at which he starred: planning.

It was not always a safe, comfortable job. In October of 1942, when General Clark undertook his secret mission to North Africa, General Lemnitzer went along as his deputy. A British submarine took Clark and Lemnitzer, with three other Americans and several British commandos, to a lonely house on the coast of North Africa to meet French officers with whom the Americans and British hoped to cooperate when the landings took place. It was a hair-raising venture for the Americans; capture by Vichy French authorities would mean long imprisonment for all of them—or even possible execution as spies. Though at times the participants were in danger of detection, the perilous mission was successfully completed. The meeting with the French accomplished much, providing the Anglo-Americans with a wealth of information regarding the strength and dispositions of French units in North Africa and confirming the soundness of the plans the Allies had made. The sheer daring of this cloak-and-dagger expedition made it the subject of widespread acclaim, immortalizing in a small way all the members of the party.

From then on, Lemnitzer's future in the Army was assured. He soon became the Allied Force G-3, a position of great prestige whose holder was charged with all the planning of future operations and the execution of those in progress. A major general by the end of World War II, Lemnitzer commanded the 7th Infantry Division during the Korean War and ascended the steps of the Army hierarchy to the highest pinnacles: commander in chief of the Far East Command in the 1950s, chief of staff of the U.S. Army, chairman of the Joint Chiefs of Staff (JCS), and finally, supreme commander, Allied Powers, Europe.

It was not always smooth going. As chairman of the Joint Chiefs, the general saw his luck run out temporarily. During the first few months of the Kennedy administration, the United States became directly embroiled in Cuba when President Kennedy launched the ill-fated invasion popularly known as the "Bay of Pigs." Lemnitzer, because of his position but not because of his actions, lost the confidence of a frustrated young president, who determined to replace those in high office with his own men. Lemnitzer's appointment as JCS chairman was not renewed in 1962, and he was free to retire.

At that point, a lesser man, realizing that he had been replaced because of events not his fault, would have gone into a sour retirement and possibly have written a bitter book about his maltreatment at the hands of the current presidential administration. But that was not Lemnitzer's way. He cheerfully recognized the president's right to have his own men in office, and when Mr. Kennedy offered him the highly prestigious post of Supreme Allied Commander, Europe (SACEUR), he accepted it and continued to serve in that post. He held it for nearly seven years, retiring from active duty in the early fall of 1969. From there, he continued to perform for nearly two decades those national services for which he was called upon.

My own association with Lyman Lemnitzer began in 1957 when the general returned to Washington from Tokyo after having presided over the dissolution of the Far East Command (FECOM). It was one of the world's most coveted command posts, and Lemnitzer was the last of a line of commanders in chief which had included such luminaries as generals Douglas MacArthur, Matthew B. Ridgway, and Mark Clark. The termination of FECOM was a sad moment for the beleaguered U.S. Army, a move perhaps inevitable with the upsurge of emphasis on naval and air power caused by the end of the Korean War and the new threat from Soviet nuclear missiles. I personally thought the termination of FECOM was unwise, and as a junior officer in the White House I expected to see a downcast General Lemnitzer come into the presidential office to make his final report. Lem, however, was far from gloomy. With his typically respectful but ebullient attitude, he reported happily on the success of the turnover ceremonies and the good will exhibited on all sides. It was there that I came to realize the source of Lemnitzer's strength: no petty considerations ever dampened his customary upbeat, optimistic outlook.

After that first exposure, I saw the general frequently when he was Army chief of staff, JCS chairman, and finally in 1969, when I, as the new U.S. ambassador to Belgium, drove from Brussels to Casteau to attend the ceremony in which he turned over his command as supreme commander to Gen. Andrew J. Goodpaster. As always, his attitude was optimistic, bursting with that disarming, boyish pride that only he could exhibit without being mistaken as egotistical. His time as SACEUR, as with other times in his career, had not been smooth. It was during his tenure that the president of France, Charles de Gaulle, removed his nation from the military part of the NATO alliance, forcing Lemnitzer to recast his war plans and, at the same time, to move his ever-growing headquarters from Versailles, outside Paris, to its current location a few miles south of Brussels. As always, General Lem told stories of his difficulties with great gusto, especially of his exasperations in negotiating administrative arrangements with the Belgians. One of the problems was to find a suitable location for supreme headquarters, made touchy by the fact that every square foot of territory was precious to the Belgians. As the general told of these experiences, I could tell that he had lost none of his zest.

I had one more exposure to General Lemnitzer. In 1980 when he was retired, he was asked by the U.S. Military Academy's Association of Graduates to wrestle with the problems of raising funds, obtaining a sculptor, and approving the design of the statue of my father, Dwight D. Eisenhower, that stands on the Plain at West Point. I was a member of the general's committee (despite his total lack of pretension, I could never call him Lem), my main function being to assist him in selecting appropriate Eisenhower quotations to be inscribed on the statue's base. I dealt closely with the general, finding him always willing to listen, never showing impatience but reserving final judgments to himself. In dealing with the committee as a whole, I observed him to be diplomatic, handling a high-powered group of men with ease and aplomb. While entertaining us at his home in Honesdale, he demonstrated, as if this were necessary, that beneath his shirtsleeves he was comfortably in charge. On the day of the unveiling, when he turned on the podium after his dedication speech and awkwardly saluted my father's statue, my eyes were misty.

I tell these personal stories for one purpose: to illustrate my very high admiration for the subject of this book. I am delighted that the memory of Lyman L. Lemnitzer is being preserved by the work of a first-class writer, Jim Binder. And I am grateful that Jim has provided me with a chance to pay tribute to a great American soldier.

John S. D. Eisenhower

$\star$ $\star$ $\star$ $\star$

ACKNOWLEDGMENTS

I am indebted to many people for their help and encouragement during the more than three years in which General Lem has been virtually a full-time member of my household. Thanks to the general's daughter Lois and his son Bill, I feel as if I have become a lifelong friend of a man whom I never knew personally. Their trust in me and their generosity in allowing me unlimited access to their father's papers, diaries, photographs, and other records have given a depth to my account of a great soldier's illustrious career that I could not have achieved without their cooperation and friendship. My guide through the thickets and valleys has been my good friend, Lt. Gen. William J. McCaffrey, U.S. Army retired, who read every word during the gestation period and made it a better book with his always astute comments and suggestions. Much of the credit for launching the project belongs to Lt. Gen. Orwin C. Talbott, U.S. Army retired, whose determination and tenacity were important factors in keeping the idea on track. I am indebted also to John S. D. Eisenhower for his friendly encouragement and for his eloquent response to my request that he write the foreword. Much deserving of my thanks is Col. John B. B. Trussell, U.S. Army retired, who was an important source of insightful information that could only come from a person who not only knew the general well but who also is a gifted observer. When a detail had to be nailed down or a gap filled, invariably the person I turned to was Chief Warrant Officer Ralph L. Chambers, U.S. Army retired, whose remarkable memory could almost always produce the answer I needed. Maj. Gen. David W. Gray, U.S. Army retired, was invaluable in helping me to piece together an accurate account of what took place during the planning and execution of the Bay of Pigs operation. Martin Blumenson made some key suggestions in generously reviewing my chapters on the Italian campaign; and Gen. Andrew J. Goodpaster, U.S. Army retired, was most helpful in answering my questions about NATO and what went on in the White House when Dwight D. Eisenhower was president. Susan K. Lemke, the superb Special Collections librarian at the National Defense University, was a godsend in helping make sense out of the over seventy-five feet of Lemnitzer papers that occupy the shelves over which she held sway. Gen. Gordon A. Sullivan, Army chief of staff when I began writing this book, was instrumental in helping to get things off to a good start by marshaling Army research support. I am also grateful for the help given me by Sally Talaga, director of the Wayne County, Pennsylvania, Historical Society; genealogy expert Richard O. Eldred; and Alexander S. Cochran, Jr. Finally, I lift a loving toast to my wife, Marge, whose gift for spotting the not-quite-right word or phrase contributed in no small measure to the lucidity of this volume.

LJB

1

★ ★ ★ ★

'BE YOURSELF'

When, in 1970, the nation was preparing to celebrate the twenty-fifth anniversary of the end of World War II, the secretary of the Army wrote a letter to the leaders of both houses of Congress, outlining plans to expand its "Big Picture Famous Generals" film series. The reason for the letter was a routine one: under a public law enacted five years before, congressional approval was required to show such documentaries to the public.

The motion pictures of the eight modern-era generals then in the series had been made before the law went into effect, but the Department of Defense wanted one more name on a list which included General of the Armies John J. Pershing; four generals of the Army: Omar N. Bradley, Dwight D. Eisenhower, Douglas MacArthur, and George C. Marshall; General of the Air Force Henry H. Arnold; and generals George S. Patton, Jr., and Joseph W. Stilwell.

The name the Army had just added was that of General Lyman Louis (Lem) Lemnitzer. Congress gave its approval and when the Pentagon went public with a widely acclaimed series originally conceived to inspire military personnel "through the patriotic example set by great men," Lemnitzer was there among his profession's immortals.[1]

The general was retired when the decision was made to include him. If he had been on active duty and still possessed the authority that belonged to a senior officer of the U.S. armed services, it is likely that he would have found a way to quietly quash the idea. Being Lemnitzer, he very probably would not have thought that he belonged in such exalted company. Moreover, a biographical film was personal publicity, an inescapable requisite of high rank that he had not suffered gladly during his twenty-seven years as a general officer. By the time he

1

found out about the film, the wheels had been in motion too long to try to stop them.

In terms of professional achievement, his record while in uniform was as impressive as those of anyone else on the list: chairman of the Joint Chiefs of Staff; supreme allied commander, Europe; vice chief and then chief of staff of the Army; and commander in chief, Far East. Only Eisenhower, when he was president and U.S. commander in chief, ranked higher in the chain of command. Five of the generals in the series had worn the wartime rank of five stars, but of these only Bradley had also been a chairman of the JCS, the senior position in the uniformed armed forces.[2] In terms of actual continuous active service, Lemnitzer topped them all with fifty-one years; only the fact that a general of the Army or of the Air Force never retires kept him from this distinction in this company.

Of the nine men singled out for special recognition in the era following the biggest war in the country's history, Lemnitzer was the least well known. A major reason, of course, was his passion for keeping out of the limelight, but there were other factors, as well: he had not held a top command in either World War II or the Korean War; he had not been a hell-for-leather field general like Patton; he had not been a highly visible adviser to Washington's mighty; and he invariably was busy somewhere else when the Army was making headlines.

Even some of his reputed strong points could raise eyebrows. When he was making his way toward the top, he was frequently described in the press as a scholar; but, though he held seven honorary doctoral degrees, he rarely read a book and his academic education had ended after two years at West Point. He became one of his country's most accomplished soldier-diplomats, but he could speak no foreign languages. His many citations invariably hailed him as a superb tactician, and he was, but his only front-line command experience in which battlefield tactics was a factor consisted of seven months as commander of an infantry division during a standoff phase of the Korean War. He was also called an outstanding strategist, and he proved it in war and on a global scale in peacetime; but strategists tend to be far-thinking, "big picture" people, and Lemnitzer's chief fame lay in his ability to deal with problems and issues as they arose. As one of his former chiefs of staff put it: "He was a strategist if that was the problem of the day."[3]

Luck is an important factor in a military career. Although a soldier may hate war, it nonetheless makes generals out of officers who in peacetime would be content to retire as colonels. World War II made one of Lemnitzer, a coast artilleryman who a few years before had finished fifteen years as a lieutenant. He was lucky, too, that men with influence spotted him as an extraordinary officer and saw to it that he got assignments that were commensurate with his abilities. A military "ticket-puncher" might say, however, that he was unlucky in his assignments: membership in a dying career branch; consignment for much of World War II to the staff of a British field marshal in a secondary theater of operations;

ordered to fill a postwar slot in which even the secretary of defense was an adversary; sent to the Far East to eventually preside over the death of a major command; elevation to the highest posts in the Army during a period in which the senior service was regarded by the administration as little more than a security force for Air Force bombers and missiles; occupancy of a chair which became a hot seat during one of the most embarrassing episodes of military adventurism in U.S. history; and, finally, command of the forces of a dissension-torn alliance whose resources were being bled white by a war thousands of miles away.

But had it not been for these assignments, Lemnitzer might not have become the giant that he was. He carried out his missions so well that he became the man the White House and the Pentagon frequently turned to when there was a tough job to do. Increasingly as he gained stature, these tasks meant stepping across service lines, always a precarious undertaking in a calling in which turf is often everything, but one in which he became eminently successful. Sometimes he had to carry out actions which seemed to be unfair slaps at his own service, as when he was in charge of transferring the Army's space responsibilities to the National Aeronautics and Space Administration (NASA). The Army, which had lifted the nation's first satellite into space, was proud of its achievements in this area and it caused bitterness, but none of it seemed to be aimed at Lemnitzer. In fact, he had been a tough, skillful, and tenacious negotiator whom even the outmaneuvered NASA bargaining team grew to admire: "This is a man we can work with," its chief said afterward.[4]

A term often used by journalists to describe Lemnitzer was "bear-like." He was a large, but not huge, man—six feet tall and two hundred pounds. He had a powerful frame and massive shoulders, but the curious would probably find more clues to the use of "bear" in his style: he did things with gusto, from his unfailing enthusiasm and booming voice to the zest with which be could smash a golf ball 250 yards down a fairway. The general loved a good story, and he had a deep, infectious laugh. John S. D. Eisenhower, the president's son, recalled "how upbeat he always was—constitutionally, a happy guy. He never talked down to anybody. If anything, he was ingenuous, as opposed to being cynical. He was uncomplicated—not always looking for a worm under every rock."[5] But despite this seemingly simple exterior, one of the qualities remembered best by his contemporaries was his extraordinary command presence, that difficult-to-define mystique that sets a born leader apart, whether on a battlefield or in an office, in uniform or out.

This unassuming man always seemed much more interested in the things and people around him than he was in the attention and ruffles and flourishes that go with high rank. Another officer wrote him after he became a full general that "it is reassuring to realize that you will wear your four stars with the same easy grace with which you wore your lieutenant's bars."[6] The general was often told that he looked like Douglas MacArthur, a compliment that pleased him. But as striking a soldier as he was, there was enough of the everyman about him that he could put on civilian clothes and stand undetected in the crowd during a "ban the Bomb" rally in London while he was supreme commander of NATO's armed forces. He explained later that he had just wanted to see what it was like.

Lemnitzer was famed chiefly for his accomplishments in high staff positions, but he was no stranger to physical peril. He was second in command of one of the most daring exploits of early World War II—a nearly disastrous, but ultimately successful secret submarine trip behind enemy lines to set up the invasion of North Africa. In a later encounter, when the bomber in which he was a passenger was riddled by gunfire from attacking German planes, Lemnitzer manned a machine gun and shot down at least one of them. Exposure to front-line hostile fire was almost a daily occurrence during heavy fighting in the Italian campaign, and he risked capture repeatedly when he went into Axis territory in disguise to arrange for the surrender of more than a million German troops. When he was fifty-one, he went through one of the Army's toughest training programs to win a paratrooper's badge and then, while commanding an infantry division in the Korean War, was decorated for coolness under enemy fire.

But the trait that did the most to make him a survivor and succeed in the "take no prisoners" world of high-level military leadership was that he was a pragmatist who thought in terms of the possible. Another general might rail at a concept like President Eisenhower's "New Look"; Lemnitzer could be just as opposed and as outspoken, but he would also be thinking of ways to do the best he could with what had been given him. A favorite expression of his when he considered that someone had gone beyond this limit was, "You're telephoning from jail," which meant that the plan under discussion didn't have a chance of being adopted and was therefore a waste of effort. At the same time he was fair, made strong use of common sense, and was capable of cutting through the knottiest of issues with solutions that left all sides satisfied or at least resigned to the fact that there was not a better one. And he could be very tough: Colonel John B. B. Trussell, his speechwriter, recalled that "the position or concession or agreement he argued for was always eminently logical and reasonable to begin with; hence, no compromise or concession on his part was called for. He did not tilt at windmills."[7] When the basic problem defied settlement, as was the case when he was trying to keep Greece and Turkey from going to war over Cyprus, he made no effort to try to deal with a dispute that was complicated by ancient antagonisms. He had been sent to head off a war; he simply told Greece while it was preparing to invade Cyprus that it couldn't possibly win a full-scale conflict with Turkey, and he informed them both that war would result in the loss of U.S. military and economic aid, leaving both countries exhausted.

Statesman Henry Kissinger, who was not a charitable judge of other men's intellectual qualities, regarded Lemnitzer as "brilliant."[8] He had the ability to move swiftly to the heart of a problem, but as military historian S. L. A. (Slam)

Marshall once observed, "he does not make himself a boor by insisting ever on doing so."[9] He was a patient listener, although on occasion he would interrupt a staff member's unnecessarily verbose approach to a point with a firm "Bottom line! Bottom line!" As a staff officer or troop leader, he was capable of quick, clear decisions; in the extended deliberations on involved issues that are the regular fare of high-ranking generals, he could sit through hours and days of complex discussion, then expertly sum up the major points and quickly reach or recommend a decision. Pressure, the fast pace of high command—especially in Washington— and incredibly heavy workloads did not seem to ruffle or tire him. He rarely, if ever, displayed temper or was caught off-guard when representing his office, although a former assistant said that he was capable of "ripping the hide off" a subordinate or staffer if the mistake at issue was serious enough. Mostly, however, these rare outbursts were directed at situations, rather than people.[10]

The general had a way of questioning an officer making a report or conducting a briefing that could be demoralizing if the officer was not familiar with Lemnitzer's methods. He usually spoke loudly, chiefly because he wanted to make sure he was understood but also because he had a hearing problem that grew worse as he got older. He was quick to spot a weak point in a presentation, but even if he agreed with his briefer's position he would ask searching questions that could give the presenter the impression that the general was trashing his product. The uninitiated might flounder or the faint-hearted retreat, but what Lemnitzer wanted was to be sure the person in his office believed in his position and had thought it through. If the officer stood his ground, he had a good chance of walking out with his plan intact and approved. Trussell recalled meeting a Marine colonel he knew as he left Lemnitzer's office when he was chairman of the Joint Chiefs. He looked shaken and told Trussell he was sure his career was ruined because of the going-over he had just received. He learned that what had happened was only Lemnitzer's way and fared much better the next time.[11]

Other subordinates, particularly those on his immediate staff, saw their general as a thoughtful and considerate man who had a staff officer's penchant for going over all details to make sure that all alternatives had been considered—another of his sayings was that "I want to be in on the takeoff as well as the crash-landing." He could be hard on those who tried to cover poor preparation with "snow jobs"; he wasn't bothered by an admission of "I don't know," but he expected an answer immediately after the briefing. The Lemnitzer of those encounters tended to point out other alternatives when he disagreed with a conclusion, quietly steering the subordinate toward the solution he considered best. He was meticulous in going over paperwork, but kind when he spotted an error; Chief Warrant Officer Ralph Chambers, his principal administrative assistant for years, recalled that instead of dressing him down for a mistake that Chambers should have caught the general would circle it with a pencil and tell him: "have those people out there fix this up."[12]

A top assistant when Lemnitzer was NATO commander remembers that "I always felt comfortable with General Lem. He wasn't an easy-going man. He had very definite ideas of what he wanted; he expected results; he was clearly a man in charge of the operation."[13] Although he insisted on excellence from his subordinates and could be very difficult until it was achieved, he was revered by those who served under him. He was a warm, caring leader who worked in his shirt-sleeves and took time to make small talk with even the most junior of those on his staff. Another stripe or a transfer was an occasion for a celebration, no matter how busy the general was at the time. He was interested in his people and their families, insisted on being kept informed of such things as illnesses and personal concerns, and made sure to mention them when he spoke to those involved. He inspired loyalty and was loyal in return, although this quality sometimes had its drawbacks: he tended to heed the advice of those who had been with him the longest, rather than that of relative newcomers with better advice.[14]

The general had the British gentleman's way of addressing male subordinates by their last names, whereas women on his staff were called by their first names or by their ranks—he always seemed to be more comfortable conversing with men than with women. His staff and other subordinates referred to him as "General Lem," although not in his presence. Boyhood friends from his hometown called him either "Lyman" or "Rocko," although his wife and equals in rank addressed him as "Lem." U.S. Representative Mendel Rivers, a stalwart on the House Armed Services Committee, called him "Lemmie."

Lemnitzer was always appreciative of kindnesses and jobs well done, no matter how modest. When he was leaving Washington to become supreme allied commander in Europe, he wrote a letter to the manager of the shoe repair shop at the Fort Myer, Virginia, post exchange, praising him for the quality of his service while the general lived on the post. His files bulged with copies of similar letters: to the drivers of his cars; to a baker in his household in Japan; to an airfield maintenance crew that had serviced his plane during an emergency stopover—each person mentioned by name and service number; to countless other persons whose efforts on his behalf he considered exceptional. Another heavy file contained his responses to requests for help from service personnel who thought the system had wronged them in such areas as promotions or assignments—in one letter to the head of Army personnel he asked that something be done for a sergeant and his wife who had called on him at his quarters after duty hours while he was JCS chairman to seek relief from excessive overseas assignments. If he thought a complaint had merit, he would usually bring the matter to the attention of the appropriate commander or department head; whether or not the grievance turned out to be justified, he would always follow up with a letter to the person who had sought his help explaining what response he had received. The services have regular channels to deal with complaints about unfair treatment, and it is probable that some of those Lemnitzer contacted thought he had no business getting into such matters. But the general seemed incapable of ignoring a plea for help. He did not pull strings—if there was a reasonable explanation for the perceived injustice or even if the aggrieved party's superior just declined to change his mind, Lemnitzer would not take the matter any further. Usually, though, an indication of interest from someone on Lemnitzer's level was enough to make things right if a wrong had been done.

The general liked soldiers and had a friendly, easy manner when he dealt with them. He played regularly on at least two predominantly enlisted men's softball teams when he commanded units and for a time was a star member of a Fort Monroe bowling team called the "Oozlefinches." He disdained making contact with troops just for show, much to the continuing displeasure of some senior staff members who thought a general should tour a post now and then to boost morale and as a public relations gesture. Modesty, not arrogance, was the reason for his reticence: the general just did not believe that when he was in high command his troops would get any benefit from seeing him. When his senior staffmen did succeed, things did not always go well, as was the case when Lemnitzer's chief of staff persuaded him, when he was supreme allied commander in Europe, to occasionally invite a low-ranking member of his headquarters to play golf in his foursome. Early in the experiment, the invitee, an Air Force officer who had been studying Lemnitzer's swing, suddenly blurted: "Sir, do you know that your club hits your left shoulder during your backswing?" There was a long silence; it isn't good form at any time to make unsolicited comments about another golfer's game while playing, and this is especially true when the person addressed is a four-star general who takes his golf game very seriously. The general who had thought up the idea of bringing the staff member along broke the tension by laughing. Lemnitzer joined in after a moment, but afterward he suggested that his chief of staff be more careful the next time he rounded out the general's foursome.[15]

Lemnitzer had a remarkable memory, a trait which enabled him to recall names and details happened upon, however fleetingly, years before. A favorite trick was to ask a member of his staff: "Do you know what I did on this day ten (or five or twenty) years ago?" He then would describe in detail what had occurred that day. Hugh M. Milton II, an assistant secretary of the Army, wrote Lemnitzer after a visit to Tokyo when he was Far East commander in chief, expressing amazement at the general's "grasp of detail. Mr. [Wilber M.] Brucker [then secretary of the Army] and I have commented numerous times that there was not a single question asked on which you did not have a thorough under-standing."[16] His gift of total recall also made him a respected congressional witness. While other officers and civilian leaders might have had to be prompted by aides or have had to promise a later answer to a question, Lemnitzer was renowned for doing his homework and remembering even the most minute details about the issue under discussion. Moreover, he believed that Congress had the right to any information he could give and he spoke in language a civilian could understand: he didn't use military jargon or acronyms, the verbal Pentagon shorthand that can render the speech of the user unintelligible to the layman. A congressman once told him admiringly after some testimony that "you're the only son of a bitch from over there [the Pentagon] that I can understand."[17]

Surprisingly for one so personable and effective in expressing himself in carrying out his duties, Lemnitzer was a poor public speaker during his active duty career. He considered most speaking to be a necessary but not very important chore and spent little time in preparing for a speech. The writing usually was done by a speechwriter like Colonel Trussell who knew the general very well and could prepare a suitable address after a brief conference on what Lemnitzer wanted to say. At best, Lemnitzer was able to find the time to go over a speech on the way to the occasion, unless the address was a particularly important one; at worst, he saw the words he was to use for the first time at delivery. He usually read the speeches in a near-monotone, looking up only occasionally; his talks tended to be repetitious—often purposely because he thought repeating points added emphasis. Ironically, he was a very effective speaker when he spoke from notes or extemporaneously. He was witty, relaxed, and interesting, something his assistants knew, but their efforts to persuade him to forego the written page were seldom of any avail. As sure as he was of himself as a general, he was also acutely aware that any slip of the tongue could embarrass the government or cause other complications. Only after he retired and spoke for himself did he become an effective speaker. A civic leader in Chicago who heard him speak without script or notes on the North Atlantic Treaty Organization (NATO) and foreign policy in 1970 likened him to master orator Douglas MacArthur in his ability to stimulate an audience.[18]

Lemnitzer had a reputation for always being well informed and, although he was firmly opposed to military personnel involving themselves in political matters, he was astute in spotting political developments that could affect his own operations—a valuable asset to have in Washington in-fighting. He read five or six newspapers thoroughly every day and was briefed daily by staff officers on news developments around the world. He kept abreast of the latest news and other current events with one of his most prized possessions, a small Toshiba transistor radio which had been sent to him as a gift by a tailor friend in Tokyo when he became Army vice chief of staff. It went everywhere with him. He also kept a crystal ball on his desk, the gift of a friend who jokingly suggested that it would help him in making decisions. It became a familiar prop to visitors: one, a reporter, recalled the general telling him that the ball was the secret of his ability to get along with the French when he was supreme NATO commander. To demonstrate, he invited the reporter to ask him any question he liked; when the reporter posed a particularly difficult one involving how France was going to respond on a thorny nuclear issue, the general made a great show of studying the crystal ball before replying with a chuckle: "It says, 'unclear at present.' See? It never fails."[19]

The general was regarded as a "workaholic," although he rarely took work home. He usually arrived at his office every morning at about nine o'clock when he wasn't traveling and left for home at half past six in the afternoon unless he had to stay in town for a social function. After dinner, he would go into his study, close the door, and spend the evening reading newspapers, news magazines, professional journals, and, occasionally, official reports (his wife commented to a *Time* magazine writer: "I don't know whether he goes in there to work, or read or snooze.").[20] His daughter Lois remembers that he liked to wear old clothes around the house and rarely talked very much.[21] He was careful about keeping his private life separate from his official one. His daily office schedule was usually hectic, increasing in tempo as the day wore on. A staff member remembered as typical a day which began with an early morning meeting with the secretary of defense, followed by a conference at the White House. From there the general went back to the Pentagon for a meeting of the JCS, then to the State Department for a working lunch. Afterward, he rushed back to his office for a half past two meeting with the secretary of defense, arriving at two twenty-nine. Glancing at a clock, he muttered to an aide: "How on earth do you suppose I'm going to manage to while away the next thirty seconds?"[22]

This pace could be hard on his schedulers and those he was supposed to meet during the day. Invariably, his itineraries had to be continually reshuffled as his planners tried to get him back on schedule. Somehow, he was able to occasionally squeeze in a round of golf, although even then his proclivity for on-the-second arrivals had its penalties. He would arrive so close to tee time that he wouldn't have time to warm up. The result was usually a badly flubbed first drive, a development the fiercely competitive Lemnitzer did not take lightly.

He could be very fussy. Each time he played golf, he kept score with a pencil stub which was given to him by an administrative assistant who, when he once went on leave, left directions with the general's chief of staff as to just what sort of pencil the general used. Watched carefully by colleagues, the chief of staff carefully ground a pencil down to what he thought was the desired length. But the morning after the general's match, the pencil appeared in the SACEUR's outbox with a piece of paper wrapped around it which said: "This pencil is too short."[23]

When Lemnitzer sat for formal photographs or was otherwise conscious of the camera, he almost always turned the back of his left hand toward the lens so that the ring on his third finger would show. It was his West Point class ring, but the reason he displayed it so prominently was that it also carried the Masonic emblem. The general took his Masonic obligations very seriously; he joined the Freemasons in 1922 when he was a young lieutenant at Fort Adams, Rhode Island, eventually became a 32nd Degree Mason, and finally attained the honorary rank of 33rd Degree. He was a member of the Masons' Shrine, whose charitable work for orphans probably helped influence his strong interest in Korean orphanages when he was Far East commander in chief. A sure way of getting the general's attention was to identify yourself as a Mason; military members of all ranks wrote to him, addressing him as "brother" and being addressed the same way in Lemnitzer's reply. Even the newest private, if he was a Mason or was just from Lemnitzer's home town, could expect a warm response if he wrote to the general, along with an invitation to stop by at his headquarters for a visit when his correspondent was in the area. Although he was raised by a devout Lutheran family in which church attendance and service to the congregation was a way of life, Lemnitzer was not a deeply religious man. His World War II diaries indicate that he attended church services regularly, as he had probably done his entire life, but it is likely that this was in deference to the wishes of his mother. After she died in 1952, his church attendance was confined mostly to Christmas and Easter.

The general loved to watch sports contests, especially football. He was an avid follower of the Military Academy's fortunes, attending games when he could get away from Washington and speculating on the contributions of individual players and the team's chances in letters to his son William, also a West Point graduate and an outstanding Army officer himself. He held a season's ticket to Washington Redskins games at a time when it wasn't easy being a fan; in a letter to his daughter in 1961 he groused about the team's current losing streak of seventeen games.[24]

Golf continued to be a passion with him well into advanced age. At seventy-three, he wrote his son about a match he and three friends played on a sub-freezing day in March with a forty-mile-an-hour wind blowing. "All four of us knew it was no day for golf, but we were all too stubborn to admit it. We went the entire eighteen holes—half-frozen and with tears streaming down our faces from the wind. The strange part, however, was that one of the group—Gen. J. Lawton Collins, then age seventy-six—played his best game of the year. The reason, no doubt, was that he was too frozen to look up."[25]

Another Americanism was his love of cars and driving. In his letters to his family, a favorite topic was the latest models, from their characteristics to their merits and drawbacks. A highly prized possession was a big green 1959 Oldsmobile "Super-88" sedan, which the penurious general bought new after considerable study and some haggling. He wrote Lois that "we are very well satisfied with it" and went on to extol its "Hydramatic transmission, power brakes, power steering and air conditioning, not to mention a rather impressive list of other items."[26] The car became a familiar sight around Fort Myer and the Pentagon, and he drove it long past the time when it badly needed to be traded in for a newer model. His daughter recalled it as a "clunker he just wouldn't let die." One of her personal projects to make it marginally presentable was to periodically launch searches for hubcaps to replace those knocked off by potholes. When the car was still almost new and Lemnitzer was chairman of the JCS, one of his principal staff officers tried to persuade him to authorize installation of a radio telephone so that he could be reached when he was on the road. The general declined on the grounds that he didn't want to be bothered while in the car, but the officer was convinced that the real reason was that he didn't want a hole drilled into the car's roof.[27]

Historian Marshall, one of the military profession's most exacting judges of its members, admired Lemnitzer. In a moving tribute to the general as he neared retirement, Marshall wrote: "Honors over the years have in no way changed him. High rank and responsibility have, if anything, made him more outgiving, and this is probably the key to the inner man. He has never been inflated with a feeling of self-importance. He agrees warmly, disagrees fairly and his playfellows are mankind. There is not a shade of hauteur in his makeup. It is not in his nature to do anything meanly.

"Some men get ahead by knowing where to cut and slash, how to play organization politics and through ruthless cunning. It is impossible to think of Lemnitzer wittingly advantaging himself at the expense of any other person. There is too much decency in him. And, besides, with his talents there was always a clean route to the top. Publicity seeking would be for him wholly out of character... he accepts the spotlight when position requires it and, though he does not try to stand aloof, such things are treated as if they were necessary nuisances."

Marshall wrote that the general had "what the Scots call 'innerliness.' He has time for small talk; he has grace and gentleness with all folk on social occasions. Not seeming to be bothered by life's small frustrations, he probably has won as much peace of mind as any main figure of our time." Alluding to Lemnitzer's problems with the John F. Kennedy administration after the ill-fated Bay of Pigs invasion of Cuba, Marshall wrote that Lemnitzer "bore unjust attacks and some popular distrust with dignity and magnanimity. To reply or reproach was beneath him."[28]

Despite his human qualities, Lemnitzer rarely afforded any glimpses of the inner man. He hated communism and no person more epitomized the West Point motto: "Duty, Honor, Country," watchwords he was always sure to cite when anyone asked him about his beliefs. He is remembered as a "doer," a practical problem-solver who dealt with the moment; strangely, he has never been accorded the stature he deserves as one of his era's most dedicated visionaries. He believed fervently in NATO, an alliance he was instrumental in creating, nourishing, defending, and sustaining in what many remember as its darkest hour. It was a crusade that he did not abandon when he took off his uniform for the last time. Until ill health forced him to curtail his activities a year or so before he died at age eighty-nine, he was still one of the alliance's most vigorous champions.

There are few clues in Lemnitzer's letters and utterances to how he felt about issues that were unrelated to the country's defense. One that was revealing was his reply to a Philadelphia schoolboy who wrote to him asking him his concept of a "great American." The general wrote back that during their lives great people "served a cause they believed in, overcoming opposition, both from honest men who disagreed with them, as well as from bitter enemies." Quoting from a pamphlet he once read entitled "They Made a Nation," he wrote: "What makes men great? Not living in the clouds, above the cares and sorrows of their fellows, but struggling with the questions of their day. If what they do is something that will make a difference ever afterwards—and if they do it well—their names go down in history because they did great things greatly."[29]

Lemnitzer would never have placed himself in such company, although others might. There was no doubt, however, that he meant himself in another observation, this one being some advice at the end of a lecture on command at the Army War College when he was nearly eighty years old:

"It is a serious error for any officer to attempt to emulate one or more qualities of our great military leaders when such qualities are lacking in his own individual makeup. Any attempts in this regard are usually so transparent that anyone, particularly the members of his command, can easily see through them.

"My advice is to turn in the very best performance you are capable of, but, above all, be yourself—be yourself."[30]

2

★ ★ ★ ★

ROCKO

The fall colors in the surrounding Pocono Mountains were at their most brilliant that sunny October day in 1961, and Clifford Ammerman, editor of the thrice-weekly *Wayne Independent*, was planning to leave early for a leisurely stroll home under the dazzling clouds of red, yellow, and orange that crowned Honesdale's stately shade trees.

As he walked to the door of his outer office, Ammerman made small talk with Dick Coyle, a paper salesman from New York City, who was also leaving. Just then, the door opened and in stepped a powerfully built, pleasant-faced man dressed in casual clothes and carrying a small camera. The visitor greeted Ammerman warmly and told the editor he had stopped by to say hello and to check on the status of his subscription. Informed after a quick check of the office files showed that it still had several months to run, the man shook hands with Ammerman and Coyle and left.

The editor asked Coyle if he had recognized the visitor. The salesman, who had heard Ammerman call the visitor "Lem" but had missed his last name in the introduction, said he thought he probably was a local businessman out for the afternoon to take pictures of Honesdale's famed autumn foliage. "Lem's from Washington," said Ammerman. "That's the chairman of the Joint Chiefs of Staff." Impressed, Coyle walked to the window and watched Gen. Lyman Louis Lemnitzer walk briskly down Eighth Street, pausing once to snap a picture of a huge old maple tree before disappearing around a corner.[1]

As a neighbor once remarked, the general "always came home,"[2] and home was Honesdale, a quiet little industrial borough of five thousand residents tucked away in the Poconos up along the extreme northeastern corner of Pennsylvania,

13

some twenty miles east of Scranton. It is one hundred thirty-eight miles from New York City; many of the city's residents have used the Honesdale area with its lakes and ski trails as a favorite vacationing spot for over a hundred years. It is also two hundred fifty miles from Washington, D.C., which was, for many of Lemnitzer's years as a general officer, the "home away from home" of Honesdale's most famous son.

Lemnitzer's devotion to the place of his birth was remarkable. He returned often, usually driving himself and his wife, Katherine, in one of the Oldsmobiles that were his favorite autos. Motoring in the mountain country of northern Pennsylvania can be a perilous undertaking, especially in late fall and winter, and the general's letters to his family contain many references to spine-tingling trips, frequently at night over slippery, snow-covered highways and through heavy fog. At other times, Honesdale was a stopping-off place when Lemnitzer was flying on military business, the touch-down spot Avoca International Airport, south of Scranton and some thirty miles from Honesdale by car.

Being a general was a busy profession, particularly in the years Lemnitzer served in Washington, D.C., and his visits were brief, often overnight affairs squeezed in on weekends. Then he would get out of the heavy, ribbon-encrusted uniform of a high-ranking Army officer, slip into comfortable civilian clothes and become just another Honesdalian. He loved to walk, and he was a familiar figure on downtown streets as he paused frequently to talk to old friends in a town where to this day residents still say good morning to strangers and where passing cars stop on the main street to let pedestrians cross.

Lemnitzer was an enthusiastic fisherman, besides being an avid photographer, and when he had time he went angling for bass and panfish in the lakes and rivers that abound in Wayne County, of which Honesdale is the county seat. The general also usually found time to play golf. His regular partners when he was in Honesdale were not the mayor or other local dignitaries; they were old friends like Edward R. Ripple and the editor, Ammerman. When he fished, it was likely to be with Frank Valenzano, who had a barbershop just off the town's main street. Another golfing companion when he was in town was Honesdale native Art Wall, Jr., 1959 Masters champion and winner of many other major tournaments. He and the general, then the newly named Army chief of staff, were honored together in 1959 as Honesdale's "Men of the Year."

But there was another reason why the general would for years wind up a grueling day in the nation's capital and spend the night driving over frequently treacherous roads to a tiny borough in Pennsylvania, why the hundreds of letters he was fond of writing to members of his family always had this reason as a recurring subject, why over the thousands of miles and enormous responsibilities Honesdale was never far from his thoughts.

In Honesdale, there is a large, once-stylish but still imposing Victorian frame house on a tiny lot at the corner of West and Fifteenth streets on the borough's near west side. Lemnitzer was born there on August 29, 1899, a few months after the house was built. He was raised there, and his father and mother and paternal grandparents died inside its walls. The general became its owner after his mother Hannah's death in 1952.

Except for visits home, the general had not lived in the soaring, three-story structure since he was seventeen, nor did he ever really dwell there in the thirty-six years after he inherited it. He purchased his brother Ernest's share in the house, insisting in their negotiations that when the estate was finally settled the house was to be exactly as it was when his mother died, inside and out, down to the last stick of furniture. Until his own death in 1988, Lemnitzer went to extraordinary lengths to make sure that those standards were kept.

In 1955, when he was commander in chief of the U.S. Far East Command, concerns about a cracked toilet bowl and such maintenance details as the proper kind of exterior paint to use were on a personal agenda that also included presiding over the military aspects of a corner of the world that was struggling to emerge from the rubble of the Korean War. A friend at home was overseeing care of the mostly unoccupied house in Honesdale, and to him the general dispatched the letters that gave instructions about what to do about keeping things shipshape.

In letters to his family over the years, Lemnitzer went into minute detail on the condition of the house. Winters can be harsh in northeastern Pennsylvania, and while he was chairman of the JCS a plunge in temperature to twenty-six degrees below zero coincided with an oil heater malfunction that resulted in extensive damage to the house's frozen water pipes. His letter to his daughter Lois about the mishap was in the paragraph below another one mentioning his having been to the White House that morning to confer with President Kennedy about an overseas crisis.

The year before, he wrote to Ernest that burglars had broken into the house through a kitchen window. No patch of rust or crack was too small to merit four-star concern during the general's stewardship. A loose piece of molding in the living room, duly reported by his attentive caretaker, brought about a letter with detailed instructions as to what to do about it. A fallen picture in the living room prompted a long letter about replacing the glass and where in the house a spare frame could be found. After a mid-September inspection when he was JCS chairman, he was able to report to his daughter and her husband Hank that the "plugging up of the holes around the attic proved to be very successful. There was not a single fly, bee or bird that penetrated the attic."[3]

Nothing having to do with the house's well-being escaped the general's attention, even the occasional labor problem. In a letter to his brother, he told of the "good job" done by a painting contractor, noting that he was "very expensive" but praising him for his attention to "thousands of small details" and the "particularly good job" done on the living-room woodwork and the kitchen door. But the project had not gone smoothly.

Lemnitzer employed a local man named Willie to help in the house's upkeep. He wrote to his brother about "quite an incident between Willie and the painters. Mr. Palmer (the paint contractor) painted only in perfect weather and he had seven painters on the job one particularly fine day when the house was suddenly engulfed in a heavy cloud of smoke and cinders from burning leaves. Willie, ignoring the fact that the house was being painted, was proceeding in his usual routine to burn them. They say it took many hours for the painters to overcome the damage done by the incident:

"As though that was not enough, there was another more violent incident a week later. Mr. Palmer had assigned his best painter to varnish the natural wood-work in front of the living room. As he was finishing, billows of smoke and ashes covered the front of the house as a result of Willie duplicating his earlier efforts. The painter was of German descent and had very strong views about things, and he told Willie in no uncertain terms what he thought of his methods and, partic-ularly, his intelligence. They had quite a shouting engagement, which, I am told, could be heard for blocks. As a result, Willie threatened to quit. I did not see him when I was up there but I understand he has cooled off and I have not heard any-thing more from him."[4]

So important was the house to him that in a sealed letter written by him while he was overseas during World War II and labeled "to be opened only in the event of my death," he cited three desires: that his son attend West Point, that his daughter go to college, and that the house in Honesdale remain in the family for as long as a Lemnitzer lived.[5] Seven years after his death, his daughter moved into the long-vacant old house, a dwelling so timeless that the ceiling of its enormous attic still anchors the rope swings Lemnitzer and his brothers played on when they were children.

Lemnitzer's copies of the *Wayne Independent* followed him everywhere he was stationed, and he apparently read them thoroughly. Deaths of local friends and acquaintances were always a subject to be touched upon in letters to his family, along with the weather extremes that seemed to be the lot of folks who lived in Honesdale and its environs. The fortunes of local businesses were favorite topics, and there was always frequent mention of the nearby Prompton and Dyberry dams, the construction of which had considerably eased the flooding problem that had plagued Honesdale for much of its existence.

Ironically, frequent heavy flooding was one of the prices Honesdale paid for the location and surrounding terrain that made it prosper during the previous century. The town lay at the bottom of a long incline along which coal from the West was transported to New York City to the east. Honesdale was regularly inundated by high water where two large streams from the higher ground came together. One of the worst rampages occurred in the spring of 1942 when some thirty Honesdale area residents died in floods, the high water mark of which reached almost to the ceiling of the Lemnitzer home's commodious first floor.

In an interview many years later, Lemnitzer commented after one of the frequent immersions of his hometown: "It occurred to me that it was kind of stupid that there wasn't some way to stop this kind of thing from happening every year." He arranged for a delegation from Honesdale to travel to Washington to present its case to the U.S. House Committee on Rivers and Harbors. Dr. K. A. Gillespie, who headed the group, recalls what happened next:

"The committee seemed to lose interest in our story until I introduced our next speaker as General Lemnitzer. Then they came to attention just like that (snapping his fingers), got their pencils and there was no more doodling."[6]

In 1957, the Army Corps of Engineers began construction of the two large dams. Although Lemnitzer never claimed any credit, it was too much of a coincidence to many townspeople that salvation had finally come while their most illustrious native was a four-star Army general. So, Lemnitzer is still generally regarded as the father of the dams, and when they were completed and dedicated, the main speaker each time was Lemnitzer.

Although the general always modestly pooh-poohed his role in bringing about construction of the barriers, there was more than a hint of consternation in his note to the Army chief of engineers after Lemnitzer learned that plans were afoot to name one of the dams after another general. Noting that the district's congressman had introduced a bill to name the Dyberry Dam after a deceased Honesdale native, retired Lt. Gen. Edgar Jadwin, Lemnitzer asked the chief of engineers what action had been taken on the proposal, adding: "I presume that the Corps of Engineers has already considered names (for the dams). I would appreciate any information you have regarding the proposals that are to be made in this regard." Lemnitzer, then the chief of engineers's immediate superior, concluded, perhaps a trifle ominously: "Rather than attempt to write up the answers to the foregoing in a fact sheet, I would prefer that you stop in my office at your convenience to discuss this matter with me."[7]

Whatever his hopes, if they ever existed, neither of the dams was ever named for Honesdale's most famous general. Congress prevailed, and the Dyberry Dam became the Jadwin Dam in honor of a general who had helped build the Panama Canal and had been a specialist in flood control projects. The Lemnitzer name lives on locally as that of a small bridge in East Honesdale and the local National Guard armory.

The town's most-visible memorial to Lemnitzer was for many years the stuffed remains of an Asian tiger that had killed three people and considerable livestock before it was hunted down and killed by a South Vietnamese army captain in his country's Hau-Duc district jungles during the war in Indochina. The captain, who was later himself killed in battle, presented it to Lemnitzer while he was visiting the area as chairman of the JCS. Mounted in a large glass case, the trophy has been on display at the general's old high school since 1962.

In 1959, when he was chief of staff of the U.S. Army, he wrote to Ernest that his speaking schedule was so heavy that "I turn down more than four out of five speeches and appearances for every one I accept." But that ratio might well have been reversed when it came to requests from Honesdale. There is no record in his letters of his ever having refused an invitation from his native town, although he more than once asked that an event be rescheduled so that he could speak. He spoke at the dedication of both dams, Chamber of Commerce meetings, Eagle Scout ceremonies, building dedications, and other community events. He belonged to local civic groups, including the American Legion and Veterans of Foreign Wars posts. Once, after he had spoken at a Wayne County Historical Society meeting while he was the Army's vice chief of staff, he noted with satisfaction in a letter to Ernest that the speech "seemed to have gone very well. They had the largest crowd they ever had at Grace Episcopal Church."

Wayne County, where Lemnitzer's German immigrant grandparents took up residence in the mid-1800s, was created in 1798 and was named for the legendary Revolutionary War general, "Mad" Anthony Wayne. Honesdale was known as Dyberry Forks in the early 1800s, and it was an important place because it was here that some financiers from New York City in 1829 established the Delaware & Hudson Canal. In gratitude, the pleasant little municipality changed its name to honor Philip Hone, a diarist of some renown and a onetime mayor of New York City who was the first president of the canal company.

Washington Irving, author of "The Legend of Sleepy Hollow" and other American classics, visited the area soon after the canal was built and pronounced it "a pretty village which has recently come into existence . . . new but very bustling. Well laid-out and prettily built." Irving is reported to have been with Hone at the time and is said to have drunk a toast to the town with spring water: "To Honesdale, a memento of an enterprising man in an enterprising age."[8]

But it was not because of Dyberry Forks's beauty that Hone and his backers chose to invest their money there. Extensive deposits of anthracite coal had been discovered on the other side of the Moosic Mountains some twenty miles west of the county, and a route had to be found to get it to New York City, a prime customer with its large population and burgeoning industry. Dyberry Forks was located in the foothills between Carbondale, Pennsylvania—the center of the mining area—and the big seaport to the east.

The coal started its journey in cars that made the trip from Carbondale to Dyberry Forks by what was called a "gravity railroad." The cars would coast down the twenty miles or so along a series of large steppes, slowing down or stopping when they reached a succession of plateaus. At these intervals, the heavily laden cars would be attached to stationary steam engines, towed to the top of the next downgrade and sent on their way again. When the coal reached Honesdale, it was loaded onto barges at the canal, and these barges were towed by mules a hundred miles to Eddyville, New York. From there the coal was transferred to other vessels for the trip south to New York. When the barges returned to Honesdale, they carried general cargo from New York.

Canal company officials thought they could improve on the laborious process of getting the coal to the canal, so shortly after the nation's first privately owned, million-dollar enterprise was formed in 1825, President Hone sent an order to Stourbridge, England, for a locomotive to speed up the journey from Carbondale. It arrived in 1829, an eight-ton mechanical marvel adorned with green paint and emblazoned with a painted likeness of a lion's head for decoration. The *Stourbridge Lion,* as it became known, put Honesdale on the map for evermore as the site of the first run by a locomotive over commercial track in America. The event was hailed with appropriate pomp and oratory, and to this day the *Stourbridge Lion* is the official emblem of Honesdale. Its likeness is everywhere, on signs and letterheads and in the town museum, where a replica is the main attraction.

But a pioneering trailblazer it was not. The *Stourbridge Lion* traveled just one mile in three attempts on one day between Honesdale and neighboring Seelyville.[9] The problem was that the English manufacturers apparently had not followed customer specifications, for the locomotive was much too heavy for the wooden tracks in use on the gravity railroad. The sad results were a trail of broken hemlock rails and a badly bogged-down *Lion.* The high-stacked little engine that couldn't was shunted to a siding to rust and was extensively "cannibalized" over the years for parts; what was left ended up in a machine shop in Carbondale. All that remains today of the onetime pride of Honesdale is a cylinder and part of the boiler in a display at the Smithsonian Institution in Washington, D.C.[10]

The American branch of the Lemnitzer family got off to a tentative start in 1851 when a German youngster named Ernst Lemnitzer left his native Saxony with some neighborhood friends at age fourteen and sailed to the United States. Whether he got homesick or became disillusioned with his new home or for some other reason, young Ernst stayed in this country only a short time and then went back to Germany. A few years later, though, in 1860, he was back for good as a man of twenty-three.[11]

The grandson who would become a famous general in the next century had a lifelong interest in his family's origins, as expressed in correspondence he would carry on from time to time with persons who would write asking if he could be a relative. To one who wrote to Lemnitzer after he had achieved prominence as a deputy Army chief of staff in Washington, the general replied that despite many efforts to find German relatives he had had no success. The closest he came was immediately after World War II, he wrote, when persons named Lemnitzer had written him from Berlin and Munich professing to have information about his family. This was after he had won worldwide fame in the war as second in command of a secret mission to North Africa to pave the way for the Allied invasion.

"Although I replied immediately, no further information was received from them," he wrote in a wistful letter to his brother Ernest in 1957. "I cannot understand their reason for failing to reply after they had taken the lead in asking for information." General Lemnitzer's quest could have been complicated by his belief that his grandparents on both his father's and mother's sides of the family had come from the same region of Germany—indeed, he apparently believed that their families had lived within some twenty-five miles of each other.[12] The region in which he concentrated his searches was the Black Forest area of western Bavaria. Census records, however, show his grandfather Ernst's home when he left for the United States as having been in Saxony, hundreds of miles north of Bavaria and along the eastern edge of Germany,[13] whereas the Black Forest is in the southwest. His wife, the general's grandmother, was from Berlin, much farther still to the north.[14]

On the voyage back to the United States in 1860, grandfather Ernst became acquainted with Louisa Grimm, whom he married shortly after they arrived in their new homeland. Sometime between when he first arrived in America and shortly after he returned, he became a U.S. citizen. The couple settled in Honesdale, site of a large German immigrant population and the main office of Ernst's new employer, the Delaware & Hudson Canal Company. In 1861, General Lemnitzer's father, William L., was born, the first of nine children.

The country was locked in the Civil War when the young couple settled down, and in February 1862, Ernst became a private in the 112th Regiment of the Second Pennsylvania Heavy Artillery. The volunteer unit spent much of its first two years manning the defenses of Washington, distinguishing itself for "its proficiency and soldierly appearance," whereas other units engaged the Confederates on the war's far-flung battlefields. Then, in 1864, the 112th was divided into two regiments and sent into southern Virginia, where it took part in such bloody campaigns as the Wilderness and Cold Harbor, and the siege and eventual capture of Petersburg. Often fighting as infantry, both heavy artillery regiments suffered heavy casualties in some of the most violent engagements of the war.[15]

But the young German immigrant was not with the regiment in the fighting. He later told his family that he had been a prisoner of war during this period. Many years later his grandson, the general, wrote to a man who had requested information about the Lemnitzer family that his grandfather had been captured at Gettysburg, confined in Libby Prison at Richmond, Virginia, and later transferred to Andersonville, Georgia, where he reported he was when the war ended.[16] In fact, however, the battle of Gettysburg was fought in July 1863, when Lemnitzer claimed to have been in prison. Further, there is no record of the 112th having fought at Gettysburg; at the time, the regiment was in southern Virginia.

The unfortunate truth is that Lemnitzer was indeed in a military prison for the last year and a half of his enlistment, but it was in the Union stockade at Delaware's Pea Patch Island, where he was confined at hard labor for desertion.

According to records in the National Archives, Lemnitzer deserted on August 9, 1862, while stationed at Fort Slocum in the District of Columbia with the regiment's Battery C. Exactly a year later, he was arrested in Philadelphia and was returned to his battery to await a general court martial. Convicted of desertion in December 1863, he was sentenced to serve the rest of his enlistment, about eighteen months, in a military prison.[17] He was lucky; other deserters, especially those who fled in the face of the enemy, were being shot. Fort Slocum was in the backwater of the Union effort, one of a ring of defensive positions established to defend the capital from a Confederate assault in force that never came.

Discharged in June 1865, Lemnitzer came home "almost a physical wreck" as a result of his professed term in a southern prison, according to his obituary.[18] Apparently, the actual story of his incarceration was never known in Honesdale and probably not by his family, at least his children and their descendents. Although it might seem strange that such a dark episode in his background would escape community notice, it could be explained that Lemnitzer was inducted in Philadelphia, far away from Honesdale, and that he could have been the only member of his unit from the town.

Lemnitzer's enlistment papers referred to him as a "laborer," and it was as such that he went to work for the canal company after his discharge. His descendants remembered him as an engineer and, in the words of his obituary, "for many years a faithful employee" of the canal company. But when the 1900 census was taken, it was evident that he had become part—undoubtedly out of economic necessity—of the flourishing glass manufacturing business that had taken root in Wayne County as the number of German immigrants grew and the fortunes of the canal company ebbed. Lemnitzer had become a glass cutter, and a son, John, a glassblower.[19] In 1898, a year before his grandson Lyman was born, the canal went out of business and the gravity railroad followed a year later.

Over the years, the patriarch of the Lemnitzer family became one of Honesdale's leading citizens. He was described as "a man of few words, quiet and reserved, but esteemed by all who knew him." Like his wife and other members of the Lemnitzer family, he was a pillar of the borough's St. John's Lutheran Church, serving for many years as president of its board of trustees.[20]

Of the couple's nine children, there are records of only four having reached adulthood: William, Mary, John, and Ernest. John, twenty-four, accidentally shot and killed himself in a hunting accident in 1889; Ernest died of typhoid fever at age thirty in 1901; and William and Mary lived into the early 1940s, when Lyman was winning fame as a World War II general. Ernst died in 1910 at seventy-two, and his wife Louisa followed him in death in 1916 at age seventy-eight.

Ernst's oldest son, William, has been described as a "shoemaker" by such sources as a May 1959 *Time* magazine cover story. More often, he was referred to as a foreman in a shoe factory. The general's father may have served in the latter position on his way up, but it is doubtful if he ever made a shoe in his life. For many years, in fact, he was superintendent, a large stockholder, and finally president of one of Honesdale's leading manufacturing concerns, the Durland, Weston Shoe Company. According to its letterhead, it was "makers of the original Honesdale shoe and manufacturers of boots and shoes and jobbers of rubbers." He entered its employ as a boy and worked there for nearly sixty years.

A devout Lutheran and a Freemason as Lyman was after him, William was remembered as a quiet and unassuming man who was busy much of his life running the shoe factory, even maintaining a separate working office in his home. He was married for fifty-five years to Lyman's mother, the former Hannah Blockberger, of Coshecton, New York, daughter of Charles and Ernestine Blockberger, of that city. Hannah was a stern-looking product of another German-American family whom her grandchildren recall frequently read a Bible that was printed in German.

The general's only son William remembered his grandfather as a gruff, dignified man with a large mustache who smoked cigars and followed with avid interest Lyman's exploits in World War II. He was not a colorful head of the household, but on occasion he could make memorable contributions to family lore with such episodes as the time he hid his company's payroll in the bottom of a flower pot at his home. His unknowing wife poured water in the top, soaking the bills into a sodden mess that had to be dried out before the shoe company's employees could be paid.

His son Lyman was careful about how he spent his money all his life, a trait that could be attributed partly to low military pay but could also have been influenced by his father's obviously prudent ways with a dollar. In one example of the latter, after his father died Lyman's letters to his family made frequent reference to a strong desire to have the spelling on his grandfather Lemnitzer's tombstone corrected, noting that the misspelled name had "bothered me for many years and I am only too glad to take care of the cost of correcting it."

The name the monument maker had chiseled into the German immigrant's headstone was "Lemenetzer," and that is the way it stayed for forty-four years; visitors walking years later through the large Lutheran cemetery where the family burial plot was located might well have wondered whether the patriarch of the family had any connection with the correctly named Lemnitzers resting all around him. In a letter to a relative in 1954, when he finally had the letters made right, the general recalled: "Years ago I asked dad how it ever happened that a monument had been accepted on which the name had been so badly misspelled. He indicated that the monument had come from somewhere 'over in the valley,' that a major expenditure would be involved to make the change and apparently he did not consider it of significant importance to have it changed."[21]

Lyman's parents also watched their money when it came to the education of their three sons. The general's son, William, who would be a general himself some day, said that there was a "real sibling rivalry" to get funding for higher education.

What help the parents gave went to Coe, the oldest son, who was Lyman's senior by six years. If scholastic merit was the criterion, Coe would have been the winner hands down: at sixteen he was valedictorian of his Honesdale High School graduating class, whereas Lyman and the youngest son, Ernest, were, at best, just good students. Coe went on to the Cornell University law school where he graduated with honors. By his mid-twenties, he was a successful attorney with a prestigious law firm in New York City. Ernest later attended a business school.

All of the sons had jobs. Coe clerked in a bank before going to law school, and Lyman delivered the *Wayne Independent,* rode his bicycle to nearby Steene's Pond or Lake Lodore each day during winter to help cut ice for a local railroad's refrigeration cars, mowed lawns, was a golf caddie, and worked as a tailor's assistant in Mike Bregstein's tailor shop in downtown Honesdale. Like the adults in his family, Lyman was active in the church, serving as the librarian of St. John's Lutheran Church.[22]

The boys were close. Coe is believed to have been a major influence in Lyman's decision to attempt to fulfill his grandfather's reputed wish that he attend the military academy at West Point, New York. Coe was to die unexpectedly after supposedly routine throat surgery at age twenty-five before his brother entered West Point. Lyman and Ernest visited each other often throughout their lives and wrote to each other regularly until Lyman's death in 1988.

In spite of their close relationship, Lyman's fame apparently was both a source of pride and a burden to Ernest, who once remarked in frustration to a close Honesdale friend, Herman Rusch: "I'm the black sheep in this family."[23] Still, his assessment of himself did not keep the opinionated Ernest from expressing his strong views about doings and people in Washington in letters to his soldier brother, a practice that often brought strong rejoinders from Lyman when Ernest attacked someone he admired.

One of those was Robert T. Stevens, secretary of the Army during the Senator Joseph McCarthy hearings in the early 1950s, whom Ernest accused in a letter to his brother of not having stood up to McCarthy. The general strongly defended Stevens as having done the opposite and concluded in his reply to his brother that "I am unable to understand why you indicate, 'Let somebody with guts take over as secretary of the Army.'"

Another time, in a letter to his son, Lemnitzer wrote that "I am sure Uncle Ernest thinks the country is going to collapse because [Ohio U.S. Senator Robert A.] Taft was not elected [president]," going on to imply that he and his brother had had some strong disagreements on who the country needed as its chief executive in the election of 1952. Despite Ernest's misgivings about his status in his family, he grew up to become vice president and chief financial officer of a prominent New Jersey construction company. When he died in 1991, after retiring to Honesdale with his wife Margaret, he was a very wealthy man.[24] He and his wife, who died in 1987, had no children.

Lyman's childhood was uneventful. It is unlikely that he ever ventured very far outside of Honesdale until he went to West Point, and much of his spare time was devoted to working for spending money. He fished in the many streams and lakes that inundate Wayne County and became a skilled marksman with the .22-caliber rifle he bought with his earnings. A favorite target range, according to Ernest, was the family attic whose windows were frequent casualties of shots gone astray. Years later, Lyman would become one of the Army's outstanding rifle marksmen. He was also a catcher on the Honesdale High School baseball team and was the treasurer of his graduating class.

Childhood friends called him "Rocko" all his life, the nickname generally believed to have been conferred on him after he rammed his head into a boulder while sledding; despite a deep, bloody gash in his forehead, he had wanted to go on coasting until playmates persuaded him to go to a doctor, who put six stitches in his scalp.[25] Another version is that he got the name because he liked to hang out with an older crowd of boys who didn't want him around. They would pummel him but he kept following them. After a particularly painful slapping around one day, he got up, rubbed his head, and kept following. "Rocko" was a form of grudging admiration. As a boy, he was small for his age: William C. Reif, a boyhood friend, recalled that "Lyman was a little runt, the type of youngster you would grab around the neck and sort of drag along because he was so good-natured."[26]

Honesdale was fertile ground for a budding coast artilleryman. Historically, the usually tranquil little area seemed to like a good explosion. Many of the residents who fought in the Civil War, like Lyman's grandfather, were cannoneers. A revered chapter in local lore is about an old Revolutionary War six-pounder that had been captured from the British, later rescued from a junkpile, and then fired at the opening of the Delaware & Hudson Canal. The cannon had a nasty predilection for going off prematurely, doing so at the ceremony that launched the *Stourbridge Lion* on its brief fling with mobility and severely injuring an onlooker. Similar early blasts at civic ceremonies over the years claimed several local fingers and an arm, caused numerous burns, and finally took a life when a Wayne Artillery Company crewman fell under its wheels. The old artillery piece met its end in 1877 when some of the town's men pushed it to a local cliff, intending to fire it one hundred times to celebrate the election of President Rutherford B. Hayes. On the sixth shot—crammed to the muzzle with gunpowder, sod, leather scraps, and rags—it blew up. Fortunately, the gunners apparently had known something about the cannon's history and had taken cover. For once, no one was injured.[27]

The militia unit that owned the cannon was also known as the German Artillery Company, its members a part of the community's large German-American population. Lyman's favorite toy was a cannon with a twelve-inch-long barrel which by some means could be made to emit a loud blast noise. Many years later, when he was famous, neighbors would remember the cannon when they recalled his boyhood. They also remembered an explosion of a more effective nature the year before he entered West Point:

He and friend Ed Rippel decided to "wake up the folks downtown," according to a local newspaper account, and put together a bomb made of a steel pipe a foot long and four inches wide. They filled it with blasting powder, covered it with a huge stone, and touched it off with a three-foot length of fuse in a woods near Honesdale's downtown. The result was much more spectacular than they expected, and for what Lyman later said seemed like minutes following the mighty explosion, the air was filled with pieces of trees, steel, stones, and dirt. Residents of nearby neighborhoods were said to have been indignant over the incident, but the future general was reported to have been highly pleased with the result.[28] It was not for lack of inspiration that after he graduated from West Point Lemnitzer opted for a career in the Coast Artillery Corps, the proud possessor of the biggest artillery pieces in the world.

Lyman was not quite the brilliant student that his brother Coe had been, but he distinguished himself enough to have been chosen to deliver an address at his high school graduation in 1917. His theme was a prophetic one: "Aviation During War." His favorite fields of study were mathematics, physics, and chemistry, and his grades were good enough that West Point's Academic Board excused him from having to take the academic examination for entrance.

But getting into the Military Academy had not gone smoothly. He had obtained an appointment from the congressman for Pennsylvania's 14th District, Louis T. McFadden, who lived in the next county and was not acquainted with the Lemnitzers. However, Lemnitzer was only the first alternate, slated to win appointment if the principal appointee failed to pass the mental and physical examinations, or chose not to accept the appointment. Lemnitzer spent a year after his graduation from high school as a deputy inspector of machine parts at the Gurney Elevator Company's plant in Honesdale while he waited to see how McFadden's first choice would do. The factory was operating around the clock seven days a week, manufacturing big boring machines for the engines of wartime Liberty cargo ships.

The prospects of becoming an Army cadet did not look promising because appointment to the military or naval academies was much sought after in those days and principal nominees usually won them. But one day at the Gurney factory a friend showed Lemnitzer an item in *The New York Times* listing the names of the young men who had been accepted for the next year's class at West Point. Lemnitzer's name was among them ("the fact that it was spelled right meant that it must be so," he recalled thinking).[29] He learned later that the principal nominee had been turned down for physical reasons. Fortunately for Lemnitzer, the only negative mark on his physical chart was for having flat feet. (By a coincidence, the New York State Army post at which he received his physical examination was

Fort Slocum, also the name of the fort in Washington, D.C., at which his grand-father had served in the Civil War before he deserted.)

Despite the Military Academy's approval of his high school record and other qualifications, Lemnitzer must have had some misgivings about how he would stack up among the elite of America's young men because he followed up his appointment by persuading his old high school teachers to help him cram for six weeks on such subjects as mathematics and physics.

When asked many years later why he chose a military career, he replied that he had always been interested in the soldier's life, and this ambition had been crystallized by the country's entrance into World War I as he was finishing high school. He recalled a burst of patriotism while watching the Honesdale company of the National Guard march off one morning to join the 28th Infantry Regiment for eventual service in France. The war also was the focus of a spirited and highly effective national campaign to arouse public enthusiasm for the war, and the slogans and reports from the battlefields made a deep impression on young Rocko. When the National Guard unit left, he joined the military home guard that replaced it.

Still, the decision to try for West Point was only made after some heavy persuading from his older brother Coe and a fellow Honesdalian, George Burkett, who was already a cadet (like a good Honesdale man, Burkett became an officer of heavy artillery after he graduated). The argument that may have been the clincher was Coe's: he pointed out that there was no other way that his brother was going to get a college education. It was a view that for years had been the initial motive that had furnished the country with many of its finest military officers.

The armistice that ended "the war to end all wars" was less than six months away when young Lemnitzer packed the few belongings he would be permitted to keep, bade farewell to his family and Honesdale, and set out to become a soldier amid the austere stone walls that for over a hundred years had echoed the footsteps of men who would become the nation's most illustrious military commanders.

It was not an auspicious time to begin a career in the armed forces. Before the year was out, being a professional soldier would become a precarious calling as America gutted its armed forces, its citizenry confident in the wake of the most devastating war in history that substantial military power would never be needed again. More discouraging for Lemnitzer from a personal standpoint, some West Point upperclassmen reportedly soon began suggesting to the new plebe that he did not have "visible leadership qualities" and advised him to quit West Point and go back to Honesdale.[30]

But he had not been dubbed Rocko for nothing. He hung in, delighted in the rigors of "Beast Barracks," the plebe's make-or-break ordeal of the first summer, and reveled in the challenge of academic work. He did particularly well in physics and chemistry, became a catcher on the West Point baseball squad, and was a crack shot on the rifle team. When he graduated, his rank was a respectable 86th out of the 271 cadets who made up the class of 1920.

Future historians searching for the spark that would explain how this young graduate from Pennsylvania's Poconos Mountains would reach heights achieved by very few in his profession would not have found it in his writeup in the West Point yearbook, *Howitzer*. Couched in the vernacular of what was "hip" among the young in 1920 and printed beneath the photograph of a solemn-eyed, stiff looking young man in a cadet uniform, the words read:

"Well, who have we here? Mr. Lemnits-sir, sir. A typical P.D. [Pennsylvania Dutchman], to say the least. He hails from Honesdale, but hates to admit it. We don't blame him much, for the only map it is on is one to the scale of one inch to the inch. A hopoid? [a cadet who liked to attend dances]. Yes, when it's a feed hop. Being a member of the Choir, he never sings, even in chapel. The only time he's happy is when he's reading some podunk [?], and the only time he is sad is when he has to attend riding. Lem was told by a member of the beast detail to put some collars in his hat. It never occurred to Lem to put them in the sweatband. Gosh, no! He put them between his hat and his skull and had to stand on his hands and drop into his hat to get it on. Efficiency!"

At best, this breezy summation probably meant that the awkward-looking new lieutenant in the photograph was well liked, or could at least take a joke, and it is improbable that even cadet paragons like Robert E. Lee, Douglas MacArthur, and John J. Pershing would have made it unscathed through the pages of the *Howitzer* edition of 1920. But the writeup of a young man who would one day wear four stars and occupy the highest military posts the nation's services had to offer? Hardly.

3

★ ★ ★ ★

THE HUMP

General Lemnitzer was past seventy years of age when he retired in 1969, and soon afterward he was invited to address the advanced classes at the infantry branch school at Fort Benning, Georgia. In introducing him to the students, the commandant remarked that, among his many accomplishments, the guest of honor had been a general for a remarkable twenty-seven years.

That was true, the general conceded as he began his talk, "but before that fact gives you too big an opinion of me I should like to point out that I also was a lieutenant for fifteen years."[1]

This typically self-effacing comment brought a round of appreciative laughter from the audience of young officers, many of whom would shortly be on their way to combat leadership posts in Vietnam. But it could hardly have been a laughing matter back in the 1920s and 1930s when Lieutenant Lemnitzer was earning his spurs in a profession that was then one of the most lowly regarded, and neglected, of society's callings.

That was not the case in June of 1918, when Lemnitzer left home to become a plebe at the U.S. Military Academy. The nation and much of the western world were at war. A citizen in uniform, even a lowly fourth classman at West Point, was a revered figure upon whom society heaped the best it had to offer, from unbridled esteem to the cream of its industrial and agricultural productivity.

Then, less than six months after the sober-faced young Pennsylvanian donned cadet gray, the "War to End All Wars" ended. Not for another twenty years would the soldier be brought in from the cold to which he had been consigned by a populace which truly believed that the nation had just fought its last war.

A year after the war was over, an Army which had boasted a total strength of

2,395,744 when the last shot was fired had fallen to 204,292. There were 130,485 officers in the Army when the armistice was signed and 19,000 in 1920, the year Lemnitzer graduated and was commissioned a second lieutenant. The total was even more dismal the next year: 16,500. The year beyond was worse for both officers and enlisted personnel, a steady trend that continued for over fifteen years.[2]

The war—and more directly a bumbling, short-sighted War Department in Washington—also nearly destroyed the august institution at which Lemnitzer and 270 of his classmates assembled in the summer of 1918. Driven by the need to rapidly expand an Army that had just 5,175 officers and 103,225 enlisted men in 1916,[3] the year before America entered World War I, the War Department ordered West Point to sharply reduce the four-year requirement for graduation. Five classes were graduated in 1917 and 1918, and when peace was declared the only cadets left on the Plain, the academy's parade field, were Lemnitzer and his fellow plebes.

They, too, were promised early graduation—the next June, to be exact, which would have given them just one year at West Point. The promise was broken—the Class of 1920 became a two-year class—but the one-year course of study was envisioned as more than just a wartime expediency by such Army luminaries as then Chief of Staff Gen. Peyton C. March who stated that "this would permit us to graduate from West Point annually over one thousand officers instead of the two hundred we are now getting from this elaborate and expensive plant."[4]

Whatever it might have meant in terms of short-changing the nation's future Army officers in their preparation, the one-year program was popular with many cadets, so much so that over a hundred resigned in 1919 because the War Department had changed its mind and was lengthening the course of study. In later years, this kind of treatment would be called being "jerked around," and Lemnitzer would experience it often in the years that followed.

Many a veteran of battle will tell you that, to a professional soldier, combat can be a snap compared to the peace that follows it. Armies are decimated, a once-adoring citizenry suddenly dislikes the sight of you, and military readiness gets tossed into the scrap heap with the guns, tanks, planes, and warships that were the tools of victory. Often reason goes on the pile, too, or so it might have seemed to the eighteen-year-old Lemnitzer as he got past his first summer with its fearsome "Beast Barracks"[5] and settled into the demanding West Point routine. Indeed, for the Corps that was assembled, that year surely had to be one of the strangest in academy history.

The cadet year started out normally enough on June 14 when two hundred nine men were admitted; more donned uniform on the seventeenth, twenty-five on July 2, and an additional fifteen straggled in at various times from June to September. Then during dinner in West Point's giant mess hall on October 1 the acting commandant of cadets made an announcement: all cadets except for the current plebe class were going to be graduated on November 1, a month away, because of a wartime need for officers. A few days later, the War Department announced further plans to add more cadets to Lemnitzer's class, graduate the latter at the end of the current year, and the latest arrivals the next June. One hundred showed up, many less than expected, and were admitted in November, just as all the upperclassmen were being graduated. It was easy to identify members of this extraordinary segment: because of a wartime shortage of cloth for proper cadet garb, they were issued enlisted men's olive drab uniforms, complete with leggings and campaign hats circled with orange hatbands. They were promptly dubbed "Orioles" by their traditionally gray-clad classmates.[6] (One of the Orioles who was destined to go far was future general Maxwell D. Taylor who, although a classmate of Lemnitzer's, went on to graduate in 1922 as the four-year course of study resumed.)

The journey of what became the class of 1920 and beyond grew still more bizarre the following month. With the war unexpectedly over (the Armistice was declared eight days after the Orioles entered Beast Barracks) and perhaps finally heedful of outcries that West Point was being ruined by the yearlong training regimen, the War Department brought back two prematurely graduated classes for six more months of education—each had been at the Academy for only seventeen months. There was one overriding problem: the returning cadets were now officers who rated salutes and other appropriate deference from the regular cadets and post enlisted men. But they were still cadets and were treated as such by the Academy's administration, a status much resented by men who already held commissions.[7]

Somehow, the academy had to make some sense out of the mess Washington had handed it, so for a time the June arrivals became "Fourth Class A," the Orioles were "Fourth Class B," and when a new plebe class was enrolled the next June it became the plain Fourth Class. When the cadets finally became used to this arrangement, the War Department struck again: the length of study would now be three years, and Lemnitzer's segment became the First Class, the Orioles were the Second Class, and the new plebes were the Third Class.

A member of the Class of 1920 recalled the academy's mess formation as the "weirdest thing that was ever seen." The Corps of Cadets had been reorganized into three battalions of nine companies, as it was originally. On the right was a battalion of five hundred second lieutenants and then the cadets in gray, olive drab, and orange. Lemnitzer's class, the de facto first classmen, were distinguished by a half-inch-wide, two-inch-long stripe on the cuff where the yearling stripe was normally worn.[8]

But the powers that be were still not through. In Lemnitzer's second year, the course was extended again to four years and all cadets were given the opportunity to stay on. Lemnitzer and his classmates who entered in June 1918 were unanimous in their decision: they would graduate in 1920 after two years at the Point.

Retired Col. Clarence C. Clendenen, a member of the Class of 1920, wrote many years later in an article entitled "The Curious Class of 1920" that in its zeal to preserve cadet customs and traditions "we were probably one of the hazingest classes ever at the Academy. It is quite likely that some of the customs that we persevered in maintaining could well have been lost . . . but we preserved what is good, too. I think we can take justifiable pride in the fact that we were the tenuous link that maintained the continuity of the Long Gray Line at a time when it was in danger of being broken."[9]

Maj. Jacob L. Devers, a West Point tactical officer and years later to become one of Gen. Dwight D. Eisenhower's principal generals in World War II, described the academy of Lemnitzer's plebe year as "an old institution with a great heritage of success and tradition, now reduced to a pitiable state as a result of action of the War Department."[10]

Morale, already at alarming levels, plummeted even further during Lemnitzer's first winter when one of the Orioles killed himself with a service rifle after being singled out for especially severe hazing because a more senior cadet had discovered that he wrote poetry in his spare time. Congress was furious, a war-weary public was calling for an investigation, and, as had happened before in the venerable institution's existence, there was an outcry in the press and other quarters for its dissolution.[11] The academy's anguish was compounded further during this turmoil when a famous president emeritus of Harvard University derided it in a speech as "an example of what a university should not be," citing as proof "the inefficiency and failure of its graduates in the World War."[12]

Shortly before this stinging denunciation, in the spring of 1919, there strode into the fray one of the most remarkable figures in West Point history. At age thirty-nine, he was the youngest superintendent since the legendary Sylvanus Thayer, the officer who is credited with taking over a barely struggling officer training post in 1817 and turning it into one of the world's foremost military academies. Just sixteen years before, the new superintendent had graduated from the Academy as first captain, his academic record the most outstanding of any cadet in twenty-five years. He was just back from France where he had been the highly decorated commander of America's famed 42nd (Rainbow) Division. His name was Douglas MacArthur.[13]

West Point had never seen anyone quite like this officer who would go on to become one of the century's most famous combat leaders. He wore a floppy garrison cap tipped at a rakish angle with the brim just above his eyes, walked about in sun-bleached puttees and other unorthodox garb, and casually returned salutes with a tip of an ever-present riding crop. Promoted over many general officers far his senior into one of the service's most coveted posts, he was under orders from Army Chief of Staff March to bring order out of what many inside and outside of the Point's imposing stone walls regarded as chaos.

An iconoclast like his famous general father before him, MacArthur wasted no time in waging a series of only partially successful battles with the academy's formidable and solidly entrenched Academic Board over a curriculum he thought was outmoded. To the chagrin of traditionalists, he did away with such hallowed fixtures as Beast Barracks. Hazed into unconsciousness in a highly publicized incident when he himself was a cadet, the young brigadier general almost succeeded in stamping out the time-honored upperclass practice of cowing, humiliating, and sometimes physically abusing lower-ranking cadets, especially plebes. No tradition, procedure, or deeply instilled belief was immune from the superintendent's attention. Many of MacArthur's innovations and adjustments did not survive long after his three-year reign. Two that did were the institutionalizing of West Point's famed Honor Code—until MacArthur's tenure a cadet-administered means of keeping cadets honest—and the Academy's emphasis on athletics.

MacArthur let it be known early who was boss. One example was after the cadet newspaper, the *Bray*, published a letter to the editor taking issue with the superintendent's trashing of traditions. Several thousand copies were in the mails when the academy adjutant issued orders that all copies of the paper were to be turned in to the administration and that there would be an inspection to ensure that they were. The inspection consisted of visits to cadet rooms and a question of whether the occupants had any copies of the *Bray*. A lie, of course, meant expulsion. (Lemnitzer, who had been injured in a varsity baseball game, was hobbling slowly to his room on crutches from the mess hall when the inspection took place, was never asked The Question, and so retained one of the rare remaining copies of the offending publication.) Some two thousand copies still at the post office were brought back and destroyed. And with that the *Bray* ceased to exist.[14]

It was an exciting time to be at the Academy, although the man responsible for making it so was a remote figure to most of the cadets. MacArthur was aloof, often seen striding briskly on his frequent solitary walks around the grounds or sitting in the back of a classroom to critique professors, an unheard of and much resented incursion into the academic process.[15] But he rarely addressed cadets directly; the exceptions were athletes, especially outstanding ones like Earl H. (Red) Blaik, a member of Lemnitzer's class and a star on the football and basketball teams. A lifelong friend of Lemnitzer's, Blaik went on to become a coaching immortal at West Point. He recalled in later years an attempt by MacArthur, bat in hand, to teach him how to hit a curve ball.

Blaik, an all-around athlete, remembered the brief one-on-one seminar as "the only failure in the general's career. After he got done with me I couldn't even hit a fast ball."[16]

If MacArthur ever took any particular notice of the slender, solemn-eyed Pennsylvanian who would one day go farther than any other member of his class, it was because Lemnitzer was a varsity catcher on the academy's baseball team. He was good enough to have been able to wear a star near his baseball letter signifying a victory over Navy. Disappointment came his second year, though, when, after getting the first hit in a game with Harvard, he tore the ligaments in his right foot while sliding into second base on a wet field. It ended his athletic career at West Point just when he had become the undisputed first-string catcher after his rival for the position suffered a split finger from a foul tip.

High cadet rank or academic achievement are sure to catch the eye of a super-intendent, no matter how haughty, but Lemnitzer was in neither of these charmed circles. He was a private when he joined the Corps of Cadets and a private in D Company when he left it, becoming one of the few members of his class not to have any chevrons on his sleeves.

Part of the problem, he thought, was that two years was too short a time "to identify yourself with any capability" and another was the lack of any military grounding in a class in which many cadets had been to military schools like Culver and the New York Military Academy or had been enlisted men. "Hell," he recalled, "I didn't even know my left foot from my right."

Among these superachievers was classmate Thomas D. White, who had gone to a good military prep school and was the youngest man in the class. He became a cadet captain and was on the "opposite side of the Corps [from me]," Lemnitzer noted. Not close friends at West Point, possibly because of the rank difference, they did become so in later years when White was a member of the JCS as chief of the Air Force. Lemnitzer was JCS chairman at the time.[17]

Lemnitzer sang in the cadet choir, but was no great shakes at it, judging from his class yearbook's comical assessment. What he did excel at was riflery, a skill that would one day distinguish him as one of the Army's best marksmen. And, of course, he was one of the school's best catchers.

He threw himself enthusiastically into the field maneuvers at the end of his first summer at West Point, when cadets marched up to eighteen miles a day and were given rifles to fire for the first time. The only military experience he had had before joining the Corps of Cadets consisted of a couple of drills with Honesdale's home guard, hastily organized to deal with local strife after the National Guard company went off to war.

Lemnitzer credited his achievement in graduating in the top third of his class to his baseball injury. On crutches for much of the spring of his graduation year, he spent all of his waking hours studying. He recalled that "I gained a great many files in those last three months," meaning that he had raised his class standing considerably.[18] Despite his injury, he was determined to march with his class at graduation—and he did, without crutches, despite excruciating pain every time his still-bandaged right foot hit the ground.

When June 1920 rolled around the War Department had still another nasty surprise for a class that it had splintered, frequently misled, and finally denied a full four-year education. Congress wanted to show some special appreciation to officers who had served overseas during the war, so an act was passed on June 4,

1920, which delayed the commissioning of members of the Class of 1920 from June 15, when they graduated, to July 2. This was to enable officers who wanted to become regulars and had served overseas to have a one-day date of rank, or seniority, over the newly graduated cadets.

For just over two weeks, Lemnitzer and his classmates were known as "graduated cadets" or mere candidates for commission. This status posed other problems, as well: under a previous congressional act, cadet service could not be counted in computing officers' longevity pay. The Army paid the class as officers for the seventeen days anyway, refusing to take the money back despite a General Accounting Office assertion that the "graduated cadets" were not entitled to it. The Army's position held, except in the case of Lemnitzer; seven years after he graduated, the government deducted $14.04 from an income tax rebate, the sum representing what he would have received if he had been commissioned when he should have been. For some unknown reason, he was believed to have been the only member of the class who had to give back his pay.[19] He lodged a formal protest, but to no avail.

The infamous "hump" of 1920 was a discouraging setback for a career soldier in a rapidly shrinking Army in which promotion was based solely on seniority. Because of it, the Class of 1920 wound up behind nearly two thirds of the officers in the entire Army on the promotion list. Lemnitzer would not receive his captain's bars until 1935. He was not alone, however; even those who graduated in later classes would suffer for years because of this bizarre jiggering of the promotion list. Maxwell Taylor, another future JCS chairman, would be a lieutenant for thirteen years after graduating fourth in his class in 1922. Alfred M. Gruenther, fourth in the Class of 1919 and future allied commander in Europe; and classmate Anthony C. McAuliffe, the doughty acting division commander who stared down the Germans at Bastogne in World War II, each wore single bars for seventeen years.

The wait might have been even longer but for the fact that many of their West Point classmates resigned their commissions and took up more promising careers. It was okay with the Army; all an officer or enlisted man had to say was "I want out" to open the exit doors of a service that would go along with anything that would help it to reduce its size.

Then, as if to make amends for singling out the Class of 1920 to take the brunt of the hump, five months after the War Department commissioned its members as second lieutenants on July 2, 1920, it promoted them to first lieutenants, retroactive to July 2.

Lemnitzer wore his silver bars for a year and a half. On December 15, 1922, presumably after discovering that a faster-than-anticipated rate in postwar cutbacks had given it a large surplus of first lieutenants, the Army reversed itself: the silver bars would have to come back. Lemnitzer and two other members of the Class of 1920 who were serving at Fort Adams, Rhode Island, got the word just after the Army area commander, a general from Boston, inspected the post and found it in a deplorable state of readiness because of the reductions. Seeking to raise morale, the general told a meeting of the fort's officers to cheer up because things couldn't get any worse. It was then that the Class of 1920 learned that its members were going to be demoted: Lemnitzer was quietly given a discharge and was immediately reappointed a second lieutenant. It would be more than three years before a vacancy in another branch would allow him to pin on silver bars again.

Having had their spirits raised and then dashed again, Lemnitzer and his class-mates wrote what he later described as a "pretty acrimonious" letter to the corps area commander in which they bitterly pointed out how wrong he had been. "We edited it and we polished it, then edited it and polished it again. Then we made one of the soundest decisions most of us would ever make for the rest of our service; we decided to tear the damned letter up."[20]

Lemnitzer's first year of commissioned service was as a student in the basic officer's course at historic Fort Monroe, Virginia, home of the Coast Artillery Corps and today a tourist attraction as the post in which Confederacy President Jefferson Davis was imprisoned following his capture at the end of the Civil War. The coast artillery was an elite branch in those days, ranking second only to the engineers in prestige. Given the mission of protecting America's shores from attack, its bases were sturdy forts located at the entrances of important harbors that could be expected to be primary enemy objectives in an invasion. Established in 1794, the coast artillery had for more than a century been regarded as the keystone of America's military defense against aggression by foreign nations. With the most likely threats to its security lying across the oceans rather than in its own hemisphere, the country lavished a great deal of money to construct forts along its coastlines and to develop the world's most advanced heavy ord-nance. Coastal defense suited the nation's isolationist traditions, its apprehen-sions about any armed force that was aggressive in nature, its insistence on as few troops as possible in peacetime, and, of course, its predilection for minuscule armed forces budgets between wars. The coast artillery offended none of these principles while affording a satisfying, and well-founded, sense of security.

A well-equipped U.S. Army coastal fort was a formidable adversary. At the height of its effectiveness, its guns and mortars had no equals among military weapons in power and accuracy. Its thick walls could withstand the assault of the heaviest naval cannon made. When a fort's weapons fired, they did so from stable, carefully laid permanent platforms, making possible an accuracy no seaborne craft or mobile land artillery battery could equal. A fort's field of fire was carefully registered so that determining the precise range and bearing of an approaching vessel could be as direct a matter as consulting a chart and set of tables.

Far from being a static lot, as membership in such a purely defensive arm might suggest, coast artillerymen of Lemnitzer's early career were innovative, highly professional soldiers who spent much of their duty time seeking ways to improve their weapons, methods, and firing positions. Their enthusiasm was stoked by steady improvements in stationary artillery and mortars and their shells over the years, although the actual fielding of such fruits of civilian enterprise could be frustratingly slow in the arms budget-pinching years between wars.

No other development in the heyday of the coast artillery—the period between the Civil War and the turn of the century—better illustrates the drive from within to advance the state of the cannoneer's art than the famed disappearing gun. Invented in Europe but perfected by two U.S. Army ordnance officers, the gun was hidden behind up to fifty feet of concrete and earthen walls, becoming visible from the target side only when it was raised up to fire. It then disappeared for reloading and sight adjustment, activated by an ingenious recoil and counter-weight mechanism. Fielded in the late 1800s to replace such Civil War era standbys as the fifteen-inch Rodman, the disappearing carriage mounted eight-, ten-, and twelve-inch guns which could hurl one thousand-pound projectiles up to eight miles, making them at least a match for any battleship in the world.[21]

This peek-a-boo cannon would have been a marvel in any age, but by 1915—four years before Lemnitzer put on the insignia of a coast artilleryman—the navies of several foreign powers had guns that could not only shoot farther than U.S. coastal ordnance but also their ability to deliver plunging fire made obsolete any emplacements that had only walls for protection.[22]

When Lemnitzer had been a cadet, with typical disdain for the sensibilities of more orthodox Army and Navy elements, MacArthur had invited one of the uniformed services' most celebrated mavericks to speak to the Corps. He was Brig. Gen. William (Billy) Mitchell, a fiery champion of air power who a few years later would be court-martialed for insubordination. It is unknown what effect, if any, Mitchell's words had on the young officer-to-be, but he would have done well to have listened carefully, for the dynamic new arm of which he spoke was about to drastically change the way Lemnitzer's future branch performed its mission.

During the 1920s the coast artillery attained an antiship capability that far surpassed what it had when the country entered World War I. Much of this resurgence was due to improvements in mount and tube design that allowed increased ranges and higher trajectories, but a bigger reason was the acquisition of various types of long-range weapons from the Navy and other branches of the Army. These included wicked-looking twelve-inch railroad mortars and guns of up to sixteen inches in caliber. The year Lemnitzer graduated, the branch became equipped with a gigantic fourteen-inch railroad gun which was developed specifically for coastal defense. The period also saw the fielding of what was then the most powerful cannon in the world, a sixteen-inch monster which could hurl a shell weighing over a ton a distance of more than thirty miles. It was believed to have been able to outshoot any battleship ever built, even the Japanese Yamato class goliaths of World War II with their 18.1-inch main guns.[23]

But despite these remarkable advances in harbor defense, the decade marked the rise of widespread interest among coast artillerymen in a new combat dimension that had not even been dreamed about when their Corps was created: antiaircraft defense. Considering the burgeoning importance of airpower, it was a prescient trend. During World War II, the branch's antiaircraft mission was much larger than the coastal defense one, and when the Corps was dissolved after the war the only component remaining was its antiaircraft artillery.

The country which the new lieutenant from Honesdale had sworn to defend as he set out for his first assignment was a turbulent place. Most young men his age were looking for jobs as America throttled down from a booming wartime economy to a peace in which at the outset jobs were few and applicants abundant. Times would get much better as the decade advanced, but in the early 1920s the nation was in what in later years economists would call a recession. Moreover, the United States was in an isolationist mood, sick of war, suspicious of anything not American, and eager for tranquility. Complicating this unrest was a wave of violent labor strikes and marches, which many blamed on a disquieting element called Bolshevism or, more familiarly, Communism.

Lemnitzer would become a fervent foe of Communism during his years as a general, and this antipathy could well have had its roots in the times of the "Great Red Scare." The bloody 1917 Russian Revolution had horrified the world and, no doubt, the patriotic and impressionable young machinery inspector in peaceful Honesdale. Army troops were called out often in the early years of Lemnitzer's career to put down riots that most War Department officials considered Communist inspired. General Leonard Wood, a former Army chief of staff who led troops sent to quell particularly bad labor riots in Omaha, Nebraska, and Gary, Indiana, undoubtedly spoke for many fellow military men when he said that all Bolsheviks should be deported "in ships of stone with sails of lead, with the wrath of God for a breeze and with hell for their first port."[24]

But postwar America and all its problems were a world away from the solid old walls of Fort Monroe to which Lemnitzer reported for study in the year-long basic officers course. As is true of all new graduates of the Military Academy, officers do not go out ready to take command in their respective branches. They are assigned to specialized branch training in courses like Fort Monroe's, and it is unlikely that any of that day were any tougher than what was taught in the venerable bastion on the lower Chesapeake Bay.

The coast artillery was the most isolated of all the major Army branches, a situation brought about largely by the fact that its bases were located far from the large mainstream posts where integrated units like divisions and regiments were headquartered. Too, whereas infantry, armor, and field artillery units functioned together as teams in battle, the coast artillery probably had a closer kinship with the Navy than it did with the other Army combat arms. This "left field" status was reflected in the West Point curriculum, which contained almost nothing about coast artillery.

As a result, the basic officer's instruction at Fort Monroe was a cram course in which brand new lieutenants had to become acquainted with the most sophisticated gunnery and equipment in the world. Coast artillery officers had a reputation for being hard workers; they had to be to keep up with rapidly changing technology and a branch tradition of constantly seeking more effective ways of performing its mission. Its officers were regarded as "gadgeteers," mechanically minded, analytical men who spent even their off-duty hours discussing new concepts or the latest development in range-finding technology. Lemnitzer remembered Fort Monroe as having had the best electrical engineering course in the Army and perhaps one of the best in the country. Its faculty included several officers who were graduates of the Massachusetts Institute of Technology and students trained on the latest technical equipment from the recent war.

The basic officer's course curriculum didn't get much attention during the 1920–21 study year because the Fort Monroe school was preoccupied with a newly established coast artillery field officer's course, into which much of the faculty's energies and resources were being poured. Perhaps in recompense or maybe because the school was at a loss as to what to do with them, the fifty-eight members of the basic class of 1921 wound up their year with a ten-day trip by reconnaissance car and truck over the ground covered by Maj. Gen. George B. McClellan's army during the Civil War's ill-fated Peninsula Campaign. Interesting though it must have been to a professional soldier, the McClellan advance on Richmond and withdrawal had nothing to do with the coast artillery, except that McClellan had launched his campaign from Old Point Comfort, near Fort Monroe. A prime purpose of the exercise, as Lemnitzer recalled, was to compile an authentic history of the Peninsular campaign, something that had not been done before. Each student was given a segment of the campaign and told to emulate the movements and actions of the participating Civil War forces; Lemnitzer's assignment was the Union side in the Battle of Seven Pines. The expedition turned up many heretofore undiscovered relics of the war, from trenches and fortifications to weaponry, while making possible the creation of the first complete official history of the campaign.

The ending of the war had made available large stockpiles of artillery and mortar ammunition, much of which was given to training centers to use in firing practice. "We had scads of ammunition just for artillery adjustment firing," Lemnitzer recalled. Busily using ranges at Fort Monroe and nearby Fort Eustis, the students indulged themselves in a rare peacetime phenomenon: almost unlimited supplies of ammunition for training which they used to fire big twelve-inch mortars, 155-millimeter cannons, and a mammoth fourteen-inch naval gun.

Lemnitzer loved it. "I learned more in that year than in any other year of education or exposure in my entire service; it was terrific," he said after he retired.[25]

While Lemnitzer and his classmates were learning how to protect America's shores, their teachers were taking stock of them and writing down their impressions in a document that has made or broken more careers than an entire Army of martinets could accomplish in a lifetime. The document is the Officer's Efficiency Report (OER), in which every officer in the service is evaluated periodically by superiors on such factors as leadership ability, intelligence, and personality traits. The range of criteria is very broad, and little escapes the practiced eyes of raters.

It would have been clear to anyone reading Lemnitzer's OER that this "phenom" with the premature first lieutenant's bars was no ball of fire in the estimation of his instructors. In an OER signed January 21, 1921, by the Fort Monroe school's assistant commandant, Colonel J. C. Johnson, Lemnitzer was an "average all-around officer" who "lacked personality." Of ten qualifications listed in the report, he was rated average in all but two: he was below average in "force" and above average in military bearing and neatness.

In the next two OERs, however, there were indications that Johnson had changed his mind: Lemnitzer was now "above average," had become a "hardworking young officer," and the damning "lacks personality" did not reappear. He now was rated as above average in intelligence, professional knowledge, and attention to duty, and below average in nothing.

Fort Monroe was a time for beginnings. One of these was Lemnitzer's first chest ribbon, emblematic of the World War Victory Medal for which he applied because—even if he was only a cadet stationed far from the fighting—he had been on active military duty during the war.[26] Some forty-five years later, the German magazine *Der Spiegel* counted Lemnitzer's twelve rows of ribbons, did some checking, and announced that the total was tops for the world, surpassing even those of such celebrated warriors as Britain's Lord Louis Mountbatten and Field Marshal Bernard Montgomery, all the senior German generals of the time, and even the then current Soviet defense minister, a marshal of the Soviet Union who lost out by one row.[27]

After completing the basic officer's course in July 1921, Lemnitzer was assigned to the 10th Coast Artillery Regiment at venerable Fort Adams. Located near Newport on Rhode Island Sound, the sprawling, pentagonal-shaped installation had since 1799 been guarding the approaches to Narragansett Bay. Lemnitzer was a range officer for one of the fort's two twelve-inch mortar batteries. Then Fort Adams's principal weapon, the mortars were grouped by battery in clusters of eight stubby tubes, each capable of hurling seven hundred-pound projectiles in high arcs onto the decks of enemy ships. Usually fired simultaneously by battery, the weapons had a shotgun-like effect that could be devastating.

The post–World War I defense cutbacks were in full swing. Any soldier, enlisted man or officer, could obtain a discharge just by asking for it, and many did. Lemnitzer recalled as "ludicrous" an inspection of his battery by the area corps commander, a major general. The battery had four or five privates, fifteen corporals, more than twenty sergeants, eight lieutenants, and three captains.[28]

New lieutenants are supposed to commit at least one quotable gaffe during their apprenticeships. Lemnitzer's occurred when he and a fellow shavetail were in charge of a convoy of trucks carrying troops back to Fort Adams after a field exercise. Asked by their commander when they returned to the post how the trip had gone, Lemnitzer reported that all had proceeded smoothly except for when they stopped along the road so the troops could take a smoke. It was a dry day, and the grass in a roadside pasture caught fire, apparently when someone threw away a lighted match or cigarette. No problem, though, Lemnitzer said: the men had quickly put the fire out and the convoy had gone on its way.

Just then, the telephone rang and the lieutenants were shooed into an outer office and told to close the door while the commander talked on the phone. After a while they were summoned back into the main office by a very red-faced colonel who informed them that, contrary to their beliefs, the fire was not out when they left and had spread to a nearby chicken coop.

Fixing the two with a fierce glare, he announced that as a result the government had just agreed to purchase over a hundred thoroughly roasted chickens from a very unhappy Rhode Island farmer.[29]

Whatever the chickens may have felt about him, the incident apparently did nothing to hurt Lemnitzer's career. His efficiency reports at Fort Adams were glowing: he was rated above average in the first report and described as an "excellent young officer." In the second, six months later, his company commander gave him a top "superior rating," supporting it thus: "I realize that I have given this officer a remarkably high rating, but in . . . comparing him with officers in his grade and of equal service (less than two years) he stands out head and shoulders above any that I have known. He has a pleasing personality and accomplishes splendid results with both officers and men."

In the summer of 1922, Lemnitzer competed for a place on the national Coast Artillery Rifle Team. After qualifying as an Expert rifleman, he was appointed to the team, a high honor in a peacetime service in which a sharp shooting eye was highly prized. He became one of the military services' top shooters. His keen eye won him a Bronze Medal in the 1923 national rifle matches at Camp Perry, Ohio, and he was also awarded a Bronze Army Team Badge. Competing against sixty-five of the country's top interservice military rifle teams, the Coast Artillery Corps team placed fifth, with Lemnitzer posting the fourth highest score on his ten-member team. The next year, while stationed at Corregidor in the Philippine Islands, he won a Gold Medal in the Philippines Department competition against the department's best riflemen. He then was named a Distinguished Marksman, a high award given to shooters who had won three or more medals in national competition.

The marksman's medal was one of his most prized decorations, and throughout his career he would remain one of the country's most forceful advocates of proficiency in rifle and pistol marksmanship. Many years later, as chairman of the JCS in a nuclear age, he would reaffirm his faith in the effectiveness of the individual small arm in a speech to the 1960 national convention of the Veterans of Foreign Wars in Detroit, in which he said: "We must not forget that the military purpose of war is to achieve control over land and the people who live in it . . . the success with which that domination is established, maintained and extended depends in large part on the soldier's mastery of his rifle."[30]

Lemnitzer completed two years of duty at Fort Adams, half of it on detached service as a member and mess officer of the rifle team (OER verdict: as a member, "superior"; as a mess officer, "average") in the summer of 1923, and was ordered to travel to San Francisco for transport by ship to the Philippine Islands.

His sailing date was delayed twice, and in late October 1923, he was granted leave. A week later, on November 6, he married Katherine (Kay) Meade Tryon at the Lutheran Church of the Advent in New York City.[31]

Lemnitzer and the attractive, fun-loving member of a prominent area family had become acquainted at the Honesdale Lutheran church both attended. Kay, who was two years younger, thought her future husband was "cute," according to her daughter Lois, but they didn't date until both had left Honesdale, she for a job in New York City and he for military service. Kay worked as a secretary for a Wall Street financial firm while Lemnitzer was stationed at Fort Adams. They began writing to each other, and soon the young lieutenant was traveling the one hundred fifty miles southwest to New York as often as his duties would permit.

The Tryons were an old East Honesdale family. The new Mrs. Lyman Lemnitzer was a daughter of Mead Tryon, a railroad clerk and the elected tax collector for the Honesdale area's Texas Township. In 1905, three years before he died, this son of a Methodist minister from New York State was the unsuccessful Republican candidate for prothonotary, a high county office that is equivalent to being chief clerk of the courts.[32] His widow was the former Anna Storm, mother of Kay and another daughter, Helen, who was Kay's maid of honor at her wedding.

It was a marriage that lasted sixty-five years and produced a daughter and a son. Katherine learned early that being a military wife required a toughness required of spouses in few other professions. Three weeks after she and Lyman were married, they set sail for his first overseas assignment. Their vessel was a troop ship, so crowded that husbands and wives traveled segregated in five-passenger cabins.[33] She later told her daughter that she was violently seasick all the way.

At the end of the voyage was Corregidor, in later years to be forever etched in U.S. history with such names as the Alamo and Bastogne as symbols of courage and steadfastness in the face of overwhelming odds. Lemnitzer would serve two tours on the island, the last ending eight years before the devastating siege that eventually silenced its big guns.

Lemnitzer had many reasons to remember Corregidor during his career: its beauty, the anguish he felt in 1942 when it was being blasted into rubble by the Japanese, the pain he suffered over the deaths and capture of many friends. But he also would have cause to look back on his service there as the pivot point that set a promising but seemingly unremarkable junior officer on the path to becoming the armed services' highest ranking officer.

4

★ ★ ★ ★

THE ROCK

There is an opening scene in the 1938 motion picture classic *The Hurricane*, in which a tourist ship glides slowly past a storm-battered island that looks like a no-man's-land rising from the sea. When an onlooker remarks that it is a "wretched-looking spot," a man who had been standing at the rail watching the hulk disappear in the vessel's wake replies: "That was once the most beautiful of all the islands that raised their little green heads above these waters . . . the most beautiful and enchanting piece of paradise in all the world."[1]

Similar thoughts might have been going through Gen. Lyman L. Lemnitzer's head in 1957 when he, too, was on a ship that was going past another island that had once also been famed for its beauty. He had been a young officer in those days; he was now on a yacht loaned to him by Ramón Magsaysay, president of the Philippines, and Lemnitzer was the four-star commander in chief of the U.S. Far East and United Nations commands. It was an emotional—and depressing—moment, for the object of his gaze was Corregidor.

World War II had ended twelve years before, but rusting cannons, shattered gun emplacements, twisted steel building frames, and heaps of blasted concrete littered the beaches and rocky hills. Artillery shells, many of them still live, were strewn across the bomb- and shell-pocked ground. As the American general watched, civilian salvagers were busy in the ruins, further dismantling and carrying away for scrap the torn reminders of what had once been the most furious battle in U.S. Coast Artillery Corps history.

In a letter to Magsaysay after his return to Japan, Lemnitzer wrote that his "return had a solemn note of sadness when I saw what the merciless bombardments of 1941–42 had done to the pleasant surroundings we once knew so well.

43

What we saw made us realize the enormity of the agony of the defenders—Filipinos and Americans, many of whom were our close friends—during those last grim days before they were overwhelmed by the enemy landing attack."[2]

Worried that the wholesale scavenging was destroying all vestiges of one of the war's historic military stands, Lemnitzer appealed to Magsaysay to halt it, predicting that not to do so would impair plans to build a monument he foresaw would "some day rank with Gettysburg, Verdun and Normandy as a great war memorial."[3]

The Philippines president was killed in an airplane crash less than two weeks after Lemnitzer wrote, and one of his last acts was to order the scavenging stopped. Today, Corregidor is indeed the site of one of the world's most moving memorials to military valor, its striking steel sculpture and "Eternal Flame of Freedom" the centerpiece of an exhibit dedicated to telling posterity what happened during twenty-seven terrible days in the opening months of World War II.

But Corregidor's moment in history was some seventeen years away when Lemnitzer and his bride sailed into Manila Bay in the waning days of 1923. The little tadpole-shaped island—two and a half miles long and thirty miles from Manila near the opening of its bay—called itself "The Gibraltar of the East," although it was perhaps better known to coast artillerymen and their families as being as close to the embodiment of the fabled tropical island of the tourist books as there was in any military post in the world. Spectacularly flowering flame and fire trees, frangipani, bouganvillaea, hibiscus, cadena di amour, orchids, and palm trees grew profusely in its rocky hills. The China Sea to the west was an intense blue in the daytime and gold when the sun dipped low. At night, officers could sit on their verandas after a late game of golf and watch the lights of Manila. A peacetime tour on the "Rock" in the 1920s and 1930s was something to be recalled with affection and nostalgia.[4]

Despite its natural splendors and air of enchantment, Corregidor—or Fort Mills, as it was officially known—was a formidable fortress. Troop units stationed there consisted of the U.S. 59th Coast Artillery and 60th Antiaircraft regiments and two Filipino regiments, one of scouts and the other of artillery. Fifty-six coastal guns and large mortars grouped in twenty-two batteries guarded the bay and approaches to the island, along with large minefields on the north and south. To the world, the best-known feature of the stronghold was the famed Malinta Tunnel, a huge, bombproof complex which Army engineers had blasted through the solid rock of Malinta Hill. Over eight hundred feet long, twenty-four feet wide, and laced with twenty-five 150-foot laterals, the tunnel became the headquarters of Gen. Douglas MacArthur, commander of Army forces in the Philippines, in the final desperate weeks before the Japanese crushed U.S. and Filipino forces in the spring of 1942.[5]

Corregidor was the largest of several islands outside Manila Bay that were won in 1898 by the United States in the Spanish-American War. The most noteworthy of the others was Fort Drum, the famed "Concrete Battleship." An acre in size and surrounded by reinforced concrete from twenty-five to thirty-six feet thick, the warship-shaped fort had two twin fourteen-inch turret mounts, four six-inch casemounts, and a pedestal-mounted three-inch gun. Teamed with Corregidor's formidable arsenal—eight twelve-inch cannons, twelve twelve-inch mortars, and other artillery pieces ranging from ten-inch down to three-inch[6]—tiny Fort Drum kept a withering fire on mainland targets and aerial attackers for nearly a month after war broke out. Its defenders gave up only when ordered to on May 6, 1942, when U.S. Lt. Gen. Jonathan M. Wainwright surrendered Corregidor and fifteen thousand U.S. and Filipino troops after the island was overrun by Japanese troops.

Twenty-seven days before, what remained of the combined American and Filipino forces in the Philippines were crushed on the Bataan Peninsula, just two miles across the water from Corregidor. Over seventy-eight thousand fighting men surrendered—sixty-six thousand Filipinos and twelve thousand Americans— many of them to be herded to prison camps via the infamous "Bataan Death March."[7] Only Corregidor, Fort Drum, and two other small nearby forts—Frank, on Carabao Island, and Hughes, on Caballo Island—were left to face the full fury of the Japanese attack. It was the coast artillery's finest hour: augmented by troops from the mainland, Corregidor's defenders fought on against staggering odds. The big guns and mortars, most of them poorly armored against aerial assault and lacking proper ammunition for the mission they were assigned, succumbed one by one to enemy fire.[8] There was little left with which to fight when Japanese ground troops poured onto the island. Wainright and those still alive were taken prisoner and, like the exhausted remnants of the forces on Bataan, were marched off to spend the rest of the war in prison camps.

Among those who were captured was Lemnitzer's Filipino clerk, when he was in charge of Corregidor's power station. In the general's papers is a letter from Sergio I. Villanueva, who wrote of being captured and the fates of others in the garrison when the Japanese conquered the island.

Lemnitzer left the island in 1934, and it wasn't until 1955 that Villaneuva finished a twenty-year quest to locate him. By then, Lemnitzer was commanding general of U.S. Army forces in the Far East. In his letter he wrote:

"Humble as it may be, yet your former clerk at the old power plant in Corregidor cannot forget his old boss who was with him in Bataan before the war catching those doing illegal logging... the fishing off the engineer dock with little Billy. My association with my lieutenant was very close."[9] ("Little Billy" was Lemnitzer's son. Many years later, a retired general himself, he recalled one of the fishing trips as the occasion for one of life's small "miracles": A long wait without a bite ended one day when he pulled in a large, very dead red snapper. Such a species is not, of course, native to Philippine waters; moreover, this one was frozen solid. When he was older, he learned that his amazing "catch" was from the post commissary, put there by an underwater-swimming fort employee in return for a small gratuity from his father.)[10]

There is ample evidence in Lemnitzer's papers that the years he spent in the Far East—in the Philippines as a junior officer and after the Korean War as a general—were special to him. A prolific letter writer, he corresponded with friends he had made in the islands, Korea, and Japan long after he had gone on to assignments in Washington and Europe. His fondness for the people, the countries in which he had served, and the good times he had spent in each come through often in his letters and notes to old acquaintances. The Corregidor upon which Lemnitzer took up station had much more serious things going on than the fragrance of tropical flowers and the easy ways of peacetime garrison life would suggest. Although much of the world might have shown little concern about long-range Japanese military intentions in the first part of the twentieth century, those Americans who took over the defense of the Philippines after the Spanish-American War had been worrying about this threat since early in the century. Corregidor, with its flanking islands, was the key to the defense of Manila, a truth of which Japan was aware, as evidenced in the considerable amount of obvious spying that went on from as early as 1910.[11]

The post was a "real going place," in his words, when Lemnitzer arrived for duty. His mission, according to his first efficiency report: "ordinary garrison duties." Whatever the mission might have looked like through the eyes of a junior second lieutenant, the fort's command was busily involved in living up to its quite awesome designation as the Philippines's "keep." In the event of attack or invasion, this was to be the ultimate redoubt, the invincible bastion to which the government would flee until the enemy could be turned back by reinforcements from the United States.[12]

Although the fort's garrison was confident that it could carry out its mission of guarding the bay from sea attack, the certainty that war would bring air assaults and artillery fire from the jungles flanking Manila Bay had convinced senior coast artillery officers that a much more effective counterbattery capability was needed and that Corregidor's gun emplacements needed better protection. The twelve-inch disappearing guns, as awesome as they could be in operation, were fixed, flat-trajectory weapons with only limited effectiveness when directed against the many valleys, ravines, and reverse slopes of Bataan. Corregidor's pride, two long-range twelve-inch guns with barbette carriages, could fire a seven hundred-pound shell 29,500 yards into the sea or jungle, but they, too, had a serious drawback: like all other main Corregidor guns, they were in open, fixed mounts. When war came, they were easy targets for Japanese howitzers and mortars on Bataan.[13]

This dilemma could have been averted, although it would have done no more than slow the inevitability of the conquest of the island. Repeated requests for armored turrets were turned down in Washington because they were expensive and hard to maintain. One measure that might have somewhat evened the odds in the coming conflict was the dispatch to Corregidor in 1921 of twelve big 240-millimeter howitzers from World War I's Western Front. With high trajectories capable of searching Bataan's ravines, they were eagerly awaited by the gunners on Manila Bay's designated "keep." But they got no further than Pearl Harbor; Washington had decided that the Japanese threat could be better cooled by diplomatic means.[14]

The Army assumed, rightly it turned out, that the most likely point from which the Japanese would concentrate an attack was the Bataan peninsula, so much of Lemnitzer's first tour was spent there in supervising the construction of roads and the laying out of defensive positions in the thick jungle. It was strenuous work, but Lemnitzer liked it—indeed, as he told an interviewer many years later, "those defensives which we were surveying and constructing, and things of that character, made military service very attractive."[15]

However ineffective Corregidor was in stemming the Japanese ground and air onslaught, in fairness it should be pointed out that in its primary mission—that of denying Manila Bay to an enemy fleet—it was eminently successful. As a seacoast defensive bastion, the Rock was exceedingly powerful, with guns and mortars that could make short work of any kind of sea assault an enemy could mount. Japanese agents had been spying on the island for years, and coast artillerymen there were convinced that no Japanese admiral would risk bringing his ships within thirty thousand yards of its guns. They were right: while Corregidor was in American hands, it never had to fire a shot in anger in support of its primary mission.

By Lemnitzer's second tour on Corregidor, in the early 1930s, the stronghold was well on its way to being written off, a victim of ineffective diplomatic agreements limiting armament improvements and America's decision in 1934 to give the Philippines its independence in 1946. The long-anticipated decision virtually halted further U.S. expenditures on improvements for installations that were soon to be turned over to a new foreign country.[16] Only when its entrance into World War II was just months away would the United States belatedly begin to bolster its Philippines forces.

The Harding administration's repeated slashings of military budgets was at its grassroots worst during Lemnitzer's first tour—from December 1923 to March 1926. While the coast artillery high command wrestled with ways to improve firepower and protection, those responsible for the day-to-day operations at the "Gibraltar of the East" had to economize to absurd lengths. Prisoners in the post stockade foraged for metal scrap to sell on the commercial market in Manila to raise money to buy barbed wire for Corregidor's beach defenses. A plan to convert the Rock hospital's coal heating plant to more efficient oil was denied because oil would cost $185 more a year than coal.[17]

Corregidor's most effective weapons during the Japanese siege were its two twelve-inch mortar batteries of twelve mortars each. These weapons were of the type in which Lemnitzer had become expert during his tour at Fort Adams. He expected to be assigned to either batteries Way or Geary where these squat and deadly mounts were concentrated, but much of his time seemed to be spent on typical junior officer tasks, aptly summed up in one efficiency report as "usual garrison duties." For Lemnitzer, these included being in charge of a riflery range, teaching small arms marksmanship, handling supply duties, and several unspecified "temporary" assignments.

His OER ratings during his first stint on the Rock gave no indication that the young Pennsylvanian had much of a future in the Army. His first OER deemed him to be "a good all-around average officer," above average only in physical endurance. An endorsing officer added that he was also above average in attention to duty and force (the latter defined in the OER as "the faculty of carrying out with energy and resolution that which on examination is believed reasonable, right, or duty").

The next report, covering a five-month period, was also lukewarm. The lieutenant was average in everything, "a faithful and hard worker—very painstaking with any task assigned him." The "average" label still stuck the next time around. His rater, Capt. Clyde L. Walker, commander of A Battery, went a little further, writing: "He is a good officer and on artillery work functions well (and) on other duties his performance is average. On some routine duties he needs supervision, as a fair performance satisfies him." The first endorsing officer, the battalion commander, concurred in the overall "average" assessment, but added his opinion that Lemnitzer was "above average" as an instructor, in military bearing, neatness, attention to duty, and intelligence.

But that was not good enough for the second endorsing officer, the 59th Coast Artillery regimental commander, who took issue with Walker's comments thus: "I do not think the foregoing report, particularly the remarks under Para. N [Capt. Walker's], gives a just impression of this young officer. He has been under my observation for the past eighteen months, during which he has shown a high degree of devotion to duty and has obtained excellent results in all his work, especially for an officer of his years. He is above average in capabilities and in the manner of performance of his duties."

The author of this unusual rebuttal was Col. Stanley D. Embick, a brilliant coast artilleryman and extraordinarily outspoken strategic planner who twelve years later would be in Washington as chief of the Army's War Plans Division. A vocal and persuasive opponent of any move that would get his country into war, Embick would in any other era of U.S. history undoubtedly have been summarily cashiered for so flagrantly venturing into an area in which, if military officers speak at all, they do so through their civilian superiors.

But that was years off, although even as a colonel Embick rarely hesitated to speak his mind on military or diplomatic affairs, no matter who was listening. In June 1925, when he wrote out his dissent of a subordinate's views regarding

Lemnitzer, he was an officer running a regiment and part of his job was to ensure that his officers were treated fairly. In righting a perceived wrong and becoming an active admirer of Lemnitzer's potential, Embick probably had a longer lasting effect on the Army than he ever had as a high-level strategic planner.

When biographers examine a successful military career, they look for factors that bring men to the top in this most competitive of professions. Often the reasons are easy to spot: success in battle or obvious all-around brilliance. More frequently, though, the impetus is a senior officer exercising a leader's duty to find promising young men and help them along. George C. Marshall was an outstanding example of such a leader: many of those who achieved high rank during World War II owed their climbs to being included in the famous notebook in which for over twenty years Marshall wrote the names of talented officers he had met during his various assignments.

Lemnitzer's name was not on Marshall's list,[18] as were those of such more senior officers as Dwight Eisenhower, Mark Clark, and George Patton, but it is clear that he was very high on Embick's—if he had one. Although Lemnitzer had to prove himself each step of the way, there can be no other plausible explanation of how this quiet, unassuming lieutenant from an insular and dying branch eventually advanced in his profession as quickly as he did.

Lemnitzer did a little better in his next OER; Captain Walker gave him an "above average" rating and conceded that he "is a good steady reliable worker who has initiative . . ." and who "is learning to accept responsibility and is paying more attention to details. He is above the average as well as one of the best of the younger officers I have had serve under me." Once again, Embick was not satisfied: in his endorsement, he gave Lemnitzer a top rating of superior for his supervision of the reconstruction of a small-arms range, citing him as above average in training recruits and instructing in small-arms. He added: "His work has been consistently of so high an order that I regard him as an unusually dependable and promising young officer."

Lemnitzer had reasons for feelings of déjà vu in February 1925, when he was ordered to appear before a promotion board and four months later became a first lieutenant again, a rank he would hold for the next ten years. Making room for first lieutenants is much easier in today's Army; back then, the event that made Lemnitzer's elevation possible was the promotion to captain of another first lieutenant somewhere in the Quartermaster Corps.

Another of the reasons Lemnitzer had to remember peacetime Corregidor with fondness was a fine nine-hole golf course. Since heretofore he could have had little opportunity to play the game, it is probable that among the facets the Rock added to his makeup was a lifelong love of golf. References to games with friends, the peculiarities of various clubs and courses, and the play of famous professionals appear frequently in his personal correspondence. One of his first moves during stops on official trips or upon arriving at a new post was to check out the local golf courses. His twelve-stroke handicap did not make him an opponent to be feared, but the powerfully built Lemnitzer was famed in Army golfing circles for his prodigious drive. His iron and greens play, though, left something to be desired, according to fellow Honesdalian Art Wall, Jr., a onetime national Masters champion with whom Lemnitzer played when both were home. Wall termed these aspects of the mid-1980s enthusiast's game as "shaky."[19]

The young lieutenant remembered his off-duty life as the most pleasant of his career up to that time. He and Kay lived on what he called "one of the nicest houses on Corregidor—right up on top of a rock six hundred feet above the China Sea." He was paid $142.50 a month, enough to afford three servants at the going rates for domestic help in the Philippines. On his second tour, when he was making a little bit more, he was even able to afford a second hand 1926 Chevrolet.[20]

He was ordered back to Fort Adams in the spring of 1926 for four months of duty as a battery commander and for "ordinary garrison training," in the words of an efficiency report that cited him as "above average" and described him as a "very efficient and reliable officer. Very industrious. Has the faculty of meeting a problem and working at it until solved without calling for assistance." He was dropped to "average" in the next report, earning this rather sour comment from the 10th Coast Artillery commander: "Intelligent. Good appearance. Somewhat unobservant and lacking in snap."

During this tour, Kay gave birth in June to their first child, Lois. "Sparky" to her friends and "Loie" to her younger brother, she shared her father's love of the outdoors, often accompanying him on fishing trips. In one of his letters, he tells proudly of her shooting a deer while hunting in New York State; in others, he tells of things they had done together in the many years that she accompanied him and her mother in his various assignments. In the early 1950s she received press attention when she made a civilian jump from an airplane at Fort Campbell, Kentucky, shortly after her father had just qualified at age fifty-one for a parachutist's badge after completing the jump course at Fort Benning, Georgia.[21] Her marriage in 1959 to a Lemnitzer aide, Lt. Henry Simpson, ended in divorce some years later.

Lemnitzer's next assignment made it clear that he had been marked as a "comer." In August 1926 he was appointed to the faculty at West Point where he was assigned to the academy's Department of Natural and Experimental Philosophy. Whatever the name might have suggested in the way of course content, the department was where Lemnitzer taught physics, mechanics, hydraulics, thermodynamics, and aerodynamics.

He did very well. In his first OER, his department head rated him as "above average" overall; a top "superior" in military bearing and neatness, and attention to duty and force; and concluded that he was "a young officer of great promise." His rating climbed to "excellent" in the next report. In the next two, his overall mark was "superior." In one, his rater wrote that in peacetime he should be a captain, in war a major. Col. C. C. Carter, his department head, called him "one of the most efficient and best young officers I have ever known. I know of none better." In his last OER he was rated "superior" in every category, and for the first time he was repeatedly lauded for a quality that was to stand him in spectacular stead in future years: the ability to interact well with civilians.

A faculty tour at the Military Academy with its scenic and historic surroundings is a pleasant existence, and there is evidence that Lemnitzer liked teaching and was popular with the cadets. Hamilton H. Howze, a member of the Class of 1930 and a future four-star general, studied mathematics under Lemnitzer and recalls that he had an extraordinary ability to reduce complicated concepts to simple and understandable terms.[22] In later years this was one of the traits most frequently mentioned by those seeking to single out the factors that contributed to his remarkable career.

The only glitch on the record during his tour was a query from the adjutant at Fort Adams as to why he had taken so long to report to West Point, the inference being that he had started out his new assignment by being absent without leave. It turned out that he was too junior for quarters on post and had been forced to scour surrounding communities by train at the last minute to find a home for his wife and infant daughter, all within the letter of his transfer orders. He finally found a place in Cornwall, some ten miles up the Hudson River, and all was forgiven.[23]

In looking through Lemnitzer's OERs from his short second stay at Fort Adams and considering its adjutant's seemingly picayune parting shot over a few hours of travel leave, one can sense a coolness that is out of keeping with the glowing reports that preceded him from Corregidor and followed at West Point. Maybe it was just that the commanders at the Narragansett Bay facility didn't find him as impressive as those at his previous and future posts. More likely he ran into some commanders who didn't like their fort being used as a brief parking place for a young hotshot who obviously had just been moved onto the coast artillery's fast track. Jealousy is not an unheard-of trait in the competitive world of military career advancement.

West Point was the birthplace in December 1928 of a son, William Lyman Lemnitzer, the "Little Billy" referred to in the letter from the father's former clerk at Corregidor. William became a soldier, too, graduating fifth overall in the West Point Class of 1951, and first in chemistry, physics, electricity, and thermodynamics. He was the second in his class to become a general (the first was Edward C. Meyer, a future chief of staff of the Army), and was involved in a brilliant career when he suffered a stroke in 1973 and was forced by disability to retire as a brigadier general. He was an artillery officer who at the height of his career was heavily involved in high-level nuclear warfare contingency planning. William was an outstanding staff officer like his father, following up extensive field duty with assignments in the Office of the JCS, in the White House as Army liaison officer to Henry Kissinger when he was national security adviser to the president, and as division chief in the Tactical Nuclear Section of the Strategic Plans and Policy Directorate. Still involved in nuclear studies as "a hobby," he and his wife, Lydia, live in Arlington, Virginia, and have three sons. One, William F., an Army artillery officer like his father and grandfather, is the only Lemnitzer still on active military duty.

When Lemnitzer's tour of duty was up in 1930, he was sent back to Fort Monroe to attend the coast artillery's nine-month battery officer's course, a necessary step for officers slated for higher command. One of the few official pictures taken of him during his early career shows him, typically solemn of face, standing in the rear ranks of the 1931 graduating class, the Army Distinguished Marksman's Medal displayed prominently on his chest.

Once again, his final OER was lavish in its praise: "An exceptionally fine officer who will perform in a superior manner any task assigned to him. He has a pleasing personality, poise, dignity and ability."

Upon his graduation, the Coast Artillery School's commandant sent a "Special School Report" to the adjutant general in Washington, noting that Lemnitzer had finished with a "Superior" rating and adding a recommendation that would turn out to be prophetic: "Believed to be specially qualified for General Staff training at the proper time."

It was signed by Lemnitzer's champion from Corregidor days, Stanley D. Embick, a new brigadier general and only a few months back from four years as executive officer of the War Plans Division of the War Department General Staff.

5

✯ ✯ ✯ ✯

BROWN SHOE DAYS

In a branch noted for its insularity and single-minded devotion to its mission of defending America's shores, Stanley Embick was, to put it mildly, an exception. To be sure, he was a superb coast artillery commander—one of the best in the arm's long history—but he is remembered chiefly for his considerable role in national strategic policy in the crucial years just before the nation entered World War II.

Like Lemnitzer, he was a Pennsylvanian who graduated from the U.S. Military Academy two months before Lemnitzer was born. His aptitude for staff duty was recognized early in his career, and by the First World War he was serving as chief of staff to the general who was the U.S. delegate to the Supreme War Council, the agency that coordinated Allied military activities in World War I. In 1935, Gen. Douglas MacArthur, then the Army's chief of staff, ordered him to Washington to head the War Plans Division, a post in which he would eventually be succeeded by George C. Marshall, America's wartime Army chief of staff.

War clouds were gathering over Europe, and there was intense discussion at the highest military and political levels over what America's role should be in a future conflict. It was not in Embick's nature to give a staff officer's salute and say "Yes, sir!" when he disagreed with a policy, plan, or superior officer, and very soon he was in the thick of arguments that had service pitted against service and government official against government official. Embick campaigned forcefully for staying out of war by getting our forces out of the Pacific beyond a line from Alaska to Oahu to Panama, even going so far as to personally give a copy of his proposal to President Franklin D. Roosevelt.[1]

Embick distrusted the French and British, especially Winston Churchill, pointing to his own experiences on the Supreme War Council in World War I and the Peace Conference after it to support his convictions that the European powers were bent on drawing America into a war in which it did not belong and for which it was not prepared. He favored appeasement of Germany's Adolph Hitler if it would prevent war and said so publicly. Some of his military colleagues and others in government agreed with him, but when it became apparent that Roosevelt was hardening the U.S. position in the Far East, Embick went outside of official channels and threw his active support to private peace organizations whose views coincided with his own.[2]

An officer of today would look on this scenario with horror. Persons in uniform, certainly not a career officer with ambition, do not go into the civilian sector in an effort to influence official policy. The wonder is that Embick's powerful espousal of his cause was permitted in the first place, even from his lofty position as head of the important War Plans Division. No congressmen called for his head nor, as far as is known, was he summoned by the Army chief of staff for a verbal dressing down and exile to the command of some far-off coast artillery outpost. One factor in his favor might have been that Douglas MacArthur, the Army chief, was a rebel, too, a proclivity that was to result during the Korean War in the most famous military sacking in the nation's history.

Embick regarded himself as a soldier-statesman, a description that would one day be attached to Lemnitzer, and with good reason. Highly regarded in the Army for his brilliance in the field of grand strategy, Embick's usually minority and often unpopular views were respected because of his unquestioned loyalty, integrity, and ability to make a strong case. The president and astute men like Marshall solicited his opinions and analyses, often agreeing with him on major points while ending up going in other directions.[3]

Pearl Harbor ended any chance that a policy of isolationism had any chance of prevailing, particularly in regard to the Pacific. But Embick was not through; after Pearl Harbor, he opposed British desires for an early landing in North Africa (ironically, Lemnitzer would be one of the chief architects of the Africa invasion plans).

Embick spent the war as a Marshall-appointed member of the influential Joint Strategic Survey Committee (JSSC), a group of three senior generals and an admiral from the Army, Navy, and Army Air Corps who advised the JCS on strategy. He retired as a lieutenant general in 1946 and, coincidentally, was succeeded on the JSSC by Lemnitzer, then a major general.

Lemnitzer apparently kept in contact with Embick over the years, possibly the last time being in 1954 when he wrote a friend: "I have not seen Gen. Embick recently but talked to him by phone. He was very exercised about the possibility of our going into Indochina. I assured him that we here at the Army were opposed to such action and I have not heard from him since."[4] Embick died in 1957.

The general held those with whom he served, particularly subordinates, to high standards. He was one of the services' foremost intellectuals, and it is doubtful that he would have been so lavish in his praise or would have pushed Lemnitzer toward General Staff duty so diligently if Lemnitzer had been merely a superior line officer. Embick took a lively interest in Corregidor's junior officers, testing and sharpening their intellectual capacities by assigning them study topics in such areas as foreign affairs, economics, and politics. The officers would then prepare reports on their subjects and present them for discussion at post meetings conducted by the general.[5]

It could be wondered if Embick would have been as ardent in his support if he could have foreseen that his protégé would one day become one of the armed forces's leading advocates of international alliances and one of their most skilled practitioners in the art of making them work. Embick was a professional, however, and it is highly doubtful that his bias toward joining in alliances would have altered his judgment of Lemnitzer's potential. Moreover, it could also be reasonably conjectured that in the power-struggle years following World War II a leader as astute as Embick would have found good reason to change his mind about the viability of isolationism.

When he had finished the battery officers' course, Lemnitzer was ordered to return to Corregidor. He, his wife, and their children sailed for the far-off station in August 1931 to begin a tour that would last until September 1934 and would encompass an assignment in which his success would seemingly clinch Embick's earlier belief that he had picked a winner in his fellow Pennsylvanian from Honesdale.

When he reported to the Rock, he was assigned to "routine guard and battery duty," which consisted of being adjutant of the 92nd Coast Artillery Regiment's Third Battalion while also serving as the officer in charge of "Barrio Concepcion." The latter assignment, in which he received special praise from Corregidor's commandant, apparently consisted of overseeing a post housing area, or "barrio."[6]

Lemnitzer came back to a fort that was trying mightily with limited resources to make itself better able to withstand a Japanese attack its officers were convinced was coming sometime soon. In 1931 a Japanese army began the conquest of Manchuria as a prelude to an all-out effort later to subdue China. The apprehensions Corregidor's defenders and their Filipino colleagues had harbored since early in the century were beginning to be realized.

Stymied in their attempts to obtain funds to protect their batteries from plunging artillery fire and air bombardment, the fort found other ways to protect its defenders. During the first year of Lemnitzer's return, the commandant, Brig. Gen. Charles E. Kilbourne, stated matter-of-factly in routine dispatches that the fort was going to build a "tunnel road" through huge Malinta Hill for the convenience of those at the Air Corps garrison at Kindley Field on the tail end of Corregidor.

In fact, the burrowing was to create an extensive headquarters and supply complex that would be protected from artillery fire from Bataan in the event of war.[7]

Kilbourne used post maintenance funds, old mine-drilling equipment, and prison labor to begin the gigantic task. Embick, who succeeded Kilbourne as commandant, carried on by lining the main corridor and cross-tunnels with concrete and adding large storage areas, all the while avoiding official notice outside of the Coast Artillery Corps. (It was said to have had the tacit approval of Maj. Gen. John W. Gulick, chief of the Coast Artillery Corps, who reportedly allowed no discussion of the project's real purpose at his headquarters.)[8] Substantially completed by 1938, the tunnel was to become famous as the last redoubt of Army forces in World War II.

While all this high-level maneuvering was going on, Lemnitzer was garnering more admiration for the way he handled his duties. His rater in early 1932 wrote: "I consider this officer to be outstanding in capacity and efficiency. He has excellent judgment, much initiative and considerable ability. He is socially inclined and has a very attractive personality." Again, he was cited for his ability to get along with civilians.

During his second tour at Corregidor, Lemnitzer apparently served in a "swing" capacity, spending never more than a few months in any single position. From battalion adjutant and barrio officer, he became, in turn, commander of Batteries E and F, earning OER ratings of "superior." Next, he was plans and training officer and then put in charge of the subsistence branch of a supply headquarters, where his work in handling a commissary and large reserve stocks brought a commendation of "excellent" from the harbor defense quartermaster. The latter tried to bring about a career change for Lemnitzer, noting that he had displayed "special qualifications" for Quartermaster Corps work and "highly" recommending that he be transferred at once to the Corps.

But that was not to be, for the fort had a new commandant who had other plans for the lieutenant's future. General Embick was back in charge of the Rock, and it was clear that once again he had his eye on Lemnitzer. But commanders sometimes have what might seem to a subordinate strange ways of showing favor to those they are bringing along. Lemnitzer stayed under the immediate command of the post quartermaster for the rest of his tour, presumably not by preference, because he kept his line officer status despite repeated indications from the quartermasters that they would like to keep him. Captain A. L. Littell, the quartermaster, termed him "an excellent officer in every respect," and put him in charge of the post's supply branch, where he received top marks for attention to duty, tact, intelligence, force, judgment and common sense, and leadership.

Embick added an interesting observation in his endorsement of Lemnitzer's next OER: "Qualified to command a battalion in peace or war"—pretty heady stuff for a first lieutenant to read considering that battalions are usually commanded by lieutenant colonels.

In 1933 Lemnitzer was given an assignment that might well have been the career clincher that assured a successful future by convincing the hard-to-please Embick once and for all that his kudos had been justified. Lemnitzer was made the officer in charge of Corregidor's diesel power plant.

In an ordinary post, this might be the sort of assignment that would be dumped off on a junior officer, along with slots like laundry or morale officer; power plant crews don't need an officer to keep their place running. But Corregidor's electricity generating plant was no ordinary one; it was at the vital heart of the island's defenses because, among other things, it supplied power to its guns and mortars.[9] Located in a ravine on the Bataan side of the island and buried under a nine-foot-thick concrete cover, the plant would become a prime target when the Japanese began shelling the island in 1942.

Like so much of the coast artillery's assets, the plant was obsolete and Embick and his commanders wanted this key part of the fort's operations to be brought up to more modern standards. Lemnitzer was given the job of supervising installation of new generators, rehabilitating the entire system and reorganizing the operation and personnel on a military basis. Considering the importance of the installation, the task assigned to Lemnitzer clearly was one that would normally have gone to an officer more senior in rank.

Although nothing in Lemnitzer's background indicated that he knew anything about electric power generation before the assignment, his written reports on progress indicate an impressive knowledge of the workings of diesel engines and allied operations. Embick wrote in an OER after Lemnitzer had assumed charge that he was performing his mission with "conspicuous success." With that, he upped his assessment of what the lieutenant should be commanding: In peace, a battalion; in war, a regiment.

When Lemnitzer finished his ten-month powerhouse stint to take charge of the island's transportation division, things were running so smoothly at the plant that Embick wrote this passage on his efficiency report: "Although an outstanding artillery officer, and with no experience in quartermaster work, he was especially selected, because of exceptional dependability, to rehabilitate the central power plant and reorganize its personnel on a military basis. He has performed this work with notable success."

Finally, Embick gave this extraordinary accolade: "He is qualified to command a regiment in peace OR war." Regiments are commanded by full colonels; by this time, Lemnitzer had been a lieutenant for fourteen years.

His superiors had one more assignment for him before he left Corregidor for good in 1934. He headed up an investigation into large-scale illegal logging by Filipinos on the island and on the Bataan Peninsula. His written reports of seeking evidence and pursuing elusive wood poachers through heavy jungle and along rocky beaches are those of a plainly frustrated junior officer who knew he would never bring his quarries to justice. And his final report indicates that, indeed, he never did.

West Point beckoned again at the end of his Corregidor tour, and he returned in September 1934 to teach, impressing the head of the Department of Natural and Experimental Philosophy as being superbly grounded in the applied sciences, and hydraulic and mechanical engineering.[10] In later years, he would look back with fondness on his teaching years at the Military Academy and Fort Monroe as a "great educational process for me. An instructor learns more as an instructor than he does as a student in a course because you have to be ahead of all the people you're teaching."[11]

West Point offered him a permanent place on its faculty as an assistant professor, a tenured position that could eventually lead to a full professorship. It was a tempting offer for an officer who had been a lieutenant for nearly fifteen years and saw no immediate hope that things would soon get any better. Choosing the academic life offered many advantages: steady, if slow promotion; security and a long career; and the satisfaction of helping prepare young cadets to become officers. But Lemnitzer wanted to stay in the Army's mainstream; he looked ahead and saw war with either Germany or Japan as inevitable. When that happened, promotions would come, and so he turned the West Point offer down.

Congress saw the same ominous signs, and while Lemnitzer was teaching at the Academy, ordered a sharp expansion of the Corps of Cadets, from 1,374 to 1,960, with a proportionate expansion in its physical plant.[12] It was an uncharacteristic move for the times; Washington's lawmakers had been ruthless in slashing defense spending and the services' officer corps to exceedingly dangerous levels. But in doing so, the congressmen had been reflecting a national antipathy toward the military, part of it a lingering revulsion from World War I and another part preoccupation with the effects of the Depression. Antimilitary demonstrations were widespread and citizen apathy toward preparedness the majority sentiment as the nation fought to survive in the Depression.

The move to beef up the officer corps was led by far-thinking congressmen who saw grim tidings for the United States in Hitler's aggressive posturing and the buildup of Germany's armed forces. In 1935 the Army's officer total had dropped to 13,470, its lowest level since the war.[13] Raising this number apparently seemed like a good place to start if something was going to be done about military readiness. The Army's enlisted strength was 126,000,[14] its heart centered in three substrength, under equipped infantry divisions whose components were spread around the country because the service lacked the transportation resources to get them together. Depleted to near-suicidal levels by fifteen years of bare subsistence because of steadily decreasing defense budgets, it was an Army that had to train using telephone poles painted black to simulate cannons while charging across fields behind trucks daubed with the word "tank" in big letters. Ammunition was a precious resource, to be doled out like diamonds for small-arms practice and usually not at all for sharpening skills on the big guns and mortars of the coast artillery. Equipment was largely World War I surplus, obsolete and worn-out.[15]

The "Brown Shoe Army" of Lemnitzer's junior officer years—so-called because regulation footwear in the 1930s was brown in color—is recalled with nostalgia today, but mostly by people who never served in it. Pay was abysmally low, even by civilian Depression standards, and what training units could afford consisted chiefly of day-after-day repetitions of routine drill, map-reading, road marches, and the "dry" loading and unloading of machine guns and cannons.[16] The cleaning and repair of equipment consumed much of the time with frequent inspections being ends in themselves. Life in the ranks was monastic; it had to be because, among other things, soldiers beneath the top grades of sergeant were not permitted to be married. Promotion was slow, and the Army could be so selective that in the Coast Artillery Corps, for one, if a sergeant who was a candidate for promotion to technical or master sergeant failed his examinations twice he was reduced in rank to private.[17]

An officer's life was better, but the promotion outlook was just as dismal. For all Embick's status and influence, he was not able to obtain for Lemnitzer the obvious reward for superior performance: promotion to the next higher rank. Even though he could state that the young man was qualified to command a regiment, there just weren't any available slots for a captain in the coast artillery long after Lemnitzer became eligible.

That ended August 1, 1935, when Lemnitzer was at last elevated to captain by order of the secretary of war. Prodded by Army Chief of Staff MacArthur, Congress passed a bill which decreed that any officer who had been a lieutenant for at least ten years would receive an automatic promotion to captain. The measure also provided that fifteen years of service entitled an officer to be advanced to major. Lemnitzer's time in a lieutenant's grade met this requirement, too, but it would be five more years before he would become a major.

The news of his promotion to captain reached Lemnitzer as he was beginning a posting that he was to remember many years later as an important turning point in his career. The assignment was the Army's Command & General Staff College (C&GSC) at Fort Leavenworth, Kansas—a "must" stop for officers slated for higher command. It was a demanding course whose subjects covered almost every aspect of command and staff functions that a company or field grade officer could expect to experience. Emphasis was heavily on "how to" because there was little time to explain "why." Infantry and cavalry combat, logistics and organization up to corps level were studied in minute detail with heavy attention to historical illustration through analysis of past battlefield successes and failures. It was an impressive and mind-boggling example of the curriculum assembler's art, an intensive nine-month cram course which must have been as formidable a test for those who finished it as they would ever face in their entire careers outside of actual battle. (It is significant and a reflection of the times that this high-powered schedule found time for daily mandatory classes in horseback riding.)[18]

Adding to the challenge was the fact that previous classes had lasted two years and, as Lemnitzer ruefully recalled years afterward, everything that had been covered in that period before was crammed into nine months for the Class of 1935–36. A Chinese Army major who was in his class expressed the general bewilderment with his comment: "Most peculiar school—many questions, no answers."[19]

Coast artillery officers who made it into the prestigious school had a reputation for being serious, hard-working students. They had to be; study was devoted almost exclusively to the infantry and cavalry arms, with some air support. These and their supporting elements, such as field and air artillery, were the heart of Army field operations, and they were accustomed to working together, as much as budget and distance constraints would permit. Until its demise after World War II, the coast artillery was a branch apart. Those who manned its guns had little or no contact with the other combat arms and needed none. It is significant that in all the courses, seminars, and exercises that made up the curriculum in the 1935–36 school year, there was no mention whatsoever of the coast artillery.

Besides having to keep up in advanced classes in unfamiliar fields, the C&GSC's coast artillerymen came from a proud branch whose remoteness from the Army's mainstream made them an odd lot in the eyes of many of their colleagues in the more conventional arms. In a sense, they were on trial when, on rare occasions like being selected to attend the Fort Leavenworth school, they were able to mingle with other officers. With the branch's honor on the line, they worked very hard to make a commendable showing.

Many years later, Lemnitzer recalled appointment to the C&GSC as a "major and dramatic development in my military education. Until that time, my military education had been devoted primarily to the study of techniques and tactics of the coast artillery. At the C&GSC, however, we studied for the first time how to employ the Army's combat arms and services in combination, and thus we became acutely aware that the coordinated and integrated use of the separate arms and services provide far more powerful and effective forces than the sum of their individual parts. You learned how to function as a team instead of being just one of the players."[20]

Lemnitzer graduated twenty-seventh with a top rating of "superior" in a class of one hundred eleven, which included seven other coast artillerymen and two future U.S. Air Force chiefs of staff: Lt. Col. Carl Spaatz, who held the post immediately after World War II, and Capt. Hoyt S. Vandenberg, who was chief during the Korean War.

For the next three years after graduating in June 1936, Lemnitzer was an instructor in the Department of Tactics behind the familiar old walls of Fort Monroe. Much had changed at the venerable bastion since Lemnitzer's last tour as a student in the battery officers course at the beginning of the decade. Two powerful hurricanes in 1933 had destroyed many of the buildings while causing extensive damage to the grounds. The same year, the post lost 60 percent of its staff and faculty to training and supervising the Civilian Conservation Corps (CCC), a Depression-spawned institution which created jobs for young men by assigning them to public works projects. Fort Monroe had also become a training center for thousands of the CCC volunteers.[21]

The installation had suffered along with the rest of the Army in obtaining funds for training and equipment, but by the time Lemnitzer arrived for his third tour the fort was on the crest of a massive building boom created by the general infusion of government funds across the country to counteract the effects of the Depression. Not since its founding had there been such extensive construction of fortifications, office buildings, housing, unit facilities, training areas, and roads. Undoubtedly to Lemnitzer's delight, Army engineers had even rebuilt the golf course that had been destroyed during the hurricanes.[22]

The future general's comment in later years that an instructor learns more about a course of study than his students was put to the test at the school's Department of Tactics. The coast artillery's increasing emphasis on antiaircraft defense that began after World War I was evident in the attention being given in course work and area field exercises. But the corps's traditional role in protecting the nation's shores against attacks from the sea was still important; Lemnitzer's son William, by then approaching his teens, can remember he and his father watching demonstrations of firepower by such old standbys as the twelve-inch disappearing gun and the newer three-inch antiaircraft cannon. Lemnitzer's three years at Fort Monroe were an invaluable grounding in the state of the coast artillery's art as it existed on the eve of America's entry into another world war.

He continued to draw "superior" ratings during his years on Fort Monroe's faculty. Among the comments on his OERs: "An unusually alert, bright officer of immaculate appearance"; "even-tempered and tactful"; "keen mentally, well-read"; "... brilliant mind, a soldierly bearing and an attractive personality.... [O]f the officers of his grade whom I have known in the service I rate him among the best."

Austria and Czechoslovakia had fallen to Hitler, and Poland was about to be crushed by the German juggernaut as Lemnitzer wound up his tour at Fort Monroe at the end of the summer of 1939. Despite the worsening war picture in Europe, America's eventual entry into any world conflict was by no means viewed as inevitable by the nation as it began to emerge from the worst of the Depression in the late 1930s. Its soldiers would be fighting in the most devastating war in the world's history in a little over two years, but in 1939 Lemnitzer's Army was largely a garrison force in which neatness, smartness in close-order drill, and, among officers, social correctness were highly esteemed qualities.

It was soon after one of the latter manifestations of the good life that the approaching war came home, after a fashion, to the officers at Fort Monroe. The social event of the summer of 1939 was a reception and party at the post's Beach Club for the officers of the British heavy cruiser HMS *Exeter*, which was making a port visit at nearby Hampton Roads. The *Exeter's* officers repaid the courtesy by inviting the Fort Monroe officers to a party at their ship, and by the time it sailed off many friendships had been made between future allies.[23]

Later in its voyage, the *Exeter* and its sister vessels, the *HMS Ajax* and the *HMNZS Achilles,* made naval history in one of the classic sea engagements of the war, the pursuit and cornering in South America of the German pocket battleship, *Graf Spee,* in December 1939. Badly damaged and outgunned in the running battle with the formidable sea raider, the *Exeter* and her light cruiser companions nevertheless hounded the *Graf Spee* so fiercely that it fled into the protection of neutral Uruguay's Montevideo Harbor. The battered warship was later scuttled outside of the harbor by its captain, who committed suicide three days later.

In less eventful times, perhaps, Lemnitzer might have served his three years in Fort Monroe's pleasant confines and gone on to another staff assignment or command as he moved up in his branch. Clearly, he was marked as an officer who was going to go a long way, and, in the normal peacetime scheme of things, ending his career as chief of the Coast Artillery Corps was not a remote possibility. But, again, perhaps this was never really in the cards: after all, General Embick, who had left the branch for bigger things himself, had early spotted Lemnitzer as General Staff material. The line from this discovery to the point at which this prediction came true was dotted with assignments that test and prepare those destined for high command.

A very big dot on such a path was then, as now, the Army War College, to which the service sent a highly select few of its most promising officers for a year's study. Lemnitzer was a forty-year-old captain in September 1939, when he made his first official trip to a city that he would come to know well in the years ahead—Washington, D.C., then the site of the Army War College. Located on an eighty-nine–acre peninsula between the Potomac and Anacostia rivers, and known then as both Fort Humphreys and the Washington Barracks, the post is today named for Lt. Gen. Lesley J. McNair, upon whose staff Lemnitzer was to serve and who was killed in Europe in World War II. Today it is the site of the National Defense University and the residences of some of the Army's most senior commanders, its quiet, campus-like atmosphere belying the bustle of the capital city around it and a lively two hundred-year-old history that included such episodes as the executions by hanging of the conspirators involved in the assassination of President Abraham Lincoln.

The mission of the War College, now located at Carlisle Barracks, Pennsylvania, was spelled out thus in War Department Regulation 350-5 (December 1927):

> a. To train officers in the conduct of field operations of the Army and higher eche-
> lons; and to instruct in those political, economic, and social matters which
> influence the conduct of war.

b. To instruct officers in War Department General Staff duties and those of the Office of the Assistant Secretary of War.

c. To train officers for joint operations of the Army and the Navy.

d. To instruct officers in the strategy, tactics and logistics of large operations in past wars, with special reference to the [First] World War.

The approaches to accomplishing this mission varied with the commandants over the years. Where the C&GSC provided a tightly structured curriculum in troop command and the techniques, tactics, and logistics of battle, the War College was concerned with a much broader picture. General of the Army Eisenhower, a graduate, defined this difference in a speech to students at the War College in 1966:

"...realizing that war involves every single facet of human existence and thinking, every asset that humans have developed, all of the resources of nature, here education deserts the formerly rather narrow business of winning a tactical victory on the battlefield; it is now concerned with the nation."[24]

Focuses on fields of study varied from year to year. From 1935 through 1940, classes in a major course on the position of the United States in world affairs were divided into five groups, each responsible for monitoring significant developments in a part of the world and reporting on them twice a week to the entire class. Visits to Civil War battlefields were part of the study, as were frequent addresses by prominent figures in government and the private sector. Spurred by increasing student and faculty interest in political and war developments in Europe, the classes of 1939 and 1940 were given regular intensive briefings on what was happening there by intelligence officers from the War Department's General Staff.

A highlight of Lemnitzer's class year was the study of the German campaign in Poland, a rare opportunity to analyze current German fighting tactics and doctrine made possible just nine months after the campaign was over by classified reports prepared by the Army's Military Intelligence Division.[25]

Committees of students made in-depth studies of issues ranging from national economic problems to such areas as the influence of public opinion on the conduct of war. There was heavy emphasis on high-level planning, in which students prepared detailed division, corps, and Army-level plans from mobilization to deployment in battle. Each student was required to present a paper during the year. Lemnitzer's presentation, again a reflection of the interest that would win him his greatest fame, urged that the State, War, and Naval departments work as a team in war planning. "Modern war is not fought on the military front alone, as was the case in wars in past centuries when professional soldiers were the only participants," he wrote. Calling for concentrated efforts by the three parties to understand each others' part in waging war, he noted that "war planning agencies will [always] be hampered in planning as long as civil heads of government fail to furnish them with concise and concrete expressions of national policy."[26]

Ironically, as it would prove in Lemnitzer's case, perceptions that America had been treated poorly by its allies in World War I were still ingrained in the officer corps of the late 1930s. There was a popular saying in the Class of 1940 that "if we have to go to war, let's do it without allies."[27]

One of the speakers during the year was Fox Connor, a wise retired major general who, as Dwight D. Eisenhower's mentor in his younger years, was credited by the future president as having been one of the most influential persons in his life. He was asked by a student after his talk if he thought Winston Churchill "is qualified to be awarded a diploma as a military and naval strategist." The British prime minister was already achieving a reputation in military circles as a not-always-welcome participant in planning strategy and tactics. Connor replied:

"Mr. Churchill was a trained soldier as a youngster and has certain abilities, but I think his abilities are political rather than soldierly. Personally, I would not sign his diploma, although it was to his credit that he admitted that a submarine might have difficulty attacking cavalry because of sand banks."[28]

Attendance at the Army War College had a significant effect on an officer's career. Fifty-two percent of all its graduates in the lean, slow-promotion years from 1920 to 1940 became generals. In 1945, considerably less than 1 percent of the over half-million officers on duty were graduates, but of the more than one thousand generals, over six hundred were graduates.[29]

Unlike at the C&GSC—generally a prerequisite for consideration for appointment to the War College—class rankings were not kept, a seemingly remarkable rule in a professional calling that places a powerful premium on competition. Maj. Gen. William D. Connor, commandant from 1928 to 1932, explained the War College rationale in his welcoming address to students in 1928:

"In a very large measure, the period of your self-development begins right now, for in this institution there are no marks applied to your daily work and there are no periodic tests or final examinations that you must undergo to show the faculty what progress you have made or what advantages you have accumulated during the year's work. From now on, you become, more than ever before, subject only to the critical judgment of your fellow officers."[30]

But the OER, as inevitable as death and traffic lights, knows no such moratoriums as those of the War College, and in June 1940, Brig. Gen. P. B. Peyton, the commandant, wrote a glowing assessment of Lemnitzer that summed up the traits most often cited by persons who would serve with him in the years ahead: "Cheerful, even disposition, patient, sense of humor, engaging personality, serious. Exceptionally good team worker, responds to leadership. Works rapidly, thoroughly, accurately, and methodically. Open-minded, appreciates views of others. Takes definite stands, determined, holds to his convictions, sure of himself. Broad-minded, views problems from all angles. Original, independent thinker, produces practical ideas, active imagination. Prompt with good judgment, clean-cut, exhibits firmness." The report rated him as "superior" academically and personally, and recommended him for general staff duty at War Department, army, corps, or division levels.

With the graduation of the Class of 1940, the War College ceased to exist as a learning institution for the duration of the coming war and beyond. In 1950 it was reestablished at Fort Leavenworth and the next year moved to its present location in Pennsylvania.

The Japanese attack on Pearl Harbor was a year and a half away when Lemnitzer, promoted to major on July 1, 1940, took command of a battalion and was also named S3, in charge of plans and operations, of the 70th Antiaircraft Regiment. Headquartered at Fort Moultrie, South Carolina, on Sullivan's Island at the entrance to Charleston Harbor, the fort was one of the most heavily gunned and oldest (established 1776) in the coast artillery system.

Lemnitzer continued to impress his raters: the fort commander, Brig. Gen. R. F. Cox, described him as an "exceptionally capable officer" ... having "a keen and logical mind" ... "his subordinates gladly put forth their best efforts for him. I would especially desire to have him under my command either in peace or war."

But this was not to be for very long. Less than four months after reporting to the South Carolina post, Lemnitzer was reassigned, this time to Camp Stewart, near Savannah, Georgia. There, he became executive officer of the 38th Antiaircraft Brigade. Among his duties was the supervision of the construction of a new training center for antiaircraft personnel. During its life, the 279,000-acre installation would be the home station for various other major Army units, one of the last the 24th Infantry Division (Mechanized), which helped spearhead U.S. units during the Persian Gulf War in 1991.

The carving out of Camp Stewart was one of the manifestations of a services-wide buildup that had begun in 1939 when President Roosevelt declared a national "limited emergency" and ordered increases in regular and reserve armed forces. By 1940, the Army totaled 270,000 officers and enlisted men, an increase of 130,000 over the totals for the previous five years. The same year, the country enacted the first peacetime draft in its history, and during 1941 the Army had a strength of 1,462,000. When the war ended in 1945, there were 8,268,000 men and women in Army uniform.[31]

The future that so many of his superiors had seen for Lemnitzer over the years was realized in May 1941, when he was appointed to the War Plans Division of the War Department's General Staff. A month later, he was a lieutenant colonel and assistant to the operations and training officer at Army General Headquarters in Washington, D.C.

On December 7, 1941, avid football fan Lemnitzer was watching a game between the Redskins and the Philadelphia Eagles when an announcement came over Griffith Stadium's loudspeakers that all military personnel were to report to their posts immediately.[32]

The eventuality for which Lemnitzer had been preparing himself for twenty-three years was beginning. It was time to go to war.

6

FIRST CHOP

West Point's Class of 1915—the one that produced Dwight D. Eisenhower and Omar N. Bradley—is famed in Military Academy annals as "the class the stars fell on" because, of its one hundred sixty-four graduates, a remarkable 36 percent became generals.[1] If it has a counterpart at the Army War College, it probably was the Class of 1940.

Seventy percent of the one hundred graduates won stars in their careers, a dazzling output when compared with the 52 percent rate for the previous twenty years and the approximately one in eight who would be making it by the time of the Persian Gulf War.[2]

A major reason for the huge percentage was, of course, the upcoming war, just as it was for the West Point Class of 1915. The country needed outstanding officers, and quickly, to lead the millions who would be in uniform before the conflict was over. In its War College graduates the Army had what it considered its best. And its timing in regard to assembling what was to be the last class of pre–World War peacetime couldn't have been more opportune.

Five of its graduates became four-star generals: Lemnitzer, Maxwell D. Taylor, Anthony C. McAuliffe, Clifton B. Cates, and Henry I. Hodes. There were also six lieutenant generals, twenty-three major generals, and thirty-six brigadier generals.

McAuliffe would become the most-quoted member of the class during World War II when, as the acting commander of the 101st Airborne Division, he growled "nuts" when the Germans demanded the surrender of his encircled division at Bastogne during the Battle of the Bulge.

Taylor, the 101st's commanding general, was in Washington when the Germans attacked, although he managed to get back to his division in a wild jeep trip through enemy lines while his troops were still engaging the enemy. A handsome, dashing commander who spoke five languages fluently, Taylor would one day become an important and, at times, troublesome figure in Lemnitzer's career.

Both would become major generals by the war's end, Taylor as the leader of one of the Army's elite combat units and Lemnitzer as a high-level planner, military diplomat, and staff officer. Of the two, Lemnitzer was the more ideal graduate of the War College with its emphasis on strategic and logistical planning. Years later, Taylor would recall Lemnitzer and McAuliffe as the outstanding members of the class,[3] an observation that seems to be borne out in class records. Both were cited frequently as being active or for having held leadership roles in various activities, studies, and projects.

Lemnitzer's brilliance as a planner brought him to the attention of another unusual officer, Col. Harry J. Malony, chief of the G-4 (supply) section of the War College's faculty. A field artilleryman, Malony was an outspoken intellectual in the Embick mold. When the War College was closed in 1940 for the war's duration, Malony was assigned to the War Plans Division of the War Department General Staff, later becoming the staff's G-3. Convinced that the War Plans Division was ill prepared for the war he saw looming, Malony sought to institute improvements. Among them was new personnel. Thirteen officers were handpicked for assignments on the staff by Malony, among them Lemnitzer, as the division was expanded.

Lemnitzer was on the Plans Division staff for two months—May and June of 1941—when he was moved up to Army General Headquarters (GHQ) as assistant G-3. Again, Malony was responsible. Now a brigadier general, he was deputy chief of staff when the GHQ became the Army's planning and operations headquarters in July 1941. At that time, seven officers were ordered transferred from the Plans Division to the newly organized headquarters, all selected as especially outstanding by Malony from his observations of the students who had passed through the Army War College during the three years before it closed.[4] All, Malony recalled later, were "first chop." Lemnitzer was one of them.[5]

The Army's growing pains spread to its highest echelons as some of its most able and strong-minded leaders labored to forge a headquarters apparatus that could cope effectively with the myriad of considerations that have to be dealt with when a nation goes to war. Malony, not the most tactful of men and a stubborn in-fighter in advancing his ideas, was in the thick of the forging process. Nine months after Lemnitzer reported for duty at GHQ, Malony was relieved as deputy chief of staff, reportedly over a jurisdictional dispute, and was transferred to the Munitions Assignment Board. He ended the war as commander of the 94th Division in Europe.

The American armed services had a great deal of catching up to do in a world that their leaders saw as approaching general war. By the time Lemnitzer got to Washington, much of western Europe had been conquered by Germany and the country had awakened to the fact that it was poorly prepared for war. Gen. George C. Marshall, the Army chief of staff, stated that the American Army ranked seventeenth in the world in size with less than 25 percent of its units ready for battle.[6]

By the summer of 1941, the U.S. Army had a personnel strength of 1,500,000 regulars, draftees, and National Guardsmen, the latter having been mobilized when the draft was instituted. It was a feeble effort, however, by a nation that was still largely unconvinced that it was in danger. At a time when German forces were ravaging the Soviet Union, under the terms of U.S. mobilization Guardsmen and draftees could not be required to serve anywhere outside the Western Hemisphere or for more than twelve months in the continental United States.[7]

Thanks largely to the persuasive powers of General Marshall, four months before the attack on Pearl Harbor the U.S. House of Representatives—by a single vote—passed the Selective Service Extension Act allowing all military troops to be sent overseas and extending lengths of service. But the closeness of the vote and such limitations as the requirement that inductees had to be released from service at age twenty-eight were among many indications that much of the country did not feel that it was in any immediate peril.[8]

Among the things that could be said about this remarkable margin on such a critical issue is that the United States was saved by one vote from legislating itself out of existence.

Relentless in his efforts to awaken the nation to prepare for the war he knew was coming, Marshall and his top generals drove the members of their staffs hard in the months after Lemnitzer and his six fellow "star pupils" from the War College were appointed to the Army's GHQ. As assistant to the staff's chief of planning and operations, Lemnitzer worked on such contingency plans as the defense of the Azores and the taking over of the defense of Iceland from the British. A month before Pearl Harbor, he was promoted to lieutenant colonel.

The nation's entry into World War II in the wake of the December 7, 1941, attack touched off a period of intense activity at all levels of the armed services. Although the Army's high command expected that Japan would be a future enemy, generals such as Eisenhower had assumed that Japan would not move against the United States until it had committed itself to the war in Europe. There was no time for detailed plans, often for any plans at all, as the War Department dispatched troops and materiel to counter a possible invasion of the West Coast. An infantry unit could be started across the continent with a telephone call. Men and equipment moved out on every available railroad car with nothing in writing to show by what authority they moved.[9] Everywhere—on both coasts, national borders, and locations vital to national security—similar activity was taking place.

The Coast Artillery Corps initially assumed an importance in the public eye that it had not enjoyed for many years. To be sure, since 1937 the country had been putting more money into coastal defenses with the worsening of the international situation; indeed, in a nation in which isolationism was still a powerful force, funds for such a clearly defensive arm as coastal protection had a better chance of congressional approval than those for armored tanks. In 1938 funds for the coast artillery were doubled to $4.5 million, to $8 million the next year, and to $13 million in 1940. The same year, one third of the graduating class at West Point chose the coast artillery for their careers, making it the most popular of all the branches that year.[10]

It was natural that the country would look to its coastal defenses in the turbulent weeks following the Japanese attack. There was widespread fear that an invasion of the West Coast would follow, and the citizenry looked to the coast artillery to defend its shores, just as their forebears had for one hundred fifty years. Forts along the coast were put on full alert, manning was beefed up, and ammunition stocks were topped off. The immediate transfer of antiaircraft units to the region was ordered during numerous false sightings by citizens of enemy airplanes.

But the Japanese followed up their strike at Pearl Harbor by opening a broad offensive in the Pacific, far from America's mainland shores. Particularly painful for Lemnitzer must have been the furious onslaught on the Philippines and his beloved Corregidor. When an army goes into battle, a professional soldier instinctively wants to be in the field with troops. So it must have been for Lemnitzer in the winter and spring of 1942 when the fighting edge of a branch in which he had served for over twenty years was engaging the enemy in a desperate struggle to defend a tiny island where he had spent six of the most pleasant and productive years of his career.

The Army had other needs of his abilities, however, and in the early months of the war he and his fellow officers at GHQ worked many hours attending to the staggering multitude of details that have to be attended to in putting an armed force onto a wartime footing. Lemnitzer's brilliance as a planner stood out, even in the company of some of the service's most outstanding staff officers. As he was leaving his post as deputy chief of staff, his champion from War College days, General Malony, issued a commendation that praised him for "loyal and efficient service" and noted:

"As Assistant to the Officer in Charge of Planning and Operations, G-3, GHQ, and later as Executive for the Assistant Chief of Staff, G-3, GHQ, you have rendered exceptional service to this headquarters. Your energy, long hours of work, good judgment, and grasp of strategy and details have been noteworthy. Your loyalty, enthusiasm and unfailing good nature have made my associations with you extremely pleasant. Your exceptional executive ability was demonstrated in the preparation of ten Theater Plans at this headquarters, most of which you coordinated."

Malony's departure coincided with dissolution of GHQ and the creation of three new commands: Army Service Forces, Army Air Forces, and Army Ground Forces. Lemnitzer became chief of the plans division of the latter under General McNair. An ironic sidelight to McNair's hand picking of his new plans chief was that McNair was reputed to have had a career-long bias against coast artillery-men as a result of branch rivalry when each Army component had its own promotion lists and budgets.[11] One of the Army's most influential generals, he was known to look on with disfavor any effort to promote a coast artilleryman outside his own branch.[12]

The Army Ground Forces command had the responsibility of organizing and training combat units. To help him in directing this task, McNair, the former GHQ chief of staff, brought with him a remarkable officer who was to become an important part of Lemnitzer's future. He was Mark W. Clark, a tall, intense infantryman from the Military Academy's Class of 1917. McNair's chief of staff, Clark later became a highly regarded favorite of Marshall and Eisenhower, who once described him as "the best trainer, organizer and planner I have ever met."[13]

Lemnitzer served in Army Ground Forces for four months, impressing McNair and Clark as a superb planner and all-around superior officer. In his last OER as a member of the GHQ staff, Col. George P. Hays, Lemnitzer's immediate superior, wrote: "I rate this officer as among the best of all the officers, regardless of grade, I have come in contact with in my entire service. He has the capacity to accomplish difficult tasks well." Underneath there was a comment by McNair: "I concur." Clark had this to say, McNair again concurring, in an OER while Lemnitzer was with the Army Ground Forces staff: "Exceptionally well-qualified temperamentally, physically, mentally for any duty, and is possessed of superior military background and experience." Recommending his immediate promotion, Clark added: "Superior results should be anticipated on any future assignment, especially as a staff officer."

Just before being transferred out of the Ground Forces staff in June 1942, Lemnitzer was promoted to full colonel. Two weeks later he was a brigadier general; he had gone from wearing the gold leaves of a major to the single stars of a general in seven months.

Despite his growing reputation as one of the Army's premier planners, the lure of troop duty was strong and in July 1942, Lemnitzer was named commander of the 34th Antiaircraft Brigade. He commanded the 34th for a year, but for much of the time in name only because a month after taking over he was assigned additional duties as assistant chief of staff for operations, Allied Forces Headquarters, England and North Africa. After participating in the planning of the invasion of North Africa, he became Deputy Chief of Staff of the Fifth U.S. Army in North Africa. Only occasionally could he get back to his brigade, commanded in his absence by an assistant brigade commander, and finally full time for a few months at the end of the North African campaign and into the invasion of Sicily.

The time-tested, nonpejorative military maxim that it's who you know—or more aptly, who knows you—had once again come into play. Mark Clark had been named General Eisenhower's deputy for the upcoming invasion of North Africa, and the planning phase for the highly complex operation was about to begin. Recalling Lemnitzer's outstanding achievements at GHQ and Army Ground Forces headquarters in Washington, he was one of the first officers Clark asked for when he began creating his planning staff.

The Allied members of the newly assembled staff knew that plans for a major operation were taking shape and there were indications that the target would be North Africa, but that was the extent of Lemnitzer's knowledge when three officers from the British War Office called on him one day. They had a document, drafted under the direction of the British chiefs of staff, which spelled out the responsibilities and the extent of the authority of the operation's supreme commander. That was to be Eisenhower, of course, and the War Office representatives wanted to know what the Allied Forces Headquarters' assistant chief of staff for operations thought of their work.

Lemnitzer recalled that the document, known in military parlance as "terms of reference," was full of caveats that would permit British forces under Eisenhower's command to appeal to their national authorities if they disagreed with an order, felt unduly jeopardized, or otherwise wanted to do things their way. It was clear that the British were trying to see how far they could go in reserving maximum authority for themselves in upcoming operations. Lemnitzer decided that Eisenhower should see the paper right away, so he made an appointment with the general and rode with the British officers to Eisenhower's offices on Grosvenor Square in London.

"I kind of looked for an exit for a rapid escape because I knew he wouldn't like it," he said years later. Lemnitzer had a healthy respect for Eisenhower's temper: "He had a short fuse. He could blow real quick when he was exasperated with something." Eisenhower began leafing through the document's pages, and it was clear that he did not at all like what he was reading. There was no explosion, but he picked up a pencil and began crossing out whole sentences and writing furiously. Lemnitzer remembered that he was "mumbling around" as he worked while the four staff officers stood "absolutely mute." Finally he said: "This is not any directive to a supreme commander. Anyone who had this simply wouldn't be a supreme commander."

Lemnitzer said, "He really tore it up, literally. He didn't like anything in it. And he was dead right." Eisenhower's reaction made it clear that he would not accept the appointment as supreme commander unless the offending caveats were removed. Three days later, the War Office staff officers returned with a new draft that incorporated every piece of editing that Eisenhower had done. "We [now] had a real supreme commander who had authority to direct national units," Lemnitzer said. "Of course, implicit in [the document] was that there was [still] a channel of communication between national commanders and their respective governments, but on operational matters he [Eisenhower] was the commander."

Lemnitzer looked back on the episode as a landmark development in establishing an effective warfighting alliance during a period when skepticism about ever again going to war with allies was still a deeply ingrained sentiment in American military circles.[14]

The North Africa campaign was an exacting test of the planner's art. No country had ever before endeavored to conduct an overseas military operation requiring the movement of troops and materiel over thousands of miles from its bases, terminating in a major assault.[15] Although it was to be primarily an American operation, other nations and their resources and territories would be involved. Even coordination of the separate U.S. armed services would become a major headache for the planners and commanders.

The target of the amphibious sea and air attack was a hostile, thousand-mile coastal area stretching from Casablanca in French Morocco on the west, east behind neutral Spanish Morocco, and through Oran and Algiers in Algeria. The choice of North Africa for the first deployment of American troops against European Axis forces was not without controversy; there were accusations back home that the United States had been pressured by England into invading an area of dubious strategic importance with insufficient time to prepare.

From a military standpoint, the African operation was regarded initially as diversionary in nature with the ultimate goals the clearing of Axis forces from North Africa, the denial of the area as sites for enemy air and submarine bases, and—through further advances to the east—the relief of the British island of Malta.[16] After American forces had occupied French Morocco and Algeria, the plan was then to quickly drive on east and conquer Tunisia before Axis troops could move in. This would give the Allies control of a strategically vital coastal region while making possible a giant pincers movement against the forces of German Field Marshall Erwin Rommel, then being forced back from Egypt by British General Bernard Montgomery's troops.[17]

Marshall and Eisenhower had serious misgivings about invading North Africa in 1942. Robert D. Murphy, U.S. consul general in Algiers and a key player in subsequent efforts to secure the cooperation of Vichy French military leaders during the operation, wrote years later that Eisenhower disliked almost everything about the expedition: its diversion from the central campaign in Europe; the heavy risks in vast, untested territory; its dependence on local forces of doubtful and probably treacherous dependability; the bewildering complexities of dealing with deadly quarrels between French factions; and such uncertainties as whether the move on her doorstep might inflame Spain to enter the conflict on the side of the Axis.[18]

But President Roosevelt, with the powerful encouragement of English Prime Minister Churchill, was adamant that the invasion was going to take place in 1942, and so the planners went to work on Torch, the code name assigned to the operation. In addition to the daunting concerns cited by Murphy, Eisenhower was faced with putting together within weeks an enormously complex military blue-print governing every detail of landing over one hundred thousand Allied troops on an enemy shore from bases thousands of miles away and sustaining and supporting them for however long it took to achieve their objectives.

Planning Chief Lemnitzer and his colleagues at Eisenhower's headquarters in London worked around the clock during the late summer and autumn of 1942 to create a plan that would put invasion forces on the beaches in early November. Recalling those feverish days at Allied Headquarters, Eisenhower noted years later:

"Grand strategy, tactics, procurement of landing craft and ships, allocation of supporting naval forces, organization of air forces, provision of staging and training areas, arrangements for early and later supply, and determination of actual composition of each element of each assault force—all these were matters that had to be handled progressively and simultaneously. Difficulty in any of these produced at once difficulties in all the others."[19]

A major handicap for the planners was the lack of information about North Africa, a situation brought on in part by the extremely short time given Eisenhower to launch the invasion. Lemnitzer said years later that as late as three weeks before the landings "our planning up to this point was quite superficial. . . . We didn't know a damned thing about North Africa. A lot of people had never heard of Casablanca, Algiers or Oran. We had no good maps, no good intelligence on what was happening there. We were planning an amphibious operation on only supposition."[20]

Of primary consideration in any military plan is, of course, the strength and nature of the opposition. French Morocco and Algeria were occupied by two hundred thousand Vichy French troops, a portion of the French Army that had surrendered to Nazi Germany in 1940. Part of a government headed by World War I hero Marshall Henri Petain, the force was nominally under the control of Germany. However, it was known that there were significant elements in the Vichy military structure whose leaders would welcome an American invasion if it would help defeat Germany.

Exploiting this spirit was crucial to the Allies. Neither England nor the United States wanted to fight their defeated former comrades in arms, desiring only to use the strategically important invaded area as a stepping stone to driving Axis forces out of Africa and the Mediterranean region. Axis elements in the region consisted chiefly of senior German officials who were there to keep their eyes on their puppet state.

But where were these friendly elements, and how were the Allies to get in touch with them? The question was answered in mid-October when General Marshall received a secret cable from Murphy, whose title of consul general was a cover; in reality, he was President Roosevelt's "personal representative" in North Africa, and he reported directly to him.[21] The message was that a spokesman for one of France's most prominent generals wanted to talk. Thus began one of the war's most remarkable adventure stories, a saga of derring-do in hostile territory that would, for a time, make celebrities of Clark and Lemnitzer in an alliance whose citizens badly needed a lift during a period in which the Allies were losing on every front.

7

☆ ☆ ☆ ☆

THE ROBINHOODS

A tiny white light appeared suddenly in the blackness that was the coast of Algeria, French North Africa. Six miles offshore, a lookout on the bridge of His Majesty's submarine *Seraph* (P-219) raised his binoculars for a better view, lowered them, and spoke softly to the officer nearby. Almost immediately the engines on the little sub began to throb as it turned and headed toward the distant gleam.

Lieutenant Norman A. A. Jewell, Royal Navy and captain of the *Seraph*, gave his helmsman a heading and sent word to awaken the submarine's passengers. Other orders were given, and quickly the compartments below were bustling with crewmen carrying out landing boats and equipment.

The eight passengers dressed briskly, finished packing their equipment, checked their weapons, and climbed up the conning tower ladder to the deck. They waited in the darkness as the *Seraph* glided slowly toward the light. Moderately heavy swells stirred the Mediterranean under a bright moon.

It was just before midnight on October 21, 1942.

Less than a week before, five of the passengers had been neatly uniformed staff officers, their surroundings one of the world's most civilized cities, all their waking thoughts monopolized by a rugged and hostile coastline hundreds of miles away. Now they were there.

The voyage of the *Seraph* climaxed an extraordinary five days that began October 16 when Eisenhower received a top secret cable from Marshall informing him that Maj. Gen. Charles E. Mast, deputy commander of the French XIX Corps with headquarters in Algiers, wanted a secret meeting near Algiers to confer on possibly cooperating in an Allied invasion of North Africa.

The development was important enough to bring Prime Minister Churchill scurrying back to London from his country estate on a weekend, convene his cabinet, and later send off the conferees with the grand pronouncement: "The entire resources of the British Commonwealth are at your disposal!"[1]

The excitement was prompted by the fact that Mast was known to be a personal representative of Gen. Henri Honoré Giraud, an authentic French hero whom the Allies considered to be the most likely soldier French forces would rally around if they invaded North Africa. If Giraud were to come to the side of the Allies, the grave probability of having to fight French forces would be solved.

Giraud had twice escaped from German captivity—in World War I and in 1940 when he commanded the French Ninth Army. The French Intelligence Service had helped free him the second time, and now he lived clandestinely in Lyons, one of the few French military leaders of stature who had no connections with either Vichy France or Nazi Germany. Other French generals had gained their release from German prisons by signing pledges not to bear arms against their conquerors; Giraud had refused.[2] Winning him as an ally—and quickly—became a matter of the most urgent priority at the highest levels of Allied governments.

As relayed through Murphy, Mast had stipulated that the Allied representatives must include a senior general officer and they must travel to North Africa by submarine. The cable from Washington also specified that the party should include someone thoroughly familiar with the details of the Torch operation, a supply expert, a naval officer, and a political specialist who could speak fluent French. It was decided that all were to be Americans; relations between France and England were very poor then, thanks in part to British attacks on Vichy French naval vessels after France surrendered to Germany and a perception by French leaders that the British had not helped enough to forestall a German victory.

Eisenhower chose Maj. Gen. Clark, deputy commander in chief, Allied Force Headquarters, to head the delegation. Clark picked Brig. Gen. Lemnitzer, chief of the Allied Forces Plans Section, as his deputy and the party's expert on Torch plans and operations. The rest of the group included Col. Archelaus I. Hamblen, assistant chief of staff for supply (G-4); Capt. Jerauld Wright, the U.S. Navy's liaison officer for Torch; and Col. Julius C. Holmes, a former U.S. State Department officer who headed up the civil affairs branch of Allied Forces Headquarters and who spoke French.

The rendezvous point was to be a private seaside villa fifteen miles west of the Mediterranean port of Cherchel, which was some sixty miles west of Algiers. Mast would meet Clark's party there with a similar number of French officers after the Americans arrived on the evening of October 21. The signal for them to disembark from their submarine would be a light beamed from a villa window and visible only from the sea.

Extreme secrecy was vital if the expedition was to succeed. The French seeking the meeting disclosed that German and Japanese sources had reported that the Allies were planning early military operations against Casablanca, Dakar, or both. Germany was urging the Vichy French to take every precaution to head these off, strongly implying that failure to do so could bring about Axis occupation of French North Africa.[3]

The Americans had less than five days from the time Marshall's cable arrived in London to fly to Gibraltar and board a submarine for the dash to the Algerian coast. The French didn't know it, but eighteen days beyond the scheduled meeting—on November 8—over one hundred thousand U.S. troops, backed by English and American warships, would invade their coast with the launching of operation Torch.

Because of bad weather between London and Gibraltar, Clark and his party didn't get off the ground until October 18. A B-17 bomber named "Red Gremlin" carried Clark and Hamblen, while Lemnitzer, Holmes, and Wright rode in another B-17 called "Boomerang II." If Clark's plane was downed, forced back, or delayed, Lemnitzer was to carry on as commander of the mission.

Led by Clark's plane, piloted by Maj. Paul Tibbetts, whose B-29 later in the war dropped the atomic bomb on Hiroshima, Japan, the group left London at dawn and arrived in Gibraltar in late afternoon. One of the party's concerns was that no plane of the B-17's size had ever landed on Gibraltar's short airport runway. While Spitfire fighters swarmed overhead, Lemnitzer's plane landed first without trouble, followed a few minutes later by the Red Gremlin.

Gibraltar, which would become Eisenhower's headquarters during Torch, was far from an ideal place to begin a secret mission. Situated on the Spanish coast across a narrow strait from Spanish Morocco, the tiny British fortress was the constant target of close surveillance by German agents located on Spanish soil. Intense security measures to shroud the comings and goings of official visitors proved effective throughout the war. In the Clark party's case, the British foiled prying eyes by bringing a large car with heavy curtains close to the planes and hurrying the visitors inside.

There was no time to lose if Clark and his team were to meet Mast's deadline. There were frustrations, beginning with the foul weather. At Gibraltar, the attitude of senior British naval officers contributed to Clark's qualms about the operation by expressing serious misgivings regarding chances for success of the "whole crazy American adventure." They warned of thick shore patrols and many spotted planes in the rendezvous area and predicted that the mission had little chance of succeeding.

Clark, who wrote later that he had already "hardly ever been less certain of the success of an operational mission in my life," said he badly needed reassurance. Finally, he told the skeptics: "Gentlemen, there is no help for this. We are going. It has been decided by our two governments, and I don't intend to call it off."[4]

The party saw its confidence bolstered considerably in a talk with the captain of the *Seraph*, a small, slow submarine whose specialty was unconventional and secret missions.[5] After Clark explained the mission to Lt. "Bill" Jewell, the self-assured young submariner commented without hesitation: "I am sure we can get you in there and off again."[6] Lemnitzer later was to praise Lieutenant Jewell as "magnificent in his skill, courage and daring on the entire trip and particularly during the difficult hours on the morning of take-off from North Africa."[7]

Accompanied by three British commandos, the five Americans boarded the *Seraph* immediately after the conference with Jewell and put to sea after dark, with a destroyer as an escort for the first fifty miles. Because of the need for speed to reach the rendezvous point on time, the young *Seraph* crew kept the sub on the surface as much as possible, steering what Lemnitzer called a "sinuous" course to thwart possible enemy submarines. On the surface, the boat could travel at from ten to twelve knots; submerged, two or three. Cherchel was four hundred miles away and the *Seraph* had forty-eight hours to get there.

Clark was perplexed when he found that no word from Murphy awaited him when the planes reached Gibraltar. Just before leaving in the *Seraph*, Lemnitzer sent a message from Clark for relay to Murphy stating that the party planned to arrive off the rendezvous point on the evening of October 21 and that the French should be at the meeting place from eleven o'clock until dawn the next day. If inclement weather should prevent a landing, the wire suggested the meeting take place on the submarine. In the event that neither plan should prove feasible, the Americans would try for the next night.[8] Confirmation of the message or changes in plans were to be radioed to the *Seraph* through the governor of Gibraltar, Lt. Gen. Sir F. N. Mason MacFarlane.

As the submarine made good time in choppy seas toward its destination, the party, ship's officers, and commandos discussed coordination of the operation after contact was made. Lemnitzer and his comrades played bridge to pass the time but they were becoming increasingly tense over the lack of any response to their message to Murphy. Lemnitzer, the expedition's designated recorder and treasurer, penciled in his notes: "No word from Gibraltar. Queer?"

That night, the *Seraph* halted to enable the group to rehearse. The landing craft were to be two-man wood and canvas kayaks used by British commandos. Propelled by double-scooped paddles, they were fast but frail and unstable, especially in turbulent water or heavy currents. When not in use, they could be folded up for stowage.

Lemnitzer and a commando, Lt. J. P. Foote, were in the second boat to be launched in increasingly choppy seas. Describing their effort, Lemnitzer wrote: "Foote and I next. Folbot (the manufacturer's trade name for the kayaks) had about 1″ of water on bottom, resulting in wet tail for me. Boat rode rollers and swells very well. Paddling a bit awkward at first. I hit gun platform on submarine with one hand trying to fend off one high swell—not hurt seriously. Got real wet by breaking waves."[9]

After Clark and commando Capt. Godfrey B. Courtney had practiced without incident, the *Seraph* got under way again. The delegation and escorts were sleeping at dawn the next morning when the submarine's klaxon went off, signaling an impending dive. Jewell had sighted the stretch of the beach at which the historic meeting with the French was to take place. But all was still not well, as Lemnitzer noted in his personal account of the mission: "Still no word from Gib [Gibraltar]. What the hell is the matter?"

The passengers played more bridge while taking turns at the sub's periscope, which was run up a few seconds at a time from a mile and a half offshore so sketches could be made of an area from which a white light had been seen burning in the early morning darkness. Two Algerian fishing boats came into view shortly after dawn and anchored off the beach. The sub moved further out to sea.

The day wore on, the air inside the packed vessel getting increasingly bad to the point that Lemnitzer recorded feeling "rather dopey" because of dwindling oxygen. Later he would recall the day underwater as the "longest" of his career and the experience as his worst of the war. Back and forth, ten miles out and return, the *Seraph* moved at a depth of thirty-two feet, moving up often to raise its periscope in a vain search for a signal. Apprehensions grew that the delegation, already a day late for the rendezvous, had missed its connection or that something else had gone amiss.

Jewell, himself a paragon of coolness under duress, was impressed with the Americans' demeanor. When the periscope revealed a plane overhead, the submarine's captain watched intently as it roared off into the distance and then ventured to Clark that it was probably a commercial craft. "Probably," agreed Clark, his brow suddenly wrinkling as if he were pondering a weighty problem. It turned out that what was bothering him was a maneuver in the bridge game: "I'll double your spades, Lem," he said, and for the first time Lemnitzer was moved to show a trace of concern.

"I had never met five such iron-nerved men who simply refused to cross bridges until the spans were underfoot," Jewell observed later.[10]

Then came the long-awaited message from Gibraltar:

"Most secret and personal—from Flag Officer Commanding North Atlantic Station. Information received that meeting cannot take place on submarine or surface vessel but must take place as previously arranged. Your parties expected night Oct 20–21 up to 0500 GMT [five o'clock in the morning]. If not contacted then you would be expected on night 23rd. The interested parties have been informed to expect you night 21–22 as well and that if no contact made to expect you night 22–23."[11]

Elated that the mission was still on, the group then devised a plan should it run into trouble: the sub was to stand offshore until the morning of October 24 if it received no radio communication from the landing party, then move to a point five miles off nearby Fountaine de Genie. If there was still no contact, on the morning of October 25 it was to return to Gibraltar without the party.

It grew dark, and still there was no signal from the shore. At half past ten, Clark and Lemnitzer went to bed in the belief that there would be no light shown that night. An hour later, they were aroused and told the light had been spotted. The little sub was turning and heading toward the rendezvous point.

When the *Seraph* got within two miles of shore, Clark's party—all in uniform—slung their carbines, picked up their packs, and climbed into the four kayaks, along with the three commandos. One boat capsized, was damaged, and had to be launched again later after it was repaired. Lemnitzer and Foote were nearly spilled into the sea when their boat was dashed under the sub's hydroplane by a swell, but they managed to right themselves and paddle off with the rest toward the beach.

Two hundred yards from the shore, the boats paused while the first, containing Holmes and commando Capt. R. T. Livingstone, went ahead to reconnoiter. The come-ahead signal, the letter *K* flashed on a flashlight in Morse code, was given, and the party came ashore. Murphy and several French officers, some in uniform and some in civilian clothes, were waiting as the party carried the boats and the rest of its gear two hundred yards along the beach to the bottom of a steep bluff. On top, two hundred feet above the beach, stood the dwelling they had come so far to visit.

The villa was a large, red-roofed white stone building built around a courtyard some thirty yards away from the main highway to Algiers. Its owner was Monsieur Henri Teissier, a well-to-do landowner and French patriot who was risking his life to provide the meeting place. As the party reached the top of the rocky path with its boats, weapons, and packs, it came upon Monsieur Teissier, described later by Clark as a very nervous, "rather frightened-looking Frenchman" who obviously wanted the whole affair to be over with quickly.

It was by now early morning of the twenty-second, and there was no chance that the group could leave again before daylight. The submarine was radioed to return at ten o'clock that night, and the eight visitors turned in to get some sleep before General Mast's scheduled visit at half past five in the morning. The boats were hidden in a room off the courtyard, and the three commandos were ordered to keep out of sight in an upper bedroom to keep the French from knowing that British officers were involved.

Mast and his chief of staff, Col. Emile Jousse, arrived at six o'clock, and over a breakfast of coffee, sardines, and bread and jam in the living room began to talk with their visitors about what they could do to facilitate an American offensive in North Africa.

The opportune timing of the meeting was due to the persistent efforts of Murphy, whose vital part in bringing about the meeting was known by only a few persons in the highest levels of American government. He had long been an advocate of seeking ties with dissident factions in the Vichy military establishment to further Allied objectives. His opportunity came when he made contact with a group of French officers who called themselves the "Robinhoods."

One of their most prominent members was Mast, a regular Army officer who, despite his high Vichy military position, was loyal to Free France.[12]

Clark and Lemnitzer were in a tough spot as they sat down to try to exploit the avenue that Murphy had opened up. They had been ordered to seek active French cooperation in North Africa and gather any intelligence they could; but, in accordance with directives that came from President Roosevelt, under no circumstances were they to reveal that an invasion was imminent or to give any indication of its nature or focus. But both knew that the day before the meeting the first elements of Patton's Western Task Force had left the United States on their three thousand-mile trip to attack the Casablanca end of the invasion beachheads.

Lemnitzer was much impressed with Mast, whom he regarded as "absolutely sincere, capable and completely engaged in setting up a French government in North Africa under Gen. Giraud. He willingly presented all his plans [for an invasion] in complete detail with maps and supporting papers. There is no doubt in my mind that this man can be trusted completely and will do everything within his power to assist our entry into North Africa. The general plan as outlined by him paralleled our own so completely that it seemed that he had read a copy of ours."[13]

Sometimes seemingly on the verge of breaking into tears, the general painted a bleak picture of French military capabilities in the region. His forces, he stated, had men but no arms, ammunition, armor, no modern airplanes, and very little gasoline to move what they had. There was not much left, he declared, but the will to prevent occupation by Axis forces regardless of the odds. French North Africa desperately needed U.S. help.[14] (There were no Axis troops in the region occupied by Vichy French forces—French Morocco, Algeria, and Tunisia— because of the terms of the 1940 armistice. In return for leaving the region unoccupied, the French agreed to protect it from invasion—at the time, the British were perceived as the only potential invaders.)

Presumably because presenting a picture of overwhelming power was necessary to clinch French cooperation, Clark was considerably less than accurate with some of his figures. When Mast, who spoke passable English, asked how many American troops would be in the invasion, Clark replied that they would total a half-million, comprising three corps of fifteen divisions. There would also be two thousand airplanes and heavy U.S. naval support. (Actually, the United States— in the war for less than a year and heavily engaged in the Pacific—had all it could do to get 112,000 troops ashore in the initial landings, and their naval support had a heavy British element.)[15]

Lemnitzer's notes of the meeting show Mast opening with the advice that the best time for the invasion would be the following spring. Clark replied with a straight face that it was "best to do something soon—we have the Army and the means." (The French general was furious when he later learned that the invasion had been imminent as they spoke. Told about the invasion three days before it began, he accused the Allies of having responded to French candor with deception.)

When Mast asked if the Allies had any intelligence about Axis intentions, Clark answered that many of its forces were massing in Lebanon, Sardinia, Sicily, and probably Spain, creating a "general picture of covetous eyes on this area."

With Clark noncommittally repeating the "need for an early operation," Mast indicated that Giraud wanted an invasion of southern France to take precedence over one in North Africa or that the invasions take place simultaneously. Otherwise, said Mast, "France will be lost." Clark replied that the invasion of southern France could come later, but that for the present, logistical conditions would not permit this. Told that there would also be British air and naval support, Mast said the French preferred that there be no British in France or North Africa at first. The French officer reported that "the French Navy is not with us—the Army and the Air Force are." Clark's comment: "If the Navy opens up on us we will not reply."

Mast suggested that the invasion concentrate on Oran and Algiers, and perhaps Bone to the east, and that Casablanca, furthest west, should be avoided because the French naval presence was strongest there. To deal with this, he urged that Casablanca be conquered from the rear after Oran and Algiers had been taken to avoid Vichy naval guns. (In planning the invasion, Casablanca had been agreed to as an objective only after long Allied discussion about whether it was necessary. Mast was right about the resistance; the fighting there between Vichy forces and those of Patton's Western Task Force was the heaviest along the entire coast.)

Mast returned to the subject of the huge force Clark had described: "Where are these five hundred thousand men to come from—where are they?" Clark: "In the U.S. and U.K."

Mast: "Rather far, isn't it?"

Clark: "No."

Told by Mast that the Axis might move troops in by the end of the month, Clark replied that if the Germans were in North Africa in force, "I don't believe we could come in here promptly."

Mast answered that if the Germans came in his troops would fight them, but that his was "an army without guns" that couldn't stop a single German division if one came in. He pleaded for arms, equipment, and supplies, estimating that with enough of these resources he could raise an army of three hundred thousand troops if U.S. forces were strong enough to hold back the Axis during the buildup.

The French general asked who the commander in chief would be. Clark said he didn't know (he did know, of course, although it had not yet been officially announced). Mast stated that Giraud wanted to command all forces in North Africa—French, as well as Allied. This was to be a major sticking point in the high-level negotiations that followed completion of the mission. At the moment,

Clark could only stall because this was a decision that would have to be made at a higher level. He knew, however, that the United States and its allies would never permit a French general to have overall command of their invasion forces.

Mast offered a draft of a letter to be dispatched to Giraud by Murphy after it had been approved by Eisenhower's headquarters in London. Among other things, the draft promised that "French sovereignty will be reestablished as soon as possible in all the territories, continental and colonial, over which the French flag flew in 1939." France would be considered a U.S. ally. A provision dealing with command was reworded at Clark's request, and the letter was put in a pouch to be taken back to London.[16]

Mast said he thought Giraud would be impressed enough by the size of the U.S. forces, as portrayed by Clark, to give his support. The French general stated that he would assume command of French troops in the region if Giraud refused the U.S. invitation. The question of how Giraud would get out of France to meet with the American commanders was answered by Clark, who promised to send a submarine to get him.

At eleven o'clock that morning, Mast had to return to his headquarters in Algiers, explaining that to stay away any longer would arouse suspicion. He left Colonel Jousse, his air officer, naval adviser, and special operations officer to continue the discussions.

Lemnitzer marveled at the detailed invasion plan laid out by Mast's deputies, observing in his notes that "it was practically a duplication of our own Torch plan." With Murphy and Holmes interpreting, the Frenchmen went over naval, air, special operations, and logistical plans, furnishing detailed copies of each for Clark's staff to take with them. The French also provided detailed information showing locations and strengths of army and naval units; told where supplies— including gasoline and ammunition—were stored; gave details about airports, where resistance would be heaviest; and supplied such information as where airborne troops could safely land. Everything the Americans were told turned out to be accurate in every respect.[17]

Late that afternoon, as Clark and Lemnitzer were beginning to speculate that too much remained to be done for the party to get away that night, the villa's telephone rang. Teissier hurried in shouting that police were on their way; they had learned of some "queer goings-on," apparently prompted by reports from local Arabs of having seen footprints on the beach and other suspicious activity. Smugglers were active along the coast, and these were what the police were looking for when they arrived.

Instantly, there was intense activity as the French gathered up their maps and the Americans crammed papers into bags and packs. "People were rushing through the house in all directions gathering up anything that might disclose our presence there," Lemnitzer wrote in his notes. "Colonel Jousse changed from uniform to civilian clothes in less time than I ever dreamed was possible."[18]

Another Frenchman leaped into his car with a suitcase and sped off toward Algiers, while others climbed out through windows to hide in brush on the beach.

In the confusion, Murphy ran into the room and asked for some of the money Lemnitzer had brought with him for emergencies like this: he would try to bribe the police, if necessary. The general gave him five thousand Algerian francs, in the process dropping and losing several gold pieces also brought along in the event that francs wouldn't do. (Lemnitzer had been issued six hundred dollars at the start of the trip: ten thousand paper francs and forty gold pieces with values ranging from five to ten dollars.)

The police drove up before Clark's party could run down to the beach with their kayaks. One commando made it to the shore and radioed the submarine to tell Jewell what was happening, while the terrified Teissier herded the other seven into a very small and dirty wine cellar located underneath the dwelling's patio. He then hastily covered the trapdoor with a rug as the police pounded on the front door. Clutching carbines and Thompson submachine guns, the delegates from Allied Headquarters knelt or sat on packs stuffed with maps, plans, and secret intelligence data and waited as police swarmed through the rooms above.

Clark's group was in a terrible spot. Capture would touch off an international incident of historic proportions, result in terrible retributions for the French involved, and gravely complicate, if not doom, the forthcoming invasion. The general ordered his group to resist arrest if the police discovered them, shooting their way out if necessary.

They hardly dared breathe as the policemen banged about a few inches above their heads, Teissier chattering excitedly all the while as he followed them. Courtney had a fit of coughing. Holding his hand over his mouth and sputtering and gasping, he finally whispered to Clark: "General, I am afraid I will choke!" To which Clark replied: "I am afraid you will not!"[19] Courtney's struggles subsided somewhat after Clark slipped him his own wad of well-chomped chewing gum.

After the adventure was over, Clark cabled Eisenhower that he and his band had hid out in what was "an empty—repeat—empty wine cellar." It was a disclosure that reportedly prompted hearty laughter from King George VI of England, who was closely monitoring the party's progress.[20] Actually, their precarious haven was not completely dry, thanks to someone's producing a private bottle of wine which was passed around as the ruckus continued above. The ever-resourceful Murphy was coping with the situation by pretending to be the mildly inebriated American consul from Algiers who was having a party at the house with French friends. To embellish the pose, he hinted that there were women upstairs, urging the police not to embarrass him by going up.

All the while, the gendarmes tramped about looking in corners and behind furniture. As Clark recalled, "Every time their feet approached our trapdoor, seven hearts popped into seven throats."[21]

Finally, after two hours the stomping and shouting stopped. Murphy opened the trapdoor and said, "This is Bob. They've gone, but they'll be back."[22] The police had told him and Teissier that they were still suspicious and that they would return after getting further instructions from the chief of police in Cherchel. Murphy expected this to be soon and advised the seven to get out of the villa as fast as they could.

Like the rest, Lemnitzer and Holmes had been given a room for their possessions and for sleep; hence, Murphy's nervousness about the possibility of the police going upstairs. The general—who had come ashore in a dark green uniform shirt and brown regulation trousers—was changing his clothes in preparation for departure when he decided to make a quick check of the conference room to make sure no evidence of their visit had been left behind. He was doing this in his underwear when one of the Frenchmen rushed in to report that a second, strongly enforced police contingent was on its way to the villa. Before Lemnitzer could get back to his room, Holmes picked up all the pair's personal belongings from the room, including Lemnitzer's pants.

While the others fled down the steep path with their boats, weapons, and equipment, Lemnitzer returned to his room for his pants, gun, and the other things he had brought with him. Finding that they had disappeared, he and Foote dragged their boat down to the beach and, nearly exhausted, joined the rest of the band on the shore. The general would perform the remainder of the shore phase of his mission in his undershorts.

A heavy wind had sprung up during the afternoon, whipping the sea into crashing eight-foot waves. By then it was dark, and it seemed to Lemnitzer and his comrades that the roaring of the surf was growing louder by the minute as they searched for a place to launch their boats. An attempt by Clark and Livingstone failed when a huge wave capsized their craft a few feet from shore. Despite fears that they had been lost, the two were rescued from the surf and pulled back to shore with their boat. The eight then dragged the kayaks and their equipment into the bushes along the beach and waited for a letup in the turbulence.

One of the traits fellow soldiers remember best about Lemnitzer was his cheerfulness and remarkable calm in time of crisis. But he had a boiling point, and he clearly was piqued with his French hosts during this part of the episode, as recorded in the personal notes compiled during the trip:

"In the meantime, all the Frogs who had been promising us the world with a fence around it, hundreds of thousands of troops, and who had assured us that the situation was 'in the bag,' had faded into thin air. Only a few remained."[23]

Clark, who had stripped to his undershorts and a shirt to launch his boat, had lost his pants, shoes, and much equipment in the capsizing, so he, Lemnitzer, and Holmes went back to the villa to find him some dry clothes. Teissier, who was very upset over the trio's return and kept trying to get them to leave as soon as possible, produced two sweaters. Holmes found Lemnitzer's trousers in his bag and handed them to Clark.

Lemnitzer returned to the beach, and Clark, who was trying to further cram his much-too-small borrowed sweaters with two bottles of wine and a loaf of bread, was about to follow when a lookout reported that the police were coming back again. Spurred on by the now almost hysterical villa owner, Clark leaped from a ten-foot wall in his bare feet and limped off to join his shivering staff in the bushes.[24]

They had signaled their location to the *Seraph* with an infrared light, and the ever-intrepid Jewell had brought his submarine to within a mile of the beach to await the boats. As the surf continued to pound the shore, Jewell was signaled to go out further to avoid damaging his vessel. The group continued its wait, its members taking turns as sentries. At one point, one of the Frenchmen from the house was sent to Cherchel with some gold pieces to try to obtain a fishing boat to take the party out to the *Seraph*. No success: the fishermen contacted were afraid to become involved in anything so mysterious.

As the *Seraph* waited, Jewell noticed an increasing atmosphere of gloom among his crew as the night wore on. He wrote later: "I doubt if we would have fallen into such a somber frame of mind if the Americans had still been on board. Their cool, carefree manner and their perfect unconcern when real danger threatened had helped us to emulate them in the matter of *sangfroid*."[25]

Throughout the night, there were several more alarms that police or Arabs were approaching, but they proved to be groundless. While Lemnitzer, still in his underwear, was standing guard, he noticed that the surf was subsiding a little and that at one point along the beach the waves seemed less ferocious than at others. They were seven feet high at four o'clock in the morning when the party decided to make another attempt to put to sea regardless of the cost. There had been indications that at any moment police would come again and discover them.

Discarding all weapons and equipment not absolutely required, the band began to launch the kayaks despite fears that loss of some lives was a certainty. Aided by four French officers and civilians who pushed from the shore, Clark and Wright made it through the surf and headed for the submarine, now back a mile offshore.

Lemnitzer and Foote were next. Leaving behind most of their equipment except for an infrared signaling device and a musette bag containing Lemnitzer's notes of the conference and an envelope full of gold coins, the two waited for several huge waves to come in and made a dash for open water. But more big breakers hit their boat, and it capsized. The general recalled being "under water longer than ever before in my life" as he and the British commando were rolled over and over in the surging waters. A strong undertow contributed to their travails in trying to get back to shore. They made it with great difficulty, only to be knocked down again by another wave and the rolling and dunking process repeated. Despite their fears that their boat's keel had been broken, it proved to be sound. As Lemnitzer wrote in his notes:

"After coughing up about a gallon of water and sand, Foote and I were ready for another attempt. This time we were successful, although on two occasions we nearly capsized again. The boat was nearly a fourth filled with water, and several ribs were broken—it was most difficult to keep it headed into the tremendous swells which were nearly ten feet high. After paddling for nearly a half-hour, we tried the infrared detector and located the submarine which, when it spotted us, started coming in dangerously close to shore, another display of daring and skill by Lt. Jewell and the crew of the P-219.

"After difficulty, we succeeded in getting aboard where Clark and Wright were waiting for us. I had no dry clothes except for the pajamas I had left aboard the preceding night. Everything in the musette bag was in a hell of a mess. The envelope with the gold had broken open and apparently many coins had been lost when we capsized. My leg was badly cut and scraped on the rocks."[26]

The other two boats containing the rest of the party also capsized, but were righted, and the men managed to get them to the submarine. However, the craft containing Holmes was dashed against the *Seraph* by a wave and it sank, its framework smashed. The occupants were rescued, but the boat went down with a weighted musette bag containing a number of letters written by Murphy, several to President Roosevelt, for delivery to England. If they were found, they would reveal that Murphy had been at the conference site, putting him and the expedition in serious jeopardy. Adding to the party's anxiety was the fact that the kayaks had air pockets at each end as safety features, which meant that the craft could have floated and been found. Top priority messages were dispatched to Gibraltar for relay to Murphy, apprising him of the problem and urging an immediate search of the villa's waterfront area. If the lost bag was ever found, it apparently did not fall into unfriendly hands.

As the boats were being folded and stowed below, Jewell saw a file of flashlight beams moving rapidly down the path from the villa on the shore to the beach. He gave orders for the *Seraph* to get under way, and as it picked up speed he saw lights moving about on the beach from which his passengers had fled. "I half-expected a volley of rifle shots," he recalled, but there were none.[27]

Safely aboard and with the submarine making full-speed toward Gibraltar, Clark surveyed his soaked and exhausted followers and decided that some kind of celebration was in order. He asked Jewell if his vessel carried the British Navy's traditional rum ration. The captain replied that it did, but that it could be drunk aboard a submarine only in emergencies. Said Clark:

"Well, I think this is an emergency. What about a double ration?"

Jewell answered that that would be all right, "if an officer of sufficient rank will sign the order."

"Will I do?" asked Clark. Jewell nodded, and a very weary and battered but happy eight American and British fighting men toasted the finish of one of the war's most storied and successful secret missions.[28] During the celebration,

Lemnitzer noticed that Clark's trousers were much too short for him—at last, the mystery of Lemnitzer's missing pants had been solved. After the exploit was made public, Lemnitzer would observe that the press seemed to give more attention to the mix-up with the pants than to what the mission had accomplished.

Clark's hardy followers would go their separate ways after bidding farewell to the crew of the *Seraph*, but in the story telling and warmth of that morning's celebration under the sea would come the only name the daring band ever had. They dubbed themselves the "Panoe Club," and, although there is mention of occasional meetings in Lemnitzer's personal correspondence, it is more likely that it prevailed chiefly as an exclusive bond to be nourished by frequent letters between members over the years.

The club's name sprang from an off-color joke told while the tired passengers were sipping their rum and sharing laughs over their experiences on the shore. The story was about three wealthy businessmen who went up to Canada on a hunting trip, to be joined later by a fourth who was still in the States. When they got into the wilderness, they hired a guide who told them they needed three punts (a small, flat-bottomed boat) and a canoe. They wired the fourth man and asked him to ship the four watercraft as soon as possible. The wording got garbled, and the next day they received a reply: "Girls are on the way, but what's a panoe?"[29]

Both Lemnitzer and Clark would go on to bigger things in their profession, but their secret trip to North Africa always occupied a special place in their memories. Years later, Lemnitzer sent a package containing the uniform he wore to a relative in his native Honesdale, asking that it be put away in the family home; it was quite valuable, he wrote, and was much sought after by museums. Clark had the conning tower of the little *Seraph* enshrined on the campus of The Citadel after he became president. It was not the only memento of the trip at the school: the other was Lemnitzer's trousers, presented this time with the compliments of the owner.

The exploit made national heroes of those who had pulled it off. A colonel who was secretary of the Allied Force Headquarters general staff wrote to Lemnitzer: "Your mission is now well-known to all. Even my little five-year-old son asks his mommie to tell him the story of Clark and his soldiers on the submarine at night before he goes to sleep."[30]

Clark was awarded the Distinguished Service Medal for his part in the mission, the other four Americans a new decoration known as the Legion of Merit (Officer Degree). Later the Officer Degree designation was dropped, the criteria for awarding it were changed, and all those who had received it were told to return it for new medals. Lemnitzer refused to give his up, stating that it had been given for a performance of which he was particularly proud and that it was wrong to take it away. He continued to wear its ribbon, along with the one provided to replace it.

His dash through its doors in his underwear was not Lemnitzer's last glimpse of the Teissier villa. Years later, the C-47 in which he was riding circled the historic meeting spot to give him an opportunity to see the twenty-five foot pyramidal monument the postwar French government had erected near the villa to commemorate the October 1942 visit. During the Algerian war for independence, Algerian rebels blew up the monument and burned the house. Teissier lost all his property and extensive vineyards during the struggle and escaped to France. Penniless when he arrived, he went into the wine business and eventually became prosperous again.[31]

With the morning sun beginning to glow beneath the horizon, Skipper Jewell gave the order to submerge, and the return trip that had begun in such haste from a dark North African shore slowed down to a maddeningly slow three knots, ninety feet beneath the sea. Once, on Clark's orders and against Jewell's wishes, the sub surfaced in heavily patrolled hostile waters, breaking radio silence to report Murphy's lost musette bag.

Submerged again, Clark, Lemnitzer, Holmes, and Wright played bridge through the day, despite severe headaches brought on by the heat inside the sub and the heavy demands on the *Seraph*'s precious air. Jewell surfaced when it got dark and the passengers spent the night drying out and sorting wet equipment, clothing, and papers. Lemnitzer finished writing his account of the venture and turned in for the night.

Gibraltar radioed that it was sending a destroyer to escort the *Seraph* into its harbor, but Clark—impatient to report to Eisenhower and to put Lemnitzer to work incorporating their hard-earned intelligence into the Torch invasion plans—took note of the now-calm seas and radioed for a seaplane. At four forty-five in the afternoon on October 24, a lookout sighted an American Catalina flying boat. By a quarter past five, the Americans—and their equipment and the remaining kayaks—were aboard.

As the Catalina taxied slowly for takeoff, the crew of the *Seraph* asked for permission to come up on deck. Five bruised, dirty, and widely smiling members of the newly incorporated Panoe Club waved farewell through the windows. Their British comrades-in-arms were waving, too, and before the airplane's engines revved up, three exuberant, British-accented "Hip, Hip, Hurrahs!" could be heard across the water—a fighting men's accolade for a job well done.

8

☆ ☆ ☆ ☆

TORCH: THE PUDDING

The Bay of Biscay was a silvery backdrop as the pilot in the leading Junker-88 dive-bomber banked to get a better look at the big warplane skimming over the wave tops hundreds of feet below. Increasing his speed, he dove until the outlines of the other aircraft stood out clearly in his windshield. At that moment, it became a target, for the stranger that had just arrived in German Lt. Erik Molder's patrol area was an American B-17 bomber.

It was an odd sight, indeed. Outlined in the sunlight beneath was one of the war's elite aircraft flying south, far away from any of its usual bombing targets and—most bizarre of all—seemingly all alone and unescorted. Moreover, it was flying less than a hundred feet above the water, so low that spray from the choppy bay was hitting its wings.

Molder radioed to the three JU-88s behind him to follow as he went in to inspect the intruder at close range. The enemy formation split into pairs, one on each side, and flew beside the bomber for several moments. Suddenly a machine gun opened fire and a stream of tracer bullets flashed toward them from behind the pilot's compartment. The JU-88s sped up, zooming ahead for a distance, then turned sharply about, came back, and opened fire with their twenty-millimeter cannons and 7.9-caliber machine guns. They made their runs from the front at first, apparently because the pilots thought both the waist and tail guns were manned.

The German fliers were eager as they pressed their triggers. The appearance of the B-17 had come at the end of a long, boring, and fruitless patrol aimed at seeking and destroying Allied ships in the Bay of Biscay. Downing an enemy bomber would be a memorable achievement in this usually uneventful backwater of the German war effort. Molder and his companions kept looking for escorting U.S. or British fighter planes as they blazed away. None appeared.

The occupants of the B-17 had been watching the JU-88s from the time they became black specks in the skies over the northern Spanish coast, but initially they were helpless to do anything but take evasive action because there were no air gunners in the bomber's crew.[1]

There was a reason why this strange-acting B-17 was carrying an abbreviated crew; an inventory of its interior would have revealed that it was short of practically everything a B-17 carries in wartime, including ammunition. The plane had been stripped to lighten it and to make room for extra fuel and key members of Eisenhower's staff, now on their way to Gibraltar over international waters to oversee the fast-approaching invasion of North Africa.

Eisenhower had left Hurn Airdrome in southern England the previous day in one of five B-17s of the U.S. 97th Bomb Group that had been similarly modified to accommodate other members of his staff. The sixth had to stay behind because of a malfunction in its hydraulic system that had nearly sent the plane crashing into the others as they lined up in single file to take off. Only frantic, last-second braking by the pilot of the heavily fueled plane had averted a fiery collision that could have destroyed all six bombers. Repairs took all day and the next night, and now that plane was winging its lonely way toward Gibraltar, keeping far away from the French and Spanish coasts to avoid patrolling enemy aircraft.

Despite the important nature of the trip, the American planes did not have escorting fighter planes because of the long distance of the flight. Eisenhower, who had previously circulated false reports that he was in Washington for conferences, was relying on extreme secrecy and stealth to get his key aides into position to direct the invasion. Maintaining altitudes that averaged a hundred feet and less, four of the five bombers made it to their destination without incident. The fifth in the main group, carrying logistician Maj. Gen. Asa Duncan and other Torch personnel, disappeared during the flight and was never found.

Now the sixth plane was again in serious trouble. The heavily armed JU-88s were turning for another pass after raking the B-17 with more bullets. The B-17 acquired a gunner: he was Brig. Gen. Lyman L. Lemnitzer, Eisenhower's assistant chief of staff for operations, a onetime gold medalist on the coast artillery's national rifle team who was thoroughly familiar with the operation of the .50-caliber machine guns carried by B-17s. For some unknown reason, such a weapon had been left in the radio compartment. Lemnitzer mounted it and opened fire.

Enemy bullets and cannon rounds raked the twisting and turning American bomber, a tracer bullet shattering windows and the instrument panel in the pilot's compartment and severely wounding the copilot, Lt. Thomas F. Lohr. At the same time, a high whine told the pilot, Lt. John C. Summers, that there was a runaway propeller on one of the plane's four engines; the danger of its coming loose and ripping into the ship's wing or fuselage was added to the perils at hand. Summers desperately needed a copilot to help him manage the bucking aircraft. Lohr, only partly conscious and bleeding badly from an arm wound, could not help.

Fortunately, the battered Flying Fortress had aboard another Eisenhower staff member who also had impressive credentials to lend a hand in an emergency of this magnitude. He was Brig. Gen. James H. (Jimmy) Doolittle, then one of America's most celebrated war heroes for leading the U.S. Army Air Corps' recent first air raid on Tokyo, Japan, and now the commander of Torch's newly formed 12th Air Force. Wrestling with the controls, Summers shouted for Doolittle, the only other flier on the plane, to come to the cockpit.

Slipping into the blood-spattered copilot's seat after Lemnitzer had stopped firing long enough to administer hasty first aid to Lohr, Doolittle followed Summers's orders and helped to slow the runaway engine. Next, he aided the pilot in performing evasive action, the plane making one maneuver that left an attacking JU-88 with the B-17's cockpit in its sights streaking off into empty air with its guns flashing. It was the first time Doolittle had ever been at the controls of a B-17.[2]

In the meantime, Lemnitzer was back firing at JU-88s that were so close he could clearly see the faces of the pilots. He saw the wings on one of the targets wobble as he poured bullets into it and then go into a dive into the sea below.[3] Then, just as it seemed that the enemy dive-bombers were about to overpower their badly out-gunned quarry, the German planes turned and flew off toward the blue coastline on the horizon. The last plane Lemnitzer had been shooting at was trailing heavy smoke as it disappeared in the distance.[4]

After the war it was found out that the JU-88s, attached to the German Air Force's *Fliegerfuhrer Atlantik* at Biarritz, France, had been at the end of their patrol when they encountered the B-17 and had barely enough fuel to return to base when they attacked about midway into the bomber's flight to Gibraltar.[5]

The U.S. bomber continued on its wave-skimming course and later landed safely at Gibraltar after approaching the Mediterranean bastion from such a low altitude that it had to climb to enter the traffic pattern.

It had been an action-packed autumn for the forty-three-year-old Lemnitzer. Two weeks earlier, he had been dodging Vichy French police and fighting for his life in treacherous coastal seas during a secret submarine mission to pave the way for the November 1942 Allied invasion of North Africa. Now, as one of the chief planners of the landings, he would have what was very close to a front-row seat for the first heavy deployment of American ground troops in a European area combat operation.

Gibraltar, a British possession, was just about everything a high echelon head-quarters should not be. Perched on a narrow strait within sight of the continent (but not the area) the Allied troops were to invade, "The Rock" was located on the southern tip of a nation which, though neutral, clearly was friendly to the Axis. German agents maintained around-the-clock surveillance from adjoining

Spanish soil, but they apparently never were able to predict that an invasion was about to take place across the straits or that this was the headquarters.

Eisenhower recalled Gibraltar as "the most dismal setting" he and his staff had occupied during the war. Offices were in subterranean passages blasted into the rock interior. "The eternal darkness of the tunnels was here and there partially pierced by feeble electric bulbs. Damp, cold air in block-long passages was heavy with stagnation that did not noticeably respond to the chattering efforts of electric fans. Through the arched ceilings came a constant drip, drip of surface water that faithfully but drearily ticked off the seconds of the interminable, almost unendurable, wait which occurs [between] the completion of a military plan and the moment action begins."[6]

In this bleak, torturously cramped setting—so close to the planned points of attack that forces and equipment streamed past in ships less than a rifle shot away—was jammed signal equipment by which the Allied commander in chief and his staff kept contact with the commanders of what was until then the biggest amphibious operation in military history. Even with the invasion date weeks away, every inch of the Rock's tiny airfield was taken up with either fighter aircraft or cans of fuel. All this activity was taking place under enemy eyes but, miraculously, there were no attacks by Axis bombers or other countermeasures; apparently the enemy, as Eisenhower had hoped, perceived the buildup as an unusually ambitious effort to reinforce the badly besieged British island of Malta.[7]

(Germany's Adolf Hitler was of the view that the goal of the Allied expedition was Tripoli or Bengasi, far to the east of the actual landings, where he thought the Allies would land four or five divisions to contribute to the destruction of Erwin Rommel's beleaguered forces in the wake of the German field marshal's defeat at El Alamein. The German Naval High Command agreed, and listed Sicily, Sardinia, and the Italian mainland in descending order as possible objectives. French North Africa was listed last. Only Benito Mussolini, the Italian premier, thought French North Africa was the target. But Hitler prevailed, and the Axis concentrated its air units for an attack on the convoys in the Sicilian straits.)[8]

As precarious and miserable as Gibraltar was, there was no other place for Eisenhower to set up his headquarters; except for Malta—an important British bastion that was under almost constant Axis air attack during this period—the Allies possessed not a single other piece of ground in all of Western Europe and the Mediterranean area.[9]

With the invasion less than two days away after his shell-pocked bomber landed on the Rock, Lemnitzer and his planning staff were on duty for long hours with little sleep as they worked out the myriad of final details of putting three major invasion forces on the beaches on the same day. The challenge from a planner's standpoint was staggering: the invasion armadas—two from England and Scotland, and one from the United States—had to arrive on a thousand-mile-long coast early in the morning of November 5, fully equipped and ready to fight.

Complicating the task even further was the heavy toll of equipment and supplies being taken by Axis submarines in raids on convoys in the Atlantic Ocean. These inroads required continuous shuffling to make the best of the resources available as losses kept mounting. Coping with this problem and a difference of opinion on what a properly equipped invasion force should carry with it brought Lemnitzer into his only known confrontation with Maj. Gen. George S. Patton, Jr., the irascible commander of the Western Task Force.

Lemnitzer and his planners were having great difficulty learning what the task force was loading in ships at Norfolk, Virginia, for the crossing to Casablanca. From what they could find out, a serious imbalance was developing. As the shipping capability to his force was being reduced, Patton was making proportionate cuts in combat and service support, medical, signal, and other backup elements while leaving his armored strength intact. Lemnitzer, with Eisenhower's concurrence, saw no justification for the huge amount of armor Patton was bringing along considering the expected strength of the opposition.

"I had the unhappy task at a commanders' conference in London of telling General Patton that his force was becoming unbalanced, that his combat and service support was very thin and that his armored strength was too heavy," Lemnitzer recalled. He remembered that Patton was "sort of standing in front of a rather large group of people" at the conference when Lemnitzer brought up his concerns. Patton listened patiently as Lemnitzer explained his reasons, and when he indicated that his presentation was ended, Patton commented:

"General, I'll do it my way. In this operation, I can't help Eisenhower and he can't help me." Lemnitzer interpreted this remark to mean that because the overall invasion was spread out so far and wide, Patton was going to do it his way and no other way.[10] And that is where the matter rested.

Being the bearer of unhappy tidings is often the lot of the military planner, and Lemnitzer had occasion to have to do this again when shipping problems made it clear to him sometime in the fall that it would be impossible to launch the invasion on November 5. Impelled by impatient men at the highest levels of the Allied governments, this timetable had been hammered out by Eisenhower and his staff during lengthy and often heated planning sessions. The target date was ingrained in every mind involved in the operation, probably the deepest in Eisenhower's. And now Lemnitzer had to tell this general with the famous temper that a minimum of three more days was needed to put the troops on the beaches, necessitating countless changes in plans from the highest to the lowest levels of the complex operation. He waited in front of Eisenhower's desk for the explosion:

"He took it very well," Lemnitzer recalled. "The idea of meeting the target date must have been bothering him, although he seldom, if ever, discussed it. His reaction, his acceptance of the change from the fifth to the eighth of November, came as a pleasant surprise to me."[11] The November 8 date stood after that, but as it approached a vital piece of business in which Lemnitzer had a key stake remained unfinished:

On the day before the Torch landings were to begin, the general was busy with his charts, lists, and the telephones in the headquarters' dimly lit planning room when Eisenhower came in. Accompanying him was a tall, erect Frenchman who, although he wore rumpled civilian clothes, could not have been taken for anything but a professional soldier. At last Lemnitzer was face to face with the man for whose cooperation in the coming operation he, Mark Clark, and a small party of others had risked their lives on a rocky shore in North Africa the month before. The visitor was Gen. Henri H. Giraud.

As Lemnitzer remembered the next few minutes, Eisenhower said to him: "All right, general, explain to General Giraud what the plan is." Using a map on his table, Lemnitzer went over in detail the operational plans for the Allied landings at Casablanca, Oran, and Algiers. Eisenhower's aim, he knew, was to arouse enthusiasm in the French general by showing him how wonderfully things were going. When Giraud made no comment after the briefing, Eisenhower finally asked:

"General, what do you think about it?"

Giraud replied: "I will be an interested spectator."[12]

Eisenhower later recalled the comment as part of "one of my most distressing interviews of the war."[13] With the start of the invasion only hours away, the Allies still had not found a leader to rally Vichy French forces in North Africa to their side. They thought they were close when Giraud agreed to be brought secretly to Gibraltar from France by British submarine (the same one that had carried Lemnitzer and his party on their mission to North Africa). But soon after his arrival, he made it known that his price was command of all forces in the operation, not just the French.

Lemnitzer was not impressed with the famous soldier: "He was terribly hard to get along with," he said many years later. "He was childish, too," he added, noting that when Giraud was finally persuaded to go to Algiers for final discussions of the matter, he refused to fly on anything but a French airplane. This had become a sticky point until the ever-resourceful Robert Murphy found a French plane someplace and dispatched it to Gibraltar to pick up the general. When Giraud got to Algiers he went into hiding.[14]

It was not the first time that Giraud had been stubborn about the nationality of his transportation. When the *Seraph* had plucked him off the shore just west of the port of Toulon, its crew had to pretend the submarine was American because Giraud, in keeping with his sour attitude toward the British, had insisted that his escape vessel had to be American or he wouldn't leave France. There were no suitable American subs available, so the crew hid every item on board that would identify it as English, and the members did their best to sound like Yankees when they had to speak. Lieutenant Jewell, the captain, even stepped aside during the voyage and nominally turned over the deck to a commando officer who looked and sounded more American.[15]

The commando was Capt. Godfrey B. (Jumbo) Courtney, the officer whom General Clark had ordered not to choke (at least audibly) when they, Lemnitzer, and four others had been hiding in the wine cellar during the previous month's submarine mission to North Africa. The popular Courtney was the target of good-natured raillery when he was selected; one U.S. staff officer who was going along suggested that the bogus skipper greet Giraud in American fashion with "Hi, Gen, what's cooking on the front burner or something democratic like that." With the news that the *Seraph* was to host still another general, Courtney had joked with Jewell that "if this sort of thing is going to continue you really should petition the Admiralty to throw out a wing on your submarine liner and install a royal suite."[16]

It had been a rough trip for the general, and his mood reflected it when he arrived in Gibraltar. It must have been harrowing just to get to the rendezvous point in unfriendly territory, and after he stepped onto the deck of the little submarine he and the three men with him—his son, Leon, and two staff officers— were nearly swept overboard by heavy seas as the *Seraph* hurried to get out of dangerous waters. Much of the long voyage had to be spent submerged to avoid enemy patrols, an oxygen-draining mode of travel which sapped energy and morale. Moreover, as General Clark had learned during his secret trip to North Africa, underwater cruising in the cramped *Seraph* was merely unpleasant for most men, but hell for those who happened to be tall. A faulty radio transmitter delayed a rendezvous with a Catalina flying boat, and when the trip ended there was no time for the weary general to get some rest: with three Allied invasion forces nearing their destinations, Eisenhower badly needed to talk right away.

Eisenhower and Clark pressed their point all day and past midnight to no avail. Once, Giraud stood up and said that if he could not command all of the Torch forces he would return to France. Clark, who could be tough in an argument and didn't awe easily, told him: "Oh, no, you won't. That was a one-way submarine. You're not going back to France on it."[17]

Lemnitzer tried his hand as well. Before Giraud finally left for North Africa after the invasion had started without him, Lemnitzer asked to talk with him at the Gibraltar's governor general's residence. The general told Giraud he had been shocked by the Frenchman's obvious disapproval of the Torch plan and asked him why. Giraud replied that the Allies had landed in the wrong place. When Lemnitzer asked where the landings should have taken place, Giraud answered: "In southern France."

Lemnitzer recalled telling Giraud that his proposal was "absurd," and asked him if he knew how many divisions it would take to make an amphibious landing on a shore as strongly defended as that in southern France. When Giraud said "twenty" Lemnitzer said "I nearly fell off my chair and I asked: 'Do you have any idea, general, of what it takes to move a division with the equipment it needs to land on a hostile shore?'" When he asked Giraud what kind of divisions he was talking about, the general answered: "Twenty armored divisions." Lemnitzer remembered that he considered the reply so "ridiculous" that he broke off the conversation and left, convinced that Giraud was no longer in touch with reality. "It was obvious that he had lost all idea of modern warfare, particularly amphibious warfare and things of this kind."[18]

Giraud finally came around and accepted Eisenhower's offer to command only the French forces in North Africa. But it would have been interesting to find out how enthusiastic he would have been had he known that in the entire Torch invasion force there was less than a single armored division.

The French general reached Algiers on November 9, the second day of the invasion. Clark was already there, even as the area was being brought under control by the Allies' Eastern Task Force. The surprise that awaited him gave birth to one of the war's memorable messages: he wired Eisenhower that "I find that I now have not only one Kingpin, but two." Kingpin was the Allied code name for Giraud. The second one Clark was alluding to was Adm. Jean Francois Darlan, commander in chief of Vichy France's armed forces.

Unaware, of course, that Algiers was about to come under siege, Darlan was in the city to be with his son, Alain, to whom he was devoted and who was critically ill with polio at the city's famed Pasteur Institute. Darlan was much despised by the Allies at the highest levels because of his Vichy connection, and under other circumstances might have been seized as a prize prisoner. But the Allies needed him badly, for it turned out to their dismay that Giraud was not the "kingpin" they had envisioned. When he made a radio broadcast announcing that he was assuming command of all French forces in North Africa and calling for them to stop fighting, he was completely ignored.[19]

No other French commander of stature would consider cooperating with the invaders, despite vigorous efforts by Clark. Their allegiance remained to Marshal Henri Philippe Petain, the leader of Vichy France, who had scornfully rejected President Roosevelt's appeal not to fire on Torch forces. The only friend the Allied command had in high places was General Mast, Giraud's emissary during the secret submarine mission to Africa, but he had just been relieved as deputy commander of the Algiers area's XIX Corps for ordering his troops to welcome the invaders as friends and to assist them in repelling any resulting attacks by the Axis. (Mast's cooperation with the Allies, before and after the invasion, was not forgotten: he later was made military governor of Tunisia after it was conquered.)

Eisenhower would later receive heavy and bitter public criticism in the press for dealing with the hated collaborationist, Darlan, but he reasoned that there was no other way to halt further bloodshed between two peoples whose friendship dated back to the U.S. War of Independence. Under heavy pressure from Clark, Darlan, acting in his capacity as commander in chief of the Vichy armed forces, issued orders to his commanders on November 10 to cease fighting. Petain promptly dismissed him as commander in chief, and when Darlan sought to rescind his orders Clark refused to allow it and placed the admiral under house arrest. Clark's brusque treatment of the high Vichy official moved Darlan to ask Murphy one day: "Would you do me a favor? Please remind Major General Clark that I am a five-star admiral. He should cease shouting at me and treating me like a junior lieutenant."[20]

When Germany overran and occupied Vichy France in response to his cease-fire order in North Africa, Darlan considered the armistice between the two nations broken, and he stepped up his cooperation with the Allies. Giraud had earlier thrown in his lot with Darlan, conceding that the little naval officer was the only leader around whom the legalistic French would rally, and was later given command of the North African military forces under Darlan. It was an alliance born of necessity and circumstances: Giraud was contemptuous of Darlan for his Vichy association and the admiral felt that Giraud was, at best, a good division commander but hardly fit for anything higher.

In December, Darlan was assassinated in his office in Algiers by a young Frenchman who gave as his reason his view that the admiral, by dealing with the Americans, was conspiring to revive the corrupt conditions that had prevailed in prewar France.[21] Allied apprehensions that the slaying would touch off an uprising among the French proved to be unfounded. However, the leadership vacuum resulting from the incident touched off a power struggle in which the apolitical Giraud eventually was pushed aside by the ambitious Free Frenchman, Charles de Gaulle. But by then the Allies had moved their forces east into Tunisia. The site of what was up until then history's biggest amphibious operation had served its purpose.

Back at D-Day plus 1, 2, and 3, despite the initial intransigence of Vichy commanders, the wealth of intelligence brought back by Clark and Lemnitzer from their covert mission to North Africa was bearing fruit. The maps and data provided by Mast and his staff were proving to be accurate. There were foul-ups, as they always are in large-scale multiservice assaults, and many could be ascribed to the inexperience of the forces involved. There were errors, some serious, in reaching landing sites and in coordination between units and services. But considering that the U.S. forces, at least, were hearing hostile fire for the first time, progress at all three beachheads went remarkably well.

The Oran landing force, under Center Task Force commander U.S. Maj. Gen. Lloyd R. Fredendall, encountered heavy resistance, particularly from naval elements. But—spearheaded by the 1st Infantry Division, elements of the 1st Armored Division and supported by the 12th Air Force and British naval units—all resistance in the Oran sector ended with the surrender of Vichy forces on November 12. It was the only one of the three task forces to achieve victory by military means alone.[22]

Algiers, the most important objective of the Torch operation, was quickly surrounded by elements of the Eastern Task Force, commanded by U.S. Maj. Gen.

Charles S. Ryder. The center of anti-Vichy activity in North Africa, Algiers had been seized by civilian anti-Axis resistance forces when the Allies landed but Vichy troops quickly regained control. However, by nightfall of the first day the city had capitulated after it was encircled by elements of the U.S. 9th and 34th infantry divisions, and the British 11th Infantry Brigade Group with heavy Allied naval and air support.[23]

As expected in the pre-invasion planning, the heaviest opposition came in the Casablanca region where Patton's Western Task Force ran into elaborate and well-established defenses. Heavily supported by the fire of strong U.S. naval forces, the task force consisted of the 3rd Infantry Division, the 60th Regimental Combat Team, and Combat Command B of the 2nd Armored Division, reinforced by the 47th Regimental Combat Team. As at the other two main invasion points, attacking U.S. forces were confronted with a paradox, created at least in part by the awareness on both sides that a cease-fire was possible at any time. The situation was that many French troops, especially those in the army, did not want to fight the Americans nor was there any enthusiasm on the American side to crush French forces. However, there was no uniformity in these attitudes: some French units, particularly those in the navy, fought back vigorously. An example of the diversity of attitudes occurred after the defeat of the French garrison at Fedala. The commander told Patton the French army did not want to fight Americans and urged that he send a party to Casablanca to ask for the port's surrender. When Patton did so, the commander, an admiral, refused to even receive the general's representatives.[24]

As the Western Task Force tightened its grip, a serious communications problem was developing involving Allied Forces Headquarters at Casablanca: well into the second day of the invasion, Eisenhower had heard nothing from Patton, despite repeated radio messages to his task force. On November 9 Eisenhower dispatched two British patrol planes to find out what was going on. Both were shot down (a subsequent investigation turned up as the probable reason that Allied gunners might have been confused by the British wing and fuselage insignia, which closely resembled that of the Vichy French).

Reports were coming in hourly from Oran and Algiers, and Eisenhower was under heavy pressure from Washington and London for information about what was happening in the Casablanca sector. On the tenth, Eisenhower told Lemnitzer that if he had not heard from Patton by the next day they were going to fly down to see what was going on. When Lemnitzer sought to dissuade him from going personally, citing what had happened to the Spitfires, Eisenhower replied: "I have to go down and see what the hell is the matter with Casablanca. If I don't I'll not be in command of this operation very much longer." Accompanied by Brigadier J. F. M. (Jock) Whiteley, the British deputy chief of staff, Eisenhower and Lemnitzer flew to the Casablanca area in an old British light bomber on the morning of the eleventh. Correctly identified this time by two planes scrambling from an American aircraft carrier, the plane landed and a clearly angry Eisenhower told Patton to start talking.

It turned out that the Western Task Force had been receiving Gibraltar's messages, but its replies were not going through. Lemnitzer said many years later that the American ships handling the communications lacked the proper transmission equipment to get messages to the Allied headquarters. Whatever the eventual explanation, communications of all kinds were a problem in the region. One possible contributing factor was the activities of a hostile station that posed to each of the Allied stations as the other and then effectively employed jamming when a way was found to get around the posing.[25]

Years later, a Lemnitzer interviewer raised the possibility that Patton had not been "exactly grief-stricken that he couldn't report each step he was taking." Lemnitzer agreed, replying "absolutely not, absolutely not."[26] Lemnitzer was convinced that if Patton had not had the situation well in hand in his sector, Eisenhower would have relieved him. As he left to return to Gibraltar, the supreme allied commander told Patton that he wanted an immediate, detailed report delivered to Gibraltar covering everything that had occurred from the time of the landings until Eisenhower's visit. Patton flew up to Gibraltar with his report the next day, arriving safely despite the fact that his C-47 had been fired upon by Spanish antiaircraft batteries when it inadvertently flew over Tangiers on the other side of the Strait of Gibraltar.[27]

The climactic and expected bloody battle for Casablanca was scheduled for the early morning of November 11. The complex struggle for Mehdia-Port Lyautey was just over with the American capture of the French fort, the Kasba, and Patton was making final plans to concentrate all of his forces for an attack on the coastal city. Then, late on the afternoon of the tenth, orders from Darlan were issued to French commanders to cease fighting.

At two o'clock on the morning of November 11, a bugle sounded outside a U.S. outpost northeast of Fedala, site of the task force headquarters, and a French staff car appeared out of the darkness, its headlights shining and white flags flying. Its occupants, two officers and two enlisted men from the French post at Rabat, were given safe passage through U.S. lines to Casablanca after being warned that unless they returned quickly with an agreement to negotiate an armistice, Patton's forces would attack. Only a few minutes before the assault was to begin, with the task force's warships already taking up firing positions, the French ordered their forces to terminate hostilities at once. Operation Torch was over at a cost of five hundred thirty Americans killed and nearly nine hundred wounded. Four members of the British forces were killed and fifty wounded. French losses were much heavier.[28]

Four days later, a weary but exultant Lemnitzer wrote his family: "I feel particularly relieved to know that the entire operation, the largest of its kind in history, went off so successfully. It was perfectly timed, we gained complete surprise and we have a tremendous start which will give the enemy plenty to ponder." Further on, he wrote: "We are working hard and about the most pleasant thing in life these days is sleep. Never thought I'd get to the stage where eight hours of sleep would mean so much."[29]

Eisenhower moved his headquarters to Algiers two weeks after the cessation of hostilities, and Lemnitzer went with him. In a letter to his family written on Christmas Day, Lemnitzer mentioned having flown in "to stay with Albert," a term he had used in previous letters and which probably was a personal code term for Algiers. In late November, he wrote home that "Everything is in confusion in Gerald's place (apparently Gibraltar)," and in another letter he reported that "I have been with Gerald for two weeks, but have also seen Casper (probably Casablanca) and Opal (Oran). They are fine and I thoroughly enjoyed my visits with them."[30] To be sure, his personal code names were undoubtedly thin and might not have made it past an official censor, but one of the privileges of rank was that he also acted as the censor of his own mail.

In another of his letters, he described the Algiers region as "a grand and glorious country—much like California. The palms, orange and tangerine trees are beautiful today. They really look like Christmas trees with trimming." Describing the area's lush farmlands, he exulted that one result of the North African campaign was that it would deny its food output to "Hitler and his lackey, Mussolini. They will have to scratch now to make up for this tremendous loss, and no doubt it cannot be made up anywhere now because we are closing in on him and he knows it."

Elsewhere in the letter, he wrote that he was "greatly relieved" that the U.S. draft age had been dropped to thirty-eight because this meant that his brother Ernest would now be exempt. Addressing his brother, he went on: "I feel you are greatly needed back there to look after your own family, mine, and the folks. You probably don't agree entirely and would probably like to get into things, too, but things must go on at home—otherwise we cannot carry on over here. We can do much better over here when we know that things are being properly looked after at home. So you handle things there, and I'll represent the family in the war." Perhaps in reference to Ernest's known envy of the publicity his brother's career was getting, he added: "I'll get some newspaper mention now and then but that amounts to very little in the long run. You people back there deserve just as much credit as we do, and all of us over here realize it only too well."[31]

With the start of the new year and with Torch forces moving east to do battle with German and Italian legions in Tunisia, Clark once again requested and got Lemnitzer transferred to his staff. Clark, now a lieutenant general, was activating the U.S. Fifth Army, and he wanted Lemnitzer as his deputy chief of staff during the organization period. There was time during this busy period to see the country; in one of Lemnitzer's letters home from Clark's headquarters at Oujda, just west of Oran, he wrote a colorful account of his surroundings: "I have now covered this entire theater of operations by automobile and air—it is never to be forgotten. Colorful Arabs, dirty Arabs, friendly Arabs, sullen Arabs, camels, donkeys (all sizes), tremendous vineyards, deserts, mountains, fertile valleys, severe sandstorms (siroccos), nights so clear you can see stars never visible in the U.S. or England, French uniforms (all kinds), Junkers 88 bombers, olive groves, dive bombers, B17s, P38s, large naval forces, convoys—never were such contrasts and so much of interest packed into one area."[32]

Lemnitzer worked diligently to help set up the new Army command, but he wanted fervently to command troops again before the war was over and made his desires known to Clark. Six weeks after joining Clark at his headquarters, he received new orders: it was time for him to put on his other hat, by now a very dusty one. He was back in active charge of his old 34th Antiaircraft Brigade, now heavily engaged in protecting strategic Allied airfields in Tunisia. Lemnitzer reached his new headquarters in the U.S. II Corps's area of operations less than a week before its elements were badly mauled by Rommel forces at Tunisia's Kasserine Pass, some thirty miles away. With no involvement, all Lemnitzer could do was listen to his post's radios and follow official reports as Rommel's desert war veterans dealt a humiliating defeat to the II Corps's green, poorly led, and ill-equipped Americans.

The disaster resulted in the relief by Eisenhower of the Corps commander, General Fredendall, and his replacement by General Patton. The battered Corps was revitalized under Patton's leadership, becoming an effective fighting force before the Tunisian campaign was over. During this period, Lemnitzer became well acquainted with Patton whom he came to regard as "probably the greatest field commander of our time," at least the equal of Germany's Rommel.[33]

It is probable that no other Coast Artillery Corps unit ever had a more distinguished combat record than the 34th, which saw heavy action throughout the war from North Africa into Sicily, Italy, southern France, and through the rest of Europe into Germany. Activated in February 1941, the brigade was made up of the 67th, 76th, and 77th antiaircraft regiments, and at the height of its strength was comprised of fifteen thousand troops. Its mission was to protect airfields, although in some of the furious fighting around the beachheads its guns were often called upon to engage ground targets as well as aircraft. At Gela, Sicily, for example, a 40-millimeter battalion saved the day by destroying many German tanks at close range when it looked as if U.S. forces were about to be driven back into the sea. In North Africa, Lemnitzer was able to report that the "pasting" German planes had been giving to Allied trains stopped when several were shot down by antiaircraft batteries carried on flatcars. In Tunis, antiaircraft guns were employed effectively against snipers. Searchlights performed missions never envisioned for them with such uses as antimine measures and in acting as homing beacons for landing bombers in bad weather after dark; the general stated in a report on the brigade's accomplishments in North Africa that in one night, thirteen B-17s were saved in this manner.[34]

Service with his own branch in wartime was obviously a source of great satis-faction to Lemnitzer, and, despite more and more assignments in top-level planning, he still regarded himself as a coast artillery professional. In a secret report to the commander of the Antiaircraft Command in Norfolk, Virginia, he wrote enthusiastically from North Africa about his brigade's experiments with using incendiary ammunition in .50-caliber machine guns. In a penned footnote he added that one of these guns had just shot down a big hedge-hopping, four-engined German bomber from a searchlight position—"a most unusual per-formance if there ever was one."[35]

In its 90-millimeter gun, the brigade and its sister units had perhaps the finest long-range antiaircraft gun of any army in the war. Developed shortly before the country entered the conflict, the gun replaced the coast artillery's three-inch gun, which had been found to be ineffective against high-flying enemy aircraft. Lemnitzer considered the 90-millimeter to be superior to the vaunted new German 88-millimeter antiaircraft gun, and all other U.S. antiaircraft equipment to be better than the enemy's. Other weapons in the brigade's arsenal were a rapid-firing Bofors 40-millimeter cannon, a 37-millimeter gun, and the old reliable, the .50-caliber machine gun, which was especially effective when mounted in clusters of four.

The brigade was based briefly in Salisbury, England, after arriving overseas, and first saw action in Oran during the invasion of North Africa. It had moved with the invading forces, protecting vital airfields and even assisting in the ground campaign with such contributions as spotting descending German para-troopers with its powerful searchlights and capturing them as they landed. When its job was done in the Oran sector, the brigade moved into Tunisia to serve with II Corps and then into Sicily.

Lemnitzer's accounts of this phase of his career always make particular mention of the fact that he was Patton's antiaircraft commander when the Seventh Army invaded Sicily in July 1943 and was involved in the general planning. It was an operation to have been proud to have been a part of, for the 34th went ashore with the assault element and distinguished itself both in the air and on the beaches before the island was conquered.

Lemnitzer's association with the brigade ended with the landing phases of Operation Husky, as the landing phase was called, and he was succeeded by Brig. Gen. Aaron Bradshaw, Jr.

In April 1943 Lemnitzer lost a proud follower of his growing wartime fame when his father died at the age of eighty-one. In a letter to his family, Lemnitzer made reference to having known his father had been very ill, but added: "I must admit that the news came as a terrific shock which, I am afraid, will last for a long time. It seems incomprehensible to me that he is gone, and it is very difficult for me to imagine Honesdale and home without him."

William Lemnitzer, the father, seemed to have been a caring, though undemonstrative parent as his son was growing to adulthood, but the war appeared to have established a new warmth in their relationship. His proud father worried about his son and read everything he could find about what he was doing. The huge console radio to which he listened to war news for hours was still in the family home's big attic after his son died. The general wrote after his father's death: "I feel very badly for not having [had] an opportunity to see him again. During my visit at the end of last July when I said good-bye he broke down and said he would never see me again. His premonition was too true."[36]

His assignment over as the Seventh Army's antiaircraft commander in Sicily, Lemnitzer received a letter from its commanding general as his forces were nearing the end of a spectacular sweep of its sector of the strategically important island. It said: "My dear Lemnitzer: "Upon relief from my command for higher headquarters, I want you to know how much I appreciate the fine job you did for me in Bizerte (which Patton's Corps captured near the end of the Tunisian campaign). Your splendid cooperation and prompt action in keeping our urgent requirements in personnel and supplies flowing to the battlefront, and your tactful handling of the many difficult and trying situations with which you were confronted, contributed greatly to the successful operations of the Seventh Army. I am sorry to lose you, but glad that the Commander in Chief, Allied Force Headquarters, appreciates and recognizes your ability and has called you for such a highly important post. I really feel as though we haven't lost you, for on your new assignment I know you will be of great assistance to me and the Seventh Army. Very sincerely yours, G. S. Patton, Jr., Lt. General, Commanding."[37]

Two days before Patton, known fondly to his men as "old blood and guts," paused during his Army's famous dash through Sicily to write his letter, Lemnitzer had been handed a new assignment. Given the tenure of the times, it was not an enviable one, and not only because he would never again command coast artillery troops. It would test him as he had never been tested before, and in passing he would take one of the most personally and professionally rewarding steps of his fifty-one-year military career.

9

THE MENTOR

The briefing was over, and the British general and his staff moved outside to the vehicles that were waiting to take them on an inspection of a mountainous sector of the Italian front held by Brazil's 6th Infantry Regiment. The unit, head-quartered in a valley near Riola, was part of a Brazilian division that had been taking a terrific pounding from big German 170-millimeter artillery pieces located at overlooking mountain sites from which gunners had a clear view of the division's positions.

The day before, twenty-one shells had landed nearby when the general and his staff were inspecting another regimental position in the vicinity. One had incon-veniently destroyed a new privy (fortunately unoccupied) that had been built especially for the general's visit.

Noticing that one of the visitors was wearing only a soft overseas cap for head covering as he walked to his car, the American liaison officer attached to the Brazilian Expeditionary Force picked up a helmet from a barrel outside the head-quarters and asked: "General Lemnitzer, do you want a helmet?"

Lemnitzer looked at him and replied in a low voice: "Christ, yes. But *he* won't wear one, and if he doesn't wear one, I can't wear one."[1]

The style-setter on this chilly November morning in 1944 was Gen. Sir Harold Rupert Leofric George Alexander, commander in chief of the Allied Fifteenth Army Group and in less than a month to become a field marshal and the supreme allied commander of the Mediterranean theater of operations. Lemnitzer, then a major general, was his deputy chief of staff.

Lemnitzer's assignment to Alexander's staff during the invasion of Sicily in July 1943 brought him into contact with one of the war's most extraordinary and admired soldiers. It also touched off a friendship that lasted until the long-retired field marshal's death in 1969, when Lemnitzer was an honorary pallbearer at a royal funeral service in England's Windsor Castle.

He regarded the more than two years he spent with Alexander as the most important in his career in terms of professional development. He became U.S. Army chief of staff sixteen years later, and two hours after being sworn in he wrote a personal letter in longhand to his old mentor. Citing the occasion as "this very important day in my life," he referred to remarks he had made in the ceremony in which he called his selection to the Army's highest uniformed post as having been "due in no small part to the associates with whom I have been privileged to serve during my military service." Then he added: "I want you to know that of this group of valued associates, I consider that you belong at the very top."[2]

On the surface, it would have seemed an unlikely friendship. Alexander, very much to the manor born, was the third son of the fourth Earl of Caledon. He was raised in the family's castle in Ireland, and, while Lemnitzer was still a schoolboy, Alexander was excelling in cricket at Harrow, winning the prestigious annual Irish Mile race and holding down the top cadet post of color sergeant in his class at Sandhurst, England's famed military academy. While his future deputy chief of staff was working in a factory and sweating out an appointment to West Point, Alexander had already commanded an Irish Guards brigade in battle, had been wounded and decorated three times, and had been extolled in print by Rudyard Kipling for his outstanding leadership qualities.[3]

A talented artist whose ambition to become a professional painter had been sidetracked by the war, he was cultured, dashing, articulate, a bit of a dandy and an individual in his military dress, and the possessor of an easy command presence that inspired confidence and respect. Behind the gentle, cultivated manner was an aggressive field commander whose overriding purpose was to "attack, attack, attack, even on the defensive. I have always aimed at the technique of the ring and the double-handed [one-two] punch." But his aggressive nature had a human side: "Always at the back of my mind when I make plans is the thought that I am playing with human lives. Good chaps get killed and wounded, and it is a terrible thing."[4] In a sense, Alexander regarded himself as a servant of his soldiers. Once when a subordinate senior general met him at an airport, Alexander took note of the platoon of motorcyclists waiting to escort his car and asked the general why. When his host said, "To clear the road," Alexander replied: "Would you mind dismissing them? I have a marked objection to clearing my own troops off the road for me."[5]

Alexander's courage and coolness under fire were legendary. He had commanded the rear guard in the evacuation at Dunkirk and was the last British soldier to leave the beaches. The sounds of German armor commander Hans Guderian's tanks were beginning to drown out the lapping of the waves on the shore as Alexander cruised along the coast in a motorboat calling out in English and French for any stragglers.[6] Only then did he board an English destroyer, which was pursued much of the way across the English Channel by *Luftwaffe* fighter planes and dive-bombers.

He later commanded in another losing cause, this time in Burma, where he took over an exhausted and outnumbered force of British and Indian troops and led them in a successful retreat into India. There, as at Dunkirk, his performance was of the stuff that inspires paintings of heroic moments in history: while his troops retreated, he drove up and down the line in a jeep with the steering wheel in one hand and a pistol in the other, urging his exhausted forces on and watching for pursuing Japanese.[7]

Next he was the commander in chief of British forces in the Middle East when, under his command, Gen. Bernard L. Montgomery's Army turned the tide for the English at El Alamein. When Allied armies launched their drive to complete the conquest of North Africa by pushing the Germans and Italians into the sea in Tunisia, he led the U.S. Third and British Eighth armies under Eisenhower, the supreme commander. Alexander apparently regarded this victory as his greatest triumph, for when he was named a viscount in 1946, he chose to be called "of Tunis and Errigal," the latter in honor of the Irish region in which he spent his childhood.

Despite the wide variances in their backgrounds, the blueblood from Ireland and the small-town shoe company president's son from Pennsylvania's Pocono Mountains took a liking to each other early in their relationship. Both were easy to like: Alexander had what the British called "no side," meaning a lack of any pretension or pomposity. Lemnitzer was the same way; those who knew him during his career remember this as perhaps his most endearing quality. Both liked sports—cricket on one side, and baseball, American football, and golf on the other; both loved a good story, each had a keen sense of humor, and they shared a lively curiosity about what was going on around them.

But their most enduring bond had to have been that both were military professionals in the highest sense of the term. Each was selfless to a fault in the performance of his mission; in their own spheres they were the best their countries could produce; and they were true gentlemen, with all that implies in a profession in which deceit of any kind is anathema. For example, Alexander's personal code, born in his formative years in the elite Irish Guards, made him chary of speaking ill to another person or a fellow officer. When he did, as was at times necessary in command, it was on an official level, and his comments were carefully couched to avoid personal observations. Lemnitzer shared that sense of honor; even in his diaries, he was restrained in his comments about persons and events that were obviously trying to his composure, but occasionally he would give vent to his exasperations, most often in letters to relatives and close friends.

Lemnitzer's regard for Alexander bordered on reverence, and years later he would remember him and Eisenhower as the greatest generals of the war. He was nearly seventy and at the end of his tenure as NATO's highest ranking officer when Alexander died, but during his life he always addressed him as "field marshal" and in tones of deep respect. To Alexander, his friend and onetime deputy was always "Lem." Recalling their first meeting, when Lemnitzer became U.S. Army chief of staff, Alexander wrote to him in a letter beginning, "My dear Lem: . . . "It was a very happy day for me when you joined me as my Deputy Chief of Staff and happier too when I learned what an able and efficient staff officer I had gained. To this I need not add what a popular and delightful companion we had found when you came to my headquarters in Italy at the beginning of that campaign. Your [new] assignment is a very popular one in our Army and will do even more to strengthen the ties of friendship between the military of our two countries."[8]

Those ties were in a deplorable state at the field and various headquarters levels when Lemnitzer became Alexander's deputy; indeed, if they had not been, the American general's future might have been vastly different. Lemnitzer's reputation and success ultimately were built on his skills in dealing with matters on an international level, and they seldom would again equal the test he faced when he reported to his new boss in Tunisia on July 25, 1943.

American troops were not highly regarded among their allied comrades in arms during the early phases of the Tunisian campaign. Green, pressed into action without being adequately trained, often poorly equipped, and—most damaging of all—frequently badly led at the highest field levels, their reputation was such that they gave rise to such slurs among the British and French as "our Italians." This low esteem stemmed from initial poor battlefield performances in Tunisia and earlier in French Morocco and Algeria.

Assigned a new commander, George Patton and later Omar Bradley, the U.S. II Corps went on to become an effective fighting force that acquitted itself well in defeating Axis forces in Tunisia and Sicily. But it took an order from Eisenhower to Alexander to take the corps out of a supporting role and give it a portion of the front. Executing a difficult movement across the rears of the mainly British forward units, the Corps then fought its way up the offensive's northern flank and captured Bizerte, a final objective of the campaign, at the same time British and French forces reached Tunis, the other major goal.

It was an outstanding performance. But Alexander still had reservations about Americans as fighting men when the American Seventh and the British Eighth armies invaded Sicily. His attitude was shared by others on his Fifteenth Army Group staff, so much so that Lemnitzer's predecessor on the staff got fed up and became party to a minor act of conspiracy that led to his relief.

Montgomery had been given the main objective of Sicily. After landing, he was to advance up the eastern coast of Sicily to Messina near the island's northern tip. Patton and his Seventh U.S. Army had the mission of protecting

Montgomery's left flank and rear. The assignment was insulting and rankled Patton. He was further incensed later when Montgomery took for his own use a road reserved for the Americans. It was then that Patton learned about a facet of Alexander's style of leadership that most subordinate American field commanders would find unthinkable of exploiting once a battle had begun: he could be made to change his mind about a fundamental decision. (Montgomery routinely took this flexibility a step further: when Patton once complained to him about what he called the "injustice" of one of Alexander's directives, the British general replied: "George, let me give you some advice. If you get an order from [Alexander's] Army Group that you don't like, just ignore it. That's what I do.")[9]

Frustrated that the immense striking power of his Seventh Army was being kept on a tight leash and that it was being confined chiefly to a flank protection mission that was no longer needed, Patton flew to Alexander's headquarters in Tunis to ask that the leash be removed. Alexander listened to his rationale and agreed with him. A fired-up Patton returned to his troops, and in five days, the Seventh Army fought its way against strong German opposition to capture the key seaport of Palermo on Sicily's northern coast. The Americans then shifted their assault to the east and in four weeks entered the Eighth Army's sector and captured Messina, winning what had become a race with Montgomery's forces for the seizure of the campaign's final objective.

Patton's spectacular series of victories gave a badly needed lift to the morale of U.S. troops, but getting respect could still be an uphill struggle in spite of the Seventh Army's success. Toward the end of the campaign, a BBC broadcast reported that Patton's army had "nothing to do except walk through Sicily eating melons and drinking wine." The BBC, which to an American soldier was likely to be synonymous with the British government, was the only source of news on the island, and the broadcast infuriated Patton's soldiers. The report was so unfair and the effect on morale so serious that Eisenhower himself intervened with a protest to Churchill:

"It is reported to me that a recent broadcast of the BBC stated in effect that the Seventh Army was lucky to be in the unoccupied western portion of Sicily eating grapes. The facts in the case . . . are that during the early stages of the invasion the Seventh Army faced at least two-thirds of the German strength on the island, that the only serious counter-thrusts made by the Germans were directed at the Seventh Army, and at least all or practically all the German tanks were at that time employed in the Seventh Army area. . . ."[10] The flap eventually blew over, and at the end of the campaign Eisenhower noted with satisfaction that Sicily had instilled a "spirit of comradeship between British and American troops in action. The Seventh Army, in its first campaign, established a reputation that gained the respect of the British Eighth, while on the American side there was sincere enthusiasm for the fighting qualities of their British and Canadian partners."[11] The real clincher, of course, had been the Seventh Army's capture of

Messina, which showed the British that the American troops were just as good as they were.

Alexander never again showed reluctance to use U.S. troops in any operation. One of the frequent questions posed to him by visiting members of the press and American and British VIPs was "who do you consider the greatest general of World War II?" He would reply that the greatest would be a combination of George Patton and Omar Bradley—Patton for his dash, his willingness to accept any challenge, and his bold, never-say-die style of leadership; Bradley for his outstanding military talents, his unassuming ways, and his quiet and reassuring leadership.[12]

Lemnitzer joined Alexander's staff soon after Patton began moving his forces north. He replaced Maj. Gen. Clarence Huebner, deputy chief of staff and commanding general of the Fifteenth Army Group's U.S. contingent.[13] The U.S. Army's official history implies that Huebner was reassigned because he overtly resented the attitude on Alexander's staff that the American soldier was inferior to the British soldier and was of little value in combat. Huebner, the account goes, "felt impelled to become the protector of American interests."[14]

Brig. Gen. Hobart Gay, Patton's chief of staff, recalled in an oral history interview years later that the specific reason for the reassignment occurred when Alexander changed his mind after his conference with Patton and issued a detailed order which, in effect, would have reattached the leash he had just removed from the Seventh Army. Gay, who had just told the U.S. 2nd Armored Division that it was free to roll, made sure Patton never saw most of the order. Huebner kept Alexander from finding out about Gay's bit of stonewalling until Patton's troops were advancing on Palermo. When Alexander discovered what his deputy chief of staff had done, Huebner was quietly transferred.[15] A distinguished combat commander in World War I, Huebner later became one of the European theater's outstanding division and corps commanders in World War II.

Lemnitzer was notified of his assignment to his new post by Eisenhower. It was an indication of high esteem on the supreme allied commander's part, for the maintaining of good relations between Allied forces was of crucial importance to him. Without such relations, Eisenhower and his superiors in Washington and London knew that the Allies could not wage an effective war against the Axis. It didn't take a major transgression of this spirit to bring down Eisenhower's wrath. One staff colonel found this out when he was sent home because he called a colleague a "British son of a bitch"; it wasn't the SOB part that bothered his boss, but the fact that the colonel specified that the target of his barb was a *British* one.[16]

Relations between the allies on Alexander's staff became much better after Lemnitzer joined it. The improvement in the Americans' performance in battle might have been a factor, but there can be no doubt that Lemnitzer made a significant contribution. Alexander wrote of him in a citation to a decoration at the end of the Italian campaign that "he has done as much as any man to cement the friendship between our two nations. The splendid spirit of cooperation that existed between the two Allied armies was largely due to his efforts."[17]

Lemnitzer regarded the field marshal and Eisenhower as the war's outstanding commanders of Allied forces, an aptitude he said "was lacking in so many senior officers of World War II."[18] Alexander devoted much of his letter to this aspect in 1964 when he penned an answer to what apparently was a cablegram from Lemnitzer on the anniversary of the capture of Rome: "What has always pleased me about it is that it was an Allied [underlined] victory, like all our successes in Italy. And unlike other theaters of operation, there has never been any arguments and recriminations as to whom the credit was due. But then we were a very happy team, thanks to the commanders and staff who all worked so contentedly together. And, my dear friend, you were yourself one of them. What a happy state of affairs, which I have always been proud and thankful for."[19]

On the day Lemnitzer was ordered to join Alexander's staff, Mussolini was deposed as Italian premier by a government whose leaders knew that the swift Allied advance through Sicily meant Italy would be the next target. Eisenhower began receiving strong indications that the new government, under the new premier, Marshal Pietro Badoglio, wanted to surrender. Badoglio proposed that the capitulation begin with a joint Allied–Italian operation to seize Rome under the noses of the Germans. Thus was born Giant II, a near-disaster that came very close to resulting in the destruction of the U.S. 82nd Airborne Division. Only a desperate, final-minutes airplane flight, with Lemnitzer standing behind the pilot firing signals from a flare pistol, saved it.

Badoglio's plan was that the Allies would air-drop a large force onto airfields around the city where they would be joined by Italian units. The Allies were assured by the marshal's emissaries that the combination of the two elements would ensure control of Rome against the German forces known to be in the area. Despite misgivings by such key personnel as Lemnitzer and the commander of the division that would make the drop, Eisenhower regarded the operation as an Italian-imposed condition of surrender. The 82nd, then in Sicily, was assigned the mission.

But Eisenhower wanted a clearer picture of what would await the paratroopers when they landed, and, besides, the Italians had been less than direct so far in their negotiations. So, Brig. Gen. Maxwell D. Taylor, the 82nd's deputy commander, and U.S. Air Force Col. William T. Gardiner were dispatched to Rome in a secret mission to determine how ready Badoglio was to receive the American division. The two left Sicily by a fast British patrol boat, were met at sea by an Italian corvette, and were escorted into Rome under the guise of being captured Allied airmen.

Taylor quickly learned to his dismay that Badoglio was beginning to vacillate and that he and his key generals were now of the mind that if Giant II was to come off at all it would have to be at a later date. The situation Taylor faced was impossible: he met with Badoglio on September 8, the very day the Italian marshal had agreed that an armistice was to begin. Unbeknownst to the seventy-two-year-old premier, the Allies were going to land on the beaches at Salerno the next day and Eisenhower was very desirous that his forces would not have to fight Italians in addition to Germans. Now, Taylor and Gardiner were being informed by the marshal and his staff that not only would Giant II now be impossible because of beefed-up German strength in the area, but that it might infuriate the Germans so much that they would take control of Rome in a bloody battle that the Italians and their American paratroopers could not win.[20]

Something had to be done quickly. Taylor sent a message to Eisenhower's chief of staff, ostensibly asking for instructions. The message contained the phrase "situation innocuous," a prearranged signal which meant that it was imperative that Giant II be canceled. When Eisenhower received the message at his headquarters in Bizerte, he issued an order calling off the operation. Lemnitzer, who was in Bizerte with Alexander, dispatched a message to Maj. Gen. Matthew B. Ridgway, the 82nd's commander, telling him of the development and asking that the message be acknowledged.

When time passed and no notification of receipt had been received, Lemnitzer suggested to Alexander that a courier be dispatched to Licata, on Sicily's southern coast, the 82nd's headquarters. Alexander passed on the suggestion to Eisenhower at a meeting. The supreme commander agreed, and both looked down the table at the junior general in the room: Lemnitzer. There was no time to change into field dress. Lemnitzer jumped into a headquarters car and sped the several miles to the closest airfield, a British one. Alerted of the urgency of the mission when the general left the headquarters, the field had available its only crew and plane, a night-flying Beaufighter. The craft had seats for the pilot and a navigator, which meant that Lemnitzer had to jam himself behind the pilot, standing while bracing himself with his hands on the cockpit's fuselage struts as he gave directions. As the plane taxied for takeoff, it suddenly swerved into the midst of a bunch of parked planes, almost crashing into several before the pilot managed to get it back on the runway for another attempt. Lemnitzer recalled that he nearly bent the struts to which he was clinging: "The pilot turned to me and said 'sorry.' He was scared to death. I told him that was the worst takeoff I had ever seen and wanted no more like it. The pilot explained that he had not flown in daylight for two weeks and was not used to daylight takeoffs. I failed to see the connection."[21]

Finally airborne after the next try, Lemnitzer's next problem was with the navigator, who could not find Licata. When Mt. Etna, Sicily's famed volcano loomed up, Eisenhower's emissary realized that they were lost because the mountain is far northeast of Licata. Lemnitzer ordered the pilot to turn around and fly along the island's southern coastline until they found their destination in late afternoon.

Sixty-two transport planes loaded with paratroopers were already orbiting over the field, and more were taking off at one-minute intervals when the Beaufighter arrived. The plane could not land because of the heavy outgoing traffic, so Lemnitzer looked up the current "colors of the day"—a signal used by fliers when a plane was in trouble. Loading and reloading the plane's flare pistol with cartridges of the proper color, the general began firing from both sides of the plane. After the fifth flare streaked across the sky, the takeoffs below stopped and the British plane was able to land. It taxied to the end of the single runway where Ridgway had set up a small field headquarters. The 82nd Division's commander was wearing a parachute and was about to board one of the transports. Lemnitzer shouted: "Didn't you get our message?"

Ridgway yelled back, "What message?"

The airborne planes were called back, and Giant II came to an end.[22]

The airdrop would have been a disaster. The Allies later learned that there were several German divisions in the landing areas with sizable components assigned to the targeted airfields. The Italian forces that were to team up with the Americans were completely unprepared for combat; they had been broken up into small detachments, and had just enough ammunition for security purposes and fuel supplies sufficient only for routine unit administration.[23]

The Italian surrender took place on schedule despite Badoglio's decision on September 8 to renege over the fear of what the Germans would do to the Italians in retribution. When the Italian premier informed him of his decision, Eisenhower replied that he was going to announce the agreed-upon surrender that day and that if Badoglio did not follow suit, his country would have no friend left in the war. Badoglio signed.[24]

For all it did to forge a tough Allied fighting force and to put the Allies within striking distance of Italy, the Sicily campaign was criticized by some military historians and generals because 110,000 enemy troops with 10,000 vehicles and 17,000 tons of supplies were able to escape across the Strait of Messina into Italy to fight again. Some critics argued that the Allies should have landed troops at Reggio Calabria, across the strait, to cut off the escape. Lemnitzer contended that the division-sized force that might have been conceivable would have been vastly outnumbered and destroyed by enemy troops on the mainland. He also contended that the Allies at that time lacked the air superiority, the landing craft, the troop strength, the experience in amphibious operations, and the time necessary to have executed a successful trap.[25]

In praising Lemnitzer's service after the war, Alexander noted that the American general had been "intimately involved" in all major actions in Italy, from Salerno to final victory on the Plains of Lombardy in northern Italy. Judging from entries in Lemnitzer's diary for the more than two years he served under Alexander, he was a steady companion on the almost daily trips the field marshal took to see what was going on in his command. Alexander rode about in a Ford V8 sedan from which the top had been removed and which had been painted with desert camouflage paint during his days in Tunisia. Lemnitzer said Alexander wanted to be in the open so that he could have an unobstructed view in all directions and, in turn, could be seen by his troops and their officers because he believed that this was important to morale. During his service under Alexander, Lemnitzer recalled: "We spent about three days of every week traveling down to battalion level. The rest of the time we would tour other headquarters or make official or political visits. We drove in the open Ford [because] he was averse to sitting in a car from which he couldn't see everything, especially in the days before we gained air superiority. Under fire he was absolutely imperturbable. I never saw him excited. He never wore a helmet, always his red-banded hat. He had great courage and a remarkable ability to talk to other ranks and extract information from them, gauge their morale, and give them information for which he knew they were hungry. When we were on tour, he would often turn aside to look at some place of historic interest or a battlefield. His curiosity was insatiable."[26]

Once when they were traveling by jeep through a Sicilian village with Lemnitzer driving, they heard someone call out in a clearly American voice, "Hi, Yank." Intrigued, Alexander told Lemnitzer to pull over because there were no U.S. troops in the area. The greeter turned out to be a local civilian from Chicago who had been deported to his native island in the 1930s for bootlegging. "He seemed quite proud of it," Lemnitzer remembered years later.[27]

From Alexander he learned to play cricket, recording in his diary that in a headquarters victory over a Royal Air Force team he scored six runs in a sterling performance that was tarnished somewhat by his un-British habit of dropping his bat after each hit, U.S. baseball style. But prowess at an English sport never turned his head; he played on a headquarters softball team and always noted the score in his diary when there was a West Point football or World Series baseball game.

Lemnitzer had a major role in planning the invasion of Salerno, located on Italy's western coast some one hundred miles south of Rome. Although Salerno was the first Allied invasion of Italy against heavy opposition, Montgomery and two divisions of the Eighth Army had slipped ashore at Reggio Calabria, to the south, six days before. With the landing at Salerno imminent, he cautiously moved his force north against delaying opposition as Axis forces watched for where the anticipated main assault would take place.

Salerno very nearly became another Dunkirk. Clark's Fifth Army, consisting of three augmented divisions, established a beachhead on schedule, but by the fourth day heavy German counterattacks had pushed back the attacking forces to within two or three miles of the beaches where they had landed. Alexander dispatched urgent messages to Montgomery in the south to bring up his two divisions to at least divert some of the savage thrusts being hurled at Clark's forces. Despite a succession of reassuring dispatches that he was on his way,

Montgomery did not arrive on the scene until after the crisis was over. Lemnitzer agreed with later criticism that Montgomery was unduly slow in trying to link up with Clark's forces at the endangered beachhead: "Monty had the tendency to get things completely end to end before he did anything, and they (the Eighth Army) were obviously taking their time about moving up and making contact with the Fifth Army."[28]

Massed German armor smashed at the invading forces, and artillery shells rained destruction from the heights above the beachhead as Alexander and his staff and Clark drove themselves to find ways to turn the tide. Throughout, Alexander maintained his legendary calm, only twice showing any emotion in Lemnitzer's presence: once while arguing for more air support and again when he was told that a subordinate was drawing up a withdrawal plan. Lemnitzer learned of the plan during one of his trips to assess how the fighting was going. The commander of the supporting naval forces had ordered preparation of a contingency procedure to evacuate the beachhead. Alexander, always sensitive to the state of troop morale, showed anger for the first time since Lemnitzer joined his staff. While conceding the need always for contingency planning, he told the admiral in command that news that the Navy was even discussing withdrawal would "spread like wildfire" ashore and that the result would be a disaster. He ordered the plan scrapped immediately.[29]

Alexander and his staff scoured the Mediterranean theater and beyond for more troops and air and naval support to throw back the furious German counterattacks and preserve the beachhead. Follow-up forces would double the initial ground strength, but it was a massive air assault that was the deciding factor in securing the victory. Obtaining the planes was a fight in itself. Lemnitzer recalls being in the room when Alexander and theater Air Chief Marshal Sir Arthur Tedder clashed over Alexander's request for more air support. Tedder, a crusty individual who had had differences with the Fifteenth Army Group commander in the past, pooh-poohed the danger on the ground and implied that Alexander was exaggerating the extent of the struggle below.

Alexander replied: "Well, Arthur, I'd just like for you to go up to Salerno, stay with the men in an infantry battalion for a month, share their life and then see what you would say." Eisenhower, who was also at the meeting, took Alexander aside after the meeting and told him not to mind what Tedder had said—that was just "his way." He added that Alexander would get the air support he needed.[30]

Following an inspection of the front on the third day of the invasion, Alexander and his generals became convinced that the Germans were about to exploit the presence of a river extending to the beachhead and try to split the Allied toehold. The fourth day the field marshal received authority to use every available aircraft in the theater to attack the enemy positions. Supported by heavy naval gunfire offshore, the planes arrived over their targets the next day and so disrupted German communications, supplies, and mobility that troops on the ground were able to regain the initiative. Nearby Naples and the strategically important airfields at Foggia fell three weeks after the initial landings at Salerno.

Years later, one of the field marshal's British biographers wrote admiringly of the invasion: "If any individual can ever be said to win a battle, Alexander won Salerno."[31] However, at least one American historian gives a major share of the credit to Clark.[32]

Lemnitzer was involved in discussions that led to the relief of a U.S. Army corps commander during the battle for Salerno. Clark became concerned about how VI Corps was being led, and he asked Alexander to visit the commander, Maj. Gen. Ernest J. Dawley. Alexander and Lemnitzer arrived at his headquarters to find that the stress and strain of battle had affected the exhausted Dawley to the extent that his hands shook, and he was unable to give Alexander a coherent account of his corps' situation, deployment of units, or what actions he planned to take next. Because the relief of a corps commander is a very serious matter—the effect on the morale of the troops alone can be staggering—the field marshal sent Lemnitzer to explain the problem to Eisenhower. After listening, the supreme commander burst out, "Well, goddamit, why in the hell doesn't he relieve him?" But Alexander had always had qualms about relieving a senior commander of another country, and so Eisenhower returned to Salerno with Lemnitzer to look into the situation himself. He met with Dawley and then agreed that he had to be relieved.[33]

Lemnitzer was the chief planner for the Allies' next major amphibious operation, the landing at Anzio. Code-named "Shingle," the invasion had as its target a small seacoast area located thirty-five miles south of Rome. Eisenhower had been lukewarm toward Shingle because he considered it to be too risky. But Churchill and Alexander (and Lemnitzer) were enthusiastic about it and they prevailed, helped by the fact just before the final decision was made, Eisenhower was transferred out of the theater to command Operation Overlord, the cross-channel invasion of northern France.

The outgrowth of an idea broached by Lemnitzer during a staff meeting, the Anzio landing was conceived as an "end run" to break up the impasse at the German Gustav Line to the south where Allied forces had been stopped cold.[34] Afterward, Lemnitzer would declare Shingle "a complete success [which] accomplished the objectives we were seeking."[35] This is a confusing claim because the ultimate achievement of Anzio was not what Alexander had envisioned. The goal, as he saw it, was to trap Field Marshal Albert Kesselring's Tenth Army or compel it to move back from the enemy's Gustav Line by placing a strong Allied force in its rear. The Gustav Line was a formidable defensive position which was standing in the way of Allied forces seeking to drive north. Possibly Lemnitzer was referring to the landing's short-term objectives when he dubbed it a success—it certainly did little, if anything, to weaken the Gustav Line. What it did do was to provide Clark with a jumping-off place for the eventual capture of Rome and, in so doing, touched off one of the war's great controversies.

Anzio and adjacent Nettuno proved to be an excellent choice, both to establish a beachhead and as a base for operations inland. The VI Corps of two divisions, one American and one British, went ashore without opposition. Not a shot was fired in the predawn darkness of the opening day—June 22, 1944—and so complete was the surprise that on the morning of the invasion Alexander, Clark, and Lemnitzer cruised to the landing site in an American patrol torpedo (PT) boat and walked four miles along a road leading to Rome without seeing a single enemy soldier.[36] The Allies were astounded by their good fortune. Harold MacMillan, the theater's resident minister, was about to board a plane for Algiers from Naples when the landings began: "Just before leaving," he wrote in his diary, "we had the first news of the landings, which sounded very good. By some miracle, the thing was a complete surprise. How they [the enemy] can have failed to see the great convoys moving slowly up the coast all day yesterday and going only about five knots, I cannot imagine."[37]

The convoys carrying troops, equipment, and supplies had slipped past the *Luftwaffe* patrols that were supposed to be watching the waters over which they traveled. The first report of the invasion to Kesselring came from a small panzer grenadier detachment that happened to be resting and retraining near Anzio. The Germans reacted quickly, however. Within two days, powerful forces were streaming into the area, many sent from France, Germany, and Yugoslavia under the orders of Hitler and the German High Command. In less than two weeks, ten of the enemy's best divisions were fighting to carry out Hitler's personal orders to "drive back into the sea and drown" an Allied invasion force that had grown to five divisions.[38]

While Alexander was preparing to drive northeast with a general offensive aimed at cutting German Tenth Army supply lines, Kesselring's forces struck. The battle raged for a week, reaching the height of its severity between February 16 and 20, with German divisions attacking in succession down the Albano-Anzio Road. The outnumbered Allied forces fought back furiously, the ground troops heavily supported by artillery, naval vessels, and air forces. At one point, they were backed up nearly to the Allies' "final defense line," but they held and surged back to preserve the bridgehead.

Lemnitzer noted in his diary that in the heavy fighting an entire battalion of U.S. Rangers was destroyed. The unit belonged to the famed Darby Rangers, commanded by Col. William O. Darby. The possessor of one of the war's most illustrious battle records in combat from North Africa through Sicily and Salerno, the battalion was ambushed during a surprise attack on the little inland town of Cisterno. It was Darby's last combat command; he was promoted to brigadier general, became assistant commander of the Fifth Army's 10th Mountain

Division, and was killed by artillery fire shortly before the Italian campaign ended.

In the around-the-clock shelling that rained on the invaders, one of the German's most formidable weapons was a 280-millimeter railway gun—dubbed the "Anzio Express"—which the enemy kept concealed in railroad tunnels in the mountains between firings. A peculiarity of the beachhead was that the ground's soft sandstone base caused a tremor in the target area when the enormous gun was fired from fifteen or twenty miles away, signaling that a shell was en route and adding to its psychological effect on the invading forces. Other dependable warnings were the regular radio broadcasts of the German propagandist "Axis Sally," who would report the precise times when the gun was scheduled to fire. What the troops in the beachhead were not told was where the shells would land.[39]

With the defeat of Kesselring's first effort to smash the invading forces, the VI Corps got another new commander when U.S. Maj. Gen. John P. Lucas was relieved by Clark. Lemnitzer said years later the reason was that Lucas had not been aggressive enough in pushing beyond the beachhead, but indecisiveness, weak battlefield leadership, poor command presence, and outspoken pessimism about the military value of the Anzio landing also were said to have contributed to Clark's decision.[40] In Lucas's defense, his health had suffered because he had been given an inoculation from a defective batch of yellow fever vaccine, and he was not physically able to command a corps in combat.[41]

Lucas's performance in exploiting his successful landing has been the subject of considerable controversy. Some historians contend that Alexander's operational orders to Lucas were to drive to the strategic Alban Hills, twenty-five miles to the northeast. Lemnitzer disputed this, contending that the corps commander's force of two divisions was understood by the field marshal and his staff to have been too small to accomplish this mission or to hold the hills after it got there.[42]

Lucas halted his corps when the bridgehead was seven miles deep to await the addition of an armored division and other reinforcements. By the time more divisions arrived, Kesselring had moved in strong reinforcements. Although Alexander said later that Lucas had made the correct move in pausing, he regarded his operations as halting and poorly coordinated, and suggested to Clark that he be relieved. The Fifth Army commander was reluctant because it would be awkward to relieve another VI Corps commander so soon after Dawley had been replaced.[43] But Alexander persisted in his indirect way, recalling in his memoirs: "His [Lucas's] appointment was entirely an American affair, and it would have been quite inappropriate for me to have intervened. However, at last, I brought myself to remark to Mark Clark: 'You know, the position is serious. We may be pushed back into the sea. That would be very bad for both of us—and you certainly would be relieved of your command.' This gentle injunction, I am glad to say, impelled action."[44]

The new corps commander was the very able and aggressive Maj. Gen. Lucian

Truscott, already at Anzio as Lucas's deputy and the commander of the 3rd Infantry Division.

Having thrown everything it had at the invading forces and been turned back during its first offensive, the enemy never again attacked at Anzio with the same vigor. The 3rd Division took the brunt of a second offensive on February 29, and during three days of fierce fighting kept the Germans from making any material gain. Resigned to the fact that he did not have the strength to break through the Allied lines during the winter, Kesselring ordered his forces to go over to the defensive.

With both lines stabilized, Anzio could now wait because the contribution Alexander had envisioned for it would come when the Allies could smash through the Gustav Line. The linchpin of the line was the town of Cassino, which lay one thousand seven hundred feet below the famous old Benedictine monastery of Monte Cassino. Both were regarded as formidable obstacles to any Allied advance north, the town because it was defended by well-entrenched elite troops and the monastery because it was believed by the Allies to be an important observation post from which the enemy could watch the movements of the besieging forces while targeting their positions for artillery fire and aerial bombing attacks. Lemnitzer and Army Air Corps Maj. Gen. Lauris Norstad were ordered to plan the destruction of the monastery and the town.

The possibility that the monastery would be attacked touched off a worldwide public outcry, including an appeal from the pope and opposition from such close associates as Clark. But, convinced that the monastery was a center of enemy activity by such subordinates as Australian corps commander Lt. Gen. Bernard Freyberg, Alexander put his planners to work. He said later: "A commander, if faced by the choice between risking a single soldier's life and destroying a work of art, even a religious symbol like Monte Cassino, can only make one decision."[45]

The historic landmark was pounded with five hundred tons of aerial bombs on February 15. When the Allies were still unable to capture the town below, a combined air-ground attack was launched a month later. In the devastating assault, Allied planes rained over eleven hundred tons of bombs on Monte Cassino and the town while troops attacked behind heavy artillery fire. They succeeded in occupying most but not all of Cassino in a battle made even more fierce because the bombing and artillery fire had created a city of rubble behind which the defenders—five thousand members of the crack 1st Parachute Division—threw back repeated assaults.[46]

The Germans stayed, however tenuously, and Monte Cassino held out until a Polish Army corps climbed higher mountains east of Cassino and came down from their crests to overpower the German garrison after the French Expeditionary Corps had broken through the Gustav Line during Alexander's Operation Diadem. The Allies then learned that the enemy had not been occupying the monastery; its fortifications were on the hill around it, although some were close enough that incoming artillery rounds would also hit the abbey. Sentries had been posted at the walls by the German corps commander for the area, a devout Roman Catholic, to prevent German troops from entering.[47]

Years later, Lemnitzer took issue with a book reviewer who had termed the bombing unnecessary. "The facts are," he wrote to a friend, "that Allied intelligence strongly indicated that the Germans were using the monastery for military purposes—particularly for observation which gave them a great advantage in the land battle taking place below. Military operations have to be conducted based on intelligence at the time, not on what history shows to be the case forty years later."[48] Inspection after the position's fall showed that the Germans had indeed been using Monte Cassino as an observation post, but their vantage points were in their own fortified works hundreds of yards away.

Alexander launched Operation Diadem on May 11 with an assault along the entire length of the Gustav Line. In five days of heavy fighting, the destruction of the Gustav Line was complete and Kesselring's forces fell back to the Hitler Line, a heavily fortified defensive position to the north. Deceived by Alexander as to the timing and thrust of the attack, the Germans were kept off-balance and were outfought and outgeneraled at every turn as the Eighth Army and elements of the Fifth Army smashed their way north. In what has been called one of the most beautifully orchestrated offensives of the war, Alexander had secretly shifted much of the Eighth Army to the eastern flank of Cassino and then launched a surprise attack, which broke the Gustav Line.

When the Hitler Line began to crumble, Alexander was ready to make the destruction of the Tenth Army complete. He ordered Clark to break out and move his six divisions northeast to Valmontone to cut the main highway to Rome, and join with the Eighth Army in a pincers movement to crush Kesselring's forces. Supported by nearly the entire weight of the theater's air forces, Truscott's corps reacted like an uncoiled spring after months of dreary siege warfare and slashed into the encircling German Fourteenth Army on May 23. Within two days, enemy troops in the Cisterna sector gave way and Truscott began driving toward Valmontone.[49] Then ensued a series of strange command developments, the circumstances of which are still being debated by military historians.

Three days before the breakout, Lemnitzer personally delivered to Clark a written order from Alexander directing him to move his forces to Valmontone and cut off the Tenth German Army. Immediately, Lemnitzer recalled ruefully, he became "the man in the middle" of what turned into a bitter argument at the highest Allied levels.[50] Although it is clear that Alexander had conceived Anzio as the base for a thrust at the Tenth Army's rear, by the time of the breakout—and probably well before—Clark had made his own plans. He wanted the troops of his Fifth Army to be the first to enter Rome. After Lemnitzer gave him Alexander's order, Clark said he was "shocked" at the field marshal's decision, although Alexander had reiterated his dedication to the Valmontone objective in a conference with Clark a few days before.[51] The Fifth Army commander told Lemnitzer that his forces could not reach Valmontone and ordered Truscott to send five divisions to seize the Alban Hills and drive on to Rome. The other division was dispatched toward Valmontone, where it was stopped by much larger enemy forces along the way. As a result, Kesselring's veteran Tenth Army lived to fight another day north of Rome.

Of his decision to move on Rome, Clark later wrote: "We not only wanted the honor of capturing Rome, but we felt that we more than deserved it; that it would to a certain extent make up for the buffeting and frustration we had undergone in keeping the winter pressure against the Germans. . . . Not only did we intend to become the first Army in fifteen centuries to seize Rome from the south [the last was the Byzantine general, Belisarius, against the Goths in A.D. 536], but we intended to see that the people back home knew that it was the Fifth Army that did the job and knew the price that had been paid for it."[52]

Clark was concerned, perhaps with reason, that the honor of capturing "The Eternal City" would go to the Eighth Army, although Alexander had assured him that as Operation Diadem unfolded Rome would be in the Fifth Army's sector. Like Montgomery, Clark apparently had learned that when one of Alexander's generals didn't like an order it was possible to ignore it and get away with it. After hard fighting in the Alban Hills, Truscott's corps entered Rome on June 4. It encountered no resistance; the German forces there had already moved out. Alexander was lavish in his public praise of Clark's deed and let the Fifth Army commander take full credit, even arranging to be elsewhere during Clark's triumphal entry into a city that was regarded as one of the great prizes of the war. When the field marshal entered, it was in a jeep as a sightseer. But, in fact, Alexander was "terribly disappointed, terribly disappointed—we all were," Lemnitzer recalled years later in reflecting on Clark's failure to trap the Germans at Valmontone.[53]

In the American Army with its tradition of strict obedience to orders, Clark's action would surely have resulted in his being sacked, even though his forces had performed a remarkable feat of arms in their advance on Rome. In Clark's favor, Alexander's laissez-faire style of leadership has been criticized as having provided fertile ground for the American general's apparent disregard of a direct, written order. Alexander's instructions and conversations with Clark during the Anzio battles had been too indefinite for a general imbued with the American way of command. Alexander appeared to have been inclined to let Clark run the Fifth Army as he liked.[54]

Alexander's approach even drew the attention of Churchill, who wrote later of Anzio that "I had hoped that we were hurling a wild cat onto the shore, but all we had got was a stranded whale." To Alexander, he commented: ". . . senior commanders should not 'urge' but 'order' . . . American commanders expect to receive positive orders which they will immediately obey. Do not hesitate to give orders just as you would your own men. The Americans are very good to work with, and quite prepared to take the rough with the smooth."[55]

The field marshal's order to Clark couldn't have been more explicit, but he did not make a determined effort to ensure that it was obeyed, trusting Clark to carry out the spirit, if not the letter, of his directions.[56] When Alexander got to the bridgehead on May 27, Clark's forces were already driving into the Alban Hills and it was too late to change direction. There are indications that the two were not in accord on the feasibility of bottling up the Germans. Writing after the war, Clark commented: "I certainly did not want to send Truscott forward until the enemy had been driven into a position from which we were certain we could force him back beyond Rome."[57] He regarded Alexander's plan to cut the Germans off and trap them as militarily unsound and impossible to execute. But the Fifth Army commander denied that he had disobeyed Alexander's order, contending that his superior had agreed to his plan to attack through the Alban Hills toward Rome while simultaneously sending a single-division "task force" to Valmontone. The latter was, of course, easily stopped by the Germans before it got to its objective. He recalled: "I know Alex didn't like the way I was doing it, but he issued no ultimatum to me to make me do it differently. He left it to me."[58]

Lemnitzer was beholden to many as he climbed in his career; most recognized his extraordinary abilities, and by their usually glowing assessments moved him into ever more challenging assignments. He learned from his benefactors as well, but, as he wrote when he became Army chief of staff, he owed the most to Field Marshal Alexander. No one was closer professionally to the British commander during his finest and most trying hours, and it is reasonable to believe that at this still very formative period of Lemnitzer's life many of the traits that took him to the top of his profession were instilled in his years with Alexander.

There was the renowned aplomb, in Lemnitzer's case whether under enemy fire in Korea or in a congressional hearing room. There were the common grounds cited before: the gentlemanliness, the warmth, the lack of pretense, the enormous personal courage, the concern and affection for subordinates of all ranks, love of a good game, and the instincts of born professionals. If staid American Army customs would have permitted it, Lemnitzer might have adopted some of Alexander's sartorial fancies, too, although it is difficult to imagine him garbed in anything but the most regulation of military dress.

Eisenhower regarded Alexander as his nation's foremost strategist and wanted to take him to England with him for Operation Overlord, but Churchill said no because he didn't want two of the Mediterranean theater's top commanders leaving at the same time. This was a high tribute to Alexander's ability, for his command style was about as foreign to Eisenhower's and the American Army's tight-rein concept of leadership as picking generals by popular vote. Although

Lemnitzer would never hold a command comparable to his mentor's in wartime, there were striking parallels in the way he exercised his leadership in the high staff posts that occupied much of the rest of his career.

MacMillan, a future British prime minister, recalled that Alexander "has the most effective way of giving not exactly orders but suggestions to his commanders. They are put forward with modesty and simplicity. But they are always so clear and lucid that they carry conviction. It is a most interesting (and extremely effective) method."[59] This style could, however, invite adventurism on the part of subordinate commanders and sometimes outright disobedience. The ever-loyal Lemnitzer was incensed many years later when he was supreme allied commander in Europe to hear that Montgomery had just remarked at a press conference that "Alex was a very good general, a very good general indeed—he did everything I told him to do." Lemnitzer called this "the most contradictory and the most vicious statement he could possibly have made."[60]

Alexander found Montgomery a difficult, irritating person to deal with, a situation which may have prompted a style in which he rarely, if ever, issued direct orders to him. His policy in regard to the Eighth Army was to get his ideas down to the staff level. In visits to the Eighth Army, he would put forth these ideas to the staff and ultimately they would come back to him from Montgomery or, later, his successors, as recommendations. Lemnitzer thought it was "very skillful and fitted the personalities very well."[61]

Another example of Alexander's policy of persuading and, when necessary, appealing to his subordinates' sense of duty and common purpose occurred during the final battle for Cassino when a highly charged dispute over command of the tactical air forces arose between the British and Americans. Unable to resolve it, Alexander's chief of staff took the matter to his superior. Alexander told him to tell the commanders concerned to come to his office: "I shall then lock the door, tell them I have letters to write and invite them to let me know when they have reached agreement." General (later Field Marshal) John Harding, the chief of staff and Lemnitzer's direct superior, recalled much later that "the matter was settled and in the right way—by agreement and 'out of court.'"[62] Harding added, though, that Alexander "could be firm and ruthless, if need be."

Finally, Lemnitzer may also owe to Alexander his nearly career-long aversion to the limelight. It wasn't always thus: before he joined the field marshal's staff, his letters home frequently asked his family to save any news stories about him; he was particularly concerned about keeping anything having to do with the submarine trip to North Africa. These kinds of requests were rare after he met Alexander.

One of his favorite recollections of his service with Alexander had to do with publicity. Part of Lemnitzer's job during the Italian campaign was to issue a press communiqué each evening that detailed the day's accomplishments of the U.S. Fifth and British Eighth armies, both commanded by highly publicity-conscious generals. He regarded it as a "very onerous, disagreeable task" because he was constantly criticized by the commanders of the respective armies for giving too much credit to the other. One day, after an especially rough going-over by the chiefs of staff for both armies—Alfred Gruenther for the Fifth Army's Clark, and Francis de Guingand for Montgomery—he was feeling disgusted, and it showed at the headquarters mess that night. Alexander noticed that he was upset and asked him why.

His deputy chief of staff cited the "terrible time" given him by Gruenther and de Guingand and told the field marshal he thought the whole system of issuing press releases was wrong. "Why should we be putting out communiqués pertaining to the Fifth and Eighth armies?" he asked. "The communiqué should be put out for the Fifteenth Army Group, Field Marshal Alexander's group." Alexander smiled and replied: "Lem, the purpose of the Army group commander is to help the Army commanders, and when things are going well, there's credit enough to go all the way around. When things are going badly or we are being defeated, it doesn't make any difference."[63]

This response, perhaps as much as any other comment the field marshal ever made on the subject, did much to explain what to many seemed an impossibly detached concept of command. But for Alexander—one of the war's most successful military commanders—it usually worked, his difficulties with Clark at Anzio notwithstanding. Perhaps no one else among the Allies' elite possessed quite the right combination of abilities to lead an army group the way he did.

The key quality in the field marshal's lesson was selflessness, its military value summed up in a maxim that a future U.S. commander in chief kept on his desk: "There is no limit to what a man can do or where he can go if he doesn't mind who gets the credit."[64] Whether it was a trait that Lemnitzer brought with him when he went to war or whether it was learned from one of the war's truly great masters of command, of all his qualities this is the one remembered best when those who knew him try to describe him to others.

10

★ ★ ★ ★

SUNRISE

Lemnitzer's dangerous penchant for putting himself in harm's way manifested itself again two days after Christmas in 1944 when the C-47 in which he was riding back from a conference strayed over enemy lines and tried to land at a German airfield. He noted in his diary:

"Error in navigation (mistaking Caesena for Forli) put us over German lines at Imola and Castel Bolognese at 500 ft. alt. AA [Antiaircraft] and small arms from entire German area opened up on us—40 mm. hit and blew off most of rudder. Finally limped back to Forli. This is the narrowest escape yet—A MIRACLE."

There the matter ended. The next entry that day noted that he had lunch with the commander of V Corps, visited Ravenna, Italy, and had dinner in the British Eighth Army headquarters mess. There was no time in the general's busy schedule to waste an hour or so resting up after nearly being shot down at point-blank range.

Lemnitzer was meticulous in recording his actions and impressions during the war. He described his days in a paperback, government-issue diary whose daily space allotment measured four inches by one-and-a-half inches, and he wrote in a tiny but highly legible longhand that made it possible to cram a remarkably broad range of information into a tiny portion of a page.

It was the journal of an enormously busy senior staff officer who seemed to be almost constantly on the move as he carried out his duties as one of Alexander's most trusted deputies. By plane, car, jeep, boat, half-track, tank, truck, and foot, he seemed to be everywhere from one end of Italy to the other, and back and forth from other headquarters as far away as London. He even made one brief trip in an Italian locomotive; it was a ceremonial run, and the hand on the throttle was Alexander's, who had earned his engineer's cap years before when the British army had taken over the nation's railroads during a labor dispute.

Entries almost invariably began with "the usual conferences," of which there were many. Besides the regular daily meetings through which headquarters business was conducted, Lemnitzer's week often was filled with high-level conferences in which the participants could be anyone from Prime Minister Churchill to U.S. Army Chief of Staff George C. Marshall. Usually, Lemnitzer was one of the conference's chief planners, and often, he was the conductor. When important people arrived at Alexander's headquarters at Caserta, Italy, it was frequently Lemnitzer's job to meet them and to act as a host, with Alexander and others on his staff at lunch and dinner.

During Lemnitzer's two years with Alexander, some of these guests included King George VI of England; Churchill (dinners for the garrulous prime minister often lasted past midnight); Prince Peter of Yugoslavia; Prime Minister and Field Marshal Jan Smuts of South Africa ("one of the most interesting and wise men of this generation," a Lemnitzer diary entry noted); future British prime ministers Harold MacMillan, Clement Atlee, and Anthony Eden; James Forrestal, after the war to become the first U.S. Secretary of Defense; celebrity Congresswoman Clare Booth Luce and various other congressmen; members of British Parliament; and practically every Allied general of any note in the Mediterranean and European theaters. The only visitor without a title that Lemnitzer mentioned in his diary was sultry film star Marlene Dietrich, to whom he was designated to be official greeter during one of her visits to entertain troops.

When these elegant evenings were over (the Caserta headquarters were in an ornate castle which in years past had been the abode of the kings of Naples), Lemnitzer turned soldier again. His quarters and office were in a "caravan," which he described in a letter to his fifteen-year-old son William as a "small house built on a two-and-a-half ton truck." He added that "when the weather gets cold, I merely add more clothes" because there was no heat. He noted, however, that he was much better off than "the boys at the front who sleep on the ground and are out all the time in the rain, sleet, and snow."[1] After the war was over and he became the Mediterranean theater's chief of staff, he finally got more palatial quarters closer to the castle in a building that had been used as a hunting lodge during the reigns of the Neapolitan monarchs.

His letters home belied the sometimes popular assumption that generals on headquarters duty lived high. He often asked for such ordinary items as toilet articles, hair tonic, and pencils. When the U.S. mails sought to limit the number and sizes of packages going overseas by requiring written requests for specific articles, Lemnitzer complied. One of his lists included a picture of a pair of shoes that he had clipped from a magazine advertisement. Some of his letters might have been written by a private at the front, so often did they carry expressions of gratitude for the chocolate bars, cookies, and other commonplace things his family had sent to him.

In March 1944 his diary noted that the War Department had requested his transfer back to Washington to serve as deputy chief of staff for operations. It would have meant a promotion, but he liked where he was. "Gen. Alex does not want me to go," he wrote in his diary, and the next day mentioned that Lt. Gen. Jacob L. Devers, then senior U.S. general for the theater, had sent a message to Washington saying that Alexander wanted him to remain on his staff. He heard nothing more of the War Department's request. Alexander followed this up a few weeks later with another request: after praising the outstanding job Lemnitzer was doing, he recommended that he be promoted to major general, a rank he stated would be more appropriate for his responsibilities. Lemnitzer began his June 23, 1944, entry: "Two stars on for first time."

Naturally inquisitive, he was fortunate to have a superior like Alexander who moved about even more than did Lemnitzer and whose interests ranged from how one of his distant regiments was deployed on line to the fine points of a famous piece of ancient Roman statuary. A typical Lemnitzer entry for a trip to the field includes the one for September 28, 1944: "Up early at new CP (command post) on Adriatic shore. Drizzling. Left 0900 [nine o'clock in the morning] with Gen. Leese [Sir Oliver, Montgomery's successor as Eighth Army commander], and Cannon [Maj. Gen. John K. (Joe), commander of the theater's tactical Air Forces] to inspect Gothic Line[2] positions. Very strong and formidable—Panther [tank] turrets, much wire, mines, many destroyed tanks of both sides, destruction of fruit and olive orchards and vineyards for fields of fire, whole villages destroyed for same purpose. Took off for Fano at 11:30. Back at [command post] for lunch. Spent afternoon cleaning up paperwork."

Alexander's zest for Italy's art treasures and the beauty of the countryside took Lemnitzer off on excursions, and one can sense from reading his daily account he would sometimes rather have foregone in the interests of getting some work done. He exclaims in wonder in his diary about the contents of Rome's museums and buildings; the glories of Florence, Assisi, and Pisa; and how much he enjoyed a performance of La Boheme in an Italian opera house. On another occasion, he describes a leisurely drive with Alexander and visiting British Foreign Minister Anthony Eden in which the highlight was a stop to pick chestnuts.

But a recurring, almost daily, theme in his notes was a frustration with the stacks of paperwork that awaited him when he returned to his hut-on-wheels after a lengthy day in a car with the field marshal or an evening of helping entertain visiting dignitaries. "Cleaning up paperwork" vied with "usual conferences" for frequency in his entries, and when the backlog would get particularly heavy, notice of this fact would occasionally be followed by an anguished, "Where does it all come from?"

One of the mandates handed to Lemnitzer when he was brought into Alexander's inner circle back in Sicily was to improve the sadly sagging relations between U.S. and British forces. His success sometimes made him the man in the middle in other relationships as well. One of these was that between Clark and Devers, who, he once observed, "couldn't be together for three minutes without getting into a fight."[3] The situation was so serious that every time Devers went to Clark's headquarters, Lemnitzer feared that the ensuing verbal brawl would result in Clark's relief because he was outranked by Devers. The upshot was that Devers would not deal with Clark directly but would have Lemnitzer take care of his dealings for him. It was an old feud, dating back to before the war. Clark was contemptuous of Devers's tactical ability and would explode in anger when he tried to interfere with Fifth Army tactical operations. Devers regarded Clark as overly ambitious and intent only on personal aggrandizement. Devers ended the war as an Army group commander and one of Eisenhower's principal lieutenants.

Meanwhile, a war was going on. Morale among Alexander's troops after Rome fell was very high and the fighting edge of the Fifth and Eighth armies was at its peak as they fought their way north against a stubborn and formidable enemy defense. But by the time they reached the Gothic Line, Alexander and his army group were feeling the effects of a new fact of life that was to take up as much of his attention as the campaign raging to his front: with the gearing up for Overlord, Italy had officially become a secondary front. The decline in status coincided with Eisenhower's departure to become supreme Overlord commander just before Anzio, but, although declaring the Italian campaign of "subsidiary" importance, he later was to concede that "the results it attained in the actual defeat of Germany were momentous, almost incalculable."[4] Still, Eisenhower viewed the Italian campaign's principal contribution as the draining of German resources and the diversion of forces that might have been used to oppose the Allied invasion across northern Europe. He did not feel that the German homeland could be attacked decisively by forces coming north through Italy.

Alexander, although agreeing with the importance of Overlord, did not share Eisenhower's opinion. He went directly to Churchill for support of his plan to defeat German Field Marshal Kesselring's armies in northern Italy and drive across the Alps into Austria and from there into Germany. The prime minister was much more sympathetic to Alexander's hopes than Eisenhower and George Marshall, but Overlord's priorities prevailed. There was nothing to keep Alexander from driving as far as he liked—except for one thing: now being a secondary theater, the Mediterranean area not only had second call on troops and supplies but also was forced to relinquish substantial amounts of what it had in these categories for deployment elsewhere.

The biggest drain was for Operation Anvil (later called Operation Dragoon), the long-anticipated invasion through southern France. Alexander flew up personally to London to argue against Anvil because it meant considerable weakening of his armies. Churchill also vehemently opposed it, using terms like "skinned and starved," "stripped and mutilated," and "mauled and milked" to depict what Anvil's demands were doing to Alexander's (and Clark's) Fifteenth Army Group.[5] But once again Overlord won; Eisenhower maintained that Anvil was vital to the success of Overlord because it would draw off German defensive resources from the north while giving Allied forces another toehold in Europe.

Anvil was launched on August 15 in the Marseille-Toulon region. Seven of the ground divisions—four French and three American—came from Alexander's Army group. The operation also gobbled up 70 percent of his group's air strength.[6] Harold MacMillan, then British resident minister for the Mediterranean region, recalls that after Anvil and its inroads on his forces, Alexander looked "rather tired, even strained" when he met with him at his advanced headquarters near Siena, Italy. "He feels rather bitterly the neglect by the powers-that-be of his campaign and the lack of support he has received. Even on the basis that everything was to be sacrificed to the operations in France, a more determined effort to rake up a little help would have meant a great deal to him . . . a single airborne brigade or a single division from the Middle East would have made all the difference. As it is, the Germans have twenty-six divisions against his twenty and have in the Gothic Line a naturally defensive position even stronger than that at Cassino."[7]

The raids on Alexander's legions did not end with Anvil. Lemnitzer's diary makes several mentions of cutbacks to satisfy the needs of operations in France. On July 19 he noted that Devers had informed him that no more combat or service troops would be available for Clark's already badly depleted Fifth Army ("very bad news, indeed."). In October, he wrote, Alexander made a personal appeal to Eisenhower for replacements and got three thousand troops from France to fill in for combat losses. It was a drop in the bucket and the troops were green, but Ike had come through, in a fashion, and a few days later they were airlifted to the divisions deployed along the Gothic Line.

Alexander and his staff were able to cobble a makeshift but woefully inadequate replacement system by reorganizing some units and nipping at the meager assets remaining in North Africa. But the situation was disheartening. Only the Poles, whose corps had contributed a great deal to the field marshal's successes in Italy, had an effective replacement apparatus; they obtained theirs from the ranks of liberated Polish prisoners of war. Lemnitzer joined his boss in scouring his theater and others for more strength. In the late spring of 1944, for example, he flew to London to ask Allied Force Headquarters (AFHQ), for the immediate transfer to Italy of the 91st Infantry Division. In an all-night session with U.S. Maj. Gen. Kingsley Rookes and others on the AFHQ staff, Lemnitzer pleaded his theater's case, but lost before the staff's unanimous view that the Germans would withdraw north of Rome to the Alps without making a stand. They proved to be wrong in this regard, but eventually Italy got the 91st. Judging from the frequency of his mention in Lemnitzer's notes, Rookes apparently was a relentless adversary in Lemnitzer's efforts to improve his army group's worsening position.

During another Lemnitzer visit to London, again in the spring of 1944, he was told that there was a strong feeling on the staff that enough forces must be pulled out of Alexander's army group to form a substantial strategic reserve for use in southern France, the Balkans, or Italy. Such a reserve is an external reinforcing element that is not committed in advance to a specific combat operation but can be deployed later in response to circumstances. This would have meant that Alexander would have lost still another large chunk of combat strength as he was preparing to launch a major offensive along the Gothic Line. It was recorded that an exasperated Lemnitzer "reacted so violently" that the scheme was dropped then and there.[8]

Italy's armed forces, now on the Allied side, were of almost no help and were not even considered as Alexander and his staff cast about for troops to beef up the forward edges of their attack forces. Many of Italy's divisions had been disarmed by the Germans before and after the surrender, and it was clear to the Allies that their former enemies had not regained the will to fight. Lemnitzer considered his new comrades in arms to be fit only for labor services. One of the few Italian units to be put into the line, an assemblage of paratroopers who had distinguished themselves as German allies in Sardinia, was mauled by the Herman Goering Division shortly after it was deployed. Lemnitzer thought that the Italian soldier's generally dismal performance in battle throughout the war was directly due to appalling leadership: "Not only did the Army have very poor equipment, but the officers were completely indifferent regarding their men—they had no regard for their feelings and hardships. A kind of squeeze operated all along the line; so much was given out for supplies, the officers took their cuts and what was left over went to the men. In the U.S. and British armies, officers were constantly on the lookout to prevent a bad morale situation from developing. In the Italian Army, nothing whatsoever was done to keep up morale."[9]

Alexander, ever-mindful of the vital importance of troop *élan*, approached the showdown at the Gothic Line with deep concerns about what effects the relegation of the Italian campaign to secondary importance would have on the spirit of his men. Not all of his colleagues agreed with his misgivings about this factor: Eisenhower felt that a high command's designation of an operation as secondary made little difference to a soldier at the front.[10]

Although Alexander and his staff had earlier reckoned that his forces would need a superiority of three to one in infantry when they reached the rugged mountainous regions north of the Gothic Line, he had only twenty divisions to the enemy's twenty-six[11] when his army group attacked the line in the fall of 1944. In setting up an Alexander-style "one-two punch," the Eighth Army was shifted secretly through the Apennine Mountains to the Adriatic coastal region. There, it broke through the enemy line's coastal sector and was at the point of entering the Lombard Plain when it was stopped by the Germans at Coriano. Next, Clark's Fifth Army attacked in the Gothic Line's center, capturing the strategically important Futa Pass before being halted in the mountain ridges beyond.

As had happened so many times before in an Alexander operation, his and his staff's carefully worked-out plans were scrapped at the last moment when a subordinate commander argued for a different approach. The original plan had been for both armies to attack in the center of the line. British General Leese, commanding the Eighth Army, argued for moving his forces east and hitting Kesselring's divisions with a surprise attack—thus, the Eighth Army's movement through the mountains to the Adriatic coast. Both Allied armies lacked the reserves to follow up their initial successes and exploit their modest break-throughs. They stopped where they were in December, not because of a reported shortage of artillery ammunition or even because of the muddied mountains that lay ahead, but simply because they badly needed to rest.[12] Alexander told his staff to prepare plans to resume the offensive early in the approaching year.

While Lemnitzer and his colleagues worked out the details of a drive that initially was to begin no later than the end of February 1945, Alexander was promoted to field marshal and made supreme commander of the Mediterranean theater. Lemnitzer moved up with him to become his deputy chief of staff, while Clark was given command of the Fifteenth Army Group and Truscott succeeded Clark as commander of the Fifth Army.

The Allied high command would have been content if Alexander had done no more until the end of the war than keep pressure on Kesselring's troops to reduce the shifting of forces to other fronts. Indeed, few thought the field marshal could do any more than this, considering the enemy's strength, a country-side strongly favoring the defense, and the steady drain on the Fifteenth Army Group's resources by requirements in northern Europe.

Early in January, Allied forces advanced to the Senio River. Three more divisions were removed from Alexander's armies the same month for reassign-ment to northern Europe, and what was later dubbed "the winter pause" began. Gone were the field marshal's plans for launching a general offensive before the end of February. While Allied planes battered enemy communications, Alexander's forces made a major contribution to Eisenhower's efforts in the north by pinning down the German Tenth and Fourteenth armies, each desperately needed in their embattled homeland.

Lemnitzer's first experience with dealing with the Soviet Union occurred during this lull. As the Allies moved east and the Russians west, there was increasing contact between them. To avoid "friendly fire" incidents, the Allies established a reporting system that was tied to the "bomb line." This line was an indication of where an army's forward area ended and the enemy's began. Commanders of air and ground units were kept informed of bomb line locations to avoid firing on friendly forces. The Allied Strategic Air Command, operating out of the air base at Foggia, Italy, had begun sending bombers north to bomb targets in Austria and southern Germany. The Allies by then had fighters of such extended range that they could escort bombers all the way to their targets and back. On their return trips their pilots were encouraged to attack ground and air targets of opportunity. Mindful that Soviet forces were operating in the regions along the way, the Allies asked the Russians to be kept informed of the locations of their bomb lines. Their repeated requests were ignored by the Soviet high command. The need for this information was made tragically apparent one day when Allied fighters spotted a long column of motor vehicles moving along a road in the Danube Valley. They attacked it with machine gun fire and bombs, practically wiping it out. The procession turned out to have been an entire Soviet corps headquarters.

Alexander and Lemnitzer, then his acting chief of staff, were in Yugoslavia shortly after the incident to discuss mutual concerns with Yugoslavia's Marshal Tito whose forces had just captured Belgrade. The Combined Chiefs of Staff suggested that this would be a good opportunity for Alexander to meet with Marshal Feodor Tolbukhin, commander of the Soviet Third Ukrainian Army Group, to discuss the bomb line problem. Alexander, who was disgusted over the absence of Soviet response on the issue, didn't want to go to the Russian's headquarters but was persuaded to do so by Lemnitzer who thought it offered a good opportunity to see what was going on in Tolbukhin's camp.

After two days of discussions about various subjects at Tolbukhin's headquarters near Budapest, Hungary, Alexander raised the bomb line issue again. The Soviet marshal got up from his chair, struck the table with his fist and shouted: "Field Marshal Alexander, I don't want to hear anything more about the bomb line! You don't have to tell me how important a bomb line is. That corps commander and his staff were very close friends of mine. I went through the military academy with the commander. I knew him, and I very much regretted that he was killed in the air attack. I know where the bomb line is, but the people in Moscow say no. So the answer is no, and I don't want to hear about it any more."[13]

While both sides settled in to watch, wait, and probe in the bitterly cold winter of 1944–45, Lemnitzer filled his diary with reports on what was happening in the battle areas in northern Europe ("Situation on Western Front looks good. Patton went thru for 30 miles. Bridgehead over Rhine seems secure"). But as the winter wore on into March, there began to appear references to something he called "the Switzerland project." On March 13 he cut his entry short with "Situation on front moving fast. 10th Mt. Div. is across Po"—the latter sentence crossed out. There were no more entries until April 5, seemingly a strange omission, for Lemnitzer was faithful about detailing every day's activities, no matter how busy he was.

The fact is that he did not slight this daily routine, because his journal for the next twenty-two days was a writing tablet in which he penciled down his activities during what became one of the most celebrated cloak-and-dagger missions of the war. The operation, in which he was to have a leading role, was "Sunrise," the highly secret mission that resulted in the surrender of over a million German troops in northern Italy.

Sunrise (or "Crossword," as it was labeled by Churchill)[14] was played out in Switzerland where Allen Dulles, ostensibly deputy to the U.S. ambassador in Bern but actually head of the Office of Strategic Services' (OSS) intelligence network for central Europe, had been approached by emissaries of a faction in the German high command who wanted to discuss the surrender of the forces facing Alexander. The leader was Gen. Karl Wolff, SS Chief Heinrich Himmler's personal representative and commander of all SS forces in Italy. Wolff, an influential and well-connected figure in the upper echelons of the Nazi party, was convinced that Germany was facing defeat. To continue the war, he stated in his first meeting with Dulles, would be a crime against the German people. His interest in bringing about a surrender coincided with appeals by prominent Italians who, along with some high-ranking German officers, feared that the departing Nazis would carry out Hitler's threats to destroy and burn in revenge for Italy's going over to the Allied side.

Dulles notified his superiors in Washington of Wolff's overtures, and they passed the information on to Alexander. It was an exciting development, and Dulles kept in contact with Wolff and his emissaries while he waited for Alexander's reaction; a surrender of forces in the field is a military matter, and the theater's supreme commander would have to call the shots. Alexander's headquarters indicated interest, so Dulles encouraged the Germans to keep in contact while he waited for the field marshal to send a representative to take over the talks. But then the OSS leader learned something that threatened to destroy any hope that a surrender could be brought about.

Although Wolff was as powerful in his own sphere as Field Marshal Kesselring, the commander of German forces in Italy, was in his, a surrender could not occur without Kesselring's cooperation. Wolff was sure that the field marshal could be persuaded to agree to a surrender and the SS general was on his way to the commander's headquarters to clinch a commitment when he found out that Hitler was said to be considering transferring Kesselring from Italy to take command of the Western Front; the report turned out to be true, and the order was issued shortly after Wolff first heard about it.

The spirits of all those involved in Sunrise were at a very low ebb on March 13 when Dulles received word from Alexander's headquarters that two officers were en route to represent the field marshal in talks with the Germans. Dulles recalled: "When I read the names and rank of the men who were being sent I was astonished. I wondered if I had made sufficiently clear just how bleak the situation was with the possibility of Kesselring's change of command. The two emissaries were the American Major General Lyman L. Lemnitzer, then deputy chief of staff to Field Marshal Alexander, and British Major General Terence S. Airey, Alexander's chief intelligence officer."[15] The two had flown by B-25 bomber from Caserta to Lyon, France, that day—Lemnitzer to take charge of the talks with the Germans, and Airey to assist him. But they could not enter neutral Switzerland in uniform or with their true identities, so the OSS took them in hand. From Lyon, they were whisked by car to the village of Annemasse, located just south of the Swiss border, where they were ensconced briefly in an OSS "safe house."

The men who emerged resembled, in face only, those who went inside. Lemnitzer wore what he later would refer to as his "OSS suit," a garish and ill-fitting pin-striped number. The usually quietly elegant Airey was garbed similarly, although his pinstripes seemed a shade more subdued. The two generals were to enter Switzerland as American Army sergeants being reassigned to the communications facilities at the U.S. embassy in Bern. Lemnitzer assumed the identity of a Sgt. Guy H. Nicholson, and Airey became Sgt. W. D. McNeilly, the names of two actual U.S. Army noncoms who had been destined for service in the embassy. Lemnitzer spent nearly eight hours picking the brain of the real Sergeant Nicholson in an effort to find out as much as he could about the man's life—family details, his hometown, where he went to school, and other scraps of information an interrogator would expect him to know. He also memorized the sergeant's dog tag number and in the whole process, he recalled, "I acquired several children and a domicile in Long Island."[16]

It was fortunate that he had prepared himself. After meeting with Dulles, who had come from Bern (Lemnitzer always referred to him in his notes and dispatches as "110," Dulles's OSS code number), he and Airey were taken by U.S. consul car to a Swiss consulate office on the French side of the Swiss border where they were issued various required in-country papers to go with their new U.S. passports. But when they crossed the border, unusually suspicious Swiss customs officials— Lemnitzer suspected that they had been alerted by a leak—subjected him to a searching interrogation about his background; Lemnitzer remembered it as the most intense grilling he had ever undergone. But his OSS preparation stood the test, and he was allowed to go through. Airey, who was behind him, got by with only a couple of routine questions, one of which concerned where he was born. Either the guards didn't have a very good ear for accents or the very British Airey was an exceptional mimic because he was passed through without comment after giving his hometown as Brooklyn, New York.

The contradictions in how readily different visitors could enter neutral Switzerland could be puzzling: a German SS general and members of his staff moved back and forth across the border, seemingly without interference, while two ostensibly genuine American sergeants were made to undergo intense official scrutiny. The factor that made the difference was a highly placed Swiss intelligence officer named Max Waibel. Captain Waibel, later major and ultimately major general by the end of his military career, belonged to a group of patriotic Swiss officers who had never forgotten the desperate days of 1940 when their country became entirely surrounded by Axis forces. There was a real fear then that Germany and Italy would invade the tiny nation, the way cleared of obstacles by an official government element that was inclined to seek compromises. Waibel and his comrades made a vow then to actively resist a Nazi invasion, no matter what course their civilian and military superiors took. Whatever his country's posture as a neutral nation had to be, Waibel knew how slim Switzerland's chances of remaining independent would be if Germany won the war. So he did whatever he could within the parameters of his authority to facilitate any activity that might result in bringing the war to an end on the Allies' terms. This included keeping an eye on a growing and surprisingly widespread feeling among Germany's military leadership that it was time for the nation to get out of the war. Out of his contacts came peace feelers, and one of these led to a meeting with General Wolff.

An affable, cigar-smoking member of the Swiss General Staff, Waibel held a doctorate in philosophy and he knew how to get things done. His authority was such that a word from him could open border barriers at any time of the day with no questions asked of the visitors who disappeared into the Swiss interior and then emerged again. He arranged for secret meeting places and saw to it that the right people reached them. He was imaginative in providing cover stories: when Wolff and his staff arrived for the general's first visit, if any strangers on their train asked questions they were to say they belonged to a German-Italian commission that was in the country to discuss with the Swiss the use of port facilities in the harbor of Genoa.

Dulles had been sending regular detailed reports of the overtures to Alexander's headquarters in Caserta, as well as to Washington and London. Alexander, who was busy with the final plans for a spring offensive in northern Italy, was willing to pursue any avenue that would reduce or eliminate the heavy toll of lives and resources that an all-out attack into the north would entail. It is a measure of his high regard for Lemnitzer that he entrusted him with the management of this historic windfall. As important as Dulles was—and he reported only to OSS Director William J. (Wild Bill) Donovan, who reported to the president—he had no authority once meetings had been set up. He and his staff could arrange meetings, move people about, provide security, suggest, inform, and persuade, but any details of capitulation, as well as the act itself, were in the province of the generals. As the personal representative of the supreme commander of the Mediterranean theater, Lemnitzer was in charge of the next move.

After they cleared Swiss customs, the two generals were taken to the resort town of Ascona, located on Lake Maggiore, ten miles from the Italian border. The small villa in which they stayed and another in which the meetings were to take place were owned by the family of one of the most intriguing figures in the whole convoluted sequence of events leading up to the actual surrender. He was Gero von Schulze Gaevernitz, Dulles's OSS deputy in Switzerland and a key mover in bringing the Germans to the discussion table. A German by birth, the tall, strikingly handsome, and debonair Gaevernitz had become a naturalized U.S. citizen who now lived in Switzerland where his cover was that he helped look after his affluent family's business interests.

Gaevernitz headed off a potentially serious problem early in the generals' stay when he noticed a small band of armed men in civilian clothes hidden in the woods around their villa. Inquiry revealed that they were OSS men who had been assigned to provide security for Lemnitzer and Airey. An alarmed Gaevernitz pointed out to Dulles that a single shot fired in the peaceful little region would alert Swiss police and doom the whole operation. The guards were removed.[17]

While Lemnitzer and Airey waited for the complicated situation brought on by Kesselring's reassignment to clear up, they shopped and went sight-seeing in the picturesque Swiss countryside. They also became fast friends with their hosts. Out of this friendship, there sprang a badly garbled story about a dachshund which was repeated so often in the press and in books that it has become an integral part of many historical recountings of the mission. Years later, Lemnitzer still winced when he was asked to tell the tale again of how he went to Switzerland, ostensibly to buy a dog, and ended up with the surrender of over a million German soldiers.

The way the press told it in the great outpouring of publicity following the surrender, the two generals had entered Switzerland disguised as sergeants with the cover story that they were there to purchase a dog. What actually happened is that Gaevernitz wanted to give his new acquaintances souvenirs of their visit to Switzerland and asked them what they would like. Airey chose a dog, a dachshund named "Fritzel," and so an unfounded and persistent legend was born.[18] The only grain of truth in the story that developed was that Airey had been looking for a dachshund as an incidental acquisition of the trip but could not afford the $125 a pedigreed animal would cost. Lemnitzer apparently asked for nothing.

(An amusing photograph, apparently taken during this waiting period of relaxation and conviviality, shows a frowning and seemingly ill-at-ease Lemnitzer sitting at a table at an outside cafe. Looking like a gangster in his terrible "OSS suit," he is staring stonily into space while a smiling Airey and Waibel stand chatting in the foreground. The usually pleasant-looking general's mien is puzzling, but a likely explanation is that Airey, who liked to show off his fluency in German, was making small talk with Waibel in that language. In short, Lemnitzer—who never learned to speak a foreign tongue—was, for the moment, out of it.)

The situation in Wolff's camp was still very much up in the air when the SS general returned to Switzerland on March 19 with several trusted aides. Gen. Heinrich Vietinghoff had been appointed to replace Kesselring, but it would take more time to feel him out about a surrender. In the meantime, Dulles told Wolff there were two "military advisers" from Alexander's headquarters he would like the German general to meet. Despite misgivings about beginning talks without any assurance that the German army would cooperate, Lemnitzer decided to meet with Wolff, partly to size him up and partly to make clear why he (Lemnitzer) was sent to confer with him.

But before they sat down to talk, there arose a problem of protocol and professional distaste. Airey told Dulles that he would not, under any circumstances, shake hands with an SS officer. Dulles did his best to avert this by bringing in the two sides at opposite ends of the meeting room and seating Lemnitzer and Airey against a wall behind a wide table, with the Germans seated on the other side. Lemnitzer said in his diary that this solved the problem, but Dulles wrote later that the extroverted Wolff bounded across the room, squeezed behind the table, seized and vigorously shook first Airey's hand and then Lemnitzer's before either could do anything to head it off.[19]

Dulles recalled years later: "The situation was unique and solemn. It was the first occasion during the entire war when high-ranking Allied officers and a German general had met on neutral soil to discuss a German surrender and talked peacefully while their respective armies were fighting each other."[20] Lemnitzer conducted the meeting with Gaevernitz acting as interpreter because Wolff (code name "Critic" in Lemnitzer's dispatches to his headquarters) could not speak English. Lemnitzer, whose name and rank were not revealed to the Germans at the table, told Wolff he assumed that the SS general considered further resistance in Italy to be hopeless ("otherwise you would not be here").[21] He stated that he had not come to Switzerland to negotiate but to help his enemy plan how it would surrender its forces in Italy. The surrender would have to be unconditional, he said, the details to be worked out at Caserta, to which the Germans would have to send plenipotentiaries representing Wolff and the commander of army forces in Italy. Only methods of military surrender would be discussed, Lemnitzer stated, and no political issues could be brought up. Unless they agreed to this outline, he added, there would be no point in their coming to Caserta.

If only Kesselring had not been reassigned, the path to the eventual surrender would have been much simpler. Vietinghoff, his successor, now had to be induced to join Wolff, and the SS leader felt the only way to do this was through Kesselring's influence. After convincing Lemnitzer that reaching Vietinghoff through Kesselring was worth a further wait in Switzerland, Wolff left to see the field marshal at his new headquarters in Germany. Lemnitzer, Airey, and their OSS hosts spent the next two weeks waiting for Wolff to return. Dulles later described the wait as "tense," and it must have been so for the OSS operatives charged with trying to keep track of the various principals involved in the surrender machinations. But for Lemnitzer and Airey, there was little to do until Wolff made his next move. They were kept informed by Dulles and were in steady contact with their headquarters, but Lemnitzer's diary shows that he and his fellow AFHQ staff member took advantage of the lull for days of shopping, relaxing, and sight-seeing.

Finally, word came that Wolff was returning on April 2. Anticipating the dropping of the last brick into place, Lemnitzer and Airey were preparing for a final presurrender meeting when an Italian emissary of the SS general came across the border with a message that the talks would have to be held up a while longer because Wolff was in deep trouble. Himmler had learned about Wolff's having made contact with the Allies in Switzerland, but it turned out later that he knew none of the details. His suspicions that Wolff was up to something had been heightened when he found out that he had moved his family into an area that was under his own command, an obvious move to protect them that was not lost on Himmler. The development that caused Wolff to break off the Sunrise talks was a telephone call from Himmler to inform the SS general that he had found out about the family's having been taken away. His chilling comment to Wolff was: "That was imprudent of you, and I have taken the liberty of correcting the situation. Your wife and children are now under my protection (back in the Wolff home in Austria)." Himmler's threat was clear: get out of line, and I have your family as hostages.[22] Fearful for his life and his family's, Wolff sent word that he would have to keep out of contact for at least a few more days.

When the emissary wound up his cryptic report and the Switzerland group had extracted meager details, there was a gloomy silence as the members digested this depressing news. Finally, Lemnitzer said, "It's not half as bad as it looks."[23] He didn't explain, although he ultimately turned out to be right, give or take several more very bad moments. There were still implications of hope in Wolff's situation, but Lemnitzer and Airey had compelling reasons to have to be back in Caserta. On April 4, they returned to the OSS safe house across the border in France, put on their uniforms again, and were flown back to their headquarters.

Lemnitzer's diary entry for April 9 began: "Today is the day." Thunderous artillery barrages shook the earth, and swarms of Allied aircraft streaked into northern Italy's mountain ridges, their bombs and guns tearing relentlessly at the long line of enemy troop concentrations stretching below. Over a half-million troops of the Allied Fifth and Eighth armies moved out of their winter positions and attacked. Alexander's spring offensive had begun.

It was a classic Alexander operation, a "one-two punch" which began with the Eighth Army attacking across difficult swamp country in the east and capturing Imola in the Po Valley within a week. Truscott's Fifth Army smashed across the line on April 14, and after a week of heavy fighting had captured Bologna and also entered the Po Valley. Vietinghoff, who had been deceived by Alexander into thinking the assault would open with a major landing on the coast south of Venice, was now threatened with having his two armies completely enveloped as the Allied forces raced northward toward the Alps foothills. Assisted by thousands of Italian antifascist partisans behind the enemy lines, Alexander wielded his combat elements masterfully—using his superiority in air power to destroy and disrupt, his armor to slice into the flanks of retreating divisions, and his ground troops to seal the rout with their hour-by-hour conquest of the historic cities of the northern plains. Similar developments were taking place in the north where Eisenhower's armies were shredding Axis resistance from the west and the Soviets were overrunning the enemy from the east.

Meanwhile, Wolff, who had hoped to head off Alexander's anticipated offensive, was still trying to bring about a surrender and in doing so very nearly paid with his life. He had finally secured Kesselring's support and permission to use his name in influencing Vietinghoff to join him in surrendering German forces. But while he was trying to make contact with Vietinghoff, Himmler's taking of Wolff's family as hostages occurred. Previously, he had been able to put the SS head off when he tried to get him to Berlin, but he had no choice now that his family was involved. He was fearful, also, that if he continued to avoid coming to Berlin he would be replaced by an SS commander less amenable to discussing surrender. Wolff knew that his chances of coming back to Italy alive were very poor because he was aware that Himmler was trying to make a case to accuse him of treason. At Himmler's headquarters near Berlin, Wolff was confronted by Himmler and the second most powerful figure in the SS, Ernst Kaltenbrunner, chief of the Security Office of the Reich (RSHA) and a bitter Wolff enemy. During hours of heated interrogation about his activities in Switzerland, Wolff skillfully defended himself, but when it became clear that his SS superiors were determined to bring him down, he demanded a personal audience with Hitler. Himmler tried to discourage such a meeting because it could take the situation out of his control, but Wolff persevered and got his audience.

The German dictator, a physical and mental wreck as his empire was collapsing around him, listened to Wolff's account of the surrender overtures. His manner was not unfriendly, but Wolf found him disturbingly critical as the general ran through his efforts in detail. One important step that he did not mention was the meeting at Ascona with Lemnitzer and Airey because he had become convinced that the only contact of which Himmler had knowledge was the initial March 8 meeting with Dulles in Zurich.

Hitler, who apparently had known something about Wolff's activities, accused him of a "colossal disregard of authority." But he listened intently as Wolff did a masterful job of making a case that took into careful consideration high-level politics, Germany's war situation, and the facets of the dictator's character and outlook that he knew so well. He concluded his *tour de force* by telling Hitler that he was happy to be able to inform him that he had opened a channel for him that led directly to the president of the United States and the prime minister of England, if he wanted to use it.

Hitler wanted time to think about what Wolff had said and told him to come back later in the day to the underground bunker complex where the dictator would spend his last living hours. The two talked some more, and finally Germany's *Reichfuhrer* told Wolff to go back to his post in Italy and keep up his contacts with the Americans. He urged him to hold out for better terms than an unconditional surrender based on vague promises. Wolff had gone to Berlin in real danger of losing his life and returned stronger than when he left.[24] Somehow, at around the time of the Berlin meetings or right after, Wolff managed to move his family back into the area under his command and out of Himmler's clutches.

As soon as he got back to his command, Wolff met with Vietinghoff who, impressed by Kesselring's endorsement, was willing to talk about a surrender. At the outset, the chance for an early capitulation did not look promising. Vietinghoff insisted that certain "points of honor" be observed, such as permitting surrendered troops to be returned to Germany rather than being placed in prison camps. There were other lesser stipulations, putting the German general's position further and further away from the Allies' insistence on unconditional surrender. When Dulles relayed Vietinghoff's desires to Lemnitzer, he replied curtly that the terms of the surrender would be handed to the German plenipotentiaries when they reached Caserta and that they would not be shown them beforehand. He made no mention of the points of honor.

Then a new and much more serious obstacle occurred which threatened any chance of an early surrender. On April 20 Dulles received a top secret message from Washington that the Joint Chiefs of Staff had directed that all contact with the German emissaries cease immediately. The message gave as the rationale that it had become clear to the Combined Chiefs of Staff (U.S. and Great Britain) that Vietinghoff was not ready to surrender on acceptable terms.[25] However, there was another and more compelling reason: the Soviet Union had learned of the talks and was insisting that it be permitted to send representatives. After much and at times very bitter discussion at the highest levels of the U.S., British, and Soviet governments, the Russian request was turned down on the grounds that the military forces involved were entirely within territory under Western Allies jurisdiction. Dulles, who had discussed the Soviets' move with Donovan, cabled Lemnitzer that it stemmed from a desire to get their hands on northern Italy and the strategically important port of Trieste before the Allies could occupy them.[26] (At about this time, German intelligence intercepted a message from the Soviet Union's Josef Stalin to Yugoslavia's Marshal Josip Broz Tito, urging him to prepare to move his forces across northern Italy to the French border. A high German official theorized that the Russian intent was for Tito to link up with communist partisans in France to create a Soviet-controlled belt across southern and western Europe; this would then be a base for the eventual communization of France and Italy.)[27] President Truman, who had just succeeded Roosevelt upon his death, wrote in his memoirs that the Sunrise talks were terminated at the urging of Churchill who wanted to avoid further friction with the Soviets.[28]

While he was in Switzerland, Lemnitzer had been aware of the Soviet desires to participate and, like his fellow movers in Sunrise, was opposed—not for political reasons, but because smuggling in the three generals the Russians wanted to send and then keeping them concealed would have been impossible and would have jeopardized the entire operation. Neither he nor Dulles knew that the controversy had taken on international proportions involving Roosevelt, Churchill, Stalin, and his sharp-tongued foreign minister, Vyacheslav Molotov, but Lemnitzer's solution may have provided the Allies with a much-needed stop-gap measure at a time when they were under tremendous pressure from the Soviets.

When a message had arrived from Alexander's headquarters informing him of the Soviet demand, Lemnitzer conferred with Dulles and wired back: "No objection to Russian member provided he wear civilian clothes and speak English." The wire urged also that the Soviet representation consist of one officer, because only a single officer could be admitted into Switzerland. Lemnitzer knew that the only Russians in Italy at the time were attached to the Allied Control Commission in Rome, and none of them could speak English. The possibility that the Russians would send only one person, Lemnitzer and Dulles knew, was very unlikely because they always insisted on sending a military commissar with every military officer on special missions. Lemnitzer was banking, too, on the unlikely event that any civilian clothing would be available in Rome on short notice.[29] No Russian showed up in Switzerland, and the only part the Soviet Union played in the surrender at Caserta was the sending of a major general and an interpreter to act as observers.

As if things were not already complicated enough, shortly after the JCS order to break off talks, Dulles received word that Wolff and a high staff officer representing General Vietinghoff were on their way to Switzerland with full powers to surrender—and Dulles was under strict orders to not even talk with them. Considering it inconceivable that the JCS would turn down an offer to surrender, Dulles appealed to his superiors in Washington, but to no avail. Then Alexander added his weight with a request to the Combined Chiefs of Staff to reconsider the order. Until that happened, though, all the Sunrise orchestrators could do was wait. It was a nerve-wracking period and another dangerous one for Wolff. He had to return to his command in Italy after several days of waiting and while there was nearly captured by Italian partisans who undoubtedly meant to kill him; only a daring rescue masterminded by Waibel and Gaevernitz got him out of his surrounded villa and to safety. Himmler, too, had resumed making threats.

The JCS ban lasted for a week; on April 27, Dulles received a "triple priority" signal telling him that the Combined Chiefs of Staff were instructing Alexander to make arrangements for the Germans to come to Caserta immediately to sign a surrender. Lemnitzer, who was also in charge of the surrender, sent a plane to Annecy, France, the border town to which Wolff's and Vietinghoff's plenipotentiaries had been taken. Once again the question of handshaking came up when the two German officers were met at Caserta by Lemnitzer and Airey. Lemnitzer decided that there would be none, he and Airey confining their greetings to curt nods as the enemy representatives were introduced.

The final talks took place in an isolated compound on a hill, the surroundings of which were shielded from the German visitors by sheets of canvas strung from tree to tree; with a war still on, it wouldn't do to let their guests see any more of Allied headquarters than they had to. The German emissaries—Lt. Col. Viktor Schweinitz, representing Vietinghoff, and Maj. Max Wenner, Wolff's adjutant— were handed the Allied surrender terms at the first meeting, in late afternoon of the day of their arrival. The terms spelled out the modifier used in every mention of surrender since the Casablanca Conference: "unconditional." In subsequent meetings, Schweinitz sought unsuccessfully to implant Vietinghoff's "points of honor," particularly the one enabling the defeated soldiers to return to Germany without being put in prison camps (earlier, the German general had wanted them also to be allowed to march back wearing their bayonets and belts, as German troops had done in 1918, to signify that it had been an "orderly surrender"). Alexander's staff members stood firm, and in the end only minor concessions were included in the surrender document. One of these permitted officers to keep their side arms to maintain order during the surrender, and another allowed the retention of motor vehicles to enable the vanquished to carry on such administrative functions as feeding their troops before they became prisoners.

Lemnitzer and his staff met through the night with Schweinitz and Wenner after their arrival, through the next day, and much of the following night in working out surrender details. Gaevernitz, who attended the sessions as an interpreter, said of the marathon meetings: "To make a fighting army put down its arms is in many respects as painstaking a task as to mobilize it."[30]

The conferees agreed that the surrender must take place as soon as possible. The date was set for noon, May 2. On April 29 Lemnitzer's diary entry read: "To bed at 0430 [half past four in the morning] after much discussion with von Schweinitz and Wenner. Much progress made—more discussion resumed after breakfast. Met again with von Schweinitz, Airey and Wenner. Finally convinced them to sign instrument of surrender and forget details. Finally agreed. Signing surrender took place in Chief of Staff's office 1400 hours [two o'clock in the afternoon] in presence of Chief of Staff. BIG DAY."

Time was vital. In order for the surrender document to get to the German headquarters in Bolzano that day, it had to leave Caserta by plane by three o'clock that afternoon, an hour after the signing. There was no time to even retype the agreed-upon document before the signatures were affixed, so Gaevernitz went through the some thirty pages, inserting the final changes by hand while Lemnitzer looked over his shoulder to make sure the wording was correct.[31]

Dulles noted afterward: "There was little if any recent precedent for the drafting of an unconditional surrender. The text of this one had been composed more or less out of whole cloth by General Lemnitzer and his staff and then shown to Field Marshal Alexander for his approval. This is all the more interesting because this text, it is reported, was used as the basis for the surrender document hastily drawn up for the over-all German surrender at Reims [France] a week later. That this was an 'unconditional surrender' was amply set forth in the opening paragraph: 'The German Commander-in-Chief Southwest hereby surrenders unconditionally all the forces under his command or control on land, at sea, and in the air and places these forces unconditionally at the disposal of the Supreme Allied Commander, Mediterranean Theater of Operations.'"[32]

There was still one more twist before the stranger-than-fiction episode that was Operation Sunrise was finally played out: after dithering his way through the surrender preliminaries, Vietinghoff was relieved of his command before he could endorse his plenipotentiary's acceptance of the Allies's terms. That was done by Kesselring in time to meet the schedule agreed upon at Caserta.

It was a remarkably smooth surrender considering the shortness of the time between the signing and the actual capitulation. Over a million fighting men laid down their arms with one tragic exception: Allied units were instructed to send surrender parties under white flags to contact enemy units across from them at the front. But when one of these groups approached the German First Parachute Division's position, the unit opened fire, killing nearly all of the delegation's roughly fifteen members.[33] The division, comprised of fanatical, die-hard young Nazis, was the unit that had proved so stubborn in the difficult siege of Cassino. It was not a mistake—the division's commanders had been officially informed of the surrender, and the fire was believed to have been intentional—but their leaders soon brought the holdouts under control, and the disarming went on.

The Allies were not universally successful in keeping their own forces in line. Lemnitzer became involved when a French division threatened to fire on elements of Truscott's Fifth Army when they sought to occupy an area assigned to them along the Italian-French border. Truscott was acting under orders of the Combined Chiefs of Staff that military jurisdictions be set up for military government purposes. Which nations eventually would occupy the regions was a political issue that would be decided later. The disputed area was Ventimiglia, a small salient near Nice on the Ligurian Sea on Italy's northwest corner, which France had claimed for many years. In the confusion of surrender, Lemnitzer recalled, "de Gaulle acted like lightning and grabbed it, just like that."[34]

When U.S. troops arrived in the area, they found it occupied by French forces whose commander refused to leave. When Truscott reached the scene, he was confronted by a French general of civil affairs who told him that if his troops tried to enter he would order his units to oppose them "by all means without exception."[35] A dumbfounded Truscott told theater headquarters about the impasse, and while the staff was trying to figure out what to do next, Lemnitzer happened to describe the situation to the OSS's General Donovan, who was visiting. Donovan was furious and sat down and wrote a message to President Truman, recounting what had happened. In the meantime, the Fifth Army moved the 1st Armored Division and the 92nd Infantry Division to the disputed region and waited for further orders. If the Americans had attacked, it would have been an unequal fight because the French were considerably outmanned and outgunned.

A major irony of the situation was that the United States was supplying everything French forces were using in the theater. After receiving Donovan's message, Truman sent authority to cut off all aid to the French in Italy until their troops got out of the disputed area. De Gaulle dispatched a senior staff officer, a General Carpentier, to look into the problem. A jovial man whom both Lemnitzer and Alexander knew, Carpentier announced when he was brought into Alexander's presence: "Bonjour, mon field marshal. I understand that there has been some kind of misunderstanding."

Lemnitzer recalled that "it was one of the few times I have seen Field Marshal Alexander change from a smile to the sternest look he could give. He said, 'General, there is no misunderstanding,' and he left it that way. Carpentier knew there was not going to be any argument, and so he went back to Paris to report to de Gaulle."[36] When Carpentier returned, he and Lemnitzer worked out a phased withdrawal in which the Americans moved in and the French moved back to where the French-Italian border had been in 1939.

Col. William J. McCaffrey, the 92nd's very young chief of staff and a future lieutenant general, chuckled years later that the peaceful settlement caused some disappointment among the U.S. troops. "They wanted to go in and kick hell out of the French," he recalled.[37]

On May 7 Lemnitzer wrote in his diary: "Germans surrendering all over Europe. Prime Minister Churchill announced tomorrow as VE Day in stirring speech. President Truman did same from U.S. and Stalin in Moscow. [Grand Admiral Karl] Dönitz [Hitler's successor] broadcast surrender of all German forces."

The next day his entry read: "VE Day—Victory in Europe. We have waited a long time for it. Work as usual."

11

'AN IRON CURTAIN HAS DESCENDED'

The *Wayne Independent*, the venerable voice of Wayne County's sedate little county seat, was in rare form on that late-summer Thursday in 1945 as it topped its front page with an account of the biggest thing that had happened in Honesdale since the disastrous floods of 1942:

> Ten thousand cheering spectators and admiring friends lined the sidewalks of Honesdale Wednesday afternoon to greet Maj. Gen. Lyman L. Lemnitzer, hero of World War II, at a "homecoming" day planned by the American Legion, David McKelvy Peterson Post, and participated in by the various civic and patriotic organizations of his home town. A half-day holiday had been proclaimed by the town's acting burgess, John F. Riefler. From all sections of Wayne County came an outpouring of populace to honor General Lemnitzer. The weatherman cooperated also and sent as fine a day for a parade and celebration as ever dawned in the Maple City. Every detail of the parade and program was carried out as planned; it was an occasion long to be remembered. Flags outlined the streets of Honesdale and waved from windows and porches of local homes. Four bands stirred the crowd with martial music; drum corps beat out a snappy rhythm with bugle accompaniment. It was a day never to be forgotten.

On the opposite upper corner of the page, a poem began:

> Hail General, back to Honesdale, Hail! . . .

Rocko was home from the wars.

The native son the townspeople cheered as he waved from the back seat of the procession's leading car was not quite the friendly little "runt" a schoolmate used to love to grab around the neck and "drag along," or the shy, solemn-eyed coast

146

artillery officer local folks might once have thought was destined to retire as a middle-aged lieutenant, so long did he wear single bars on his shoulders.

The general who got out of his car and made his way through the applauding crowd to the speaker's stand in front of the courthouse was, in some ways, the same old Rocko: the infectious laugh, the enthusiasm when spotting an old friend, the love of a good story, the total lack of any pretense, and his obvious deep interest in everything going on around him. But he had changed—considerably. There was a worldliness and quiet self-assurance that had not been there when he went away to war; it showed in the way he moved, the way he responded to the greetings of Wayne County's leading citizens, and in the way he spoke. Fit and slender to the point of gauntness, his chest a blaze of colorful ribbons, he had the look of a soldier who had seen battle and who had more than once been very close to having been one of its casualties.

Three years of daily contact with the war's greatest generals and statesmen are bound to have an effect on the way a person handles himself, and this showed when he got up to give his speech. Delivered without notes or any trace of the nervousness that might be expected while addressing the people he grew up with, Lemnitzer's stirring three thousand-word tribute to the war just ended—its goals, its sacrifices, and those who fought in it—was probably at least the equal of any being given any place in the country in that early postwar outpouring of public thanks that the bloody conflict was over. It was Lemnitzer the speaker at his best, as he always was when he spoke from the heart:

The general paid homage to the more than one hundred local residents who were killed or were missing in the war—"a terrific toll in an area the size of Wayne County"—and cautioned against a precipitate reduction in the nation's military strength in the postwar period. It was a warning, a futile one, that Lemnitzer and fellow military men would reiterate may times, at the end of this war and the two more in which the country would fight before he retired. He said:

"We have emerged from this war as the most powerful nation on earth—we must see that we remain so. I do not refer only to military power; I refer to the important teammates of industrial power, moral power and the power which stems from a great people united in their outlook on life and their ideals. If we are to shape a world molded on the American way of life—if we are to enjoy the peace we as Americans desire on this earth, we must remain strong and show the world that we mean to achieve and maintain these ideals. We cannot provide the necessary leadership to point the way if we are a weak nation; no weak nation in history has ever accomplished anything great in this world. We must have force available and we must have the courage and intelligence to use it if the situation demands. Much of the cost of this war could have been avoided if we had been willing to use force on our recent aggressors when they were embarking on their program of world conquest."[1]

A hometown parade in one's honor must rank very high in the American Dream as a trapping of success, but if it did on that fifth day of September in 1945 it is not reflected in Lemnitzer's laconic entry in his diary: "Big Day—Homecoming. Judge Bodie [Clarence E., master of ceremonies] came to house at 1:30—open cars for Mother, Bodie and me. Lois, Katherine and Bill in another—Ernest & Margaret [his wife] in another. Excellent parade—well organized and run. Ceremony at Court House. Received life membership in Eagles. East Honesdale bridge named for me. Speeches by Judge Bodie, Rev. Kelpfer [Albert F., main speaker] and me. Cocktails."

The parade and the week of golf, fishing, and socializing that followed were the highlights of a much-needed break in a fast-track schedule which, judging from Lemnitzer's diary, had been running at high speed at least ten hours a day, seven days a week since the war began. Only occasional lapses, such as when he accompanied Alexander on sight-seeing trips or when he was waiting for surrender developments in Switzerland, offered chances to escape for a while from the crush of heavy routine. Even if the boss is relaxing, though, it does not mean that the staff member who goes along with him is doing likewise: helping keep things carefree for the man who runs the show can be a full-time job in itself.

Lemnitzer went on leave, probably at Alexander's insistence, for the first time in three years on August 28, the day before his forty-sixth birthday. A departure for leave does not ordinarily call for a guard of honor or a band. Lemnitzer got both and a send-off at the airfield by Alexander, four of the theater's senior generals, and the rest of the field marshal's staff. The gesture was probably as much a tribute to the American general's popularity as to his exceptional record as a key member of Alexander's staff.

The trip to the States was not uneventful after his plane reached Casablanca, as his diary indicates: "Took off in C-54 from Casablanca en route to Santa Maria, Azores. Breakfast and look around. Took off again in C-54 at 0800 [eight o'clock in the morning]. Three hours out No. 2 engine sprang oil leak and had to shut down as it got rough. Turned back to Santa Maria with 3 engines. Transferred to another plane filled with nurses and WACs all in various degrees of pregnancy. Long flight toward Stephensville, Newfoundland. Arr 2330 [half past eleven at night]." The next day: "Arrived Mitchell Field, NY, 0600 [six o'clock in the morning]. Breakfast, phoned Ernest. Discharged all patients and proceeded to Washington. Arrived at 0700 [seven o'clock in the morning]—met at field by Kay, Lois and Bill."

The end of the fighting in Europe had brought little slackening in the volume of Lemnitzer's responsibilities over the previous four months. If, as his old Sunrise comrade, Gaevernitz, had observed, surrendering an Army can be as complicated as mobilizing it, then sending one home must run a close third. An Army motion picture sequence taken during this period shows a beaming Lemnitzer standing at dockside in Naples bidding an official farewell to a wildly waving shipload of homeward-bound members of the 85th Division and then stepping down from the speaker's stand to salute them as their vessel got under way. Perhaps only he of all those there had any idea of how high the mountain of paperwork and the hours of planning it required to get them aboard the *West Point* (in peacetime, the luxury liner *America*) that day.

And then there was Venezia Giulia, a region mentioned often in Lemnitzer's diary in the weeks after the surrender in Italy. Alexander's deputy chief of staff was deeply involved in resolving a dispute over this northeastern Italian region that grew so serious that the Americans and British were preparing to march on the armies of Marshal Tito. What caused American and British ire is that Tito's partisan forces had marched in and occupied Venezia Giulia and Carinthia in southern Austria in violation of an agreement the Yugoslavian leader had previously made in negotiations with Alexander and Lemnitzer in Belgrade. In the case of Venezia Giulia, the Yugoslav army had been merely "leaning against the front" when the Germans surrendered. When the front gave way, Tito's troops rushed forward, but the Germans surrendered to the American-Anglo armies,[2] and the Yugoslavians were supposed to get out. The problem first was mentioned in Lemnitzer's diary the day after the German surrender in Italy: "Venezia Giulia looks bad and is getting worse." Two days later: "Message from Tito—situation much improved." On May 9 Tito rejected Alexander's request that he leave Italy, but two weeks later pulled out of Austria. Lemnitzer's penned comment: "One victory for us—now how about Venezia Giulia?"

In the meantime, Lemnitzer began to draw up plans to redeploy Allied units for movement against Tito's forces. He also drafted a message from Alexander to his troops explaining the impasse. The latter step was thought necessary to prepare them for the possibility that they might have to fight respected comrades in arms. The field marshal's sensitivities about his armies' sentiments prompted a message which brought a rare sharp rebuke from Churchill. In a message marked "personal for the Prime Minister," Alexander had written: "If I am ordered by the Chiefs of Staff to occupy the whole of Venezia Giulia by force if necessary, we shall certainly be committed to a fight with the Yugoslav Army who will have the moral backing, at least, of the Russians. Before we are committed, I think it as well to consider the feelings of our own troops in this matter. They have a profound admiration for Tito's partisans, and a great sympathy for them in their struggle for freedom. We must be careful therefore before we ask them to turn away from the common enemy to fight an ally."

The field marshal sent a copy to the Combined Chiefs of Staff, and somehow it was leaked and made public. Churchill was furious and wrote to Alexander: "The wide circulation given to your message has done much harm. I hope that in the changed circumstances produced by President Truman's telegram [The U.S. president had wired Churchill that 'If Tito takes hostile action and attacks our Allied forces anywhere, we would expect Field Marshal Alexander to use as many troops of all nationalities in his command as are necessary.'], you will find it possible to give me the assurance that the army under your command will obey your orders and its customary sense of duty and discipline. I have been much distressed by this paragraph of your message, and wish that, as far as the British troops are concerned, it had not been given such a wide circulation."[3]

Lemnitzer's almost daily mention of the nip-and-tuck situation extended into June when Tito, apparently convinced that the Allies were not going to back down and unwilling to risk an armed clash with overwhelmingly superior forces, finally withdrew his troops from the disputed territory. Whether Stalin would have backed Tito with force if he had chosen to fight can only be conjectured, but it is doubtful if the Soviet leader would have involved his troops in so minor a cause if it meant going to war with the Western Allies.

Lemnitzer had also been at Alexander's side early in 1945 when the field marshal was trying to settle two major Allied concerns: Trieste and Yugoslavia's cruel treatment of German prisoners of war (POWs). In the case of Trieste, this was an Italian coastal city in Allied territory that Tito had seized and refused to give up. Only threats of U.S. and British military action eventually forced him out, but this occurred long after the talks with Alexander and his staff. The Allied officers had no success either with the German POW issue. When he and Alexander arrived in Belgrade in bitter cold in February, Lemnitzer saw German prisoners standing outside dressed in burlap sacks, their only footwear pieces of wooden boards tied to their feet with field wire. General Arso Jovanovich, Tito's chief of staff, refused to discuss the matter, asserting that the prisoners deserved the treatment because of German 1st Mountain Division brutality toward Yugoslavia residents.[4]

Lemnitzer's final summer in Italy, as described in his diary, seemed to have been a fast-paced welter of unremitting paperwork, late hours in the office of his drafty "caravan," and a long succession of ceremonies for departing theater superiors and colleagues. He got away once to spend the day with Maxwell Taylor, then commander of the 101st Airborne Division, visiting the division sector's "showplace": Hitler's and other high Nazi leaders' mountain homes near Berchtesgaden. This area in Germany's southeast tip held a special attraction for Lemnitzer because it was to have been the command post of a "national redoubt" in which it was feared that Hitler and die-hard Nazi followers would stage a last-ditch stand which could have prolonged the war by months. The possibility that the German forces facing Allied troops in northern Italy would escape to this redoubt was among the reasons why Alexander and his staff had been so anxious that Lemnitzer's mission to Switzerland succeed.

During another trip after the fighting had stopped, an inspection tour with Alexander wound up at the end of a busy day at the villa of deposed Italian dictator Mussolini, on Lake Garda, near Verona. Lemnitzer spent the night in the bedroom belonging to Claretta Petacci, Mussolini's mistress who had been slain with him and their bodies hung upside down for public display after they were captured by Italian partisans in the waning days of the Italian campaign.

His diary references to the sea of paperwork in which he always seemed to be adrift grew more frequent a month before he went on leave when he became Alexander's chief of staff, while retaining his deputy chief of staff's workload, and also chief of staff of the Mediterranean Theater of Operations, U.S. Army (MTOUSA). Two days after his return to Caserta from leave, he wrote in his diary: "Sunday, Sept. 30. Up early. To Marcianese where many troops (Br & US) drawn up in review for the Field Marshal. Beautiful weather. Excellent ceremony but very gloomy one for me as it means break up of fine associations with Field Marshal Alexander since 25 July 1943. Plane took off at 9:00 [nine o'clock in the morning] escorted by 10 Spitfires." Alexander was leaving to become governor-general of Canada, a post much coveted by Field Marshal Alan Brooke who wanted Alexander to succeed him as chief of the Imperial General Staff. Alexander could have had either position but was urged by Churchill to take the Canadian one because "it was much more important."[5] After over six very successful years as governor-general, he became British minister of defense in 1952 after Churchill returned to power as prime minister.

General Sir William D. Morgan, Alexander's successor at Caserta, returned from London late in October after having been knighted by King George. Morgan told Lemnitzer that at the ceremony the king had asked him: "Is Lem still with you?" Informed that he was, the king said: "Give him my best regards." Three days later, Morgan made him a Companion of the Bath in the name of the king. Noting in his diary that the accompanying citation had been written personally by Alexander, Lemnitzer called the award "a very great honor and I am most grateful for it."[6] His medals during his years on Alexander's staff bore impressive testimony to his accomplishments as the field marshal's representative in dealings with foreign armies. In addition to his U.S. decorations—the Distinguished Service Medal, Legion of Merit (Officer's Degree), and Legion of Merit (Legionnaire)—he wore six campaign stars on his Mediterranean theater ribbon, was a Companion of the Bath, a Commander of the British Empire, had been made a Cavalier of the Great Cross by Prince Umberto of Italy, and had been awarded Brazil's Medalha de Guerra, Poland's Gold Order of Merit with Swords, France's Legion of Honor–Degree of Officer, France's Croix de Guerre with Palm, Yugoslavia's Royal Order of the White Eagle–Class II, and Czechoslovakia's Medal of Merit–First Class.

Lemnitzer followed his mentor out of the theater a month after seeing him off at the airport. A farewell ceremony in the huge courtyard of Caserta Palace took place in front of ranks of American and British troops. With a veteran staff officer's eye for the caliber of official amenities, he noted in his diary: "Very impressive and well-arranged."

When Lemnitzer returned to Washington in November 1945, he was assigned to the Joint Strategic Survey Committee (JSSC), a high-level group of officers who during the war had advised the JCS on strategy. He succeeded Lt. Gen. Stanley D. Embick, his benefactor and mentor from his early career, as the panel's senior Army member. With the war over, the committee's deliberations turned to the problems of peace. Soon after reporting for duty, Lemnitzer was assigned to write papers on disarmament and Japanese government reforms, each of which was then put through various reviewing processes, returned for a series of redrafts and presumably then submitted to the Joint Chiefs to use in their planning. The tempo and responsibilities were a far cry from those of the past two years, and it is reasonable to conjecture that Lemnitzer might at this climactic point of his career have been giving some serious thought about his future.

He had been in the Army for twenty-seven years and wore victory ribbons from two world wars. Many other officers with less service were retiring, just leaving, or were being forced out as the armed forces were going through the most extensive downsizing in the country's history. In less than two years after Lemnitzer returned from Europe, the Army would be reduced from a force of over eight million to less than seven hundred thousand with a proportionate drop in the number of officers. In the spring of 1946 Lemnitzer received a letter from the Army's assistant chief of staff for personnel that must have caused him to sit up when he read the first paragraph: "In providing for the interim Army it has been necessary to reduce a number of general officers. This action was reluctantly taken since it affected some of our outstanding leaders of the war, but it was inevitable."[7] But then he must have breathed easier when he read further because, for the time being, at least, he was not going to be one of these postwar casualties. Those to be separated were chosen from a "master merit list," compiled from ratings submitted by the Army's principal commanders. Lemnitzer, who had never received a rating on his OERs of less than "superior" since his days as a junior officer, was high enough on the merit list to be retained. However, the letter made it clear that he was not going to be promoted for the foreseeable future either, if ever at all, for the letter went on to say: "It is now expected that you will hold the grade of major general for a considerable time."

Judging from some earlier family correspondence, however, he had not always seen himself as a soldier when the shooting was over. Three years before, apparently in response to his brother's expressed hope that he would return to the family house in Honesdale after the war, he had written: "Your remarks about my getting back home to retire in the Lemnitzer home certainly hit a very agreeable note with me—it cannot happen any too soon for me and I would like nothing better than just that. Unfortunately, however, I do not see any possibilities along that line for years to come. We must win this war first and that may take a long time."[8] He might have also been worried that the family would sell the commodious old dwelling, now occupied only by his seventy-eight-year-old mother, because he wrote further down: "Under no circumstances count on selling the house—no matter what happens, because I have always wanted to do just what you suggested [probably settle in Honesdale] and the longer this war lasts the more anxious I am to do it." Maybe he was feeling a little homesick the day he wrote Ernest or he was basing his gloomy predictions on his estimate to his family when he went overseas that the war was going to last at least another ten years. As it turned out, it would be twenty-six more years before he went back to Honesdale as a civilian.

The entries in Lemnitzer's diary for the final months of 1945 might have been written by another person, so different are they from those for the previous two years. Where the daily fare then was made up of often-hazardous comings and goings to the outposts of a theater of war or to high-level strategy conferences involving some of the conflict's most illustrious names, now the pages read like those which might have been written by any of a million other veterans just back from the war. An event like trying to flag down a taxi or having to stand all the way to Philadelphia on a crowded train were worth mention. A faulty car which defied repair became a daily subject until a mechanic discovered it needed a new battery. His son's accident in school, which resulted in two broken front teeth, was duly noted and followed through treatment to mending, as was the fact that brother Ernest and King George VI both celebrated their birthdays on December 14. And, like the problem facing many another soldier home from the war, there was house hunting. His two stars were of no help at all as he scanned the pages of Washington newspapers daily for a place to rent ("Spent evening looking for a place to live. Am positive that only way we can get a house is to buy one"). Finally, that is just what he did, paying a thousand dollars down, much of it loaned to him by his brother. Intended to provide shelter during a severe postwar capital housing shortage, the modest brick house at 3286 Worthington Street on Washington's northwest side became wife Kay and the general's main dwelling until they died.

Lemnitzer's vantage point as a senior adviser to the chiefs of the armed services gave him a front seat at the spectacle of an enormous fighting force being reduced to a fraction of its wartime size in less than three years. In September 1945 the Army had ninety-one divisions, all trained and ready; by 1948 there were ten, all understrength with only two organized for combat. During the same period, the Navy was reduced from a top World War II total of 1,166 combat vessels to 343; the Marines Corps from six combat-ready divisions to two, both understrength. The Army Air Force fell from sixty-three operational groups to eleven. When hostilities ceased in 1945, there were more than 12,000,000 troops under arms; at the end of demobilization in 1947, the total was less than 1,600,000. In 1946 the approved military budget ceiling was forty-two billion dollars; the next year it was fourteen billion dollars.[9]

Lemnitzer had seen it before and would see it again: the military professional's dreaded involvement in still another postwar, head-for-the-exits gutting of

America's defenses. This one wasn't supposed to be as willy-nilly as the cutbacks after World War I—there were few illusions in 1945 that the country had, at last, fought a "war to end all wars." But America wanted its veterans back home; the resulting slack was to be taken up by the influx of young men that were to don uniform when Uniform Military Training (UMT)[10] kicked in. Buoyed by a surge in enlistments right after the war and expecting prompt passage of a UMT law, Congress and President Truman did not renew the Selective Service Act when it expired in 1947. But Congress rejected UMT, enlistments did not keep up with requirements, and soon a manpower problem that had been bad got steadily worse. By mid-1947 the services had once again become all-volunteer forces made up mostly of young and inexperienced recruits.

The period from 1945 to 1948, when rebuilding was begun in response to the perceived challenges of the Cold War, was a turbulent time for the services, whose primary mission had turned from war fighting to demobilization and occupation duty. Both took heavy tolls of resources, even at a time when peacetime military budgets were the highest in U.S. history. Trying to maintain U.S. forces in a state of readiness kept the lights burning nights in the JCS offices at the Pentagon as the chiefs, their staffs, and Lemnitzer and his fellow advisers wrestled with the onslaught of peace. The newly chartered United Nations was supposed to be the world's guarantor of that peace, its member nations acting in concert to deal with any threats to the hard-earned tranquillity. One of the first problems laid in the laps of Lemnitzer and his JSSC colleagues was to draft a plan for a UN peacekeeping force. As Lemnitzer recalled: "We had a hell of a lot of problems within our own government as to what we would come up with. There were lots of arguments but agreement was finally reached." The U.S. contribution would consist of an army corps, a naval task force, and a tactical air task force to support the ground corps. The nation's strategic air forces would not be a part of the UN commitment but would be available for support if necessary. "After we put this recommendation together," Lemnitzer said, "the British did the same thing. France didn't have much of a voice in it because they didn't have a capability at that time, and the Russians were supposed to be doing the same thing. And what happened? At the United Nations Security Council meeting which considered the peacekeeping force, it got six straight vetoes from the Soviet Union, which killed the concept entirely."[11]

The Russians also vetoed another U.S. plan, which Lemnitzer remembered as "the greatest offer for peacekeeping the world has ever seen and ever will see." This was known as the Baruch plan, named after U.S. elder statesman Bernard Baruch, and under its terms the United States would have placed its nuclear capability at the disposal of the UN to use to keep the peace. When the Soviets said *nyet* again, Lemnitzer remembered, "they were, at the time, using every means—fair and foul—to obtain information regarding our nuclear capability and know-how and were developing their own capability."[12]

Lemnitzer's performance on the JSSC impressed a rater whom he would one day succeed as supreme allied commander in Europe (SACEUR). Maj. Gen. Lauris Norstad, director of plans and operations on the War Department's General Staff, wrote in one of his OERs: "One of the outstanding general officers in the Army" and in another: "... qualified for the highest command or staff position by virtue of his exceptional intelligence, professional skill, wide experience, sterling character and capacity for open-minded analysis and unbiased judgment." An added comment was prescient: "Particularly qualified by character, ability and experience for high-level staff work, and for assignments involving heavy responsibilities in politico-military matters."

Lemnitzer's busy tour of duty with the JSSC lasted three months short of two years. In August 1947 he moved across town to familiar surroundings, Fort Lesley J. McNair, where he had been a student at the Army War College on the eve of World War II. The post on Washington's waterfront was now the site of the recently founded National War College (NWC), of which Lemnitzer was the new deputy commandant. The NWC had come into being as one of a number of major early postwar institutional changes accompanying establishment of the Department of Defense, the National Security Council (NSC), and the Central Intelligence Agency (CIA). Founded in July 1946, its mission was to prepare military officers for the highest level of joint staff duties and to foster mutual understanding between them and other federal agencies involved in national defense. James F. Forrestal, then secretary of the Navy and an enthusiastic supporter of the college, wanted its joint course to be "the culmination of the formal education of military and naval personnel."[13]

Its launching and early years were watched closely at the highest levels of government and the military services, for the war had shown a deep need for the infusion of the college's goals into the thinking of the officer corps. When Vice Adm. Harry W. Hill became the first commandant, Army Chief of Staff George Marshall told him: "I have just issued orders today for the best man in the Army to be your deputy—his name is [Maj. Gen. Alfred M.] Gruenther."[14] The next year, Gruenther became director of the Joint Staff of the JCS, and Eisenhower, Marshall's newly appointed successor, told Hill that "as a replacement for Gruenther I'll give you any man in the Army you want."[15] The commandant chose Lemnitzer who, from his post at the JSSC, had taken a personal interest in helping get the college started, even participating in many of the classroom discussions during its first year.

Lemnitzer, while serving as the college's chief of staff and its senior Army representative, also directed the NWC lecture program, a wide-ranging forum which during its first year had established the fledgling school as a center for the discussion of defense issues. Besides the college's students, the lecture program attracted nearly four thousand senior officials from both the civilian and military branches of government yearly during the first few years. Cabinet members,

members of the U.S. Senate and House, academicians, and others with interests in defense affairs flocked to the normally quiet little military post to listen and then participate in the often lively question and answer periods which followed the lectures. The speaker could be anyone from a high-level government leader or congressman to a university professor, writer, statesman, or other acknowledged authority in a particular field. During Lemnitzer's first year as deputy commandant, the stream of visitors included President Truman, who rode over from the White House to hear a lecture on "The Political Strategy of the Axis" by Dr. Raymond J. Sontag, chief of the State Department's German War Documents Project. The chief executive was an animated participant in the spirited discussion session that followed.[16]

The more than two years he spent at the NWC were among the most enjoyable of Lemnitzer's career. Besides overseeing the lecture program, the former two-time U.S. Military Academy instructor took an active interest in the curriculum and in the hundred or so military officers and government civilians who made up the annual classes. The college's objectives were, after all, something he had believed in long before ecumenism among the military and other branches of government became institutionalized at Fort McNair. Indeed, the term paper he had written for his year at this very post when he was a student at the Army War College before the war could well have been the model when the NWC's mission was spelled out: its theme was the importance of teamwork between the country's army, naval, and state departments in war planning.

Despite the college's heavy class and lecture schedule, there was time for fun. Lemnitzer was the catcher on one of the softball teams, and he quickly earned a reputation as a fearsome competitor who could swing his bat with as much zest as a young lieutenant or get as indignant over an umpire's call as a major league manager. When he played, there was no need for an opposing player to worry about knocking the catcher down during a vigorous slide into home plate because it was understood that the general always kept his stars in his pocket when his team took the field. He also became a kind of godfather to one of the military establishment's most unusual golf courses. To this day, Fort McNair's nine-hole layout is a marvel of efficiency which holds no mercy for the duffer who slices, hooks, or can't gauge distances. Its fairways—as narrow as the streets they parallel—weave in and out and back and forth between buildings. A ball knocked across a street or into a river—any shot that is less than right on dead center can do it—is out of bounds. If that prospect isn't daunting enough, then perhaps the awareness that an errant ball can very likely bounce off the person or car of a passing general or admiral is what keeps Fort McNair golfers among the sport's most disciplined. Nor are the numerous brass or windows the only objects about which to be nervous—the course's most inviolate rule is written on all scorecards in bold lettering: "Let Helicopters Play Through." The course badly needed some sprucing up when Lemnitzer became deputy commandant, so he became a sort of overseer-at-large, an unofficial calling he never really relinquished despite intervening years in assignments overseas. When he was in Washington, even on visits, he was sure to stop by to run a stickler's eye over how well the fairways and greens were being maintained. If everything didn't measure up, someone would hear about it.

Lemnitzer was SACEUR when Lt. Gen. Andrew J. Goodpaster became the college's commandant in 1967. In the capital for a conference, Lemnitzer made it a point to ensure Goodpaster's appreciation of the course by inviting him to play a round with him. His tip to Goodpaster to follow his lead and "choke up" on his driver so as not to overshoot the hole well over two hundred yards away was as much a tribute to Lemnitzer's formidable hitting power as it was to the fact that this was no ordinary little "pitch-and-putt" course, as Lemnitzer once referred to it in a letter to a friend.[17]

Lemnitzer and the first commandant made a good team. Admiral Hill wrote of his deputy in his first OER: "An unusually capable and efficient officer, who is exceptionally well-informed regarding high-level policy and problems. Combines a fine personality and sound judgment with a strong and decisive character, which fit him particularly well for independent duty."

The war college remained Lemnitzer's favorite Army institution long after he had left it. He designated it the repository of his papers, which today occupy seventy-six feet of shelf space in the Special Collections section of the National Defense University, of which the NWC is a part. Whenever the college needed some help in high places, it could always count on its former deputy commandant. Shortly after the Kennedy administration took over, for example, then JCS Chairman Lemnitzer learned that the new regime in the State Department wanted to substitute something with a more peaceful connotation than the word "war" in the college's title. The general appealed personally to Kennedy to leave it the way it was, and the president agreed. This wasn't the first time that there was a high-level struggle over the college's name. After it was founded in 1946, it was to have been called the "College of National Security," but when Secretary of War Robert P. Patterson heard of it a half-hour before it was to be announced at a press conference he declared his emphatic disapproval of any title containing the word "security." He preferred National War College, and that is what it became.[18]

Lemnitzer was nearing the end of his first year on the pleasant little campus on the Potomac when something happened—call it fortunes of war, in this instance the Cold one—which would put an end to any dreams he might still have had of going back to Honesdale and living a comfortable life as a retired major general. More than at any other time in his career, his performance in this new test would put him on a fast track that would take him to the very pinnacles of his profession. The general had just finished packing for a fishing trip to Alaska with Gen. J. Lawton (Lightning Joe) Collins, Army vice chief of staff, in July

1948, when he telephoned Collins to confirm their departure time. Collins told him, however, that there had been a new development: "You're going on a trip, all right, but you're not going where you think you are." To Lemnitzer's query, "What the hell do you mean?" Collins replied: "I think Mr. Forrestal wants to see you."[19] When Lemnitzer arrived at the defense secretary's office in the Pentagon, Forrestal commented on the considerable experience the general had in Europe and asked if he was familiar with the Brussels Pact. When Lemnitzer replied that he was, Forrestal told him that he was assigning him to a top secret mission. He was going to London to sit in on the meetings of a group called the Military Committee of the Five Powers.

The committee represented the defense establishments of the five European nations that earlier in the year had banded together to sign the Brussels Pact: Great Britain, France, Belgium, the Netherlands, and Luxembourg. The motive for forming the alliance was the growing fear in Europe that the Soviet Union was bent upon domination, if not the subjugation, of the continent.

The signs were ample. Tensions between the Soviets and the western Allies had begun to materialize even before the war ended. One of the earliest signs of outright hostility had been Stalin's truculent charges during Sunrise, the Lemnitzer-managed secret talks leading to the surrender of German forces in Italy, that the United States and England were negotiating with the Germans behind the Soviets' backs. President Roosevelt had come to believe in the Soviets's good faith after Allied summit meetings at Tehran and Yalta, and Stalin's insulting denunciations gave the president his first nasty jolt in his relations with the Russians.[20] As the war ended, the range of disagreements grew. There were East-West disputes over the organization of the new United Nations; the termination of lend-lease, surrender terms for Germany; and the status of Eastern Europe where pro-Soviet, military-backed regimes violated United States-Soviet understandings regarding the right of the countries involved to political self-determination. So obvious and blatant were the Soviet aims that Churchill in May 1945 wrote a grim assessment to President Truman in which he early articulated his famous phrase, "Iron Curtain."[21]

As its grip on eastern Europe tightened, the Soviet Union began making a series of moves in western Europe and other places that were clearly aimed at exploiting the economic and political disarray left by the war in order to bring about the installation of communist regimes. Efforts to pressure the western Allies into leaving Berlin began; Norway and Finland were bullied to sign "mutual assistance" treaties that would allow Soviet troops to pass through and fortify certain parts of their territories; heavy Soviet troop buildups were taking place along East Germany's borders; and Moscow was pushing campaigns to put communists in control of European governments.

Any uncertainties about the Soviet Union's ultimate intentions were removed in February 1948, when Czechoslovakia broke under heavy Soviet pressure and became a communist state; during the coup, Jan Masaryk, the Czech foreign minister and son of the republic's founder, died and was believed murdered. The takeover was the catalyst that finally shocked Great Britain, France, and the Benelux nations into forming the kind of protective alliance that had been under increasing discussion between the five countries and the United States. In March the Brussels Pact was signed, establishing what came to be known as the Western Union.[22] In time this union would become one of history's most successful alliances, the North Atlantic Treaty Organization (NATO).

The Western Union came into being with strong, behind-the-scenes encouragement of President Truman and Secretary of State Marshall, who also foresaw the need for a larger alliance to combat the communist menace. Advocates of such an organization had to move cautiously, for the country's isolationists still had considerable power in government. However, an important precedent had been set in 1947 with the United States's agreement to be a party to the Rio Pact, an important departure from the nation's historic aversion to entering into international alliances in peacetime. The pact, adhered to initially by most independent Latin American countries, pledged its signatories to consider a military attack on one nation an attack on all. But the Rio Pact did not provide for a permanent military organization to support it; so, while Truman and Marshall could point to the pact as a precedent and its one-for-all action provision as a model, they had to be careful about stressing military commitments. That was a major reason why Forrestal, the administration's leading get-tough advocate in the Cold War, put so much emphasis on the need for strict secrecy in sending Lemnitzer to London.

The NWC's deputy commandant had been selected for the mission by the JCS the day following Truman's approval of an NSC recommendation that the United States support, but not join, the Western Union while exploring the possibility of creating a larger mutual defense agreement involving the United States, members of the Western Union, and other North Atlantic countries. The president also approved an NSC recommendation that the United States initiate military assistance to prospective alliance members and take part in Western Union planning.[23]

The top secret NSC initiative had made its way slowly through the concerned institutions of government, prompting enthusiasm in some places and serious reservations in others, such as in the Joint Chiefs. Among other things, the JCS worried about the impact on U.S. defense resources and requirements. The action that broke the logjam and became the cornerstone for the eventual creation of NATO was Senate approval of the Vandenberg Resolution in June 1948. Sponsored and pushed through the upper chamber by Senator Arthur Vandenberg, Michigan Republican, the resolution notified President Truman that the Senate favored the country's entering into a mutual defense agreement with other nations. Three days later, the NSC overcame JCS qualms with a recommendation that any military assistance be prohibited that would "jeopardize the fulfillment of the minimum materiel requirements of the United States armed forces, as determined by the JCS." The report further provided that assistance "should not be inconsistent" with JCS strategic concepts.[24]

The choice of Lemnitzer to serve as the assistance program's "point man" probably was prompted by his extensive allied experience in World War II, since this was cited by Forrestal in their initial meeting. It is possible, also, that his selection had been suggested by the Western Union's military committee because the defense secretary noted that Lemnitzer was acquainted with the British air marshal who headed the committee and with whom the American general had served on a staff level in the war. And, finally, the Joint Chiefs, who picked him, had had two years to watch him at work as a member of the JSSC.

Probably few envisioned the assignment as anything more at the outset than the routine dispatch of a competent and experienced staff officer to size up a situation and then return to his regular duties at the NWC. No one could have foreseen at this stage that what was, in essence, a fact-finding mission would turn into a job that no ambitious general in his right mind could have wanted. Before Lemnitzer moved on to the next stage of his career, he would find out what it is like to work for a cabinet officer who was openly contemptuous of the goals he was charged with accomplishing. He would be a target of the dark suspicions of uniformed superiors in rank, and even those he was trying to help would, at times, look upon his efforts with distrust or try to cheat the government he represented. He would be woefully underranked in his new post, carrying on with his two stars in frequently hostile territory against an army that would include every kind of chief from a secretary or senator to the head of a foreign state. It is doubtful if even four stars would have been sufficient, if rank was all that was needed.

The fact that the Pentagon's powers-that-be did not select a full general adds a new dimension to the question of "why Lemnitzer?" As had others in his past, it is not inconceivable that somewhere in the highest levels of government some far-thinking visionary had seen in Lemnitzer the makings of a future Army chief of staff and had decided to test his mettle as it had never been tested before.

12

∗ ∗ ∗ ∗

MINDER OF THE ARSENAL

Short of actually attacking its wartime allies, the Soviet Union could have heightened the urgency of Lemnitzer's mission no more dramatically than it did in the spring of 1948 when it launched a bold campaign to force U.S., British, and French forces of occupation out of Berlin.

When he arrived in London, the Western Allies were using every available transport aircraft to airlift food and other essential supplies into the German city to thwart a ground blockade thrown up around the former capital by communist troops. Berlin had been divided into east and west portions after World War II, with Soviet troops occupying the east while the United States, Great Britain, and France held sectors in the west.

When the confrontation of 1948 occurred, West Berlin had for months been the target in a series of increasingly militant harassing incidents involving forces of the Western Powers. Located one hundred ten miles inside Soviet-held East Germany, West Berlin could be reached only by crossing communist territory. There was very real concern at the White House and the Pentagon that the United States and its wartime communist ally might soon be at war, a conflict for which the Western powers were ill prepared.

Official accounts of Lemnitzer's mission to the Western Union's military committee give it a formal flavor that was not reflected in the general's recollections years later. The JCS recommendation outlining the mission specified that he was to head up a delegation of "not more than seven officers" who were to participate on a nonmember basis in talks about military plans and supplies.[1] Lemnitzer received his instructions from Forrestal, who may have toned down the JCS plan. He told the general he was to go as an observer and that Canada was sending a brigadier who would have the same status. Lemnitzer had one objective, he recalled, and that was to find out what the Western Union's five member nations needed in the way of military equipment and supplies.[2] At the time, the existence of the military committee was a closely held secret and when Lemnitzer checked into the Dorchester Hotel he did so as a civilian in town for a personal visit. The communist threat was so pervasive at the time that participants in the meetings, held at London's Horse Guard headquarters, were not allowed to carry away any documents or notes when their sessions recessed or adjourned. The reason for the extreme security was that the French government, a participant in the talks, was shot through with communists at the time. When delegates returned home, they had to brief their superiors from memory.[3]

Lemnitzer was recalled to Washington after six weeks, his mission accomplished, but before he returned he borrowed a small airplane and two Royal Air Force pilots from the British government for a brief trip into the continent. After a meeting in Paris with Averell Harriman—head of the Marshall Plan in Europe and a leading Truman administration advocate of foreign military aid—he flew to West Germany to watch the Berlin airlift in operation. It is probable that he was acting as a fact-finding emissary for Forrestal because he was met at each stop by U.S. commanders, including Lt. Gen. Curtis E. LeMay, commander of U.S. Air Forces in Europe, and Gen. Lucius D. Clay, U.S. military governor in Germany. The latter meeting took place in Berlin at the end of a foggy trip from Wiesbaden by C-47, with the only other "passenger" being a ten-ton cargo of flour. The cloud ceiling at Berlin's Tempelhof airport was less than two hundred feet that day.

Lemnitzer regarded the mission to London as "one of the simplest assignments I ever had in my life. My instructions were to find out what the Europeans needed most to build up their forces as quickly as they could afford to. The first day I sat in with the committee I found that they needed everything—it was just about that simple."[4] Forrestal listened intently to his report of the trip when he got back to Washington and remarked, "Well, you met some people and you know what their organization is." The general recalled that "he [Forrestal] knew at the time that they were thinking about a NATO or something like it. This was the beginning of it, but he didn't say that."[5]

His contribution seemingly over, Lemnitzer returned happily to his duties at Fort McNair. But Forrestal was not through with him, and four months later, he was summoned again to the secretary of defense's office. Forrestal told him that work had begun on the drafting of a treaty that would create a mutual security organization involving the United States, the Western Union nations, and others with reasons to fear Soviet aggression. Forrestal told Lemnitzer that "we're going through with this alliance [but] it's no use of the United States government having an alliance with only weak allies, and all our allies are weak. I want you to begin thinking about putting together a military assistance program." The creation of what would become NATO was at an extremely delicate stage and

Forrestal cautioned that Lemnitzer's role would be "super top secret. You can't even breathe about this—you can barely think about it."[6] The general could recall no issue in his memory—with the possible exception of the Manhattan Project that produced the atomic bomb—that was shrouded in so much secrecy. "We were told time and time and time again that under no circumstances could this matter be surfaced unless and until this country subscribed to the Atlantic Alliance." The official rationale was that if Congress or the nation's citizenry knew that any thought was being given to military assistance, the ratification of a NATO treaty would be seriously jeopardized.[7]

Thus began a two-year tour of duty—half of it off the record—of which Lemnitzer remembered: "I never worked so much alone in my whole service."[8] Forrestal told him to obtain any help he needed from Gruenther, director of the JCS Joint Staff, who assigned him a room in the Pentagon's D Ring, a cubicle with no windows and no furniture. "So I got a table and chair and moved in," he recalled years later, and then he said to Gruenther, "well, goddam it, I've got to have some assistance. So he loaned me 'Ham' (Lt. Col. Hamilton) Twitchell."[9] The concept of military assistance, as envisioned by Forrestal in his sketchy charge to his new helper, was so new that the first thing Lemnitzer and Twitchell (who retired as a major general) did was to sit down and try to define from a military standpoint such issues as what assistance was, why it was, and how it could be implemented. These questions were also on the minds of Lemnitzer's new civilian colleagues on the just-created Foreign Assistance Correlation Committee (FACC): John H. Ohley, of the State Department; and Alexander Henderson, and later Edward Dickinson, of the Economic Cooperation Administration (ECA). The committee was headed by Ernest A. Gross, assistant secretary of state, and later by Lloyd V. Berkner, also of the State Department.

Perhaps partly to conceal the existence of the committee and its purpose, Lemnitzer retained his title as NWC deputy commandant. On mornings, he carried out his duties at Fort McNair, and after lunch he went to his Pentagon office, often working until midnight and later to help get the assistance program and a North Atlantic alliance off the ground. His first task was to assume a key role in drafting legislation to set up the program. He and his colleagues on the FACC used as their model the Marshall Plan, a program named after Secretary of State George C. Marshall whose aim it was to use U.S. funds to rehabilitate the war-torn nations of Europe. "Our problem was quite similar to the Marshall Plan," he recalled, "except that we were going to provide military equipment to our allies. We had equipment running out of our ears from World War II."[10]

The Marshall Plan was in trouble when the military assistance program was first being discussed. While the United States was introducing huge amounts of money and resources into Europe, the nations there were not making investments of their own. The reason was that they felt that there was no security on the continent—the Soviets could walk across Europe to the English Channel anytime they pleased. The nations were not going to invest their meager resources in anything that could be swept away in communist takeovers. "So it was considered essential to rebuild some military strength in Europe as soon as possible," Lemnitzer said.[11]

On April 4, 1949, the representatives of twelve nations convened in Washington and signed the North Atlantic Treaty. It took until July 21 for the treaty to be ratified, and hours after President Truman signed it on July 25 he asked Congress for approval of a comprehensive military aid program. Military assistance would be extended to non-European nations under the plan, but the timing of its inception and the weighting of its initial allotments made it clear that the principal beneficiaries were to be America's new postwar allies in Europe. Indeed, without the plan it was clear that creation of an effective alliance would not have been possible. The administration wanted swift approval, but it took Congress nearly three months to pass an authorization bill and another three weeks to approve the appropriations for Fiscal Year 1950.[12]

Through the tough congressional struggles and into the unsteady months when what came to be known as the Mutual Defense Assistance Program (MDAP) was finally implemented, Lemnitzer was in the middle of every fight, earning a reputation as a tireless, always well-informed, resourceful, credible, and courageous campaigner. Much further into his career, when he was in a particularly bruising political donnybrook in the nation's capital, he would occasionally be stereotyped as too straight an arrow, too politically naive to do battle on the fields favored by congressmen and government officials. It was an impression that rarely lasted long and wouldn't have surfaced at all if the nay-sayers had ever seen him in action at the forge that hammered out the nation's first real "entanglement" in an international alliance.

An early test of how well he could stand the heat came during the early months of 1949 when there reappeared in Washington's upper government circles a man who was destined to become perhaps the most despised secretary of defense ever to hold the office. He was Louis A. Johnson, a former assistant secretary of war who led by bombast and an arrogant forcefulness that paid little heed to the feelings of either peers or subordinates. A large, intensely ambitious man who had been a successful lawyer from Virginia, Johnson had been a founder and national commander of the American Legion before joining the campaign to elect Franklin D. Roosevelt in the early 1930s. In 1937 he became assistant secretary of war under Secretary Harry H. Woodring, serving until 1940. He and Woodring feuded incessantly during a period regarded as one of the most turbulent in the War Department's history.[13] Now, in the early months of 1949, he was back in the wake of a successful Truman reelection campaign in which he had achieved a spectacular record as a fund-raiser.

Forrestal had resigned, probably under pressure from the White House. It was known that Truman was not satisfied with his performance in office, and there had begun to appear signs of the depression and acute paranoia that would culminate in his mental breakdown and assumed suicide within two months of his leaving office.[14] Still another compelling reason was that the very persuasive Johnson wanted badly to be the secretary of defense (and, many believed, the next president), and Truman owed him a great deal for his support in the election campaign. If Truman had been able to hand-build a person who would be the direct opposite of his first defense secretary in practically every way, he couldn't have done better than Johnson. The quiet, hard-working Forrestal was an intellectual—creative, idealistic, an introvert, apolitical, publicity-shy, and a firm believer in teamwork. He was also, in Truman's estimation, indecisive and suspect in his party loyalties. Johnson was outgoing, loud, brash, flashy, a superb salesman, a slick political in-fighter, and a loyal Democrat. He was also considered a light-weight as far as military knowledge was concerned, and his style of leadership seemed to have been aimed more at alienating and dividing subordinates than at uniting and inspiring them.

Ohley remembered that during the Forrestal tenure "One had a sense of mission and purpose, of being part of an important constructive undertaking." Najeeb E. Halaby, manager of the Pentagon's Office of Military Affairs (OFMA) and a close associate of Lemnitzer's, wrote of Forrestal: "The too-brief time I spent working for him was one of the most exciting and stimulating periods of my life."[15] This was definitely not the kind of atmosphere that prevailed during Johnson's stewardship. Although Forrestal was said by an associate to have been "just galled" to "think that an office he had created to be above and beyond politics would become a spoil of the 1948 campaign," he made every effort to ensure that the change in Pentagon leadership would be smooth and efficient.[16] The transition period lasted two months, and during this time Lemnitzer had his first encounter with a man who could send tempers soaring just by entering a room.

Forrestal called Lemnitzer one day and told him he wanted him and Halaby to come to his office because "Mr. Johnson is going to come down to visit us and we want to tell him a little about these important international activities in which you and Halaby are engaged."[17] As Johnson and Forrestal sat on one side of the secretary's conference table and he and Halaby on the other, Lemnitzer began: "Well, the first thing of extreme importance is the question of developing some kind of alliance to stop the rush of international communism that is sweeping across eastern central Europe. To that end, we are engaged in drafting what would be the preamble to some kind of an Atlantic treaty."

"That," as the general recalled it, "was as far as I got." Johnson hit the table with his fist and, as Lemnitzer remembered his words, shouted: "General, what the hell are you talking to me about an alliance for? Don't you know that two weeks ago I gave an address to the Daughters of the American Revolution (DAR) at Constitution Hall in which I took violent exception to foreign alliances?" Lemnitzer said, "I sat there and I thought that Mr. Forrestal should answer this one," but he added that the secretary was well into the mental decline that led to his being hospitalized in the spring of 1949. (Since Johnson took office on March 28, the briefing must have taken place about March 18. Forrestal either jumped or fell to his death at the U.S. Naval Hospital in Bethesda, Maryland, on May 21.) Forrestal "just sat there and didn't say a thing," Lemnitzer recalled. "So, seeing that I was not going to get any help from anybody, I said 'Yes, sir, we all know about your talk to the Daughters of the American Revolution; but when you become secretary of defense ten days from now you're going to be the second witness before the Senate Foreign Relations Committee on the ratification of this particular treaty.' That ended the conference. He blew up and went out."[18]

Johnson based his stance on George Washington's opposition to any U.S. involvement in foreign alliances, and Lemnitzer felt that he never changed in his personal bias against either the North Atlantic Treaty or the military assistance program. But both were key elements of administration policy, and some way had to be found to get the intemperate secretary-designate off the hook. The word from Capitol Hill was that members of the Senate Foreign Relations Committee, especially the Republicans, were sharpening their knives for Johnson's appearance at the ratification hearings, scheduled to begin within two weeks after he formally took office. Lemnitzer had already drafted much of the secretary's testimony, but he had prepared it for Forrestal, who had been expected to remain in office longer than he did. He recalled that he received no guidance on what to do, so "I came to the conclusion that there was only one way to meet this [problem] and that was to meet it head-on." He changed the opening part of Johnson's testimony to have him conceding that he had indeed given the DAR speech but that since then he had been given access to intelligence about Soviet activities and had changed his mind.[19] He put the new testimony into an envelope, gave it to Louis Renfrow, a Johnson assistant, told him "this was going to be a very tough one," and asked him to get the secretary to look at it as soon as possible.

No one wanted to approach the bad-tempered Johnson directly on an issue which had elicited such a violent outburst at Lemnitzer's briefing, so Renfrow put the amended testimony in the in box on the secretary's desk and waited for his response. Days went by and there was no indication from Johnson that he had even read the testimony—the draft had gone into his out box, but it contained no initials or any sign as to whether the secretary had approved or disapproved it. Because of Johnson's strong feelings about the causes Lemnitzer represented, the general tried to stay out of his sight as much as possible during their association, so he and Renfrow devised a system of signals through which the aide would indicate whether the secretary was in or out when Lemnitzer made his nightly stops at the door of his outer office to check on his script's status. When the signal was that Johnson was in, the general disappeared; when Johnson was out, he and Renfrow would slip into his office and scan his desk for an indication of where things stood. While this was going on, developments on Capitol Hill and elsewhere made necessary frequent updating of the testimony. Each time Renfrow would retrieve it, Lemnitzer would make the changes and back it would go into the secretary's in box, often several times a day. Just as regularly it would be back in the out box with no indication that Johnson had even looked at it.

The general sent word to Johnson through Renfrow that the Senate Foreign Relations Committee required copies of testimony at least twenty-four hours before it was to be given. Still no word, so Lemnitzer had two hundred fifty copies made and gave them to the committee's staff. Johnson and Lemnitzer rode up on the elevator together the day the secretary was to appear. "He didn't indicate that he had ever seen the goddam thing," Lemnitzer said later.[20] The secretary gave the testimony exactly as Lemnitzer had prepared it. It took the edge off the opposition, and Johnson got through without incident in what could have been a very thorny hearing. Reflecting on the bizarre episode, Lemnitzer recalled: "Riding back from the Hill, did he ever say anything about it? How well it went? What a good job that was done? And the fact that it was all right? Not a word, not a goddam word."[21]

The general's precarious relationship with the mercurial defense boss was further complicated by Johnson's bitter running feud with Dean Acheson, the secretary of state. The bad feeling between the two men assumed such proportions that Johnson issued orders that the only contact between the two departments was to be at the secretarial level. It was an impossible situation for Lemnitzer, who had to work closely with representatives of the State Department in setting up the assistance program and drafting NATO legislation. At the Secretary's thrice-weekly meetings of key staff members, Johnson would reprimand Lemnitzer frequently for not following his orders. As the general remembered it: "...he'd come to me and say, 'General, I understand that you've agreed to such and such a part of this legislation that's being drafted. Don't you understand that I put out that I was the only contact with the secretary of state?' I would say, 'Mr. Secretary, what am I supposed to do? I'm on this committee [FACC] as your representative. Should I come to you for every little detail, then you deal with Mr. Acheson? The thing won't work that way.' We used to go through this about every goddam meeting."[22]

Actually, there was another Pentagon official authorized to deal with the State Department; he was retired Army Maj. Gen. James H. Burns, who carried the title of assistant to the secretary of defense for foreign military affairs and military assistance. He was aware of the difficulties Johnson's order imposed on Lemnitzer and Halaby, but he neither officially condoned nor condemned the only way the two could do their jobs: they simply worked around or disregarded Johnson's edict on contacts. They managed to get their work done but under conditions many officials of the two departments regarded as outlandish.[23]

Burns, who had been Johnson's executive officer when he was with the War

Department, very nearly resigned in a rage over the defense secretary's conduct at a briefing Lemnitzer had tried to hold at a meeting of the Armed Forces Policy Council. Lemnitzer had been elated because the council was made up of all the top Pentagon officials, including the JCS, and this would give him a rare opportunity to explain what he considered a badly misunderstood assistance program. Normally, such a briefing would be an integrated, comprehensive presentation with each piece being carefully fitted with all the others. But Lemnitzer knew that Johnson hated briefings and that therefore his stint on the podium might be short, so he selected ten major issues and arranged them in descending order of importance. By the third item, the general noticed that Johnson was beginning to fidget in his chair. He got through the fourth issue and was beginning the fifth when Johnson said, "Okay, that's all. We've heard enough." Lemnitzer picked up his papers and went back to his seat for the rest of the meeting. On his way out after the meeting, he walked through Burns's office and found him sitting at his desk writing furiously and muttering to himself. When Lemnitzer asked what was wrong, Burns replied with an angry tirade against Johnson which concluded with, "Anyone as rude as that I simply won't work for. I'm writing out my resignation." Lemnitzer remonstrated with him: "Now, look, general. I batted nearly .500 in there and, as an old baseball player, I know that's a pretty good average. It's batting very high in this league on briefings and you know that better than I do." Burns finally cooled off and tore up his resignation.[24]

Nor were Lemnitzer's miseries confined to the civilian side of government. The JCS still had deep misgivings about the military assistance concept, chiefly because they feared the drain on materiel would seriously impair U.S. military readiness. Lemnitzer would complain years later about the lack of staff support, by individual services and at the JCS level. In those days, when the Department of Defense was going through intense reorganizing, interservice bickering could get brutal. An example of how a combination of these factors affected Lemnitzer's operation occurred during congressional hearings on the military aid bill. The House Foreign Affairs Committee had requested that it be given a comprehensive intelligence briefing on the world military situation. Pressed into service on the assistance program because its Senate counterpart was busy with other issues at the time, the House group had not previously come into contact with military activities and, Lemnitzer recalled, "their curiosity regarding them was just beyond belief."[25]

Lemnitzer took the request to the Joint Staff of the JCS where it ran into a series of roadblocks brought on by the fact that the services could not agree on what should go into the briefing. "The Navy didn't agree with the Air Force," he remembered, "and the Army didn't agree with either one." Lemnitzer needed to pre-brief the Chiefs before presenting the briefing to the congressmen, but he could not get anything from the Joint Staff without an agreement among the Chiefs, and it wouldn't do to go before a congressional committee with a split position. The day scheduled for the briefing arrived, and Air Force Maj. Gen. W. E. Todd, the Joint Staff's chief of intelligence, told Lemnitzer an agreement had not yet been reached. Lemnitzer's next move expressed a great deal about the style that would make him one of the services' most effective and respected congressional spokesmen in the years ahead. It also was an eloquent underscoring of the abilities that would soon put him on a fast track into the upper echelons of the Army's uniformed leadership. "Everyone expected that I was going to ask for a postponement," he reminisced after his retirement. "What the hell; I didn't do any such thing. I went up and I gave them an intelligence briefing right from the top of my head—top secret, super top secret, restricted data, anything else, because I had come to the conclusion that if you gave them nothing you'd get nothing."[26] After the war in Korea broke out, Lemnitzer took it on himself to give the information-hungry committee a daily morning briefing on what had happened since the previous morning. He never told Johnson or his other superiors that he was doing it, but each day for six days a week he would gather up what information he could obtain from official sources, pick up his map case, and go over to the Hill to tell committee members how the war was going.

Widespread suspicions that he was the tactical commander of a damaging assault on military supplies sometimes made him the target of pointed comments from fellow officers who often outranked him. One such encounter that disturbed him particularly was with General Collins, the Army vice chief of staff, who said to him one day: "Lem, I understand you're up there doping out all the equipment that you're going to take away from the Army and give to our European allies. When are you going to tell us something about it?" Collins made similar biting comments on other occasions. Lemnitzer could only reply as he did the first time: "Look, I'm not the boss of this particular program—the secretary of defense is. I'm working on a military aid program for the secretary with representatives of the secretary of state and the ECA."[27]

One reason Lemnitzer was such an effective champion of military aid and NATO is that he believed in it, strongly. He was convinced that the creation of an alliance was imperative if the communist threat was to be stopped, and the aid plan was not only a necessary prop but it made it possible for the United States to modernize its own forces. This was financed by military aid funds which U.S. services used to replace equipment sent overseas from World War II stockpiles. But JCS skepticism remained a factor even after the aid program became law, although it was a peripheral one in the face of its strong administration support. JCS Chairman Omar N. Bradley was called upon frequently to testify as the bill made its way through Congress with Lemnitzer accompanying him to provide factual information and present the nitty-gritty after Bradley had given the main testimony. He didn't always have one of the Defense Department's big guns to rely on, though. Once while Forrestal was still in office, he called Lemnitzer to his office where he was having lunch with Carl Vinson, chairman of the House

Armed Services Committee. Planning on the aid program was in its early stages, and Forrestal wanted the general to brief this very powerful congressman. When he finished, Vinson unexpectedly asked him how much it would cost to implement the plan. "Well, I had never thought about the thing," Lemnitzer said, "so I just gritted my teeth and said, 'About two billion dollars, Mr. Chairman.'" Vinson looked at the ceiling for a moment and commented, "Well, I think that's reasonable."[28]

By the time Truman signed the Mutual Defense Assistance Act on October 6, 1949, this figure had been so kicked about by various committees and agencies that when the Bureau of the Budget (BoB) got through with it and sent it to the president, only nine hundred million dollars remained. Convinced that the plan needed a minimum of one billion dollars to work, Lemnitzer gritted his teeth once more and went to see Johnson while his colleagues on the FACC appealed for help to their bosses in the State Department and the ECA. The latter, in turn, went to Truman, who overruled his BoB, and when the act became law it had $1.314 billion to take it through its first year of operation.

The job that had rarely seemed like a job ended the following month when Lemnitzer doffed his other hat and left the NWC's pleasant confines to become the first director of military assistance in the Office of the Secretary of Defense. His chief function: the "unified direction and authoritative coordination of the military phase of planning, programming, logistic and training activities in connection with military assistance."[29] It was a tough assignment, for Congress had made no effort in the assistance act to spell out how the program would be organized and managed. A State Department official, James Bruce, was in overall charge of the program, and Burns was the top man in the Defense Department. But it was Lemnitzer who was on the firing line, the man who, seemingly, everyone turned to for interpretations of the act's provisions, its implementation, and about every other concern having to do with getting the program off the ground.

The general's journal for 1950 shows a daily calendar packed with meetings, congressional appearances, visits, and telephone calls from persons interested in benefiting from the aid program, overseas trips to recipient nations, requests for clarifications and decisions, interviews with editors and reporters seeking information, and a surprising number of applications for employment. (Throughout his career, Lemnitzer was not the best government contact to hit up for a job, invariably telling the seeker he was not the proper person to see or sending him or her off—without recommendation—to see someone else. Among those who didn't get anywhere when Lemnitzer directed the aid program was a man whose employment had been urged on the general by both the White House and his boss, General Burns. He told each that the man was not qualified to fill either of the "one or two positions" available, and there the matter ended.)[30]

Because of the lack of guidelines in the assistance act, Lemnitzer pretty much had to carve out on his own how his part of the program was to be implemented and managed. Neither Johnson nor Burns seemed to have been of much help— Johnson wanted to have as little to do with the program as possible, and Burns, whose heart problems made him almost a part-time official, was content to let Lemnitzer and Halaby run their operations their own ways. Moreover, in its early days the program was little understood outside of Lemnitzer's small circle, and in a profession in which even the top generals had negative feelings there wasn't a long list of career officers eager to have anything to do with it.

Time and again, Lemnitzer's journal refers to instances in which he was called upon to voice opinions on such matters as whether a particular country could receive aid or what kind. Having been thoroughly involved in the concept ever since it was nothing more than an idea, he was versed in its intricacies as were few others in government. He appeared to be scrupulously fair, standing on his interpretations of the assistance act's provisions and offering logical rationales of why he supported a particular course of action. When he was opposed to a proposed move, he said so and would indicate that he was prepared to follow through with his opposition if the proponent persisted. And he could be very firm, as this diary entry suggests:

"Mr. Ohly called. Discussed development of supplemental program. He said the supplemental programs won't be firmed up until October or November. McNeil and Bendetsen said 22 October was the earliest date. I told Ohly I would not accept this date, that it would have to be sooner. Ohly quoted McNeil as saying 'things they are going into production on were, for the most part, common to what would be required in MDAP.' I told Ohly if it is done with certain objectives in mind we have no objection. Army will have to justify it on a project-by-project basis before I will approve the general use of funds for that purpose."[31]

That the general was the pivot man in the assistance program was an understatement. No question was too small or too large, it seemed, to properly belong in his bailiwick. One day, he would be addressing a message to Gruenther at the Joint Staff protesting a quartermaster general's exertion of pressure to include food and clothing in the aid program, and the next day he would be investigating why Norway had been ruled ineligible to receive radar equipment. He also kept a close eye on how assistance funds were being spent and found out that the services were capable of doing "some pretty fast footwork in calculating their price tags." One instance was in the procurement of jeeps. "Everyone wanted jeeps," he recalled, "and the Army had loads of them." When he looked into why the assistance program was getting so few for its money, he found out that the Army was computing what a new jeep would cost, which by this time was 25 percent more than the wartime price, and adding the cost of putting it back into top condition. The result was that the price for the reconditioned jeep was more than twice its original cost. He recalls that "I took violent exception to that" and "had a pretty interesting time" with the secretary of the Army and his assistant secretary for logistics before the situation was corrected.[32]

Hopes that final passage of the assistance act and authorization of supporting funds would soon see huge shipments of money and equipment flowing into the defenses of beneficiary nations had to give way to the realization that it wasn't that simple. First, in the case of NATO, assistance could not begin until the new alliance had adopted a strategic plan. A much stickier aspect was the requirement that bilateral agreements had to be reached first with each nation requesting assistance. The chief reason for these agreements was that Congress and the administration wanted to know how the requested assistance would be used and if it was justified under provisions of the act. This meant making surveys, examining military budgets, inspecting armed forces, and otherwise poking U.S. noses deeply into the internal affairs of often resentful erstwhile recipients.

Getting signatures on bilateral agreements was a State Department job, although Lemnitzer was deeply involved in an aspect of the diplomatic side of the program that caused as much controversy as any other. This was the requirement that Military Assistance Advisory Groups (MAAG) be assigned to participating nations to supervise the disposition of aid. European countries were annoyed and felt humiliated that Americans were setting up headquarters in national capitals to monitor what they did with their aid. To such countries as Norway and Denmark, the sending of large staffs wearing uniforms brought back memories of German occupation and made Americans look like conquerors. National pride was also an issue; honor made France, for example, ask to have the word "advisory" struck from the MAAG title. Part of Lemnitzer's job was to ensure that suitable personnel were sent overseas and that the groups be as unobtrusive as possible.[33] Despite the obstacles and red tape, the first shipment of MDAP equipment—naval aircraft for France—left Norfolk, Virginia, on March 8, 1950, aboard the French aircraft carrier *Dixmude*.

As had been the case so often in Lemnitzer's career, France proved to be a difficult client in the early days of the assistance program. As the principal contributor to armed power in Europe, it received special attention,[34] but its conduct could well have given the impression that it was the giver rather than the receiver. Anxious to get their share of the aid, the French made high-handed requests for preferential treatment and opposed aid to European nations not belonging to the Western Union.[35] At one point, Lemnitzer had to field a demand from France that the United States also underwrite the cost of shipping the materiel it was sending to France. He said no—that wasn't in the agreement.[36] The general's diary is peppered with notations regarding special French requests and objections. Once at a meeting in Ohly's office regarding assistance in Southeast Asia he apparently became so exasperated about French complaints of delays that he noted: "Vigorous representations were made by Mr. Dickinson and myself to send a strong dispatch to Mr. Acheson in Paris to document the French wavering and indecision re equipment in Indochina in order that responsibility for delays should be placed squarely on those responsible; i.e., the French."[37]

A high-level French request for help in the fall of 1950 forced the United States to make a decision that denied a squadron of twenty-one B-26 light bombers to United Nations forces in Korea. George Marshall had just succeeded the fired Johnson in October when he received an urgent request from France for the aircraft, said to be needed desperately by its forces in Indochina. The request was delivered personally by French Foreign Minister Robert Schuman and Defense Minister Jules Moch at a meeting attended by Marshall, Acheson, Treasury Secretary John Snyder, ECA Director Paul Hoffman, and Lemnitzer.

As it happened, that morning Marshall had received a message from General of the Army MacArthur stating that B-26s were urgently needed as soon as possible by beleaguered United Nations forces in Korea. Only two squadrons of the aircraft were available at the time, so Marshall—after what Lemnitzer later described as "an agonizing appraisal"—decided to give one of the squadrons to MacArthur and the other to the French.[38] Lemnitzer thought it was a good solution. "I would have preferred that both of them had gone to Korea in our own self-interest," he reflected years later, but, ever the internationalist, he added: "But here was an important ally of ours that was in deep trouble in Vietnam and desperately needed help."[39]

It was during Lemnitzer's tenure that the United States began making its first substantial contributions to a struggle that twenty years later would claim over fifty-five thousand American lives and billions of dollars while plunging the nation into one of the most devastating domestic crises in its history. This was the war in Southeast Asia in which France was trying to regain control of its pre-world war colony, Indochina, against strong resistance from well-organized indigenous forces led by future American nemesis Ho Chi Minh. The United States had followed a hands-off policy toward the French campaign until 1949 when China became communist. The "domino theory"—which held that communism was contagious and that if one critically situated nation fell its neighbors would fall as well—gathered credibility, and suddenly Southeast Asia became strategically very important to U.S. policy makers. During the same period, France's military position began to deteriorate rapidly despite its massive infusion of troops and materiel into the struggle. The United States rushed to help stem the tide, and by May 1950, shipments of aid to Indochina were given the highest priority in the assistance program.[40] Lemnitzer and others involved in running the aid plan were opposed to the new order of precedence because "we were anxious to build up the strength in Europe and we hated to see the large amounts of money that we were fighting so desperately to get into the program going to Indochina."[41] Too, the MDAP director was suspicious about how effectively the French were using the millions of dollars in equipment being sent to them.

Because the French had resisted the assignment of a MAAG to Indochina (ostensibly on the grounds that there was already one in Paris), Lemnitzer had no way of knowing what was happening to U.S. equipment. So he obtained the loan of a Marine Corps lieutenant general, Graves Erskine, and dispatched him to Indochina to see how the aid was being used and how the war was going. His visit touched off what Lemnitzer remembered as a "frightful argument" in Washington. Erskine sent back a message to Lemnitzer in which he declared that it was going to be impossible for the French to hold on and control the situation in Indochina if they insisted on fighting from their *"Beau Geste* towers." The expression infuriated the French and dismayed the U.S. State Department, both of which sought unsuccessfully to have Erskine reprimanded and relieved.[42]

Lemnitzer agreed with Erskine, whom he called a "heck of a fine marine," and recalled that many other U.S. military officers felt the same way. "The French controlled the countryside and the people during daylight and then went back into their *Beau Geste* towers at night. The people who were building roads in the daytime were blowing them up at night."[43] It was a lesson that Americans would learn the hard way when it became their turn to fight the same enemy on the same ground.

Despite Lemnitzer's misgivings about how the aid was being used, the French argued that "we've been in this country a long time; we know how to fight this war and what we want is the aid without supervision." The general recalled years later, "And that, unfortunately, was the policy that was adopted and agreed to."[44] France suffered a disastrous defeat at Dien Bien Phu on May 7, 1954, and two months later its war ended when it signed a peace agreement dividing Vietnam at the seventeenth parallel. Afterward, hundreds of millions of dollars worth of MDAP equipment still lay piled in open fields, all of it still packed in its shipping crates. Frank Higgins, assistant secretary of the Army for logistics, later went to Indochina to make a survey of what had not been used and sadly dubbed the towering mass "the acre of diamonds" after the huge commercial jewel displays in Bangkok, Thailand.[45]

MDAP efforts to build up its allies in Europe suffered another blow on June 25, 1950, when powerful communist forces from North Korea invaded South Korea. Neither South Korea nor the United States were prepared for the onslaught. South Korea had five lightly equipped combat divisions designed to provide internal and border security, some light artillery pieces, but no tanks or other modern equipment other than what U.S. forces had left them after World War II. The American units the United States was able to mobilize when Truman committed the nation to South Korea's defense were—for the most part—green, understrength, and poorly equipped.

One of the first things Lemnitzer did was to sit down and write a memorandum to Johnson urging that he submit an immediate request to Congress for a supplemental MDAP appropriation of four billion dollars to provide aid to South Korea. "I don't know what got into me to do this," he recalled years later, "but I felt that we were going to have to rearm the Republic of Korea . . . and that anything less than four billion dollars would not be enough."[46] The general was out of line, and he knew it; major generals at his level did not make those kind of recommendations to the secretary of defense. He said later: "I thought this was going to bring down the roof. I expected an explosion when the secretary found out that I had the nerve to put it up to him and to suggest that he carry the ball on a program that he was not particularly enthusiastic about."[47] But the only result was what Lemnitzer described wryly as a "thunderous silence." Johnson never mentioned the memo, then or later, or even that he had received it. The only information about it that he could obtain from repeated queries to Renfrow was that the secretary had "put it in his pocket." As it happened, four billion dollars was the amount that the president eventually asked for and got from Congress to beef up the grossly overmatched South Koreans and the rest of the aid program.

As an appalled America read the news accounts of North Korea's first swift thrusts into the south (Lemnitzer likened the advances of the Soviet-supplied T-34 tanks to "hot knives running through butter"), congressmen were asking the Pentagon's director of military assistance what the United States was sending in the way of weapons and equipment. No MDAP program had yet been approved for Korea, or any other nation, at the time of the attack; further, Korea had not been high on the list of priorities because it had not been considered vital to U.S. strategic interests in the Far East.

The administration and Congress were moving as quickly as they could to provide the needed funds for a buildup in Korea, and other machinery was in motion to bolster its defenses. But in the meantime, Lemnitzer had to answer some hard questions. They grew particularly pointed in his morning situation briefings to Congress as his maps showed communist forces pushing the defenders back at an alarming rate. It made no difference that South Korea's five divisions were not even combat units—the lawmakers persisted in asking: couldn't we find *something* over there to give them? Weary of facing the frustrated congressmen every morning with no progress to report, Lemnitzer's staff put out some frantic messages to MacArthur's headquarters asking if there was anything that could be released from the command's military stocks. The headquarters replied that the Koreans needed communications wire, so the services combed their depots in Korea and found two hundred and twenty miles of field wire. Special authorization to transfer it was needed from the U.S. secretary of defense, and this was quickly done. Soon afterward, the House committee told Lemnitzer that it wanted a complete list of every piece of military equipment that had been sent to Korea by the next morning. He went back to his office hoping he could find something substantial to report but the only thing was the communications wire. So he told the committee about that, and rued it for the rest of his days on the assistance program and beyond. It was leaked to the press, and he became the instant target of such needling as "In the face of the Korean War, the great military aid program and the director of that program have provided the Koreans with two hundred and twenty miles of field wire. That certainly ought to stop the communists." As he recalled, "I was snarled up on that goddam field wire for about two years."[48]

Johnson got much of the public blame for the deplorable state of U.S. forces in the early days of Korea, although it should be pointed out that Truman was giving the orders to tighten defense budgets and Congress had been going along with him. The secretary had been assuring everyone that the services were in great shape while he was cutting strength to what most military leaders regarded as suicidal levels. Lemnitzer recalled that Johnson had been especially active at the time the North Koreans invaded in an effort to trim a shocking two billion dollars from a thirteen-billion-dollar defense budget. "On the twenty-fifth of June, five days before the end of the fiscal year, he did some horrible things," Lemnitzer recalled. "He was closing hospitals, closing stations, cutting back the forces, stretching out procurement programs and so forth. And he got his two billion dollars."[49]

When Johnson was fired in September and replaced by George Marshall, the abysmal state of U.S. readiness was a major reason. But he might have weathered the avalanche of criticism had it not been that he was simply a terrible man to get along with. Truman, Acheson, and Bradley—to mention a few—all expressed the view at one time or another that he had mental problems; Acheson suspected a brain tumor.[50] Johnson's personal vendetta against Acheson—which was highlighted by at least two angry tirades to the secretary of state's face in the presence of such persons as presidential confidant Harriman and Lemnitzer—was believed by many in upper government to have been an even more influential factor. There was little to cheer about in the ranks during the grim autumn of 1950, but the news of Johnson's sacking was probably at least the equivalent of driving the enemy back fifty miles. James H. Dill, an artillery officer aboard a ship bound for Korea, recalled that "cheers broke out all over the ship. Soldiers slapped each other on the back and clapped. . . . We hated Louis Johnson. We hated that man with the hatred of a blood feud. We damned him day and night. We damned anyone anywhere who would not damn him. He had cut the Army to the bone and then scraped the bone to the quick. . . . To us a simple proposition presented itself. We were apt to get killed—and had already had so many friends killed—because that man cut our strength so much."[51]

Lemnitzer deserved to experience how an MDAP director's life could be under a secretary of defense of General Marshall's professionalism, ability, and even temperament, but this was not to be. Within a month of Marshall's taking office, Lemnitzer was at Fort Benning in training to jump into combat from an airplane as the commander-designate of the 11th Airborne Division. It was an assignment that had been approved before Marshall succeeded Johnson. Although his new tour of duty would remove him from a cause to which he was devoted just when it was becoming a success, it is difficult to imagine him having felt anything but great happiness when he received his orders. Most military officers love troop duty—Lemnitzer had some of the most professionally satisfying days of his career when he commanded the 34th Antiaircraft Artillery Brigade—and he was long overdue for such an assignment. Doubtlessly, a command of some kind was something he had requested, and probably pushed hard to get during his bruising two years in Washington. But it is also likely that it was in the cards anyway because command of a division is almost a prerequisite for an officer slated for the Army's senior leadership. If it hadn't been for Johnson's intervention, he would have been given command of the 82nd Airborne Division the year before. The Army had selected him for the prestigious post; however, while conceding in a memorandum to the secretary of the Army that "I well understand your desire to round out his experience," Johnson wrote that "General Lemnitzer is thoroughly familiar with the [assistance] program, and to replace him at this time might unnecessarily delay carrying its provisions into effect." Johnson concluded his memo with the hope that "you will give him consideration for this or a similar assignment when we can let him go from his present duties."[52]

Lemnitzer's departure from Washington did not go unnoticed. In an editorial headlined "A Man of Vision," the *Detroit News* commented: "By one of those changes of assignment which are routine in the military profession, Maj. Gen. Lyman L. Lemnitzer has been relieved as director of the Defense Department's Office of Military Assistance and given duty at Fort Benning. That news conveys very little to the country. But it was Lemnitzer who had the courage and vision to see in the first place that an alliance with Western Europe was the main hope for American military policy and who played a main hand in winning the Pentagon to this conviction even before the Congress began to move toward the treaty and the aid program."[53]

Acheson, who was one of the hardest persons in the Cabinet to please, wrote a lengthy letter to Marshall in which he said that Lemnitzer's "imminent transfer to a troop command leaves us with a feeling of very great loss . . . he has made a tremendous contribution to the conduct of American military policy, demonstrating a remarkable breadth of approach and an ability to grasp, and look objectively at, the variety of complex and interrelating political, military and economic factors involved in the [assistance] program. These factors, together with the wealth of wisdom and experience which he has brought to bear on every problem, have contributed in large measure to the development of balanced and practical solutions to the many difficult questions of policy and administration which are inherent in this complicated operation. In his many dealings with the political and military leaders of foreign countries, General Lemnitzer has repeatedly demonstrated his ability as a diplomatist and has won their universal admiration and respect."[54]

Marshall added his own glowing letter of commendation to Lemnitzer's personnel file and, congratulating him on a "job well-done," the secretary of defense wrote this in sending him a copy of the secretary of state's letter: "I do not have to tell you that you have my personal good wishes and those of the entire Department of Defense in your new assignment. I have a sneaking suspicion that you will find your paratroop training at Fort Benning considerably less arduous than that you have been exposed to in recent years here in Washington. I envy you."[55]

Burns wrote him: "The difficulties involved in your work have been many and great and your burden has been heavy.... [Y]ou have performed [your tasks] with ability, vision, patience, enthusiasm, firmness, good nature and as a very loyal team player. Above all, you have achieved success.... [Y]ou are a real soldier-statesman."[56] Marx Leva, the Pentagon's chief counsel and its top legislative contact who worked closely with Lemnitzer on the assistance program, wrote to Army Secretary Frank Pace that "... I have never seen anyone perform a task of equal complexity with anything approaching the skill, sense of duty, drive and general competence which General Lemnitzer has displayed."[57] Even Johnson added his comments to the flood of laudatory letters in a memorandum to Pace just before he left office: "He has demonstrated outstanding ability, initiative, leadership and judgment of the highest caliber.... [T]he more I have watched his performance, the more respect I have for his ability. General Lemnitzer has done a magnificent job which reflects great credit upon the United States and the Department of Defense."[58]

The final assessment was a verbal one and it came in early 1953, a few days before Eisenhower was to take office as president. Lemnitzer, by then the Army's deputy chief of staff for plans and research, received a telephone call from Harriman asking him to come to the White House because President Truman wanted to see him. When he got there, he recalled that Truman "gave me one of the most cordial receptions I have ever received—commending me for my work in the drafting of the NATO treaty and getting the military aid program under way. He couldn't have been nicer."

Then the president took a paper off his desk, handed it to Lemnitzer, and said, "I thought you'd like to keep this for your files." It was the general's memorandum to Johnson urging the immediate addition of four billion dollars to the military assistance program following the invasion of South Korea. On the bottom was the notation: "Approved, HST."[59]

13

★ ★ ★ ★

KOREA

Officers in the Army's combat arms take off their branch insignia when they get their first star—and in 1950 Lemnitzer had been a general for eight years—but he must have felt a deep pang of sadness that year when the Army announced that the grand old lady of the nation's harbor defenses had ceased to exist as a military force. The demise of the Coast Artillery Corps and the incorporation of its antiaircraft functions into a new artillery branch came as no surprise—the wonder is that the execution had taken so long. Not since Corregidor and the valiant stand of the "Concrete Battleship" had a U.S. coastal gun been fired in anger, and when the end finally came the last of the Corps's big guns had been scrapped the year before.

Loyalty to the branch that came with the gold bars is a powerful relationship, ranking with service, comrades, and unit as qualities that bind an Army into an effective fighting force. No matter that the coastal protection aspect of his branch was well on its way to becoming a relic of a bygone era when he joined it upon graduation from West Point, Lemnitzer had been a proud wearer of its insignia for over twenty years—the span of an entire career for most professional soldiers. But the general, the most astute and objective of men in assessing how best to get a job done, must have known years before that the glory days of the disappearing guns and monster cannons and mortars were over. There were those who seriously thought until the end of World War II that coast artillery still had a major place in the nation's defenses, even as such major developments as aircraft carriers, long-range bombers, amphibious landings, and V-2 rockets were burying it deeper in obsolescence. By then, by intent or luck of the draw, Lemnitzer had gone on to excel in the aspect of the coast artillery's mission that was very much geared

179

to modern warfare: antiaircraft defense. He never lost his love for this vestige of his old branch, and when what was left was resurrected in 1968 as the air defense artillery branch it is very likely that he had something to do with it.

But this was 1950, a war was on, and Lemnitzer traded one branch for another when he left Washington for Fort Benning to become qualified as a parachutist. It was a skill he had wanted to acquire for many years and one for which, he quipped when he reported for jump school training, he was eminently qualified "because I'd been in the Pentagon for five years and I was used to jumping."[1] There was a deeper purpose to the training, however, than merely the thrill of floating in the sky and acquiring a parachutist's badge to wear. Lemnitzer was slated to take command of the 11th Airborne Division, and a prerequisite was to be jump qualified.

Airborne training was, and is, among the toughest in the services. During the month-long course, the fifty-one-year-old general got up at dawn every morning and ran five miles with a class made up of men less than half his age before going through a day devoted largely to testing the physical and mental limits of men who aspired to be paratroopers. So demanding were the requirements that the washout rate at the school averaged 35 percent. The only part of the daily routine the general was spared, speculated retired Col. Albert Garland, a Fort Benning area resident and former editor of *Infantry* magazine, was having to police up the grounds and pull KP duty.[2]

Lemnitzer climaxed his three weeks of rigorous training by making the required five jumps, one of them at night. It was an accomplishment of which he was immensely proud, and as the 11th Airborne's commander, he was a stickler for maintaining the skill's high standards; during his tenure, for example, he was under strong pressure for a time to waive the five-jump rule and allow a parachutist's badge to be awarded to a popular division chaplain who had become ill after two jumps and couldn't finish the requirements. The general refused, stating as his reason that "any relaxation of the requirements whatsoever" would cheapen the badge and "would be a serious blow to the prestige and morale of Airborne officers and men."[3]

Lemnitzer assumed command of the 11th Airborne on December 1, arriving at its headquarters at Fort Campbell, Kentucky, at about the same time as his classmates from Fort Benning who had been assigned to the 11th and could now boast that they had learned to jump with the "old man." The Lemnitzer family's year in the placid, friendly, and small-community atmosphere of an Army post seemed to have been a welcome respite from the years of war-forced separation and the frenetic pace of duty in the nation's capital. Lemnitzer had been a general officer since early World War II, but for the first time his wife Kay could enjoy the singularly pleasurable experience of being a military post's first lady. Son William was finishing up his last year at the U.S. Military Academy and would graduate a brilliant fifth in his class of four hundred seventy-five cadets. Daughter Lois helped manage the post's hobby shop, took up skydiving with Fort Campbell's parachute club, and, to the expressed displeasure of some members of the general's staff, spent much of her spare time with the club's enlisted members—in the eyes of rank traditionalists not a seemly association for the post's commanding general. But her father, she said years later, didn't mind a bit. It was a pleasant year for Lemnitzer, who undoubtedly felt considerably more at home in the Honesdale-sized surroundings of Fort Campbell than in the impersonal pressure cooker that was Washington. His letters to his family after he went to his next assignment sound like they were written by a talkative member of a small town's country club set—gossipy, concerned about the comings and goings of former colleagues and their families, and fretful about such details as how well his successor's family was going to take care of his old post dwelling.

The 11th Airborne was the possessor of an outstanding combat record in the Pacific in World War II, and there were plans in Washington to send it to Korea. While it waited for the call, the division trained under the watchful eyes of a commanding general who seemed to be everywhere and who appeared to like nothing better than to suit up with a unit and add another jump to his record. During the year, the division traveled to North Carolina to participate in training operation Southern Pine and one of its regiments, the 188th Airborne Infantry, went to Nevada to receive training in combat on an atomic battlefield. Lemnitzer continued to receive enthusiastic OERs at Fort Campbell. In his last OER as the 11th Airborne's commander, Maj. Gen. Clift Andrus, Second Army deputy commander, called him "top flight in every respect," describing him as "a fine-appearing, alert, vigorous officer. He is endowed with an unusual intelligence, possesses tremendous drive and evidences unusual qualities of leadership. He has a balanced mind and a sense of realism. He has a high sense of integrity and appears to be in fine physical condition. Should be given command of a division in combat earliest." The endorsing officer, Lt. Gen. Edward H. Brooks, Second Army commander, concurred and recommended that he be given either a division or a corps in combat.

Lemnitzer got his corps, the XVIII Airborne, and was its acting commander for a month. But neither the corps nor the 11th ever went to Korea as combat units, and in December 1951, Lemnitzer became the commanding general of the 7th Infantry Division. He had no doubts about the division becoming involved in a conflict he wanted very much to join: it was already there, a battle-hardened outfit of seasoned veterans who had been through some of the toughest fighting of the war. The fact that Lemnitzer was given command of such a unit was a tremendous vote of confidence on the part of the Army. His previous experience as a commander in combat had consisted solely of the World War II leadership of an antiaircraft brigade whose support mission was not at all akin to the command of an infantry division on line. Not the least of the obstacles he faced was winning the confidence of the experienced leaders and troops now under his command.

A former Washington staff officer with a coast artillery background and a scant year in command of a stateside airborne division had a lot to prove. That he turned out to be a superb, much admired 7th Division general was described by a former regimental commander as a "truly remarkable achievement."[4]

Activated in World War I, the 7th Infantry had one of the Army's most distinguished combat records, seeing action in France in 1918 and in heavy fighting during World War II from the Aleutians to Okinawa. It was assigned to occupation duty in Japan after the war and had come ashore in Korea with the 1st Marine Division in MacArthur's tide-turning landing at Inchon. It had fought as far south as Pusan and as far north as the Yalu River, on the Manchurian border, where it was the first UN unit to erect a U.S. flag on the river's banks. Its elements were among the first American units attacked when the armies of the People's Republic of China entered the war in force in November 1950. Trapped and surrounded by vastly larger forces of advancing Chinese in the Chosin Reservoir, the battered 7th Division units joined with the 1st Marine Division in fighting its way free in one of the classic retreats of U.S. military history. The division was put aboard ships at the seaport of Hungnam on North Korea's eastern coast and was taken by sea to regroup near Pusan where it joined the rest of the Eighth Army in fighting its way back north. Its frequent style of fighting in the bloody hill-by-hill, valley-by-valley offensive won the 7th the designation "Bayonet Division" because of its success in driving the enemy from well-fortified positions with bayonets, grenades, and hand-to-hand combat.

It has been said that no one hates war worse than professional soldiers because they are the first to have to put their lives on the line when it breaks out and the first to know such hardships as having to leave families behind for the battlefield. Lemnitzer's exceptional devotion to his family was well known to those with whom he served, but in none of his letters home or other available records of his feelings on the eves of his departures for war duty are there any expressions of regret. He was a professional, and a professional's job is war. But, duty aside, it helps if you believe in the cause for which you are fighting, and Lemnitzer endorsed very strongly Truman's rationale that if the free world's armed forces did not fight communist inroads in Korea they would have to fight them all over the world. The general had been one of the first in his profession to have been recruited into his country's campaign against communist aggression when he was called from his desk at the NWC to sit in at the birth of NATO. He got into the struggle during his enthusiastic management of the military aid program. Now he had the opportunity to face directly a foe whose creed he truly hated and would oppose by word and deed for the rest of his life.

If Lemnitzer had any negative thoughts about the conflict, they were about what he called the "disgraceful state" of U.S. preparedness, a typical American between-wars condition that became a recurring theme in his speeches and congressional testimony over the years. The Eighth Army had taken the field when the war began with regiments consisting of only two battalions and with battalions made up of just two companies. "It was a bobtail Army, an occupation Army," he recalled. "It wasn't a combat Army at all. Equipment-wise, it was just horribly badly off."[5] Of the armed services, the Army was in the worst shape to deal with an emergency of the magnitude posed by the invasion of South Korea. It had ten divisions and separate regiments, all understrength except for the one division then in Europe. All four of the divisions on occupation duty in Japan when the war broke out were below their authorized peacetime strengths of 12,500, a level which itself was just 66 percent of wartime strength. After the massive drawdowns of post–World War II, the Army had emphasized a minimum reduction of combat units and a maximum cutback in "fat"—in other words the support units that are essential for sustained combat. To raise its vulnerability even further, equipment modernization had suffered badly in Army budgets in which funds went largely to pay, allowances, and maintenance. The bulk of troops deployed overseas were young, inexperienced, and, for the most part, soft from relatively undemanding occupation duty.[6]

The situation had changed considerably by the time Lemnitzer took command of the 7th Division. In the year and a half the United States had been in the war, Washington had dipped deeply into its general reserve for men and equipment, the dormant Selective Service System had been revived, National Guard and Reserve forces had been activated, and Congress had voted a heavy increase in defense spending. When Lemnitzer arrived in "The Land of the Morning Calm," replenished and now battle-experienced UN forces had driven the Chinese and North Koreans back above the thirty-eighth parallel, the prewar demarcation line between the Koreas. The 7th Division was deployed in the center of the line with the X Corps in a mountainous region containing such heavily fought-over areas as the Punchbowl and the Mundung-ni and State-ri valleys. The division occupied positions along Heartbreak Ridge, so-called because of the many times it had been captured, lost, and recaptured during the war.

Lemnitzer succeeded Maj. Gen. Claude B. Ferenbaugh, a West Point classmate who had returned to the academy as a commissioned cadet after having been graduated prematurely during the officer shortage of World War I. The division's outstanding fighting reputation was due largely to his leadership, and now he had just been assigned to the truce talks at Panmunjom. Truce negotiations had begun the previous July, but had ceased in late August when the communists broke off the talks. General James A. Van Fleet, commander of UN forces, then launched a limited offensive to straighten and improve his lines. The 7th Division came out of reserve to drive the enemy from well dug-in positions on five hills in some of the bitterest fighting of the war. By mid-October, the Chinese and North Koreans had been defeated and they again asked that truce talks be reopened.

When Lemnitzer reached his new command on December 5, the division had come through a month of heavy patrol activity and bunker construction as the front lines on both sides settled in to await developments in the peace talks. The negotiators then agreed to keeping front line activity strictly defensive in nature, and for Lemnitzer's first month in command his division's ground patrols were forbidden to pass north of a line five hundred meters in front of its forward edge. Enemy forces were under similar restraints. The agreement apparently did not pertain to artillery fire, however, for Lemnitzer's diary reports various instances of shots being fired by both sides during the "break."

In his first letter home, written on the day he assumed command, he claimed "some kind of record for speed" in reaching the front. He left Fort Campbell on November 28 and, traveling on four different aircraft, reached his division on December 4. He explained the haste: "In view of the fact that I was the key element in an elaborate shift of generals in this area, it was important that I come through as quickly as possible."[7] Another likely reason is that the general didn't want to waste any time in getting into action.

The division got the worst of one of Korea's infamous winters, with heavy snow and sleet; high, bitterly cold winds; and temperatures ranging to twenty-five degrees below zero. The highest position in the 7th's sector was over a mile above sea level, "so there is perpetual snow and frost," he wrote home. "Right now in the valleys, we are in that difficult period of freezing nights and thaws during the day. This is the damnedest country—when it goes above freezing the mud is terrible. When it stays frozen the dust is equally bad."[8] The division's troops lived largely in wooden bunkers that they had built into the hillsides and heated with kerosene and charcoal stoves. As in Italy, Lemnitzer lived and worked in a van— a hut on wheels, so difficult to heat, he said, that it was "almost impossible to keep water in liquid form"—even the ink with which he wrote would freeze. He expressed admiration for a resourceful member of his staff who faced the problem of being unable to put his partial dentures in a glass of water when he retired for the night because they would be frozen in solid in the morning. He solved his dilemma by acquiring a small refrigerator, leaving it open during the day when the temperatures got above freezing and putting his teeth and water glass inside while he slept at night.

As the general had learned from Alexander in Italy, a major part of a field commander's job is visiting his troops. A sharp-eyed leader finds out a great deal during these visits, from the state of readiness and morale to how effective a particular officer will be when his unit closes with the enemy. The signs can be no more blatant than a poorly presented briefing or the way a noncom or a private responds to a question. If they don't measure up, an experienced observer starts looking for more fundamental flaws, and invariably finds them. Such inspections work both ways. Lemnitzer had learned his battlefield demeanor from a master who believed that it was vital for morale and unit *esprit* that troops see their general up where they were fighting. And, also like Alexander, Lemnitzer knew that a touch of theater went a long way. For the first time, one of his OERs praised him for "showmanship," a tribute, perhaps, to his practice of venturing calmly, and seemingly in utter disdain of the shooting going on around him, into the most exposed forward positions with no more outer protection than a parka and a regulation fur cap. He always carried an automatic pistol in a shoulder holster outside his parka for an added bit of dash, and no enemy soldier with a pair of field glasses could ever have mistaken the significance of the two silver stars fastened to his cap. Officers are not always encouraged to display their rank in forward areas because of the danger of snipers but, like Alexander with his ever present red hatband, Lemnitzer wanted his men to know who he was. Less than two weeks into his command, the stars apparently attracted the attention of a Chinese sniper who took a shot at him as he was standing near the command post of the 17th Infantry Regiment's third battalion. The bullet missed him, struck a tent, and knocked a mess kit from the hands of one of his drivers. A week later he wrote in his diary of visiting a forward tank position on an exposed ridge and making a study of the Mundang-ni Valley through a spotting scope. "Drew considerable incoming 76 mm fire," he noted laconically.

The division's rugged surroundings and the fierce weather often made a simple visit the most arduous of his duties; he noted in a letter to his wife that it could take as much as two hours of climbing steep trails up ridges and mountains to reach one of his outposts: "It certainly is a workout to inspect a front line position and I find that I can do no more than one battalion a day. The long climbs, especially with the snowdrifts getting deeper with each storm, take a lot of time—not to mention the time to walk to the front line positions, many of which are located in the most inaccessible places."[9] He frequently expressed frustration at how little those at home, and even fellow officers who had never been to Korea, knew about the conditions under which U.S. soldiers lived and fought. He mentioned receiving a Christmas card from a friend that "made me mad as hell." His correspondent wanted to know what he thought of the "Coca Cola Army" and wrote that the Army had "spoiled" its soldiers. "I am going to write him a few facts of life regarding the conditions under which we are fighting in this area and how it is not a Coca Cola Army and how the men are not spoiled."[10]

The division's complement of 16,500 troops included Ethiopian and Colombian battalions in addition to some 8,000 Korean volunteer soldiers who were integrated into division units as KATUSAs (Korean Augmentation to the U.S. Army). Lemnitzer was particularly impressed with the Ethiopians, all members of Emperor Haile Selassie's personal honor guard whom he described as among the best troops in the theater. (In all, sixteen nations sent troops to help South Korea.) But his respect did not extend to driving. Noting that his area's icy roads were causing a record number of accidents, he observed that the worst offenders were the Ethiopians "...who had never seen snow before, so you can imagine how their driving on snow and ice goes."[11] The general also admired the fighting qualities of his KATUSAs, so much so that he requested through official channels that they be made eligible to receive the U.S. Army's Combat Infantryman Badge, awarded to enlisted troops who have seen action. Turned down, he ordered the creation of a special division combat badge for his Korean troops.

As the lull in the fighting continued, the division prepared to celebrate Christmas. In a letter to his family, he marveled at the resourcefulness of his troops in creating a holiday atmosphere under the guns of the enemy: "The men have done wonderful things with the pine trees and Xmas trimming sent from home. I was up at a position less than 50 yards from the enemy trenches the other day and the men had a nice tree, well-trimmed in their bunker. They had about 10 Xmas packages stacked near it waiting for Xmas day to open them."[12]

Francis Cardinal Spellman, Roman Catholic archbishop of New York, flew in by helicopter on Christmas Day to say a mass near the headquarters of the 31st Infantry Regiment, located, the general wrote, "in the highest and most rugged part of Korea." Over three thousand troops attended the mass, he told his daughter. "They came down from the front and all units of the division. The cardinal delivered a fine sermon—one of the best I have ever heard. It began to snow as the mass opened and it was a real Xmas picture. Nearby artillery kept firing during the ceremony and that, with the snow and the towering mountains, really made a wonderful setting."[13] Afterward, the cardinal's helicopter could not take off because of the heavy snow, and he, General Van Fleet, and Lemnitzer rode the twelve miles back to 7th Division headquarters in open jeeps. When one would get stuck on the steep grades, the occupants would climb into another, doing this several times until they reached the division headquarters. The prelate and Van Fleet then continued their journey by sedan, intending to visit other units, but were stopped by snow for the night at a hospital ten miles away. Two days later, eleven enemy artillery rounds landed on the spot at which the cardinal had conducted his Christmas mass. "They wounded three men," he wrote to his wife, "but if it had happened during the mass it would have been a shambles."[14]

New Year's Day was "quiet," he wrote, "except that at exactly midnight every gun along the [UN] front fired a round to let the enemy know that the war was not over and if they want it to be they'll have to be more cooperative and agreeable at the talks at Panmunjom. As a matter of fact we are going to become more aggressive so as to give them a greater sense of urgency. So far they have done a remarkable job of stalling."[15] He reported a month later of having read in Army General Orders that his son, now a second lieutenant of antiaircraft artillery, was being assigned to duty in West Germany. He wrote to his son, "Maybe if we get a Lemnitzer in Europe, as well as Asia, we might be able to get this world situation under control."[16]

Exasperated with the communists' stalling tactics at the truce table, UN forces resumed aggressive patrolling in January with the objective of maintaining contact with the enemy while fixing the location of his defenses and monitoring his movements. In ordering his patrols to be more attack oriented, Lemnitzer touched upon a problem which was bedeviling commanders all along the front lines: as the war wore on, experienced officers and enlisted men were constantly being rotated back to the United States and their places taken by men with no combat experience. The general observed in his diary: "Present inactivity along front and loss of combat experience through rotation is making everyone too defensive-minded." In one five-week period he reported rotating over five thousand men back to the United States—"a great loss of combat experience, which hurts"—and integrating an equal number of replacements.[17]

The day after Lemnitzer's order to be more aggressive, a combat patrol from the 31st Regiment penetrated deeply into enemy lines and drew over a hundred rounds of artillery and mortar fire while, the general noted in his diary, killing and wounding "substantial" numbers of the enemy. The same day, another patrol ran into heavy opposition, suffering twelve wounded while killing seven and wounding ten of the enemy. And so it continued through the early winter with continual probing of enemy defenses and frequent firefights as the opposing forces made contact. The enemy to the front was made up largely of Chinese units that responded to the 7th's forays into their lines with a succession of company and battalion-sized attacks, all of which appeared to have been easily beaten back. One of these occurred on February 13, and the general wrote to his wife: "I have had several very busy nights as a result of a special operation we are conducting. Last night, 450 Chinese hit my front at 3:05 AM in a snowstorm and when it was over 225 of them were killed or wounded—many of them in our wire and mine fields. The activity since indicates they might try it again tonight with even a larger force but we'll be ready for them. In last night's fight, we did not lose a single man."[18]

Discovery of any kind of enemy activity would often bring the general himself to the scene. He would watch while Chinese troops attacked his positions, and he would often personally order artillery responses to enemy activity. Once after ten to fifteen of the enemy were spotted trying to erect a command post, he ordered the position to be destroyed by artillery fire. The delivery of the fire was poorly executed, and the shells missed. "Sorry exhibition," Lemnitzer noted in his diary and returned the next day to observe another attempt. This time the rounds apparently landed where they were supposed to because he made no further comment. His diary entry for February 16 noted that it was snowy and reported: "To Hill 605 to observe effects of CLAM UP [a division operation involving a surprise artillery attack]. New and much better camouflage. Took several pictures of Mundung-ni valley. Artillery and mortar fire received from the enemy."

An X Corps headquarters account of the general's actions that day were less matter-of-fact. He was awarded the Silver Star, and the citation that went with it stated: "Major General Lyman L. Lemnitzer, O12687, 7th Infantry Division, United States Army, distinguished himself by gallantry in action near Mundung-ni,

North Korea, on 16 February 1952. General Lemnitzer, who as division commander exposed himself daily in the front lines, went on this day to an exposed forward observation post to observe and direct an intense surprise attack by fire following a lull of several days intended to make the enemy careless. The enemy in retaliation opened a very heavy concentration of mortar and artillery fire on General Lemnitzer's observation post and adjacent positions, obviously making General Lemnitzer's position a particular target. With characteristic disregard for his own safety, General Lemnitzer remained in his exposed position to observe the effectiveness of the firing and ensure coordination of the infantry and artillery elements. His calm, unruffled bearing at the spot where danger was greatest aroused the enthusiastic admiration of his men and enhanced the aggressive tradition of this fine division. After completing his planned activities in this area, General Lemnitzer moved to other front-line positions, intent always on gaining first-hand information concerning the enemy situation and capabilities. The gallantry displayed by General Lemnitzer reflects great credit upon himself and is in keeping with the highest traditions of the military service."

Four days after the exchange of fire at Mundung-ni, Lemnitzer's division was taken out of the front line and ordered into reserve in the Kapyong area. The town, located in the central part of the Korean peninsula, had been the scene of heavy fighting the year before, but now it was far enough away from the action to provide the division with some badly needed rest. So serene were parts of it that the general wrote in his diary after a reconnaissance trip by jeep into Kapyong's "very rough and primitive" back areas that "the people there had probably never seen a white man before." Another trip turned up a "very beautiful valley—the war did not hit it at all."

The general's letters home did not always make it clear that his division had gone into reserve. On March 6 he wrote to Kay: "We know well that the news of Korea is off the front page—it almost seems as if only those of us in Korea know that there is a war on over here. In addition to our fighting, we are carrying on an intensive training program in this division to get our many new men ready for the heavy fighting that may break out this spring. I don't know what the Reds are going to do, but it is quite possible that they may try it again when the weather gets better and the ground thaws and dries out." Another time he wrote: "The truce talks continue to drag out badly. Most of the officers and men have given up hope of anything happening in that field."

While the division rested, refitted, and trained, its commander indulged himself with a new hobby: photography. He announced in a letter to his daughter that "I have finally gone into the photographic business," explaining that it was brought about by "a combination of factors"—the many interesting things in Korea to photograph and the fact that he was "able to get a whale of a bargain" through the division's post exchange on a new thirty-five-millimeter Zeiss Contessa. Not a man to spend money on frivolous things, he seemed to be trying to justify his purchase by pointing out in his letter that because he could obtain the camera at less than half its U.S. retail purchase price, he had little choice but to buy it. He was seldom seen without a camera, during his tour in Korea and in later assignments. His pictures of battle areas and Korea's towns and countryside fill boxes and albums at the family home in Pennsylvania. The hobby carried over into his years in Washington, where he could write at one time to a friend that he had photographed just about every important site in the nation's capital. "I ought to have a fairly complete photographic record of my Korean service when I am finished up over here," he wrote to Lois. "If I had only had this camera during World War II I could really have gotten some fine pictures. I also could have used it to fine advantage at Campbell."[19]

Much of his correspondence home while he was in Korea dealt with details of keeping the house in Washington in good shape. His wife and daughter had to make the move from Fort Campbell by themselves, usurping the family to whom the Lemnitzers had rented the house when they were living in Kentucky. No matter was too trivial; in one letter he might fret about some drains he had installed or the merits of putting in an attic fan, in another the location of flower beds or the proper place to put wall insulation. He cautioned Kay to keep track of everything she spent on the house "because that is an important income tax deduction which I can make when I figure up my tax for this year." He made all the house and car payments from his command post in Korea.[20] The status of the family car was frequently a topic of concern, the general inquiring often about the state of its repair and giving detailed instructions on keeping it running. He got nervous when Lois wrote of her plans to drive to Fort Campbell, urging her to have the oil changed regularly and pointing out that it "has to last us for quite a while—it hasn't been paid for and won't be for some time."[21] But the prospect didn't keep him from starting to think about a successor, for the next month he wrote his daughter that "I have seen the new Olds in the ads and it looks fine. They really have stepped up the power."

The general seemed hardly less occupied when his division was in reserve than when it was on the line. It was time to award medals, attack the piles of paperwork that had accumulated while his troops were engaging the enemy, and to inspect. On one day, he noted in his diary, he inspected every tent, every mess hall, and every single one of the more than five thousand men in the Ethiopian battalion and the 32nd Infantry Regiment. "Finished up at dark," he wrote. "Regt in fine shape."

In Korea, as in the United States, the big news in the spring of 1952 was the campaign for the Republican nomination to president, eventually won by his old boss, Dwight D. Eisenhower. Lemnitzer wrote to his wife: "Everyone out here follows the primary results closely. I would say that the sentiments of the troops are far and away in favor of Gen. Eisenhower. From the latest returns, especially from Pa., N.Y. and Mass. it looks as if he will be able to go to the convention in

Chicago with at least as many, if not more, votes than [Senator Robert] Taft, which should help in forestalling the professional politicians controlling the nomination."[22]

In late April, the division was back on the line again, this time in the IX Corps sector to the west of its old location in the Chorwon-Humwha area known as the "Iron Triangle." With the move came spring, and Lemnitzer wrote his wife that "it is a great relief to see winter fade out of the picture. The mountains, which I have only seen covered with snow, are now a blaze of pink azaleas, which look wonderful."[23]

For several weeks, Lemnitzer had been wearing two hats: one of a division commander and the other as deputy commander of the Eighth Army. In the latter capacity, he was Van Fleet's representative at a series of financial and economic meetings between the U.S. and Republic of Korea governments in Pusan. The assignment necessitated frequent travel, mostly by air, between his headquarters in the field and Pusan, Seoul, and Tokyo. During one of these trips, when bad weather kept him from flying, he got an early look at the trappings that go with life in the upper military echelons. He wrote to Lois: "Last Saturday the weather really closed in and I had to come down by train. It was an overnight trip and was not too bad considering the poundings these railroads have taken since the Korean War began. As Deputy Army Commander, I had a private car for myself and my aide, which wasn't too hard to take."[24]

He had frequent contact with Van Fleet during this period. At one of these times, he sat next to the UN commander at a ceremony in the 7th Division sector marking the creation of a new Korean army corps. South Korean President Syngman Rhee and U.S. Ambassador John J. Muccio were there as bands played and troops from both nations put on elaborate marching displays in honor of what was regarded as a truly significant milestone in making the Republic of Korea (ROK) Army self-sufficient. Lemnitzer described the ceremony to his daughter and added: "The thing that impressed me [most] was that I sat next to Gen. Van Fleet and I was with him all the time. He did not give the slightest information or clue that just before he left his headquarters in Seoul, General Everest of the Fifth Air Force had informed him that his flier son was missing in a B-26 strike in North Korea the night before." It was learned later that Air Force Captain James A. Van Fleet, Jr., a West Pointer like his father, was killed when his plane was shot down.

Visits by superiors in uniform were frequent during the Bayonet Division's days on the line and in reserve, but rarely did anyone else make it to the craggy sectors where Lemnitzer's unit kept its vigil. There had been the cardinal, of course, and two USO troupes—one starring actress Betty Hutton and the other actor Paul Douglas and his actress wife, Jan Sterling. Another visitor was U.S. Congressman Olin E. Teague, Texas Democrat, whom Lemnitzer spent a great deal of time showing around the division area. Somehow the general learned later—possibly from his wife who may have read about it—that Rep. Teague had said on his return to the United States that what the forces in Korea needed was more cocktail spreads. Probably the remark was meant to be facetious, but it irritated Lemnitzer, who wrote Kay: "If Congressman Teague could only suggest we needed some cocktail spreads, he missed the boat and was dumb. Out here we need those like a hole in the head."[25]

A much happier memory was left toward the end of his tour by his old World War II commander, retired Field Marshal Alexander, who had recently been installed as Great Britain's minister of defense and was in Korea on an inspection tour (his nation had sent a division to fight in the war, the largest UN contingent next to those of South Korea and the United States). When he visited Lemnitzer's division, its commander noted with satisfaction that Alexander was wearing a uniform from his Italian days that had been made from material that the U.S. general had found for him. "It was like Italy and World War II all over again with Gen. Clark and Alex here," he wrote Kay.[26] He was referring to Gen. Mark Clark, who in May 1952 succeeded Gen. Matthew B. Ridgway as commander of the Far East Command. By all accounts, the reunion of the three veterans of the Italian campaign was convivial, with a great deal of reminiscing about things that had happened and men they had known as their armies drove north in some of the hardest-fought and bloodiest fighting of the war. But Alexander could well have had reason to recall Anzio afterward because once again he and Clark, his old Fifth Army commander, had a communications problem.

When the British defense minister stopped in Washington on the way back to London, he was told by JCS Chairman Bradley that the UN had just bombed the huge communist hydroelectric works at Suiho on the Yalu River. It was the heaviest raid of the war, and it had been ordered by Clark to give teeth to the UN's negotiating position at the Panmunjom truce talks. The British government regarded the raid as needlessly provocative while peace talks were in progress and wanted to know why it wasn't consulted, particularly when its defense minister had been in Korea on the eve of the raid. Clark stated that he had not been authorized to tell Alexander of the bombing plans, but the defense minister drew criticism in England that he did not have the confidence of his old subordinate of the Italian campaign.

Alexander made the situation worse for himself by saying while still in Washington that he was in favor of the bombing, thus prompting a demand from the opposition in Parliament for his resignation. The water got even hotter a little later when the defense minister, speaking at a Dominion Day dinner of the Canada Club in London, stated that his visit had convinced him that there were "weaknesses in Korea"; pressed for an explanation, he replied that "I would be very much happier if General Van Fleet had a little more reserve in his own hand." This raised a public outcry when the press picked it up because it was taken as a breach of military security, not to mention bad form. Prime Minister

Churchill called Alexander at three o'clock in the morning for an explanation, and the former field marshal told him he had thought he was speaking in private. Churchill spent some uncomfortable hours in the House of Commons defending his defense minister before the matter died down.[27]

In May Lemnitzer received word that he was going back to Washington as deputy chief of staff for plans and research. It would mean another star, and Lemnitzer was anxious that the word not get out before the Pentagon reported it. In breaking the news to Lois, he wrote: "You cannot say a word about it to anyone until it is officially released. That is very important because it could easily get off the rails if anyone talked about it." There was another hitch, as well: he could not take up his new duties until he was relieved by a new 7th Division commander. Although the general knew in early May that he was slated for the new job, he was not relieved until early July by Maj. Gen. Wayne C. Smith. "They have been expecting an attack in this (the 7th Division's) sector for the last few months," he wrote to Kay and Lois, "and I suspect that Corps and Army are not anxious to have a change in command any sooner than absolutely necessary."

Although both sides were continuing to carry on their strange defensive struggle while the truce talks dragged on, the general wrote to his wife and daughter in mid-June that "Our front is really getting hot these days—the artillery fire and fighting increase each day. It could be that the Chinese are going to launch another offensive. If they do they'll get the shock of their lives because they'll take heavier losses than ever before, and that's a lot. We are certainly ready for them." The Korean rainy season began early in 1952—it normally starts in July—and with it Lemnitzer's division conducted a series of what he described in a letter as "surprise attacks" that "have cleaned out quite a few of their positions facing us." The Chinese did not attack in force before Lemnitzer left Korea, but the division's defensive posture ended three months later when it drove the enemy out of the Triangle Hill complex north of Kumwha in Operation Showdown. The 7th later saw action in heavy combat on such epic battlefields as Porkchop Hill and Old Baldy before the fighting finally ceased in July 1953.

Five years later, when he was wearing the four stars of a full general, Lemnitzer sent a message to the division congratulating it on just having completed ten years of service in Korea. In it he stated: "One of the greatest honors that has come to me in my entire military career has been the privilege of serving as commanding general of the 7th Division in the fighting which occurred in Korea in late 1951 and 1952 during which period the division added new laurels to its already brilliant record at Heartbreak Ridge, the Punchbowl, Mundung-ni Valley, Chorwon and Kumhwa." It must have been a frustrating period. No American field commander—especially one who had learned his way around a battlefield from a field marshal whose credo was "attack, attack, attack"—could have been happy with the static kind of warfare the 7th was forced to wage most of the time under his command. How he must have longed to have been there when his old division went on the offensive three months after he departed!

Lemnitzer's imaginative use of his limited offensive tools and leadership impressed the commanders of the two corps in which his division had served during his tenure. Maj. Gen. Williston B. Palmer, X Corps commander and one of the hardest men in the Army to please, wrote in his OER: "One of the ablest major generals in the US Army. Physically youthful-looking and well-groomed, very active, vigorous, and courageous; mentally alert, imaginative and thorough, with a good sense of showmanship. Very cooperative; a team player, not a prima donna. I would be happy to serve under his command." Lt. Gen. Willard G. Wyman, commander of the IX Corps, made this judgment: "An officer whose superior qualities are so well-known that further descriptive comments are really redundant. His service for the period in IX Corps only verifies previous reports and adds to his stature as a field commander. In all respects, he is outstanding." It must have gratified Lemnitzer to know that, although he had carried out important staff duties as Van Fleet's deputy, the qualities most mentioned in assessments of the months he served in Korea during the war had to do with his ability to command troops and to lead a division in action.

Rhee personally awarded him South Korea's Order of Military Merit Taiguk, noting that "despite extremely rugged and unfavorable terrain and adverse weather conditions, General Lemnitzer, through his rare diplomacy, superior knowledge of military tactics and superlative leadership, has been instrumental in molding the troops comprising his command into a formidable fighting force." Equally satisfying to a general whose reputation before he went to Korea was built on his brilliance as a staff officer had to have been some of the phrases included in the citation that went with the award of his second Distinguished Service Medal.

Praising him for his "mastery of military science and superior leadership," the citation noted that "despite severe cold, treacherous terrain, seemingly insurmountable logistical problems and drastic losses of key personnel, General Lemnitzer, through his adroit application of combat tactics, executed and directed aggressive defensive maneuvers which inflicted maximum casualties and material damage to a determined enemy. Later when the division was in a reserve status, he integrated numerous replacements into the command and initiated a vigorous training program, maintaining constant combat readiness, confidence and a high state of *esprit de corps*. General Lemnitzer's professional acuity, brilliant exploitation of the capabilities of his command and superior performance of duty materially furthered the United Nations campaign against aggression in Korea."

On July 8 the general left Tokyo for home. Four days later in Washington, his diary notes, he watched television as General Eisenhower became the Republican candidate for president on the party convention's first ballot. The entry the next day in a diary that a short time before had been chronicling the comings and goings of the commander of a division in the line read: "Cleaned gutters."

14

★ ★ ★ ★

BASTARD AT THE REUNION

Lemnitzer's future with the new administration's civilian defense officials did not look at all promising on that spring day in 1953 when Secretary of Defense Charles E. Wilson asked him his views on a proposal to end the war in Korea. As the general remembered it, "I was the bastard at the family reunion on that occasion, believe me."

Lemnitzer, the Army's recently confirmed deputy chief of staff for plans and research, had been invited at the last minute by Army Secretary Robert T. B. Stevens to sit in on a briefing by a civilian committee that had been convened by Wilson to find a solution to the impasse in Asia. Halting the war, then still in a stalemate while the two sides argued at Panmunjom, had become something of a crusade to the newly elected President Eisenhower, who had promised an end during his election campaign. Before he took office, he had fulfilled a pledge to visit the Korean battlefields, and the committee that met in Wilson's office was one of several groups named by the administration to advise it on how to terminate hostilities.

As Lemnitzer recalled the briefing, the chairman of the eight-member committee of industrialists and business leaders replied to Wilson's requests for its recommendations in these words: "Pretty simple, pretty simple—use the atomic bomb." Lemnitzer winced, and Stevens apparently noticed the pained expression on his face because he told Wilson that the general had commanded a division in Korea the year before and had seemed "surprised" at the committee's recommendation. Lemnitzer, now a lieutenant general, remembered that he had not wanted to speak but the secretary of defense asked him to comment. He replied that he didn't agree with the recommendation and asked the committee chairman what targets he proposed to bomb. The chairman answered: "Hell, general, that's not our problem; that's for you military people to work out."

The general addressed his response to Wilson: there were, in his opinion, only two suitable targets for an atomic bomb in Korea—Pusan and Inchon, both of which were controlled by UN forces. There were no large concentrations of materiel in North Korean territory, no functioning railroads or operational airfields. Troops were dug into hillsides, bunkers, and trenches, mostly in mountainous terrain in which an atomic explosion would not be effective. His assessment was received without comment, although he remembered that there was a noticeable chill in the room when he sat down. Eisenhower was informed of the committee's recommendation but, as was seen, did not accede to it.[1]

Despite Lemnitzer's disdain for its suggested course of action, the committee's thinking fit in very well with that which prevailed in national defense circles during the Eisenhower years. The use of the bomb on the battlefield and against civilian targets was not only thinkable but assumed. It was a concept that was to cause the Army a great deal of trouble in the years ahead. Serious consideration to using atomic weapons had been given before, notably when UN forces were bottled up at Pusan. Later, there was talk about employing them to rescue the besieged French at Dien Bien Phu and in the late 1950s to defend the offshore Taiwanese islands of Quemoy and Matsu against Communist China. There were no suitable weapons or sufficiently accurate delivery systems in the first two instances; any blast would have also destroyed friendly forces. In the third, it was decided that atomic weapons were unnecessary.[2] "In those days," Lemnitzer recalled, "there was a tendency in this country to think that the nuclear weapon was a panacea for all military ills. And it definitely proved not to be."[3]

The possibility of using atomic weapons gathered impetus in early 1953 when the United States test-detonated its first tactical nuclear device of a size that could be fired by artillery. Soon after, the JCS urged their employment as a means of ending the war and in May went even further by recommending direct air and naval action, including the use of nuclear weapons, against China and Manchuria. Secretary of State Dulles added his support to using the bomb unless China and North Korea agreed to a truce. Eisenhower also seriously considered it, although, like Lemnitzer, he had reservations about the limited number of tactical targets. Whether or not the new president would have risked probable severe international censure for using nuclear bombs in a stalemate situation will never be known. However, enemy awareness that U.S. leaders were thinking about it has been credited with speeding up the pace of the peace talks at Panmunjom.[4]

The presidential and congressional election campaigns of 1952 had begun and Congress was in recess in August when Lemnitzer was appointed deputy chief of staff. The Senate did not get around to confirming the appointment until the following March, when he was approved without fuss and his date of rank as lieutenant general officially made retroactive to the previous August 1. He was one of three deputy chiefs, all lieutenant generals, who served under the chief and vice chief of staff and just above the general staff (G-1, personnel; G-2, intelligence; G-3, operations and training; and G-4, logistics).[5] When Lemnitzer's predecessor, new Army Vice Chief of Staff Gen. Charles L. Bolte, had held the position it had been designated deputy chief of staff for plans. At Lemnitzer's request, "research" was added because he felt there was a close kinship between the two areas and because of a keen interest in research and development that he probably owed to his days as a coast artillery officer.

It was a good combination if a soldier wanted to be in the thick of things in the 1950s, for this was the era of the "New Look," the Eisenhower administration's formula for dealing with the Soviet threat. Its core was "massive retaliation" with nuclear weapons, a posture that minimized the importance of ground troops in war despite the development of tactical warheads. Indeed, the Army's very survival as a major component of the defense team sometimes seemed to have been at stake in the often bitter internecine struggle that ensued before the New Look ran its course. Planning and research were at the heart of the Army's campaign to stay on the playing field.

Assessing the contributions of a staff officer, especially in an area like planning, is difficult because final decisions are made by commanders and chiefs of staff. How much or what the staffer at even the highest levels can be credited with originating often is hard to identify after everything has been put together and a course of action decided. The staff member's value usually lies in how well he or she helped a superior to accomplish a mission. An OER is one way of evaluating this; another is in a personal letter, such as one written to Lemnitzer by Gen. J. Lawton Collins, Army chief of staff, when Collins left office:

> Dear Lem:
>
> I could not end my tour as Chief of Staff of the Army without making my appreciation of your invaluable assistance as a matter of formal record. I consider myself most fortunate indeed to have had the benefit of the counsel of an officer in whom are combined your keenness of intellect and your outstanding qualities as a soldier. In addition, the knowledge that I could always rely upon your splendid cooperation and staunch support has been a source of constant assurance to me.
>
> Faced as the Army was with the necessity of "fighting a war in peacetime" [Korea] and developing a posture of readiness for a possible general war, your function as Deputy Chief of Staff for Plans and Research has been one of the utmost importance. The splendid manner in which you have correlated our strategic plans with our research efforts has always been such that you are justified in feeling the greatest satisfaction. Your insight and your objective understanding have not only contributed significantly to the great success which has been achieved but have done more than I can say to ease my own task.[6]

Collins, who earned the nickname "Lightning Joe" as a fast-moving corps commander in World War II, left office and retired a year after Lemnitzer joined his staff and less than a month after the fighting in Korea ended. He was succeeded by Gen. Matthew B. Ridgway whose 82nd Airborne Division had been saved from probable destruction by Lemnitzer's timely delivery of an abort order in Sicily during World War II. Both chiefs of staff had been on the faculties when Lemnitzer was a student, Collins at the Army War College and Ridgway when he was a cadet at the Military Academy.

The first six months of Lemnitzer's tour was a wait-and-see period. Heavy combat flared up in Korea during the fall, but the stalemate continued. A war-weary country elected a president who as a candidate had said that bringing the troops home would receive a high priority in his administration. The Army wrestled with the problems of keeping fielded a million-and-a-half-member force in which draftees served only two-year terms and in which frequent rotation in and out of the war zone continued to be a major headache for combat commanders.

One of Eisenhower's first major undertakings in the field of defense after he assumed office in 1953 was to reduce Truman's budget request for the approaching fiscal year by nearly ten billion dollars, more than half of it in national security programs. One of his next steps was to launch a sweeping study into the nation's options in foreign and security policy. It was called "Solarium," and Lemnitzer was one of some two-dozen persons picked personally by the president to make up the study's three task forces. These teams each consisted of about eight members, all selected because their backgrounds in government or the civilian sector made them exceptionally well qualified to contribute to the study. The project was supervised by the National Security Council, and it addressed three options: containment, roll back, and drawing a line. Each task force was assigned one of these options and was expected to make the best case it could for its adoption when it delivered its final report. In containment, essentially the nation's policy since the late 1940s, the United States would protect vital areas of economic and military power, such as Western Europe and Japan, from Soviet expansionism. Roll back called for pushing back Soviet influence and causing disruption and division through covert operations and propaganda. Drawing a line meant telling the Soviets that any attempt to expand communist control would be met by nuclear attack.

Drawing on the full resources of the government for its information, the committee worked in strict secrecy through the summer of 1953 in the main building of Washington's National War College, which was not in session at the time. When the group was finished, the teams presented their positions in the White House library before an audience made up of the president and his top men from the State and Defense departments and the CIA. Lemnitzer's task force was headed by Soviet State Department specialist George F. Kennan who argued for containment. Rear Adm. Richard L. Connolly, president of the Naval

War College, directed the roll back study, and retired Air Force Maj. Gen. James McCormack headed up the task force on drawing a line.

The three-hour report touched off an extended debate among the president and his national security advisers. In the end, Eisenhower laid down a policy based essentially on containment but which carried a threat of retaliation if the challenge merited it. The Solarium presentation set the stage for an Eisenhower *tour de force* which Kennan later remarked admiringly "showed his intellectual ascendancy over every man in the room."[7] Speaking for nearly an hour without notes, the president summarized and evaluated the complex reports, cutting to the heart of each argument and subjecting each task force to searching questioning about its conclusions. Eisenhower's masterful analysis was as remarkable for its strong signal of who was going to be boss as it was a display of his grasp of intricate foreign policy and security principals. No president before or since was better qualified by background and ability to run—and, as importantly, understand— the huge Defense Department. It was an example worth considering as having been a factor when Lemnitzer went through the worst ordeal of his professional life under another president in the Bay of Pigs debacle eight years later.

There was considerable expectancy in Army ranks that with one of their own now installed as commander in chief, the service could expect to receive warm treatment in the defense budget and in such areas as roles and missions. These hopes were dashed when the administration followed up the Solarium study and the end of the Korean War with the unveiling of the New Look in the late summer of 1953. Predicated as it was on the early use of massive nuclear retaliation in the event of a Soviet attack, the New Look meant that the bulk of defense resources would go to the service charged with carrying out an atomic strike against the Soviet Union, namely the Air Force. In the eighteen months following adoption of the new policy, the Army lost a half-million soldiers and saw its share of the shrinking defense budget fall from 33 percent to 25 percent. The Air Force's allotment rose from 39 percent to 47 percent. A substantial portion of the cutbacks was the result of the windup of the war, but it was clear that the new order of things in the budget was due to Eisenhower's reshaping of national security policy.[8]

There was no lack of reminders to compound the Army's misery. Exultant champions of the Air Force asserted that airpower could handle just about every-thing in a war and Treasury Secretary George M. Humphrey, one of Eisenhower's closest advisers, said of massive retaliation toward the end of the administration: "That and that alone, I am sure, kept peace in the world. And all the rest of these soldiers and sailors and submariners and everything else, comparatively speaking, you could drop in the ocean and it wouldn't make too much difference."[9] The New Look would not be fully implemented until 1957, when Lemnitzer returned to Washington from the Far East to become the Army's vice chief of staff. Fitting the Army into this nuclear age posture would occupy most of his waking hours when he came back, but for this tour he was a subchief whose job it was to help keep the Army running. Years later, he would say that he had been very much in accord with those who were outraged by the Army's diminishing share of the defense load. However, a deputy chief of staff was in no position to actively oppose a commander in chief's policy. For the Army, that fell principally to his boss for most of his present tour, General Ridgway. A persistent but low-key opponent of what the New Look was doing to the Army, Ridgway was out of presidential favor when he retired after a single two-year term as chief of staff.

The Army had been busy with atomic weapons long before the Eisenhower administration took office. Three months after Lemnitzer became head of research and development, the Army showed off for the first time its new atomic cannon, a 280-millimeter monster capable of firing an atomic or conventional artillery round twenty-five miles. Another spectacular battlefield performer fielded at about the same time was the electronically controlled "Skysweeper," a 75-millimeter antiaircraft gun which could fire forty-five rounds of high explosive shells a minute at low- and medium-altitude aircraft. Spurred by the new administration's fixation with atomic weaponry, Lemnitzer pressed researchers and developers to come up with missiles and delivery systems. Improved mobility and increased, more effective, and longer-range firepower received high-level emphasis. A new M-48 tank, a 175-millimeter gun, a 106-millimeter recoilless rifle, and the rapid-fire antiaircraft Vulcan were in development or were fielded. Lemnitzer was also an enthusiastic supporter of an element which in the next decade would be as common a sight on the battlefield as a tank: the helicopter.

His tenure also saw the introduction or further development of a whole family of missiles, some with the capability of carrying nuclear warheads: the surface-to-air Nike; and the surface-to-surface Honest John, Little John, Corporal, Redstone, and Jupiter. A radical idea then but not so far-fetched today in an era in which manned space flights are commonplace, the Army borrowed a scenario from the future "Star Wars" initiative with sketches of a missile which would carry troops into battle. Whole units would have been loaded aboard a missile under the design, blasted off into a trajectory reaching one hundred thirty miles above the earth, and lowered to the ground up to five hundred miles away by means of a large parachute and reverse-thrust rockets.[10] The general took much of the press media heat during his term when the Army canceled a program to field an antitank missile known as the Dart. In development when he came to Washington, the Dart had already cost over one hundred million dollars and was still not operational. When the figure reached two hundred million dollars and the missile continued to fail to meet Army field requirements, it was abandoned in favor of a French wire-guided missile, the SS-10. Lemnitzer was the Army's man up front in the public hullabaloo that arose. To press accusations that the Army had wasted two hundred million dollars, the general could only say that the Dart was not working out, but "we learned a hell of a lot and got some valuable experience...."[11]

Lemnitzer was the only military member of an advisory committee appointed in the fall of 1953 by Secretary Stevens to come up with a plan to reorganize the Army. After three months of what the general recalled as "very strenuous duty," the five-member group submitted to Stevens and Eisenhower a plan which Lemnitzer reported "represents our unadulterated views of action required to give the Army an organization that will not have to be changed if we get into a large shooting war—something we had to do in 1917 and 1942."[12]

The committee's proposal called for sweeping organizational changes through-out the Army's upper echelons while restructuring the way various agencies and commands accomplished their missions. It strengthened the offices of Army secretary and the chief of staff, created two new assistant secretary positions, added a second vice chief of staff (for supply), established the Continental Army Command to head up the six continental Army commands and training, urged creation of a supply command, and redefined the responsibilities of hundreds of offices and positions. Lemnitzer predicted that "a great many people—particularly in DoD—will not like certain features of it,"[13] and he was right. This aspect was especially wearing on Lemnitzer because he was the only member of the committee remaining in Washington after it issued its report and thus the only one available to defend its recommendations. Despite considerable flak from many persons whose oxen stood to be gored, most of the group's proposals were adopted and the *Combat Forces Journal* declared editorially that its twenty thousand-word report was "a reasoned and responsible handbook for those who would work in the garden of military organization." It praised the committee as "the men with green thumbs."

The Army prizes soldiers who work well with civilians, especially influential ones, and Stevens was pleased when he received a letter from the committee chairman praising Lemnitzer's contribution. Paul L. Davies, president of the Food Machinery and Chemical Corporation, referred to him as "in many ways the most outstanding member of our group," a panel which consisted of three corporation chief executives and a major auto company vice president. Davies was particu-larly impressed with Lemnitzer's objectivity, a word which appeared often in his OERs and citations for superior career accomplishments. "I am sure that most of the committee members felt as I did . . . that General Lemnitzer would strongly be inclined to view the organization of the Army from the viewpoint of the pro-fessional soldier. I am happy to advise you that at no time during the course of our long deliberations was General Lemnitzer's viewpoint influenced by any personal considerations or by his deep loyalty to his fellow officers. His conclusions were always arrived at on the basis that what was best for the country was best for the Army, and I am sure in many cases his viewpoint was more detached and his thinking sounder than was mine on subjects where normally a civilian would have been expected to have the sounder judgment." Davies concluded: ". . . he has made four real and lasting friends who now feel very close to him and will continue to do so because of the warmth of his personality, his keen sense of humor and his very real desire to do more than his part in making the report of our committee something that in the years ahead hopefully might contribute to strengthening our country's defense program."[14]

The crystal ball that became a desk fixture was sent to him by a former member of his staff after the reorganization plan was announced. He responded by writing that "it was just what I needed. I keep it on my desk and when one of those hot questions are fired at me I look into it to the great amusement of the 'Indians.'" He went on to write that "we have been having a rugged time here in the Department of the Army, as you can imagine from the press and radio. I do not know why we seem to get into these situations but we certainly succeed. Between my defending the Organization Committee's report, the McCarthy issue and problems connected with the New Look by the JCS, I am really getting a workout."[15]

The "McCarthy issue" referred to congressional hearings then being held by Joseph R. McCarthy, a free-swinging Republican senator from Wisconsin who was prominent in the early and mid-1950s for his charges that the federal government was riddled with communists. The Army got involved when McCarthy publicly maligned one of its officers, Brig. Gen. Ralph W. Zwicker, after the senator accused the service of bungling the discharge of an Army dentist suspected of having been a communist. The controversy got uglier when Secretary Stevens took issue with McCarthy over his rough treatment of Zwicker. Later, in a counterattack believed to have had the backing of Eisenhower, the Army accused the senator and his counsel, Roy Cohn, of exerting pressure to get favored treatment for G. David Schine, an Army private and a Cohn associate on McCarthy's investigating committee.

Lemnitzer was not involved in the hearings, but he admired Stevens, and when his brother Ernest wrote him that he thought Stevens had backed down in his fight with McCarthy, the general stoutly defended the secretary. He noted that Stevens had prevented any further attacks on Zwicker by the senator and that Stevens "is not backing down one iota" in the Schine investigation. "All in all," he wrote his brother, "it seems to me that the secretary has done an outstanding job in battling McCarthy and has done something that no previous official in government has dared to do."[16] The general and the mild-mannered, gentlemanly Stevens became lifelong friends after the secretary left office, frequently exchanging letters about events in Washington over the years.

McCarthy fared badly in the widely publicized Army hearings which are regarded to have been the catalyst that started a disastrous decline in his credibility and eventual censure by the Senate. McCarthy was removed as chairman of the subcommittee on investigations and was succeeded by Sen. John McClellan. He and the majority counsel, Robert Kennedy, sought to persuade the U.S. attorney general's office to prosecute Zwicker for committing perjury on the witness stand but it refused to do so. Two weeks later, in 1957, Zwicker was promoted to major general and appointed assistant chief of staff for personnel in the headquarters of U.S. Army Forces Far East and Eighth U.S. Army. The event prompted a letter from his new boss, Commander in Chief Lemnitzer, who expressed regret at having missed him at a conference in Japan and wrote: "I wanted to extend personally my hearty congratulations to you for the way things went in Washington and on your promotion to major general. I believe the action by the Congress in this regard is the final repudiation of Senator McCarthy on the entire Army-McCarthy issue."[17] Less than three weeks later, McCarthy died at Bethesda Naval Hospital in suburban Washington of acute hepatitis.

Lemnitzer got the opportunity to renew his ties with the British military establishment when he was selected to deliver the Army's prestigious Kermit Roosevelt Lectures for 1953. Inaugurated after World War II by the widow of a son of President Theodore Roosevelt who had served in both the British and American armies, the lecture program is an annual exchange in which a British general is sent over to speak at leading U.S. military schools such as West Point and the Army War College. The American general goes to places like the Royal Military Academy at Sandhurst, the Royal Military College of Science at Shrivenham, and the Joint Services Defence College at Greenwich.

The New Look with its sapping of Army strength and its demoralizing effects on traditional directions persuaded Lemnitzer during his Washington tour that the service needed all of its resources to survive. He saw its salvation in the Association of the U.S. Army (AUSA), a nonprofit, Washington-based educational foundation with grass roots and high-level ties between the country's military and civilian sectors. He wrote a friend in 1955: "My experience as Deputy Chief of Staff for Plans and Research has further convinced me that in light of present conditions and those immediately ahead, the Army has got to close ranks and become a unit with a single, powerful voice if it is going to survive at all. To me, the fragmentation of the Army into branches, components and societies of various types makes no sense at all and is doing the Army harm. Many of our officers are far more interested in their branch or component than they are in the Army as a whole. In the ruthless competition in Washington with the other services we cannot maintain our position if these divisive elements are permitted to continue."

He added that "as you may detect, my foregoing comments are not totally unrelated to the drastic reduction now being made in the size of the Army. We are having some terrific problems here in adjusting our plans and programs to meet these drastic cuts. I hope we will be able to minimize the impact on the European area, but Army forces in other parts of the world are going to have to be drastically reduced."[18]

Lemnitzer had sought for several years to merge his own Antiaircraft Association with AUSA, which he saw as the spokesman for the U.S. Army, especially in the civilian sector. Five years before he succeeded, AUSA had been formed by a merger of the Infantry and Field Artillery associations. He was president of the antiaircraft group when it voted to approve the merger in 1955, and the same year he was elected president of AUSA. He had earlier become an AUSA vice president with the merger, and he was not long in making known his presence in the organization's upper levels with a letter to the publisher of its professional magazine, the *Combat Forces Journal*. It was a protest against a speech given in England by retired Field Marshal Montgomery, a commander for whom he had little use since serving on the staff of Montgomery's superior, Field Marshal Alexander, in World War II. Referring to the journal's reprinting of the speech, Lemnitzer wrote:

"For some reason or other, Field Marshal Montgomery has gone completely overboard on the Air Force aspects of future war. As almost an independent operator he is able to sound off on his concepts completely without restriction. Those of us on active duty cannot express our views as freely as [he] is able to do. Many of us who have studied the problem vigorously disagree with the view that small regular armies are needed in the future as is concluded by Field Marshal Montgomery. I consider that his speech in the main is definitely anti-Army and pro–Air Force. Therefore, I would not have recommended its reproduction in the Army *Combat Forces Journal*."[19]

Lemnitzer was compelled under the AUSA constitution to resign the same year he was elected president when his new assignment as commander in chief of the Far East Command prevented him from attending Executive Council meetings regularly. In his letter of resignation, Lemnitzer wrote that ". . . I take this step with considerable regret because of my keen interest in the Association and the objectives which I hope that it can in time accomplish."[20] In 1970, after he had retired, he was awarded the association's highest honor, the George Catlett Marshall Medal, "for selfless and outstanding service to the United States."

The pundits are not infallible, but the word had been out since the Korean War and probably further back that Lemnitzer was a future Army chief of staff. *The Washington Post*, for example, commented in a May 17, 1955, editorial that "General Lemnitzer has a reputation as one of the coming men of Army command." The general was not a "ticket puncher," a disparaging term conferred on inappropriately ambitious officers who seek just the right combination of assignments that will bring successive promotions; no such climber would seek some of the posts Lemnitzer had held. But he had distinguished himself so well in each—as director of the thorny military assistance program, for example—that whatever ticket punching was going on was being conducted by others. That he had lived up to expectations in the key deputy chief of staff slot was clear in his OERs during his tour.

General John E. Hull, vice chief of staff, wrote: "An officer of great vision with a fine analytical mind, especially well-qualified for high level planning and command responsibilities." General Collins, then chief of staff, concurred, with this addition: "General Lemnitzer has rounded out his acknowledged ability as an exceptionally able planner and staff officer with a fine performance as CG of an Infantry Division in action in Korea. Combined with his broad staff experience during WWII and subsequently, he is now fully qualified for top-flight command or staff responsibilities." Bolte, Hull's successor as vice chief, wrote: "General Lemnitzer... possesses all the qualities, capabilities and experience to perform in a superior degree any assignment appropriate for a four-star general. If he had not already been so nominated, I would heartily recommend it. I would gladly serve under his command in peace or war." Chief of Staff Ridgway, the endorsing officer, added: "Viewed from the aggregate of his personal character and professional qualifications, I know of no finer officer in our service, or of one of greater potential value to the nation."

Lemnitzer must have breathed more than one sigh of relief in May 1955, when he was awarded his fourth star and packed up to leave the fractious headwaters of the New Look to become commanding general of U.S. Army Forces, Far East, and Eighth Army. But he would be back, and the ride the next time would make the last one look like a cakewalk.

Left: The future general, circa 1903.
Above right: The family home during the disastrous floods of 1942.

William and Hannah Lemnitzer, Lyman's parents.

Cadet Lemnitzer on sentry duty at West Point.

A serious-faced young lieutenant on his first assignment as a company officer at Fort Adams, Rhode Island.

Kay and Lyman shortly after they were married.

A vacation trip to Honolulu with son, Bill, and daughter, Lois, in the early 1930s.

Lemnitzer's early career was spent in the coast artillery, and he served in the Philippines in the twenties and thirties. Here one of Corregidor's famous twelve-inch "disappearing" guns is fired.

Members of the "Panoe Club" after their secret submarine trip to North Africa to prepare for the 1942 invasion. *From left:* Col. A. L. Hamblen, Col. J. C. Holmes, newly promoted Lt. Gen. Mark W. Clark, Lemnitzer, and Capt. Jerauld Wright.

— U.S. Army Signal Corps

The British submarine *Seraph* just after it unloaded members of the secret mission into a Catalina flying boat in the Mediterranean Sea.

Lemnitzer sits aboard a PT boat as it moves ashore after the landing at Anzio. Gen. (soon to be field marshal) Harold Alexander sits on his right.

Lemnitzer *(right)* and Alexander check a map during the Allied drive to capture Cassino, Italy. British generals Richard McCreary, Alan F. Brooke, and John Hawksworth are on the left.

Alexander congratulates Lemnitzer after Gen. Joseph T. McNarney *(background)* awarded him the first of his six Distinguished Service Medals.

Lemnitzer and Alexander with Yugoslavians Marshal Josip Broz Tito *(second from right)* and Lt. Gen. Jovanorre *(far right)* during a dispute over Tito's incursion into territory assigne the Western Allies when the war ended.

Lemnitzer *(first row, second from left)* poses with the 34th Antiaircraft Brigade's softball team while he was commanding the brigade during the North African campaign.

Wearing his "OSS suit," Lemnitzer sits outside a house in Switzerland where he was in charge of secret negotiations that led to the surrender of more than a million German troops in Italy. Swiss army Capt. Max Waibel stands at the left; British Maj. Gen. Terence S. Airey is on the right.

King George VI of Great Britain makes Lemnitzer an Honorary Commander of the Most Excellent Order of the British Empire in a ceremony in Italy during the war.

Lemnitzer meets Winston Churchill at an airfield in Italy during a tour of Fifth Army positions by the British prime minister.

The former "Rocko" beside a float built by his high school graduating class for the 1945 parade in his honor.

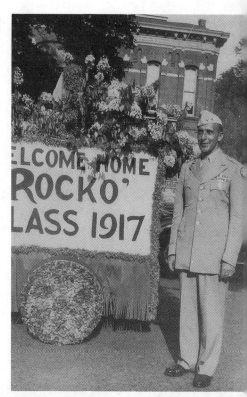

A final check of the general's parachute as he prepares for a jump while commanding the 11th Airborne Division in 1950 at Fort Campbell, Kentucky.

With President Harry S Truman during a presidential visit to the National Defense University in 1949, when Lemnitzer was deputy commandant. Vice Adm. Harry W. Hill, commandant, is at right.

At the front while in command of the 7th Infantry Division during the Korean War.

The Lemnitzer family at the
general's swearing-in as Army
chief of staff on July 1, 1959.
From left: Army Secretary
Wilber M. Brucker; sister-in-
law, Margaret; brother
Ernest; Kay; Lemnitzer; Bill
and his wife, Lydia; son-in-
law, Henry E. Simpson, Jr.;
and Lois

— U.S. Army Photographic Agency

The general inspects the South
Korean front lines in 1959 while
serving as Army chief of staff.

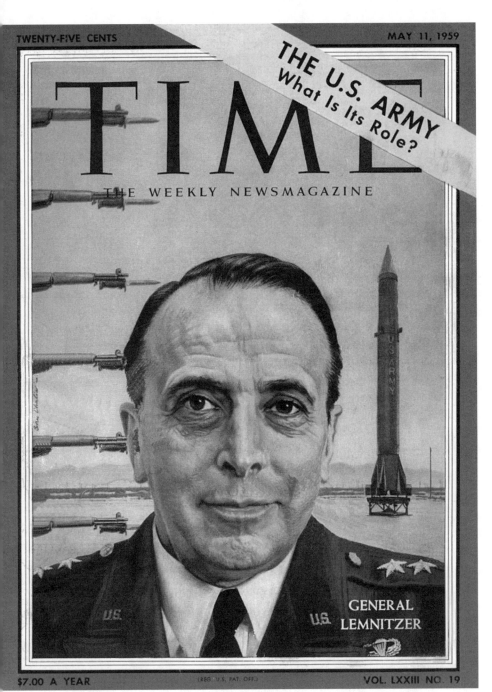

Time magazine cover, May 11, 1959.

Lemnitzer and Kay, with Robert S. and Margaret McNamara, chat with British Adm. Lord Louis Mountbatten at a NATO reception.

Lemnitzer and Gen. Maxwell Taylor shake hands at the White House after President Kennedy (*far left*) awarded Lemnitzer another Distinguished Service Medal following his term as chairman of the Joint Chiefs of Staff. Robert Kennedy is at right.

Wearing a different uniform, the general leads a formation of Shriners. Lemnitzer maintained close ties to his hometown throughout his career.

The Joint Chiefs of Staff meet with President Kennedy shortly after the Bay of Pigs fiasco. *Seated, from left:* Air Force Gen. Curtis E. LeMay; Lemnitzer; Kennedy; David Shoup, commandant of the Marine Corps. *Standing:* Gen. George Decker, Army chief of staff; Adm. Arleigh Burke, chief of naval operations.

The general talks with President Lyndon Johnson during a visit to Washington while he was supreme allied commander, Europe.

President Richard Nixon listens as the general addresses guests following a White House ceremony in which he was presented the Distinguished Service Medals of all three services.

Son Bill receives the stars of a brigadier general from his father and his wife, Lydia. Bill suffered a stroke a year later and was forced to retire, ending a career that many expected to be as distinguished as his father's.

Lemnitzer delivers the principal address at the dedication of the statue of a man he revered, the late General of the Army Dwight D. Eisenhower, on May 3, 1983, at the U.S. Military Academy at West Point, N.Y. *Others, left to right:* George F. Dixon, Jr., president of the Association of Graduates; Lt. Gen. Willard W. Scott, Jr., academy superintendent; and John S. D. Eisenhower, the general's son.

President Ronald Reagan congratulates the retired general in 1987 after conferring upon him the Medal of Freedom, the highest award the U.S. Government can give to a civilian.

15

* * * *

THE RINGMASTER

The general had a temper, although few outside of his immediate staff ever saw him lose it. If he had been easy to anger, it is highly unlikely that any president in his right mind would have sent him to the Far East to hold the world's most militant communists in check and ride herd on Syngman Rhee.

The wily South Korean president, whose machinations had kept blood pressures in the UN high command at unhealthy levels since the shooting war had ended two years before, wasted no time in testing the mettle of the new commander in chief of the Far East and United Nations commands. A month after Lemnitzer assumed command, Rhee issued an ultimatum: throw the inspection teams monitoring the truce out of the Republic of Korea by midnight of August 13 "or else." The teams belonged to the Neutral Nations Supervisory Commission (NNSC), which was set up after the armistice to ensure that both sides complied with its terms. The UN named Sweden and Switzerland as its choices; the Communists selected Poland and Czechoslovakia, both members of the Communist bloc and by no stretch of the imagination neutral.

Rhee regarded the Polish and Czechoslovakian inspectors as spies for the communists, and Lemnitzer agreed with him. The JCS and then the UN command had protested the inclusion of the two nations on the NNSC, but when the UN representative at Panmunjom told his communist counterparts that they were unacceptable, they replied that unless they were accepted there would be no armistice. The result was another stalemate in the talks, but by this time ending the war had become a major issue in the 1952 U.S. presidential election campaigns. "It wasn't long thereafter," Lemnitzer said, "that we in the military were directed to accept the communist terms. And since the military only recommends and the political authorities decide, this was a political decision that we had no alternative but to carry out. We sent word back to our representatives at Panmunjom that we would accept the communist nominations."[1]

Soon after the NNSC began its work, principally at ports of entry in North and South Korea, Rhee began compiling evidence that the communist representatives were sending out information on military matters in violation of the truce agreement. Unsuccessful in his efforts to change the makeup of the commission, Rhee organized large citizen protests at ports of entry in the south in an effort to force rejection of the communist element in the NNSC. Lemnitzer went to the scene of five of the largest demonstrations as his command brought up additional troops to control the crowds. At Pusan, where there were over twenty-five thousand demonstrators, he recalled years later that he saw "Russian tommy guns" in the crowd. "I feel certain to this day that if a shot had been fired we would have had a shambles there."[2]

It is not clear what the South Korean president meant by "or else," but if he thought the region's affable new military commander could be pushed around he was mistaken: "I don't like the neutral nation inspection teams in South Korea any more than President Rhee and the ROK do," he wrote to his brother Ernest, "but the government certainly overstepped itself when it gave me an ultimatum in the form of a statement that the teams had to be out of there by midnight of the 13th. I immediately reinforced all of the security forces that are spread all over Korea and was able to keep the situation under control, but with considerable difficulty. President Rhee and I had some stormy sessions, but I had to let him know that he could not issue orders to the UN Command to do something by a certain time."[3]

Understandably, a government can get uneasy when one of its generals has to get tough with the head of a foreign state, especially a friendly one, and the most nervous of all is apt to be the department responsible for foreign relations. But Secretary of State Dulles was highly complimentary regarding the way Lemnitzer had met his first major challenge in the volatile Far East. Three days after Rhee's deadline and with Lemnitzer strongly in charge, Dulles wrote to Secretary of Defense Wilson: "Now that the crisis in Korea is, we hope, somewhat abated, I want to express the appreciation which I and my associates in the Department of State feel for the conduct in this period of General Lemnitzer and those under him. I have been in constant touch with this situation and have followed closely General Lemnitzer's cables, and I believe he has exercised very fine judgment. Also, the troops under him have acted with a combination of firmness and strength under very trying conditions." Wilber M. Brucker, secretary of the Army, added in a letter to Lemnitzer: "Secretary Wilson and I wish to express our sincere appreciation for the superior performance rendered by you and the men under your command in the very difficult situation occasioned by the demonstrations in Korea against the Neutral Nations Supervisory Commission. I wish also to express my great admiration for the splendid example which you and your subordinates are showing in the exercise of a most difficult responsibility."[4]

A bigger headache than the espionage factor for those charged with making the truce work was an inspection procedure which made it possible for the Communists to carry on flagrant violations of the agreement's curbs on increasing military strength. The UN command, acting on a recommendation by the U.S. JCS, had insisted when the truce's ground rules were being worked out that inspections would be carried out promptly after each side requested them, the object being to make them cheat-proof. The Communists refused, contending that inspections could be conducted only upon unanimous agreement of the four NNSC members. Considering the commission's makeup, unanimity was impossible if China and North Korea didn't want an inspection. When the UN command opposed this provision during the truce talks, the communists replied that then there would be no truce. Once again, Washington stepped in and ordered the negotiators to agree to the Communists' terms.

Lemnitzer was still serving in Washington when the UN command was compelled to give in to the Communists' demand, but he remembered being "appalled" when he learned of it. "There was a great willingness to do almost anything to stop the war, almost anything," he recalled.[5] Lemnitzer said the requirement for unanimity rendered the truce agreement "useless" because it allowed the Communists to either conceal violations completely or delay an inspection until the transgression could be covered up. One such instance that occurred during Lemnitzer's tour in command involved an airfield in North Korea. The UN command had photographs of every airfield in enemy territory, taken by reconnaissance planes on the morning of the day the armistice went into effect in 1953. Two years later, Lemnitzer was shown clear evidence that several wings of military jet aircraft were sitting on one of the airfields. The general demanded an immediate inspection because the presence of the planes was a serious truce violation. The Swiss and the Swedes argued vigorously for an immediate visit to the site. The Poles and Czechs replied that they had reliable "sources" in the vicinity who said there were no aircraft there. The argument lasted for three days, and finally the naysayers said: "Well, if you insist." But when a team was dispatched to the airfield, the planes, of course, were no longer there, having had plenty of time for a leisurely getaway, probably back across the Yalu River into China.[6]

Along with a continuing stream of violations that dated back to when the truce was signed, the south was the frequent target of North Korean infiltration teams that slipped across or tunneled under the demilitarized zone (DMZ) between the two countries to spy, assassinate, demoralize, exert political pressure on local governments, and undercut the economy. Lemnitzer was visiting the DMZ when a UN patrol captured a typical team; as he watched, his troops took custody of one hundred thousand dollars in large U.S. bills, twenty-five pounds of heroin and opium (intended for use as bribes), and what he called "some of the finest communications equipment that I am sure existed anywhere." The Communists would also infiltrate using fast motorboats along the coasts. Firefights between opposing patrols were frequent as the South sought to halt the troublesome penetrations.[7]

Lemnitzer arrived in Japan in March 1955, where he became the commanding general of U.S. Army Forces, the Far East, and the Eighth Army. Three months later, he was named commander in chief of the Far East Command and the United Nations Command, succeeding Maxwell Taylor, who was leaving to become the Army chief of staff. Lemnitzer's main missions in his new job were to maintain the defensive strength of UN forces in Korea and direct the buildup of ROK military forces and the Self-Defense Forces of Japan. If only it could have been that simple: Lemnitzer once likened his job to a "three-ring circus," the rings consisting of Japan, Korea, and the Ryukyu Islands, the latter of which he was appointed governor by President Eisenhower shortly after taking command in the Far East. In a letter to his brother following the near-riots over the truce commission activities, he wrote:

"I have just returned from a long trip to Korea. I seem to be spending most of my time over there recently. There are so many military and economic problems, both of which are in my area of responsibility, that it takes an unusual amount of time to keep things moving properly. Many other problems are backing up in Okinawa [the main island in the Ryukyus] and here in Japan. . . . I spend a great deal of my time commuting between the three areas."[8] He also once told Taylor that the job was akin to "having to paint a train while it was in motion."

Despite Lemnitzer's problems with the restless Rhee, the two enjoyed a warm friendship that lasted long after the general had gone on to other commands. Ralph Chambers, a retired chief warrant officer who used to be Lemnitzer's principal administrative assistant, thought they got along so well because "they understood each other." Moreover, he added, Lemnitzer "knew the Eastern mind,"[9] which might have further explained why the general was able to stay on good terms with a manipulative despot whose path as head of the South Korean government was littered with the bones of U.S. military and civilian officials who had gotten in his way. Still another factor might have been, as he wrote in a personal letter to the general at the end of Lemnitzer's tour, that "we realize that your love for Korea is very deep-seated."[10]

Rhee had been working for Korean independence since before Lemnitzer was born. He hated the Japanese, who ruled his country when he was a young man and who imprisoned him for his activities the year the general came into the world. The holder of a doctorate from Princeton, he had spent much of his life in the United States as president of a provisional government in exile. When World War II ended, he returned to Korea and after being elected president in 1948 assumed dictatorial powers, which included ruthlessly pushing aside or removing any person or political party that opposed him. Among Lemnitzer's papers is a report, stamped "secret," in which a U.S. officer who saw the president frequently (possibly during a liaison assignment) described him as a "dynamic man, warm and friendly, and extremely self-centered and egotistic. He commands the respect of all Korean officials and all appear to be much afraid of him." The report said Rhee's frequent threats to send South Korea's armies north to renew the war were a means of causing concern among U.S. leaders and creating a desire to placate him by acceding to his various demands [Rhee's government, unhappy with the terms of the armistice that ended the war, in the end had not opposed it but had refused to sign it]. Rhee regarded the UN as "worthless" and, according to the report, "he tolerates the U.S. because of his appreciation of the fact that Korea couldn't exist without U.S. aid, but he actively dislikes the present administration, freely and frequently calling Eisenhower and Dulles 'fools,' 'cowards,' etc."[11]

Fortunately, Rhee liked Lemnitzer and military men in general. One of the tokens of his high regard was his gift to the general and his family of a Korean Toy Shepherd puppy, an offspring of the president's favorite pet dog. Dubbed "Mr. Brady" by its new owners,[12] the friendly little animal lived for fifteen years, and after it died Lemnitzer wrote to an Army enlisted man from his hometown, that "we were terribly distressed" because "he was a member of our family in all respects."[13]

Lemnitzer had to step in again in late 1955 when South Korea established a "Peace Line" (but more popularly known as the "Rhee Line") to keep Japanese fishing boats out of Korean coastal waters. The line paralleled the shore much further out than the U.S.-recognized international limit of three miles, but Rhee argued that the longer limit was necessary to prevent the Japanese from ruining Korean fishing resources. His joint chiefs of staff backed up his claim by issuing a warning that South Korea's navy would fire on any fishing boat that crossed the Rhee Line, including those that might be under the protection of the Japanese navy. When Lemnitzer learned of the warning, he wrote a letter to Sohn Won II, the South Korean minister of defense, in which he cited a past UN directive to the ROK navy that its patrol function "does not include interference with or seizure of peaceful fishing vessels operating in international waters." The letter went on: "It is not my intention to project myself into the unfortunate fisheries controversy between the Republic of Korea and Japan. However, you must realize that I cannot overlook the announced intention of Republic of Korea military leaders to take actions which are contrary to existing United Nations Command instructions. Accordingly, I request that you inform General Hengkun Lee [chairman of the ROK JCS] and the Chiefs of the Armed Forces that I cannot permit Republic of Korea armed forces under my command, which are equipped and are being supported by the United States, to be employed against an ally of the United States for the enforcement of the Republic of Korea's unilateral claim over international waters, which the United States does not recognize."[14]

The South Korean navy did not carry out its threat, but two months later Rhee proved, as he had before, that he was not averse to performing an "end-around" to get his way. When Adm. Arthur W. Radford, chairman of the U.S. JCS, paid a visit to Korea in early 1956, Rhee raised the issue again and Radford politely told him that in the eyes of the JCS, Lemnitzer's decision stood. The Korean leader went outside of channels once more two months later in a letter to Adm. Felix B. Stump, commander in chief of the U.S. Pacific Command, in which he complained about violations by Japanese fishermen of the Rhee Line while bitterly denouncing Japan for, he said, failing to make proper restitution for crimes allegedly committed against Korea during the occupation in World War II.[15] There was nothing Stump could do, even if he had wanted to, except send a copy of Rhee's letter without comment to Lemnitzer, who was not under Stump's command and was equal to him in rank.

The eighty-year-old president also sought Radford and Lemnitzer's support in compelling North Korea to vacate the Kaesong-Ongjin Peninsula-Han River estuary area north of Seoul. Situated just south of the Thirty-Eighth Parallel in the demilitarized zone (DMZ) between the two Koreas, the area contained the city of Kaesong, which North Korea had shelled so heavily on the eve of the war that its occupants deserted it. When the two sides were discussing opening truce talks, Kaesong was picked as the site. The Communists promptly brought in substantial forces and turned the city into an armed camp, whereupon the UN command asked that the talks be moved to Panmunjom. As a result, the estuary area went to the Communists by default, posing a military threat to the capital city of Seoul, a few miles away, and depriving the south of an important center of ginseng production. Once again, Lemnitzer had to say no, asserting that the Communists would pay little or no attention to such a demand. The UN was committed to respect the DMZ's military demarcation line, the point of contact between opposing forces when hostilities ceased. As for the defense of Seoul, the general pointed out that with two U.S. infantry divisions and an ROK marine division deployed in the sector, the region was the most heavily defended part of the DMZ. And again, that is where the matter rested.[16]

As exasperating as Rhee could be at times, Lemnitzer respected men who let nothing stop them in their pursuit of what he regarded as worthy goals, as he would prove again years later when his protagonist was the equally single-minded Charles de Gaulle. He regarded Rhee as "tough and uncompromising," but felt that "it takes that kind of individual to run Korea."[17] Lemnitzer was Army chief of staff in 1960 when Rhee was forced to resign after charges of vote fraud in the 1960 elections ignited violent and widespread civilian demonstrations. He wrote to his daughter and her husband: "We, too, were very much distressed about recent events in Korea. I think they made a serious mistake in forcing President Rhee out of office and I am concerned lest the government fall apart without his strong leadership. I have sent him a long letter of encouragement, knowing that he certainly needs it these days."[18] Rhee died in exile in Honolulu, Hawaii, in 1965.

The general took very seriously his responsibilities as governor of the Ryukyus, a strategically important archipelago of some sixty islands lying south of Japan between the western Pacific Ocean and the East China Sea. Its main island, Okinawa, had been the site of one of the bloodiest battles of World War II, and after the war ended it became the location of several major U.S. military bases. Japan and China had vied for dominance over the Ryukyus for centuries, and in 1879 the Japanese dethroned the local ruler and turned Okinawa, then called Luchu, into a Japanese prefecture while claiming title to the rest of the islands in the group. The United States assumed control with the conquest of Japan, governing them as part of the military occupation of Japan. When the United States and Japan signed a peace treaty in 1951, the United States insisted on a provision keeping Okinawa as a military base because of its importance to U.S. strategic interests in the Far East. Military occupation of the Ryukyus had given way to a U.S. civil administration the year before the treaty was signed, but overall charge was placed in the hands of the commander in chief of the U.S. Far East Command.

Nothing in Lemnitzer's background—with the possible exception of the days when he was waging a multifronted battle against friend and foe to get the foreign military aid program off the ground—had prepared him for the tussle that was going on over Okinawa. At the core of the problem was mounting Japanese government pressure for return of the islands. There was substantial similar sentiment among the residents of Okinawa, one of the Far East's most thickly populated regions, with nearly two million people living in a 458-square-mile area. Stoking this feeling was the desire to get back all or some of the precious land being used by the U.S. military for bases, airfields, and supply areas.

Further complicating this problem was a running dispute between the U.S. Defense and State departments over the administration of the islands and their reversion to Japanese control. There were strong feelings in U.S. diplomatic circles that the islands should be returned to Japan without further delay, but that while they were in U.S. control they should be under the jurisdiction of a civilian governor rather than a military one. The issues had stirred up considerable controversy in and out of the government back in the United States, a factor Lemnitzer felt had encouraged reversionists and opponents of military control to the point that his stewardship was being undermined. It was a situation that was to last until shortly before he relinquished his command when President Eisenhower issued an executive order designating the Army as the executive agency with all powers of administration, legislation, and jurisdiction over the islands. Laid down as the United States was preparing to dissolve the Far East Command, the order more clearly defined U.S. responsibilities in the Ryukyus than a presidential directive of August 2, 1954, which it replaced. The Department of Defense had pressed strongly to keep executive powers, and

Lemnitzer's performance as governor was credited as having been an important factor in the president's decision to leave them with Defense. Army Chief of Staff Taylor wrote to Lemnitzer after the order was issued: "I was happy to note the reference by both secretaries [Dulles, State; and Brucker, Army] to their high opinion of the past conduct of the civil administration of the Ryukyus. Your efforts in this regard have, of course, accounted in a significant degree for the Army's success in this area."[19] (As Lemnitzer's predecessor, Taylor must have felt that he, too, deserved a share of the credit.)

While both sides were waiting for the order, Lemnitzer wrote a letter to one of his generals which touched upon the tension between the region's military and diplomatic authorities: referring to an impending U.S. visit by Japanese Prime Minister Kishi Nobusuke to press for reversion, Lemnitzer stated that "Personally, I believe he [Kishi] is going very far out on a limb but he seems determined to make a sharp issue of the Okinawa problem. In this connection, I have been having considerable disagreement with Ambassador MacArthur regarding the Executive Order. He has taken the position, and has so recommended to Washington, that the issuance . . . now be deferred until six or eight weeks after Kishi returns to Tokyo. I have expressed my strong disagreement with this position and I am so informing the Department of the Army and the Department of Defense. It seems to me, and I have so informed the ambassador, that the embassy and State always seem to be able to find a reason to delay some action we propose to take to improve our administration of the Ryukyus. . . . The ambassador and I agreed to disagree and the matter is now in the hands of the authorities in Washington."[20]

Lemnitzer and the Defense Department won their point: Eisenhower signed the executive order in early June, the same month Kishi visited the United States. Unfortunately, the order didn't help Lemnitzer's own situation much because it went into effect the month before he went on to another assignment. The president agreed with Lemnitzer's position that the military was the appropriate authority to govern the islands because America's only reason for maintaining a presence there was security. The general's efforts to convince those who lived there that their security was at issue, too, were not successful. He stated at one point: ". . . there would be fewer conflicts of opinion if the Japanese and the Ryukyuans understood that our present policies are necessary for their own security as well as ours. Unfortunately, I can see little hope in the immediate future of convincing them that this is true. Their outlook is fundamentally emotional and therefore not likely to be swayed by logic, particularly when the logic is premised on a communist threat which they do not really believe in. Japan is strongly attracted by the naive dream of becoming an Oriental Switzerland, neutral, prosperous, and immune from attack."[21]

Lemnitzer was critical of Japanese leaders for exploiting sharp and well-publicized divisions of opinion within the U.S. government on the Ryukyus issue: "So long as we insist on airing our Ryukyus policy disputes in the press, we will continue to be at the mercy of this type of pressure. By contrast, the Soviets, who have a potentially similar problem with their retention of certain of the Kurile Islands group,[22] are experiencing no difficulty whatsoever due to their firm and solid-front attitude which leaves the Japanese no openings and discourages constant public discussion of this issue. The Japanese know they will not get anywhere with the Russians if they try to discuss it, so they make no attempt to do so."[23]

While the Okinawans were trying to get back military land, U.S. forces continued to need more space. Okinawans would provide it, but only as high-priced rental property instead of selling it, as the Americans preferred. Still, Lemnitzer was able to report to Eisenhower when he returned from the Far East in July 1957 that a land reform program, under which all land not strongly needed by U.S. forces was being returned to the civilian economy, was well under way.[24] Lemnitzer took exception to an article in *The New York Times* in 1957 which charged that Okinawa had a "colonial administration." Whereas colonization means exploitation, he asserted, the United States had done just the opposite, spending over two hundred million dollars on an "unparalleled recovery from the ravages and misery of the war." New industries had been introduced and old ones restored, he pointed out; incomes were much higher; thousands of new houses had been built; harbors and transportation facilities had been vastly improved; power generation and communications systems had been revamped; and, with the construction of new schools and hospitals, education and medical standards had been raised. When the Far East Command ceased to exist with Lemnitzer's departure, the title of governor was changed to "high commissioner" and the task of running the islands given to the senior U.S. military commander in the Ryukyus. Much later, in 1972, the islands were returned to Japan with the United States retaining possession of its military sites.

Lemnitzer's prime mission in Japan itself was to assist it in rebuilding its armed forces. It was a formidable endeavor with which his successors would also be wrestling for years after he left the theater for other challenges. As he explained years later, "the building up of military strength in a nation that has been completely defeated is an enormous undertaking."[25] Their armed forces shattered and what remained disbanded after the war, the Japanese in 1947 adopted a constitution which declared in part: "The Japanese people forever renounce war as a sovereign right of the nation and the threat or use of force as a means of settling international disputes." It was a reflection of a deep-felt fear of resurgent militarism and of memories of the terrible destruction of World War II, among other things. As laudable as it was, however, this provision placed a big burden on the United States, which became responsible for the nation's defense and internal security. Lemnitzer told Eisenhower when he returned to Washington in 1957 that he felt that the Japanese were content with being under U.S. protection and were using their constitution as an "excuse" to avoid meaningful rearming.[26]

In 1950, a movement toward limited rearmament began and a national "police reserve" of seventy-five thousand men was created for internal defense. The title was changed to "National Safety Force" and expanded to one hundred ten thousand in 1952, and in 1954 it became the "National Defense Force" with an army, navy, and air force whose total size was approaching two hundred thousand when Lemnitzer left.

Still, the postwar surge to pacifism was a powerful deterrent to building an effective defense force, and when the general reported on the situation to Eisenhower after he returned to Washington in July 1957, he had to say that the Japanese forces were still far from being able to provide for their nation's security—this at a time when the United States was preparing to move all of its combat units out of the country.[27] One of Lemnitzer's arguments against returning the Ryukyus to Japanese control was that this would extend to the islands the same problems he was experiencing in Japan: "Inability to obtain essential land for airfield extensions, constant labor disputes, disagreement over the use of ship repair facilities and training grounds by third-state vessels and personnel, lack of legal protection for military secrets, constant pressure for the relinquishment of facilities, disputes over conditions under which facilities and maneuver areas can be used, and limitations on the introduction and storage of modern weapons."[28]

Relations between the United States and Japan and the U.S. Army and the American public received a rough jostling during Lemnitzer's last year in the Far East when the "Somagahara Shooting Incident," as it was known in Japan, was dropped into his lap. So volatile were the repercussions that a Far East brigadier general known for his savvy regarding military politics was heard to say privately: "There goes the career of a future [U.S. Army] chief of staff."[29] Lemnitzer recalled the case as having demanded more of his time than any other occurrence during his tenure in the Far East.

The January 30, 1957, shooting involved a soldier, Specialist Third-Class William S. Girard, of Ottawa, Illinois, who was accused of killing a Japanese woman while she was picking up brass cartridge cases on an Army firing range near Somagahara, Japan. Girard, twenty-two, was a rifleman assigned to Company F of the 1st Cavalry Division's 8th Cavalry Regiment, and he and a fellow soldier, Specialist Third-Class Victor N. Nickel, had been ordered to stand guard over a machine gun and some field jackets awaiting pickup at the end of a training session at the range. The security was necessary because the range was being swarmed over by some one hundred fifty local Japanese residents who were busily picking up shell cases and whatever else they could find that could be sold later as scrap. The scavenging was a popular way of making money despite posted warning signs that the activity was illegal and very dangerous. The range was located in a part-time maneuver area which, when it wasn't being used by American and Japanese defense forces, was farmed by local civilians.

The two soldiers were not authorized to fire on the civilians in the range and, in fact, had no live ammunition because their company commander had ordered unit members to turn theirs in after deciding that further target practice would endanger the persistent scavengers. The unit was then issued blank ammunition to use in a training exercise scheduled for later in the day. While the two soldiers stood watch in a foxhole, Girard attached a grenade launcher to the muzzle of his Garand rifle, inserted an expended rifle cartridge, loaded a blank round into the weapon's chamber and fired toward the civilians. The cartridge struck Mrs. Naka Sakai, forty-six, in the heart and killed her instantly. Girard claimed that he had fired from the hip, intending only to frighten her and the others.

Nickel testified, however, that the victim had been lured into point-blank range by Girard's shouts of encouragement to approach and pick up empty cartridges that the two soldiers had been deliberately throwing increasingly closer to their foxhole. When an old man, woman, and two boys got close, according to Nickel, Girard got out of the foxhole, raised his rifle to his shoulder and fired toward the man. He missed and the group fled, but Nickel testified that they and several others were coaxed back by Girard through gestures and Japanese words signifying that he would not shoot again. When the Japanese resumed picking up cartridges, Nickel stated, Girard put another empty cartridge into his launcher, loaded another blank, and ran toward one of the women. When she fled, he raised his gun to his shoulder, fired again from about ten yards away and struck Mrs. Sakai in the back.[30]

The aspect of the case that stirred up the biggest storm in the United States was not the incident itself, but the question of jurisdiction in the ensuing legal proceedings. Public outrage over the incident was high in Japan, whose government wanted Girard turned over to a Japanese court under the status of forces agreement it had reached with the United States in 1953. Such agreements govern the administration of troops stationed in allied sovereign nations. The possibility that a U.S. soldier might be placed at the mercy of a former enemy nation's court system touched off an avalanche of protests, with congressmen, veterans groups, and members of the public angrily demanding that Girard be tried by his own country. U.S. Congressman George S. Long's comments in a letter to a member of Lemnitzer's staff were typical, if considerably more restrained than many: "Surely, the time has not come when the United States government will release its fighting men to be tried by a foreign country and former enemy. The woman involved was where she had no right to be and the soldier was acting under orders."[31]

Lemnitzer overruled several of his top commanders, many members of his staff, and "practically all of the lawyers who have studied this case" in recommending to Washington that Girard be tried by U.S. military court martial.[32] His position was that Girard was officially on duty at the time of the shooting and thus was subject to U.S. jurisdiction under the status of forces agreement. Japanese authorities and other proponents of turning him over to Japanese courts contended that the soldier's action in firing the shell cases was outside the scope of his guard duties and therefore was not done in the performance of his official duty. The Department of the U.S. Army, the executive agent in the case, accepted Lemnitzer's recommendation, but, as he explained in a letter to Admiral Stump, commander in chief of the U.S. Pacific Command, "only so long as it did not run into serious objection which, of course, was impossible." Japan did indeed object, vigorously, and in a decision by Secretaries Dulles and Wilson, Lemnitzer was overruled and the United States waived its right to try Girard. Lemnitzer strongly resented the reversal, but the aspect that vexed him the most was the fact that his civilian superiors let him take the blame for turning Girard over to the Japanese. He wrote in his letter to Stump that he was "bothered very much because the dispatches out of Washington make it appear that I recommended turning Girard over to the Japanese courts for trial, whereas I did just the opposite. It was the decision taken in Washington and in consultation with the Department of State that overrode my position and directed the procedure which resulted in the action which has and will continue to raise so much hell." He was especially disturbed that his deputy chief of staff, Rear Adm. Miles H. Hubbard, his representative in U.S.-Japanese discussions over the issue, was "literally being crucified . . . for merely carrying out the action directed by Washington."[33]

A U.S. Federal District Court judge in Washington, D.C., issued a ruling that the decision to waive jurisdiction was unconstitutional, but he was reversed by the U.S. Supreme Court after the Justice Department appealed. Tried by a three-judge Japanese court on a charge of causing death by wounding—the least serious homicide charge for which he could have been indicted under Japanese law—Girard was given a three-year suspended prison sentence when the court held that he had fired accidentally. The ruling was considered far more lenient than Girard would have received had he been tried by a U.S. military court. Lemnitzer had predicted that Girard would fare much better with the Japanese—particularly if he showed repentance, which he did. The Japanese government filed a claim for 800,000 yen—about two thousand dollars in U.S. money—for damages on behalf of the slain woman's husband. The actual amount of the final settlement was not disclosed but was believed to have been between 600,000 and 700,000 yen.

Many people were still furious when the general got back to Washington for his next assignment two months before the Girard verdict was reached. Secretary Wilson sent him to the American Legion's annual convention at Atlantic City to attempt to get the big veterans' group to tone down some "very rough language" in a proposed resolution condemning status of forces agreements of the kind that covered the Girard incident. The general gave the government's position before the Legion's security and foreign policy commissions, and remembered it as "without doubt the most antagonistic and belligerent audience that I had appeared before in a long time."[34] How well Lemnitzer succeeded in his toning-down mission is debatable: the resolution that passed was still very "rough."

Home front indignation of another kind aroused Lemnitzer's ire early in his Far East tour when the chairman of the U.S. House Foreign Affairs Committee's subcommittee on the Far East was widely quoted in the press as having said following a trip to Japan that U.S. servicemen were engaging in rampant illicit sex because of a lack of adequate recreational programs in the command. The general objected in a letter to Chairman Clement J. Zablocki, Wisconsin Democrat, that "the serious and harmful results of such publicity upon the morale of my command are extremely detrimental to the accomplishment of my mission in the Far East and affect adversely, at a most critical time, United States-Japanese relations." Pointing out that prostitution was legal in Japan, Lemnitzer denied that illicit sex was widespread and was, in fact, limited to a "very small minority" of the largely draftee force that made up his command. He asserted that "young men who don the uniform and bear arms in defense of their country should be treated as adults," and added that "those individuals, military or civilian, who seek and find illicit sex relations here would find them in the United States and elsewhere in the world."[35]

Whatever one might think of the congressman's identification of the root problem, the general's accompanying list of recreational facilities in the command was impressive: 638 movie theaters with an average monthly attendance of two million, over one thousand libraries and craft shops, and two thousand athletic facilities. Moreover, he wrote, theater commanders and chaplains, through educational and character guidance programs, were "making vigorous and comprehensive efforts to further the moral development of their men." The commander in chief wanted Zablocki to correct the "erroneous impression" caused by his remarks. There is no record that he ever did so.

Later in his tour, Lemnitzer raked a future four-star general over the coals following a visit from another congressman, Rep. J. Leroy Johnson, California Republican. The officer, Maj. Gen. John H. Michaelis, was the Army's chief legislative liaison officer in Washington and would normally have been in charge of setting up such a VIP trip. In this instance, the visit required special treatment because the congressman was a member of the important and powerful House Committee on Armed Services.

In a letter which began, "Dear Michaelis," Lemnitzer went into detail on what his command had laid on for the lawmaker: a personal, hour-long briefing by the commander in chief, extensive briefings by his senior generals and component commanders, visits to theater commands, and a VIP lunch in his honor. Lemnitzer delayed an important and urgent trip to Korea to preside over the visit.

When Johnson arrived, he announced, with what Lemnitzer described as "astonishing frankness": "Well, I'm out. I got licked in the election. The Committee staff thought it would be a good idea if I took advantage of the opportunity and did some traveling before 1 January, 1957, so here I am." The general recalled that it was "immediately apparent from the foregoing and many other remarks he made that Johnson was primarily interested in shopping and sight-seeing and not in the activities and problems of this command." Because it was too late to cancel the itinerary that had been arranged, the program went on with the congressman interrupting repeatedly with "irrelevant comments that made briefing difficult and further indicated his lack of interest in the subjects of the briefings."

Lemnitzer objected to the waste of time and money that had been expended on the visit and, among other comments, he wrote Michaelis: "I urge that in the future you and your staff determine the *real*, repeat *real*, purpose of such visits before-hand and that commanders concerned be informed accordingly so that plans can be made to fit the purpose of the visit."[36] Michaelis wrote back a week later to apologize but he pointed out that responsibility for the visit had been assigned to the Air Force by the Defense Department and that the Army did not get involved when another service had been designated as executive agency for a trip. On the outside of the file containing copies of the exchange of letters, Lemnitzer noted: "I badgered Michaelis unnecessarily—the message did come from the Secy of the Air Force—[signed] L."

Lemnitzer's official residence was an imposing brick dwelling in Tokyo known as Maeda House. Formerly the property of Count Maeda, a member of the Japanese aristocracy, Maeda House was in a walled compound in which there were two smaller houses occupied by principal members of the general's staff. The compound was a short car ride away from his headquarters in Pershing Heights, an office and living complex that had been the site of a major Japanese military headquarters during the war. Kay and Lois lived with him in Maeda House, and it is clear from comments in his correspondence that, despite the complexity of the problems with which his command had to wrestle, his two years at the helm in the Far East were the most personally enjoyable of his career. He was especially fond of Korea and its inhabitants, and had many friends there and in Japan with whom he corresponded long after he had gone on to other assignments. When he served in Washington and Europe, and even into retirement, he remained intensely interested in Far Eastern affairs, particularly those involving Korea, frequently writing to old acquaintances to comment on developments reported in the news. The family home in Pennsylvania teems with mementos of the general's travels and assignments, and by far the most prominently displayed are those from the Far East.

As the commander in chief of a United Nations command, Lemnitzer had to entertain frequently. The family had a staff of Japanese servants, and his post even came with a small yacht, the Q-611, which he apparently rarely used but which he sometimes loaned to hospitals and charitable groups for excursions. Far Eastern dignitaries tend to entertain lavishly and often, a situation that put

Lemnitzer at a disadvantage because of the paltry sums provided him by the Department of Defense for this purpose. To a query from the U.S. Army deputy chief of staff for personnel in 1957, he reported that for the previous eight-month period he had spent $460 on visiting foreign officials, $130 on members of the U.S. executive branch other than members of the military, $65 on members of Congress, $400 on assorted dignitaries, and $1,400 on military and civilian members of the Department of Defense. Over $1,000 came from his own pocket. He took issue with the fact that although he was the senior military official in the region, he was unable to entertain Ethiopian Emperor Haile Selassie, while he was in Korea to visit his country's troops, and other high officials of nations with forces in the theater. By contrast, he added, the State Department provided annual entertainment funds of $7,000 each to the much lower-ranking heads of its military assistance advisory groups in Japan and Korea.[37]

Lemnitzer and his wife were very fond of children, a trait which was badly needed in war-torn Korea whose formidable task of rebuilding included caring for thousands of orphans, crippled children, and those of mixed blood who had been fathered by UN troops and left behind. Both were active in overseeing and raising funds for orphanages and hospitals which had been built in places like Pusan through the efforts of UN personnel and the governments of countries with troops in Korea. In replying to a letter from famed blind writer Helen Keller regarding the plight of Korean children blinded in the war, Lemnitzer wrote: "I am indeed proud to be able to tell you that the service men and women of the United Nations command in Korea have devoted great expense and unremitting labor to care for thousands of these homeless and destitute little children, many of whom, as you point out, are blind. Our armed forces during and since the fighting have contributed millions of dollars to provide shelter and food for these little ones. With the help of our government, through the Armed Forces Assistance to Korea Program, they have accomplished much in rebuilding the schools, orphanages, hospitals and other public buildings which were destroyed in the fighting and which are now so urgently needed."[38]

The general became personally involved in the program, contributing his time and personal funds. Kay—a warm, motherly woman who, a former staff officer observed, treated everyone as if they were neighbors from her old hometown in Pennsylvania—spent many hours during her husband's tour in raising money, enlisting volunteers, and helping out in the Choong Hyun Babies' Home in Seoul and the Maryknoll Sisters' Orphanage in Pusan. So energetic was she in soliciting money for various causes that the general's staff presented her with a tin cup as a gag gift at a party. The Lemnitzers were active in the establishment of the famed Pusan Children's Charity Hospital, which was built in one of Pusan's poorest sections during the general's tenure. The hospital, the successor to a clinic belonging to an orphanage that had been started by U.S. servicemen to house refugee children during the war, was constructed by the U.S. armed forces and its operation financed by organizations and individuals in the United States. The hospital occupied a special place in the Lemnitzers' attentions long after they had left the Far East for other assignments. In a letter to a general who had supervised its construction when he was Eighth U.S. Army surgeon, Lemnitzer wrote on the eve of his leaving Washington to become supreme allied commander in Europe: "Although we are getting ready to live in Europe, we have no intention of decreasing our interests in Korea, particularly the Pusan Children's Charity Hospital. I have sent word to this effect to the various governmental officials in Korea and also to Ambassador Chung and the Korean Embassy officials here."[39]

Kay's efforts on behalf of Korean children and her position as honorary president of the Far East Red Cross took her from Maeda House, where she sponsored benefit garden parties, to such places as the former scene of fighting north of Seoul where the Army helicopter in which she was once riding was forced to make an emergency landing beside the Han River when it developed engine trouble. Her daughter remembered that afterward her mother, who was not injured, laughed about the incident and the considerable fuss it stirred up in high military and government circles. An account of the near crash was carried by the Associated Press (AP), prompting a letter to the general from the chief of the AP's Tokyo bureau: "We had a story last night on Mrs. Lemnitzer's escape in a helicopter accident. I would like you to know that we are all glad that your final days in the Far East were not marred by any mishap to you or yours. Flying accidents are certainly the occupational hazards of generals and newspapermen—and their wives.... [C]ongratulations to Mrs. L, and please be careful! There are some stories we really don't like to write."[40]

The Lemnitzers' devotion to the care of orphans was the beginning of a life-long friendship with Jane Russell, a sultry motion picture star of the period whose interest in the plight of homeless children brought her to the Far East to perform at benefit performances. The three corresponded frequently over the years; in a typical exchange, Lemnitzer congratulated the actress on receiving an award for her work from the Philadelphia Club of Advertising Women. Miss Russell wrote back expressing "my fondest regards to you and your Dear Lady."[41]

Another hazard of travel in Korea was the food, which often contained toxins or bacteria which presented no problems for Koreans but could cause severe intestinal upsets for persons not accustomed to eating it. Commenting to his brother after the current U.S. ambassador had decided to resign because of having been ill with dysentery and other digestive ailments ever since his arrival in the country, Lemnitzer wrote: "As a matter of fact, I attended some of the same official functions he did, after which I also got a severe case of dysentery. This is one of the principal problems in Korea. We try to avoid eating anything when we are invited to official functions but we are not always able to do so. It is therefore necessary to keep dysentery remedies around at all times."[42]

The general had no similar qualms about his favorite tropical fruit: mangoes.

Possibly an acquired taste from his years of service on Corregidor, the mangoes were flown in on military flights from the Philippines, often following a letter prompting a colleague to get things moving. In a letter to the chief of the head of the U.S. MAAG in Manila, he led off a rundown on his plans for an important forthcoming trip with Japanese leaders to Okinawa with these very precise instructions: "I would appreciate it if you would have one of your aides or a member of your staff purchase a basket of approximately 50 mangoes for me and send them on a USAF plane from Manila or Clark AFB to Kadena AFB in Okinawa, arriving at Kadena not later than the evening of Tuesday, 12 March. I would like to have the very best mangoes selected and graded from slightly underripe to completely green, so that they will gradually become ripe by natural processes. As you know, I employed this method in purchasing approximately the same number of mangoes during our brief stop-over at Manila prior to my flight to Hong Kong and as a result we were able to have mangoes throughout the remainder of the trip to Tokyo and for a considerable period after we arrived there."[43]

When he could find time, he played golf, his position carrying with it a guest membership in the prestigious Tokyo Golf Club. He also fished, setting a record and prompting this ecstatic account to his brother: "On the 4 July weekend we went up into the mountains near Nikke to get out of the heat in Tokyo. I tried my hand at fishing for rainbow trout and had the most phenomenal luck. Although I had never fished for rainbow before I caught a 27-inch rainbow that weighed 6 ¼ pounds. It took me 18 minutes to land him and it was the largest rainbow ever caught by a member of the armed forces in Japan." This feat with a light fly rod broke the previous record of 26 ½ inches set by one of Lemnitzer's Far East Command predecessors, his old friend Mark Clark. He mused: "I don't believe he will be very happy when he hears I topped his catch."[44]

In mid-1957 Lemnitzer was named vice chief of staff of the U.S. Army, succeeding Gen. Williston B. Palmer in a position which Lemnitzer likened to being the chief of staff's "alter ego." But before reporting for his new assignment, Lemnitzer carried out an order which ordinarily would be among the saddest a commander could execute: he was to dissolve his command. The Far East Command would be no more, and after he left the UN flag would fly over Korea. His successor would be a future Army chief of staff, Gen. George H. Decker, who would bear the title of commander in chief of UN forces and commanding general of U.S. forces in Korea and the Eighth Army. Army forces in Japan, Korea, Hawaii, and the Ryukyus were placed under a new command, the U.S. Army Pacific, commanded by Gen. Isaac D. White, who came under Admiral Stump's headquarters. The Ryukyus became the direct responsibility of Lt. Gen. James E. Moore, whose post as commanding general of the Ryukyus Command and the IX Army Corps carried with it the title of high commissioner.

It is questionable whether Lemnitzer felt any real regret over the inactivation, which constituted little more than a transfer of headquarters. The Japanese had been difficult hosts in many ways, increasingly so since the peace treaty had been signed. Korea, understandably more attuned to the need for maintaining large armed forces, was more hospitable and tolerant of the military point of view in matters involving its citizenry. Still, the move was viewed with misgivings by such people as Lt. Gen. Elmer J. Rogers, Jr., a former member of Lemnitzer's senior staff and then inspector general of the Air Force. He wrote to Lemnitzer following the announcement that the command was going to be dissolved: "The news that this fate was to overtake the Far East Command brought us [Rogers and his wife, Wilma] a great pang of regret and left us more than a little sad. It seemed to us that your superb administration of that command fully justified another and more deserving fate. Moreover, I feel certain that the Japanese segment of the redistribution, by its swiftness and extensiveness, will be taken as an indication of waning United States interest. In the Far East area in general and in Japan in particular, it will, in my view, be almost certain to result in a diminution of U.S. influence over Japan, not only in matters of the buildup of Japan's Self Defense Forces but in other areas of mutual interest, as well."[45]

One of Lemnitzer's last acts as commander in chief was to inform President Rhee that U.S. forces in Korea were going to be equipped with more modern weapons and the Korean air force given enough jet aircraft for a second fighter-bomber wing as part of a decision in Washington to bolster the UN's retaliatory capabilities. In a confidential "talking paper" the general left with Rhee, a plan was also outlined to reduce the size of Korean ground forces. The rationale for the latter was that current strength levels imposed too high a drain on the nation's economy and reductions would permit greater emphasis on economic development.[46] What the paper did not mention was that another driving force for this streamlining—perhaps the most dominant one—was the drain the South Korean force levels was having on the U.S. economy.

Despite the delivery of the talking paper, the reductions did not begin immediately because Rhee was opposed to any cutbacks in his nation's forces until North and South Korea were united, an eventuality whose chances for fruition in the foreseeable future were regarded in most places as on a par with teaching a shrimp to whistle. Lemnitzer had been in his new job in Washington nearly two months when Rhee wrote him that the matter still had not been settled. "I told President Eisenhower that until we have a unified Korea we feel compelled to maintain the present level of our defense forces. However, if the maintenance of the present military strength can be accomplished through the introduction of modern weapons, we would give serious consideration to a reduction in our manpower. I advised the President that until information was made available to us concerning the modernization program contemplated, and plans are made for delivery to our forces, the present level of forces must be maintained."[47]

Although Lemnitzer's talking paper had not gone into detail on the specifics of the upgrading, "modern weapons" meant atomic ones. When the general met with Eisenhower to report on the termination of the Far East Command, Lemnitzer urged that the country get on with deploying the 280-millimeter atomic cannon and the nuclear-capable Honest John missile in Korea. Notes taken during the meeting quoted the president as saying he felt that "such actions . . . should simply be taken without making a great public announcement about them. General Lemnitzer said he strongly supported exactly the same procedure—if people saw new weapons around and asked about them they should be told that specific details as to timing, numbers, etc., were and should remain classified. The president strongly endorsed this procedure."[48]

The cannon and the Honest John and Lacrosse missiles, all capable of delivering nuclear warheads, were later deployed to American forces in Korea. The North Koreans found out about the weapons—as the United States and its allies undoubtedly counted on their doing—and protested, to no avail, that deploying them was a violation of a provision of the armistice which banned the introduction of new weapons. The UN had, in fact, suspended this provision, citing its repeated violation by the Communists. The suspension, declared Decker as he prepared to assume his new command, was "merely an effort to try to equalize our position."[49] Although calling up nuclear weapons undoubtedly enhanced the south's defensive capability considerably, it is interesting to note that their introduction with an accompanying one hundred thousand-man reduction in South Korean conventional forces fit in well with the economy-minded Eisenhower's bigger-picture posture in the States: nuclear weapons were cheaper than keeping large bodies of troops under arms.[50]

Before he left for his new assignment, Lemnitzer traveled the length of Korea's 155-mile front making farewell calls at each of the five corps headquarters and that of the First Republic of Korea Army. The UN command's senior generals were waiting at each stop, and Lemnitzer was able to write his brother afterward that "thus I was able to talk to every senior commander and staff officer of the Republic of Korea Army and the British Commonwealth, Turkish, Thailand, French, Greek and Ethiopian forces."[51] He wrote in the same letter that he took a group of UN liaison officers with him and "practically wore them out" in a whirlwind week of farewells, which included calls by him and his wife at hospitals and orphanages in Seoul and Pusan, a dinner with the Rhees, first-time visits to the Ryukyu islands of Miyako and Ishigaki, and an address to the Okinawan legislature.

A year earlier, when he was halfway through his tour in the Far East, Lemnitzer received a letter from his longtime friend, General Ridgway, which read: "I often think of you, particularly when the major issues still boiling in Washington get back on the front pages of the newspapers, and I am glad that you are at least temporarily out of it. I haven't the slightest doubt, however, that this is a temporary respite. . . ."[52]

As he packed up once again and prepared to turn over his "three-ring circus" to other ringmasters, it is not likely that Lemnitzer would have picked "respite" to sum up his two years in the Far East. But considering what the next few years would bring, his former Pentagon boss couldn't have chosen his words much better.

16

★ ★ ★ ★

THE VICE

General Lemnitzer had wanted it to be named "Top Kick" after that Army stalwart, the first sergeant. But less-parochial heads prevailed, and the ballistic missile that lifted America into the space age will forever be remembered in history as Explorer 1.

The Army deserved and needed to be at least a little parochial in those early days of 1958 and the months before when it had at last been given the mission of firing a satellite into space. The blastoff at ten forty-eight on the evening of January 31 was the culmination of over two years of frustrating efforts to convince the nation's leadership that it had the capability to do so.

The story goes back to the closing days of World War II when the Allies were overrunning Germany. Wernher von Braun and his team of rocket scientists, developers of the Third Reich's V2 missile, surrendered to the U.S. Army, along with over a hundred rocket experts and three hundred boxcars of captured rocket equipment from the V2 development center at Peenemünde. Whisked away to Fort Bliss, Texas, and finally in 1950 to the Army's Redstone Arsenal at Huntsville, Alabama, the Germans became the core of the nation's premier rocket development group.

Despite Army claims as early as 1954 that it was ready to proceed with the launching of a satellite, the mission for achieving this long-sought objective of the scientific world was assigned to the U.S. Naval Research Laboratories. As Lemnitzer remembered it, Defense Secretary Wilson ordered the Army missile-men to put their hardware in a warehouse and "get on with developing military hardware" because space was "none of their blankety blank business."[1]

Lemnitzer, now Army vice chief of staff, or "the vice" as the position was called, was visiting the Redstone Arsenal on October 4, 1957, with Neil H. McElroy, Wilson's incoming successor as secretary of defense, and Army Secretary Brucker. During the tour, von Braun and Maj. Gen. John B. Medaris, commander of the Army Ballistic Missiles Agency (ABMA), used every opportunity during the briefings to stress that the Army had the means of putting a satellite into orbit. "But that was sort of a subject of bad odor around there," Lemnitzer recalled, so "we'd immediately get back on the track and brief about military hardware."[2]

That night, while the four were dining at the arsenal's officers' club, the telephones began ringing with calls from the press that the Soviet Union had just put Sputnik I into orbit. "And that dinner went right out the window," the general said. "There was consternation and exclamations and everything else. It just broke up the works."[3] Similar reactions were taking place around the country as the realization set in that the Russians had beaten the United States in a field in which it was assumed that it had no rival.

"It's almost impossible in this day and age to imagine, a quarter of a century later, the psychological blow to this country, all segments of the population, at the Soviets beating us in this great scientific accomplishment," Lemnitzer said after he retired. "You can't imagine it unless you lived through it."[4] The next morning, McElroy asked Medaris and von Braun how long it would take for the Army to put its own satellite into space. After considerable discussion, the two told him four months. When McElroy took office a few days later, the Army was ordered to get its rocket ready as a backup to the Naval Research Laboratories' project, Vanguard, then being readied for orbit in December. In November, the Soviets put up another satellite, this one carrying a dog, and the same month the Army was given a definite firing date: January 29, 1958.

National pride took another powerful slap on December 6 when the Vanguard fell back to the earth in flames at its launching. Only the Army Explorer 1 was left and it came through, its four-month schedule off by only two days, and that because of adverse last-minute weather conditions. Propelled by eighty-three thousand pounds of thrust, Explorer 1's Jupiter C rocket performed flawlessly after liftoff, placing a 30.8-pound satellite in orbit. It was a great moment for a service whose self-esteem had been taking a bad beating in the New Look priorities of the 1950s. There were more triumphs in the two years ahead: a satellite in orbit around the sun; deep space exploration and radiation experiments; and a trip into space and back by two monkeys, "Able" and "Baker."

No one was prouder of this new jewel in the Army's crown than Lemnitzer, who was acting chief of staff during much of the pre-launch period while General Taylor was on an extended trip overseas. But less than a year after the historic Explorer 1 launch, Lemnitzer would be given what had to have been the most unpopular task in the Army: that of turning over its space mission to another government agency. In October 1958 NASA was created by an act of Congress, and the general was put in charge of the Army's part in the transfer. The assignment put him in the line of fire of some of the armed services' most powerful opponents of the move. Without naming names, he recalled being "confronted by several senior officers in the top level of the Army who maintained that we should continue to fight."[5] Among the most prominent of the critics was Medaris, who later retired and wrote a book in protest.

But Lemnitzer agreed with Eisenhower's decision that space exploration was foreign to the Army's mission ("I had no problem after the president made his decision—I had no problem within myself.")[6] At issue now was what the Army would lose in the transfer. NASA wanted the Army's two principal centers of rocket development: the Jet Propulsion Laboratory (JPL), operated for the Army by the California Institute of Technology, and much of its Ballistic Missile Agency at Redstone Arsenal. The Army was willing to give up the JPL, but Lemnitzer dug in his heels in regard to Redstone because this would have meant, among other things, giving up the von Braun team. It was an awkward situation because the Defense Department had agreed to the transfer, apparently without consulting the Army. As Lemnitzer wrote to his brother: "Without our knowing anything about it, both of these [Redstone and the JPL] were practically handed over to NASA.... [W]e have objected vigorously to such action and since the middle of October [1958] I have been the principal Army negotiator to hammer out an acceptable solution to both sides. After many hours of discussion and preparation of staff papers we did reach a satisfactory solution on this problem which, as you know, was announced by the President after the meeting of the Space Council on Wednesday, 3 December. We have been gradually reducing our activities in JPL and they are anxious to get into space work, so that part of the problem was not difficult to handle. The Ballistic Missile Agency at Huntsville, however, was our key missile facility and we simply couldn't have our team, which includes Dr. von Braun and the German scientists, broken up and dissipated. We were able to prove to everyone involved that this would not be the way to handle the matter and we were able to keep this installation and the personnel in the Army."[7] The final decision to let the Army keep Redstone was made by Eisenhower.

Army victories were rare in the often brutal Washington in-fighting of those days, and the *Washington Evening Star* gave the credit for this one to "the brilliance of Army maneuvering" during the transfer negotiations.[8] Under the agreement, the Army continued to completion space projects in progress at Redstone while NASA did likewise for Army projects under way at the JPL. Long-range missilery became the responsibility of the Air Force. There are indications in his letters to his family that, at least initially, Lemnitzer shared in the indignation over the transfer, and he may have even voiced his feelings to those above him, according to this observation made years later: "It has always been my policy at this level of government that when you're in the discussion phases you speak your mind freely, candidly, frankly and fearlessly. But when the decision is made by the proper authority you get behind it to carry it out effectively and efficiently and do your best to make it a success. If you can't live with that, then you don't belong in your particular position."[9]

Lemnitzer must have shaken his head over a newspaper clipping sent to him by a friend when it was announced that he was going to be the Army's next vice chief of staff. The item speculated that Lemnitzer was chosen to spell Taylor at capital social functions because the current vice chief—Gen. Williston B. Palmer—"is a fearless field commander who won't flinch in the face of the enemy but runs like a rabbit from cocktail parties." "The Army chief finally decided he'd had enough," the article continued. "He ordered 'Willie' transferred to Europe and the more social Lemnitzer brought to the Pentagon as vice chief."[10] The friend who sent the clipping wrote in an accompanying note: "It's certainly an original version of why vice chiefs are changed. Didn't know Willie was such a meek mouse at cocktail parties."

The vice chief is far more than the chief's stand-in at receptions, of course. In a sense, he is the executive who "runs" the Army, the degree depending on the chief. During the Taylor-Lemnitzer reign, the vice chief's share was enormous because Taylor was the Army's "up-front man" during a period when the service chiefs' JCS responsibilities had become so demanding and time-consuming that Eisenhower practically ordered them to turn over their services' internal operations to their deputies. This relationship was made binding in the Defense Reorganization Act of 1958, which clearly defined the chiefs' primary concern as their JCS duties. Although the office of vice chief had been created only nine years before Lemnitzer took over, the concept that leading the Army had become a two-man operation had become solidly entrenched. Frank Pace, a former secretary of the Army, wrote Lemnitzer in a congratulatory letter that "it certainly seems to me the team of Taylor and Lemnitzer, which I knew so well, is magnificently qualified to lead the Army in its new and vital responsibilities."[11] Maj. Gen. Paul D. Harkins wrote: "I cannot imagine any better combination than you and Max running the top echelon of the Army. It will be a wonderful team, and we in the field will have full confidence in all decisions made."[12]

Despite these and other seeming inferences that Taylor and his new "vice" were a proven combination, their only previous working relationship had been when they were students at the Army War College and during the three months when Lemnitzer commanded Army forces in the Far East and Taylor was commander in chief. They would have been members of the same Military Academy graduating class, always a strong bond among Army regulars, had fellow cadet Lemnitzer elected, as Taylor did, to take four years at West Point instead of two. Taylor had been impressed with Lemnitzer when they worked together in the Far East, judging from his glowing officer efficiency report. This brief connection, Lemnitzer's growing reputation as a commander and team player, his solid achievements as head of the Far East Command, and, perhaps, a nudge from President Eisenhower were undoubtedly factors in Taylor's decision to bring him back to Washington.

They were not much alike. Taylor was a "loner," an icy-eyed and reserved man who spoke several languages and played a fine game of tennis. He was impressive in appearance and demeanor, was regarded as brilliant but not particularly creative, had little time for small talk, did not suffer fools gladly, and was intensely ambitious. Lemnitzer was warm, outgoing and hearty, and was excellent company. He had a quick, analytical mind, possessed an extraordinary memory, was flexible in his thinking where Taylor tended toward rigidity, and was never happier than when he was discussing football or baseball with a group of friends. Taylor was meticulous about his work surroundings and uniform; Lemnitzer worked in shirtsleeves and his desk was notorious for its clutter. The two rarely socialized on a personal level, although Lemnitzer's son remembers that they were always good friends, even through the trying Bay of Pigs period ahead when one sat as the judge and the other as one of the accused.

Comparing them, Eisenhower once said: "Lem is a hell of a lot smarter than Max."[13]

Taylor needed a strong hand at the Army controls because the New Look was reaching full bloom when Lemnitzer returned to Washington. The Army was still fighting to keep the ground soldier in the forefront of the country's defense posture, putting its eggs in a Taylor-fashioned basket called the "pentomic division." It was to be the fighting edge of a hard-hitting Army which he envisioned as being capable of proportioning "its blows to fit the case—from the force of the M.P.'s truncheon to the kilotons of atomic weapons."[14] Taylor made no bones about the fact that "pentomic" was a Madison Avenue–style buzzword which was given to the new unit partly in response to a Wilson complaint that the names of the equipment used by the Army—rifles, machine guns, trucks, and unsophisticated aircraft—lacked glamor. The defense secretary once sent a budget back to him suggesting that he substitute what Taylor called "newfangled items with public appeal instead of the prosaic accoutrements of the foot soldier."[15]

The pentomic division consisted of five battle groups and was intended to fight either an atomic or conventional war. Smaller than the triangular-patterned tactical division that it eventually replaced, it was designed for flexibility, high mobility, and withering individual firepower.[16] A prime feature of the new division was that it could readily adapt to the addition of atomic weapons still undeveloped (in 1956, when the division was unveiled, the Army had only the 280-millimeter cannon and the cumbersome Honest John missile in its atomic arsenal). As Taylor pointed out in his book, *Swords and Plowshares*, "nuclear weapons were the going thing and by including some in the division armament the Army staked out its claim to a share in the nuclear arsenal."[17]

As the Army's "inside man," Lemnitzer presided over the final conversion of all combat divisions to the pentomic concept by early 1958. Taylor's creation had a short life, lasting until the early 1960s when the Army began replacing it with a more traditional version of a ground division under Lemnitzer. His successor as chief of staff, George Decker, who didn't think the pentomic division was strong enough to sustain itself in combat, continued the conversion. Lt. Gen. James M. Gavin, a deputy chief of staff under Taylor when the new unit was inaugurated, termed the pentomic division "a mess" and was surprised when Taylor adopted it. "They only had something like a battery of artillery with each battle group," Gavin scoffed. "God, if you've ever had to use artillery you knew it was grossly lacking in artillery."[18]

Taylor's JCS duties and his efforts to stem the New Look's steady sapping of the Army's strength made the vice chief's office a busy place. Lemnitzer was serving as acting chief almost from the time he walked in the door, and was even temporary chairman of the JCS for a time during his first autumn in office when the chiefs were out of town. In a letter to a friend in the early months, he wrote: "I arrived back in Washington on 11 July and was in business as vice chief of staff on the 22nd. Shortly thereafter, General Taylor went to Europe for a long tour, so I found myself back in the Pentagon whirlwind very quickly. As you know, it is possible to ease into this kind of work or to jump in—I did the latter." In the same letter, he expressed his unhappiness with the country's defense posture: "The problems we are facing in all the services, but particularly in the Department of the Army, in connection with budgets and expenditure limitations are worse than I have experienced in past years, and I have been through this business many times in the past. Frankly, my main concern stems from the fact that I find it impossible to reconcile international developments with the actions we are taking to cope with them."[19]

The first major issue involving the Army after Lemnitzer returned to the Pentagon was the school integration crisis at Little Rock, Arkansas, in September 1957, when Eisenhower ordered a thousand-man task force of the 101st Airborne Division to hold back unruly crowds seeking to block the enrollment of nine black students at Little Rock High School. The operation was successful, but the use of federal troops to force integration was resented by some southern segregationists who turned their ire on the Army. As part of a congressional inquiry into the use of the troops, Sen. Richard B. Russell of Georgia demanded that the Army turn over to the Senate a copy of its operational orders for Little Rock. Lemnitzer drafted a Taylor memorandum for Brucker in which the chief of staff protested any release of the orders. Asserting that "an important matter of principle was involved," the secret memorandum stated: "I will admit that Congress, in appropriate cases, has the right to inquire into acts performed by certain executive officers. It is one thing to investigate specific actions after they have occurred; it is a different matter for the Congress to be able to require the release of orders affecting current and delicate operations and thus invite an investigation of commanders and staff officers while they are still engaged in important activities. It would be a most serious matter to disturb the self confidence of our commanders in the field by calls from Washington either for information or for direct testimony. . . .

"While the orders requested by Congress in the Little Rock situation contain no elements of which we need be ashamed, still some portions are not suitable for publication in the present racial climate in the nation. For example, some of the essential elements of information in the G-2 [intelligence] Annex of General [Edwin A.] Walker's Operational Order could be seized upon by the less thoughtful element of the nation as being provocative."[20] Brucker agreed and refused to release a copy of the orders in a letter to Russell in which he also indicated his approval of the way the troops had conducted themselves at Little Rock. Russell chose not to pursue the matter further.[21]

Lemnitzer's tenure as vice chief also saw enactment of the Defense Reorganization Act of 1958, a major piece of legislation which was personally crafted and guided through Congress by Eisenhower. Among its sweeping changes was the establishment of unified commands in the field under the secretary of defense and operated by him through the JCS; elimination of the JCS's Joint Staff's committee system, thus making it a truly operational staff; and, of course, the strengthening of Lemnitzer's own position by making it possible for service chiefs of staff to delegate major responsibilities to their vice chiefs. A prime aim of the reorganization was to beef up the secretary of defense's control of the department (and, not incidentally, the commander in chief's). A key provision in Eisenhower's proposal was to channel all defense appropriations through the secretary rather than to the individual services. Congress balked, however, although the president got almost everything else he wanted.

Lemnitzer spent a great deal of time on the president's plan, as did all elements of the Army staff in 1958—a commander in chief's personal interest can be a powerfully compelling force. The vice chief wrote to his brother in the spring: "We are very much engaged in reorganization here and it takes a fantastic amount of work to get some of these bills up on the Hill, especially when so little time is given for their preparation. I note that in your letter you indicate that if the President can get away for the weekend I should be able to do the same. Unfortunately, that is not the way Washington operates. Top officials can sometimes get away but the staffs have to stay behind and many of them work over the weekend to prepare for the coming week."[22] He wrote later: "General Taylor appeared before the Armed Services Committee of the Senate on Thursday and his testimony was very well received by the committee. As I had previously told you, we in the Army are not generally opposed to the reorganization plan, assuming of course that some common sense will be used in administering it. The really tough opposition comes from the Marine Corps and the Navy."[23]

The year also saw the only overt international military intervention of Eisenhower's presidency when he ordered fourteen thousand Army and Marine

Corps troops into Lebanon to shore up the pro-Western government against a threatened overthrow by Arab nationalists. Like Eisenhower, Lemnitzer saw the turmoil, inspired by Egypt's Gamel Abdel Nasser, as part of a communist drive to control the Middle East. He wrote to his brother: "Needless to say, I have had a very busy time here in Washington. General Taylor left for the West Coast Friday and the developments leading up to moving into the Middle East occurred while he was there. Typical of one of my days at the office, I had lunch at 4:30 in the afternoon and dinner at 10:30 that night. The decision to move into Lebanon was, we felt, overdue. It was either a question of losing the Middle East and all that would mean to our position [there] or stepping in and stopping this Russian-Nasser movement which was receiving tremendous success in its use of murder and force to take over the entire Middle East. . . ."[24] U.S. forces—which included eight thousand Army troops comprising an airlifted battle group and a reinforced tank and engineer combat battalion—stayed in Lebanon for fourteen weeks, losing one man to hostile fire before the crisis was settled by negotiation.

Aside from issuing the necessary orders to get Army forces into the country, Lemnitzer had no part in conducting the Lebanon operation. But this didn't keep him from erupting in anger when a picture appeared on the front page of a Washington newspaper showing a U.S. soldier being marched away at gunpoint for interrogation after he and several companions had driven their jeep into a rebel stronghold in Beirut by mistake. The humiliating spectacle was in sharp contrast to two other photographs in the same issue of Marines exuding readiness and alertness. "Here in the DA [Department of the Army] we are getting rather fed up with the press coverage in the Middle East operation," Lemnitzer wrote Gen. Henry I. Hodes, a fellow member of the Military Academy class of 1920 and, in his capacity as commander in chief of U.S. Army Europe, the senior officer to whom Army commanders in Lebanon reported. "If a deliberate attempt was made to cast adverse reflection on the Army, I don't see how a more effective job could be done than by the publication of this photograph. We can't control the press nor the pictures they take, but we can alert our own people to be on the alert so as to avoid presenting opportunities to the press to photograph [troops] under circumstances that reflect adversely on the Army."[25]

In his mention of the favorable pictures of Marines, Lemnitzer was touching on an old problem: invariably, the more publicity-conscious Marine Corps captures the early headlines and pictures in high-profile operations. Frequently being trumped in this increasingly important aspect of military endeavor gave rise years ago to this rueful Army joke: "How many men in a marine rifle squad?" The answer: "Nine riflemen and a photographer."

U.S. troops were still in Lebanon in August 1958 when a new foreign military crisis arose: the Communist Chinese began shelling the offshore Taiwanese islands of Quemoy and Matsu. While seeking to restrain Chiang Kai-shek, leader of Nationalist Chinese armies on Taiwan, from retaliating with an attack on the

Communist Chinese mainland, Eisenhower and some military leaders have been reported by some historians and in the press as having considered using nuclear weapons against the Communists, a move which would have risked armed confrontation with the Soviet Union. Lemnitzer, however, denied that any top government or military official had given any serious thought to using nuclear weapons "in such a relatively minor military situation." The nuclear weapons then available, he added, were improved models of the bombs used at Hiroshima and Nagasaki in 1945 and not suited for use in the tactical requirements prevailing at the time. Lemnitzer had inspected Quemoy and Matsu and was convinced that no amount of communist artillery bombardment could have overcome the rock-embedded fortifications on the two islands. "I also felt," he stated, "that the Red Chinese did not have the amphibious resources to capture the islands, particularly if the U.S. Navy provided even a modest amount of support...."[26] The situation calmed down by October—at least to the point where the Communists reduced the shelling to every other day—when Secretary Dulles persuaded Chiang to issue a statement in which he foreswore the use of force to recover the mainland.

The Army was more directly involved in the next communist gambit. This time, the antagonist was the Soviet Union's bumptious premier, Nikita S. Khrushchev, who announced in November 1958 that he wanted the Western powers to get out of Berlin. Located one hundred ten miles behind the border dividing East and West Germany, West Berlin was the only enclave behind communist lines still occupied by the Western powers. Khrushchev gave the Western allies—the United States, Great Britain, and France—six months to negotiate a settlement that would end the occupation of West Berlin and turn it into a demilitarized free city, leaving East Berlin the capital of East Germany. The Soviets followed up their premier's ultimatum by stopping an American convoy bound for West Berlin from West Germany. They released the column after eight hours, but General Norstad, the supreme allied commander in Europe, wanted to test the Russian resolve by immediately sending another convoy along the auto-bahn and then using "the minimum force necessary" to secure its release if it was stopped. Despite the hearty endorsement of the plan by the JCS, Eisenhower said no, both to Norstad's proposal and to a subsequent JCS recommendation to send a division along the convoy route. It was a tense period, but the president kept a rein on his military advisers, asserting that the Berlin situation was not a crisis but a continuing problem that could eventually be solved by calm and deliberate action rather than by risking war. By the end of six months, the tension had eased, although Berlin would remain a problem long after Eisenhower had ceased to be president.

The New Look continued to thrive despite the obvious fact that massive retaliation would have been of no use whatsoever in Lebanon or in Germany if the Soviets had chosen to use force. When in January 1959 Eisenhower sent Congress his budget for the coming fiscal year, he cut Army personnel strength by fifty thousand, the sixth year in a row that the senior service had taken sharp cuts. There were vehement congressional protests against such a reduction during a time of international tension, but Eisenhower countered that the soldiers were unnecessary because of the nation's heavy reliance on nuclear deterrence. He also told critics like Democratic Senators, J. William Fulbright, of Arkansas, and a future president, Lyndon B. Johnson, of Texas, that any efforts to match the Russians in conventional forces would lead to a garrison state.[27]

Earlier, in mid-1958, Lemnitzer wrote his predecessor, General Palmer: "We have completed the FY 59 budget hearings and there are, of course, several very important unresolved issues. From our point of view, one of the most interesting and sensitive is the appropriation by the House for a 900,000-man Army and a 700,000 Reserve and National Guard strength, with the Secretary of Defense stating flatly that he does not propose to use any of the funds to support a strength above 870,000 for the Army and 630,000 for the Reserve and National Guard."[28] Clearly, few of the nation's movers outside of the Army shared Taylor's firmly held conviction that the only acceptable level for active Army forces was one million.

Near the end of his tour as vice chief, Lemnitzer's strong stand at a meeting of the National Security Council was instrumental in throttling an effort by the Bureau of the Budget to sharply cut back U.S. support to the Republic of Korea from sixteen divisions to twelve. Supported by the Defense Department, but opposed by the State Department and the JCS, the cutback was being pushed vigorously by Maurice H. Stans, the bureau's director, as a cost-saving measure. During a spirited discussion involving Eisenhower, Vice President Richard M. Nixon, and the principal Cabinet members, Defense Secretary McElroy asked that Lemnitzer be permitted to express his views. The general, who was attending the June 25, 1959, meeting as acting Army chief of staff, was adamantly opposed to any reduction below the then current level of 630,000 troops. His view, given added credence by his experience as Far East commander in chief, was that the force level was essential to hold back North Korea and protect the DMZ from continued communist infiltration. Stans, supported by a report issued by a study group called the Draper Committee, had urged that the United States and South Korea seek like reductions by North Korea. Lemnitzer argued that because the North Koreans had repeatedly broken promises having to do with the war truce it would be impossible to reach a valid agreement in this regard. Eisenhower agreed with Lemnitzer, stating that "if it was the mature military judgment that we need the number of ROK forces that we now have to hold the line in South Korea, I can think of nothing more costly than to proceed to cut the ROK force levels." He ordered the current levels maintained and, as Lemnitzer recommended, that they be modernized with phased-out U.S. equipment.[29]

Taylor's views on what the New Look was doing to his service were shared by one of the most charismatic members of the Army's upper echelons, a general who had little use for Taylor himself and who was disdained by the chief in return as a maverick.[30] The officer was General Gavin, famed commander of the crack 82nd Airborne Division in World War II and then the highly visible chief of Army research and development. This had been in Lemnitzer's area of responsibility before he left for the Far East, and at least one colleague wished he hadn't left. "I sure miss you—Gavin operates like a lone wolf," wrote Lt. Gen. Walter L. Weible, deputy chief of staff for operation and administration.[31] Bright, articulate, and outspoken, Gavin had been vocal in his opposition to the transfer of the Army's space functions to NASA and he was deeply resentful of what was happening to the Army. He opted for retirement in March 1958, declaring that he planned to oppose the administration's massive retaliation policy as a civilian. Lemnitzer, who remained on good terms with Gavin after he left the Army and became a business executive, had no problem with his attitude toward the New Look, but he was dismayed that he chose to leave military service: "We in the Army deeply regretted the retirement of this able and experienced military commander and staff officer. We [knew] that he was unhappy with the direction our defense policy was taking at the time, particularly with regard to the emphasis being placed on nuclear weapons by the administration, the Congress, the Department of Defense and the Joint Chiefs of Staff. This feeling of concern in this regard was not limited to General Gavin, however, but it was shared by the Secretary of the Army, the Chief of Staff, myself, and most of the other officers in the Department of the Army.

"It was obvious to us that General Gavin was extremely frustrated because his views were not being accepted at higher levels, but so were all of us. In the light of this situation he felt that he could exercise far greater and more effective influence on the outcome of these policy problems if he were outside the Army and not in it. We disagreed strongly with his views in this regard. Accordingly, when he insisted on leaving the Army for these reasons, it was generally considered that he was walking out on the Army at a very crucial time."[32] Later in 1958, Gavin wrote a book, *War and Peace in the Space Age*, in which he elaborated on the issues that had prompted him to choose retirement instead of a proffered fourth star and command of the Seventh Army in Europe after another year as research and development chief. The book impressed a future president, Sen. John F. Kennedy, who appointed Gavin ambassador to France after he was elected.

The stir caused by Washington's loss of one of its best-known and seemingly most promising generals had scarcely subsided when another bombshell rocked the Pentagon: fed up with his failure to make significant headway against the New Look, General Taylor had decided to retire after two terms as Army chief of staff. Offered nomination to a third term by Secretary McElroy, he turned it down to write his own book. *The Uncertain Trumpet*, published shortly after Taylor retired, took issue with administration defense policies, especially that of massive retaliation. In its place, the former chief of staff proposed a policy of "flexible response," which would put increased emphasis on conventional forces as a key ingredient in a military posture tailored to the nature and strength of the threat. As in the case of Gavin's book, it was a volume read with keen interest by the senator who would become the next president of the United States—and with considerable chagrin by the one he would succeed. Taylor was the second chief of staff in a row to retire and lambast Eisenhower's defense policies. Ridgway, whose resentment over the Army's diminished role had drawn a presidential comment that he was too "parochial," was highly critical of the New Look in his memoirs, which appeared first in the *Saturday Evening Post,* and then in a book.

In March 1959, *Time* magazine carried an item that began: "Like any ranking Army officer, General Lyman Louis Lemnitzer, 59, has a soldier's talents for open warfare, but like few he has a diplomat's deft touch for the quiet, unsung victory. Last week President Eisenhower, no mean soldier-diplomat himself, picked General Lemnitzer as the next Army chief of staff to succeed retiring General Maxwell Taylor, 57."[33] On July 1, Lemnitzer took office.

The promotion brought with it membership in one of Washington's most exclusive clubs—the Joint Chiefs of Staff. Lemnitzer was the only new service chief when he attended his first meeting as a full-fledged member, and to mark the occasion his new colleagues had arranged a welcoming ceremony. Adm. Arleigh A. Burke, chief of naval operations and a longtime Lemnitzer friend, made a few remarks and then handed him a long, gift-wrapped wooden box while his fellow chiefs applauded. Inside was a shiny, four-foot-long ceremonial bugle lavishly adorned with flowing gold tassels and carrying a sign that read:

"The *Certain* Trumpet."

17

✮ ✮ ✮ ✮

THE CHIEF

In its May 11, 1959, cover story, *Time* magazine called him "just the steady old pro the Army needed to get back on solid ground and carry on from there." The *Los Angeles Examiner* enthused editorially that his nomination by the president to become chief of staff was a "superb choice" and that he "could not have named a better man."[1] The future that had been forecast for General Lemnitzer at least ten years before had arrived.

He was typically matter-of-fact about the *Time* article, which was set off by a striking artist's likeness of him painted against a backdrop of leveled rifle bayonets and an Army missile. "By now you know that I finally did make this week's issue of *Time*," he wrote to his brother. "I am glad that it finally came out because sometimes it happens that after all the work is put into the preparation of a story other more newsworthy events come along and the subject gets pushed off the cover and out of the magazine. This is precisely what happened to General Collins when he was chief of staff. Although he was chief for four years he never did get such coverage."[2]

Earlier, he had written to his brother that although he had been recommended by both McElroy and Brucker to succeed Taylor he was not at all sure that Eisenhower would nominate him. Perhaps a reason for his uncertainty was that, in his own way, he was just as critical of the emphasis on massive retaliation as Taylor was, and there is no reason to doubt that the president knew it. Despite his qualms, Lemnitzer wrote his brother later, he learned that Eisenhower had never had any doubts about selecting him. Lemnitzer made it clear where he stood about Taylor's views during a confirmation hearing before the Senate Armed Services Committee. Asked to spell out the Army's role in the nation's

1959 defense posture, he replied: "To protect people on this earth you need to hold the land with forces on the ground. The addition of nuclear or thermonuclear types of weapons does not in any way replace the requirements for good manpower."[3] The committee gave its unanimous approval to his appointment within five minutes after he left the room. The full Senate endorsed the committee's action by a similar vote.

Congressional concern about the administration's defense priorities was very high during Lemnitzer's tenure as chief of staff, and he frequently found balancing his loyalty to the Army with that due the commander in chief to be sticky going. He wrote Ernest after his brother had sent him an article from the *Newark* (New Jersey) *Sunday News* which read: "The question now being asked around the Pentagon is how long General Lemnitzer, the present chief of staff, will last." Noting that the item had given him "a laugh," the general commented: "I have been involved in some very rugged hearings before seven congressional committees since you sent the clipping and I think about it on each occasion. We have to walk a very narrow path in telling the truth to the various committees and at the same time keep out of trouble with the administration. On several occasions, I had to take issue with decisions that were made by the administration on some of the positions I have made on behalf of the Army. This presents some real problems during congressional hearings when members of the committee ask me, 'What did you recommend, why didn't the secretary of defense approve it, and are you satisfied with the decision?' All of the chiefs of staff are constantly in hot water over the answers they must give to this type of question."[4] Once during a Senate hearing, a senator noted that Eisenhower had just criticized what he termed "parochial" officers who think they know more than their "bosses," and asked Lemnitzer if he felt that military commanders should voice dissent. The general replied that they should express their views to "proper authority."[5]

Despite his policy of speaking his mind, Lemnitzer somehow steered the Army away from becoming ensnarled in the kind of confrontational relationship that his predecessor had with the president and his fellow Chiefs of Staff. An unidentified Defense Department official predicted as the new chief of staff took office: "Lemnitzer isn't a yes man, but you won't see him bucking Ike on policy. He will present his requirements effectively, but he'll accept higher decisions as the final word. He's a team player all the way."[6] Also working for him was his knack for being able to prevail or at least hold his own in a hard-fought dispute over an issue without incurring the enmity of his opponent. A former superior once commented that this ability was partly due to the fact that his positions always seemed so "reasonable." Eisenhower apparently agreed: minutes and memoranda of National Security Council and White House staff conferences show him invariably concurring with positions taken by Lemnitzer.

Still another factor in why he did better than Taylor in getting along with the president was that toward the end of his administration Eisenhower began changing his mind about the importance of conventional forces. General Goodpaster, his former staff secretary, recalls that the president "was almost driven to recognize that there was more to it than just nuclear weapons, that problems were arising in the so-called 'third world' that introduced the requirement for conventional military strength and a conventional military position. And this also existed to a degree in NATO...."[7] Eisenhower's changing attitude was attributed also to Secretary of State Dulles, who had been influential in establishing massive retaliation as the U.S. defense policy early in the Eisenhower administration, but who in 1958 was beginning to believe that it needed to be supplemented by a buildup in conventional capabilities. His rationale was that new developments in Soviet strategic weapons had made U.S. allies skeptical that the United States would actually use its own.[8] There are indications, however, that when Dulles spoke of more reliance on conventional forces he may have been talking about tactical nuclear weapons rather than foot soldiers.

One sign that the president's views were shifting occurred during the National Security Council meeting in which Lemnitzer had successfully beaten back the effort to reduce South Korean armed forces. Eisenhower read a cable received that morning from Averell Harriman in which the veteran presidential envoy reported that he had just had an interview with Khrushchev which he had found "positively terrifying." The Soviet premier, whom Harriman said seemed an even more dangerous enemy than Stalin, had talked threateningly of what he would do if hostilities arose over Berlin or Formosa. He boasted that the Soviet Union had an effective intercontinental ballistic missile (ICBM) whereas the United States did not. He had also bragged that the Soviets had given rockets to China which could destroy the U.S. Seventh Fleet, then in Formosan waters. Eisenhower commented that Khrushchev's tirade was further evidence that the country could not be weak anywhere in the world. An added observation was significant: although the president realized that the nation was trying to match the Soviets in missiles, it could not afford to let itself become weak in other areas of the struggle.[9] This concession did not translate into any appreciable increase in the Army's budget during the rest of Eisenhower's second term, however, and he remained devoted to massive retaliation as the first line of defense. When confronted with the argument that the nation also needed forces to fight a limited war, the president would reply that if the United States had enough power to fight a big war it also had enough for a little one.[10]

Despite the administration's relegation of the Army to what one news magazine termed "stepchild status" among the services, Lemnitzer's regard for his World War II commander bordered on reverence. He admired Eisenhower's strong control of the Department of Defense and his intimate knowledge of its workings. Lemnitzer had been an outspoken critic of massive retaliation from the time it was implemented, and he was on record as a firm supporter of Taylor's concept of flexible response. But the professional soldier is expected to express his reservations on a course of action when it is in the discussion stage, if he has any, but then fully support whatever decision his superior reaches; this procedure was as deeply ingrained in Eisenhower's outlook as it was in Lemnitzer's. And this is just what Lemnitzer did in the case of massive retaliation, although he continued to protest against the Army's diminishing role in defense. When Lemnitzer was serving in Korea, he had expressed dismay that Eisenhower's promise to end the war when he was elected hurried the UN command into making unwise concessions at the peace talks. But he was never known to have criticized Eisenhower himself. A year into his term as chief the general received a note from the president wishing him a happy birthday. The letter Lemnitzer wrote back two days later was what one might have expected from a young captain to a much higher-ranking mentor many years his senior: "... I have always been most thankful that I had the privilege and opportunity to have been associated with you in the early days of World War II when we were preparing for and conducting Allied operations in North Africa, Sicily and Italy. It was a never-to-be-forgotten experience which has been valuable to me in subsequent years. The procedural, organizational and operational principles which you initiated in those turbulent days of 1942–43 have successfully stood the test of war and time and are as sound today as when you established them."[11]

With two years as vice chief behind him, much of it as acting chief, Lemnitzer was off and running in coming to grips with the many problems facing the Army in mid-1959. More than any of the services, the Army's main strength lies in the number of its personnel. Four years before, there were 1,109,000 men and women in its uniformed ranks; when Lemnitzer became chief of staff there were 870,000. No matter what the nature of the world threat, the Army had not been able to increase its share of the defense budget by so much as a percentage point. "We are having a particularly strenuous time this year in hacking out the principal features of the FY 61 budget," a frustrated Lemnitzer wrote to a friend a month after taking office. "DoD [Department of Defense] has given us practically no guidance except that each of the services must budget on their end FY 59 strengths and the FY 60 budget. There is practically no semblance of a requirements budget left in the process. We object strongly to the freezing of our resources in the pattern that has prevailed since 1954, i.e. 23% of the DoD budget. Our problem is particularly complicated by the high cost of the Nike-Zeus program [an antiballistic missile (ABM)]. I must say, however, that our efforts to get out of the straitjacket have met with practically no success to date."[12] Nor did the percentage change during Lemnitzer's tenure. One of the Army's goals when he was chief was to raise the active total to 925,000, but when he left office the authorized strength still stood at 870,000, and the service had lost another division, cutting its size to fourteen operational divisions. The authorized Army National Guard strength stayed steady at 400,000 and the Army Reserve at 200,000, whereas the civilian work force decreased slightly to 390,000.[13]

The services were the target in early 1960 of a series of hearings by a Senate preparedness subcommittee headed by Lyndon B. Johnson. A highlight of the proceedings was a clash of views on Army readiness between Lemnitzer and his retired former boss, General Taylor. Lemnitzer knew that he was going to be under fire. Before he began to testify at the various defense hearings scheduled by both houses of Congress that year, he wrote to former Army Secretary Stevens: "Practically every member of the committees before which I will appear has a copy of Max's book and no doubt I will be called upon to discuss practically every question raised therein which, of course, I am prepared to do."[14]

Taylor asserted in his testimony that the United States was in danger of falling far behind the Soviet Union within a year unless the defense budget was increased from the $41 billion allotted for Fiscal Year 1961 to from $50 billion to $55 billion for the next five years. He charged that civilian budget makers had usurped JCS decision making, called for an overhaul of the country's strategy-making machinery, and said that the long-range missile force was too small and of uncertain reliability. Major reliance on weapons of massive retaliation was no longer justified, he contended, because there now was a greater danger of limited war than general war. Lemnitzer conceded that the Army did not get all it wanted in the military budget for the coming year, but he told the senators: "Assuming that we carry out military progress at the present rate, we will have the capability of deterring general or limited war for the next two or three years." Lemnitzer termed himself "satisfied" with the administration's decision to give the Army only $43 million of the $382 million Congress had appropriated to the services for weapons modernization.[15]

In its conclusions, the subcommittee called for a military force capable of defeating an enemy "through the entire spectrum of warfare from limited war in its many forms to global all-out nuclear warfare." The report also criticized the slowness with which the leanly funded Army was getting new weapons into the hands of troops. These included the M-14 rifle, the M-60 machine gun, the 90-millimeter recoilless rifle, the M-113 armored personnel carrier, the M-60 main battle tank, and the 105-millimeter self-propelled howitzer. The subcommittee's concern gave added impetus to efforts to field these items, along with the UH-1A Iroquois (Huey) helicopter of later Vietnam fame, during Lemnitzer's tenure. The Senate group noted that the United States had 870,000 active Army troops and 175,000 Marines against the Soviet Union's 2,700,000 ground troops, and that the Soviets had completed the re-equipping of these forces with modern individual weapons.[16]

Lemnitzer became incensed after the hearings when a New York Times reporter wrote that the chief of staff had been taken to task by Senator Johnson for not having fought hard enough for greater Army funding. The general called the accusation "completely false" and, backed by senators who had been at the hearing, complained to the newspaper's editors. As Lemnitzer told it later, the reporter had not been at the session at which Johnson was supposed to have admonished him and had relied on information given to him by someone who supposedly had been there. The reporter straightened out the record to Lemnitzer's satisfaction in a later article, a development which had the general crowing happily to friends afterward that this was the first time anyone with whom he had talked about the matter could remember *The Times* ever publishing such a "retraction."[17] His only gripe was that whereas the first story was on the front page, the corrected version was buried inside.

Three months after Lemnitzer became chief of staff, Eisenhower undid what had been perhaps the general's most significant achievement as vice chief: von Braun and his team of scientists were transferred to NASA, along with some more of the Army's ballistic missile functions. But Lemnitzer professed not to be dismayed, contending that he did not expect the decision to have any effect on the Army's missile program. "We have not been in the big missile [function] for a long time and were merely doing work for other agencies of government," he wrote to his son. "This decision will merely put all of the big boosters talent under NASA. One of the great criticisms here in Washington is that no single agency has been responsible for big booster development. . . . They have the ball now and the resources. They won't be able to alibi any more if they are unable to do some catching up on the Russians."[18]

Lemnitzer might have been able to roll with this new punch, but one of the other principal warriors in the fight to keep von Braun and the original Huntsville missile responsibilities would not. In 1960, General Medaris—then chief of the U.S. Army Ordnance Missile Command, successor to the Army Ballistic Missile Agency—retired in disgust. The same year he finished *Countdown for Decision*, which took sharp issue with the administration for, among other things, taking the Army out of space exploration and otherwise reducing its role in missile development. As in the cases of Taylor, Gavin, and Ridgway, the Medaris attacks stung the president, and during a conference with Gen. Nathan F. Twining, chairman of the JCS, Eisenhower directed him to look into the legal aspects of a retired officer writing such a highly critical book. Eisenhower cited the previous cases of two other generals whom he said had been informed that they would be "fired" from their retired status unless they toned down the virulence of their criticism of the government. He ordered Twining, who wholeheartedly agreed with the president's reasoning, to discuss the matter with Defense Secretary Gates and then bring it to the attention of the U.S. attorney general.[19] Retired military personnel are subject to recall to active duty and thus can be court-martialed for violations of military laws, just as they could while in uniform. Criticizing the president and other superiors, as Medaris did in his book, could constitute violations and thus trigger application of this rarely used aspect of military retirement. Nothing ever came of the inquiry, and Medaris went into private business, later becoming an Episcopal priest and eventually an archdeacon in the Anglican Church.

Lemnitzer never made any secret of his approval of the flexible response concept, although for some reason it was a term he did not like and even banned from use when he became supreme allied commander in Europe. His own favorite buzzword while he was chief of staff was "forward strategy," which he defined as "a plan to dispose our military power so that we, together with our allies, could meet and repel promptly Communist military aggression if it occurred along the periphery of the free world, as well as anywhere else it might occur. Preparations to execute this strategy include, among other measures, the positioning of military forces overseas, together with the development of a capability to project our military power rapidly to areas beyond our borders when it becomes necessary."[20] In the late 1950s, 40 percent of the Army's strength and half of its operational forces were deployed overseas.

In outlining an Army role that clearly was at odds with the New Look, the general declared that limited war was more likely to occur than general war. He saw a limited conflict as raising two major requirements: "The first is for quick reaction to enemy aggression so as to limit the extent of his gains. The second . . . is for means to apply that degree of force needed to defeat the enemy without inflicting undue losses on noncombatants or risking expansion of the war into a worldwide conflagration. Versatile, dual-capable ground forces which can fight either nuclear or nonnuclear war are especially well-fitted to fulfill this second requirement. This is because they can employ a variety of types of force against an enemy appropriate to the occasion. In other words, they can exterminate the rats without destroying the neighborhood infested by the rats."[21]

Despite his dismay over what the New Look was doing to the Army's role in defense, Lemnitzer never lost any of his high regard for Eisenhower. If the president was convinced that massive retaliation was the best course for the country, a soldier's job was to do his best to make it work. Eisenhower expressed consternation when his son John once told him about the depth of the Army's resentment over the low priority assigned to it in the New Look; "He thought they would see the big picture," the son recalled.[22] It was a point of view that Lemnitzer, the pragmatist, understood and could live with. As its chief of staff, Lemnitzer had an important responsibility to speak up for the Army, but much more than service loyalty was involved: he considered the New Look a poor defense posture and said so while carrying out his responsibility to help implement it.

As careful as the president was in selecting his service chiefs and as much as he wanted them to share his strategic and organizational convictions, he never quite attained their unqualified cooperation during his years in the White House. The exceptions were the JCS chairmen—Radford and Twining—and usually the Air Force chief, all of whom shared his strategic views. While Eisenhower wanted to politicize the Chiefs and secure their support of his strategic policies in their corporate capacities as members of the JCS, they regarded themselves as professionals and apolitical. "Eisenhower was asking too much," wrote Douglas Kinnard, a university professor and author. "A service chief can never adopt such an approach (unless his service views coincide with the administration's) and still remain a chief. Paul Hammond has put it well: 'A service chief remains in control of his service only so long as he maintains its confidence; and nothing can cause the loss of that confidence faster than his abandonment of the role of service spokesman in the JCS.'"[23]

The president was a master of organization, an ability that is ingrained in the professional soldier and, in Eisenhower's case, honed to a high degree by such experiences as his command of allied forces in World War II. There was never any doubt among his generals and military executives as to the extent of their authority, and when they wandered away he would rein them in, in very positive terms. Goodpaster recalled that he would say, "Now, wait, my boys. That's not a staff matter; that's a policy matter. If we're going to consider that, I want it brought before the NSC or the cabinet. Or I want to take that up with the Secretary [of Defense]." On the other hand, he did not want nonprofessionals influencing military decisions. "Where military strategy and operational issues were involved," Goodpaster said, "he always wanted to talk to the chiefs, to the chairman of the Joint Chiefs, not to the civilian leadership in the Pentagon."[24]

The Army's active and reserve component divisions had completed the changeover to the pentomic mode when the service shifted gears again in still another twist in what seemed to be a constant state of reorganization. Out went Taylor's answer to the atomic battlefield and in came a substitute with the ungainly name of Reorganization Objective Army Divisions (ROAD). The ROAD division was structured along the lines of the triangular World War II division (infantry, armor, and artillery), with added features to give it more mobility and versatility than its wartime cousin.

The Army's doctrine of forward strategy depended strongly upon being able to move forces quickly to where they were needed. This required a long-range airlift capability that the services lacked. In pressing his argument for improvements before the other chiefs, Lemnitzer pointed out that with the current resources, it would take a week just to assemble the planes necessary to fly a single battalion and its equipment into the Caribbean. It is interesting to note that one of the chief opponents of his efforts to improve the Army's airlift capability was West Point classmate Thomas D. White, Air Force chief of staff. White, whose service was getting twice as much of the defense budget as the Army, was a fierce proponent of air power who shared the aviator's traditional disdain for ferrying troops.

When Lemnitzer was unable to get any support from the JCS and the Defense Department, he took his case to Congress. The result was the creation of a subcommittee to study the airlift problem. The group, headed by Rep. L. Mendel Rivers, South Carolina Democrat, met nearly every day for two months, and Lemnitzer attended every meeting. His determination and conduct at the hearings drew high praise from Robert W. Smart, chief counsel of the House Committee on Armed Services: "While you would be the last to acknowledge it, I am totally convinced that your high degree of interest in the hearings, your outstanding participation as an informed and objective witness, and your continuing presence throughout all of the military proceedings, placed a high degree of character on the proceedings and removed them far beyond the realm of political partisanship or single-service interest."[25] As a result of the study, Congress appropriated a billion dollars for airlift research and development. The product of this effort led Rivers afterward to call Lemnitzer the "father of the C-141," the workhorse transport plane which for years was the mainstay of U.S. troop deployment.[26]

Thanks to roots that took hold more than thirty-five years before, when he was one of the Army's top marksmen, Lemnitzer always had a special interest in shooting and that most basic of infantry weapons, the rifle. When he became chief the Army was still using the World War II-vintage M-1 Garand, a heavy, cumbersome weapon which had been one of the world's best in its heyday but was now obsolete when compared with the lighter, faster-firing rifles being used by communist forces. The Army had begun fielding the M-14, a light, automatic, 7.62-millimeter rifle that was more in the same league with weapons being carried by Soviet ground forces. Lemnitzer began pushing hard to get it into the hands of troops as soon as he took office. A *Parade* magazine cover of the time shows him standing in his office holding an M-14, his chest below his ribbons displaying his rarely worn Distinguished Marksman's Badge. (When the magazine's photographer had wanted the general to pose with the rifle, a spirited search turned up the embarrassing fact that in the entire Pentagon, the world's largest military headquarters, not a single M-14 could be found. The general's staff finally obtained one from nearby Fort Myer.)[27]

A military policy based on the assumption that a war between the world's great powers will involve long-range atomic missiles is more than just a matter between uniformed armies. Civil defense was a major national concern in the 1960s as the country sought means of survival in the event of a Soviet ICBM attack on the continental United States. Shelters, both individual and public, were built across the country and provisioned so that those who survived the blasts could outlast the atomic fallout outside. There was no question in the minds of the public that many thousands, even millions, of civilians would die in a nuclear attack; what was not clear was how order would be restored afterward. As late as 1960, military planners pegged this aspect of an atomic war to the vague hope that someone else (presumably civil authorities) would deal with the domestic chaos that would follow the widespread ruin caused by an atomic missile. Mark S. Watson, military correspondent for the *Baltimore Sun*, wrote that "observation over recent years has banished any such hope from the minds of thoughtful people at the Pentagon."[28] Lemnitzer led the Army into this vacuum in 1960 when he announced that his service would assume a major role in restoring order after an attack and in returning as much normalcy as possible in civilian regions. The chief of staff stated: "As proved by the handling of lesser peacetime disasters over and over again, the surest means of broad-scale relief and recovery is the nation's military organization—organized, disciplined and of all establishments the best equipped for that urgent responsibility."[29]

The Army was responsible for continental air defense out to a hundred miles (where the Air Force took over), and Lemnitzer placed a high priority on development of an antimissile missile during his tenure. If the Soviets were to develop such a weapon and the United States did not, he reasoned, the nation would be at a serious military disadvantage in the event of a Communist first strike because the Soviets could defend against a U.S. retaliatory strike. Efforts to develop the Nike-Zeus ABM were sped up while he was chief of staff.

Lemnitzer got along well with the press, especially in one-on-one situations and in press conferences where his candor and ability to think on his feet were impressive. He was always relaxed, had a good sense of humor, and he admired and trusted professionals like Hanson Baldwin, military editor of *The New York Times*. But he didn't always understand why members of the media did what they did sometimes. A case in point was their handling of what he considered one of the JCS's most important accomplishments during his time as Army chief. One of the most divisive disputes within the JCS in this period was the role of the various services in strategic nuclear operations. It was an enormously complex issue involving mostly the Air Force and the Navy. The squabble had been going on for months and had been narrowed down to some twenty questions which, if answered, would have broken the impasse. But the JCS couldn't reach an agreement on any of them. Finally, Lemnitzer convened the Chiefs and the services' unified commanders from around the world at the headquarters of the Strategic Air Command (SAC) at Omaha, Nebraska, to try to thrash out a solution. Such a concentration of brass attracted the attention of the press, but all the Chiefs could say was that they were discussing some important defense issues. The areas of disagreement were reduced during intense, often-heated debate and then turned over to Defense Secretary Gates for decisions. He made them on the spot, they were accepted by the Chiefs with the concurrence of the unified commanders, and the result was the Single Integrated Operational Plan (SIOP). Aside from its importance to the nation's defense posture in the dangerous nuclear age, the plan was remarkable in that it represented a coming together of minds at a time when complete agreement between the services on any issue was a rarity.

Gates and Lemnitzer telephoned the president, who listened to their account of the agreement's terms and the discussion that went into them. Eisenhower then said: "Add my name to the list of approvals. It's approved by the commander in chief." The JCS issued a news release spelling out the plan's details and emphasizing that all parties were unanimous in approving it. "We came back and expected it to be headlined in the Washington and New York papers—all the papers," Lemnitzer recalled. "But there was not a single word in any newspaper about it. I think maybe it was explained in the Omaha papers." The general called the experience one of the "greatest lessons in press relations I ever learned. The conclusion I came to about there being nothing in the papers was because [the plan] was something we agreed to and there was no dissent. If there had been a lot of controversy and people were tearing each other up we'd have made the headlines in every paper in the country."[30]

Lemnitzer was nonpartisan to a fault regarding party politics—even his immediate family didn't know how he voted, although after he retired he registered as a Republican. But being apolitical in his professional life didn't mean that he was not keenly interested in how the political winds were blowing and who was going to be in power in Washington after a national election. In the summer of 1960, he wrote his son, then a captain commanding an Honest John missile battery with the 1st Cavalry Division in Korea: "I attempted to stay up to see all of the activities of the Democratic convention because I wanted to be thoroughly familiar with everything that took place, inasmuch as those of us in the JCS may have to deal with some of the commitments that were made. The late hours due to the convention being on the West Coast really wore me down. I am glad that the Republican convention will be two hours earlier."[31]

In his next letter to his son, he wrote: "Well, the Democratic convention is over and the ticket is [John F.] Kennedy and [Lyndon B.] Johnson, which is not a surprise to many people. There were doubts that Johnson would accept the nomination for vice president because of reported statements that he felt that he has a more important job as Senate majority leader. Next week, the scene changes to Chicago where it looks like Nixon is a sure pick."[32] (Richard M. Nixon was nominated for president and Henry Cabot Lodge for vice president.)

One day during the next month, Lemnitzer, who was rarely ill, had stayed home to recover from a severe summer cold when the telephone rang in his rooms at Fort Myer's Quarters One. The caller was Col. Orwin C. Talbott, the general's executive officer, who had just received a call from the White House. The president wanted to see him the next morning. Still feeling miserable, Lemnitzer bundled up and rode to the White House with Talbott. On the way, he worried aloud about why he was summoned and looked anxious as he entered the executive mansion. But when he emerged from his meeting with Eisenhower a while later, he was "bouncy" and smiling, according to Talbott. He said nothing about what had happened at the meeting, however, and some weeks later when it was announced that Lemnitzer had been nominated to become chairman of the JCS, Talbott asked him if the president had broken the news that day at the White House. The general said that he had.

Veteran Washington hand though he was, the Army chief of staff was probably the only person in upper military and congressional circles who had any doubt that he would be the first Army general since Omar Bradley to head the Joint Chiefs. In a letter to his brother, he wrote: "As you now know, the president sent my nomination to the Senate last night, so the information is now official after many months of rumors. I have had no word from the Senate Armed Services Committee, which is charged with considering the nomination and before which I shall probably have to appear when they consider it. I know and have a high regard for most of the members of the committee and have always gotten along well with them whenever I have appeared before them. This occasion could be quite different in view of the political tensions [probably the spirited presidential election campaign of that year] but I have enough confidence in the committee to believe that they will not make an appointment such as chairman of the Joint Chiefs of Staff a political football."[33]

Afterward, he reported the questioning by the committee as "very thorough" and without "even one minor note of politics."[34] He was confirmed without trouble, and on October 1 he succeeded General Twining. It was the first time since 1953 that the JCS had a chairman who was not a vigorous supporter of massive retaliation. His confirmation prompted an editorial in the *Los Angeles Times* which headlined, "Who Envies Gen. Lemnitzer?" and began:

"The most important military job in the world was taken over last week by Gen. Lyman L. Lemnitzer, the new chairman of the Joint Chiefs of Staff. A man highly regarded among service and civilian officials for his fairness, diplomatic skill and incisive mind, Gen. Lemnitzer in the years to come may be required to face some of the most critical problems and decisions ever presented to a military planner." The editorial went on to assert that the nation was falling "dangerously behind" in its power to wage strategic and limited war, and that the fielding of new weapons was lagging because of "interservice squabbles, bureaucratic dominance, and political boondoggling." Touching upon a long list of other deficiencies, the editorial put the blame on "the proliferation of bookkeepers, bureaucrats and assistants to assistants who have replaced the leaders and strategists as key men in the defense program."

The editorial writer concluded: "No one expects that the mess can be straightened out in a short time, or that one man can do the job, least of all a military man in a field legally under civilian control. But Gen. Lemnitzer brings to the chairmanship of the JCS the prestige and respect which might be the biggest factor in shaking the Congress, the executive and the office of the secretary of defense into action. His task is not an enviable one. It is made even more trying by the fact that time is rapidly running out."[35]

The service chiefs when Lemnitzer took over were the Army's Decker, who had been Lemnitzer's vice chief of staff; reappointees Burke and White; and recent appointee Gen. David M. Shoup, commandant of the Marine Corps. Although the Chiefs had the right to go individually to the president if they chose, Eisenhower routinely dealt only with the chairman on matters involving the JCS. He was expected to speak for the JCS and to keep the commander in chief informed on each service chief's views. The chairman also represented the JCS at meetings of the National Security Council, although all of the Chiefs frequently attended when important issues were on the agenda. Under the Defense Reorganization Act of 1958, the Chiefs were required to reply fully and frankly to questions when testifying before a congressional committee, whether or not their answers coincided with official positions of the Department of Defense. In matters like the budget, Eisenhower often met with all the Chiefs, as he did one memorable time during Lemnitzer's membership when the president was spending a golfing vacation at Augusta, Georgia. In budget discussions there are issues that can only be decided by the president, so the Chiefs and the secretary of defense flew down to submit the final recommendations and sticking points for decisions. Eisenhower issued these in what Lemnitzer recalled as "rapid-fire order," so much so that the Chiefs were able to get in a round of golf at the Augusta National Golf Course before returning to Washington. Eisenhower, an avid golfer, was unable to play with them because of an attack of bursitis, prompting the Chiefs to joke among themselves that the speed with which the president had rendered his decisions earlier was not attributable to the merits involved but to the bursitis.[36]

Individually and as a corporate body, the Chiefs commanded nothing but their staffs, their principal function being as a group to provide advice to the president in his role as commander in chief and to the secretary of defense. As the JCS, they also functioned as a kind of committee inserted between the secretary and the nation's unified and specified commands to advise him, provide staff assistance, and, when authorized by the secretary, to issue orders to the commands in his name.[37] Taylor, who would become chairman after Lemnitzer, believed that the officer in that position should be sympathetic to the military policy of whatever administration was in office.[38] Lemnitzer disagreed in a letter written years after his retirement: "I feel very strongly that the chairman (or the other chiefs) should not be changed when the political administrations change. . . . Such action would deeply politicize the military and we would have Republican generals and admirals and Democratic generals and admirals à la the banana republics of Latin and Central America and Africa." He added his conviction that the election of a new political leadership is not intended to change the nation's military leadership "which is and always should be responsive to the political leadership elected by the people."[39]

During the four months Lemnitzer served under Eisenhower as chairman, an increasing proportion of their official dealings was consumed by an area of the world whose troubles would eventually drag the United States into the century's most divisive war. The region, of course, was Indochina, the target since the early 1950s of a determined Communist drive to conquer a vast peninsula, which was just gaining its freedom after years of French and Japanese domination. After the Communist defeat of the French at Dien Bien Phu in 1954, the Geneva Accords of the same year created Laos, Cambodia, and a Vietnam divided at the seven-teenth parallel with a Communist government in the north and a republican one in the south—the division to last until elections, which never took place.

The first fighting in a conflict that eventually engulfed much of the peninsula occurred in Laos, where three opposing factions were fighting each other for control. The United States, chiefly through the CIA, was backing a right-wing strong man named Phoumi Nosavan while seeking the ouster of Prince Souvanna Phouma, the Laotian ruler and a neutralist whom the United States thought was too close to the third faction, the communist Pathet Lao. Backed by heavy military and technical assistance from the Soviet Union, communist China, and North Vietnam, the Pathet Lao steadily pushed back opposing forces and by early 1961 controlled most of the country. The situation was of deep concern to the Eisenhower administration, which had given massive aid to the anticommunist government forces in keeping with U.S. policy to contain communist expansion in Southeast Asia. A month before Eisenhower left office, Phouma, under heavy pressure from the United States to leave office and in trouble militarily and politically in his own country, fled to Thailand. The military leader of his neutralist forces, Kong Le, then joined the Pathet Lao to fight against General Phoumi's army.

The ominous rumblings in Indochina were being heard by senior military and other government leaders long before Pathet Lao forces began closing in. In mid-1954, when he was deputy chief of staff for plans and research, Lemnitzer wrote his son: "The Indochina situation has been causing us a lot of pain. The situation looks quite sour out there and the outlook is not too good."[40] This was the year in which the United States and six other nations—France, Great Britain, Australia, New Zealand, Pakistan, and the Philippines—established the Southeast Asia Treaty Organization (SEATO). In a separate protocol, the United States extended SEATO protection to Laos, Cambodia, and South Vietnam, establishing the latter as an independent noncommunist state in defiance of the Geneva Accords. Although Eisenhower avoided the direct use of American force during this period, the United States helped the budding nation with military and economic aid, technical assistance, and covert operations. At the same time, the administration also extended its support to its prime minister, Ngo Dinh Diem, one of the most controversial figures in the long series of moves leading up to American troop involvement in the Vietnam War.

Now, in 1960, a thorny prelude to this commitment was being played out in the final days of the Eisenhower administration; when U.S. forces finally entered South Vietnam in strength, Lemnitzer would be stationed on the other side of the world but right then he was the president's chief adviser on military operations and a participant in all White House talks about the worsening situation in Laos. Despite his strong reluctance to use U.S. military force, three weeks before he was to leave office the president told a meeting of top military, State Department, and

Central Intelligence Agency (CIA) advisers that the United States could not stand by and permit Laos to fall to the Communists. The time could come when the country would have to bring up its Seventh Fleet with its complement of Marines. Lemnitzer told the meeting that U.S. military forces in the region had been placed on readiness "Condition Two," meaning an alert in place. Ready to go into Laos when the president gave the word, he said, were the Army's 503rd Airborne Battle Group on Okinawa, and a Seventh Fleet task force consisting of the aircraft carrier *Lexington*, a helicopter carrier, and one thousand four hundred Marines.[41] A condition of committing these armed elements and others available in the region was that the United States would have to prove open intervention by forces of another nation, such as bordering nations Red China and North Vietnam. This was something that it had not been able to do despite Lemnitzer's comment that the movement of troop columns on the country's fringes should be sufficient (he estimated that 80 to 90 percent of the in-country communist forces were Pathet Lao with a hard core of noncommissioned officers and technicians sent in by Viet Minh forces in North Vietnam). The general also felt that Soviet airlifts had to be stopped because Pathet Lao units could not function without aerial resupply. He suggested the use of B-26 bombers when Eisenhower raised the possibility of destroying the airfield being used by the Russian planes.

U.S. forces were not committed. Still determined to head off a Communist takeover by peaceful means, the president charted a course consisting of seeking stronger French and British support of the U.S. position, alerting the SEATO Council to the danger in Laos, and placing U.S. forces in a state of readiness that would maximize their ability to intervene. He also directed that the U.S. ambassador in Moscow inform Khrushchev that this country viewed the situation in Laos with "grave concern" and was redeploying its forces to ensure that the legitimate Laotian government would not be destroyed. In one of his last comments on the subject as president, he told Lemnitzer and other advisers as they left the room after a meeting at the White House that Laos could not be allowed to fall to the Communists, even if it meant war.[42] But the Laotian struggle would become the problem of a new administration in a few days. Just before Kennedy was inaugurated, he and Eisenhower met and Southeast Asia was one of the major topics. The president told his successor that North Vietnam was building up its forces and that the situation in Laos was "very, very dangerous," not only for Laos but for South Vietnam.[43]

The transition was the main topic of conversation during Eisenhower's weekly meetings with the JCS chairman as his remaining time in office dwindled to days. At their January 11 meeting, they discussed the issues Lemnitzer should raise in a pre-inauguration briefing that he had offered to give to the president-elect to inform him about such things as the locations of secret command shelters, to outline emergency procedures, and to answer any questions he might have. The chairman also briefed the incoming secretary of defense, Robert S. McNamara, and his deputy, Roswell Gilpatric, reporting to Eisenhower afterward that he thought they were now aware of "what they will be taking on in the way of operational responsibility on January 20." He added that "both expressed themselves as tremendously reassured to know of the arrangements that have been in effect." The president commented that Lemnitzer should stress to the new defense officials that the secrets they had just learned had to be guarded carefully.[44]

Lemnitzer remarked at the meeting that the new administration's staffing of top Pentagon positions seemed well advanced, but that it was having a "terrible time" finding a secretary of the Army. He told the president that General Gavin had been under consideration and that Kennedy may, in fact, have already decided upon him. Eisenhower—who had never forgiven Gavin for going public with his criticism of massive retaliation after he retired—expressed "very great concern" over this possibility and said that if there was any way of preventing Gavin's appointment this should be done. He regarded the former general as a maverick and remarked that one benefit of his selection would be that the Joint Chiefs would be forced to work closer together to avoid "improper secretarial action."[45] The post went to Elvis J. Stahr, Jr., a lawyer, Rhodes Scholar, and president of the University of West Virginia, and Gavin became the U.S. ambassador to France.

It had been a long time since Eisenhower had worn a uniform, and his stern treatment of his former service had alienated many old colleagues and had created an impression that he no longer considered himself a soldier. But his demeanor during the last few days Lemnitzer knew him as president did not fit this picture. "War stories" and nostalgic recollections from the past when all were in uniform together were the main topics of conversation when the president was the guest of honor at a luncheon Lemnitzer hosted for him and the Chiefs. The mood of the occasion was enhanced by the surroundings: the luncheon was held in Lemnitzer's official residence, Quarters One, located at venerable Fort Myer in the Washington suburb of Arlington, Virginia, and once Eisenhower's own quarters when he was Army chief of staff right after World War II. The only serious note in this relaxed gathering of old comrades in arms was Eisenhower's warning in a short talk that the JCS would destroy themselves as an organization if they failed to agree. The president clearly enjoyed himself, telling the chairman at his last weekly meeting with him that he had "tremendously enjoyed" the occasion and, in fact, could not remember when he had enjoyed one more. He told Lemnitzer that it came as "quite a shock" to him to realize that he was breaking his association with the JCS for the first time since 1945, even maintaining ties when he was president of Columbia University. As the meeting ended, he expressed the hope that Congress would give him back his rank of general of the Army.[46] It did.

In his final report to his departing commander in chief, Lemnitzer said that the Joint Chiefs constituted a "truly vital carryover" in the change of administrations.

Young officials, able but of limited service, are coming in, he said, and the Chiefs would be able to help them greatly while they were getting themselves informed.[47]

It was a noble ambition, but if the JCS chairman ever had occasion to recall his remark after the year ahead it might well have been with a rueful smile.

18

★ ★ ★ ★

BOPO

The paper's title was provocative: "The Decline and Fall of the Joint Chiefs of Staff." Written by an Army major as a thesis for a master's degree at the Naval War College, it assigned a substantial share of the blame for this alleged dive from grace to the infamous Bay of Pigs invasion of Cuba.

In the second chapter, the paper reviewed the JCS role in selecting a landing site and cited a passage from one of the many books written about the fiasco: "The Joint Chiefs . . . agreed that Zapata seemed the best . . . but added softly that they still preferred Trinidad."[1]

A pencil mark extended from the underlined "added softly" to a comment in the bottom margin. It said "Nuts!"

This mild expletive would have had journalists scribbling furiously if it had been uttered at a press conference because the person who penciled it in was General Lemnitzer, who had just strayed briefly from behind a self-lowered curtain of silence surrounding the most trying experience of his career. As it was, he jotted it down as a note to himself while obliging a young officer who had asked him to read his paper and comment.

The recently retired general went no further in this instance, but "Nuts!" and worse must have frequently come to mind during the early months of 1961 when the Kennedy administration was planning and then executing a bizarre attempt to overthrow Cuban Dictator Fidel Castro.

The expedition is known in history books as the Bay of Pigs invasion. Officially, it was referred to as Operation Pluto. The government staffers who followed it through its convolutions called it BOPO (Bay of Pigs Operation).

Cuba became a U.S. problem in early 1959 after a revolution that toppled

Premier Fulgencio Batista from office and brought Castro to power. The large island off Florida's coast, once a staunch U.S. friend, quickly became Communist and the government increasingly anti-American. Castro expropriated U.S. property, established strong economic and other ties with the Soviet Union, and boasted of his plans to spread Communism throughout Latin America. Relations with the United States rapidly worsened, and in his last month in office Eisenhower severed diplomatic relations.

In March of the previous year, the president had launched a paramilitary campaign patterned after one which had driven a pro-Communist regime from power in Guatemala. Intended to bring about the same fate for the Castro regime, the program included sabotage, the infiltration of anticommunist exiles into Cuba, U-2 spy plane surveillance, and the parachuting of arms and supplies to guerrilla groups already operating from strongholds in the country's Escambray Mountains. When these forces were strong enough, the plan envisioned, they would overthrow Castro and install a provisional democratic government.

The CIA was in charge of these activities under the overall direction of a super-secret coordinating body known as the "Special Group" (also the 5412 Committee) which was made up of men from the highest levels of the State and Defense departments, the CIA, and Eisenhower's National Security Affairs office. The range of options discussed was wide and included such measures as Castro's assassination.

Despite these efforts, Castro's political and military power continued to grow and the Special Group became progressively less confident that the dictator could be beaten with guerrillas alone. These forces needed help, and it was then that the United States turned to Brigade 2506.

This unit, named after the serial number of a member who had died during training, was an amphibious and airborne assault force of anti-Castro Cubans which had been assembled in Guatemala to train for an invasion of Cuba. Well equipped and intensely motivated, the brigade was made up largely of civilians who had left their country when Castro came to power. Those in its ranks came from many walks of life and included students, professional people, farmers, skilled and unskilled workers, businessmen, and a few former members of Batista's armed forces. Their instructors were mostly U.S. military personnel who had been loaned to the CIA by the Defense Department.

Three months after Kennedy took office, the brigade's one thousand four hundred fighting men landed at the Bay of Pigs (*Bahía de Cochinos*) on Cuba's swampy Zapata Peninsula. They fought valiantly and well against vastly larger forces led personally by Castro, but by the end of the third day the brigade ceased to exist as a combat unit. Most of its members were taken prisoner and more than a hundred were killed, ending one of the most humiliating episodes in U.S. history.

The valor of the assault force was a rare positive note in an operation which embodied, to an astonishing degree, the fatalist notion that if anything can go wrong in an endeavor it will. Miscalculation, ineptitude, abysmal coordination and leadership at all levels, misplaced priorities, execrable communication, ignorance, and appalling luck all played parts in this textbook example of what not to do when one nation means another harm.

Before the last report was written and the final hearing held, two U.S. senators would call for Lemnitzer's scalp, and the standing of the powerful group he headed would sink to the lowest level in its existence—especially with the president of the United States. Curiously, Kennedy, the person who took the blame for the comedy of foul-ups, emerged more popular with the public than before and, except for an internal shake-up at the top, the agency in charge was relatively unscathed.

The invasion began in the early morning of April 17 and soon after it was smothered by Castro forces, the JCS chairman left Washington on a long-scheduled trip to various world capitals. When he returned, his colleagues were still fuming among themselves over reports from administration insiders that Kennedy was faulting the Joint Chiefs for not having been more forceful about their reservations in regard to the invasion planning. There had been criticism in the press and even an attempt by presidential partisans to put a major share of the blame on the JCS. The president was indeed unhappy with the Chiefs, but no more so than with the CIA and some others involved. He publicly assumed full responsibility for everything that happened.

The atmosphere was grim when Lemnitzer arrived to preside over his first JCS meeting since coming back from overseas. He told his colleagues that he had met with nearly all the chiefs of state of the nation's allies during his trip and that they were not disturbed over the invasion or its failure, but were distressed over the dissension it had fomented within the U.S. government.

"I do not see how the JCS can tell its side of the story without adding to that dissension," he was reported to have said, "and I can't see how adding to the dissension can possibly be other than harmful to the national interest. Brickbats are a hazard in our profession; therefore, we will not make any statements concerning our position in this matter.

"And, gentlemen, you may regard this as an order."[2]

A chairman did not have command authority over the Chiefs, but the forcefulness of Lemnitzer's leadership and his good sense broke the tension and nipped any thoughts of going public with the JCS side of the Bay of Pigs disaster. It was a commitment that was honored by everyone in the room, and no one was more faithful to this unspoken pledge than Lemnitzer, who went to his grave without ever publicly expressing his feelings about Kennedy's Cuban misadventure.

The general had high-level backing. Indeed, Kennedy's order to those involved to put the failed operation behind them by saying as little as possible about it could well have been the impetus behind his admonition to the other Chiefs. The president was known to have suspected that the Pentagon was the source of leaks to the press about who was to blame for the failed operation, since the Chiefs themselves were barely mentioned in early stories.[3] It is conceivable that Lemnitzer was called to the Executive Mansion and told to cool it, although it is highly doubtful if the general himself was the source of the alleged leaks.

Throughout the rest of his life, the general was frequently asked to talk about the Bay of Pigs. If the interested party was a journalist, he avoided an answer. There were many letters from private citizens, most expressing the belief that the JCS was not to blame for the fiasco. He wrote to one supporter, a Connecticut woman whom he didn't know: "It is not easy for those who bear high military responsibility to remain silent while faced with ignorant and unfounded criticism. However, I do not think that the national interest is served by prolonging the sorry spectacle of public name-calling to which the country was exposed."[4]

He was somewhat less circumspect with friends like retired Army Gen. I. D. White, who had asked him to comment on an article someone had written about what had gone wrong in Cuba: "Generally, the article refers to a phase of the Cuban operation that the JCS knew or heard very little about until it was too late. All we knew was that a most important and critical air attack at daylight on the morning of the landing was called off for some unaccountable reason. We were not consulted about it nor were we even told why it was canceled. It was very typical of the way in which the entire operation was handled, or rather mishandled, by those in command and in charge (both of which did not include the JCS, unfortunately)."[5]

To one of his former speechwriters, he wrote after he retired: "The one firm decision that I have made to date is that I will not write my story of the 'Bay of Pigs' as a separate project but will include it in my memoirs."[6]

The general never wrote his memoirs, but he did write an account of the Bay of Pigs, which this book's author found among his personal papers six years after he died. Written in longhand on legal stationery, the account covers fifty-two pages and is written in the third person in a narrative style, which could indicate that he intended it for publication, perhaps under a pseudonym, or at least to be read some day to set the record straight. Entitled "The Cuban Debacle," it is undated and unsigned, but that it is in Lemnitzer's handwriting is unmistakable. It has never been published.

The onetime JCS chairman's description of the succession of events from the time Brigade 2506 was conceived until it met disaster along the swampy shores of the Bay of Pigs conforms quite accurately to the most dependable versions that have been published over the years. Much of what has been accepted as the thinking and actions that led up to the invasion is also confirmed in Lemnitzer's account. The new details and observations he suppressed while he was alive do not completely absolve the Chiefs of the principal charge that they did not speak up sharply enough when Cuba was being targeted in 1961. But they make more understandable the reasons why what voices they were allowed to have were not heeded.

Eisenhower maintained after he left the presidency that the Cuban brigade was being trained in case a decision to oust Castro should be made, but that no commitment or understanding to use this force had ever been made by his administration.[7] However, Lemnitzer wrote that in late November 1960, the president "ordered that everything feasible be done to assist the project with all possible urgency." On the day the country ended diplomatic relations with Cuba, January 3, Eisenhower directed that the size of the brigade be increased "as much as possible," and nine days later a "State-Defense Working Group" was created to "assess whatever additional measures might be required."[8] Additional instructors, including thirty-eight members of the U.S. Special Forces (Green Berets), were dispatched to Guatemala to intensify the training and help handle an influx of new recruits.

Eisenhower's order to step up the tempo followed by twelve days a November 17 briefing in which President-elect Kennedy was told of the brigade's existence and purpose by CIA Director Allen Dulles and Richard M. Bissell, Jr., the agency's deputy director for plans who was in charge of the operation. Kennedy must have also given the word to proceed because in December the CIA drafted a plan to land the brigade near the town of Trinidad on Cuba's southern central coast the following March. The force, consisting of from six hundred to seven hundred men, would then move into the nearby Escambray Mountains and act as a catalyst for a general Cuban uprising.

If the invasion was to succeed, the CIA asserted, it would be "inadvisable" for it to take place any later than March 1. One reason was that the government of Guatemala was growing nervous over the presence of the Cuban freedom fighters, and President Miguel Ydigoras Fuentes was pressing for their removal by early March. Another was that the trainees, who had been in camp for months under austere and restrictive conditions, were getting restive, and conditions were ripe for large-scale desertions. Still another factor was the desirability of avoiding Cuba's rainy season, which begins in May and would have handicapped both air and ground operations.

Finally, the United States would have to strike soon if it were to be able to deal with Castro before he became too strong to halt by a paramilitary operation alone. To the threat posed by the large quantities of medium and heavy tanks, artillery, and other military supplies already sent to Cuba by the Communist bloc nations was added the imminent likelihood that it was going to have an all-weather jet intercept capability. New Soviet fighter planes were believed to have been delivered and still in crates, their deployment awaiting only the one hundred or so Cuban pilots who were about to complete their flight training in Czechoslovakia.[9]

The Joint Chiefs became involved January 11 when Maj. Gen. Charles H. Bonesteel III, Lemnitzer's special assistant, and Brig. Gen. David W. Gray, chief of the JCS's Joint Subsidiary Activities Division, were given a full briefing by the

CIA on where matters stood on plans to overthrow Castro. Gray, whose Joint Staff section was responsible for liaison on sensitive matters between the JCS, CIA, FBI, and other agencies, prepared a report reflecting the JCS views. The gist was that the only course of action that was certain of success would require overt U.S. military intervention, either unilaterally or in conjunction with Cuban volunteer forces.

Two days after Kennedy's inauguration, Lemnitzer and Dulles met with senior cabinet officers, with the JCS chairman presenting a "concept of operations" report outlining seven options for dealing with Castro: assorted nonmilitary pressures, an internal uprising, a Cuban volunteer invasion force with covert U.S. support, the employment of guerrilla forces with covert U.S. support, an invasion by Cuban volunteers backed by overt U.S. support, a U.S. invasion supported by Latin-American volunteers, and a unilateral U.S. invasion.

Five days later, the Chiefs sent to McNamara a paper recommending "forceful action" to prevent Cuba from going completely Communist, an eventuality which the paper stated would have "disastrous consequences" for the hemisphere. The primary U.S. objective should be Castro's "speedy overthrow," the statement said, followed by the establishment of a friendly government.

The JCS paper was critical of the CIA's Trinidad plan because it did not provide for U.S. direct action that might be needed to avert failure, nor did it include follow-up efforts to exploit success.[10]

The next day the new president presided over what Lemnitzer termed a "seminal" meeting on the Castro problem, attended by Vice President Lyndon B. Johnson; Rusk; McNamara; McGeorge Bundy, Kennedy's special assistant for national security; Paul Nitze, assistant defense secretary for international security affairs; Lemnitzer; and Dulles.

At the meeting, the CIA director outlined his agency's activities in combating Communist domination in Cuba. His report that there had been a great increase in popular opposition to Castro's regime was received skeptically, but apparently silently, by Lemnitzer, who had in his files a JCS paper that appraised the internal situation quite differently. It stated: "In view of the rapid buildup of the Castro government's military and militia capability *and the lack of predictable future mass discontent* [emphasis Lemnitzer's] the possible success of the [CIA's] paramilitary plan appears very doubtful."[11]

The meeting ended with an order for what Kennedy termed "a continuation and accentuation" of CIA activities in the areas of sabotage, propaganda, and political action. The president also directed the Defense Department and the CIA to assess the Trinidad plan and report their conclusions to him.

Three days later, the CIA described the Trinidad plan to General Gray, who had been named the JCS contact for all actions involving their agency. The plan called for a diversionary attack elsewhere and an air-sea assault on Trinidad area beaches a day after B-26 bombers had attacked Castro's airfields, patrol vessels, communications centers, and tank and artillery parks (the World War II U.S. surplus B-26s were selected because Castro's Air Force used them). The object would be to establish a beachhead and attract local support in an area in which there was considerable anti-Castro activity. If the beachhead held and anti-Castro activity began spreading, a new provisional government made up of Cuban exiles would be brought in from the United States, paving the way for overt U.S. assistance. Should the beachhead become untenable, the invaders were to escape into the mountains and become guerrillas.

The JCS assessments of this and subsequent plans were to become key points in the controversy that followed the invasion. Two days after Gray heard the CIA presentation, McNamara received the JCS evaluation. It stated that the plan could be carried off without overt U.S. intervention if the various criteria were met; it also said that the Trinidad landing site was the best in Cuba for achieving success because of its isolated location. Airborne and amphibious forces should be able to overcome light opposition, the report stated, but logistical support against moderate and determined resistance looked to be marginal. Because the Escambray Mountains lie between Trinidad and the Havana area, where most of Castro's troops were located, the brigade could probably hold the beachhead for four days before a coordinated counterattack could be launched by the Cuban dictator (other estimates ranged from two days to seven).

But unless a substantial uprising occurred or large follow-on forces were provided, Castro's troops would eventually wipe out the beachhead, the appraisal asserted. Ultimate success would depend on one or both of these factors being present, it added, and concluded: "Despite the shortcomings pointed out in the assessment, the JCS consider that timely execution of the plan has a fair chance of ultimate success and, even if it does not achieve immediately the full results desired, could contribute to the eventual overthrow of the Castro regime."[12] McNamara verbally endorsed the appraisal's conclusions the same day.

(While the prospect of substantial uprisings was a key condition of each JCS assessment, it did not figure in CIA Director Dulles's thinking, a fact that was not made clear until after the invasion had failed. He told a Senate subcommittee that the CIA had not counted on an immediate uprising, but expected invading forces to be swelled by "accretions" from anti-Castro elements of the Cuban population.)[13]

The term "fair chance" in the JCS evaluation's conclusion was inserted by Lt. Gen. Earle G. Wheeler, director of the JCS's Joint Staff, who wanted an assessment of the plan's chances of success to be included. He asked Gray for an estimate, but because "there were simply too many imponderables . . . I refused to guess about it," Gray recalled years later. For example, Gray had been unable to get the CIA to gauge the strength of the anticipated uprising.

Wheeler asked if "fair chance" would be accurate, to which Gray replied: "What do you mean by fair?"

The Joint Staff director responded: "30-70."

Gray asked: "Do you mean 30 in favor of success?"

When Wheeler said yes, Gray answered: "That is about right, based on what we know."

The 30-70 figure was not included in the written evaluation, an omission Gray called "a major blunder on my part, one that had a profound influence on continuing preparations instead of killing the plan then and there."[14]

Why Wheeler equated the word "fair" with as dismal a ratio as 30-70 is not known. If the figures had been reversed, "fair" might have been closer to the actual risk, but Gray had made very clear with his question that Wheeler meant thirty chances out of a hundred. Oddly, the paper got through without anyone asking that the evaluation be spelled out in percentages.

To make sure that the brigade was capable of carrying out the attack, the Chiefs sent an evaluation team of three U.S. officers to Guatemala. The ground evaluator was deeply impressed with the readiness, leadership, physical fitness, and equipment of the assault forces, but the logistics evaluator had grave reservations about the brigade's capabilities in his specialty. An experienced logistics instructor was sent to try to correct this weakness.

A U.S. officer, whose identity was classified and who had also visited the brigade, disagreed in testimony before a presidential inquiry board after the invasion. He testified that he had stated in the JCS evaluation that "physically, they were in good shape.... [H]owever, in a fight it would be like putting our marines against Boy Scouts." He gauged the chances for military success as "about 15 percent" and that "logistically the operation would likely fall apart." Transportation was inadequate because trucks were assigned to individual commanders instead of being under central control, there was no fuel capability to support air operations, there were no floodlights to enable the beaches to be worked at night, there was no bridging equipment, the only maintenance equipment consisted of hand tools, and plans for distributing supplies from dump areas were "practically nonexistent."[15]

The air evaluator for the JCS team was sure that the brigade's seventeen B-26s and their crews would be combat-ready by March 15, but he reported that base security was so poor that the odds against achieving surprise were 85 to 15. The mayor of the closest town, Retalhuleu, was a card-carrying Communist, and it was no secret, either in Guatemala or in Cuba, that the brigade was being trained for an invasion; the only question in Castro's mind was when and where this would take place. The evaluator, Lt. Col. B. W. Tarwater, pointed out that local spies would tell Castro when the brigade left and about when it would arrive in Cuba. Since surprise was an important element in the operation, Tarwater recommended that an air attack be made instead of an amphibious landing. The Chiefs turned Tarwater's recommendation down.[16]

Then, during the first part of March, Kennedy began to worry that the

Trinidad plan was "too spectacular," too much like a World War II invasion to keep the world from knowing the United States was involved. This preoccupation with masking U.S. sponsorship would be taken to extraordinary lengths before the operation was over and, more than any other factor, would doom it to failure. Under no circumstances, the president would reiterate time and again, would there be any overt U.S. intervention until a provisional government was in place. The United States would then be justified in "going public" with its assistance, the reasoning went.

Kennedy told the CIA to come up with other alternatives, and on March 14, two weeks past the original deadline for launching the invasion, Bissell's planners presented five new proposals for evaluation to the JCS's Interdirectorate Working Group. This unit was made up of Gray and Joint Staff representatives from the intelligence, operations, supply, and civil affairs sections and each of the services.

By evening, the Working Group completed its evaluation and, in Lemnitzer's words, "by an unknown alchemy reduced the alternatives to three." The next morning, the group presented its opinions to the chairman and the Joint Chiefs in a twenty-minute briefing. The Chiefs immediately approved the group's findings and passed them on to McNamara. Lemnitzer remembered: "Probably no JCS paper of this period proved more controversial and surely none did greater damage to JCS reputations."[17]

One alternative was to change the Trinidad plan to a night landing and discard the airborne assault and D-Day air strike. The JCS evaluation gave this plan a "fair" chance of initial success, but because of the lack of air support, the difficulty of resupply during darkness, and the danger of daylight enemy air attacks, the JCS held that it had a "small chance of ultimate success."

The Chiefs also saw little merit in another plan to invade Oriente Province on Cuba's eastern end. This alternative would have begun with an air assault followed by the landing of the brigade's main body. Air support would come from a captured enemy air strip on the following day. The JCS saw numerous shortcomings in this plan: the presence of Cuban regular troops near the landing site, an inadequate airfield, difficulties in providing logistical support, and the fact that the site's long distance from Havana would diminish the operation's psychological impact, deemed a necessary ingredient in inspiring widespread uprisings.

The third alternative was the Zapata plan, so called because the landing site was in the swampy Zapata Peninsula, located one hundred twenty miles southeast of Havana and eighty miles west of Trinidad. This region had two airfields capable of landing B-26s, a feature that would satisfy State Department desires that brigade aircraft begin using Cuban airstrips as soon as possible so as to perpetuate the illusion that the invasion was an internal affair. Air and ground troops would make night landings, as in the original Trinidad plan, and light opposition was expected in an area the planners considered remote and difficult for defenders to reach. General Gray estimated that Zapata reduced the chances for the mission's success to at most 20-80, a ratio he stated years later should have made him recommend to the Chiefs that the operation be canceled.[18]

Somehow in all this effort, those in overall charge either ignored or didn't pay enough attention to the JCS evaluation's conclusion: of the alternate concepts, Zapata was considered the most feasible and most likely to accomplish the objective. But none of these options was regarded to be as likely to achieve success as the original Trinidad plan.[19] The Chiefs said later that this preference for Trinidad was passed on to McNamara, but it apparently was never made known to the president, who got the impression that the Chiefs favored the Zapata plan over all others. On March 16, Kennedy told the CIA to go ahead with fleshing out the Zapata plan, reserving the right to cancel the whole operation up to within twenty-four hours of the landing.

The CIA executives heading up the operation were old acquaintances of Lemnitzer's. Dulles and he had worked closely in helping bring about the surrender of the German armies in Italy in World War II. Bissell, a brilliant former Yale economics professor who was in charge of all CIA covert operations, had been associated with Lemnitzer when the general headed up the Mutual Defense Assistance Program, and Bissell was acting administrator of the ECA (Economic Cooperation Administration). When the general left the program, Bissell wrote him a highly complimentary letter expressing a "great sense of personal loss" at his departure and stating: "Innumerable obstacles have had to be overcome, and have in fact been overcome, in large part due to your energetic and intelligent administration of a major share of the operating burden of the program."[20]

The three got along well during the Cuban operation, as did the CIA and JCS staffs, but the intelligence agency's way of doing things was far different from the ECA's and certainly the Pentagon's. In Lemnitzer's world, teamwork, detailed plans, and copious documentation were fundamental to any endeavor. In Bissell's, the players avoided writing things down as much as possible and individuals were supposed to know only those parts of a plan for which they were responsible. These characteristics could well have been among the reasons for the JCS chairman's often-repeated complaint over the years following the Bay of Pigs that he was never kept fully informed.

Kennedy assembled the operation's key movers at a conference in the State Department on April 4 where a decision was made to invade on either April 15 or April 17. Lemnitzer wrote later that before the meeting, he "argued vigorously" against the Zapata plan with Thomas C. Mann, assistant secretary of state for inter-American affairs. When Mann replied that the president had made up his mind, the general said he asked why the decision was made without JCS consultation or concurrence. Mann, a career foreign service officer who had earlier questioned the legality of the operation, answered that "political considerations were overriding." In any case, he added, the president had made his decision.

The JCS chairman then observed, still in his curious third-person style:

"General Lemnitzer therefore refrained from raising this issue with the chief executive."[21] Lemnitzer did not indicate why he directed his comments to Mann, although, like the general, he was a "holdover" from the Eisenhower administration and was known to be an opponent of an invasion. Possibly the occasion was just a talk between old friends before the meeting started or the general might characteristically have been seeking a reading on how the winds were blowing from a top official of the department who seemed to have considerable influence with the president in this particular operation.

In his personal account, Lemnitzer cited a Gray memorandum of record of the April 4 meeting as noting that Secretary of State Dean Rusk opposed the Zapata plan whereas McNamara supported it (Lemnitzer wrote that he recalled no such debate).[22] The president repeated an earlier interest in sending in two hundred- to two hundred fifty-man infiltration teams at various points along the Cuban coast instead of concentrating the forces. He stopped pressing for this approach, however, when one of the operation's chief military advisers, Marine Col. Jack Hawkins, asserted that such a course would alert Castro and allow him to easily crush each group one at a time.

This meeting was also memorable because a highlight was a spirited denunciation of the invasion by a senator whose stature made him impervious to presidential influence and pressure. He was William J. Fulbright, Arkansas Democrat and chairman of the Senate Foreign Relations Committee, who argued that the action was untrue to American traditions. The senator's "brave, old-fashioned American speech," recalled special Kennedy assistant Arthur M. Schlesinger, Jr., "left everyone in the room, except me and possibly the president, totally unmoved."[23]

The Chiefs met four times between March 15 and the invasion's start, finally scheduled for April 17, to review progress and prospects; Gray's working group met much more often. The CIA "continued to exude confidence," Lemnitzer recalled, with Dulles and Bissell reiterating that Cuba was ripe for revolt and that at least a quarter of the populace would rally behind the brigade.[24]

Toward the end of March, Gray began to realize that the CIA had been unable to organize a viable subversive movement in Cuba, "as they had promised." As in previous detections of weaknesses, he regretted not recommending "that the Chiefs encourage cancellation, since the internal uprising was an essential part of the plan."[25]

The CIA kept revising the invasion plan as D-Day approached, and the Chiefs still did not know all the details on April 12 when McNamara and Lemnitzer went to the White House to listen as Bissell gave a final briefing to the president. As the briefing approached, Gray and his staff became increasingly concerned about the adequacy of vital air support, and they wanted to make sure that this was addressed at this important briefing. They were especially apprehensive about Castro's T-33s, as it turned out the only jet airplanes that were used in the operation on either side. Gray rode to the executive mansion with McNamara and Lemnitzer and, Gray recalled, "I stressed in the strongest terms" the importance of destroying the fast jets on the ground with air strikes. McNamara and Lemnitzer agreed.

At the meeting, "Bissell put on his usual stellar performance," Gray recounted, "but never gave the complete briefing we had begged for and never once mentioned the air strikes. I was surprised and disappointed that neither General Lemnitzer nor McNamara raised the question or asked to make a statement."[26]

Of all the misfortunes that befell Brigade 2506, none was ranked higher by the Chiefs than Kennedy's lack of appreciation of the vital importance of air support to establishing a beachhead at the Bay of Pigs.

As the president was being briefed on April 4, the first elements of the invasion force were moving from their base in Guatemala to a staging area at Puerto Cabezas, Nicaragua. From there, they would travel by ships to the Bay of Pigs. In revealing the invasion site to brigade leaders on April 14, CIA advisers told them that two hundred guerrillas were waiting near the beaches to join them and five thousand more would follow them during the first two days of the landing. Castro, the advisers said, would not be able to gather enough forces to counterattack for at least seventy-two hours. One adviser was quoted by Lemnitzer as having said: "We will be with you for the next step but you will be so strong, you will be getting so many people on your side that you won't want to wait for us. . . . [Y]ou will put your hand out, turn left and go straight into Havana." Not mentioned during the pep talk was the possibility that the survivors would have to become guerrillas if the invasion was defeated, apparently for fear that this would damage morale.[27]

Free at last after months in the confines of their training camp, that evening one thousand four hundred euphoric freedom-fighters boarded ships, confident that they would soon win back their native land. It is possible that few other military forces in history ever looked forward more eagerly to a fight. Their objective: to establish a beachhead forty miles wide and twenty miles deep, hold it for ten days, install a new provisional government, and then move on to final victory. The invasion forces would include Manuel Artime, a member of the Cuban Revolutionary Council, an organization of former Cuban leaders then in exile in the United States that was expected to provide a new government under former Premier Jose Miro Cardona.

On May 16 the day before the main attack was to take place, President Kennedy formally approved the invasion. But the operation had already begun on schedule: the day before, eight B-26s bombed and strafed three Cuban airfields, their pilots returning to Nicaragua afterward to claim that over 70 percent of Castro's air force had been destroyed. The raids were to coincide with a diversionary attack by one hundred sixty brigade members on the coast of Oriente Province, thirty miles east of the U.S. naval base at Guantánamo Bay. The intent was to draw Castro forces away from the Bay of Pigs, far down the southern coast.

But things did not go well: of Castro's partially operational air fleet of thirty-seven combat and fifteen transport planes, only five were destroyed by brigade pilots, a count verified by high-altitude U.S. photo reconnaissance. The diversionary force never landed; unaware of the importance or significance of its mission and under the impression it was only supposed to infiltrate, the force withdrew when it spotted a jeep and two trucks on the shore. A second attempt was aborted because the surf looked to be too heavy to land boats. The U.S. after-action verdict credited the failure to "weak leadership."[28]

Then, on the evening before the invasion, politics and Kennedy's obsession with the U.S. pose of noninvolvement stepped in to throw still another obstacle into the path of the main force then approaching Cuba's shores by sea. The president called off an air strike that had been set for dawn on D-Day to destroy the rest of Castro's Air Force. The decision followed an appeal by Rusk, who was getting heat from the United Nations and the U.S. ambassador, Adlai Stevenson, over a badly staged CIA effort to depict the B-26 raids as the deeds of Cuban defectors who had stolen some planes in Cuba and attacked the airfields. In an effort to give credence to this claim, a ninth B-26 carrying Cuban air force markings had been flown by a brigade pilot from Nicaragua to Miami at the time of the Cuban air raids. The cover story was that the plane had been hit by ground fire in Cuba and the pilot had flown to Miami because he was low on fuel.

Reporters were permitted to talk with the pilot and inspect the plane, but there were obvious contradictions in the account: among other things, the pilot was not wearing a Cuban uniform, the B-26's machine guns had not been fired, and the plane's nose was of metal, whereas Castro's B-26s were of plastic.[29] Occurring as it did at a time when there was increasing speculation in the press that the United States was about to invade Cuba, the incident triggered suspicion in the United Nations, despite Stevenson's insistence on the UN floor that the defection was genuine. The UN ambassador, it turned out, had not been told of the Cuban operation or the phony flight.

Worried that the U.S. role in the approaching invasion was in danger of being discovered, and undoubtedly anxious to placate a furious Stevenson, Rusk urged Kennedy to cancel a D-Day air strike aimed at knocking out the rest of Castro's air force. The secretary wanted air support to resume only after the brigade had captured an airfield in the Bay of Pigs area so that it could be used as proof that the attackers' aircraft came from Cuban soil. The president agreed, but left a window open by adding "unless there are overriding considerations."

Dulles was out of town, and when Air Force Gen. Charles P. Cabell, the CIA's deputy director, was told of the cancellation by Bundy, he and Bissell hurried to Rusk's office to protest that the action could spell disaster for the invasion. The secretary of state telephoned Kennedy—who was staying at Glen Ora, a family hideaway in nearby Virginia, for the weekend—and told him of the two CIA officials' objections, adding that he himself stood by his original position. Again, the president concurred with Rusk. While he was still on the phone, Rusk offered to let Cabell voice his views directly to the president. The general declined, expressing the opinion that he would not be able to make Kennedy change his mind. The brigade's pilots were in their cockpits waiting to take off when the cancellation order was received.

At midnight, Cabell contacted Gray to ask about the feasibility of providing early warning (EW) coverage and combat air patrol (CAP) in the invasion area. The EW support would have come from radar-equipped U.S. destroyers. The CAP, which would have been intended to fend off attacking Cuban planes in the invasion area, would have been made up of jets from the carrier *Essex* which, with seven destroyers, was lying far out at sea. Gray said both EW and CAP were available and, once again, Cabell talked to Rusk, who again telephoned the president. The secretary then gave the phone to Cabell to make the request directly; Kennedy said yes to the early warning surveillance and no to the combat air patrol.

There is a conflict in available accounts of when Lemnitzer was made aware of the cancellation of the D-Day air strike. The Chiefs were neither informed nor consulted on this aspect ahead of time, according to Lemnitzer,[30] an assertion with which other reports agree. Peter Wyden's well-regarded book, *The Bay of Pigs—The Untold Story*, states that the chairman was told about the cancellation by Wheeler and Gray when they went to his quarters at Fort Myer and awoke him around two o'clock in the morning. It sounded so unbelievable, this account held, that Lemnitzer called the JCS situation room in the Pentagon to confirm it. He was quoted as having told his visitors that the cancellation was "absolutely reprehensible, almost criminal."[31]

The book and Gray state that Lemnitzer was consulted about EW and CAP at that time and that he agreed they should be implemented. The JCS chairman wrote in his own account, however, that he recalled "quite vividly that [I] did not learn about these developments until 0700 [seven o'clock in the morning] when General Wheeler came to his quarters at Ft. Myer bearing the news."[32] By then, the invasion was nearly seven hours old.

Gray insisted many years later, however, that Lemnitzer was told about the cancellation and CAP and EW requests "a little before 0200 [two o'clock in the morning] or a little after" when he and Wheeler walked to the chairman's quarters from Wheeler's residence, which was also at Fort Myer. Gray recalled:

"Neither I nor General Wheeler would have violated a basic military tenet, which is to inform those above you and below you of significant events immediately as they occur. We would never have sat on that information all night."[33]

The assault force arrived outside the Bay of Pigs shortly after midnight on April 17, the first elements quickly landing east of the bay's opening in an area dubbed Blue Beach. A landing scheduled for the west side of the opening was diverted when it was discovered that the sea bottom identified in intelligence reports as seaweed was actually a large, shallow coral reef. Another landing was made at Red Beach, eighteen miles inland at the tip of the Bay of Pigs.

The element of surprise was lost when the landing was spotted by local militia. Castro learned of the attack at three-fifteen in the morning and headed for the area to assume personal command. At dawn, the brigade came under heavy attack from Cuban air force planes, and at half past nine in the morning a missile from a Sea Fury sank the freighter *Rio Escondido*, which carried ten days of ammunition, vital communications equipment, and aviation fuel. That morning, another ship, the *Houston*, was hit and it ran aground five miles from Red Beach, stranding one hundred eighty troops who never got into the fight, and rendering a large cargo of ammunition unavailable for use ashore.

The enemy attacks marked the debut of the T-33, a small jet trainer which carried two .50-caliber machine guns and had been outfitted with rocket launchers. Assigned little importance in prelanding appraisals of Castro's resources (an early JCS appraisal didn't even mention them in a detailed list of Cuban weaponry), the three T-33s easily outfought the obsolete B-26s and inflicted heavy damage on ground forces and shipping.

Adding to the invaders's woes were mechanical problems with the aluminum landing boats—of nine employed by one battalion at Red Beach, only two were usable for the twenty-minute run from the *Houston* to the beach. Radios were soaked when troops had to wade through deep water, cutting off communication in the beachhead areas. The tendency of green troops to fire their arms exces- sively when in combat for the first time quickly depleted ammunition supplies to crisis levels, a situation that would not have occurred if the brigade could have counted on replenishment from the sunken *Rio Escondido* and the grounded *Houston*. Follow-on supply vessels were too far away to be of any help (two of the largest had fled far out to sea when the *Rio Escondido* was sunk, and only headed back, too late, toward the fighting when they were intercepted by U.S. warships).

Castro reacted far faster than the CIA had expected. Besides his planes, large regular forces led by Soviet tanks and supported by artillery were soon engaging the men on the beachheads. By the next day there were twenty thousand regular troops in the area, heavily supported by police and elements from the two hundred thousand members of the Cuban militia. The uprisings and guerrilla assistance the CIA had counted on never materialized: Castro had moved quickly and arrested many thousands of known dissidents. The Escambray Mountains, center of the main guerrilla strength, were eighty miles away across heavy swampland and on the other side of the large Castro forces ringing the invaders.

The brigade was well equipped with 4.2-inch and 81-millimeter mortars, .50- caliber and .30-caliber machine guns, and 75-millimeter recoilless rifles, whereas individual weapons were largely M-1 rifles. There were also five M-41 light tanks whose crews had been trained secretly at Fort Knox, Kentucky.

The T-33s shot down four B-26s on D-Day, while brigade antiaircraft fire destroyed two of Castro's Sea Furys and two B-26s. Impressed by the ease with which the jet trainers downed the B-26s, the CIA—this time with Kennedy's permission—sent six B-26s to attack the San Antonio de los Baños air base in an attempt to destroy the jets and the rest of Castro's air force. Bad luck once again: the planes were unable to attack because of heavy haze and low clouds.

The air support did better the next day when U.S. civilian contract pilots, pressed into service because Cuban pilots were either too tired to fly or refused to do so, attacked a long column of tanks approaching Blue Beach along a coastal road from the north. Bombs, rockets, and napalm were used in six sorties to destroy seven enemy tanks and caused one thousand eight hundred casualties.[34] But the brigade's planes still were flying from Nicaragua and back because the one usable airstrip, located in the Blue Beach sector, quickly became vulnerable to enemy fire.

At the end of the second day, Kennedy met in the Oval Office with his senior advisers, including Lemnitzer, to review the rapidly deteriorating situation. Bissell and Burke argued ardently for an air strike from the *Essex* to knock out the T-33s and allow the brigade's B-26s to attack Castro's tanks. When Rusk strongly opposed this, Kennedy compromised and authorized a jet escort from the carrier to defend the B-26s without attacking ground targets. Six unmarked jets were waiting on the deck for the bombers when they passed over the *Essex* on the way from Nicaragua early the next morning. But once again, a miscalculation occurred, dooming this last effort to turn the tide at the Bay of Pigs. The four B-26s were on Nicaraguan time, and the *Essex* was in a different time zone. The jets were warming up on the flight deck when the bombers flew over, and by the time the U.S. planes arrived over the beachhead two of the B-26s had been destroyed by T-33s and the others had returned to Nicaragua.

The gallant defenders of the Red and Blue beaches inflicted heavy losses on Castro's troops, many more than they suffered, but the vastly superior forces opposing them and rapidly dwindling supplies of ammunition forced them to keep pulling back. On the last day, D plus 2, the troops at Red Beach retreated under attack by Castro tanks to Blue Beach. With their backs to the sea, they fought for every foot of ground. At midday, a radio message was received from the brigade commander, Pepe San Román: "We are out of ammo and fighting on the beach. Please send help. We cannot hold."[35] Navy Rear Adm. John A. Clark reported at noon that the Blue Beach beachhead had shrunk to a mile and a quarter wide to a quarter of a mile deep.

The last message from San Román was transmitted at two thirty-two in the afternoon. It said: "Am destroying all equipment and communications. I have nothing left to fight with. Am taking to the woods. I can't wait for you."

"By nightfall," the Taylor Commission's report noted, "resistance in the beachhead had ended."[36]

Dropping one final pretense of U.S. noninvolvement, Kennedy ordered two destroyers to the area to evacuate survivors. The ships passed a private Cuban yacht carrying an undetermined number of members of the brigade to safety; a message from the vessel reported that there was nothing left to salvage and Castro was waiting on the beach. The destroyers moved to within gun range of Blue Beach and then left at flank speed when they were straddled by shells from shore artillery and tanks. U.S. vessels cruised along the coast until April 26 but found only a few survivors.

Of the 1,400 men who landed at the Bay of Pigs, 114 were killed and 1,189 were captured, including San Román. About a hundred were unaccounted for and were presumed to have been unable to land, and so made their way to safety in or outside of Cuba.[37] Those imprisoned were released in December 1962 for a ransom of sixty-two million dollars worth of food and drugs from the United States.

The brigade killed 1,250 members of Castro's forces and wounded more than 2,000.[38]

The president moved swiftly to find out what had gone wrong. The day after San Román's force was overrun, Kennedy appointed General Taylor to head a commission to question witnesses and issue a report on its findings. Besides the retired general, the group included the president's brother Robert, the U.S. attorney general; Dulles; and Burke.

The commission heard fifty witnesses, including Lemnitzer, and made its report to the president in mid-June. Among its criticisms were that the invasion was a military operation that should have been assigned to the Defense Department instead of the CIA and that too much emphasis was placed upon the well-nigh impossible task of concealing U.S. participation. Although finding that Kennedy's cancellation of the D-Day air strike was ill advised, Taylor expressed his own feeling that this would not have materially affected the outcome of the landings because there were too many other factors working against their success.[39]

Gray agreed. "After Castro concentrated all his aircraft and air defenses at one base it would have been almost impossible to destroy all three of the T-33s. Only a combat air patrol [CAP] would have stopped Castro's air attack."[40]

Taylor's group was sharply critical of the Joint Chiefs for not presenting more forcefully their objections to the Zapata plan. Taylor summed up the commission's findings in this regard:

"Piecing all the evidence together, we concluded that whatever reservations the Chiefs had about the Zapata plan, about the propriety of having the CIA continue to conduct a military operation of growing complexity, or about the erosion of military requirements by political considerations, they never expressed their concern to the president in such a way as to lead him to consider seriously a cancellation of the enterprise or the alternative of backing it up with U.S. forces."[41]

Lemnitzer, as the JCS's spokesman and usually the only chief present in meetings with the president, must bear the major blame for this alleged omission if the commission's conclusion was justified. The chairman's position was that the Chiefs were not kept informed as the invasion plans progressed and that their advice was often ignored: "Without consulting or informing the JCS, they changed the concept of the operations from a covert landing to a conventional amphibious assault, switched the landing site from Trinidad to the Bay of Pigs, canceled the D-Day air strikes—and then blamed the JCS because things went badly."[42]

In regard to the Chiefs, the commission concluded that "whatever their handi-caps—and they were many—the Chiefs had certainly given the impression to their colleagues of having approved the Zapata plan and of having confidence in its feasibility. They gave no clear warning to the president of possible failure."[43]

The JCS chairman took issue with this point in a lengthy rebuttal, which followed his receipt of a draft of the commission's conclusions prior to their being put in final form. His position was that the JCS were only asked to appraise the plan, not approve it.

"Approval," he stated, "carries with it the connotation that the JCS believed that the operation had a strong chance of succeeding. The Chiefs never went beyond an appraisal that with control of the air and surprise the force could establish itself ashore, but ultimate success would depend on popular support."[44]

Lemnitzer also strongly objected to a draft conclusion that the Chiefs had given short shrift to the Trinidad alternatives at their March 15 meeting. Contending, too, that it was unfair to level this charge at the Chiefs when no determination was made elsewhere in the Taylor commission report of how long other agencies took to reach decisions, the JCS chairman stated: "This disregards the fact that the Chiefs were by this time fully conversant with the overall aspects of the operation and had been pre-briefed on it. Personally, I had spent hours studying on the map all the proposed solutions and discussing these with my principal Joint Staff advisers. . . . [U]nder such circumstances, a well-organized military briefing can cover much detail in twenty minutes. In this particular instance the issues were clear-cut and the time allotted was sufficient to deter-mine that Zapata was the most feasible alternative. Also, at this time Zapata was just an alternative. The record is clear that once Zapata was decided upon the Chiefs considered the Zapata concept for longer periods and as often as neces-sary."[45] The commission agreed with Lemnitzer's objection, and the conclusion was removed from the final document.

When the commission completed its draft, General Gray was required to carry a copy to each member of the JCS and remain in their presences while they read it, something he remembers as a "most embarrassing procedure." When Admiral Burke finished his reading, he said to the general in what he recalls as "a rather fatherly tone": "You know, Gray, we never thought some parts of this operation through very well." Gray replied that he agreed but that the Joint Chiefs should never admit it. "I later regretted that I did not add that if a fall guy was needed I was the obvious candidate," he stated years later. "For the Chiefs, this was just one of the many problems they handled each day. I was more intimately involved in all aspects of the plan than anyone else in the Defense Department."[46]

The Chiefs never conducted a comprehensive critique on what went wrong and why, but two weeks following the submission of Taylor's report to the president, Burke sent Lemnitzer a list of observations. Among them were that the Bay of Pigs was a military operation and should have been conducted by the military; that while the plan was "not bad," the failure to adhere to it was; that the whole operation should have been terminated when the D-Day air strike was called off; and that the Chiefs were naive in not appreciating how "ignorant" the new administration was in regard to military operations.[47]

General Gray had other ideas of why the operation turned into a fiasco. An assertive and intelligent officer who had been assigned to the JCS after a tour as assistant commander of the 11th Airborne Division, Gray could remember at least five times as the plans unfolded when he should have recommended cancellation to the Chiefs.

Gray thought the fact that the four senior Army officers involved—Lemnitzer; Wheeler; Gray; and Decker, the Army chief of staff—were primarily staff officers was a factor in the JCS's performance during the operation's planning. Aside from the Marine Corps's General Shoup, these four would be expected to know the most about landing troops on a foreign shore. "[However] staff officers are more inclined to accept a plan and do or die to make it work," he stated. "Officers more combat-oriented are more likely to view a plan from the standpoint of whether it is totally sound and, if not, that it should be abandoned."[48]

Gray was surprised at the equanimity with which the Chiefs received his briefings, "accepting what I presented with few questions or comments." Lemnitzer and Burke's positions were always "positive." Decker "was by nature taciturn and said little." White, the soon-to-retire Air Force chief of staff, was "almost gone and his successor, General [Curtis] LeMay was feeling his way— amphibious assaults were hardly his cup of tea. General Shoup was the puzzler: He seemed to give the impression that he had strong reservations but he never expressed them, certainly not in my presence."

Despite this disparity in outlooks and styles, Lemnitzer could report afterwards that the Chiefs were always unanimous in the actions they were required to make during the Cuban operation.[49]

Another general who figured in Lemnitzer's calculations of what was going on in Dulles's camp was Cabell, the CIA's deputy director. The JCS chairman felt that as long as the CIA had a four-star general in its inner circle the military aspects of its operations should be well in hand.[50] However, Cabell, a 1925 West Point graduate, was an Air Force staff officer with no experience in ground or sea operations. His role in the planning and execution of the Bay of Pigs operation was marginal at best.

One of the reasons for the Chiefs' "detached attitudes," Gray speculated, was that the JCS and the CIA had a long-standing way of doing things in which the Chiefs had always had an input into significant CIA activities through a high-level interdepartmental committee. But once decisions were made, the CIA normally conducted the operation without questions or advice from other departments. These operations had been basically nonmilitary in nature and "kibitzing from the military was neither needed nor wanted."

"But," the general continued, "for the first time the CIA was conducting a basically combined arms military operation, so it could be assumed that the Joint Chiefs would take more interest in the operation than normal. Instead, it appears they more closely followed their normal 'hands-off' approach and so did not attempt to monitor the CIA's planning or operational activities."[51]

One other aspect that could have contributed to the Bay of Pigs failure was the Chiefs' intense desire to see Castro deposed. The establishment of a Soviet-backed Communist state ninety miles from U.S. shores, the only one in the Western Hemisphere, was viewed as an outrage in Washington military circles. It is not unlikely that this eagerness for some kind of move that would topple the Cuban dictator from power may well have caused the Chiefs to look the other way when military fundamentals were being violated.

Still, even the best conceived and conducted operation can only be as effective as its intelligence; in BOPO, this was the CIA's responsibility and in its own area of expertise it failed miserably. The substantial anti-Castro "accretions" of which Dulles spoke never materialized to rally to the invaders' cause. They never really had a chance to do so even if they had existed in any significant numbers. The fact is that the Cubans found communism to be a whole lot better than anything that had happened before Castro came to power. They were not yet disillusioned enough to revolt. The CIA may not have considered a widespread uprising as essential to the invasion's success, as Dulles indicated, but the Chiefs did, and they were misled.

The best, and believed only, detailed records of what happened in the JCS during the planning stages were Gray's meticulously kept notes of all meetings and actions. No one else kept any records, he recalled, bringing to mind the CIA's proclivity for putting nothing on paper.

But Lemnitzer ordered him to destroy these notes after the Bay of Pigs. The chairman did not explain why but Gray believed, since these were the only detailed records, that the chairman did not want the JCS to be the centerpiece for what was looming as a full-blown Senate investigation.[52]

The inquiry did not occur, possibly because of adroit political maneuvering by the White House, but there were hearings on smaller scales than the sweeping public sessions that no one in the administration wanted. One of these was a closed meeting on May 19, 1961, of the Senate Foreign Relations Committee's subcommittee on American republics affairs.

Accompanied by General Gray, the JCS chairman was questioned by a panel of thirteen lawmakers whose incredulity at the scope of the debacle grew steadily as Lemnitzer told of what had happened. At this time, details of the invasion were still top secret and the senators were hearing information that would not be made public for years. Among the aspects that particularly bothered the subcommittee were that a military operation would be turned over to a civilian agency (the CIA) and that the success of the mission would depend on an obsolete aircraft like the B-26.

Despite the shroud of secrecy at the hearing, the usually cooperative Lemnitzer seemed stilted, legalistic, and evasive in his testimony. He disclaimed any knowledge of some aspects of the operation, asserting that they were the CIA's responsibility. But he must have been familiar with most of the details, if only in hindsight, just as he had to have known the answer to the frequently asked question of who canceled the D-Day air strike and why.

In fairness to him, his was, at best, only a secondary portion of the operation, and these questions might have been more properly addressed to the CIA or the administration. The invasion had taken place less than a month before, its details were still top secret, and the general was bound by presidential and self-imposed bans on discussing its details. Finally, as a street-smart Capitol Hill hand, he had little faith that everything said behind congressional doors could be expected to stay there, no matter what the security classification. Indeed, Sen. Wayne Morse, Oregon Democrat and the outspoken chairman of the subcommittee, had stated in a previous Bay of Pigs hearing that the CIA considered Morse himself a security risk. (Morse, long a critic of CIA policies, told his colleagues that Dulles "is very fearful of me.")[53]

Morse was impressed with the general's performance at his hearing, calling him "as objective, correct, truthful and detailed as any witness I have heard in my years in the Senate."[54] Morse, however, could not be regarded as a completely impartial observer—at the hearing, he was Lemnitzer's chief champion, standing up for him when questioning got sharp and praising him often.

The general needed Morse's support because before the meeting was over subcommittee member Albert Gore, Tennessee Democrat, called for his ouster. The senator left before the others and told reporters that, based on the chairman's testimony, he was convinced that "we need a shakeup of the Joint Chiefs of Staff. . . . [W]e direly need a new chairman, as well as new members. . . ."

Gore was the only subcommittee member to call for Lemnitzer's firing. Sen. Homer E. Capehart, Indiana Republican, commented: "I didn't hear anything in there that suggests we need to replace General Lemnitzer any more than we need to replace the president or anybody else. They were all in this together."[55] A month later, Sen. Russell Long, Louisiana Democrat and not a subcommittee member, also urged Lemnitzer's ouster.

Regret, compassion for the lost brigade, and self-recrimination reigned among the BOPO principals in the wake of the invasion, but Gray remembers that Lemnitzer "said little or anything" afterward. "He never admitted it was a mistake, never tried to excuse failure and never chastised me for not having served him better. In this respect, I believe he was following the principle that in his position the less said about failure the better."[56]

In most published accounts of the Bay of Pigs, there is a curious lack of any assertive contribution on the part of McNamara, whom special presidential assistant Arthur M. Schlesinger, Jr., seems to excuse on the grounds that he was then "absorbed in the endless task of trying to seize control of the Pentagon."[57] Of the cabinet members involved, Rusk dominated in participating in the major decisions and McNamara seemed rarely to even comment during presidential meetings. The defense secretary was heard from in the important April 4 conference when, in response to a poll by Kennedy of those in the room, he said he was in favor of the Zapata plan. (McNamara made no mention of the Chiefs' reservations, although he had been informed by the JCS that they still favored the Trinidad plan.)

Lemnitzer, however, wrote years later that "in every phase of planning, McNamara played an extremely active part. He wanted to know what arsenals the weapons were being drawn from and what the methods and routes would be—and he was distressed that General Decker did not have these facts at his fingertips."[58] Gray thought that the secretary was aware of his own lack of expertise in the military operations involved and so relied on the Chiefs to react as necessary. But he was very active in matters involving logistical support, personally reviewing every request from the CIA in this area and sometimes increasing the amounts to make sure they were sufficient. "On several occasions," the general recalled, "I heard him say that if the operation failed it wouldn't be for lack of support from Defense."[59]

During the first few days after the failed operation, when the Chiefs needed some high-level civilian backing, McNamara was silent. Finally, ten days after the brigade was defeated on Zapata's beaches, the defense secretary told a news conference that he (McNamara) was responsible for "the actions of all personnel in the [Defense] department, both military and civilian," and that if any errors were committed they were his. But he did not deny allegations that the Chiefs shared in the blame for the disaster and told reporters he looked forward to a "long and pleasant association" with them.[60]

Throughout Lemnitzer's testimony before Congress, there is the impression that he felt the CIA should be making the statements since it was the intelligence agency's operation. This reticence could be hard on subordinates, as was the case when he was testifying before the Senate Armed Services Committee. Gray, who was with him, stated that Lemnitzer sat listening but made few comments as the senators took turns excoriating the Defense Department.

Senator Stuart Symington, Missouri Democrat, cut loose with an especially blistering critique and then got up to leave as Lemnitzer sat impassively. Gray recalled that "I couldn't stand it any longer and blurted out that 'I would like the opportunity to answer the senator.'" Senator Symington paused and as the committee members stared at this upstart, the committee chairman asked Symington to sit down and listen.

"I then refuted each of his charges in pretty hard, sharp language," Gray said, "showing that none of the critical decisions had been made by the Joint Chiefs of Staff and in several instances I directly involved the White House—a no-no for a low-level subordinate." Symington commented that "you seem to know a lot about this operation," to which Gray answered: "Yes, sir, I do."

Lemnitzer was pleased with his contribution, Gray remembered, but not so the Defense Department. That afternoon the word came over from the Pentagon that Gray was not to testify at any future hearings. Gray, who had just received a second star, was slated to leave the JCS Joint Staff for an assignment that normally would lead to a three-star post later on. But a major investigation into the Bay of Pigs affair was still a strong possibility, and Gray, with Lemnitzer's encouragement, elected to take a less-promising JCS staff position in Washington so that he would be available to help out. The investigation failed to materialize, and Gray went on to other assignments.

Later the Army tried to authorize him another star but the effort was stymied by a new Defense Department technicality involving general officer promotions that made him ineligible for advancement to lieutenant general. As disappointing as this turndown was at the time, it may have saved Gray's life because in the very thorough physical examination that officers have to undergo at retirement doctors discovered that he had cancer. If it had been detected three months later, they told him after surgery, it would have been too late to save him.[61]

In a book published two years after his death in 1994, Bissell disputed the Chiefs' assertions that they were not kept informed of the invasion plans as they progressed or that they did not have opportunities to make their reservations known to Kennedy. Of Lemnitzer, Bissell recalled: "I found [him] a very good colleague. Throughout the discussions, I felt that he was an honest and objective observer, critic and reporter. He was trying (as the best of U.S. military officers often do) not to pronounce on or make a policy decision, which the decision to do something about Castro was. I never regarded him as overly or improperly critical."

The former CIA official attributed the reticence of McNamara to speak up more forcefully in presidential meetings to "an unwritten rule that one respects the prerogatives of those who 'have the action.' The Joint Chiefs did not have it. The operation was not theirs; they acted as advisers to the president. It is therefore not surprising that they would be reticent to comment too harshly on what another agency was doing." The Bissell book quoted presidential adviser Bundy as having observed in an interview: "It's the other fellow's property. . . . [T]he Joint Chiefs really didn't regard this as their main business, and if they responded honestly and straightforwardly to the president's questions, they didn't have a campaigner's need to go on and say, 'Please don't do this.'" Bissell added: "Kennedy's intense interest only heightened the potential cost of dissent."[62]

Dulles and Bissell resigned under presidential pressure. Bissell was offered a lesser CIA post but turned it down and returned to private life. All of the Chiefs stayed on, but, as Lemnitzer wrote years later, "seldom had their standing with the commander in chief [Kennedy] been so low."[63]

On May 27 Kennedy took the unusual step of going over to the Pentagon to tell the Chiefs what he expected of them in the future in a presentation that became the text of a National Security Action Memorandum (NSAM No. 55) issued by the White House a month later:

First, he regarded them as his principal military advisers and expected to receive their views "directly and unfiltered," promising also to set aside two hours a month to talk with them alone and without records being kept.

Second, he wanted them to provide "dynamic and imaginative leadership in contributing to the success of military and paramilitary aspects of Cold War programs."

Third, he expected the JCS to "present the military point of view in governmental councils in such a way as to ensure that military factors are clearly understood before decisions are reached."

Fourth, the president said: "While I look to the Chiefs to present the military factor without reserve or hesitation, I regard them to be more than military men and expect their help in fitting military requirements into the overall context of any situation, recognizing that the most difficult problem in government is to combine all assets in a unified, effective pattern."[64]

In short, NSAM No. 55 gave the Chiefs the authority to insist on thorough briefings and an insider's role in all U.S. paramilitary and clandestine operations. It was clearly an admonishment, to be sure, but it was a message to the Chiefs that if they ended up on the president's bad side for the same reasons in future operations they would have only themselves to blame.[65]

Meanwhile, outside the capital life went on. A Gallup poll taken in early May, after he had taken the blame for the Bay of Pigs, showed that 82 percent of the country liked the way the president was handling his job, an increase over the previous poll. He was quoted as commenting:

"The worse I do, the more popular I get."[66]

19

✯ ✯ ✯ ✯

McNAMARA'S BAND

Longtime Honesdale friend Clarence E. Bodie knew the general needed some cheering up. Bodie, presiding judge of the borough's Court of Common Pleas and the master of ceremonies for the big hometown celebration of Lemnitzer's return from World War II in 1945, wrote on June 6, 1961:

"Dear Lyman: Don't be Hi-Jacked by Kennedy, Gored by a Tennessee bull, Dulled by a Dulles or Addled by Adlai; just keep on leading McNamara's band. You are doing a good job. If it was forty-five or fifty years ago, we could get our uptown gang together and I am sure that gang could successfully invade Cuba. Hattie is continuing to improve and sends her best. Hope to see you in Honesdale sometime this summer. Honesdale is with you. Clarence."

It was the kind of note that must have drawn a deep chuckle from the country's chairman of the JCS. Heaven knows, there was little to laugh about in those highly charged days following the Bay of Pigs invasion. Emboldened by the new administration's blunders in Cuba and seeming faint-heartedness in other areas of foreign policy, the Soviet Union's Khrushchev was stirring up trouble in Europe and Africa. The Communist threat in Southeast Asia was worsening, and Congress, inflamed anew by Russia's launching into space of the world's first astronaut five days before the Bay of Pigs spectacle, was yelling bloody murder about another missile gap. It was a time for late hours in the Pentagon and a schedule that precluded any weekends at home, let alone a summer visit to the soothing confines of Honesdale.

Those who were becoming familiar with the way McNamara did things might well have wondered why the Chiefs were needed at all as a corporate body. The former Ford Motor Company president had brought with him a hand-picked

278

group of figures-obsessed men from the civilian world who s[...] as the "Whiz Kids." Named after a team of young cost and org[...] installed at Ford by McNamara when he joined the company [...] War II, they were characterized by a *New York Times* corresp[...] faced lads who seek pretentiously to ladle the fog of war w[...] precise measuring cups."[1] The most vexing to those in unif[...] w... ... ... effectiveness and operations analysts," men who had eyes for little else than cost and efficiency. "Some, like Kennedy's own White House people, had been children when the generals and admirals they were arguing against had already fought two wars. Backed by their charts and slide-rule figures, [McNamara's] bright, tireless assistants challenged military assumptions about proper weapons, proper organization and proper procedure."[2] Functioning just below the secretarial level, the Whiz Kids ignored the advice of their uniformed brethren and behaved in such a manner that Lemnitzer recalled years later that the new administration's "civilian hierarchy was crippled not only by inexperience but also by arrogance arising from failure to recognize its own limitations. The problem was simply that the civilians would not accept military judgments."[3]

The most prominent offender was McNamara himself, who during Lemnitzer's tenure was increasingly much more apt to accept the recommendations of members of his civilian staff than of those in uniform. It could not have been an easy pill to swallow for a distinguished general with over forty years of service, but no one who worked with Lemnitzer knew about the resentment that surfaced only after he had been long retired. Even his letters to his family gave no indication that there must have been times when he would have liked to walk out of the Pentagon forever. A member of Lemnitzer's staff, in noting that during one stretch almost every recommendation the chairman made to the secretary was disapproved, told the general one day he thought the mounting string of rejections was putting the military in an "embarrassing rut." Lemnitzer replied that "I am the senior military officer—it's my job to state what I believe and it's his job to approve or disapprove." The staff officer, a future Army inspector general, said that "McNamara's arrogance was astonishing. He gave General Lemnitzer very short shrift and treated him like a schoolboy. The general almost stood at attention when he came into the room. Everything was 'yes, sir' and 'no, sir.'"[4]

The former auto industry executive impressed Lemnitzer when he showed up at the Pentagon two weeks before Kennedy's inauguration to begin learning about how the Defense Department functioned. He told President Eisenhower so and in a letter to General Taylor, then retired and living in New York, wrote: "Mr. McNamara has been here in the Pentagon since January 3 and is working hard getting acquainted with the Defense Department and its activities. I have spent a great deal of time with him and find him to be most capable, hard-working and impressive. I believe we are most fortunate to have him as Tom Gates' successor."[5]

A slender, no-nonsense former Harvard professor with slicked-back hair and less gold glasses, McNamara had served on the Army Air Corps Headquarters staff in World War II and was a newly discharged lieutenant colonel when he applied for an executive position at Ford. A condition of his joining the Dearborn, Michigan-based firm was that Ford also hire a team of smart young managers with whom he had worked during the war, the original Whiz Kids. Augmented with dozens of Harvard Business School graduates brought in by President Henry Ford II, they formed an elitist group which eventually held most of the power at Ford.

Lee Iacocca, later a Ford president himself and finally board chairman of Chrysler Corporation, remembers McNamara as "one of the smartest men I've ever met, with a phenomenal IQ and a steel-trap mind.... When you talked with him, you realized that he had already played out in his head the relevant details for every conceivable option and scenario.... [U]nlike anyone else I've met, he could carry a dozen different plans in his head and could spin out all the facts and figures without ever consulting his notes." The hard-driving, extroverted Iacocca also characterized McNamara as aloof, "never one of the boys," and not always easy to get along with. He once told Iacocca that he never expected to become president of Ford because he and Henry II never saw "eye-to-eye on anything," a kind of disconnect with which Lemnitzer would become all too familiar during his own relationship with the steely eyed defense secretary.[6]

McNamara and the general were frequent travel companions during the early months of the Kennedy administration as the new secretary sought to acquaint himself with the complex domain he had inherited. Early in McNamara's stewardship, Lemnitzer wrote to his brother: "We had two intensive days at the Strategic Air Command Headquarters and returned to Washington at 7:30 last night. Secretary McNamara works hard and fast. As a result we covered, with briefings and visits, what would normally take four days."

Once the secretary had examined the territory, he began ordering studies, usually setting unrealistically early deadlines for detailed answers to fundamental military issues the Pentagon had been puzzling over long before McNamara came aboard. His civilian assistants inundated the Chiefs with so many requests for studies that they and their staffs had time for little else. Two months after McNamara took office, Lemnitzer wrote a memorandum in which he took strong issue with McNamara's plans to give the Air Force a virtual monopoly in military space projects, such as satellites. After reading McNamara's draft of the enabling directive, Lemnitzer objected to the other services being left out and to the fact that the Chiefs had not been adequately consulted. Despite the JCS chairman's protest, the directive was issued four days later. The press obtained a copy of the chairman's message to McNamara contesting the move and speculated that Lemnitzer had been bypassed by his new civilian superiors. The general was furious, charging that the leaking of his classified comments was a "reprehensible, disloyal and criminal" act, adding that his views had been deliberately misinterpreted in the

press. He ordered an investigation to find out who had leaked the m
"culprit," as the general described the guilty party, was never idei
The flap could not have helped in Lemnitzer's worsening .
McNamara, a man who did not like to be taken to task by a subordinate or to
have department controversies aired in public. He also did not care to be crossed,
no matter how trivial the offense: Adm. Harry Felt, Pacific commander in chief,
who had been chiding Lemnitzer for not standing up to McNamara, once attended
a JCS conference with the defense secretary while the admiral was in
Washington. Felt had come to the meeting to discuss a certain item on the agenda,
but McNamara had deleted it. When Felt brought it up anyway, the secretary
angrily tore up the agenda list and stalked out of the meeting, leaving the admiral
speechless.[8] The secretary further displayed the low regard in which he seemingly
held his uniformed subordinates by assigning four major studies in military policy
and strategy to his new civilian assistants instead of to the military, as had been
the practice in the past. For example, Charles J. Hitch, the new Pentagon con-
troller and a former Rand Corporation executive, was assigned the basic study on
nuclear war strategy.[9]

Lemnitzer had deep respect for the principle of civilian control of the military,
and he considered the working arrangement he had achieved with Gates,
McNamara's predecessor, as ideal. This was an understanding under which the
Chiefs recommended a course of action and the secretary of defense made the
decision after taking into account individual member differences when they
occurred. The general was jubilant when McNamara told him early in their relationship that he liked that idea. He could not have known then to what lengths his
new boss would take this concept or that much of the time the secretary's
decisions would be based on his own calculations and those of civilian newcomers.

The JCS chairman had been acquainted with Kennedy when he was a senator
and Lemnitzer was a frequent spokesman on military matters before the various
congressional committees. He wrote to Ernest: "I knew the president quite
well. . . . [I]n my contacts with him before the inauguration, I found him to be
very able, knowledgeable and understanding. I thought his inaugural address was
one of the best I have ever heard and he handled the televised press conference
that night in a masterful way." Noting that he and Kay had joined the president
on the inaugural parade reviewing stand, he added that "he and his family seem
to be most cordial and easy to talk to."[10]

But he was less sanguine about Kennedy's military qualifications. In his notes
to himself on what to say at a luncheon with other members of the JCS during
the final days of the Eisenhower administration, he wrote: "Emphasize importance
of solidarity—last time a Pres with mil exp available to guide JCS." At another
time, he said of Kennedy: "Here was a president with no military experience at
all, sort of a patrol boat skipper in World War II."[11] (The president had commanded a Navy patrol torpedo [PT] boat after whose sinking in the Pacific

Theater's Solomon Islands he distinguished himself in the rescue of other crew members.)

As the inauguration approached, Lemnitzer was anxious that the young president be ready to assume the enormous responsibilities that went with being a national commander in chief in a world in which nuclear destruction of apocalyptic proportions could be unleashed with a single word. In his final meetings with Eisenhower, he frequently stressed to the president the importance of informing Kennedy, and he took great care in preparing the briefing he gave to Kennedy two days before he was inaugurated. Conducted at the private dwelling at which the president-elect was staying in Georgetown, the briefing concentrated on national emergency procedures, from the stages of preparing to go to war to ordering the launching of nuclear warheads.

The aspect of his briefing that seemed to concern Kennedy the most, Lemnitzer recalled, was "the likelihood of the president's being required to come up with a decision to launch our retaliatory [nuclear] effort almost without any warning. He was rather deeply worried about [the time factor in responding to a Soviet first strike]" and continued to probe into the details after his inauguration in talks with Lemnitzer following National Security Council meetings and talks at the White House. Lemnitzer remembered: "While this [launching a second strike] was a considerable possibility at the time, we in the Joint Chiefs of Staff did not consider it likely, with the available intelligence we had, that this [requirement to respond] would come as the complete surprise the president had in mind. During his subsequent association with military and nuclear problems I feel he became more and more appreciative of the fact that the requirement for a snap decision was not as likely as he first had the impression it would be."[12] In the months after he was elected, the president's anxiety was alleviated by improvements in U.S. missile retaliatory capabilities, the hardening of missile silos against incoming missiles, and the ability of SAC to dispatch atomic bomb-bearing aircraft to enemy targets within fifteen minutes of being alerted. At least half of SAC's bombers could be in the air during that time, thus precluding the complete destruction of the U.S. retaliatory capability by a Soviet first strike.

Of all the innovations Kennedy brought with him to Washington, none caused Lemnitzer and his fellow chiefs more problems than what Gordon Gray, Eisenhower's former assistant for national security affairs, described as Kennedy's "yo-yo form of government."[13] Kennedy conducted administrative affairs by what came to be known after his presidency as an "adhocracy" approach under which issues and problems were assigned to specially appointed task forces rather than being turned over to appropriate parts of the existing government structure. Adhocracy, said the person credited with coining the term—Harvard Professor Roger Porter, President Bush's domestic affairs adviser—"minimizes reliance on regularized and systematic patterns of providing advice and instead relies heavily on the president to distribute assignments and select whom he listens to and when."[14]

Although this approach has such advantages as flexibility and the nourishment of new ideas and policies, it tends to discourage debate and dissent, promote inconsistency, is error prone, and undermines morale. On the latter fault, more than anyone in the nation's capital, Lemnitzer must have known that his Chiefs were being bypassed and ignored by superiors who were more influenced by the advice of civilian newcomers without experience in military affairs. But there was little that an officer in Lemnitzer's position could do, except perhaps resign or retire. Complaint or open rebellion were out of the question, so when he had to comment his response would likely be along the lines of that he made to a New York resident who had just read an article in which *New York Times* correspondent Hanson Baldwin had written that the Chiefs were being ignored. The general wrote: "Despite a rash of somewhat similar newspaper stories, I can find no honest justification for the idea that the Joint Chiefs of Staff organization, or its chairman, are being bypassed or downgraded by the secretary of defense or the White House. On the contrary, my relations with the senior leaders of the Department of Defense are close and intimate. I see the president on an average of three or four times a week and am quite certain that my statutory responsibilities to the secretary of defense and the president have in no way been downgraded."[15]

Shortly before he left his position as chairman in 1962, Lemnitzer reported that the Chiefs agreed 99 percent of the time on the issues brought before them.[16] This was a remarkable record, but it was not achieved because JCS members just naturally thought alike or that they were trying conscientiously to place individual service loyalties behind the common good. On the contrary, each of their services still came first, but the members were able to work together to craft positions satisfying these parochial loyalties while fulfilling their corporate obligations to act in the best interests of all the services and the country. Unanimity on such a scale was a way of closing ranks against McNamara and his civilian aides. Another approach was gathering unassailable facts and arguments that defied reversal. These were often the products of the uniformed establishment's own whiz kids, new staff members who were also systems analysts and just as bright as those in McNamara's office. The services had adapted to the new rules quickly and in doing so made a discovery that also fit in well with the new order: by making certain assumptions, one could make the answer come out just about any way that was desired.[17]

Of all the members of the JCS, Lemnitzer was the most consummate "purple suiter," service slang for officers who serve in interservice assignments. To be able to reach a unanimous decision on an issue was regarded as a superior achievement, and the chairman worked hard toward this end. He had a good rapport with the Chiefs and tried to resolve as many potential sticking points as possible before going into the "tank," the JCS conference room down the hall from the chairman's office. He disliked surprises, and he didn't like to surprise others. The defense secretary was uncomfortable with consistently unanimous decisions and so was Taylor. When the new chairman assumed office in September 1962, he and McNamara encouraged split recommendations instead of "pallid compromises" because, the secretary reasoned, this gave him the opportunity to consider more than one side of an issue before making a decision.[18] With the hand-picked Chiefs that took office with Taylor, dissent found fertile ground and the number of split papers reached forty-two in 1963, forty-seven in 1964, and forty in 1965—still not very many, however, considering that the Chiefs issued over a thousand major decision papers a year. In 1966, however, the splits dropped to seven, and to six in 1967.[19]

Despite press reports that Lemnitzer was permanently in Kennedy's doghouse as a result of the Cuban mess, those who worked closely with the general could recall no outward display of Kennedy coolness, before or after the Bay of Pigs. The president addressed him warmly at meetings, and his relations with McNamara, at least when others were around, seemed cordial, if formal.

Surely one of the classic unsung military confrontations of the period had to have been that between the Kennedy administration's ways and those of the military men who had been in the Pentagon when Eisenhower was in office. Like Kennedy, the Republican president had had his circle of close advisers, but it was an administration in which the responsibilities of organizations and individuals were clearly defined—civilians in the defense department stayed out of matters assigned to uniformed professionals, and the latter were not permitted to stray into the provinces of the civilians. The chain of command, so fundamental to military functioning, was strictly observed by Eisenhower and his officials in the Department of Defense. It is inconceivable that during Eisenhower's years in office the commander in chief would have personally issued an operational order involving an ongoing action in the field, as did Kennedy when he canceled the D-Day air strike while forces were deploying to invade Cuba.

Even deeper ingrained in the makeup of a military professional was the way one carried out a staff assignment. At the Army's Command and Staff College, students were taught that when a commander gave an officer a problem to solve, he studied it thoroughly and then recommended a course of action. At the same time, the officer was expected to cite all the reasons why his recommendation should be adopted and all the reasons why it should not. The commander would then make his decision based on what he had been told. But Kennedy did not want a recommended course of action. He wanted to be given several plans— McNamara called them "fans of plans," and five or more was not unusual—with alternatives. William J. McCaffrey, then a colonel and the Army member of the Chairman's Staff Group, recalled that "we were supposed to crank in politics, culture and anything else that came in. He [Kennedy] told us not to say we were not politically involved—'you *are* involved,' he would state. 'When you go into the Bay of Pigs, for example, I want the whole nine yards. The money is important, the politics are important, the enemy is important—I want all those in there and I want several ways of doing it.' In the military, you argue to a point and then you put everything behind it. You are not supposed to say, 'that SOB in the White House said do this—I don't agree with it, but we'll go ahead.' You are supposed to say that the president, in all his brilliance, decided this and then put everything you have into making it work."[20] When Eisenhower made a decision, all argument ended. Lemnitzer likened Kennedy's policies in this regard to the way things might be done at a college seminar: "Decisions were reviewed and changed up to the moment of execution. Thus the JCS would think matters were settled when actually they were still open to discussion and revision."[21]

Despite Kennedy's insistence that the Chiefs consider all aspects of an issue in their planning, not just the military ones, soon after the new administration took over, McNamara's office canceled a speech by Admiral Burke because it dealt with a subject outside of the military sphere, namely the internal political situations in Cuba, Laos, and Africa. "As a result," the chairman recalled, "during National Security Council discussions, the JCS members were reluctant to volunteer opinions on matters beyond their own professional cognizance."[22]

The status of the Joint Chiefs was further complicated two months after the Bay of Pigs invasion when President Kennedy persuaded General Taylor to return to active duty and appointed him to the new post of Military Representative of the President. In the two years since his retirement, Taylor had held two jobs: board chairman of the Mexican Light and Power Company in Mexico City, and then president of New York's Lincoln Center for the Performing Arts, the post he held when the president asked him to head up the investigation into the Bay of Pigs failure. Taylor had earlier turned down a Kennedy offer to appoint him ambassador to France.

Taylor and Lemnitzer both professed to seeing nothing awkward about a four-star general being interspersed between the president and the JCS. Taylor noted that he and the chairman had been friends since cadet days and wrote that he told Lemnitzer that he did not intend to act as a White House "roadblock" to JCS recommendations. He suggested to Lemnitzer that he and the Chiefs have an "early exchange of views on important matters prior to sending final papers to the White House so that I can develop my views concurrently and inform the chairman in advance of any possible conflict." In turn, he said, "Lemnitzer promised to do all he could to prevent anyone from driving a wedge between us, a trend already visible in some of the press comment on my appointment."[23] Lemnitzer recalled that "we in the Chiefs had no particular objection [to Taylor's appointment]; we got along with General Taylor very well."[24] To the press, he said that he regarded Taylor's appointment as supplementing, rather than infringing on, JCS powers. To a Tennessee high school teacher who wrote asking his opinion of Taylor, he replied that "he is a brilliant and able officer and I have the highest personal regard for him. . . . [H]is judgment and experience will undoubtedly enable him to serve the president usefully."[25] But in a letter to his brother about job pressures, he wrote of "the problems regarding General Taylor's appointment" without being specific.[26]

Taylor wrote that his appointment caused no friction "that I was aware of, although I am quite sure that the Chiefs as a body never cared for the 'Milrep' [Pentagonese for the title of his new position] as an institution." McGeorge Bundy, the president's special assistant for national security affairs, was something else: still feeling his way in a post without clearly defined responsibilities, Bundy was unhappy because Taylor's presidentially mandated involvement with intelligence, Berlin, and Southeast Asia cut sharply across activities Bundy had been directing.[27]

There was little Lemnitzer could do about Taylor's appointment, even if he had wanted to, and if his indication of equanimity years later was sincere it is doubtful if he ever voiced any reservations to the president or McNamara. The fact is, however, that the JCS chairman was supposed to be the chief uniformed adviser to the president. Lemnitzer had partially rationalized Taylor's presence as good because of the president's limited experience in military affairs. But Taylor's responsibilities to the president went far beyond filling in gaps in the chief executive's knowledge. While Lemnitzer still met with the president, the JCS pipeline went through Taylor at his office in the Executive Office Building, located next to the White House, and then to the president. Indeed, judging from his suggestion to Lemnitzer about consulting with him in the formulation process, Taylor was, in effect, also acting as a second—and certainly more influential—chairman before JCS actions even started on their way.

The urbane and intellectual author of *The Uncertain Trumpet* fitted in well in the atmosphere of Camelot, as the White House's inner circle was called during the Kennedy years. His book made him enough of a rebel to give him credibility with the new wave of young iconoclasts; he worked hard, was articulate and responsive in the Oval Office, handled himself very well socially, and cut an impressive figure. He and Robert Kennedy became particularly close, enough for the president's brother to name a new son "Maxwell." Taylor's uniform was no handicap either when he succeeded Lemnitzer as JCS chairman the next year. Where Lemnitzer came to McNamara's office with alacrity when the secretary wanted to talk to him, Taylor, as often as not, would say something like, "Fine, Bob, step down to my office and let's discuss it." Taylor was not awed by McNamara's power and treated him as if he were at least his equal and even his mentor. Those who saw the transformation figured an important reason was that Taylor had a "constituency" in the White House, i.e. the president, his brother, and the others over there in whose company he moved easily and confidently.[28]

Lemnitzer had no sooner swallowed the pill of watching his obvious eventual successor move into the presidential compound when the press took offense over

Pentagon plans to refurbish his family living quarters in an aged brick building at Fort Myer. Unfortunately, the authorization of funds came in the wake of a rash of news stories about generals' fancy dwellings and offices—one of the most circulated was about a general who had his office walls covered with expensive silk wallpaper (ignored was the fact that he had paid for it himself). The renovation of the Lemnitzer quarters was needed and, although the improvements were extensive, they were not elegant. Still, the Pentagon thought it best to give the project a low profile. "We were able to avoid any publicity for an unusual period of time," he wrote to his brother. "[But] as you would expect, such a project cannot be kept secret. The service journals, as well as the Washington and Virginia papers, wrote some really nasty articles about it, implying that this was an unnecessary expenditure being undertaken to meet my personal requirements."[29] In the end, the work proceeded as scheduled and as planned, and still another Washington flap was soon forgotten.

When Lemnitzer briefed the Morse subcommittee about the Bay of Pigs, he was asked if he knew of any Defense Department plans for a direct U.S. invasion of Cuba. He replied that he did not, but the general was being less than candid (he was not testifying under oath). In fact, Kennedy and McNamara had ordered the Chiefs to begin preparing plans for military action the day after the Bay of Pigs operation collapsed. The Pentagon continually draws up and updates contingency plans for every conceivable situation in which U.S. military forces might be involved. The vast majority never get off the shelf, but Kennedy gave off indications that this might be one that had a good chance of being implemented. One sign Lemnitzer saw as significant was a comment the president made in a speech before the American Society of Newspaper Editors on the day he ordered the plans. The Bay of Pigs operation was the top news of the day and had to be addressed, no matter how much the president wanted to put it behind him. Kennedy told the editors: "Any unilateral American intervention would have been contrary to our traditions and international obligations. But let the record show that our restraint is not inexhaustible."[30]

In response to the president's wishes, McNamara called Lemnitzer in and issued a rush order: the secretary wanted a detailed analysis of alternatives, such as an invasion or a naval blockade; an assessment of Cuban military strength and how the residents would behave if the island was attacked; a detailed description of forces needed; specific actions considered necessary; the amount of time required to complete the conquest; anticipated casualties on both sides; and an analysis of U.S. capabilities to cope with conflicts that might break out elsewhere in the world as a result of the U.S. actions. This was an assignment that conceivably could take a large staff an entire summer to do well, but the Chiefs had a forty-two page paper on McNamara's desk in six days which spelled out the information he had ordered. The Chiefs recommended an invasion "so swift and overwhelming as to present the remainder of the world with a *fait accompli*." The plan that McNamara and Burke presented to Kennedy on April 29 provided that within twenty-five days sixty thousand troops would invade the island and subdue its defenders in eight days. Units selected for the operation, which would commence with an air assault on Havana, were the 82nd Airborne Division, 3rd Armored Cavalry Regiment, 2nd Infantry Brigade, and the 2nd Marine Division, in addition to supporting Air Force and naval elements. The operation should take place before the end of July to avoid having to fight in the hurricane season. The JCS suggested also that the United States create an "incident" that would justify the overthrow of the Castro government. "Such an incident," the recommendation said, "must be carefully planned and handled to ensure that it is plausible and that it occurs prior to any indication that the U.S. had decided to take military action against Cuba."

One idea considered by the Chiefs would have begun with an "ostentatious withdrawal" from the U.S. naval base at Guantánamo of a reinforced U.S. rifle company, artillery battery, and tank platoon that had just been sent in to bolster the marine garrison. Introduced for discussion by the Marine Corps's Shoup, the goal would be to entice the Cubans into committing an aggressive act by marching on the U.S. base, thus justifying retaliation in the eyes of the world. There was distaste in Lemnitzer's comment years later that "although this proposal was never pursued, it starkly reveals the straits to which General Shoup and his colleagues [in the JCS] felt themselves reduced."

The Chiefs thought the Cubans would be unable to offer an effective sustained resistance against U.S. forces. Only about a third of the Cuban population—"lower income groups, hard-core communists, hoodlums, and immature teenage persons"—completely supported Castro, the JCS plan said, while the rest would adopt a "wait-and-see attitude" toward the invaders—"although secretly approving." The Chiefs saw little likelihood that Russia would provide direct support or take military action for fear of touching off a general war.[31]

Kennedy agreed with the outline of the plan, but after its review by the National Security Council nothing ever came of it. Under continuing pressure from McNamara, the Chiefs worked to reduce to five days the response time from when U.S. forces were alerted to deployment, while discussing the feasibility of pre-positioning units for use when needed. In a short time, however, the plan ended up gathering dust in one of the secret crannies in which the Pentagon stores its carefully worked-out scenarios of campaigns that might have been.

Kennedy took seriously Eisenhower's warning that things looked very bad in Laos. The turmoil in the Southeast Asian region was the main topic of the new president's first meeting with the Chiefs on January 27, 1961, when he brought up the possibility of sending in U.S. troops and/or introducing counterinsurgency elements to train and lead pro-American forces. Of the problems with which he dealt during his two months in office, he probably spent more time on Laos than any other.[32] It wasn't much of a war. Rusk testified before the Senate Foreign Relations Committee that the forces involved "are not fighting as we think of fighting. A few shots make a large battle. If one side has 60-mm mortars and the other side has 81-mm mortars, the 81-mm mortars tend to win because they make a larger noise. It is not easy to get soldiers to lower their rifles to the horizontal and fire at someone rather than in the air." General Phoumi once refused to go to a place on the battlefield where he was needed because he said that a broken lifeline on his palm was a warning that he must not do so.[33]

But the caliber of the conflict was not commensurate with Laos's importance to the United States and the free world. If the line against Communist aggression was not drawn there, then the rest of strategically important Southeast Asia and adjoining areas were in danger. Should the mountainous little country fall to the Communists, under Washington's "domino theory" it would set in motion a succession of similar defeats until Cambodia, Thailand, and South Vietnam were also under Soviet control. Already Laos was being used by North Vietnam as a walk-through and staging area to support Communist guerrillas in South Vietnam. Lemnitzer and the Chiefs were not in favor of committing major U.S. forces to Laos, he told Kennedy, but preferred supporting indigenous elements with training and supplies.[34] The Chiefs' reluctance could be blamed partly on the armed services' experiences in Korea where commanders felt that their troops had been sacrificed for limited political objectives, and partly on the fact that the cutbacks and depletions of the Eisenhower years had cut the services to the bone, particularly the Army. One general told the president that "if we put as many as 125,000 [troops] into Southeast Asia, we wouldn't be able to fight a war in Florida."[35]

(The JCS chairman may not have been the original source of a term that became an integral part of the nation's Cold War lexicon in the Kennedy years, but the president had fun with his use of it during a White House meeting. When diplomat Charles E. Bohlen had given his views on possible Soviet reaction to U.S. mobilization during the Laos standoff, Kennedy got a laugh at a meeting when he turned to Lemnitzer and asked: "General, what is this word 'escalation' you've invented?" Lemnitzer reportedly did not smile.)[36]

At another conference early in the administration, White House staff members brought up the possibility of a quick airborne strike into the Laotian Plain of Jars, a site of frequent fighting, and Kennedy asked Lemnitzer if he could get paratroops into the area. "We can get them in all right," the JCS chairman replied. "It's getting them out that worries me." Eventually, the Chiefs said they would need 250,000 troops to enter Laos. When Lemnitzer was asked at a National Security Council meeting what would happen if Communist China or even the Soviet Union entered the conflict, he was said to have replied: "We'll take care of that." After NSC members pursued the matter, it became clear that what the general meant was the use of nuclear weapons.[37]

The United States did not commit major forces to Laos, and the situation there eventually became chiefly a State Department concern. The several factions stopped fighting for a while in early 1961 and agreed on a cease-fire. But in May 1961, this brief period of peace was broken by the communist Pathet Lao and the fighting resumed. McNamara and Lemnitzer were in Athens, Greece, for a meeting of NATO defense ministers in May when Kennedy wired them of the new development and sent them to Laos to see what was happening. They flew to Bangkok, Thailand, transferred to a Thai air force transport plane owned by the Thais to reach Laos, and flew along the Mekong River, site of much of the fighting and the frequent dividing line between the warring factions. Any troops in the area must have pulled back or were not inclined to fire on the visitors because the plane flew two hundred feet above the ground along the length of the river and back without drawing fire. Lemnitzer and the defense secretary spent two days in Thailand inspecting Laotian border defenses and advising the Thais how they could keep the resurgent Pathet Laos from invading.

In northern Thailand, the U.S. leaders detected heavy infiltration activity from Laos, which Lemnitzer blamed on a bold move by the Soviets, "goosing these people along to move into Southeast Asia. We felt that the United States simply couldn't stand by and do nothing." Therefore Lemnitzer recommended, and McNamara approved, the immediate dispatch of two American garrisons to the region. Kennedy backed the deployments, despite strong opposition from some of his advisers, and soon a U.S. Army infantry battalion and a marine battalion supported by two tactical air squadrons were dispatched for stationing at two northern Thailand air bases.

Eventually, the United States, the Soviet Union, and Red China reached a tacit understanding that Laos was not worth risking war over, and the conflict became largely a local one. Leaders, factions, boundaries, and causes changed back and forth with bewildering regularity long past the time when Lemnitzer had gone on to other responsibilities, but never again while he was in uniform would Laos hold the importance it did during the early months of the Kennedy administration.

McNamara and the JCS chairman stopped in South Vietnam on their way back to Washington from Thailand to talk with Prime Minister Diem and members of the U.S. MAAG (Military Assistance Advisory Group) about the worsening communist threat there. After conferring with the MAAG commander, Lt. Gen. Lionel G. McGarr, Lemnitzer sent a top secret message to the service Chiefs in Washington expressing grave concerns about U.S. efforts. Although Kennedy had given general approval to a request by Diem to increase his armed forces by twenty thousand troops, the general wrote that things were going badly because the United States and South Vietnam were arguing about which should fund it. The U.S. ambassador to Saigon, Elbridge Durbrow, thought South Vietnam should finance it and could afford to do so. Diem's position was that his country could not. "The result," Lemnitzer stated, "is an impasse with little or no real action taken to implement the increase in authorized strength. When I was in Saigon, only 4,000 to 6,000 of the increase had been raised and the entire effort was grinding to a dead halt with critical loss of time in initiating the long training period involved."

He also declared: "The problem of Vietnam from the U.S. point of view is very simple and very clear. Does the U.S. want Vietnam to follow the path of Laos (with the effect that will have on the rest of SE Asia) or does the U.S. really want to maintain Vietnam as an independent non-Communist state closely aligned with the West? Stated another way, does the U.S. intend to take the necessary military action now to defeat the Viet Cong threat or do we intend to quibble for weeks and months over details of general policy, finances, Vietnamese government organization, etc., while Vietnam slowly but surely goes down the drain of Communism, as North Vietnam and a large portion of Laos have done to date?" His report concluded: "In view of the very real enemy threat . . . and the fact that in the eyes of the world, and particularly in the Far East, the international prestige of the United States is literally at stake, I feel that we must avoid the marginal and piecemeal efforts that too often have typified the past and build into our program sufficient support in men, material and money to definitely assure that we do not lose Vietnam."[38]

McNamara received a copy of Lemnitzer's message and presumably he discussed its contents with the president. But for the time being, the problems of Southeast Asia had to be put on hold while the leader of the free world prepared for his first meeting with the rambunctious chief of the Communist one. Kennedy went to Vienna in early June 1961 for a summit meeting with Khrushchev, which he hoped would result in eased tensions between the two world powers. In the little more than three months that Kennedy had been in office, Cuba, Laos, and Berlin had drawn the wrath of the truculent Soviet premier who was given to boasts about his country's military superiority and how he would use it if the United States pushed him too far.

The JCS chairman's uneasiness with Kennedy's paucity of experience in military matters showed in a top secret memorandum Lemnitzer handed him before he left for the meeting. The Chiefs had been in Europe for a NATO military exercise in mid-May when Lemnitzer came up with the idea of preparing a paper about U.S. readiness to support the president in his expected tough talks with Khrushchev. The memorandum went through many drafts before Lemnitzer signed it and gave it to the president. Dated May 27, 1961, it read:

Memorandum for the President

Subject: Military Posture of the United States

In your conversation with Premier Khrushchev, be assured that you may speak from a position of decisive military superiority in any matter affecting the vital security interests of the United States and our allies.

Anticipating your meeting, the Joint Chiefs of Staff have reviewed the most current estimates of the forces opposing us and have considered U.S. capabilities and plans to combat these forces.

From this review it is the considered judgment of the Joint Chiefs of Staff that the military forces under your command are ready and capable of carrying out their assigned missions. Their plans are realistic and current. They can achieve decisive military victory in any all-out test of strength with the Sino-Soviet bloc to the extent that the United States will retain the dominant power position in the world. Thus in your discussions be assured you may represent the national interest with confidence and without fear or reservation.

The military forces of the United States reaffirm their dedication to your command and wish you Godspeed in your mission.

For the Joint Chiefs of Staff

L. L. Lemnitzer, Chairman

It was an unusual document, written at a time when there was a great deal of speculation in the U.S. press that Soviets had eclipsed the United States in military power. Lemnitzer said later that the Chiefs would have provided this assurance to any president in the same circumstances, but that Kennedy's short time in office was a compelling factor. Citing the many other issues with which a new president has to deal, the general explained: "We felt that he was just not in a position, and no human being could have been in a position, to really fully comprehend the military power of the United States to the degree that we wanted the president to comprehend it and use it at this important conference."[39] Although the statement bore the imprimatur of the Chiefs, it was inspired and drafted by Lemnitzer; no better example exists of his sensitivity and remarkable perception of what was going on in the world at any given moment.

Earlier in the month, Lemnitzer had told the House Armed Services Committee essentially what he had told the president. In a closed session of the committee, he said: "I do feel without any doubt, and other members of the Joint Chiefs would agree with me . . . that we do have at the present time the power to destroy the Soviet Union."[40]

The Vienna meeting had not gone well. The Russian leader had been arrogant, blustery, and intractable. As Lemnitzer recalled, Kennedy "came back absolutely furious. Khrushchev was goddamned rude to him and he didn't like it worth a nickel."[41] If anything, the meeting had left the two nations even further apart. It ended with an exchange of words over Berlin, which Khrushchev was determined to place under Soviet control whereas Kennedy was just as determined to prevent him from doing so. As the meeting broke up, the Soviet premier said, "I want peace, but if you want war that is your problem." Kennedy replied: "It is you, and not I, who wants to force a change."[42]

Khrushchev had been making threats over Berlin since 1958, and at the time the two leaders met, their countries were at odds over a Khrushchev demand that the United States and its allies—Great Britain and France—vacate their sectors by the end of 1961. Allied military vehicles and aircraft crossing through the one hundred ten miles of Communist territory leading into West Berlin were continually harassed: convoys were frequently stopped for long periods of time on technicalities or for no reason, and planes were subjected to near-miss passes by communist military aircraft. It was what Lemnitzer described as a "goddanged sensitive situation," which worried Kennedy because of the possibility that an exasperated soldier on either side could begin shooting and start World War III. Only the rigidly enforced self-control of allied troops, and apparently those on the other side as well, kept at least several confrontations from becoming shooting fights. In an effort to keep allied planes from flying in, the Soviets would announce that they were going to hold a military exercise over the area and that it would be unsafe to fly. "We just decided that we were going to fly anyway," Lemnitzer recalled. "We let them know that they were not blocking us out of our rights of access."[43] NATO planes could defend themselves from air attack, but Kennedy raised the question in a meeting of whether they could shoot back when they were fired at by antiaircraft weapons on the ground. Lemnitzer and Taylor argued strongly in favor of firing back, but the president agreed with McNamara that Washington would have to be consulted first.[44]

To back his Berlin demands, the Soviet premier ordered a resumption of nuclear bomb testing, breaking a mutual moratorium that had been in effect since 1958. The first atmospheric explosion in a series of such blasts occurred over Siberia in early September, presenting a problem to the U.S. administration, which was dedicated to bringing about a treaty that would ban testing. The Chiefs were opposed to a complete ban, Lemnitzer saying so at a National Security Council meeting that had been called to hear a report by Kennedy's Science Advisory Committee (SAC). Convened in early August amid rumors that Russian testing had resumed, NSC members were told by the group that there was no evidence that this was so and that there was not an urgent need for America to begin testing again. Lemnitzer summarized a JCS paper questioning the premises and conclusions of the report by saying: "I would like to emphasize that we are not advocating atmospheric testing. Our memorandum is at fault if it suggests otherwise [presidential special aide Schlesinger commented 'as indeed it appeared to do' in his book, A Thousand Days]. And we have no objection to a reasonable delay in the resumption of testing. But we do see urgency in testing for small-yield weapons development."[45] The Soviet tests had no effect on

Western powers resolve in Berlin, and when more blasts followed, the United States resumed its own testing.

Just before the tests resumed, the Americans noticed some unusual construction activity near the dividing line between East and West Berlin. It turned out to be a concrete wall, and the Allies didn't know what to make of it; considering the increasing bellicosity of Soviet statements and actions, the barricade could be the start of a new offensive move. "It created a crisis of the highest magnitude as to what they were up to [and] what to do about it," Lemnitzer stated.[46] Kennedy sent McNamara and Lemnitzer to Europe to confer with Supreme Allied Commander Norstad. From this visit came a U.S. decision to augment the Berlin garrison with a one thousand six hundred-man battle group, send two more divisions to central Europe, and put pressure on other NATO members to bolster their own forces and logistical support. Among other measures considered by the Chiefs was simply knocking the wall down. The battle group moved into Berlin along the autobahn from West Germany through Soviet-held territory. The Americans followed standard, agreed-upon procedures providing for the movement of troops and equipment across East German ground and had told the Soviets in advance that they were going to do so. "They didn't attempt to block that one," Lemnitzer said. "There would have been a real crisis if they had," he added, noting that there were twenty Soviet combat divisions in the area.[47] Lemnitzer's personal notes recall that when he proposed sending the brigade into Berlin along the autobahn at a White House meeting "all of the president's other advisers assailed it as needlessly provocative." It was, he wrote, one of the worst confrontations to take place at this level during his tenure as chairman. Despite this opposition, Kennedy approved the move and, the general remembered, his estimate of the commander in chief "took a sharp upward turn."[48]

The purpose of the strange new barrier (infamous in history as the "Berlin Wall") became apparent only as construction progressed. It had been put up by Khrushchev to halt the exodus of thousands of East German residents to the West to escape harsh Communist governing methods and abysmal economic conditions; in July 1961 alone, over thirty thousand refugees fled into West Germany. By the time it was finished, the twelve-foot-high barrier stretched one hundred three miles; illuminated by floodlights and tended by armed troops, electronic sensors, explosive mines, and sentry dogs, the wall was a sinister symbol of Communist oppression for nearly thirty years before it was torn down in 1989 after the two Germanys were united. It turned out that the catastrophic drain on the population of his Eastern Europe satellites was what was bothering Khrushchev the most about Berlin. In October, he told the Twenty-Second Congress of the Soviet Communist Party that because the western powers were cooperating in seeking a solution to the Berlin problem "we shall not insist on signing a peace treaty absolutely before December 31, 1961."[49] Another nail-biting brush with war was over.

Meanwhile, the situation in South Vietnam was continuing to get worse. By the summer of 1961, Diem controlled only 40 percent of his country and 85 percent of his one hundred seventy thousand-man army was tied down in fighting the insurgents. Communist forces and supplies were infiltrated with impunity along the length of the so-called "Ho Chi Minh Trail," a network of roads running along the Communist-controlled borders of neighboring Laos and Cambodia. In October, Kennedy ordered Taylor to Saigon to assess the situation and recommend solutions. With him he carried a JCS analysis of South Vietnam's manpower requirements in internal security, defense against conventional attacks by North Vietnam, and defense against infiltration across its borders. Taylor, who had been accompanied on the trip by Walt Rostow, Bundy's expert on South Vietnam, returned to Washington with a series of recommendations calling for a heavy influx of U.S. help in a broad range of areas, from military assistance to nation building. The key and potentially most thorny proposal was the introduction of a U.S. logistical task force whose mission it would be to provide a "military presence" for Vietnamese morale purposes, support military operations or flood relief, and serve as an emergency reserve in a military crisis. McNamara and the Chiefs studied Taylor's recommendations and gave their support with several major—and prescient—reservations. The U.S. contingent of eight thousand troops needed to implement the program was too small to be convincing and decisive. The proposals amounted to a useful first step, the Chiefs suggested, but it was one which could lead to much deeper military involvement. If North Vietnam sent in its regular forces and Communist China intervened, the United States would have to commit up to six divisions. Before taking the first step, the McNamara/JCS memorandum continued, the administration should decide whether or not to commit itself without reservation to preventing the fall of South Vietnam and what price it was prepared to pay.

The memorandum, which was given to the president, recommended that the government assume this commitment and support it with the necessary military actions. The possibility of intervention by outside forces would not be the compelling factor in deploying U.S. forces: South Vietnam was unlikely to be able to win a war against infiltrated forces, and thus the United States must be prepared to introduce its own combat resources.

McNamara and Rusk incorporated their recommendations, which contained the essentials of Taylor's proposals, into a National Security Action Memorandum, and the president signed it on November 15, 1961. His approval put into motion a great wave of activity by the principle agencies that would be involved—the State and Defense departments, the CIA, the Agency for International Development (AID), and the U.S. Information Agency (USIA).

The country, and even those who set the sails, didn't know it then but the United States had just gone to war.

20

★ ★ ★ ★

VIETNAM

The people were already becoming used to the "whup-whup" of helicopter blades, so the villagers didn't pay much attention when still another Huey landed in a big cloud of whirling dust beside the others that had arrived earlier. Besides, they were preoccupied with another sight that morning. After alighting from their craft, McNamara and Lemnitzer walked to the village's center where the bloody corpses of eight South Vietnamese civilians were laid out on the ground. Two had been school teachers, one was a doctor, another was the mayor. Their throats had been cut a few hours before by members of the Viet Cong.

It was a scene often duplicated during a war of terror that had been unleashed by the communists under Ho Chi Minh in a ruthless campaign to bring the south under North Vietnam's control. The murderers were guerrillas, either infiltrators from the north or inhabitants of the region who carried on ordinary lives during the day and were cruel enemies of the state and their neighbors by night.

The two U.S. military leaders were on an inspection visit to South Vietnam in the spring of 1962 when they were flown into a countryside of rice paddies and tiny hamlets to view this macabre example of warfare, Viet Cong style. Lemnitzer estimated that similar nighttime tactics had brought about the murders of seventy thousand pro-Diem government local leaders during the period. Ho Chi Minh's aim was to frighten the people into becoming pro-Communist and to eliminate local leaders so that they could be replaced with communists. Weapons, supplies, and training personnel were being funneled into the country in an increasing volume during these early days of the buildup. The decision to go the whole way in keeping South Vietnam out of communist hands had been made, the Chiefs had supported it, and now their chairman was checking up on how well things were going.

The secretary and the JCS chairman arrived as the Pathet Lao went on the offensive again in neighboring Laos, breaking another cease-fire and sending Royal Laotian Army troops fleeing a hundred miles past the cease-fire line to the border of northern Thailand. President Kennedy had just ordered another four thousand troops sent to pro-West Thailand, bringing to five thousand the number of U.S. soldiers and Marines assigned to ensure the country's security.

In South Vietnam, more than six thousand members of the U.S. armed services were engaged in advising, training, and supporting Diem's forces against the hit-and-run raids and terrorist attacks of the Viet Cong. Another thousand American troops were on their way, along with more shipments of weapons and materiel. But despite the growing U.S. military presence, except for isolated brushes with guerrillas the United States was adhering to its policy of avoiding the introduction of combat forces. Still, an increasing number of Americans were getting killed, although these occurrences were still rare enough to be front-page news in the United States. One of these incidents happened when Lemnitzer was in the region: it involved two U.S. Army sergeants who had been wounded and captured by Viet Cong members during an ambush while they were on a training mission with a Vietnamese civic action platoon. They were shot and killed, apparently because their wounds prevented them from keeping up with their captors.[1]

However, McNamara was so satisfied in general with the way things were progressing that as he and Lemnitzer boarded their plane to return to Washington, he told reporters he doubted that any more U.S. military personnel would be sent to Vietnam or that the flow of war materiel would have to be increased—he added a caveat, though: barring unexpected setbacks in the domestic struggle or overt aggression from the communist bloc.[2] But of course the escalation of the communist commitment continued and less than two months after McNamara's comments, as many as three thousand well-equipped guerrillas had moved into South Vietnam from Laos. The heavy influx was in anticipation of the onset of the rainy season when helicopter and tactical air support would be limited. By that time, there were believed to be twenty-five thousand organized guerrilla forces in the country, supported by thousands of members of South Vietnam's general population.[3] The United States estimated that of South Vietnam's twelve million residents, four million were communists—a significant ratio because guerrilla warfare cannot succeed without the active support of the people in providing concealment, recruits, food, intelligence, and medical attention. The gradual shift from being mere advisers to becoming comrades in arms had begun. In 1964 the United States began bombing North Vietnam and the next year its troops became combatants after the north started sending down regular forces in a stepped-up drive to subdue the south. By early 1969, the year

Lemnitzer retired, there were nearly five hundred fifty thousand American troops in South Vietnam.

Vietnam was never Lemnitzer's war—the buildup was only beginning when he moved on to a new assignment. If there was a uniformed "point man" at this stage, it was Taylor, who initiated the plan to support Diem's government, saw it through its development as Lemnitzer's successor, and wound up running matters on the scene as the U.S. ambassador to South Vietnam. It was McNamara and Taylor, not Lemnitzer, to whom the president and his civilian lieutenants turned as they eased into the current that would send their nation tumbling into war. Vietnam had been Taylor's show even before the buildup began, and it was to him that Kennedy handed the ball as Vietnam moved steadily upward on the agenda in the Oval Office.

As Washington began stepping up its support in late 1961, Kennedy approved McNamara's recommendation that the U.S. command structure in South Vietnam be upgraded from an advisory group to a military assistance command headed by a four star-general. Since the decision had been made not to introduce combat troops, the Chiefs had what Lemnitzer described as "serious doubts" about making such a change. However, as the chairman wrote to McGarr, the Chiefs were not consulted; McNamara and Rusk "agreed that they personally (and not, repeat *not*, their staffs) would work out a final recommendation for submission to the president." The letter was a thoughtful gesture on Lemnitzer's part: McGarr was a very insecure person of modest abilities who used to dispatch long, handwritten letters to Lemnitzer expressing his cares, problems, and concerns, and seeking the chairman's approval. The primary reason for the change, Lemnitzer wrote to McGarr "is to impress Diem that we are entering a new era in U.S.-Vietnamese relationships in which the U.S. will be giving him increased support and be expecting him to pay increased heed to our advice and suggestions."

While working out the details of a reorganization to which he was opposed, Lemnitzer also had the unpleasant task of informing McGarr that he would now report to a newly promoted four-star general, Paul D. Harkins. McGarr had done a good job under very trying conditions, and Lemnitzer wrote to him: "The JCS and I have complete confidence in you and have been thoroughly satisfied with the results you have achieved in the face of great handicaps, obstacles and frustrations. All of this, I know, adds up to something less than a Christmas present for you, but you are too good a soldier to let it bother you for long."[4]

Despite an interest in the Far East that lasted for many years after he served there, Lemnitzer had long been skeptical about the prospects of settling the problems of Southeast Asia. In 1954, when he was Army deputy chief of staff for plans and research, he wrote to a friend soon after the fall of the French garrison at Dien Bien Phu: "As you can well imagine, the cease-fire in Indochina is causing us a great many problems. The present tendency is to build up SEATO in Southeast Asia, but we in the military are not impressed by such an idea. We feel there is little power to build on in that part of the world and it just adds another large military commitment when our limited military resources are already stretched to the breaking point. We are having enough trouble in making ends meet in NATO insofar as military forces and equipment are concerned."[5]

Still, he was the chairman of the JCS and he had his own ideas about how the communists should he handled. He must have thought the likelihood of the United States becoming involved in a shooting war was high because his plan called for putting American troops into North Vietnam. Roger Warner, an assistant secretary in the State Department and a future ambassador to Laos, recalled: "Lem had been a great friend and protégé of Eisenhower's and Kennedy didn't consider him fully sympathetic to the Kennedy approach to things. Lem knew that he was going to be shelved fairly soon and he asked for an opportunity to present personally his view of how he thought a military campaign should be conducted against North Vietnam, if we were going to conduct one. I suppose he wanted to present it to the president [but] finally it ended up being presented in Bob McNamara's office. Bundy came from the White House, I came from State and I think Alex Johnson [deputy undersecretary of state for political affairs] was there, possibly Paul Nitze and somebody from the Agency [CIA]. Anyway, it was a small group."[6]

Lemnitzer knew that the Ho Chi Minh Trail would be a major problem in an all-out war, just as it was in the limited military action then taking place. Extending south from North Vietnam along the edges of neighboring Laos and Cambodia, it proved to be the lifeline of the communist supply effort and the march route to the south for the Viet Cong and North Vietnamese regular forces. So porous were the national borders that men and materiel could be slipped into South Vietnam practically at will along the trail's entire eight hundred-mile length. The trail started in North Vietnam at the Mu Gia Pass, located in a four hundred-foot high karst (an irregular limestone formation with sinks, underground streams, and caverns). The JCS chairman proposed landing amphibious forces near Vinh on the Gulf of Tonkin, driving the fifty miles across North Vietnam to the Laotian border, and setting up a strong fortified position north of the Mu Gia Pass. The objective would be to plug the trail and starve out North Vietnam resources in the south. The move would necessitate sitting upon North Vietnam's two southern provinces, which Lemnitzer saw as bargaining chips in negotiations. If the North Vietnamese pulled back everything they had sent into South Vietnam, the plan envisioned removing U.S. forces from the two provinces and returning the dividing line between the two nations to the seventeenth parallel.

Warner thought Lemnitzer's plan made good military sense and so did several retired French officers who had come to Washington with the same idea. Each with extensive experience in Southeast Asia, they had flown over on their own volition to offer advice when they saw the United States becoming increasingly involved. When Warner became ambassador to Laos, he sent a cable to

Washington suggesting that Lemnitzer's plan be put into effect because he was convinced that this was the only way to win the war militarily. "And I am still convinced of that to this day," he said after the war.[7] Nothing ever came of Lemnitzer's idea. The United States generally stuck to a policy of keeping its ground forces inside South Vietnam's borders, a rule it violated in force only in the final stages of the war when the United States and its allies got fed up and sent troops into Cambodia to destroy some of the Communists' most notorious supply sanctuaries.

Lemnitzer applauded the Cambodian incursion when it occurred years later. He had thought that President Johnson, Kennedy's successor, made a "colossal and unbelievable blunder—one of the most stupid mistakes possible in warfare"— when he announced publicly in 1965 that the United States had no intention of invading North Vietnam. "It made North Vietnam (except for periodic air bombing) the greatest sanctuary of them all and enabled Hanoi to turn loose all of its divisions to invade South Vietnam, Laos, and Cambodia. They did not have to keep any at home for defense." The general felt that "the conditions for fast-moving and hard-hitting amphibious operations along the coast of Vietnam were ideal because the enemy had no navy or air force to speak of. Furthermore, I felt that the best way to get Hanoi to bring its invading forces home was to keep North Vietnam under constant threat of an amphibious landing under the complete air superiority we had throughout the war."[8]

When Lemnitzer was nearing the end of his term as chairman in mid-1962, any serious prospect of engaging in a large-scale war with combat troops had not entered the heads of America's senior military leadership. He recalled: "During my direct association with activities in South Vietnam as chief of staff of the Army and chairman of the Joint Chiefs of Staff, I don't think we ever reached a point where we didn't believe it couldn't be dealt with by military aid, the advisory groups, assisting in training and so forth. It was generally felt that this would be adequate, and it would have been if the north hadn't resorted to the use of their regular military forces."[9] There was no "hard pressure" in Washington, that he recalled, to move in U.S. forces and engage in combat on the mainland of Asia. "As a matter of fact, the feeling was just the opposite," he said, with most of those in power firmly in agreement with the earlier views of Eisenhower and MacArthur that the United States should not get involved in a war in Asia.[10]

Lemnitzer's disapproval of the way the war was being fought was summed up in 1970 in his foreword to *Alternative to Armageddon*, a book on big war strategy: ". . . [T]he past quarter of a century has seen the evolution of a widespread misconception that there is only one military alternative to nuclear holocaust. That alternative is held to be a campaign in which military objectives and the methods of seeking them are sharply restricted and the military forces are politically shackled. In application, this approach has been marked by steady and protracted attrition, to no end except qualified success at best—paid for in wasted blood and treasure. It has forced us to fight on the enemy's terms, not ours; it has represented ineffective and inefficient use of our capabilities; and in the poverty of its results compared with the cost, it has degraded our world stature, encouraged our antagonists and disheartened our people."[11]

Nevertheless, he always defended the Vietnam War as having been consistent with U.S. foreign policy aims. After his retirement, he devoted much of his time to giving speeches on military issues. The conflict in Vietnam was still going on then, and a much-used phrase among critics was "immoral war," a term that would make him bristle if it was used when he answered questions from the audience after his speeches: "I [had] detected from where I sat on the military aid program nothing but support for the programs started under President Truman, and carried out under President Eisenhower, to assist newly emerging nations throughout the world in establishing themselves as free, independent and sovereign nations. It was a noble objective and that's why I object so violently to the people who, in my lecture and speaking tours, start off their questions with 'Now, about this immoral war in Vietnam, general.' That's as far as I ever let them get. I said, 'what's immoral about it?' and then I asked them if they knew how we got into Vietnam to start with." He would then go back to 1954 when the French withdrew from Southeast Asia and trace U.S. involvement step by step to the commitment of its armed forces in supporting his view that the war was a "noble cause."[12]

In addition to the U.S. failure to take the war into North Vietnam, Lemnitzer blamed antiwar sentiment in the United States for the ultimate defeat of South Vietnam and its allies: "The collapse of both the Vietnamese and our own forces was largely due to the general attitude back home. There's no reason to believe that our war was supported," he recalled, likening the feeling to when he commanded a division in Korea: "There, too, we were losing the war on the home front." The Communist victory notwithstanding, admitting defeat did not come easily for many senior U.S. military officers. A view that received considerable license in 1975 when the communists routed South Vietnamese forces and compelled them to surrender was, "We won the war and then we left and the South Vietnamese lost." "I wouldn't agree with that," Lemnitzer said. "We lost the war. The South Vietnamese were not capable of dealing with the enemy."[13]

Fallout from a previous war caught the JCS chairman in its dust during another trip to the Far East in April 1962. Congressmen, veterans' organizations, and people in general were angry when he personally awarded the U.S. Legion of Merit, in the degree of commander, to Gen. Minoru Genda, retiring chief of the Japanese air force. Genda, then a naval officer, had a key role in drawing up the plans for Japan's attack on Pearl Harbor. To add to the public indignation, Genda had been quoted as having said the year before receiving the award that "we should not have attacked just once. We should have attacked again and again."[14] The U.S. Air Force had recommended that Genda be given the award, the highest military medal that could be conferred on a foreigner, in recognition of his cooperation with the United States after the war and for his outstanding work in building up the Japanese air force. It was approved in Washington, and authorization was given to the U.S. ambassador to Japan to present it. Lemnitzer was in Tokyo at the time and was at the award ceremony. As a courtesy, the ambassador invited the JCS chairman to make the award and he did—willingly, because he knew the Japanese officer and appreciated the support he had given the United States since the war. Possibly the resulting furor would have been less if the ambassador, as a civilian, had pinned on the medal, but, as one letter to *The New York Times* stated, the decoration was given "by no less a person than Gen. Lyman L. Lemnitzer, chairman of our Joint Chiefs of Staff."[15] The gesture touched off a storm of protest, including denunciations from such organizations as the American Legion, Veterans of Foreign Wars, and the Gold Star Mothers. Among the individuals who wrote to the general to voice their displeasure was Eleanor Roosevelt, widow of President Franklin D. Roosevelt.

"I have received quite a number of letters raising hell over this award and I am taking the pains to reply to every one of them," Lemnitzer wrote to his brother. Of his reply to Mrs. Roosevelt, he wrote that the former First Lady was satisfied with his explanation. He also told his brother: "You must remember that in top-level assignments such as I hold at the present time, one does not select the duties which have to be carried out. My participation in the award to General Genda was a part of my official duty and there was no sidestepping it."[16] In fact, he could have sidestepped it, but he respected Genda, who was running for election to the Japanese Senate, and thought he would be an influential friend of the United States if successful (which he was, serving with distinction as a member of the Japanese parliament until his death). McNamara's office, which had approved the award, made matters worse when Gilpatric issued a statement saying that in the future "the exact procedure" laid down by regulations would be followed. Retired Col. John B. B. Trussell, then of Lemnitzer's staff, noted: "Of course, the exact procedure had been followed meticulously in this case, but the dishonest implication that something had been slipped through the system was clear—and intentional."[17] Kennedy was more supportive, however. When asked to comment on the award at a press conference, the president said he thought it was appropriate because Genda had been a distinguished flier and in "his relations with the United States [he] had been extremely cooperative." Noting that Genda had been acting as a military officer under orders when he helped plan the 1941 attack, Kennedy said: "The days of the war are over. While we all regret Pearl Harbor and everything else, we're in a new era in our relations with Japan."[18]

Although Lemnitzer may have regretted the passing of the Eisenhower era with its orderliness and deft hand on the tiller, he must have been pleased with Kennedy's high regard for conventional forces. The president wanted multiple options in the power struggle with the Soviet Union and the concept of flexible response, with its heavy reliance on ground forces, was a better alternative than massive retaliation. Kennedy made it clear early in his administration that the country must be willing to pay whatever was necessary for adequate security. Defense budgets climbed into the fifty billion dollar range, in contrast to the thirty-eight billion dollars spent by his predecessor. Treasury Secretary George Humphrey had said at an NSC meeting during the Eisenhower administration that the American people would never stand for another thirty-eight billion dollar budget, but the Berlin crisis was being played out during Kennedy's term, and the country accepted the higher outlays without serious protest. McNamara was responsible for charting the buildup, but Taylor described him as "strangely reluctant to increase the forces on a permanent basis, insisting instead on a temporary incremental expansion." It took him nearly a year to expand the Army from fourteen to sixteen divisions, and the defense secretary did it only after Kennedy insisted on it. But at the same time, he set a ceiling of nine hundred sixty thousand on Army uniformed personnel strength despite what Taylor called "clear evidence that about a million men would be needed to maintain sixteen combat-ready divisions."[19]

Kennedy had a deep interest in counterinsurgency from the time he took office, and he devoted considerable time in his early meetings with the Chiefs to finding out about what the services were doing in this area and in pressuring them to step up their emphasis. Southeast Asia was a compelling factor, but the president also saw roles for U.S. trainers in guerrilla and counterguerrilla warfare in South and Central America and in Africa. Khrushchev had been a factor in the attention counterinsurgency began to receive because Kennedy had listened closely to a speech the Soviet leader had given just before Kennedy was inaugurated. In it, Khrushchev had outlined three kinds of conflict between the East and West: nuclear wars, conventional wars, and wars of national liberation. He had discounted the first as too dangerous and the second as possibly leading to nuclear war, but he saw wars of national liberation as an acceptable way of spreading world Communism. The struggles in Laos and South Vietnam were such conflicts.

When the president asked what the armed services were doing in the area of counterinsurgency, the Army told proudly of its Special Forces, whose mission it was to go behind enemy lines and train guerrillas. The president became fascinated with the Special Forces, which he saw in the field for the first time during a visit to Fort Bragg, North Carolina, with Lemnitzer and other defense officials. Originally intended to operate behind front lines in Europe, the Special Forces consisted of tough, highly skilled soldiers who, besides being experts in weapons and tactics, also spoke in a wide range of foreign languages and were proficient in intelligence, communications, and medical care. The key unit was an "A-Team" of twelve men capable of training up to five hundred foreign personnel at a time, customarily in the back country areas where guerrillas normally function. As impressed as he was, Kennedy wanted the Special Forces to be more than just trainers. He directed the Army to increase their size substantially and to change their mission from training to one of fighting insurgencies in countries friendly to the United States. Army Chief of Staff Decker thought the changes would impair the Special Forces's effectiveness and preferred that the Army develop a general capability in this area. The Army did what the commander in chief ordered, but Decker's reluctance was so obvious that it was believed to have been a factor in his serving only one term as the Army chief of staff instead of the customary two.[20]

At a key meeting to discuss increasing counterinsurgency capabilities, the president asked General Shoup what the Marine Corps was doing in this respect. The commandant replied that the Marines preferred to be their own guerrillas and heretofore had not wanted to train others. Kennedy's response was that it was not always possible to take direct action and that the armed forces would have to be satisfied with training residents of other countries to perform their own guerrilla and antiguerrilla operations—"realizing, of course, that this would disappoint the Marine Corps, but that into each life some disappointment must fall."[21]

The number of Special Forces units was increased substantially, with more and more being sent to South Vietnam as the war there picked up tempo. Little known to the public before Kennedy became president, the Special Forces became famous in story and song as the "Green Berets," in tribute to the then unorthodox (for U.S. armed forces) headgear they were authorized to wear, largely through the influence of the admiring chief executive.

Kennedy's focus on counterinsurgency as a prime means of combating communist inroads resulted in the creation of still another ad hoc organization, this one designated as the Special Group Counterinsurgency (CI). This top-level unit was headed by Taylor and included among its members Robert Kennedy, Lemnitzer, Bundy, CIA Director John McCone, Gilpatric, the State Department's Alex Johnson, USIA Director Edward R. Murrow, and AID Administrator Fowler Hamilton. Among the CI's main functions was to assure recognition throughout the government that subversive insurgency was a political-military conflict equal in importance to conventional warfare, and to keep under review the adequacy of U.S. resources in dealing with insurgency. Initial top priority was given to Laos, South Vietnam, and Thailand. Group members could not be accompanied to meetings by members of their staffs, obliging them, in Taylor's words, to "do their own homework and speak their own minds.... [T]hey knew the eye of the president was constantly upon them and that their chairman reported their day's work to him immediately after each meeting." At least some sessions must have involved a certain amount of arm-twisting to bring everyone in line with the new priorities because Taylor wrote of Robert Kennedy as being the guarantor of "unusually candid testimony" from those called before the group. "Bob was a bit rough on evasive witnesses," the general recalled.[22]

Spurred by the Kennedy brothers, the Special Group followed what the chairman described as a "feverish" pace in the early months of its existence. Among the Group's means of making sure military personnel got the message was its no-exceptions enforcement of a presidential order that any colonel being considered for promotion to general officer rank be required to have had either training or experience in counterinsurgency. By the end of 1962, counterinsurgency courses had been added to the curricula of the war colleges and elsewhere in the military school system, and fifty thousand officer-grade military and civilian officials were involved in the various training programs.

Lemnitzer's involvement in the complex deliberations and preparations that preceded America's decision to fight in Southeast Asia ended in September 1962, after Kennedy nominated him to succeed Norstad in Europe as SACEUR. Taylor was named his successor as chairman of the JCS, and General Wheeler, deputy commander in chief of the U.S. European Command, was selected to succeed Decker as Army chief of staff. Except for Shoup, Kennedy now had a JCS of his own choosing. Air Force Chief LeMay and Adm. George W. Anderson, chief of naval operations, were both his appointees. In picking Taylor, the president had not followed the traditional rotation between the services; if he had, the new chairman would have been an admiral.

Without mentioning Lemnitzer, after his retirement Taylor wrote that he had been pleased with the new JCS lineup because "an incoming president is well-advised to change [his] Chiefs"—in particular the chairman because he should be a "true believer in the foreign policy and military strategy of the administration he serves. . . . Moreover," he asserted, "I have come to understand the importance of an intimate, easy relationship, born of friendship and mutual regard, between the president and the Chiefs. It is particularly important in the case of the chairman. . . ."[23] Not said but inferred was that Kennedy now had such a man in the person of his former military representative. Also unstated, but clear, was Taylor's belief that his predecessor had not had this kind of rapport.

Ever the unswerving military professional, Lemnitzer always eschewed such reasoning as violating the principle that senior officers should be apolitical in their dealings and outlook while in uniform. Although firmly believing that military officers should be responsive to the country's political leadership, he thought that changing the chairman or any of the Chiefs with administrations would deeply politicize the military. Taylor used to feel the same way; at least that is what he wrote in his book, *The Uncertain Trumpet*, when he took Eisenhower to task for replacing all of the Chiefs after he became president.

It must have been clear to Lemnitzer that he was not going to be appointed to a second term as JCS chairman long before his first term expired. Perhaps he did not want the customary second tour because he revealed to a friend in the spring of 1962 that he was considering some job offers in the private sector. Later he accepted one of the offers and planned to enter the employ of Ryan Aeronautical Company when he retired. It is not clear in what capacity he would have served, but he recalled years later that the pay would have been nearly twice that of what he received as JCS chairman.[24]

There was a complication regarding any future service: he would be able to serve less than half his second two-year term as chairman because he would become sixty-four, the Army's mandatory retirement age, on August 29, 1963. If Kennedy had really wanted to keep him on, for another year or even another full term, there were ways of doing it, as will be seen. But Taylor's name had been on the chairman's chair from the time he got back into uniform, and there is little doubt that his performance over his first year had more than met the president's expectations.

Good soldier that he was, Lemnitzer probably would have stayed on if Kennedy had convinced him that he was needed, but after forty-four years in uniform he was ready for a rest. The prospect of a good salary, far less pressure, and more time at home was very appealing, and with just six months left in his term of office he happily began making plans for retirement. It had been a long time since he had been able to get in a round of golf or head north for a weekend of fishing in Honesdale.

The first glimmer that this might not come about right away occurred in the spring of 1962 when he was in London for a meeting. He and Kay had been invited by his former World War II commander, retired Field Marshal Earl Alexander, to come out to his home near Windsor Castle for Easter dinner. The earl was no longer the British minister of defense, but he was still influential in government affairs, and he was a lifelong friend of Harold Macmillan, the prime minister. While the two were walking in his garden, Alexander asked the general about his retirement plans. When Lemnitzer said he was considering several offers in the private sector, Alexander asked him if he had ever thought of succeeding General Norstad as NATO's supreme allied commander. Lemnitzer said he was surprised and replied: "Hell, no. I've never even thought about it. As far as I know, Larry [Norstad] is doing well there and I've never given it any consideration. Why do you ask?" Alexander answered that Macmillan, with whom Lemnitzer had been acquainted when he served with Alexander in Italy, had asked him to bring up the subject and inquire if the general was interested. The two went on to talk about other things, and Lemnitzer put the conversation in the back of his mind until he returned to Washington, when he received a visit from an officer on the military attaché's staff at the West German embassy who said he was acting on behalf of Chancellor Konrad Adenauer. He posed the same question as Alexander's, to which the JCS chairman replied that he had already made his retirement plans and was not interested.

The next move came from Kennedy, who talked to Lemnitzer after an NSC meeting in June and told him he wanted to nominate him to succeed Norstad, who, he said, had asked to retire in the fall. The highly regarded Air Force general, who had served six years in the NATO post, had suffered a mild heart attack and had also had some serious policy differences with McNamara. The offer was compelling. Lemnitzer had played a pioneer role in establishing NATO and had always been one of its most enthusiastic supporters among the military. But there

was a formidable obstacle to his serving: because he was facing mandatory retirement, any service beyond his first year would have to be as a retired general and
he was strongly opposed to a retired officer holding the SACEUR post. Kennedy
answered, "Oh, there's no problem with that. I'll take care of it." Lemnitzer
recalled replying, "Well, I don't know how you're going to do it," and then left the
matter up to Kennedy. Years later, he remarked: "Well, he *was* the president of
the United States."[25]

The next time he saw the president, McNamara was with him and told the
general, "if you agree to take the post I will ensure that you will be retained on
active duty for as long as you are SACEUR."[26] The general then raised another
issue: the SACEUR was paid $4,300 less a year than the JCS chairman, a not
inconsiderable sum when the chairman's yearly pay was $30,625 ($23,640, salary;
$2,412, quarters; $575, subsistence; and $4,000, personal allowance). McNamara
promised to seek introduction of a bill in Congress that would raise the
SACEUR's pay to that of the JCS chairman. He kept his word, but the bill was
turned down by the Senate after winning passage in the House. By then,
Lemnitzer was in Europe.

The other fourteen members of the alliance had learned before Lemnitzer's
talk with Alexander that the United States was planning to nominate Wheeler
to succeed Norstad. After a tour as director of the JCS's Joint Staff, the urbane,
soft-spoken Wheeler had been named deputy commander in chief of the U.S.
Europe Command in early 1962, apparently to prepare him to eventually take
over as SACEUR. Lemnitzer had helped in choosing him to become the eventual
supreme commander and admired him, as did McNamara who saw him as a gifted
planner to whom facts and cold logic, not service loyalties, were guiding principles.[27] But despite Wheeler's impressive qualifications, he was not well known
among NATO civilian and military leaders. The allies sent word to Washington
through the U.S. ambassador to France, James Gavin, that they wanted someone
with more prestige and experience in NATO affairs. Lemnitzer's name was the
one most mentioned as the next SACEUR when the alliance was informed that
Norstad was retiring. Lemnitzer held the highest military rank in the United
States, and no other general still on active duty was as closely identified with
NATO as he was: he had represented the United States at the meetings that led
to its creation, had helped draft the treaty on which it was founded, and had
given it teeth as the first U.S. director of military assistance.

Another factor, Lemnitzer wrote in a letter to former Army Secretary Brucker,
"was that I had just completed a year as chairman of the NATO Military
Committee in Chiefs of Staff Session during which I handled some very controversial and complex items without the explosions that everyone expected."[28]
Adding to Lemnitzer's credentials were the respect and support of longtime
friends Macmillan and Adenauer, two of the most powerful leaders in the
alliance. This had to have put considerable pressure on Kennedy, who surely had

not given the prospect of sending Lemnitzer to Europe a thought up to that time.

NATO was going through a period of internal squabbling in the early 1960s, much of it fomented by French President de Gaulle who, among other things, was raising questions about whether the SACEUR had to be from the United States. It was important to nominate a general who could achieve universal acceptance. Moreover, Lemnitzer wrote to Brucker, "It looked as if NATO was drifting toward real trouble when the matter of a new SACEUR appointment came up. This could be disastrous for the alliance and at the very time when NATO solidarity was needed more than ever." Regarding his decision to accept the nomination, he wrote the former Army secretary: "I had made complete plans to retire at the end of my present term as chairman . . . and was looking forward to doing so, taking up one of the many attractive offers I have received. The developments in the NATO situation, however, changed all that. I felt that only one decision was possible under the changed circumstances. While there were many personal aspects which made it difficult for Kay and myself, I considered that the U.S. national and NATO implications were so important that it was clearly my duty to accept the appointment."[29]

Wheeler's career was not adversely affected by what happened. After serving as Army chief of staff, he succeeded Taylor and went on to perform with distinction as chairman of the JCS.

The president formally nominated Lemnitzer to become the new SACEUR in July 1962, and five days later the nomination was unanimously approved by NATO's Council of Permanent Representatives. Some observers interpreted the delay as indicating that there was some opposition within the Council to the choice or that its response had been lukewarm. However, the reason was that before the vote de Gaulle wanted to talk with Lemnitzer about his views regarding matters of concern to the alliance, thus exercising a rarely executed right held by member nations to interview nominees to high NATO positions.

Lemnitzer turned over the chairmanship of the JCS to Taylor on October 1 in a ceremony in the White House's Rose Garden, at which President Kennedy presented the departing chairman his third Distinguished Service Medal and praised him for carrying out "the grave responsibilities of his office in an extremely outstanding manner. In the nation's highest military office, he distinguished himself as a dynamic leader whose exceptional competence in strategy, diplomacy and politico-military relations contributed significantly to the successful accomplishment of United States objectives of great national and international importance. During a period of grave international tensions, his sound judgment, breadth of vision, foresight and strength of character have been of inestimable value to the president of the United States and the secretary of defense."

The president noted that during Lemnitzer's tenure the armed services had "reached a new peacetime level of strength, flexibility and effectiveness." Forward deployments of U.S. forces were increased "significantly" in Europe and

Southeast Asia under his chairmanship and "the balance between conventional and nuclear forces was greatly improved to cope with a wide variety of threats to our security. General Lemnitzer's performance of duty reflects great credit upon himself and upon the United States of America and is in keeping with the highest traditions of the military service."[30]

The general was scheduled to take up his new duties in a change of command ceremony in Paris on November 1, giving him a month to wind up unfinished JCS business, attend briefings on his new responsibilities, and see to his personal affairs in preparation for an indefinite stay in Europe. Then, two weeks into this hiatus, something occurred that took up much of his attention for the rest of his time in Washington and set back his assumption of his new command until the coming year: on October 14, a U.S. spy plane took photographs showing Soviet atomic missile sites being built in Cuba. Along with much of official Washington—and, indeed, the entire country—Lemnitzer was suddenly caught up in the chilling "Thirteen Days," a historic confrontation between the world's leading powers that brought them very close to nuclear war. Thirty years later, McNamara recalled the period as the most frightening of his tenure as defense secretary: "There was a moment on Saturday night, October 27, 1962, when, as I left the president's office to go to the Pentagon—a perfectly beautiful fall evening—I thought I might never live to see another Saturday night."[31]

Lemnitzer's JCS experience was put to use as the White House and the Pentagon deliberated on how to cope with this new threat to world peace. The president's chief advisers during the crisis were members of a cabinet-level executive committee (EXCOMM) of the NSC, whose meetings Lemnitzer attended. He also sat in on some of the JCS conferences on the crisis. The Chiefs appeared to have had little influence on Kennedy's eventual decision—to impose a partial blockade to prevent more missiles and launching equipment from reaching Cuba. The JCS favored a massive air strike to destroy the missile sites, some IL-28 bombers the Soviets had also sent to Castro, and the country's entire air defense system. As to a blockade, the JCS wanted a complete one that would halt all imports, especially the petroleum products upon which its economy depended heavily.[32]

The meeting that stood out most in Lemnitzer's memory of the Thirteen Days was one which was called while he was watching a football game between West Point and George Washington University in the nation's capital. Summoned to the White House, he hurried over to where the National Security Council was convening to discuss a Khrushchev offer: the Soviet Union would take its missiles out of Cuba if the United States would remove its intermediate range Jupiters from Turkey and Italy. The proposal followed by a day a somewhat disjointed message from the Soviet leader agreeing to remove or destroy its missiles if Kennedy would remove the U.S. blockade and promise not to invade Cuba.

Vice President Johnson was at the meeting in the president's place, and he thought the mutual removal of missile sites was "a good deal that would go a long way toward solving this particular problem." Lemnitzer recalled that he was aghast, and during a break following the vice president's comment he went over to him and said: "Look, Mr. Vice President, it is not a good deal. These are NATO missiles, not United States missiles, and we would make the greatest mistake in the world to say [to Russia], 'Yes, we agree to bring them out' without consulting our allies." The general had been one of the movers in persuading first NATO and then "Greece and Turkey to put their fates on the line and agree to become targets by putting the missiles in their countries. I had been through all the meetings—the defense ministers' meetings, the military committee meetings, the [NATO] Council meetings, both around Washington and over there. I remember those arguments—they were long and difficult." But Johnson was unmoved. "God, he couldn't see it worth a damn," Lemnitzer said.[33]

In his reply to Khrushchev, Kennedy accepted the Soviet leader's first pro-posal—not to attack Cuba in exchange for removal of the missiles—and seemingly ignored the second one about taking out the U.S. missiles in Turkey. Cuba-bound Soviet ships carrying missile equipment turned around and headed back to Russia, and the technicians building the missile sites began to dismantle them. By October 28, the missile crisis was over.

Rusk, McNamara, and four other members of Kennedy's inner circle revealed twenty years later that a few hours after Johnson and Lemnitzer had their argument, the president sent his private assurance to Khrushchev that the missiles in Turkey would be withdrawn after the Cuban crisis was resolved. The promise was made by Robert Kennedy in a secret meeting with Soviet Ambassador Anatoli Dobrynin on the evening of October 27. The assurance was not to be regarded as part of a Cuban crisis "deal," the president's brother told Dobrynin; any attempt to do so would nullify the assurance.

The Rusk-McNamara statement reported that Kennedy had reached the conclusion early in his administration that the one thousand five hundred-mile range Jupiters were obsolete and vulnerable to attack. Rusk had approached high Turkish officials about their removal in the spring of 1961. The Turks asked that the action be delayed until submarine-launched Polaris missiles could be deployed in the Mediterranean, and the United States had not pressed the matter since the Rusk meeting. According to Rusk and McNamara, the Cuban crisis reinforced the president's conviction about removing the Jupiters and the secret promise to Khrushchev was the result. Kennedy's pledge was kept secret, the former secretaries stated, because "any other course would have had explosive and destructive effects on the security of the U.S. and its allies. If made public in the context of the Soviet proposal to make a deal, the unilateral decision by the president would have been misread as an unwilling concession granted in fear at the expense of an ally." "Deal" or not, the assurance was "helpful in making it easier for the Soviet government to decide to withdraw its missiles." The next year, after Lemnitzer had taken over as supreme commander, the fifteen Jupiters in Turkey and the thirty in Italy were removed—with the concurrence of NATO allies—and replaced by the Polaris.[34]

This brush with nuclear war had an unsettling effect on America's NATO allies and on international relations in general, so the alliance decided to postpone the installation of a new supreme commander until tensions died down. Lemnitzer was to go to Europe in November and put on Norstad's other hat—commander in chief of the U.S. European Command (USCINCEUR). Then, on January 1, 1963, Norstad would step down and Lemnitzer would also become SACEUR.

Two weeks before Lemnitzer had ceased to be chairman, he received a letter from Hanson W. Baldwin, the Pulitzer Prize-winning military editor of *The New York Times* and an astute chronicler of the stampede of McNamara and the Whiz Kids. Baldwin did not expect to be back in the capital to pay his personal respects before the general left, so he wrote:

"This is just to say thank you for all your kindnesses and courtesies to me and *The New York Times* during your tour as chairman of the Joint Chiefs and to congratulate you on the loyalty, faithfulness, good humor, common sense and integrity with which you have carried out your duties during a very difficult time.

"You have carried yourself like a soldier and I know of no higher praise."[35]

21

★ ★ ★ ★

SUPREME COMMANDER: THE FRENCH DISCONNECTION

"First they send us a tranquil ambassador and a restless general; now they've sent us a restless ambassador and a tranquil general."[1] Despite the sour ring to his pronouncement, the president of France held no rancor or disrespect for the men involved. It was just that about everything the United States did in regard to Europe in the 1960s was apt to prompt some kind of negative response from Charles de Gaulle. This particular comment was piffling; he could be more cutting with entire nations or groups of nations.

The events that prompted the French leader's cynical assessments were the arrival in Paris of veteran diplomat Charles (Chip) Bohlen to replace Gavin as U.S. ambassador, and General Lemnitzer's becoming the successor to NATO's Norstad. De Gaulle had done his homework in regard to the unflappable Lemnitzer, just as he had with Bohlen, a hard-driving former ambassador to the Soviet Union who had a reputation for not being easy to push around. Norstad had earned firsthand the adjective the French leader had attached to him.

Lemnitzer had known de Gaulle since World War II when the American general was on Eisenhower's staff during the invasion of North Africa and de Gaulle was emerging as the leader of Free France. Later he had seen the French leader's storied stubbornness up close when, as deputy chief of staff to Field Marshal Alexander, he had been only partially successful in overcoming de Gaulle's refusal to send more troops at a critical moment in the battle for Rome (de Gaulle wanted to save them for the invasion of France). They had both been at the historic Casablanca conference in 1943, Lemnitzer as a low-profile staff general and de Gaulle as a principal without portfolio who was soundly snubbed by the other Allied leaders.[2]

Five months before Lemnitzer succeeded Norstad, the French president summoned Lemnitzer to Paris for an interview following his nomination by Kennedy. The heads of NATO member nations had the right to interview high-level nominees, but in the nuance-conscious world of international politics, such a move could be construed as harassment—and, indeed, it was so viewed. Only de Gaulle of the alliance's fifteen heads of state asked for such a meeting. Lemnitzer did not resent having to pass personal muster and said that he would have willingly met with every head of state in the alliance if asked: "They had the right—this is the name of the game."[3]

Any American would have been subject to the same scrutiny, for Lemnitzer arrived on the scene at a time when de Gaulle was becoming increasingly resentful of U.S. dominance in NATO, was envious of the U.S.-British monopoly on the alliance's nuclear capability, and was obsessed with providing France with its own nuclear weaponry—an asset he considered essential to military power in the modern era. At the moment, he was also miffed at the United States because it had not consulted its European allies before Kennedy issued his ultimatum to Khrushchev in the Cuban missile confrontation. De Gaulle's anger at not having been consulted on a matter he felt could have brought NATO into a nuclear war gave rise to a sardonic question that Lemnitzer was to hear often when he had occasion to talk with de Gaulle about a NATO issue involving the United States: "Am I being consulted or informed?"[4]

The two disagreed on many issues, from the proper makeup of conventional forces and the intentions of the Warsaw Pact to de Gaulle's desire that a European—a Frenchman, in particular—be named the supreme allied commander, instead of it always being an American. Any meeting of minds with a world figure who seemed to be on a course of obstinacy for the sake of obstinacy seemed impossible, especially when an American was involved. Lemnitzer tried to bridge the gaps: to de Gaulle's comment that the SACEUR was controlled by Washington, Lemnitzer pointed out that he carried out only policies that had been unanimously approved by NATO's ministers. When de Gaulle objected to French forces serving under the U.S. flag, the SACEUR replied, "But you did that during the war [World War II] and you did pretty well." Reminding the French president that a French general commanded the main NATO sector, Central Europe, also had no effect on de Gaulle's insistence that a Frenchman should be in overall command.

Ironically, they did agree on a topic that was closest to de Gaulle's heart in terms of military readiness. Good soldier that he was, Lemnitzer probably never told de Gaulle about it, but when he was Army chief of staff, he and the other service chiefs had strongly urged that the United States help France in its nuclear research efforts. The Chiefs' position was that the Soviets already had the know-how the French were seeking and the huge amounts of money they were spending on research could serve NATO better if they were spent on conventional forces. But the Eisenhower administration, at Norstad's insistence, said no.[5]

Despite their differences, the two got along well. SHAPE (Supreme

Headquarters Allied Powers, Europe) was located just outside of Paris, and Lemnitzer and de Gaulle conferred often, met socially, hunted together, and the American general was occasionally invited to accompany de Gaulle at official functions. He was with him in August 1964 when the French leader was the near victim of an assassination attempt, the seventh of his career up to that time. Lemnitzer was standing close enough that he very likely would have been killed, too, had the effort succeeded.

Lemnitzer and de Gaulle had gone to the southern coast of France for a series of celebrations marking the twentieth anniversary of the allied landing in southern France in World War II. The U.S. general, accompanied by Ambassador Bohlen, was there for ceremonies commemorating an American airborne attack, and de Gaulle was to officiate at a series of observances honoring the performance of a French corps. The invasion had been a glorious moment for France, and de Gaulle had been determined that his segment would not be sullied by any reminders that there had been other allied troops in the invasion or that it had been commanded by an American general (Jacob Devers).[6]

Surprisingly, the French president invited Lemnitzer and Bohlen to join his official party for the windup of the French celebration in Toulon. Despite several days of heavy rains, thousands of French citizens lined the coastal city's streets to watch as de Gaulle led the singing of the French national anthem. There was a big parade, a review of allied ships in the harbor, and then a long walk up a steep hill where the French had built a museum to commemorate the invasion. Lemnitzer and Bohlen stood with the French cabinet and other French dignitaries while a band played, and de Gaulle took an honor guard's salute prior to touring the museum. During the ceremony, the official party stood in front of a four-foot-high *jardiniere,* an ornamental stand holding flowers in honor of the occasion. Two days after the ceremony, the display burst into flames. Investigation revealed that it had concealed a large bomb that had been too dampened by rain to explode when the would-be assassin had tried to detonate it by a radio signal from behind a nearby tree. When the bomb dried out, it apparently had lost its explosive properties and caught fire when the detonating equipment the would-be bomber had left behind finally did its job.[7]

De Gaulle's comment that Washington had sent a "tranquil" general to become NATO's supreme commander already became flawed when Lemnitzer put on his SACEUR hat after two months as commander in chief of U.S. forces in Europe. The general regarded the brief hiatus as a valuable opportunity to inspect his future command at the unit level, and one of the places he wanted most to see was West Berlin. But he soon found that this presented a problem: if he went as USCINCEUR, NATO's civilian ministers had no objection, but he was also the SACEUR-designate and they feared that a trip across more than a hundred miles of Soviet-occupied territory into a trouble spot like West Berlin could be provocative and dangerous. These qualms were made known to him as "innuendos," he reported years later, and never were expressed directly at the ministerial level. But the signals were strong enough to make him so furious that he considered resigning if the issue was pressed. "I got so concerned about this I decided that if I was going to be told by political authorities what I was going to do as a military commander they had better look somewhere else for a SACUER/CINCEUR. My policy had always been that a commander visits the troops in the most remote and dangerous positions first, and that was Berlin."[8] The U.S. European Command that he now headed comprised over four hundred thousand American personnel and was one of seven unified field commands operating under the JCS.

A prime factor in Lemnitzer's desire to go to West Berlin was that as USCINCEUR he also was "White Oak," the code name for the general assigned to take direct command of U.S., British, and French forces in Berlin should a shooting conflict break out with the Warsaw Pact. He had been in West Berlin many times, but with U.S.-Soviet differences as volatile as they were in late 1962 he felt that a personal visit was important. The upshot was that he flew into the former German capital, inspected the U.S. garrison, and heard nothing more about the matter afterward from the doubters in NATO.

The episode came very close to testing a complicated command arrangement in which the SACEUR answered to NATO and the USCINCEUR to the president of the United States through the JCS. But the same person normally held both posts—the temporary separation in late 1962 was a unique situation brought on by world tensions during the Cuban missile crisis. Lemnitzer reasoned that NATO's Council of Ministers did not have the authority to prevent him from going to Berlin, but President Kennedy did while he was wearing only his CINCEUR hat. If the ministers had pressed the point with Kennedy, Lemnitzer had in his files a paper for the president setting forth his reasons for wanting to go to Berlin, intending then to abide by whatever decision the president made.[9] It did not come to that, but it gave Lemnitzer an early glimpse of what it meant to be the supreme allied commander in terms of allegiance. As the SACEUR, he was responsible to NATO's civilian leadership and not to any authority in the United States; to create even the suspicion that he was being influenced by Washington would have seriously damaged his credibility. Washington should have understood that, and had—at least through the Eisenhower administration— but some of Kennedy's chief lieutenants had difficulty in reconciling themselves to the fact that they could not give orders to a U.S. general when he wore his SACEUR's hat.

Norstad recalled giving a fleeting thought to punching a U.S. cabinet secretary whom he thought had questioned his loyalty to the United States during a meeting at SHAPE. He did not identify the official, who was one of two secretaries at the meeting, but it is probable that the secretaries were McNamara and Rusk. With the coming to power of the Kennedy administration, Norstad had been receiving increasing pressure to implement American decisions independently of the NATO nations. His visitors wanted him to carry out some action he thought was wrong, and he told them: "But even if it weren't wrong, I couldn't and wouldn't do it because I have obligations. I've been around here for ten years [including previous alliance assignments] and in the course of time these governments have done things because I asked them to do it. Many times they've done it solely because I asked them to do it. Every time I've done that I've taken on an obligation, and I respect that obligation." Norstad said that one of the cabinet officers then asked: "That's the question we have: just to whom do you have an obligation?" The general said that "in other words, he was challenging my loyalty. My first instinct was to hit him and I thought that wouldn't be very dignified, so I didn't do that. I just stood there and I tried to smile and cool off a bit and I gave him a short explanation of what NATO meant and what the supreme commander meant in the whole picture. And I said, 'Well gentlemen, I think that ends this meeting.' Whereupon, I walked out and slammed the door."[10]

Brilliant, politically astute, and charismatic, Norstad believed that the supreme commander was the "heart" of "this, the greatest alliance that ever existed." At the meeting with the U.S. cabinet officials, he made a statement that probably summed up the thoughts of every man who had ever held the SACEUR's post: "The people of Europe . . . believe in NATO more than they ever believed in anything, and they believe in it because they feel that we have demonstrated that the supreme commander, though an American, thinks of their interests and has an obligation to them as well as to his own country. If you take that away, you destroy the alliance. And I'm not going to destroy it; I've spent too much of my life in this and it's too important to the world." After the meeting, Norstad convened his senior staff and said, "Gentlemen, we aren't going to be together very much longer. If they can't put up with me after this and I can't put up with them . . . one way or another, it's going to come to an end."[11] Eisenhower, as the first SHAPE commander, had understood and respected Norstad's position; those around the new president clearly did not. Norstad was convinced, too, that he was considered a Republican partisan and that the Kennedy administration regarded him as a reminder of the Eisenhower administration's success in NATO. "The new government didn't necessarily take kindly to that," he observed.[12]

When Washington announced Norstad's retirement in mid-1962, the public explanation was that he had requested it for health reasons—he had suffered a mild heart attack the year before. But the general, still fit and at the height of his abilities at fifty-five, had not wanted to go. Retired Lt. Gen. William J. McCaffrey, then assigned to the office of the chairman of the JCS, recalls running into Norstad in the Pentagon when the supreme commander was in Washington to see the president. McCaffrey, who had served under Norstad at SHAPE and admired him greatly, was aware that a concerted effort was under way in the Secretary of Defense's office to get rid of him as SACEUR, so he followed him into a men's rest room opposite the chairman's office to tell him that "a fix was on." As McCaffrey remembered his response, Norstad said, "Bill, the president and I have very similar views on how to handle the situation in Europe. I am aware of the differences with Defense and State, and I am confident the president will support me."[13] This support, if it ever were extended, was not enough, however; Norstad was too strong for McNamara's taste, too ready to take issue with the secretary's initiatives, and he had to go.

Norstad's watch was a hard one to follow. Described by Eisenhower as "one of those rare men whose capacity knows no limit," he had a reputation for having a strong personality and the ability to make decisions quickly and clearly.[14] He liked delving into NATO politics, and his stature and judgment were such that the civilian leadership into whose areas he often strayed tended not to challenge him. Norstad and Lemnitzer were outstanding supreme allied commanders, each highly effective in attaining objectives and of like minds on such issues as NATO's nuclear posture and forward defense. But they were different men in terms of approach, style, and personality.

When Lemnitzer retired, the West Germany newspaper *Frankfurter Allgemeine Zeitung* lauded him as having been a "patient and tough admonisher and warrior" in his dealings with NATO allies and who had known how to "multiply and improve what had been entrusted to him." Comparing him with Norstad, the paper attributed his success to "persistence rather than clever impulses" and to "his paternal, critical patience rather than the disarming brilliance and penetrating intelligence that had been his predecessor's."

One of the fundamental differences between the two was in their attitudes toward civilian control. Norstad respected this—he had to because the ultimate power in NATO lay in the North Atlantic Council, the supreme authority, and the alliance's Military Committee. But Norstad got away with taking political matters into his own hands; Lemnitzer, a seasoned veteran of over a dozen years of high-level Washington skirmishing, did not try and was always careful to make clear to such third parties as the press that he took his orders from his NATO superiors. His predecessor considered the SACEUR the embodiment of all the alliance stood for; Lemnitzer did not.

NATO was nearly fourteen years old when Lemnitzer became its fifth supreme military commander.[15] His command stretched three thousand six hundred miles along a line from the northern tip of Norway to the eastern reaches of Turkey and from the borders of West Germany on the east to France's Atlantic shores on the west. Fifty-three ground divisions in varying degrees of combat readiness, backed by more than five thousand tactical aircraft and powerful sea elements, were assigned to Lemnitzer when he took command, with another six divisions scheduled to be committed in the central sector within six months.[16] It had taken NATO nearly ten years to reach this goal, set in 1954, when it became apparent that the original target of ninety divisions could not be met.[17]

Created after World War II as a defense against communist efforts to dominate Western Europe, NATO had inspired the Soviets in 1955 to establish a NATO counterpart: the Warsaw Pact. The Communist alliance was made up of the Soviet Union and seven Eastern European satellites. It was a powerful military force, the core of which was twenty-six of the best armored and motorized divisions in the USSR's one hundred sixty-division army. It was an operational army, not an occupation force, and it was equipped with the latest tanks and weaponry, whereas the tactical air forces supporting it were among the most modern in the Soviet air force. The satellites—East Germany, Poland, Hungary, Romania, Czechoslovakia, Albania, and Bulgaria—provided sixty more divisions in varying and sometimes dubious degrees of training and readiness.[18]

A successful supreme commander had to be many things—an inspiring and charismatic leader, strategist, tactician, logistician, manager, business executive, diplomat, public relations expert, father figure and—despite Lemnitzer's conviction that such things are best left to civilians—a superb politician. All of these facets were brought to bear on what he considered his most important mission: the maintenance of effective combat readiness throughout his command. In a letter to his successor, Gen. Andrew J. Goodpaster, Lemnitzer wrote in reply to Goodpaster's request for an outline of priorities: "The planning and operational sides of combat readiness are absolutely vital factors. The requirements insofar as SACEUR are concerned are formidable and require his constant attention. It involves personally checking plans, visiting subordinate headquarters and units, attending exercises and maneuvers and pressing national authorities to remedy the most glaring deficiencies in their respective forces."[19] He also placed a premium on choosing outstanding senior personnel. Assignment to the SHAPE staff carried considerable prestige in member countries, and competition for appointments was intense. In his advice to Goodpaster, Lemnitzer cited something he had heard Gen. Omar Bradley say: "When you have the right senior personnel available in the right spots of command and staff, a commander's operational and other problems are largely 'in the bag.'"[20]

Whereas the supreme allied commander answered to the alliance, it was also a fact of life that he could be effective only as long as he had the support of its most powerful member, the United States. He lasted six and a half years in the post, more than anyone before him, so Washington must have been at least satisfied with the way he was doing his job. Lemnitzer's identification with a previous administration was even stronger than Norstad's, but McNamara undoubtedly found it easier to get along with him than his outspoken predecessor. Lemnitzer was a better diplomat; he and the defense secretary had worked together closely—if stiffly—for nearly two years; and, most importantly, the even-tempered and pragmatic Lemnitzer could get along with just about anybody.

Their relationship was tested early in Lemnitzer's tenure. McNamara and Paul H. Nitze, assistant secretary of defense for international security affairs, set up a meeting in the U.S. embassy in Paris at which the SACEUR was told that the two officials had decided that he should reorganize the SHAPE staff into separate nuclear and conventional sections. Lemnitzer refused, citing a study he had made when he was chairman of the JCS showing that separating these functions was unworkable. For example, it was impossible to separate a tactical aircraft that could drop either a nuclear or a conventional bomb; there was artillery that could fire both nuclear and conventional weapons; and intelligence could not be separated into nuclear and conventional. The general told McNamara that he would start such a reorganization only if he was ordered to by the North Atlantic Council. "But I also pointed out that if I got such a directive from the council it would have to get a new SACEUR." Walter Stoessel, Lemnitzer's adviser on international affairs who was at the meeting, thought his boss was going to get fired, but he stayed on and the secretary did not press the matter again.[21] Lemnitzer's one concession was that he appointed to his staff a deputy for nuclear affairs, an Italian general whom he completely ignored.[22]

Fueled by de Gaulle's frequent indications of unhappiness with Europe's military dependence on the United States, there was growing unrest among its allies about such questions as whether Washington would really be willing to risk nuclear retaliation at home by countering with atomic weapons a Soviet attack on a member nation. Massive retaliation was still the strategic policy in NATO when Lemnitzer took over; it had been an effective deterrent in the 1950s, but now that the Soviet Union also had a powerful nuclear capability, the U.S. shield was not the awesome factor that it had been.

McNamara and others, first in Kennedy's administration and then Johnson's, went to sometimes ludicrous lengths to show that Washington regarded its allies as equal partners. Lemnitzer took sharp issue with McNamara's desire that there be as many Greeks and Turks as Americans on the staff of Land Forces Southeast. The Greeks and Turks were far short of having the necessary expertise to handle the staff work, but McNamara never gave up in his efforts to pressure the SACEUR to reorganize this staff. Another idea that earned Lemnitzer's scorn was a relic of the last years of the Eisenhower administration which, fortunately, suffered a deserved death while he was SACEUR. Conceived during U.S. efforts to encourage creation of a "multilateral force" (MLF), the plan envisioned manning U.S. nuclear submarines with mixed crews made up of personnel from various NATO nations. "That fell flat on its face," Lemnitzer said, "because the idea of having a Polaris crew made up of Greeks, Turks, British, Americans and so forth living together for sixty days at a time under the ocean was impossible."[23] A subsequent proposal to integrate the crews of surface warships also went nowhere.

Although the general believed in integrated staffs—and, in fact, during World War II became one of the military profession's pioneers in making them work— he was convinced that "integrated forces of various nationalities at the lower levels was unfeasible, undesirable and ineffective."[24] The only real implementation of MLF was in the area of missiles because this gave NATO allies the feeling that they were involved in nuclear operations, but Lemnitzer always took a dim view of efforts to extend integration further. The MLF concept never received the necessary support among such powerful allies as Great Britain and France; Johnson lost interest, and when it was permanently shelved in late 1964, only staunch supporter West Germany mourned.[25]

One successful, though qualified, exception to the SACEUR's anti-integration views was the elite ACE (Allied Command Europe) Mobile Force. Hailed by Lemnitzer in 1965 as a significant milestone in MLF efforts, the brigade-sized force consisted of five thousand troops whose mission it was to quickly deploy to any area threatened by invasion, particularly in the lightly defended northern and eastern flanks of the alliance. Equipped with nuclear weapons, the force was a balanced land unit of brigade strength backed up by six air squadrons. Integration was by national unit—infantry; artillery; helicopter; armored reconnaissance; combat support; and administrative elements from Belgium, Canada, West Germany, Italy, Luxembourg, Great Britain, and the United States.[26]

While he was chairman of the JCS, Lemnitzer inaugurated an information program designed to acquaint allied military officers with the nuclear weaponry the United States had deployed in Europe. The program, which took a year to implement because much of the material was classified, had been inspired by a comment from a Belgian general who told Lemnitzer he was always embarrassed when he returned to Brussels after a NATO meeting to have to reply to King Baudouin's questions about the alliance's latest nuclear developments that "I don't know a damned thing about it except what I read in the newspapers."[27] Until early 1962, West Germany's government had no idea of what kind or how many nuclear weapons were on its soil.[28]

A heavily guarded airplane carrying briefing teams was assigned to the project and flown throughout the command to provide information on the alliance's nuclear capabilities. But McNamara decided that more was needed to convince the allies that they were being treated as partners. He told Lemnitzer that he wanted to form a nuclear committee at the political level made up of representatives of NATO's five principal nations; his plan was to call it the "Select Committee." The general recalled responding, "Geez, that's a lousy name for it." The secretary looked surprised and asked why. Lemnitzer replied: "Look, you're talking to an organization of fifteen nations; it's going to be easy to select five nations for the committee, but it's going to be damned hard to select ten of them off." McNamara saw his point, and the choice of a name was still up in the air the next time the secretary came to Europe. Lemnitzer told him, probably tongue in cheek, that he and his staff had thought of a name: the "McNamara Committee." He said McNamara "went straight up through the overhead [ceiling]." Eventually, the committee became known as the Nuclear Plans Group,[29] which was made up of permanent members United States, Britain, West Germany, Italy (France had by this time left the alliance), and two other nations represented in rotation. This group and the Nuclear Defense Affairs Committee, membership in which was open to all allies, dealt with problems of target selection, warhead allocation, and command coordination.[30]

Like Norstad before him, Lemnitzer sought diligently to persuade Washington to deploy a midrange ballistic nuclear missile (MRBM) in Europe. "We considered it one of our most important requirements," Lemnitzer said. "However, our strong recommendations were never approved because a serious impasse developed between the U.S. Defense Department and the Senate Armed Services Committee over the effectiveness of missiles versus bombers and the mobile missile we proposed fell by the wayside." The result was that NATO had nothing to compare with the hundreds of Soviet SS-20 mobile missiles which came to be one of the Warsaw Pact's principal weapons.[31]

While Lemnitzer was the Army's deputy chief of staff for plans and research, he had pushed research on a low-yield nuclear missile called the "Davy Crockett," which could be fired from a shoulder-launched, bazooka-type weapon. By the time he became SACEUR, the Davy Crockett had been thoroughly tested and was being issued to U.S. forces when the Pentagon ordered that deployment be stopped. The stated reason, Lemnitzer said, was that "we did not want some sergeant starting a nuclear war." The supreme commander protested, but to no avail: "That decision, made against military recommendations, was faulty because it was made on the false premise that sergeants would be carrying nuclear weapons around on a belt and using them promiscuously. It showed a complete ignorance of the very, very strict rules involved in the nuclear weapon release procedures in effect throughout the alliance. However, the Davy Crockett was withdrawn and was never added to our arsenal."[32]

Lemnitzer felt the same way about giving launch responsibility to generals. He was appalled to learn during the 1964 presidential election campaign that a plank in Republican candidate Barry Goldwater's platform called for giving the SACEUR authority to use tactical nuclear weapons in Europe whenever he thought it justified. The deployment of "tac nukes" was a hot topic then, and the general was besieged by reporters when he arrived in the United States on official business shortly after the platform was announced. He declined comment on the grounds that the subject was highly classified, but after he retired he said he "very strongly opposed such a policy because I felt that the initial decision to employ tactical nuclear weapons in NATO would be one of the most profound, important and far-reaching decisions in history. It should not be regarded solely as a military decision, because it encompasses vital political, moral and psychological issues, as well as military."[33] Under the policy then in effect, the supreme allied commander was empowered to recommend the use of nuclear weapons, but authority to use them was vested in the North Atlantic Council with its representatives of the fifteen heads of state. Since the decision would have to be unanimous, the United States would also have to give its consent.[34]

McNamara disdained mobile ground-based tactical nuclear weapons as being of negligible importance in combat, vulnerable to detection and countermeasures, and inciteful of a preemptive first strike by enemy long-range missiles. The administration's alternative to the MRBMs urged by Lemnitzer was the commitment to NATO of several fully operational submarines equipped with Polaris A1 missiles (SLBMs) which could fire six hundred-kiloton nuclear warheads 1,380 miles from underwater launching positions. These were assigned specifically to the supreme allied commander. The United States still considered the defense of Europe on a "global basis," however,[35] which meant that it was ready to use intercontinental missiles (ICBMs), such as the Atlas and Titan I, which could fire three- or four-megaton warheads over nine thousand miles. By the mid-1960s, America was turning out the much more accurate solid-fuel Minuteman, which carried multiple warheads (MIRVs), each with from one hundred fifty to three hundred fifty kilotons of explosive power.[36]

Although massive retaliation as a defense strategy was becoming passé as early as the waning days of the Eisenhower administration, it remained the official strategy in Europe for much of Lemnitzer's tenure. He had been an advocate of flexible response since he had been Army vice chief of staff, and he had the backing of the Kennedy administration, JCS Chairman Taylor, and most of the NATO allies in adopting it as a much more realistic policy than one which no longer made any sense in light of Russia's advances in nuclear weaponry. Further, Lemnitzer said of his own wars on the subject in Washington in the 1950s: "We couldn't believe that because a few Russians crossed the border we were going to go to all-out nuclear war."[37] But de Gaulle strongly opposed changing the strategy, and it wasn't until December 1967 that the alliance's ministers were able to get the necessary unanimous vote to adopt the strategy of flexible response. The vote followed the Military Committee's first comprehensive review of NATO strategy since 1956.

Substantial conventional forces were a necessary ingredient in sustaining a credible flexible response strategy and during Lemnitzer's tenure NATO had improved these forces so that the alliance could, at last, establish an effective forward defense. Six months after he became SACEUR, Lemnitzer declared that a major goal during his tour of duty would be the deployment of forces along the Iron Curtain, enabling direct resistance to enemy attack as soon as its forces entered NATO territory. This had long been a NATO objective, but until the 1960s the alliance did not have sufficient conventional resources in Central Europe to deploy its forces forward of the Rhine River, deep in its own territory. "If it is accepted that general war could start from an enemy miscalculation," the general told NATO leaders, "an inadequately guarded frontier is a prime invitation to make such a miscalculation. An adequate physical defense is a plain demonstration that an incursion cannot be made cheaply. From a tactical point of view, pushing the defense to the Iron Curtain should enable us, in case of an attack, to make an earlier assessment of the scale and intention of the enemy's moves."[38]

Whatever the figures seemed to say, it is doubtful if any SACEUR who held command before the Soviet Union collapsed in the 1990s ever was satisfied that he had enough strength to stop the Warsaw Pact in its tracks with tactical ground and air forces. A case might be made on paper that NATO and Pact forces were about equal if one did not take into account the one hundred thirty-five divisions back in the Soviet Union and all the other military power the USSR had at its disposal. Yet, McNamara made some calculations and announced at a NATO ministerial meeting in December 1964 that the widely held belief that Warsaw Pact conventional forces were overwhelmingly superior to NATO's was simply not true. In fact, the secretary declared, his figures showed that NATO's capabilities might be superior to those of the Pact.[39] Lemnitzer believed that his forces were sufficient in 1964 to deal with the Warsaw Pact itself, but only at the minimal level to accomplish the missions of deterrence and defense.[40] However, McNamara's comments did not make any easier the SACEUR's continuing task of trying to keep member nations faithful to their force commitments in the face of shrinking defense budgets and waning concern about the possibility of Warsaw Pact aggression.

The secretary's complacency may also have given U.S. Senator Mike Mansfield his first idea that U.S. forces in NATO would be a good target for substantial cuts. Introduced in late 1966 with forty-three Senate cosponsors, Mansfield's resolution calling for sharp decreases in force levels was the start of increasing congressional pressure for drastic drawdowns in Europe. Lemnitzer strongly opposed any cuts in congressional testimony, but in 1968 supporters of the reductions very nearly succeeded when Senator Stuart Symington announced his intention to seek a ceiling of 50,000 on U.S. troops in Europe. Before the move could come to a vote, however, the Soviet Union invaded Warsaw Pact ally Czechoslovakia, and Mansfield and Symington dropped their plans for cuts, at least for the duration of Lemnitzer's tour as supreme commander. Nevertheless, when he retired in 1969, there were 285,000 members of the U.S. forces in Europe, a drop of 125,000 from when he took over in 1963.[41] In the meantime, Soviet forces in Europe had increased from 475,000 to 500,000.[42]

The U.S. contribution to the alliance suffered during the war in Vietnam—so great were its demands on troops, leaders, and materiel that the hard-pressed commanders and staffs tasked with maintaining combat readiness referred to the U.S. European Command as Southeast Asia's "staging area." Lemnitzer conceded that the heavy drain on personnel and U.S. stockpiles in Europe was seriously impairing the allied mission. But he gave short shrift to press criticism and complaints from within his command that the United States was wrong for depleting resources that had been assigned to NATO:

"We were thin all over the world and the right thing to do was to move what we had and what we needed to where the fighting was going on," he said years later. "It never bothered me, except that I didn't like to see our forces getting a lesser capability. But when I heard the media or some of our allies pointing out that we were weakening the situation [in Europe] I just bluntly told them that this was American equipment, bought and paid for and placed here to serve NATO, but there's a war on and they desperately need this equipment in Southeast Asia. We had damned well better accept giving it up until it could be properly replaced. Period."[43] Lemnitzer successfully resisted efforts to move whole units to Vietnam, accepting levels that were far less than authorized full strengths rather than permit the instability that would result from removing units. An important factor in plugging the gaps left by the drawdown was the continuing buildup and improvement of the twelve divisions contributed by West Germany to the alliance.

The war had its most serious effects on U.S. forces in Europe in the first few years after Lemnitzer retired. Sparked by intense and widespread revulsion over the war, the United States was a turbulent place in which drugs, violence, racial problems, and a deterioration of moral values spread to the military services. Morale plummeted to historic lows as the U.S. public turned its disenchantment with the war and the draft upon anyone wearing a military uniform. Depleted and ignored as the war wound down, the U.S. European Command became a troubled organization in which such cornerstones as the U.S. Seventh Army were in danger of being ripped apart by widespread drug use, racial unrest, deplorable living conditions, and violent crime so pervasive that in many military compounds it was unsafe for soldiers to venture outside after dark.

Another problem that threatened NATO force levels was the high cost of maintaining U.S. forces in Europe, a factor which seriously affected America's balance of payments and which was one of the chief incentives for Mansfield's demands that U.S. force levels be drastically cut. Lemnitzer could watch apprehensively while his country and the alliance's civilian leaders thrashed out "offset agreements" providing for such things as the purchase of U.S. military equipment, but balance of payments was a ministerial matter. So was standardization, in some of its aspects, but the supreme commander became deeply involved in this issue, and not always with pleasing results.

Standardization was a goal, an elusive one, that would enable the allies to use the same sizes of ammunition, standard weaponry, compatible communications equipment, and on down the list of items armed forces need to be operational. Achievement of this objective, even in one category, would have tremendous advantages: allied forces could function in battle with truly compatible equipment, thus reducing confusion, promoting cohesion, and decreasing production costs. But the obstacles were formidable: nations had different and often irreconcilable concepts about what the ideal tank, artillery round, or antiaircraft missile should be. National pride and financial considerations—even such basic differences as measurements used in manufacturing screws and bolts—also played important roles. So it was regarded as a major, even a miraculous, accomplishment when the United States hammered out an agreement to adopt 7.62 millimeters (.30 caliber) as the standard size for rifles and their ammunition in NATO.

Before he became SACEUR, Lemnitzer was the U.S. representative to a NATO committee charged with deciding on a standard rifle size. The British, French, Belgians, and Dutch held out strongly for 7 millimeters throughout a long series of frequently heated negotiations. Lemnitzer argued for the larger .30 caliber (7.62 millimeters) to no avail until it came time for a final vote. "I had to go in and say that we recognized their desires for a 7 millimeter cartridge, but the United States had hundreds of millions of dollars invested in industrial equipment to make caliber .30 machine guns, rifles and ammunition, and we simply could not and would not junk this vast amount of equipment unless they could prove that 7 millimeters had a decisive advantage over 7.62. Well, they couldn't and so we agreed on the 7.62. In my opinion, this was the greatest standardization move in the history of NATO and the U.S. military aid program."[44]

But the story wasn't over: while Lemnitzer was SACEUR, he kept pressuring the allies to keep increasing their supplies of the 7.62 ammunition. They complied, gearing their production of small arms and ammunition to the adopted standard size and building up their stocks of the new round. A serious small arms problem seemed to have been solved when an aghast Lemnitzer learned that the United States had shifted gears: it had decided to equip its own forces in Europe with the new M-16, a rapid-firing automatic rifle whose smaller .228 caliber Lemnitzer did not consider as effective in the European environment as the .30-caliber M-14. "It was incredible," the general observed, "that we, the advocates that turned them all to the 7.62 caliber, were now responsible for sabotaging that important standardization program by introducing a new caliber small arms round."[45]

There was no shortage of ideas back in the States about how the country could save money and still keep a military presence in Europe. One of these that drew Lemnitzer's fire was the concept of "dual-basing" under which units would remain dedicated to NATO's defense but be based in the United States. Their combat equipment would be stored in Europe and the units brought over by air and sea when they were needed. McNamara and politicians liked the idea but not NATO commanders or the SACEUR, who said: ". . . there can be no major reliance placed upon a Big Lift type of operation to ensure the prompt return of U.S. troops to Europe in a time of crisis. Our reinforcement capability is no substitute for forces actually on the ground. While dual-basing does not reduce the troop commitment to NATO, it does degrade our 'in-theater' capabilities and therefore reduces our readiness to meet an attack with little or no warning."[46] Nevertheless, portions of the U.S. command became involved in such variations of the dual-basing concept as stationing a single "brigade forward" in Europe, with the rest of the division remaining in the United States, and a rotation policy under which U.S.- and Europe-based units traded places for periods of time.

Combat equipment for units sent over for reinforcement during crises was permanently stored in Europe under a program known as POMCUS (Pre-positioning of Materiel Configured to Unit Sets).

Although the Soviet Union had dropped its demands that America and its allies remove their troops from West Berlin, harassment by Russian and East German forces continued during Lemnitzer's tenure. Motor columns traveling in and out of the city along the main highway to West Germany often were stopped and held up for long periods of time on technicalities and then allowed to move on. Frequently, the Russians would serve notice that they were going to conduct military exercises and that while they were doing so it would be dangerous for allied planes to fly in the air corridors leading into the city. Often the allies' response to this harassment was to inform the Soviets that their vehicles and planes were coming through anyway, a practice that brought charges that the allies were engaging unnecessarily in "brinkmanship." The SACEUR conceded that this was so, but he contended that it was justified "in every sense of the word. If we had yielded on some of these things, we'd have gone through the 'salami machines.' I think the allies have given up some of their rights in order to avoid difficulty, but it didn't avoid difficulty. When I took over command I reached the stage where I could not agree to any yielding to East German or Russian pressure on any subject."[47]

The numerous brushes and near-brushes along the borders rarely resulted in shots being fired, although there always was the worry that a soldier with a gun would get angry or careless and fire a shot that would provoke a major confrontation. One encounter that cost lives occurred in January 1964, after a U.S. Air Force T-39 Sabreliner, a utility jet trainer and light transport plane, strayed into East Germany and was shot down by two Soviet fighter planes. Three lieutenant colonels were killed in an incident that touched off an angry exchange of notes between Washington and Moscow. The United States maintained that the plane got lost during a training mission; the Russians implied, but never proved, that the craft was on a photo reconnaissance mission and that its pilot had ignored orders to land.[48]

Lemnitzer, who termed the incident "absolute murder," had to answer criticism in Congress and the press that only NATO planes seemed to stray over the border. He responded that Warsaw Pact aircraft did likewise, but that NATO planes were permitted to fire only when the intruder clearly had hostile intent. He sought to make his point by publicizing an incident that occurred six months after the T-39 was shot down. A West German reconnaissance plane was taking photographs fifteen miles inside its own country's border when two Soviet fighter planes suddenly appeared on both sides of the plane. The West German pilot notified NATO air defense, which sent some jet interceptors to the scene and chased the Soviet craft back across its own border. Seizing the incident as an opportunity to answer skepticism over NATO border protection policies, Lemnitzer had a press release prepared and, because of the political considerations, submitted it to the NATO Council of Ministers for clearance. "Believe it or not, the council mulled this over for nearly a week to ten days and then took no action on the basis that this was a West German problem and not a NATO problem," the general recalled, citing the experience as illustrative of why "frustration and exasperation" in dealings with the council were endemic to the post of supreme commander.[49]

The general's diplomatic skills were tested to their limits in early 1964 when he was dispatched to the far eastern reaches of the Mediterranean Sea to attempt to head off a war between Turkey and Greece. Turkey was preparing to invade Cyprus, a large, formerly British-held island located forty miles from Turkey's coast. An independent nation for less than four years, 80 percent of Cyprus's population was of Greek origin and most of the rest was Turkish. Their mother nations were ancient enemies, and in late 1963 widespread violence erupted over what the Turkish minority charged were Greek majority efforts to weaken governing rights guaranteed under the Cyprus constitution and to annex the island to Greece.

Turkey and Greece were mainstays of NATO's vital southeastern flank, thus making the possibility of a war between them a matter of deep concern to the alliance's supreme commander. Clearly, the crisis called for a negotiator with Lemnitzer's skills, but the factor that twice propelled him into the heart of negotiations aimed at calming things down was his personal friendship with Gen. Cevdet Sunay, chief of the Turkish Defense Staff and a future president of Turkey. They had known each other since the days when both had been chiefs of their respective army staffs, and Lemnitzer had worked closely with Sunay in helping him to reorganize the Turkish army along U.S. Army lines. The SACEUR regarded him as "one of my best friends in the international area."[50]

The telephone in the SACEUR's quarters near Paris rang at half past two in the morning in late January 1964. McNamara was calling to tell him that after several months of heavy violence between Greek and Turkish Cypriots, Turkey was threatening to go to war and President Johnson wanted Lemnitzer to fly to Ankara immediately to talk with Sunay and Prime Minister Ismet Inonu. This was no time to quibble over the question of Johnson's authority to issue such an order to a SACEUR, but as soon as McNamara hung up, the secretary general of NATO, Manlio Brosio, telephoned with a directive to get in his airplane and go.

Lemnitzer recalled that "I used every type of persuasion that I knew how to use" in trying to defuse the situation. He told Inonu and Sunay that an invasion would antagonize the rest of the free world, leaving the Turks with few friends and bringing an end to the U.S. military and economic aid that had been so important to the great strides the nation had made since World War II. Any military action would have to involve U.S. equipment, all of which had been provided for use against NATO enemies, not allies, and violations of this trust would almost certainly result in suspension of further aid. Before he returned to

Paris, the supreme commander stopped in Athens and made similar arguments in urging Greek officials to try to restore order in Cyprus. He told the Greeks, as he had the Turks, that the two sides risked a "difficult war" that would leave both countries exhausted in a short time because of the resulting cutoff in American resources. Furthermore, he stated, Greece would be foolish to go to war with Turkey. "The Turks were so much stronger," he reported telling Greek leaders, "that there could only be one outcome."[51] The Turks did not attack.

Later, Cyprus's president, Eastern Orthodox Archbishop Makarios, rejected NATO's offer of a peacekeeping force but accepted one from the United Nations as internal island hostilities continued into the spring. Whatever effect Lemnitzer's visit in early 1964 might have had in forestalling an invasion, he went back to Ankara in June on another emergency mission. The Greek Cypriots had launched a large-scale assault aimed at wiping out Turkish Cypriot villages along Cyprus's northern coast and had been attacked by elements of the Turkish air force. Determined to end once and for all what it regarded as government oppression of Turkish Cypriots, Turkey had assembled an invasion fleet at Iskenderun and was preparing to send a regiment of troops to Cyprus when once again Johnson called Lemnitzer to the rescue.

The Turkish troops were already going aboard their amphibious vessels when Lemnitzer arrived in Ankara in his air deputy's small, two-engine aircraft which had been pressed into service because the SACEUR's own longer-ranged plane was being repaired. "Nobody ever thought I could make it," the general recalled. "I didn't either; I think we were running on fumes at the end—it was that kind of an emergency." The prospects of cooling things down looked dismal: shortly after he arrived, Prime Minister Inonu told his nation by radio: "Our decision is final. We have to provide an unshakeable security for the future of Cypriot Turks."[52] The SACEUR conferred again with the Turkish premier and chief of the defense staff, presenting the arguments he had used before with even more fervor this time because the situation was much more urgent. The invasion was called off, but Lemnitzer wired Johnson that he was convinced that this was the last time the Turks could be talked out of invading if tensions escalated to the same stage a third time.[53]

How much influence Lemnitzer had in persuading Inonu and Sunay to hold back their troops is not known; the fact that his visits to Ankara were followed closely with suspensions of invasion activity indicate that his efforts were important factors. More probably, they were the decisive ones—Lemnitzer thought so—for the personal friendship between Lemnitzer and Sunay was strong, and in those days the army was the real ruler in Turkey. But the United Nations and the U.S. State Department were also involved in trying to head off a war, and the clincher the second time may have been a sharp letter to Inonu from Johnson in which the U.S. president warned that unless Turkey backed off, the United States might suspend its NATO obligation to defend Turkey if it were attacked by the Soviet Union.[54]

It was a brutal slap that probably undid whatever goodwill Lemnitzer had tried to preserve in his negotiations. Turkey regarded the United States as a close friend and its cause in Cyprus as just. The two sides agreed on a cease-fire in August 1964, but the Turks never forgot nor forgave Johnson's rough treatment. In 1967 war was again averted by diplomacy, but in 1974 after Lemnitzer had retired, Turkey finally sent in its troops, overrunning 40 percent of the island before agreeing to an armistice. In 1975 the United States punished Turkey with an embargo on all military goods. Although neutral in his dealings with both sides while on active duty, in retirement Lemnitzer was fiercely partial toward Turkey in seeking a lifting of the embargo. The ban was eventually dissolved, but not before serious damage was done to the military readiness of a nation whose land units made up the largest national force in NATO and which tied down a total of some thirty Soviet and Bulgarian divisions.[55]

Although he was frequently in Washington to testify in Congress and to deal with NATO matters requiring his presence there, Lemnitzer rarely had any contact with Johnson. The president was becoming increasingly preoccupied with the war in Southeast Asia and seemed to regard NATO problems as an annoyance. While Johnson exercised his authority and influence when it was required of him, Lemnitzer felt that he did not have the grasp of NATO affairs that Kennedy had. After Kennedy was assassinated in November 1963, the visits by McNamara and Rusk became much less frequent.

NATO's most worrisome member climaxed seven years of obstructionism and displeasure with practically everything the alliance did or tried to do when France announced in March 1966 that it was withdrawing its military forces from NATO. The allies were given exactly a year to remove their troops, installations, the various headquarters, and all possessions from French soil. The list of grievances that prompted the bombshell was long, including President de Gaulle's contention that the Warsaw Pact no longer posed an immediate threat to Western Europe; by implication, that America's preoccupation with the war in Southeast Asia had turned it away from NATO; and that the United States had already adopted a strategy of flexible response to replace massive retaliation without consulting the other NATO members. This issue was assigned prime importance by Premier Georges Pompidou, who criticized flexible response as "being specifically conceived on the basis of America's geographical position . . . limiting the atomic battlefield by sparing the territory of the Soviet Union, and therefore the territory of the United States, and thereby creating a psychological risk, that of making it believed that the war could remain localized between the Atlantic and the Polish frontier in the East—that is to say, in Europe, but in a Europe doomed to destruction."[56]

It was a stunning blow for an alliance that was struggling to stay alive while its members all seemed to be pulling in different directions, and critics were gaining credibility with their assertions that NATO had outlived its usefulness. The ranks of ardent believers in its importance to free world security—like Lemnitzer—were thinning. Even he feared that the bloc might not survive what he termed the "defection" of an alliance linchpin whose size, involvement, and strategic location made it what Lemnitzer once referred to as the "keystone of the NATO arch."

Had the Soviet Union decided to take advantage of this massive fragmentation of the heart of the NATO command structure, the result could have been the start of World War III at the worst and the disintegration of the western alliance at best. Massive retaliation was still the official response policy in regard to any advances on NATO soil, no matter how small; launching missiles would have meant war and not doing so would have seriously, perhaps even fatally, eroded the faith in U.S. resolve that kept the alliance alive. For a field commander, the situation was appalling: General Andrew P. O'Meara, U.S. forces commander, told a fellow officer in jest that if the Warsaw Pact attacked, he would have no recourse but to turn his army to the west and attack the French to open supply routes to St. Nazaire, then turn back and fight the Soviets.

But de Gaulle had made up his mind, and now there was work to be done. Lemnitzer's task was to preside over what was regarded as the largest peacetime relocation of military resources in history. Involved were the general's own headquarters (SHAPE); those of the U.S. European Command (USEUCOM); Allied Forces Central Europe and subordinate commands; hundreds of army, air force, and naval bases; and numerous supply installations. Over one hundred thousand military personnel and their families had to be moved, along with over a million tons of equipment and supplies—almost all of it belonging to the United States. Dubbed FRELOC (Fast Relocation of U.S. Forces from France), the operation was conducted largely by rail, sea, and road, often at night to avoid causing congestion.[57] The coordinator of the massive operation was U.S. Air Force Gen. David Burchenal, and USEUCOM carried it out.

The relocation itself was accomplished in less than six months, a time compression forced on the movers by diplomatic and political haggling and indecision over such issues as where the many components would be sent. Not the least of the obstacles was McNamara, who found fault with all of USEUCOM's original proposals on where to relocate. He insisted on "fans of plans" so that he could pick and choose. Months went by, and the allies were able to clear out by the deadline only by dumping supplies and equipment in open fields or abandoning them. The French were auctioning off various facilities well before the expiration of the scant year of grace de Gaulle had given to his allies.[58] That the vast bulk of NATO's assets made it to their destinations in good order and on time has to rank as one of the great military logistics triumphs of all time.

Lemnitzer was determined not to go "hat in hand" to the French premier and ask for an extension of the April 1, 1967, deadline he had been given, and at five o'clock in the afternoon on March 31, 1967, he declared his new headquarters at Casteau, Belgium, to be open and the old one at Rocquencourt, France, closed. In France the next day, a front-page feature article in *L'Aurore* began: "It was a simple farewell. A few military marches. Two brief speeches. Then the fifteen flags which descended slowly to the ground to a single drum beat that sounded like the tolling of a knell. This is SHAPE and it is no longer SHAPE which on 30 March, 1967 has left French soil. That to which we have had to say good-bye is a brotherhood of arms without which our country would no longer exist today." The article concluded: "Women, certainly, but also men wept. Some fifty children of SHAPE families—boys and girls, white and black—linked hands and began to sing 'Auld Lang Syne.' They sang it in our tongue—French, with all the range of harsh and soft accents. Their lips trembled."[59]

In another poignant ceremony earlier in the month, de Gaulle had presented Lemnitzer with the Grand Cross of the Legion of Honor, the highest award that could be conferred upon a foreigner. The event took place in the courtyard of the Hôtel des Invalides, adjoining Napoleon Bonaparte's tomb, where France honors its great soldiers. Dressed in his brigadier general's uniform, de Gaulle kissed the SACEUR on both cheeks and said: "Be assured that you personally leave the best possible memory, and that everything you have accomplished in the exercise of your command has only added to the attachment that my country has for yours. As for myself, let me say that I shall regard you in the future, as I have done in the past, as my friend."[60] De Gaulle's ouster order was generally approved by the French public, but historic U.S.-French ties were still strong, especially among those who remembered the First and Second World Wars. One of those was an unidentified elderly woman who was waiting outside the Invalides's gates with a bouquet of red roses, white carnations, and blue irises. She had wanted to present them to Lemnitzer and tell him that "the French do not forget." But the crowd was thick, and the general's car passed quickly. A SHAPE officer, who was leaving the ceremony on foot, saw her weeping, and when he found out why he saw to it that the flowers were taken to the SACEUR's office and placed on his desk. Deeply touched, Lemnitzer issued a statement to the press thanking her, but he never learned her name.[61]

The readjustment prompted by de Gaulle's move, so pervasive that it could be likened to rebuilding the alliance from scratch, had been placed under the direction of "The Fourteen," a group made up of representatives of the remaining members of the alliance (former Secretary of State Dean Acheson was the U.S. delegate). Belgium was selected as the new SHAPE site, and the USEUCOM headquarters were moved to Stuttgart, West Germany, and Allied Forces Central Europe (AFCENT) was assigned to Brunssum, Holland. Air units were relocated to Germany, England, and the United States in one of the biggest realignments in U.S. Air Force history. Further reshuffling of locations, especially in West Germany, followed as Lemnitzer's planners made room for the "exiles."

It had taken six months of frequent meetings between the SACEUR and the Belgians to agree on a location for SHAPE. The Belgians were hard bargainers—a U.S. officer who served on the USEUCOM staff recalled that Lemnitzer would work out the details of an agreement at one meeting, only to have the Belgian officials disavow everything the next time they met.[62] The general wanted a site as close to Brussels as SHAPE had been to Paris, but the new host country held out for Casteau, situated thirty miles away. The Belgian intransigence probably stemmed from economic considerations—Casteau, near Mons, was a depressed area in need of jobs and income that construction of a new headquarters complex would generate. Lemnitzer protested long and vigorously, but in the end he had to settle for Casteau.

The general was even less successful in finding an appropriate dwelling for himself and future supreme allied commanders. He and his staff inspected over eighty homes in trying to find a place close to both Casteau and Brussels. When they came across something they considered suitable, the Belgians found reasons to turn it down. Finally, the general was offered the Château Gendebein, an abandoned, decaying old masonry structure which had been used during World War II as bachelor quarters for German SS officers and since then as a leaky shelter for tramps and winos. Despite his protests that it was ten miles farther from Brussels than his already excessively distant headquarters in France, the Belgians persisted, insisting that extensive repairs would make it suitable for Europe's highest ranking military officer. Incredibly slow and shoddy workmanship and inexplicable government dawdling delayed completion of the chateau until after Lemnitzer retired from the Army.[63] The general, Kay, and Lois lived in a modest, prefabricated house near the chateau. So, for quite a while, did his successor, General Goodpaster, who wrote some weeks after taking command: "Progress continues on the chateau, although the time for completion seems to remain unaltered at 'a few more weeks' no matter how many days go by. I am, of course, adhering to the stand that the chateau must be completed in a way that will 'meet SACEUR's requirements as determined by him' before it can be accepted."[64]

His major commands scattered over three countries, evicted from the ideal geographical location for conducting a defense of Europe, and beset with a succession of frustrations in setting up a new headquarters, Lemnitzer's fabled optimism was undergoing a stern testing. While he was still pondering the seemingly impossible task of getting NATO forces out of France in twelve months and politicians were still arguing over where to go, McNamara's team in Washington was cranking out press statements to the effect that France was not vital to NATO interests and that, indeed, its departure might be beneficial to the alliance. Lemnitzer growled to a *New York Times* correspondent: "One more 'benefit' of this sort and we'll be out of business."[65]

But NATO did hold together and, in fact, much better than it had when France was a full partner. An issues paper prepared by the ministers after the move was completed noted that NATO was "enjoying a period of intense and constructive activity," which it attributed to the fact that "France is now much less an inhibiting factor in the alliance deliberations. Other countries are less apt to avoid necessary decisions for fear of provoking dramatic action by de Gaulle."[66] The SACEUR had an additional rationale for the improvement: the crisis and its threat to NATO's survival influenced member nations to consider what their futures held for them if the alliance were dissolved. "I saw country after country making an evaluation of its security position as an individual nation with no NATO against that enormous military machine of the Warsaw Pact. They all came to the same conclusion: it was to their advantage from a security and political point of view to maintain the integrity of NATO. I had been having a hell of a time with people cutting back forces, lowering defense budgets, arguing about trivialities and not paying attention to the important aspects. [But then] the NATO nations closed ranks and solidarity was greater than at any time during the previous four years."[67]

From a military standpoint, however, there was almost nothing good that could be said about the move, and the SACEUR took on the task of making it clear to the NATO members that the alliance's readiness had been seriously impaired. Ironically, the seeming ease with which the gigantic repositioning had been accomplished had contributed to lulling the allies into a false sense of security when, in fact, NATO's ability to respond to a crisis had been weakened. The French withdrawal was followed by a period of economic setbacks in member nations, which forced further curtailments in troop levels, leading Lemnitzer to tell the North Atlantic Assembly (NAA) in an address in November 1967 that the early use of nuclear weapons in the event of hostilities was a distinct possibility.

If a popularity poll on world leaders had been taken in the United States in 1966, de Gaulle would have ranked somewhere just above the Soviet heads of state; President Johnson was reported to have used some especially colorful language when referring to him. But the general who bore the brunt of the French president's boot admired him as a great patriot and one of his closest friends, even while he was scrambling furiously to keep the alliance from coming apart. Like Norstad before him, Lemnitzer respected and liked de Gaulle personally while differing sharply with him on his attitudes toward NATO.

Eisenhower once told Lemnitzer that de Gaulle was a curious combination of the medieval and modern, whose mental picture of the conduct of world affairs was the "meeting of Napoleon and Alexander [the Great] on a raft in the Dnieper River."[68] De Gaulle corrected people when they referred to him as a soldier—he insisted that he was a politician. Yet he probably liked and trusted military men more than politicians, judging from the many kindnesses he extended to both Lemnitzer and Norstad during their tours as SACEUR. It is significant that he put on his uniform, last worn on duty when he commanded a French armored division in World War II, to personally present the Grand Cross of the Legion of Honor to Lemnitzer. Despite his "defection," military obligations were still important to him: in his notification to Johnson that he was pulling out his forces, he pledged that France would still "fight on the side of [our] allies in the event that one of them should be the object of unprovoked aggression."[69]

Noble though it was, this promise produced still another set of stormy and difficult negotiations—these between Lemnitzer and Gen. Charles Ailleret, the French armed forces chief of staff, to work out contingency plans to be used if France decided to fulfill de Gaulle's pledge. A major sticking point before an agreement was reached was Ailleret's brassy insistence that France retain the same access to U.S. nuclear weapons that it had before it took its forces out of NATO. The French general gave up after the SACEUR told him that the subject was such a heated one in the United States that "if I went back to Washington today and I wanted to get run out of town quickly, all I would have to do is go before the joint atomic energy committee of Congress and advocate that the French have the same access to U.S. tactical weapons outside of the integrated [military] structure as they had before."[70]

The two generals finally agreed on a contingency plan, but this did little to ease Lemnitzer's mind. He told the NAA at its November 1967 session, "No matter how one rationalizes it, the French withdrawal from NATO's integrated organization makes ambiguous what help its land or air forces would provide the center of Allied Command Europe; it affects not only operations but also flexibility to carry out operational missions. This potential loss is from a vital area—one [in] which I considered the existing forces to be only of marginal strength before this action was taken."[71]

Lemnitzer probably got along much better with de Gaulle than he did with the other heads of state and their representatives on the NATO Council. Queried during an interview after he retired, Lemnitzer could not remember a single secretary general who impressed him. At one time he uncharacteristically went public with his displeasure when in December 1967 the alliance's defense ministers finally approved the strategy of flexible response. Key to the strategy was increased emphasis on conventional forces and the need to prolong conventional operations as long as possible to avoid using tactical nuclear weapons. Then, the SACEUR recalled, the ministers turned around and voted merely to *take note* of the plans of five nations with forces in Central Europe "to reduce the very conventional forces on which they had just placed greater emphasis—and all of this [while] knowing full well that we were already seriously deficient in conventional forces." In the ensuing months, Lemnitzer spent much time giving background briefings (which permitted no attribution) to the press and making public speeches to underscore his contention "that the NATO ministers by their contradictory actions were placing their NATO military commanders in impossible positions.

My actions in this regard brought forth much flak from the political authorities, but in the end—coupled with the invasion of Czechoslovakia—produced some very worthwhile results."[72]

The invasion of Czechoslovakia on August 21, 1968, by troops of the Soviet Union and four other Warsaw Pact nations sent a chilling message to the world about how far the communists were willing to go to keep subjugated countries in line. Red tanks rolled through Prague, crushing resistance with gunfire and forcing the overthrow of government leaders, all because a spreading democratic reform movement was threatening Soviet control. Across the border, NATO's supreme commander watched and waited . . . and waited. Lemnitzer remembered it as one of the most frustrating periods of his tenure.

The general had been following the preinvasion sparring between the Soviets and Czech reform leader Alexander Dubcek, and as tensions increased he was aware of the possibility that the Soviet Union might use troops to impose its will. When the first shots were fired, NATO alerted its forces in the region, but covertly—the supreme commander did not want to make a move that would enable the Russians to say that they had moved into Czechoslovakia because NATO troops were threatening its satellite. For the same reason, he ordered two West German divisions who were planning maneuvers in the area to move their operation farther back from the border.

There was nothing more he could do. Soviet envoys quickly informed NATO member governments that the invasion would be limited to Czech territory and would pose no threat to the alliance.[73] But such an action so close to the NATO border was of major military significance, and Lemnitzer needed guidance from his civilian superiors. Urgent telephone calls to the North Atlantic Council offices in Brussels produced no results—August is vacation time in Europe, although the council was able to convene enough members to issue a condemnation of the invasion as being a "clear violation of the United Nations charter and international law."[74] But the ministers did not issue any guidance to the SACEUR. He remembered wondering what the U.S. JCS was doing; the answer, he recalled, "was that the Chiefs weren't doing anything—there was a lot of low-key accepting [in Washington] of what the Russians were doing." After Lemnitzer asked what President Johnson was thinking in regard to the crisis, he finally got an answer through the Chiefs: "We're going to stand by and see what our European allies decide to do."[75]

The SACEUR then dispatched a memorandum to Secretary General Broslio, who was vacationing in Italy, indicating that the situation was becoming "intolerable and dangerous." Despite Soviet assurances that the military action was an internal Warsaw Pact matter, the chances of the fighting spilling over at the border and the occurrence of other repercussions were enormous. The Soviets, carrying out what one NATO commander called an "almost classical pattern of a military deployment in logical sequence," had just placed large, combat-ready, and immediately responsive Soviet forces much farther to the West than at any time in recent years. Extensive mobilization of troops, communications, and transportation had taken place to sustain these forward-deployed forces. "The military balance in Central Europe has been very significantly altered to the disadvantage of the West," the general said.[76]

Lemnitzer stood practically alone in speaking for NATO as world outrage made itself felt in a deluge of press queries: what were the alliance's forces going to do?—were they going to stand by again, as they did when Hungary was invaded, and do nothing? Some of his senior staff officers wanted to move a division to the border to show the Soviets that they could go no further. Even his own commanders were pressuring him to take measures he was not authorized to take. He could only reply over and over to critics from outside his command that NATO was a defensive alliance and there was nothing he could do about Czechoslovakia's plight. Those who should have been fielding these questions were on vacation or otherwise unavailable. As it was, Lemnitzer's covert alerting of his forces and his precautions against inflaming the situation were about as far as he could go, even if NATO's ministers had been in charge. Unable to put any blame on alliance military actions, the Russians spread the word in the United Nations that the crisis had arisen because of a NATO plot to interfere in Czechoslovakia's internal affairs.[77]

One of Lemnitzer's best intelligence sources in the aftermath of the invasion was Shirley Temple Black, the onetime actress and future U.S. ambassador to Ghana and Czechoslovakia. She had been in Prague when the invasion began, as chief of a United Nations children's mission, and was there for a week while Soviet airborne troops and tanks—supported by forces from Poland, East Germany, Hungary, and Bulgaria—quickly stifled Czechoslovakia's experiment with democracy. Lemnitzer asked her to come to his headquarters after she left Prague, and she gave him and his staff a comprehensive and accurate report on what happened, the kind and quantity of weaponry involved, how it was used, and other details. "She had developed a magnificent ability to remember things," he recalled. "She proved to be an exceptionally competent observer and reporter of the events that took place and which she had personally observed."[78]

The SACEUR was disgusted with his lack of support during the invasion, remarking to members of his staff after failing to get any guidance from Washington or Brussels: "That was a hell of a fine exhibition of leadership on the part of the United States and NATO. That's the worst I've seen since I've been over here."[79] At another time, he called the episode "one of the most serious breakdowns in the political-military mechanisms of the alliance that occurred during my tenure as SACEUR."[80]

There is evidence that if NATO had been more resolute the Soviets might not have invaded. General McCaffrey, who headed up the U.S. European Command's operations directorate at the time, recalled that the Soviets knew the allies were aware of rising tensions and an invasion could occur. The Soviets waited patiently to see if NATO would intervene. When communist intelligence found no signs that would indicate NATO was ready to do battle, Pact tanks poured into Czechoslovakia.[81]

However impotent and inept it had looked while the Soviet Union was clamping down on Czechoslovakia, NATO was a better alliance afterward. Pressure to bring U.S. troops home ceased, and other member nations were more ready to fulfill their obligations to supply forces and funds. Vexing illusions that the Communist nation had no aggressive intentions disappeared. One casualty of the awakening was de Gaulle, who had not believed that the Soviet Union was a threat to peace and who had held the hope after leaving the alliance's military structure of brokering a détente with Russia that would eliminate the need for NATO and the Warsaw Pact. A de Gaulle aide told Lemnitzer that the French statesman's views in this regard "were completely blown apart" by the Czech invasion. The by-then former president "went down very rapidly—mentally and physically—after that," Lemnitzer observed years later.[82]

The general considered the move from France to have been the most momentous event of his tour as SACEUR, and when it had been accomplished without destroying the alliance he began thinking about retirement again. He had gone to Europe expecting to spend three years and he had been there for more than five in late March 1968, when, during a trip to Washington, he told McNamara and JCS Chairman Wheeler that he wanted to retire. The appropriate person to inform was the president, so the secretary arranged a meeting for April 4 while Lemnitzer was in the capital to testify before several congressional committees on NATO matters. The night before the meeting was to take place he was stricken with appendicitis and underwent surgery the next morning for the removal of his appendix. When he was wheeled back to his suite at Walter Reed Army Hospital afterward, there was a large vase of flowers on a table and a card that read: "I've heard of lots of alibis to avoid a meeting with the president, but this one takes the cake. LBJ."

There is no record among Lemnitzer's papers that would indicate he ever saw the president about the matter or, indeed, ever again. The word got through, of course, but then came Czechoslovakia—NATO did not like to change SACEURs in times of crisis—and it wasn't until over a year later that he was able to turn over his flag to General Goodpaster.

The ceremony, as was the case with any occasion in which Lemnitzer could set the rules, was simple: six hundred troops representing all fifteen nations marched past a reviewing stand in front of his headquarters, a squadron of planes flew over in tribute, and the walls of the compound he had created echoed to the blasts of a seventeen-gun salute. His remarks as he said good-bye to his last command were brief, and at the end he said:

"And now the time has come for Mrs. Lemnitzer and me to say farewell. It has been a long road that we have traveled together since I first climbed the hill at West Point on June 14, 1918. She has been at my side in many parts of the world; she has awaited my return when war prevented our being together. I am deeply grateful for her support over these many years. From West Point and 1918, to SHAPE, Belgium and 1969, has meant service in all parts of the globe. It has meant friendships with some of the world's finest people, it has meant seeing sacrifice and death, but greatest of all it has meant the opportunity to serve the cause of security, peace and freedom within the North Atlantic Treaty Organization as supreme allied commander, Europe. It is with the greatest pride that I turn over command of Allied Command Europe to General Goodpaster. Good luck and farewell."

As the general and Kay got into the back of his car for the ride to the airport and home, a U.S. Army band played "Auld Lang Syne."

He had been SACEUR for six and a half years. It had been an arduous tour, but because it was in the service of an alliance in whose ideals he believed with all his heart, it unquestionably was the most professionally satisfying of his over fifty years as a soldier. His capstone contribution to his country and its allies was summed up thus by Lawrence S. Kaplan and Kathleen Kellner in the book *Generals in International Politics:*

"His role may not have been as a conceptualizer or as a strategist or as a political leader—others have made their contributions in these areas. His role was as a manager who could contain crises and turn them on occasion to the advantage of the alliance. Although [he] does not trumpet his experience with the crisis of 1966–67 as his crowning achievement, his greatest service to NATO was to take up the challenge imposed by France's demands upon its allies and to lay it down four years later with minimal damage."[83]

22

★ ★ ★ ★

WARRIOR WITHOUT UNIFORM

High-profile commanders like Patton and MacArthur probably wouldn't have cared much for President Richard M. Nixon's accolade if either had been the center of attention that summer day in the White House's Rose Garden. Nor would the words have fit them, but they were just right for the man who stood before the nation's commander in chief on July 11, 1969, and heard him say: "He is one who could best be described as a work horse rather than a show horse."[1]

Citing some of the high points of the general's many years of service, Mr. Nixon added: "... in all of these capacities, when something had to be done that required hard, diligent work without the publicity and all the glamour that goes with the other types of assignments, General Lemnitzer was a man we so often turned to. In all of our armed forces today there is probably no man who is more respected by all the services for his professional capacity than General Lemnitzer."

With Pentagon colleagues, close friends, and family members looking on, the former SACEUR received from the president his fourth Army Distinguished Service Medal (DSM) and the Distinguished Service Medals of both the Navy and Air Force. As the president noted, it was the first time in U.S. history that all three had been awarded at one time—indeed, at that time Lemnitzer became the only person to have ever worn all three medals. The DSM is awarded for "exceptionally meritorious and distinguished services in the performance of duties of great responsibility."

Secretary of Defense Melvin Laird read the accompanying citation, which stated in part: "Evidencing an unshakable faith in the principles and objectives upon which NATO was founded, General Lemnitzer sacrificed the privileges and freedom of retirement which he had long since merited in order that he might further serve the alliance by assuming the duties of SACEUR/CINCEUR. Remaining in uniform for an additional six and one-half years, he tirelessly and selflessly contributed to the cause of NATO and thereby to the security interests of the United States and the Free World."

The general's response was typically modest. Looking over the large gathering that had been invited to the White House for the ceremony, he said: "Many of the people who are here I have known for many years and associated with them. If I have ever accomplished anything in my military service, it is largely due to the leadership, example, and the support I have received from them, among many others." As SACEUR, "I merely built upon the base and the refinements of my eminent predecessors, Generals Eisenhower, Ridgway, Gruenther, and Norstad." He praised the selection of General Goodpaster, "an old friend and associate of many years' standing," as his successor, and paid tribute to an organization to whose support he would devote the rest of his life: "As for NATO, I consider it one of the greatest, most successful alliances in the history of mankind. It has carried out its principles and objectives in a remarkable way. There has not been one square inch of territory lost to international Communism. There have been wars in other parts of the world, in the Middle East, in Asia and Africa, but not in the NATO area in the last twenty years."[2]

In less than two months, the general would hang up his uniform for good; until then, he served out a presidential appointment as special assistant to the chairman of the JCS—a position created at his own request to permit him to complete unfinished NATO work, be debriefed by the White House and State Department, and ease his transition to civilian life. He retired on September 1, two days past his seventieth birthday. It had been fifty-one years, two months, and sixteen days since he arrived at the U.S. Military Academy to become a cadet. Of the two hundred nine classmates who reported that day, he alone was still on active duty, a distinction he had borne for over eight years.[3]

One of the first orders of business when he settled back into the family home in northwest Washington, D.C., was to straighten out his retirement status. Back in 1963, when he reached the mandatory retirement age of sixty-four, he had been quietly retired and immediately put back on active duty by order of President Kennedy. This was the solution the president and McNamara had come up with after Kennedy told Lemnitzer that he "would take care of it" when the general expressed doubt that he could be kept on active duty after he reached his sixty-fourth birthday. Lemnitzer, it will be recalled, had declined to occupy the NATO post as a retired general.

There was a hitch, though: no one told Lemnitzer exactly what the president had done, or so the general always maintained. Orders placing him on the retired list and concurrently ordering him to continued duty as SACEUR, effective September 1, 1963, were issued August 6, 1963, more than ten months after he left for Europe. Nothing was said to Lemnitzer, and he assumed that the president had made good on his promise to keep him on active duty; when Kennedy was in Europe just prior to the fall when he was assassinated, he confirmed to Lemnitzer that "the matter had been taken care of."

But for reasons unknown, the retirement and reinstatement orders did not reach Lemnitzer, and he saw them for the first time in August 1969, a month before he finally retired. His first inkling that a change in his status might have occurred came in mid-1965 when the Army's finance center informed him that he was over $1,700 in arrears in his payments to the Retired Serviceman's Family Protective Plan (RSFPP), an Army-administered insurance program for which he had signed up before he accepted the assignment to Europe. Despite his argument that there had been no break in his active duty status, the finance center contended that he had "technically retired." In the end, he paid the disputed amount and agreed to make regular monthly payments because "I felt that it was advisable to avoid an open controversy on even the technical retirement issue, which was so politically sensitive that it would only be detrimental to my SACEUR active duty status."[4]

Because U.S. relations with its European allies were still under considerable strain at the end of Lemnitzer's first nine months as SACEUR, it was important to Washington that it avoid any controversy that might undermine American military leadership, as represented by Lemnitzer. The allies had confidence in their new SACEUR, and the Kennedy administration wanted to keep it that way; a public flap over reaching into the retired rolls for a supreme commander or having to bring Lemnitzer home after less than a year on the job would give credence to de Gaulle's increasing pressure to give the post to a European.

Kennedy soon learned that there could be no exceptions to the law establishing sixty-four as the ultimate retirement age. The president had the authority to return a retired general to active duty for an indefinite period, and when he did so in Lemnitzer's case, the step from retirement to recall was as brief as the link between successive paragraphs in the same orders. But, as one Army legal officer wrote in one of the numerous memoranda preceding the action, despite the president's order calling the extension of service "continued duty" there could be no continuation "even if the break is but a matter of a split second."[5] For the record, and apparently unbeknown to him, Lemnitzer's first career ended at forty-five years, two months, and sixteen days, and immediately a new one began.[6]

Normally, the retirement of a four-star general is a matter of congressional concern, as is the appointment of a military officer to a high command post. But the administration wanted to avoid any publicity regarding Lemnitzer's retirement status, so the Defense Department researched the regulations and the law and determined that congressional approval was not required. Senator Richard B. Russell, chairman of the Senate Armed Services Committee, concurred after receiving a letter from Deputy Defense Secretary Gilpatric outlining the

Pentagon's opinion and stating that "we believe it important that General Lemnitzer be kept in Europe at this time." Nomination to become SACEUR had not required congressional endorsement, but, ordinarily, retirement in the grade of full general does; three- and four-star ranks are usually temporary ones whose holders have a lower permanent rank that they assume upon retirement unless the president, with Congress's approval, elects to retire them at the highest rank they held while on active duty. Lemnitzer's permanent rank was major general, but as a former Army chief of staff and JCS chairman he was entitled by law to retire as a full general without any further action by Congress. And so it was done.

The staff memoranda generated by the White House's effort to keep the SACEUR in Europe frequently mentioned the desirability of avoiding publicity. Ordinarily, such a rare occurrence as keeping a senior general in a high position after the mandatory retirement age would not have escaped the notice of the Washington press corps, but the administration had done its job so well that the news did not hit the newspapers until early 1964. In reply to a series of questions from reporter Charles W. Corddry, the Pentagon admitted that the retirement-recall had occurred and that the other NATO allies had not been told. Corddry speculated that the "mysterious" secrecy regarding the move was invoked to "avoid stirring up new problems over command arrangements," expressly the issue of the SACEUR always being an American.[7]

Even if all other avenues of official communication had failed or been closed, it still seems incomprehensible that as sharp-eyed a monitor of the news media as Lemnitzer would not have seen the Corddry story and the spate of similar reports it touched off. But he maintained until the year he left the Army for good that he had never been informed officially that he had been retired,[8] nor had he ever gone through the other steps of the retirement process, such as a retirement physical examination. The reason he got so far in arrears in his RSFPP payments, he asserted, was that he had not been notified that he had to make them, a further indication to him that there had been no break in his active service.

Lemnitzer never paid much attention to administrative details, preferring to leave these to his staff; he was very busy with his duties as SACEUR; and SHAPE headquarters was thousands of miles away from the Pentagon with its well-run internal communications system. But none of these factors could adequately explain why a four-star general served for over five years without being officially notified that he had been retired. It could well have been that Lemnitzer did not want to know and that the administration did not want him to receive official confirmation. A deception had occurred and, although Washington could have placed the blame for not notifying him or the alliance on a bureaucratic over-sight, it would not do for NATO's supreme commander to knowingly have been a party to it. Strangely, however, there was no outcry from the NATO allies when the story was made public, and the episode was soon forgotten.

There are indications that the general knew of his service status at least as early as nine months before his final retirement, when JCS Chairman Wheeler informed him of his retired pay options in a "confidential—eyes only" memorandum, apparently in response to a Lemnitzer query.[9] The options were not as generous as they would have been if there had been no break in his service, so after he retired he appealed to Congress for passage of a personal relief bill that would permit his pay to be based upon over forty-nine years of "uninterrupted and continued active duty" as a commissioned officer.[10] The bill, which would have given Lemnitzer another $180.87 a month, was passed by the House but turned down by the Senate in conference committee. Army doctors more than made up for the rejection, however, when they discovered that he had suffered a 20 percent hearing loss during his service in Europe; added to the 10 percent loss he had already had when he became SACEUR, this disability would have rendered him unfit for further service had he not retired voluntarily.[11] The disability added five thousand dollars a year to his retired pay.[12]

At an age when most men were well settled into retirement, Lemnitzer returned to a segment of society to which he had not belonged since he had been a teenager back in Honesdale. He was a civilian again after spending over half a century in uniform and more than twenty-seven years as a general. The "perks" and deference due a senior military officer are awesome, and the transition for those who have worn stars can be difficult. No more is there a large and attentive staff outside the door to deal with the general's every wish and command. The cars and aircraft that used to wait with their motors running for him to appear are at someone else's beck and call now. The spacious, well-furnished quarters with their cooks and housekeeping staffs are occupied by others, and there no longer is a uniform to rate a salute.

Some officers never quite get over that heady period of their lives. Not so Lemnitzer, whose tenure as a general had been longer than the entire careers of most soldiers. Never entirely comfortable with the trappings of power anyway, he took easily to life beyond the sentry gates and briefing rooms. While mildly bemoaning the Lemnitzer house in Washington as being "far too small to hold the many items we have accumulated during our service,"[13] the general happily moved back, taking Kay and Lois with him and displacing another of the several families who had rented it from him during years when he and his family were away from the city or living in government quarters.

But retirement also brought the realization of a dream that went back to World War II, when he wrote his brother that he wanted nothing more after the war than to go back to the family home in Honesdale and live out his years as a retired soldier. That had been nearly thirty years ago, but the home was still there, and it was to the big Victorian dwelling in Pennsylvania's Pocono Mountains that he returned in the fall of 1969. Except for occasional visits by Lemnitzer and other members of his family, it had not been lived in since his mother died nearly twenty years before. In keeping with the general's wishes when he purchased his brother's share after her death, almost nothing had changed since the days when he and his brothers were growing up. The furniture, the pictures on the walls, even the plates and silverware his grandparents used many years before were still where they were when he went off to war in 1942. The huge attic, which was really a third floor without interior walls, still held his childhood toys and the possessions of three generations of Lemnitzers, a family that apparently disliked throwing things away. To the many stacks of trunks and boxes he added the mementos of over fifty years of soldiering—papers, records, photographs, books, uniforms and decorations, and gifts and acquisitions from all over the world. A parlor in the rear of the house became his study, and his desk was the ancient rolltop at which his father sat when he brought work home from the shoe factory.

Honesdale had always been his voting address—the only difference, he wrote to a friend, is that "we don't have to send away for absentee ballots anymore." The house on West Street became home for four months of the year until the mid-1980s, when declining health made the trip from Washington too arduous for both the general and Kay. His routine was to drive up in late June, staying through the summer to get away from the heat in the capital, and then on into November to enable the couple to savor Honesdale's exquisite autumns. He and Kay liked to sit on his home's big open porch, reading, talking, and exchanging conversation with neighbors walking by on the sidewalk less than ten feet away. Much of the rest of the time he worked on speeches and the many projects he took on in Washington in retirement, played golf with chums from boyhood, or fished on nearby lakes, often with Lois who still shared her father's enthusiasm for the outdoors. Lemnitzer was also a prolific letter writer who carried on a heavy correspondence with friends, former military colleagues, and members of the public who frequently wrote to him seeking his comments or information on various issues.

But as stimulating and fulfilling as these sojourns to his roots were, they were not enough, or he would have lived in Honesdale the year around. At seventy, Lemnitzer looked, sounded, and moved like a man of fifty. He had excellent health, the energy of a drill sergeant and, like so many other generals when they doff their uniforms, the conviction that he still had something to give to his country. He decided that the cause under whose banner he could be most useful was the one that had occupied his last years on active duty and whose birth with his help he regarded as one of the high points of his career. He became one of the nation's most vigorous champions of NATO which, despite its success or perhaps partly because of it, was a favorite target of U.S. cost cutters and Vietnam-era antiwar elements.

Lemnitzer was at the zenith of his fame when Nixon decorated him before the network television cameras and the Washington press corps. As do most prominent persons in the public eye, the general received many invitations to speak;

that the clamor continued to be strong long after he wore four stars was a measure of the high esteem in which he was held by the country, his profession, and the government. He wrote to a former colleague a month before retiring that "I am being swamped with requests for speeches, after-dinner talks, etc."[14] But he liked to speak, and he had a theme. His first major speech was at the 1969 annual convention of the Veterans of Foreign Wars; his only stipulation was that the key subject of his address be NATO.

His talk was well received by the VFW delegates, and Lemnitzer decided to spend the first year of his retirement in taking to the stump for the organization to which he had devoted so much of his efforts during his career. He needed help, though. He no longer had a staff and couldn't afford a full-time secretary. Then he found a solution: the SACEUR had an office in the Pentagon to use when he was in Washington, and most times it was occupied only by a liaison officer and a secretary. Any former SACEUR was free to use it, so Lemnitzer moved in with Goodpaster's approval and in later years that of the SACEURs who followed him.

What was to have been a year's crusade grew to two, then three, and never really ended until poor health forced him to cut back on his activities in the mid-1980s. Two years after he retired, he wrote to a British friend that he had given one hundred fifteen talks in appearances in nearly every state in the union.[15] In 1976 the total reached three hundred seventy-five, and before the end of the decade it climbed above five hundred. The general did not profit personally from his speeches, unlike celebrity fellow officers who were receiving thousands of dollars a speech after Lemnitzer had died. He required only his expenses, those usually underwritten by the organizations that invited him. "This is entirely a no-profit venture of my own," he wrote to British Field Marshal Sir John Harding in early 1972. "I speak from my own convictions, which avoids my being accused of sounding a party or administration line. I find that I am far more effective that way. I only speak where I am invited. During the past year, the volume of invitations is so great that I am able to accept only one in three."[16]

The war in Southeast Asia had hurt NATO. U.S. public attention in regard to military matters had focused on Vietnam at a time when the Western Alliance was still beset with internal bickering and under attack by critics who were arguing that the union had served its purpose. The Soviet Union was perceived in many places as having abandoned its aggressive ways, making unnecessary the stationing of large forces in Europe. Renewed initiatives to cut more troops and further reduce expenditures were surfacing again in Congress. Antimilitary feelings generated by the war were adding to the negative attitudes toward NATO. It was a time, Lemnitzer was convinced, when it was more vulnerable to Soviet exploitation than at any time in its history. Clearly, in Lemnitzer's mind, his usefulness to the alliance had not ended when he stepped down as SACEUR.

The Soviet Union had not become less eager to conquer, he held, only "smoother" in its relations with other nations. "Underneath the polish," he told a House subcommittee, "the steel of Soviet determination is as cold and hard as ever." Reducing U.S. troop strength any further could have grave results, he asserted, both in terms of readiness and in its effects on the resolve of allies. During its existence, "not one square inch of NATO territory has been lost to communist aggression" during a period when there had been fifty-one wars in other parts of the world, he said. "To dismantle or weaken such a proven success-ful structure . . . would be to repay success with great risk and folly."[17]

This was the message he hammered home for years in speeches before civic organizations, government bodies, veterans groups, educational foundations, military schools, college and university audiences, and just about anyone else who invited him and he could fit into his busy schedule. The invitations kept coming, and he kept speaking for more than fifteen years. To be in demand that long past retirement had to depend on something more than the aura associated with a four-star general and supreme commander. The fact was that Lemnitzer had become a good speaker. Freed from any concern that a slip or departure from his script could cause official problems—and no longer able to rely on a full-time speechwriter—the general had to speak from his own notes or without any notes at all. As his staffs had told him for years, to no avail, he was superb at this kind of delivery—sharp, precise, amusing, personable, and likable. Moreover, at least at first, he knew his subject, perhaps better than anyone else in Washington.

He was especially persuasive and adroit in press conferences and after his speeches when he invited questions from his audiences. With the press, he was candid and direct, and with his audiences attentive and genuinely eager to be helpful. There were also listeners with axes to grind; antimilitary feelings ran high in the 1970s, and any military speaker was fair game for hostile listeners, particu-larly in colleges and universities. With his quick mind and remarkable memory, Lemnitzer was a formidable target if the questioner wanted to get in a few licks at the military. The verbiage from the floor could get very cutting and unfair, but no one remembers Lemnitzer ever losing his cool. The closest he would come is when somebody referred to America's motives for going into Southeast Asia as "immoral." When a reporter questioned the desirability of high defense costs in an era of inflation and public pressure for tax cuts and more social programs, he retorted: "We can afford to survive, whatever the cost."[18]

To a friend he wrote: "Occasionally, I have a flareup in the college and univer-sity areas, but nothing serious. In each case, I encourage the dissenters to come up to the platform and explain what they disagree with in my comments—which they generally are unable to do because they have not been listening. In other cases, I ask them to set forth their proposals against mine on NATO and here, also, they are unable to be very effective."[19]

Although his beloved NATO always occupied the center stage in his attentions, the general had strong opinions on many other issues that fell into the military sphere. In speeches, congressional testimony, and letters to friends and former colleagues, he opposed turning over the Panama Canal to Panama; deplored the ending of draft registration; was against plans to withdraw the bulk of U.S. troops from South Korea; thought the United States was wrong in considering the return of the Ryukyu Islands to Japan; and favored Mutual and Balanced Forces Reduction (MBFR) and Strategic Arms Limitation Talks (SALT) with Russia, but criticized early proposed agreements as being weighted in favor of the Soviets.

He was appalled in 1974 when Congress imposed an arms embargo on Turkey after it invaded Cyprus. Turkey was justified in taking the action as a coguarantor of Cyprus independence, Lemnitzer contended, because it was launched in response to the seizure of the government by Cypriot National Guard troops under the command of Greek army officers. Although it was generally viewed as a prelude to an effort by Greece to annex the island, the Turks were regarded by a congressional majority as aggressors who had violated restrictions on the use of U.S.-supplied weapons. Since the United States was the sole supplier of weapons and their spare parts, the embargo threatened to cripple the defenses of an important NATO ally and seriously impair U.S. relationships with one of its staunchest friends.

Lemnitzer testified before Congress, made speeches, and wrote letters to senators and representatives in a vigorous personal campaign to persuade lawmakers to support a Jimmy Carter administration effort to rescind the embargo. Backed by former fellow SACEURs—Ridgway, Gruenther, Norstad, and Goodpaster[20]—Lemnitzer argued forcefully that the embargo-caused deterioration of Turkey's armed forces had weakened NATO's vital southeastern flank. After a furious legislative battle in which congressmen were heavily lobbied by partisans of both sides of the issue, Congress voted in 1978 to cancel the embargo.[21]

The initiative against the embargo was one of the few things the Carter administration did that Lemnitzer liked. The armed services were undergoing heavy cutbacks in personnel, weaponry, and equipment in the wake of the war in Southeast Asia, and Lemnitzer was also disturbed about what he perceived as an alarming trend toward isolationism in national foreign policy. By 1977 he had been making speeches and testifying for seven years. In December he wrote a friend: "At holiday time each year I attempt to sit back and review the developments that have taken place during the past year to determine whether or not I should continue my national security lecturing and public speaking undertakings or reduce the pace of my activities.

"Unfortunately, this year I find myself more deeply concerned than in past years with the way things are going and have [decided] to continue the march [speaking] indefinitely. I am deeply concerned by the obvious efforts of the new administration to withdraw from the world and downgrade our leadership responsibilities for leading the Western World." He was depressed about talk in Washington of withdrawing U.S. forces from Korea, contending that this would "seriously destabilize Northeast Asia after all we have done to obtain and maintain stability in that area." Although "strong declarations are being made to support NATO," he asserted, "I find great difference between words and actions." Of the administration's position in the ongoing SALT II talks, he thought that "obtaining an agreement with the Soviets is regarded as more important than the content of that agreement." He also saw the move to relinquish control of the Panama Canal as "another withdrawal by the U.S. from an important area of the world."[22]

When another friend sent him a newspaper clipping quoting Harold Brown, Carter's secretary of defense, as having said the armed forces were ready for war if it came, Lemnitzer wrote back that he was "shocked and dismayed. In my opinion, we have seldom been less prepared for war than we have during the past four years and are today." In the same letter, he commented on the election of Ronald Reagan as president: "I am, of course, very pleased with the election results and hope that my talks on national security issues and NATO contributed to the welcomed outcome. With the loss of prestige and influence in the foreign policy field, the deterioration of the capabilities of our armed forces, and the frightful state of the economy, a big change was absolutely necessary—and soon—if this country was ever going to regain the position and stature it had in the world during the period following World War II."[23] His hopes were justified, and the following year he stated: "It is certainly a relief to see the new approach of the Reagan administration toward foreign policy, military strength, economic planning and almost every aspect of government that has been dealt with so indecisively and weakly during the past four years. The president has made an impressive start and I hope he will be as successful with the economy as he has in the budget and spending fields."[24]

The general lived comfortably on his retired pay and the income he had made from investments over the years. These were principally in stocks and bonds and, coupled with his frugal ways, enabled him to leave a substantial estate to his heirs when he died. As far as is known, the only other income he had beyond his speech expenses was the honorarium he received for three years as a member of the Advisory Board of Ryan (later, Teledyne Ryan) Aeronautical Company. The San Diego-based aerospace firm was a major developer of missile systems, electronic battlefield reconnaissance systems, electronic countermeasures, drones, and other high-tech defense products.

Lemnitzer received about ten thousand dollars a year and expenses to, as a top executive described his mission, "help top management . . . in the time frame of two or three years ahead as far as investing in new projects and new ventures."[25] Besides being available for consultations as needed, Lemnitzer had to attend a four-day meeting each year at the company's facilities in California. The meetings seemed to be made up largely of touring Ryan plants and conferring with the company's top management. The general's notes for the November 3–7, 1969, meeting—his first—consisted of detailed observations and suggestions about the future of various Ryan defense programs in the post–Vietnam War period.[26]

He seemed to take a special interest in Ryan's drone, a pilotless aircraft used principally for reconnaissance, but which could be equipped with explosives for offensive or defensive purposes or even used for such ordinary purposes as target practice. The remotely or automatically controlled devices were especially suited to Army operations and are believed to be the area in which Lemnitzer would have been occupied had he retired in 1962 instead of becoming SACEUR. Ryan offered him a position at that time, and some of his letters and oral histories dealing with that period indicated that he had either accepted a job or was planning to do so. What the position would have been is not known, but his references to it described it as "attractive" and inferred that it was financially rewarding.[27] The same could be said of his membership on the board, inasmuch as the honorarium constituted more than a third of what he received from the government in retired pay.

During his three years on the board, he appeared to perform exactly the same function as had been outlined to him before he accepted the post: he served as a high-level adviser to Ryan management. The only suggestion in his files that he might have gone beyond this was a "Personal and Confidential" letter to General Goodpaster praising the Ryan drone program, noting that several NATO nations were interested in finding out more about it, and suggesting that briefings could be set up for intelligence and operational members of the SHAPE staff if Goodpaster desired.[28] There was nothing improper in this offer nor are there any indications in Lemnitzer's papers that the matter went any further.

The government commission posts and other appointments that often come to high-level generals after retirement did not come Lemnitzer's way until 1975, nor did he seek any such assignments. He had never acknowledged allegiance to any political party, but it became clear as he got into retirement that he leaned toward the Republicans, and undoubtedly that is the way he voted, especially in 1980 when Democrat Jimmy Carter was up for reelection. When Nixon was still president, he had an opportunity to follow up the kind words he spoke at the general's retirement ceremony when the Greek government urged through channels that Lemnitzer be made the U.S. ambassador to Athens; the Greeks wanted a military man because they thought such an envoy would be more sympathetic to their problems than one without a military background. The Greeks were also familiar with the general's diplomatic skills when he had been SACEUR and had served as President Johnson's special negotiator during the dispute between Greece and Turkey over Cyprus in the 1960s. Lemnitzer hadn't sought the ambassadorial post, didn't particularly want it—and didn't get it.[29]

The general was elected president of the prestigious Washington Institute of Foreign Affairs in 1974, succeeding a fellow former SACEUR, General Gruenther. The Institute was an important capital sponsor of discussions on international relations and public speeches by the world's leading statesmen. He also was a director of the Atlantic Council, a private and nonprofit educational foundation devoted to furthering understanding of NATO. He succeeded Gruenther in the mid-1970s as president of the SHAPE Officers Association, an influential NATO support group made up of former SHAPE personnel from NATO member nations. One of the most difficult parts of Lemnitzer's duties as head of the association seemed to have been in persuading the U.S. Defense Department that the association's work on behalf of NATO was important enough to merit a ride in an Air Force plane to its General Assembly in Europe each year. Despite all the pressure the general, his predecessors, and successors could muster, reluctant approval would often come only at the last minute. At least once during Lemnitzer's presidency, the desired transportation didn't come at all, and the U.S. delegation had to stay home.

President Gerald R. Ford appointed him to the eight-member Rockefeller Commission, which was created in 1975 to investigate charges that the CIA had engaged in such illegal activities as plotting the assassinations of foreign trouble-makers like Fidel Castro. The investigation led to a series of sweeping changes in the CIA's organization and management and the way it operated overseas. Lemnitzer also served as a member of Ford's presidential Foreign Intelligence Board.

Because of his long association with Eisenhower, from World War II through his presidency, Lemnitzer was asked in 1980 by the U.S. Military Academy's Association of Graduates to head a drive to erect a memorial to the late general of the Army on the grounds of his alma mater. Then over eighty years old, beginning to tire more easily but still very busy with his speaking schedule, Lemnitzer took on the job because, as he wrote a friend, "I have always considered General Eisenhower as the most outstanding military officer of World War II and I was willing to do anything to emphasize that point in history."[30] Whereas another committee concentrated on raising funds, Lemnitzer chaired an oversight committee whose job it was to handle all other details, from the selection of a memorial and its site to the planning of the ceremony.

"I never knew how much detail is involved in such a project, but I am learning fast," he commented as the committee plunged into the task of deciding what kind of a monument would do justice to one of West Point's most illustrious graduates. The group, which was made up largely of Eisenhower's son John, former cabinet officials, and military officers, first met at Lemnitzer's family home in Honesdale and agreed that the center of the memorial should be a bronze statue of Eisenhower as he looked when he was commanding allied forces in World War II. He was to be wearing an Eisenhower trademark—a waist-length "Ike jacket"—and be standing with his hands on his hips, a typical Eisenhower stance.[31]

When the monument was dedicated on May 3, 1983, Lemnitzer was the principal speaker. He had owed a great deal to Eisenhower, the fellow military professional who had recognized his gifts as a planner when he was a young general and had pushed him along to the very top of his profession. Lemnitzer's gratitude and esteem were expressed in a speech that covered the former president's career and accomplishments, and ended with a quotation that could also have been a summary of Lemnitzer's own values.

Written by Eisenhower six weeks before his death in 1969, it stated: "In these times, some Americans seem to think that intricate and superbly engineered machines have diminished the role of the individual in all sorts of enterprises, from the management of a shop to the conduct of war or the preservation of peace; that a man's character is of less account that the sophistication of the instruments surrounding him; that such concepts of duty, honor, country are outmoded relics of a simple and even primitive past. Those who think so are dead wrong. Hardly a day passes that I do not hear or read a new proof that, in the hour of grave crisis or severe challenge, character is the chief resource of men and their nations. . . . [T]oday, even as it was a century or a millennium ago, the final index to a nation's destiny is within its people; in their commitment to principles and ideals; in their willingness to sacrifice for the common good; in their determination ever to bear themselves with courage, whatever the challenge or threat."[32]

The Reagan administration's emphasis on building up and modernizing the armed forces, while strengthening the U.S. presence in Europe and elsewhere overseas, was reducing the number of targets in Lemnitzer's long campaign for improved readiness. But this surge in attention to defense requirements brought with it a drive to reorganize the JCS. A key issue in what became a heated and prolonged debate at the highest levels of Washington officialdom was whether the JCS chairman should have more power. The congressional bill authorizing the move gave the chairman a much stronger voice in military decision making at the presidential level and strengthened his control over the JCS Joint Staff, the heart of the organization's planning and day-to-day operations. To Lemnitzer, the changes would, in effect, be creating a single chief of staff for all the services at the expense of the influence and authority of the service chiefs. It was a concept to which he had been vehemently opposed since before he became a JCS chairman himself, so he plunged into the controversy. But his speeches, letters, congressional testimony, and op-ed article in The New York Times[33] were of no avail: the changes in the chairman's status became law in the Defense Reorganization Act of 1986. The general was on the losing side in the last public fight of his life.

The amazing health that had sustained him through a schedule that would have sidelined much younger men began to deteriorate when he got into his eighties. When he was eighty-three, tests at Washington's Walter Reed Hospital revealed the presence of prostate cancer. The disease seemed to respond to an extensive series of chemotherapy treatments, but later a trip to Walter Reed for what was intended to be minor hernia surgery turned up evidence that the cancer had not been cured. As time went by the disease spread, and in 1985 Lemnitzer had to abandon his lengthy yearly stays in Honesdale because of the need to be close to Walter Reed and its treatment facilities. He continued to make speeches, but less often as the cancer and its treatment took its toll on his vitality.

One of the last requirements of strength to go was golf, although at age eighty-seven he blamed his reluctant farewell to the game he loved to a shortage of partners. He wrote to a Honesdale friend in 1987: "I have not played any golf during the past year. I live quite close to the Chevy Chase [Maryland] Golf Club, but most of my former golf partners have disappeared in recent months—have moved away, are ill or have died. The situation has emphasized that golf is a game for friends. It most certainly is not an attractive game to play with strangers."[34]

When the Lemnitzers were young, Kay suffered a broken right hip in a fall, and throughout her life had been afflicted by a steadily worsening case of osteoarthritis. It was a painful ailment which made walking increasingly difficult, forcing her eventually to use canes and then a walker. After her husband's death, she was unable to walk at all and spent the last six years of her life in bed under constant nursing care at the Lemnitzer home in Washington. The couple's medical problems placed a heavy burden on daughter Lois who kept things going in the home, did the driving, and cared for her parents. "Lois is living with us and is the general manager of our household," Lemnitzer wrote a friend in 1981. "Otherwise I could not be engaged in all the activities I am engaged in at the present time."[35]

In June 1987 Lemnitzer was awarded the Presidential Medal of Freedom, the highest award the president could make to a civilian. As the general stood during the presentation ceremony at the White House, President Reagan read from the citation: "A brave and dedicated military officer, who served our nation in peace and war. General Lemnitzer's skill as a tactician, planner and negotiator was instrumental in the Second World War. He fought in Korea, served as U.S. commander in chief in Europe [sic], and eventually became chairman of the Joint Chiefs of Staff. His life has been marked by high military skill and unselfish devotion to country."

A little over a year later—in September 1988—he became gravely ill from the effects of the cancer and was taken to Walter Reed for the last time. An official Army "Special Interest Casualty Report" issued soon afterward noted: "progress—not expected, morale—fair, diet—IVs [intravenous], ambulatory— no, surgery—no, life support—no." So seriously sick and heavily sedated that much of the time he could not recognize what few visitors were permitted to see him, he died two months later—on November 12—of kidney failure. Hardly able to move anymore, Kay nevertheless attended the funeral services at Fort Myers' Old Chapel, but left immediately afterward, unable to keep out of bed long enough to accept the customary condolences that follow the services. Bedridden from that time forward, she died six years later. She and her husband of sixty-five years are buried side by side at Arlington National Cemetery.

Even in death, Lemnitzer made sure that the old home in Pennsylvania would stay in the family, just as it had for ninety years. He left it to Lois, "because," she said, "he knew I would live there."[36] A few months after her mother died, she and her brother sold the house in Washington, and Lois moved back to Honesdale. Once again, the Lemnitzer family had come home.

Lemnitzer had been dead for less than three years when the Soviet Union, that ruthless empire against whose sinister ambitions he had fought for forty years, crumbled, splintering the once mighty military power into hapless fragments and banishing Communism from the ruling centers of government.

It was a day the general would have given a great deal to have been alive to see.

NOTES

Author's Note: The chief primary sources of material included in this book are the Special Collections section of the National Defense University's library in Washington, D.C., where General Lemnitzer's papers are stored; and unfiled, uncatalogued papers, photographs, and other documents found by the author among his personal possessions after his death and used with the permission of the general's family. Extensive reference is made to oral history interviews; transcripts of those conducted by the Army War College are in the archives of the U.S. Military History Institute at Carlisle Barracks, Pennsylvania, or are in the general's personal papers. Other oral histories are on file at the institutions under whose auspices they were conducted or in Lemnitzer's personal papers.

Chapter 1: 'BE YOURSELF'

1. Letter from Army Secretary Stanley Resor to president, U.S. Senate; speaker, U.S. House of Representatives.

2. Others on the list would undoubtedly have held this office, but the JCS was not formally established until 1947; prior to that, there was no all-services equivalent. All generals of the Army but Bradley were promoted to their ranks during World War II, largely to put them on an equal footing with foreign field marshals. Two men have held generals of the armies rank: Pershing, who was invited to choose his own insignia but decided to keep his four stars; and George Washington, who was authorized the rank by Congress in 1799 but was not awarded it until 1976 when it was conferred by a joint resolution of Congress with the approval of Gerald R. Ford.

3. Gen. Theodore W. Parker, U.S. Army retired, Lemnitzer's chief of staff at SHAPE, and his special assistant when he was JCS chairman.

4. St. Louis Post-Dispatch, March 22, 1959. (Quoting Dr. Keith Glennan).

5. Eisenhower to author.

6. Letter from Maj. Gen. C. T. (Buck) Lanham, March 31, 1955.

7. Trussell to author.

8. Kissinger letter to Julius Klein, May 11, 1970.

9. Marshall, *The Overseas Weekly*, April 20, 1969.

10. Lt. Gen. Orwin Talbott, U.S. Army retired, to author.

11. Trussell to author.

12. Chambers to author.

13. Maj. Gen. Hamilton A. Twitchell, U.S. Army retired, to Alexander Cochran.

14. Trussell to author.

15. Twitchell to Cochran.

16. Milton letter to Lemnitzer, January 11, 1956.

17. Chambers to author.

18. Klein letter to Lemnitzer, April 3, 1970.

19. Robert T. Hartmann, *Los Angeles Times*, January 6, 1963.

20. *Time*, May 11, 1959.

21. Lois Lemnitzer to author.

22. Trussell letter to Gen. Matthew Ridgway, U.S. Army retired, September 15, 1961.
23. Talbott to author.
24. Letter to Lois, August 21, 1961.
25. Letter to Bill, March 23, 1973.
26. Letter to Lois, May 13, 1959.
27. Talbott to author.
28. Marshall, *The Overseas Weekly,* April 20, 1969.
29. Letter to Steven R. Mattis, September 17, 1962.
30. Lecture, "Philosophy of Command," Army War College, August 16, 1978.

Chapter 2: ROCKO

1. Ammerman to author; *The Wayne Independent,* July 17, 1962.
2. *The Wayne Independent,* November 14, 1988.
3. Letter to Lois, November 14, 1961.
4. Letter to Ernest, December 3, 1954.
5. Private papers.
6. *Philadelphia Sunday Bulletin,* January 21, 1973.
7. Letter to Maj. Gen. E. C. Itschner, July 6, 1959.
8. Wayne County Historical Society, Honesdale, Pennsylvania.
9. Although other sources are unanimous in putting the total distance traveled as a single, crunchy mile, Horatio Allen, who was at the controls, claimed to the local newspaper editor over fifty years later that the *Lion* went six fault-free miles that day—three miles out and three miles back. Allen, a driving force in obtaining the *Lion,* was a civil engineer whose first and last experience as a locomotive engineer occurred at the debut. He was alone that day: "The only sound to greet my ears until my safe return, in addition to the exhaust steam, was the creaking of the timber [rail] structure." *The Wayne Independent,* August 3, 1954.
10. Wayne County Historical Society.
11. *The Wayne Independent,* May 27, 1910.
12. Letter to Adrian Jaffe, May 17, 1960.
13. U.S. census, 1900.
14. *The Wayne Independent,* May 27, 1910.
15. Samuel P. Bates, *History of Pennsylvania Volunteers, Vol III* (Harrisburg, Pa.: B. Singerly, State Printer, 1870), 1059–61.
16. Letter to Carl F. Lemnitzer (no relation), March 6, 1955.
17. National Archives, Washington, D.C.
18. *The Wayne Independent,* May 27, 1910.
19. U.S. census, 1900.
20. *The Wayne Independent,* May 27, 1910.
21. Letter to Louise Rudolph (cousin), September 25, 1954.
22. *The Wayne Independent,* November 14, 1988.
23. Rusch to author.
24. Last will and testament, filed at the courthouse in Wayne County, Honesdale, November 10, 1987.
25. *The Wayne Independent,* November 14, 1988.
26. *Anchorage Daily News,* July 11, 1967
27. Thomas J. Ham, *Honesdale Citizen,* October 6, 1904.
28. *The Wayne Independent,* September 6, 1945.
29. Oral history interview, Army War College (hereafter cited as AWC), Richard A. Hatch, March 8, 1973.
30. *The Wayne Independent,* November 14, 1988.

Chapter 3: THE HUMP

1. Talbott to author.
2. *Historical Statistics of the U.S. Bureau of the Census* (Washington: U.S. Government Printing Office, 1968).
3. Ibid.
4. D. Clayton James, *The Years of MacArthur* (Boston: Houghton Mifflin, 1970), 262.
5. "Beast barracks" was a harsh indoctrination period through which new plebes had to pass to prove to upperclassmen that they were cadet material. Conducted by upperclassmen, the month-long ordeal brought the plebes to the point of mental and physical exhaustion through emotional torment and exacting physical requirements.
6. Thomas J. Fleming, *West Point* (New York: William Morrow, 1969), 304.
7. Ibid., 306.
8. Col. Clarence C. Clendenen, U.S. Army retired, *The Assembly,* June, 1974.
9. Ibid.
10. James, *The Years of MacArthur,* 263.
11. Fleming, *West Point,* 305.
12. Ibid., 311.
13. James, *The Years of MacArthur,* 305.
14. Oral history interview, AWC (Hatch) March 8, 1973.
15. Ibid.
16. Fleming, *West Point,* 273.
17. Oral history interview, AWC (Hatch), March 8, 1973.
18. Ibid.
19. *The Bulletin,* U.S. Military Academy Class of 1920, May 1930.
20. Oral history interview, AWC (Hatch), May 4, 1973.
21. Emanuel Raymond Lewis, *Seacoast Fortifications of the United States* (Washington: Smithsonian Institution Press, 1970), 79.
22. Ibid., 101.
23. Ibid., 111.
24. James, *The Years of MacArthur,* 260–1.
25. Oral history interview, AWC (Hatch), May 4, 1973.
26. Application for Victory Medal, October 8, 1920.
27. *The Wayne Independent,* November 14, 1988.
28. Oral history interview, (Hatch), May 8, 1973.
29. Son William to author.
30. *V.F.W.* magazine, August 1960.
31. *The Wayne Independent,* November 10, 1923.
32. *The Honesdale Citizen,* January 2, 1908.
33. *Time,* May 11, 1959.

Chapter 4: THE ROCK

1. Thomas Mitchell, *The Hurricane,* Samuel Goldwyn, Inc., Ltd., 1938. The fictitious island was "Manikoora."
2. Letter to Ramón Magsaysay, March 5, 1957.
3. Ibid.
4. James H. and William M. Belote, *Corregidor: The Saga of a Fortress* (New York: Harper and Row, 1967), 9.
5. Ibid., 11.
6. Mark A. Berhow, *Modern American Harbor Defenses* (San Pedro, Calif.: Fort MacArthur Military Press, 1992), 42.
7. Stanley L. Falk, *Army,* April 1967.
8. Capt. John Gordon IV, *Army,* March 1986.
9. Letter to Lemnitzer, June 4, 1955.
10. William Lemnitzer to author.
11. James and William Belote, *Corregidor: The Saga of a Fortress,* 16–7.

12. Ibid., 18–9.

13. Ibid., 19.

14. Ibid., 18.

15. Oral history interview, AWC (Hatch), May 21, 1973.

16. James and William Belote, *Corregidor: The Saga of a Fortress*, 25.

17. Ibid., 22.

18. Forrest Pogue to author.

19. Art Wall, Jr., to author.

20. Oral history interview, AWC (Hatch), March 8, 1973.

21. *Associated Press*, September 14, 1951.

22. Letter from Russell A. Gugeler, October 8, 1976.

23. Letter from Fort Adams adjutant and reply, October 31, 1927.

Chapter 5: BROWN SHOE DAYS

1. Ronald Schaffer, *Military Affairs*, October 1973.

2. Ibid.

3. Ibid.

4. Letter to Col. Erle Cress, August 1, 1954.

5. Oral history interview, AWC, Walter J. Bickston, November 3, 1973.

6. Officer's Efficiency Report (hereafter cited as OER), February 18, 1932.

7. James and William Belote, *Corregidor: The Saga of a Fortress*, 23.

8. Ibid., 28.

9. Ibid., 7.

10. OER, August 28, 1935.

11. Oral history interview, AWC (Bickston), November 3, 1973.

12. Fleming, *West Point*, 320.

13. *Historical Statistics of the U.S. Bureau of the Census.*

14. Ibid.

15. Col. John M. Collins, *Army*, January 1972.

16. So-called because either no ammunition or dummy rounds were used.

17. Collins, *Army*, January 1972.

18. Class schedule, Command and General Staff School library, Fort Leavenworth.

19. Letter to Gen. Isaac D. White, U.S. Army retired, February 19, 1974.

20. Letter to Brig. Gen. Robert H. Foreman, January 19, 1981.

21. Richard P. Weinart, Jr., and Col. Robert Arthur, *Defender of the Chesapeake* (Shippensberg, Pa.: White Mane Publishing Co., 1989), 250–1.

22. Ibid., 253.

23. Ibid., 256.

24. Ibid., 137.

25. Ibid., 130–3.

26. Capt. L. L. Lemnitzer, *State Department Cooperation with the War and Naval Departments in War Planning*, Army Military Institute Archives, Carlisle Barracks, Pa.

27. Trussell, file copy of Lemnitzer-approved biographical sketch.

28. U.S. Army Military History Institute Archives.

29. Col. George S. Pappas, *Prudens Futuri*, 136.

30. Ibid., 127.

31. Ibid., 131.

32. The teams finished their game, with the Redskins winning 20-14.

Chapter 6: FIRST CHOP

1. Fleming, *West Point*, 291.
2. U.S. Army Military History Institute Archives.
3. Taylor oral history interview, AWC, October 19, 1972.
4. Internal confidential Army memorandum of interview with Malony, January 10, 1944. Unsigned. National Archives.
5. The others were Alfred M. Gruenther, general and supreme commander, Allied Powers Europe, 1953; Gordon DeL. Carrington, brigadier general who died of natural causes in 1944; Hubert R. Harmon, lieutenant general and first superintendent of the Air Force Academy; George P. Hays, lieutenant general and commander of U.S. Forces Austria; and Paul McD. Robinett, retired as a brigadier general after being severely wounded.
6. Martin Blumenson, *Mark Clark* (New York: St. Martin's Press, 1984), 48.
7. Dwight D. Eisenhower, *Crusade in Europe* (Garden City, N.Y.: Doubleday, 1949), 3.
8. Ibid., 5.
9. Ibid., 14.
10. Kenneth E. Hamburger, *The Technology, Doctrine and Politics of U.S. Coast Defenses, 1880–1945*. (Ph.D diss., Duke University, 1986), 281.
11. Brig. Gen. Thomas R. Phillips, U.S. Army retired, *St. Louis Post-Dispatch*, March 22, 1959.
12. Gen. McNair was killed during an inspection visit near St. Lo, France, seven weeks after D-Day when Allied planes accidentally bombed the U.S. position he was visiting.
13. Blumenson, *Mark Clark*, 69.
14. Oral history interview, Columbia University, David C. Berliner, November 21, 1972.
15. Eisenhower, *Crusade in Europe*, 77.
16. Ibid., 72.
17. Lemnitzer interview, *Military History*, Joseph P. Hanrahan, October 1986.
18. John S. D. Eisenhower, *Allies: Pearl Harbor to D-Day* (Garden City, N.Y.: Doubleday, 1982), 133.
19. Dwight D. Eisenhower, *Crusade in Europe*, 77.
20. Lemnitzer interview, *Military History*, October 1986.
21. John S. D. Eisenhower, *Allies: Pearl Harbor to D-Day*, 129.

Chapter 7: THE ROBINHOODS

1. Gen. Mark Clark, *Calculated Risk* (New York: Harper, 1950), 72.
2. John Eisenhower, *Allies: Pearl Harbor to D-Day*, 133–43.
3. Clark, *Calculated Risk*, 121.
4. Ibid., 74.
5. The *Seraph* was believed to have been the vessel that set adrift the famed "man who never was," a body carrying false papers intended to mislead the enemy about the invasion of Sicily. Blumenson, *Mark Clark*, 80.
6. Clark, *Calculated Risk*, 75.
7. Lemnitzer's personal notes of mission.
8. Ibid.
9. Ibid.
10. Norman A. A. Jewell, *Secret Mission Submarine* (Chicago-New York: Ziff-Davis, 1945), 25.
11. Lemnitzer notes.
12. Lemnitzer interview, *Military History*, October 1986.
13. Lemnitzer notes.
14. Ibid.
15. Clark, *Calculated Risk*, 81.
16. Lemnitzer notes.
17. Clark, *Calculated Risk*, 81–2.

18. Lemnitzer notes.
19. Clark, *Calculated Risk*, 83.
20. Blumenson, *Mark Clark*, 87.
21. Clark, *Calculated Risk*, 83.
22. Ibid., 84.
23. Lemnitzer notes.
24. Clark, *Calculated Risk*, 85.
25. Jewell, *Secret Mission Submarine*, 33.
26. Lemnitzer notes.

27. Jewell, *Secret Mission Submarine*, 42–3.
28. Clark, *Calculated Risk*, 87.
29. Blumenson, *Mark Clark*, 85; and Lt. Gen. William J. McCaffrey, U.S. Army retired, to author.
30. Letter from Col. Dan Gilmer, March 9, 1943.
31. Lemnitzer letter to John S. D. Eisenhower, March 30, 1979.

Chapter 8: TORCH: THE PUDDING

1. Glenn Infield, *Man's Magazine*, June 1961.
2. Jimmy Doolittle, *I Could Never Be So Lucky Again* (New York: Bantam, 1992), 310–3.
3. Trussell, Lemnitzer biographical sketch.
4. Doolittle, *I Could Never Be So Lucky Again*, 313.
5. Infield, *Man's Magazine*.
6. Eisenhower, *Crusade in Europe*, 95.
7. Ibid., 96.
8. George Howe, *U.S. Army in World War II—Northwest Africa: Seizing the Initiative in the West* (Washington: Office of the Chief of Military History, 1957), 186.
9. Ibid., 96.
10. Oral history interview, AWC, Harold C. Deutsch, February 13–14, 1984.
11. Ibid.
12. Ibid.
13. Dwight Eisenhower, *Crusade in Europe*, 99.
14. John Eisenhower, *Allies: Pearl Harbor to D-Day*, 187.
15. Jewell, *Secret Mission Submarine*, 50–1.
16. Ibid., 48–51.
17. John Eisenhower, *Allies: Pearl Harbor to D-Day*, 176.
18. Oral history interview, AWC (Deutsch), February 13–14, 1984.
19. Dwight Eisenhower, *Crusade in Europe*, 104.

20. John Eisenhower, *Allies: Pearl Harbor to D-Day*, 191.
21. The assassin, Bournier de la Chapell, twenty-one, was a self-styled monarchist who police believed became befuddled by the wartime atmosphere in normally peaceful Algiers and decided that France needed some kind of new regime. He was executed.
22. Howe, *Northwest Africa: Seizing the Initiative in the West*, 168.
23. Ibid., 161.
24. Ibid., 158.
25. Ibid., 168.
26. Oral history interview, AWC (Deutsch), February 13–14, 1984.
27. Ibid.
28. Howe, *Northwest Africa: Seizing the Initiative in the West*, 170–3.
29. Letter to "Dear Folks," November 15, 1942.
30. Ibid., November 21–24, 1942.
31. Ibid., December 25, 1942.
32. Ibid., January 26, 1943.
33. Oral history interview, AWC (Deutsch), February 13–14, 1984.
34. Lt. Col. Tom W. Sills, *Coast Artillery Journal*, July–August 1946.
35. Report sent May 13, 1943.
36. Letter to Ernest, April 27, 1943.
37. Patton letter to Lemnitzer, July 27, 1943.

Chapter 9: THE MENTOR

1. Vernon A. Walters, *Silent Missions* (Garden City, N.Y.: Doubleday, 1978), 122.

2. Letter to Alexander, July 1, 1959.

3. Rudyard Kipling, *The Irish Guards in the Great War*, Vol. II (London: Macmillan, 1923), 44.

4. *The London Times*, June 17, 1969.

5. Nigel Nicolson, *Alex* (London: Weidenfeld and Nicholson, 1973), 239.

6. If Alexander's boat had cruised west instead of east, his voice might have reached thirty thousand French soldiers who were waiting behind the beaches to embark while another fifty thousand were further back covering the English retreat. Twenty thousand French troops escaped to Dover that night, leaving ten thousand behind. Nicolson, *Alex*, 113.

7. *London Telegraph*, June 17, 1969.

8. Letter to Lemnitzer, June 16, 1959.

9. Nicolson, *Alex*, 197.

10. John Eisenhower, *Allies: Pearl Harbor to D-Day*, 326.

11. Dwight Eisenhower, *Crusade in Europe*, 179.

12. Lemnitzer letter to J. V. Herd, January 23, 1980.

13. The group got its designation by totaling the numbers of its armies, the Seventh and the Eighth.

14. Albert N. Garland and Howard McGaw Smyth, *U.S. Army in World War II—Sicily and the Surrender of Italy* (Washington: Center of Military History, 1993), 56.

15. Geoffrey Perret, *There's a War to Be Won* (New York: Random House, 1991), 192.

16. Mark Clark, *Calculated Risk*, 69.

17. Honourable Companion of the Most Honourable Order of the Bath, 1945.

18. Letter to Field Marshal Lord John Harding, December 18, 1985.

19. Letter to Lemnitzer, June 21, 1964.

20. Maxwell Taylor, *Swords and Plowshares* (New York: W.W. Norton, 1972), 54–64.

21. Letter to Ridgway, June 20, 1983.

22. Ibid.

23. Oral history interview, AWC (Deutsch), February 13–14, 1984.

24. Dwight Eisenhower, *Crusade in Europe*, 186.

25. Oral history interview, AWC (Deutsch), February 13–14, 1984.

26. Nicolson, *Alex*, 257–8.

27. Lemnitzer personal notes.

28. Oral history interview, AWC (Deutsch), February 13–14, 1984.

29. Ibid.

30. Oral history interview, National War College (hereafter cited as NWC), Sidney T. Matthews, January 16, 1948.

31. W. G. F. Jackson, *Alexander of Tunis as Military Commander* (New York: Dodd-Mead, 1972), 265.

32. Blumenson to author.

33. Jackson, *Alexander of Tunis as Military Commander*, 271.

34. Oral history interview, AWC (Deutsch), February 13–14, 1984.

35. Letter to Edward L. Freeman, April 19, 1982.

36. Ibid.

37. Harold Macmillan, *War Diaries—The Mediterranean 1943–1945* (New York: St. Martin's Press, 1948), 368.

38. Nicolson, *Alex*, 233.

39. Edmund F. Ball, *Staff Officer* (New York: Exposition Press, 1958), 301–2.

40. Oral history interview, AWC (Deutsch), February 13–14, 1984.

41. Lt. Gen. William C. McCaffrey to author.

42. Oral history, AWC (Deutsch), February 13–14, 1984.

43. Jackson, *Alexander of Tunis as Military Commander*, 267–8.

44. Harold R. L. G. Alexander, *The Alexander Memoirs, 1940–45* (New York-London: McGraw-Hill, 1962), 148.

45. Nicholson, *Alex*, 245.

46. Official U.S. Army report: *The Bombardment of Cassino*, March 15, 1944.

47. Nicolson, *Alex*, 245.
48 Letter to Edward L. Freeman, April 19, 1982.
49. Jackson, *Alexander of Tunis as Military Commander*, 288.
50. Letter to Robert K. Dawson, June 20, 1984.
51. Clark, *Calculated Risk*, 351.
52. Ibid., 352.
53. Oral history interview, AWC (Deutsch), February 13–14, 1984.
54. Jackson, *Alexander of Tunis as Military Commander*, 289.
55. Winston Churchill, *Closing the Ring* (Boston: Houghton Mifflin, 1951), 431–2.
56. Jackson, *Alexander of Tunis as Military Commander*, 289.
57. Clark, *Calculated Risk*, 352.
58. Nicolson, *Alex*, 252.
59. Macmillan, *War Diaries—The Mediterranean 1943–1945*, 374.
60. Oral history interview, AWC (Deutsch), February 13–14, 1984.
61. Ibid.
62. Harding, *The London Sunday Times*, June 22, 1969.
63. Oral history interview, AWC (Deutsch), February 13–14, 1984.
64. Attributed to President Ronald Reagan by William Safire, *New York Times Magazine*, January 22, 1995.

Chapter 10: SUNRISE

1. Letter to son from "In the field—Italy," November 14, 1943.
2. German defensive position one hundred seventy-five miles north of Rome, launching place of the Allies' last Italian offensive.
3. Oral History interview, Office of the Chief of Military History (hereafter cited as OCMH), Sidney T. Matthews, January 16, 1946.
4. Dwight Eisenhower, *Crusade in Europe*, 190.
5. Winston Churchill, *Triumph and Tragedy* (Boston: Houghton Mifflin, 1953), 261.
6. Macmillan, *War Diaries—Mediterranean 1943–1945*, 522.
7. Ibid.
8. Oral history interview, OCMH (Matthews), January 16, 1948.
9. Oral history interview, OCMH, Howard M. Smyth, March 4, 1947.
10. Dwight Eisenhower, *Crusade in Europe*, 206.
11. Alexander biographer Nigel Nicolson put the total at twenty-two. *Alex*, 263.
12. Nicolson, *Alex*, 266.
13. Oral history interview, AWC (Deutsch), February 13–14, 1984.
14. The prime minister reveled in selecting resounding titles for major WWII operations. Lemnitzer, as deputy to a British commander, always referred to it as "Crossword," as well.
15. Allen Dulles, *The Secret Surrender* (New York: Harper and Row, 1966), 105.
16. Personal diary.
17. Gero von Gaevernitz, *Operation Cross-word-Sunrise*. (Unpublished manuscript, 1965), 117.
18. Ibid.
19. Dulles, *The Secret Surrender*, 122.
20. Ibid., 123.
21. Letter to Ross Pensa, November 15, 1978.
22. Dulles, *The Secret Surrender*, 35.
23. Ibid., 131.
24. Ibid., 160–81.
25. Ibid., 162–3.
26. Ibid., 162.
27. Ibid., 147.
28. Harry S. Truman memoirs, *Vol. I, Year of Decisions* (Garden City, New York: Doubleday, 1955), 200–1.
29. Oral history interview, AWC (Deutsch), February 13–14, 1984.

30. Gaevernitz, *Operation Crossword-Sunrise*, 156.
31. Dulles, *The Secret Surrender*, 207.
32. Ibid., 210.
33. Oral history interview, AWC (Deutsch), February 13–14, 1984.

34. Dulles, *The Secret Surrender*, 210.
35. Personal diary.
36. Ibid.
37. McCaffrey to author.

Chapter 11: 'AN IRON CURTAIN HAS DESCENDED'

1. *The Wayne Independent*, September 6, 1945.
2. Oral history interview, OCMH (Smyth), March 4, 1947.
3. Nicolson, *Alex*, 279.
4. Oral history interview, Office of the Secretary of Defense (hereafter cited as OSD), Doris Condit, March 4, 1976.
5. Nicolson, *Alex*, 283.
6. Personal diary. The Companion of the Bath, established in 1725, is Great Britain's third-oldest order for chivalry.
7. Letter from Maj. Gen. W. S. Paul, April 12, 1946.
8. Letter to Ernest, May 20, 1943.
9. Steven L. Reardon, Vol. I *History of the Office of the Secretary of Defense, The Formative Years* (Washington: Historical Office, OSD, 1988), 12.
10. Drafted by a presidential blue-ribbon committee, the plan would have required every able-bodied seventeen- or eighteen-year-old male to receive six months of military training, followed by service in the Reserves or National Guard. Ibid., 14.
11. Oral history interview, OSD, Alfred Goldberg, March 21, 1974.

12. Ibid.
13. *General Plan for Postwar Joint Education of the Armed Forces*, ANSCOL A3-1 (080).
14. Oral history interview, *The Reminiscences of Adm. Harry W. Hill*, Oral History Research Office, Columbia University, 887.
15. Ibid., 941.
16. Ibid., 938.
17. Goodpaster to author.
18. George J. Stansfield, *History of the National War College, 1946–1956*. Unpublished manuscript.
19. Oral history interview, AWC (Bickston), May 4, 1972.
20. Dulles, *The Secret Surrender*, 146.
21. The term was later popularized by Churchill on March 5, 1946, in a speech at Westminster College, Fulton, Mo., in which he said: "From Stettin in the Baltic to Trieste in the Adriatic, an iron curtain has descended across the continent."
22. Rearden, *History of the Office of the Secretary of Defense, Vol. I*, 459.
23. Ibid., 462.
24. Ibid., 464.

Chapter 12: MINDER OF THE ARSENAL

1. Rearden, *History of the Office of the Secretary of Defense, Vol. I*, 467–8.
2. Oral history interview, AWC (Bickston), May 4, 1972.
3. Ibid.

4. Oral history interview, OSD (Goldberg), March 21, 1974.
5. Oral history interview, AWC (Bickston), May 4, 1972.
6. Ibid.

7. Oral history interview, OSD (Goldberg), March 21, 1974.

8. Oral history interview, AWC (Bickston), May 4, 1972.

9. Ibid.

10. Ibid.

11. Oral history interview, OSD (Goldberg), March 21, 1974.

12. Rearden, *History of the Office of the Secretary of Defense, Vol I*, 503–5.

13. Ibid., 44.

14. Clay Blair, *The Forgotten War* (New York: Random House, 1987), 14.

15. Rearden, *History of the Office of the Secretary of Defense, Vol. I*, 61.

16. Ibid., 46.

17. Oral history interview, AWC (Bickston), May 4, 1972.

18. Ibid.

19. Ibid.

20. Ibid.

21. Ibid.

22. Ibid.

23. Rearden, *History of the Office of the Secretary of Defense, Vol. I*, 71.

24. Oral history interview, OSD (Goldberg), March 21, 1974.

25. Ibid.

26. Oral history interview, AWC (Bickston), May 4, 1972.

27. Oral history interview, OSD (Goldberg), March 21, 1974.

28. Ibid.

29. In a directive signed November 25, 1949, by Secretary Johnson.

30. Personal diary, March 13, 1950.

31. Ibid., September 19, 1950.

32. Oral history interview, OSD (Goldberg), March 21, 1974.

33. Lawrence S. Kaplan, *A Community of Interests: NATO and the Military Assistance Program, 1948–1951* (Washington: Historical Office, Office of the Secretary of Defense, 1980), 61–2.

34. Ibid., 56.

35. Chester J. Pach, Jr., *Arming the Free World* (Chapel Hill, London: University of North Carolina Press, 1991), 205–6.

36. Lemnitzer diary, June 8, 1950.

37. Ibid., May 10, 1950.

38. Oral history interview, OSD (Goldberg), March 21, 1974.

39. Oral history interview, OSD (Condit), March 4, 1976.

40. Rearden, *History of the Office of the Secretary of Defense, Vol. I*, 271.

41. Oral history interview, OSD (Goldberg), March 21, 1974.

42. *Beau geste* means "beautiful gesture" in French. The reference here was to two popular motion pictures of the same name in which the French foreign legion fought in the desert while headquartered in forts.

43. Oral history interview, OSD (Goldberg), March 21, 1974.

44. Ibid.

45. Ibid.

46. Ibid.

47. Ibid.

48. Ibid.

49. Oral history interview, AWC (Bickston), May 4, 1972.

50. Dean Acheson, *Present at the Creation: My Years in the State Department* (New York: Holt, Rinehart & Winston, 1959), 117.

51. Blair, *The Forgotten War*, 234–5.

52. Memorandum for the Secretary of the Army, August 26, 1949.

53. *The Detroit News*, November 23, 1950.

54. Acheson letter to Marshall, November 3, 1950.

55. Marshall letter to Lemnitzer, November 14, 1950.

56. Burns letter to Lemnitzer, November 10, 1950.

57. Leva letter to Pace, November 15, 1950.

58. Johnson letter to Lemnitzer, September 18, 1950.

59. Oral history interview, OSD (Goldberg), March 21, 1974.

Chapter 13: KOREA

1. Oral history interview, OSD (Condit), March 4, 1976.
2. Garland to author.
3. Letter to Maj. Gen. Wayne C. Smith who had sent him a copy of a letter in which he (Smith) had refused to grant a badge to another general who had made only one jump, January 5, 1955.
4. McCaffrey, who had commanded a Seventh Division regiment just before Lemnitzer took command.
5. Oral history interview, OSD (Goldberg), March 4, 1976.
6. West Point Military History Series, *Arab-Israeli Wars, the Chinese Civil War and the Korean War*. Edited by Thomas E. Griess (Garden City Park, N.Y.: Avery Publishing Group, 1987), 74–5.
7. Letter, "Dear Family," December 5, 1951.
8. Ibid.
9. Letter, "Dear Family," January 3, 1952.
10. Letter to Kay, January 6, 1952.
11. Letter to Kay, February 2, 1952.
12. Letter, "Dear Family," December 23, 1951.
13. Letter, "Dear Family," December 26, 1951.
14. Letter, "Dear Family," January 3, 1951.
15. Ibid.
16. Letter to Lois, February 2, 1952.
17. Letter to Kay, April 30, 1952.
18. Letter to Kay, February 15, 1952.
19. Letter to Lois, March 17, 1952.
20. Letter to Kay, February 2, 1952.
21. Letter to Lois, February 21, 1952.
22. Letter to Kay, April 30, 1952.
23. Ibid.
24. Letter to Lois, May 6, 1952.
25. Letter to Kay, February 14, 1952.
26. Letter to Kay, June 17, 1952.
27. Nicolson, *Alex*, 309–10.

Chapter 14: BASTARD AT THE REUNION

1. Oral history interview, OSD (Goldberg, Condit, Lawrence Kaplan), March 4, 1976.
2. Ibid.
3. Ibid.
4. Max Hastings, *The Korean War* (New York: Simon and Schuster, 1987), 318–20.
5. The other two deputy chief of staff positions were comptroller, and operations and administration.
6. Collins to Lemnitzer, August 11, 1953.
7. Gen. Andrew J. Goodpaster, U.S. Army retired, letter to author, September 8, 1995.
8. Chester J. Pach, Jr., and Elmo Richardson, *The Presidency of Dwight D. Eisenhower* (Lawrence, Kans.: University Press of Kansas, 1991), 80–1.
9. Douglas Kinnard, *President Eisenhower and Strategy Management* (Washington, New York, London: Pergamon-Brassey's, 1989), 27.
10. *Army*, December 1956.
11. Oral history interview, AWC (Hatch), May 21, 1973. Despite the Army's apparent rejection of the Dart, it remained in development by the Army Ordnance Corps.
12. Letter to son William and wife Lydia, January 4, 1954.
13. Ibid.
14. Letter to Stevens, December 21, 1953.
15. Letter to Lt. Col. M. N. Kadick, February 27, 1954.
16. Letter to Ernest, March 27, 1954.
17. Letter to Zwicker, April 14, 1957.

18. Letter to Brig. Gen. Robert J. Wood, January 5, 1955.
19. Letter to Col. Arthur Symons, U.S. Army retired, January 4, 1955.

20. Letter to Symons, October 22, 1955. (Symons was association secretary.)

Chapter 15: THE RINGMASTER

1. Oral history interview, Columbia (Berliner), December 19, 1972.
2. Ibid.
3. Letter to Ernest and wife Margaret, August 26, 1955.
4. Message from Brucker, August 30, 1955.
5. Oral history interview, Columbia (Berliner), December 19, 1972.
6. Ibid.
7. Ibid.
8. Letter to Ernest and wife Margaret, September 14, 1955.
9. Chambers to author.
10. Rhee letter to Lemnitzer, September 9, 1957.
11. "Summation of Debriefing of Captain Krant." Date unknown.
12. Because the dog's Korean name was long and virtually unpronounceable in English, Lois named it after a young staff enlisted clerk's odd habit of referring to any Korean with a difficult name as "Mr. Brady."
13. Letter to Specialist Fourth Class Richard Leslie who had written him asking how to get permission to bring home a pet dog from Vietnam, April 10, 1970.
14. Letter to Sohn Won II, November 23, 1955.
15. Rhee letter to Stump, October 4, 1956.
16. Lemnitzer memorandum for record, January 15, 1956.
17. Letter to Ernest, April 29, 1960.
18. Letter to Lois and husband Hank, May 24, 1960.
19. Taylor letter to Lemnitzer, June 28, 1957.

20. Letter to Lt. Gen. James E. Moore, commander. Ryukyus Command and Ninth Corps, April 21, 1957.
21. Personal letter to Adm. Arleigh A. Burke, chief of naval operations, April 23, 1957.
22. The Soviet Union seized four islands in the Kuriles, on Japan's northern coast, in 1945.
23. Letter to Moore, April 21, 1957.
24. Brig. Gen. Andrew J. Goodpaster, *Memorandum of Conference with the President,* July 25, 1957.
25. Oral history interview, Columbia (Berliner), November 21, 1972.
26. Goodpaster, *Memorandum of Conference with the President,* July 25, 1957.
27. Ibid.
28. Personal letter to Adm. Burke, April 23, 1957.
29. Trussell to author.
30. Statement of Specialist Third-Class Victor N. Nickel to U.S. Army criminal investigator Felix B. Garrett, June 10, 1957.
31. Letter to Rear Adm. Miles H. Hubbard, May 24, 1957.
32. Personal letter to Adm. Stump, May 22, 1957.
33. Ibid.
34. Letter to William, September 17, 1957.
35. Letter to Zablocki, December 13, 1955.
36. Letter to Michaelis, January 8, 1957.
37. Letter to Lt. Gen. Donald P. Booth, Army deputy chief of staff for personnel, May 1, 1957.
38. Letter to Miss Keller, March 1, 1957.

39. Letter to Maj. Gen. Floyd L. Wergeland, September 30, 1962.
40. Letter from John Randolph, June 26, 1957.
41. Exchange of notes, February 1961.
42. Letter to Ernest, November 7, 1955.
43. Letter to Maj. Gen. Joseph H. Harper, March 5, 1957.
44. Letter to Ernest, July 11, 1955.
45. Letter to Ernest, August 14, 1956.
46. Talking paper, June 21, 1957.

47. Letter from Rhee, September 9, 1957.
48. Goodpaster, *Memorandum of Conference with the President,* July 23, 1957.
49. *United Press,* June 26, 1957.
50. The reduction, effective in fiscal year 1959, reduced the authorized strength from 720,000 to 630,000.
51. Letter to Ernest, June 17, 1957.
52. Letter to Ernest, July 6, 1956.

Chapter 16: THE VICE

1. Oral history interview, Columbia (Berliner), December 19, 1972.
2. Ibid.
3. Ibid.
4. Ibid.
5. Ibid.
6. Ibid.
7. Letter to Ernest, November 21, 1958.
8. William Hines, *The Washington Evening Star,* October 29, 1958.
9. Oral history interview, Columbia (Berliner), December 19, 1972.
10. *Washington Post and Times Herald,* April 10, 1957.
11. Letter from Pace, April 12, 1957.
12. Letter from Harkins, May 14, 1957.
13. John Eisenhower to author.
14. Address before Quantico, Virginia, defense leaders conference, July 16, 1955.
15. Taylor, *Swords and Plowshares,* 171.
16. A pentomic battle group was made up of five rifle companies, a headquarters company, and a combat support company, in addition to artillery and tank elements. A standard triangular division consisted of three regiments of three battalions each, four artillery battalions, a division tank battalion and a tank company for each regiment, a 4.2-inch mortar battalion, and various supporting units.

17. Taylor, *Swords and Plowshares,* 171.
18. Gavin oral history interview, AWC, Donald G. Andrews and Charles H. Ferguson, April 16, 1975.
19. Letter to Brig. Gen. Charles H. (Tick) Bonesteel, October 16, 1957.
20. Draft memorandum, signed by Taylor, September 30, 1957.
21. Draft letter to Russell. Undated.
22. Letter to Ernest, April 17, 1958.
23. Letter to Ernest, July 5, 1958.
24. Letter to Ernest, July 17, 1958.
25. Letter to Hodes, July 24, 1958.
26. Letter to Bradley Biggs, February 28, 1975.
27. Pach and Richardson, *The Presidency of Dwight D. Eisenhower,* 202–3.
28. Letter to Palmer, July 9, 1958.
29. *Memorandum of Discussion, 411th Meeting of National Security Council,* June 25, 1959.
30. Gavin considered Taylor to be "cold, calculating and ruthlessly ambitious." Oral history interview, AWC, April 16, 1975.
31. Letter from Weible, June 17, 1955.
32. Letter to Bradley Biggs, February 28, 1975. Later reprinted in a Biggs book, *Gavin* (Hamden, Conn.: Shoe String Press, 1980), 101.
33. *Time,* March 30, 1959.

Chapter 17: THE CHIEF

1. *Los Angeles Examiner,* March 20, 1959.
2. Letter to Ernest, May 7, 1959.
3. *Time,* May 11, 1959.
4. Letter to Ernest, March 3, 1960.
5. *Washington Post,* February 5, 1960.
6. *Newsweek,* March 30, 1959.
7. Goodpaster oral history interview, Eisenhower Library, Thomas Soapes, June 26, 1975.
8. Kinnard, *President Eisenhower and Strategy Management,* 87.
9. *Memorandum of Discussion: 411th Meeting of the National Security Council,* June 25, 1959.
10. Kinnard, *President Eisenhower and Strategy Management,* 135.
11. Letter to Eisenhower, August 31, 1960.
12. Letter to Lt. Gen. Williston B. Palmer, August 8, 1959.
13. Official U.S. Army summation of major issues while Lemnitzer was chief of staff.
14. Letter to Stevens, January 16, 1960.
15. *New York Herald-Tribune,* February 5, 1960.
16. Senate Committee on Armed Services; Report on the Preparedness Investigation Subcommittee, Eighty-Sixth Congress.
17. Letter to Murray Snyder, assistant secretary of defense, March 3, 1960.
18. Letter to William, November 7, 1959.
19. Lt. Col. John Eisenhower (the president's son was assistant to Brig. Gen. Andrew J. Goodpaster, the president's staff secretary), *Memorandum of Conference with the President,* September 19, 1960.
20. Speech at the Annual Meeting of the Association of the U.S. Army, September 1960.
21. Ibid.
22. John Eisenhower to author.
23. Kinnard, *President Eisenhower and Strategy Management,* 131–2.
24. Goodpaster oral history interview, Eisenhower Library, Malcolm S. McDonald, April 10, 1982.
25. Letter from Smart, August 8, 1960.
26. Robert Previdi, *General Lyman L. Lemnitzer, Chief of Staff,* 46–7. Unpublished manuscript.
27. The cover was on the May 15, 1960, issue of *Parade.* A "red-faced" Lemnitzer was twitted about the incident in the March 14, 1960, issue of *The Insider's Newsletter,* published in Washington.
28. Watson, *Baltimore Sun,* August 8, 1960.
29. Ibid.
30. Oral history interview, Columbia (Berliner), December 19, 1972.
31. Letter to William, July 12, 1960.
32. Letter to William, July 16, 1960.
33. Letter to Ernest, August 16, 1960.
34. Letter to William, September 27, 1960.
35. *Los Angeles Times,* October 2, 1960.
36. Oral history interview, Columbia (Berliner), December 19, 1972.
37. Comprising the nation's combat units, unified commands are made of forces from more than one service, whereas specified commands consist of those from a single service.
38. Taylor, *Swords and Plowshares,* 175.
39. Letter to Brig. Gen. Theodore C. Mataxis, U.S. Army retired, February 4, 1981.
40. Letter to William, July 7, 1954.
41. Goodpaster, *Memorandum of Conference with the President,* December 31, 1960.
42. Ibid.
43. Goodpaster oral history interview, Eisenhower Library (Soapes), June 26, 1975.
44. Goodpaster, *Memorandum of Conference with the President,* January 18, 1961.
45. Goodpaster, *Memorandum of Conference with the President,* January 11, 1961.
46. Goodpaster, *Memorandum of Conference with the President,* January 18, 1961.
47. Ibid.

Chapter 18: BOPO

1. Mario Lazo, *Dagger in the Heart; American Policy Failures in Cuba* (New York: Funk and Wagnalls, 1968), 243.
2. John B. Spore, *Army*, July 1969.
3. Peter Wyden, *Bay of Pigs—The Untold Story* (New York: Simon and Schuster, 1979), 305.
4. Letter to Mrs. Arthur F. Davies, Jr., July 17, 1961.
5. Letter to Gen. Isaac D. White, U.S. Army retired, June 8, 1971.
6. Letter to Trussell, April 25, 1975.
7. Goodpaster oral history interview, Columbia University, Ed Edwin, April 25, 1967.
8. Lemnitzer, *The Cuban Debacle.* Unpublished manuscript.
9. CIA memorandum to White House: *Policy Decisions Required for Conduct of Strike Operations against Government of Cuba*, January 4, 1961.
10. Ibid.
11. Ibid. (Paramilitary forces are distinct from regular armed forces, but resembling them in organization, equipment, training, and mission.)
12. Lemnitzer, *The Cuban Debacle.*
13. *Briefing on the Cuban Situation*, Subcommittee on American Republic Affairs, of the Senate Committee on Foreign Relations, May 19, 1961.
14. Maj. Gen. David Gray, U.S. Army retired, letter to the author, December 7, 1994.
15. *Memorandum for Record*, Taylor Board of Inquiry on Cuban Operations, Conducted by CIA, April 27, 1961.
16. Lemnitzer, *The Cuban Debacle.*
17. Ibid.
18. Gray, letter to author, December 7, 1994.
19. Ibid.
20. Letter from Bissell, November 10, 1950.
21. Lemnitzer, *The Cuban Debacle.*
22. Ibid.
23. Arthur M. Schlesinger, Jr., *A Thousand Days* (Boston: Houghton Mifflin, 1965), 251–2.
24. Lemnitzer, *The Cuban Debacle.*
25. Gray, letter to author, December 7, 1994.
26. Ibid.
27. Lemnitzer, *The Cuban Debacle.*
28. Wyden, *Bay of Pigs—The Untold Story*, 171–2.
29. Ibid.
30. Lemnitzer, *The Cuban Debacle.*
31. Wyden, *Bay of Pigs—The Untold Story*, 205.
32. Lemnitzer, *The Cuban Debacle.*
33. Gray, letter to author, April 1, 1996.
34. Taylor Board of Inquiry Report, June 13, 1961.
35. Lemnitzer, *The Cuban Debacle.*
36. Taylor Board of Inquiry, *Memorandum No. 1*, June 13, 1961.
37. Wyden, *Bay of Pigs—The Untold Story*, 303.
38. William M. Crabbe, Jr., *National Security Crisis Management: The Bay of Pigs.* Unpublished student paper (Washington: Industrial College of the Armed Forces, National Defense University, 1978), 31.
39. Taylor, *Swords and Plowshares*, 186.
40. Gray, letter to author, April 1, 1996.
41. Taylor, *Swords and Plowshares*, 188.
42. Lemnitzer, *The Cuban Debacle.*
43. Taylor, *Swords and Plowshares*, 189.
44. Lemnitzer, *The Cuban Debacle.*
45. Ibid.
46. Gray, letter to author, December 7, 1994.
47. Lemnitzer, *The Cuban Debacle.*
48. Gray, letter to author, December 7, 1994.
49. Lemnitzer briefing remarks, *Briefing on the Cuban Situation, Subcommittee on American Republic Affairs of the Senate Committee on Foreign Relations*, May 19, 1961.
50. Lt. Gen. Orwin C. Talbott, U.S. Army retired (then Lemnitzer's executive officer) to author.
51. Gray, letter to author, December 7, 1994.
52. Ibid.

53. Transcript, meeting of the *Subcommittee on American Republic Affairs of the Senate Committee on Foreign Relations*, April 28, 1961.

54. *Associated Press*, May 19, 1961.

55. Ibid.

56. Gray, letter to author, December 7, 1994.

57. Schlesinger, *A Thousand Days*, 235.

58. Lemnitzer, *The Cuban Debacle.*

59. Gray, letter to author, January 27, 1995.

60. *New York Times*, May 27, 1961.

61. Gray, letter to author, January 27, 1995.

62. Richard M. Bissell, Jr., with Jonathan E. Lewis and Frances T. Pudlow, *Reflections of a Cold War Warrior* (New Haven: Yale University Press, 1996), 198–9.

63. Lemnitzer, *The Cuban Debacle.*

64. *New York Times*, January 17, 1995.

65. General Taylor claimed credit for the substance of Kennedy's charge to the Chiefs, writing that he "ran into [the president] by chance as he was leaving the White House to meet with the Chiefs. Taylor said Kennedy told him what his mission was and the general "by pure luck had a working paper in my pocket which bore precisely on the subject on his mind—the responsibility of the Chiefs to the president in the Cold War." Kennedy put the paper in his pocket, "rushed off to the Pentagon and, as I learned later, used it extensively in his discussion with the Chiefs." *Swords and Plowshares*, 189.

66. Schlesinger, *A Thousand Days*, 273.

Chapter 19: McNAMARA'S BAND

1. Jack Raymond, *Power at the Pentagon* (New York: Harper and Row, 1964), 288.

2. Carl W. Borklund, *Men of the Pentagon* (New York: Praeger, 1966), 208.

3. Oral history interview, Joint Chiefs of Staff historian Walter S. Poole, February 12, 1976.

4. McCaffrey to author.

5. Letter to Taylor, January 16, 1961.

6. Lee Iacocca and William Novak, *Iacocca* (New York: Bantam, 1986), 43–7.

7. Associated Press, March 24, 1961.

8. McCaffrey to author.

9. Raymond, *Power at the Pentagon*, 283.

10. Letter to Ernest, January 26, 1961.

11. Oral history interview, Lyndon B. Johnson Library, Ted Gettinger, March 3, 1982.

12. Oral history interview, John F. Kennedy Library, Joseph E. O'Connor, November 3, 1966.

13. Gordon Gray oral history interview, Eisenhower Library, Hugh Hedo and Anna Nelson, June 11, 1980.

14. Richard N. Haass, *New York Times Magazine*, May 29, 1994.

15. Letter to James A. McFarland, November 28, 1961.

16. Address at the annual dinner of the National Security Industrial Association, Washington, September 27, 1962.

17. Gen. Curtis E. Lemay, *America Is in Danger* (New York: Funk and Wagnall, 1968), 301.

18. Taylor, *Swords and Plowshares*, 253.

19. Lloyd Norman, *Army*, February 1968.

20. McCaffrey to author.

21. Lemnitzer, *The Cuban Debacle.*

22. Ibid.

23. Taylor, *Swords and Plowshares*, 197.

24. Oral history interview, Johnson Library (Gettinger), March 3, 1982.

25. Letter to Victor Ashe III, August 22, 1961.

26. Letter to Ernest, July 19, 1961.

27. Taylor, *Swords and Plowshares*, 198.

28. McCaffrey to author.

29. Letter to Ernest, July 19, 1961.

30. Schlesinger, *A Thousand Days*, 269.

31. Lemnitzer, *The Cuban Debacle.*

32. Schlesinger, *A Thousand Days*, 308.

33. Meeting of the Senate Foreign Relations Committee, April 11, 1961.

34. Goodpaster, *Memorandum of Conference with the President,* January 25, 1961.

35. David Halberstam, *The Best and the Brightest* (New York: Random House, 1972), 89.

36. Frank L. Kluckhohn, *America: Listen!* (Derby, Conn.: Monarch Books, 1963), 121.

37. Halberstam, *The Best and the Brightest,* 89.

38. Message to JCS, May 8, 1961.

39. Oral history interview, Kennedy Library (O'Connor), November 3, 1966.

40. Jack Raymond, *New York Times,* May 18, 1961.

41. Oral history interview, Johnson Library (Gettinger), March 3, 1982.

42. Schlesinger, *A Thousand Days*, 348.

43. Oral history interview, Johnson Library (Gettinger), March 3, 1982.

44. Schlesinger, *Robert Kennedy and His Times* (New York: Random House, 1985), 447–8.

45. Schlesinger, *A Thousand Days*, 442.

46. Oral history interview, Kennedy Library (O'Connor), November 3, 1966.

47. Oral history interview, AWC (Hatch), December 18, 1972.

48. Lemnitzer personal notes. Date unknown.

49. Schlesinger, *A Thousand Days*, 372.

Chapter 20: VIETNAM

1. *New York Times,* April 11, 1962.

2. *New York Times,* May 12, 1962.

3. *New York Times,* July 14, 1962.

4. Priority message, "Top Secret for General McGarr from Lemnitzer," December 5, 1961.

5. Letter to Maj. Gen. A. Franklin Kibler, August 26, 1954.

6. Warner interview with William A. Sullivan. Date and circumstances unknown.

7. Ibid.

8. Letter to Gen. Isaac D. White, U.S. Army retired, February 2, 1973.

9. Oral history interview, Columbia (Berliner), December 19, 1972.

10. Ibid.

11. Col. Wesley W. Hale, U.S. Army retired; Gen. Isaac D. White, U.S. Army retired; Gen. Hasso E. Manteuffel, German army retired, *Alternative to Armageddon* (New Brunswick, N.J.: Rutgers University Press, 1970), vii, viii.

12. Ibid.

13. Oral history interview, Johnson Library (Gettinger), March 3, 1982.

14. *New York Times,* April 7, 1962.

15. *New York Times,* April 15, 1962.

16. Letter to Ernest, April 19, 1962.

17. Trussell to author.

18. *New York Times,* April 11, 1962.

19. Taylor, *Swords and Plowshares,* 207.

20. William A. Hamilton III, *The Decline and Fall of the Joint Chiefs of Staff;* Unpublished thesis: Naval War College, Newport, R.I., April 15, 1971.

21. Brig. Gen. Chester V. Clifton, Jr., *Memorandum of Conference with the President,* February 23, 1961.

22. Taylor, *Swords and Plowshares,* 201–2.

23. Ibid., 252.

24. Oral history interview, AWC (Hatch), November 13, 1972.

25. Ibid.

26. Letter to Senator John C. Stennis, chairman, Senate Armed Services Committee, February 5, 1970.

27. Lloyd Norman, *Army,* April, 1970.

28. Letter to Wilber M. Brucker, August 28, 1962.

29. Ibid.
30. From the citation accompanying the award of the Distinguished Service Medal, Second Oak Leaf Cluster, October 1, 1962.
31. McNamara interview by Carl Bernstein, *Time*, February 11, 1991.
32. Taylor, *Swords and Plowshares*, 269.
33. Oral history interview, Johnson Library (Gettinger), March 3, 1972.

34. "The Lessons of the Cuban Missile Crisis," *Time*, September 22, 1982. Authors: Rusk; McNamara; George C. Ball, undersecretary of state; Gilpatric; Bundy; and Theodore Sorensen, special assistant to Kennedy.
35. Baldwin letter to Lemnitzer, September 16, 1962.

Chapter 21: SUPREME COMMANDER: THE FRENCH DISCONNECTION _____

1. *U.S. News & World Report*, December 31, 1962.
2. De Gaulle was said never to have forgotten the humiliation of having been virtually ignored at the historic conference. Lemnitzer attributed the slight to the fact that the French leader "had no chips," i.e. forces, materiel, and a base. "They didn't pay a lot of attention to [him]," the general recalled, "because we were in the crucial stages of trying to turn the tide of defeat everywhere in the world, and the people who had some chips were the ones calling the shots." Oral history interview, AWC (Hatch), November 13, 1972.
3. Ibid.
4. Oral history interview, OSD, Maurice Matloff, January 24, 1984.
5. Ibid. Also, Norstad oral history interview, Eisenhower Library (Soapes), November 11, 1976.
6. De Gaulle rejected several plans for the French celebration as "too much American, too much American" before being presented one he liked. Lemnitzer oral history interview, OSD (Matloff), January 24, 1984.
7. Ibid.
8. Oral history interview, AWC (Hatch), November 13, 1972.
9. The SACEUR's second in command was the deputy SACEUR, usually a U.S. Air Force general when the SACEUR was an Army general. The deputy had command, less operational control, of all U.S. forces in Europe.

Day-to-day operations of U.S. forces were run by the U.S. European Command and the SACEUR assumed operational control only after the outbreak of war. He was kept advised of major decisions and could, if he chose, override any decision made by his deputy.
10. Norstad oral history interview, Eisenhower Library (Soapes), November 11, 1976.
11. Ibid.
12. Ibid.
13. McCaffrey to author.
14. *New York Times*, July 21, 1962.
15. Previous commanders: Eisenhower, Ridgway, Gruenther, and Norstad.
16. Commitments in Northern and Central Europe sectors: United Kingdom, three divisions; United States, five divisions and three armored cavalry regiments; France, two divisions; West Germany, nine divisions with three more being organized; Belgium, two divisions; Netherlands, two divisions; Canada, one brigade. Southern Europe: Turkey, fourteen divisions; Greece, eight divisions; Italy, seven divisions. Source: *The Military Balance* (London: Institute for Strategic Studies, 1962–63).
17. *New York Times*, June 7, 1962.
18. Alastair Buchan, *NATO in the 1960s* (New York: Praeger, 1963), 16–7.
19. Letter to Goodpaster, September 5, 1969.
20. Ibid.

21. Oral history interview, OSD (Matloff), January 24, 1984.

22. In a May 24, 1976, letter to a former administrative assistant, retired Chief Warrant Officer Ralph Chambers, Lemnitzer remembered the deputy, Gen. Nino Pasti, as a "complete disaster" who wrote articles and made comments to the press without first clearing them with Lemnitzer. He threatened to fire Pasti if he kept this up, and when Pasti left SHAPE in 1968, Lemnitzer abolished the deputy position. Pasti later ran for the Italian senate as a communist.

23. Ibid.

24. Ibid.

25. Lawrence S. Kaplan, "The U.S. and NATO in the Johnson Years," *The Johnson Years, Vol. III,* Edited by Robert A. Divine (Lawrence, Kan.: University Press of Kansas, 1994), 119.

26. Lawrence S. Kaplan and Kathleen A. Kellner, "Lemnitzer: Surviving the French Military Withdrawal," *Generals in International Politics,* Edited by Robert Jordan (Lexington, Ky.: The University Press of Kentucky, 1987), 101–2.

27. Oral history interview, OSD (Matloff), January 24, 1984.

28. Kaplan and Kellner, *Generals in International Politics,* 67.

29. Oral history interview, OSD (Matloff), January 24, 1984.

30. Kaplan and Kellner, *Generals in International Politics,* 101.

31. Lemnitzer speech at conference on "Leadership in NATO—Past and Present," Eisenhower Library, October 15, 1982.

32. Ibid.

33. Ibid.

34. *The London Times,* October 6, 1963.

35. McNamara, commencement speech at the University of Michigan, Ann Arbor, June 16, 1962. The secretary put the Polaris submarine total at five; other reliable sources placed it at three.

36. *Facts on File Dictionary of Military Science,* 238.

37. Oral history interview, Kennedy Library, David Nunnerly, February 11, 1970.

38. Speech before Assembly of Western European Union, June 7, 1963.

39. National Security Council "scope" paper, "The Troop Problem and Burden-Sharing: A New Planning of NATO Forces," Johnson Library.

40. Oral history interview, AWC (Hatch), March 8, 1973.

41. Ibid.

42. Richard Hart Sinnreich, "NATO's Doctrinal Dilemma," *Orbis,* summer, 1976.

43. Oral history interview, Johnson Library (Gettinger), March 3, 1982.

44. Oral history interview, OSD (Goldberg), March 21, 1974.

45. Ibid.

46. Hanson W. Baldwin, *Strategy for Tomorrow* (New York: Harper and Row, 1970), 141.

47. Oral history interview, Kennedy Library (Nunnerly), February 11, 1970.

48. *New York Times,* January 30, 1964.

49. Oral history interview, AWC (Hatch), December 18, 1972.

50. Ibid.

51. Oral history interview, AWC (Bickston), February 17, 1972.

52. *New York Times,* June 5, 1964.

53. Oral history interview, AWC (Hatch), December 18, 1972.

54. Z. Michael Szaz, "NATO, Turkey and United States Strategy," Studies on NATO Defense Policies, American Foreign Policy Institute, Washington, 1978.

55. Ibid.

56. Speech to French National Assembly, April 30, 1966.

57. *Stars and Stripes,* June 10, 1990.

58. McCaffrey to author.

59. Serge Groussard, *L'Aurore,* March 17, 1967.

60. *New York Times,* March 17, 1967.

61. *Le Figaro,* March 17, 1967.

62. McCaffrey to author.

63. Lemnitzer report to JCS, OSD, State Department on "SACEUR's Residence, Belgium," June 28, 1969.

64. Goodpaster letter to Lemnitzer, July 14, 1969.

65. Comment to Cyrus L. Sulzberger, June 8, 1966.

66. Position paper, NATO ministerial meeting, Luxembourg, June 13–14, 1967.

67. Oral history interview, AWC (Hatch), March 8, 1973.

68. Goodpaster, *Memorandum of Conference with the President,* January 9, 1961.

69. *France under de Gaulle,* Edited by Robert A. Diamond (New York: Facts on File, Inc., 1970), 154.

70. Oral history interview, AWC (Hatch), March 8, 1973.

71. Kaplan and Keller, *Generals in International Politics,* 121.

72. Letter to Goodpaster, September 5, 1969.

73. *New York Times,* August 22, 1968.

74. Ibid.

75. Oral history interview, OSD (Matloff), January 24, 1984.

76. Speech, Annual Meeting of the Association of the U.S. Army, October 28, 1968.

77. Summary notes, 590th National Security Council Meeting, September 4, 1968.

78. Lemnitzer, remarks at conference on "Leadership in NATO—Past and Present," Eisenhower Library, October 14, 1982.

79. Oral history interview, OSD (Matloff), January 24, 1984.

80. Remarks at conference on "Leadership in NATO—Past and Present," Eisenhower Library, October 14, 1982.

81. McCaffrey to author.

82. Oral history interview, OSD (Matloff), January 24, 1984.

Chapter 22: WARRIOR WITHOUT UNIFORM

1. It is doubtful if Lemnitzer liked being termed a "work horse," either. Nixon's words were given prominent attention in an eloquent fifteen-page file biography the general authorized his longtime speech-writer, Col. John B. B. Trussell to write, and which he read carefully afterward. The word "horse" does not appear anywhere.

2. *Weekly Compilation of Presidential Documents, Vol. 5, No. 28* (Washington: U.S. Government Printing Office, 1969), 971.

3. Classmate Gen. Thomas D. White, Air Force chief of staff, retired in 1961.

4. Letter to Senator John C. Stennis, chairman, Senate Armed Services Committee, February 5, 1970.

5. *Memorandum for Record,* Lt. Col. R. F. Askey, General Officer Branch, U.S. Army, July 31, 1963.

6. It will be remembered that a similar "split-second" break in service occurred in 1922 when Lemnitzer was demoted from first to second lieutenant.

7. Corddry, *United Press International,* January 23, 1964.

8. Chief Warrant Officer Ralph Chambers, who handled Lemnitzer's correspondence, confirmed to the author that he had never seen the order retiring and concurrently reinstating Lemnitzer to active duty. A copy of the order, signed by the Army's adjutant general, was found in the general's personal files after he died. A hand-written, unsigned notation at the bottom said: "Gen. Lemnitzer saw this letter for the first time on/about 1 August, 1969. Original never reached him."

9. Dated January 18, 1969.

10. Letter to Stennis, February 5, 1970.
11. Soon after the diagnosis, Lemnitzer began to wear a hearing aid.
12. The general's base pay with the addition of the disability payment was set at $26,400 a year on October 26, 1972. Letter to Lemnitzer from Brig. Gen. R. G. Fazakerly, U.S. Army Finance Center.
13. Letter to retired British Fleet Adm. Earl Mountbatten, September 5, 1969.
14. Letter to Brig. Gen. Harold H. Dunwoody, SHAPE, August 20, 1969.
15. Letter to retired British Field Marshal Sir John Harding, February 9, 1972.
16. Ibid.
17. Hearing-symposium on "National Security Policy: The Exercise of Military Power" before Subcommittee on National Security Policy, House Committee on Foreign Affairs, May 31, 1972.
18. Louisville, Kentucky, Courier-Journal, May 19, 1979.
19. Letter to Harlan Cleveland, July 17, 1970.
20. In addition to other support, all signed a June 1, 1978, letter to Congress.
21. Despite the presence of a UN peace-keeping force, Turkish troops overran 40 percent of the island and the coup collapsed. Greece mobilized its armed forces but did not intervene. Cyprus remained a republic after Turkish forces left, but continued to be wracked by unrest in the years that followed.
22. Letter to Harry Darby, December 19, 1977.
23. Letter to Gen. Isaac D. White, U.S. Army retired, December 5, 1980.
24. Letter to Harry Darby, August 17, 1981.
25. Letter to Frank G. Jameson, Ryan executive vice president, August 21, 1967.
26. Lemnitzer notes on Ryan Advisory Board conference, San Diego, California, November 3–7, 1969.
27. Source: Lemnitzer's son William to author. Lemnitzer description of offer in Chapter Twenty.
28. Letter to Gen. Goodpaster, August 8, 1972.
29. Letter to Frank G. Jameson, January 19, 1970.
30. Letter to Harry Darby, June 15, 1981.
31. Ibid.
32. Written to be read at West Point's Founder's Day, 1969.
33. New York Times, June 19, 1984.
34. Letter to William C. Reif, May 20, 1987.
35. Letter to Mrs. Leland S. Smith, April 8, 1981.
36. Lois to author.

INDEX

Entries under "Lemnitzer, Lyman Louis (Lem)" contain only information related to General Lemnitzer's family and personal life. His career activities can be found under specific separate entries.

★ ★ ★ ★

ABOUT THE AUTHOR

L. James Binder, spent twenty-six years in Washington, D.C., and Arlington, Virginia, as editor in chief of *Army* magazine before retiring in 1993. Born in Jackson, Michigan, he is a graduate of central Michigan University and has been an editor at the *Wayne Eagle, Pontiac Press,* and *The Detroit News,* all in Michigan; a newspaperman for the *Associated Press,* and a writer for the old *National Observer.* He served on a destroyer with fast-carrier Task Force 58 in the Pacific in World War II and held a commission in the U.S. Army Reserve. He has been a contributor to various national and international publications, and was the editor of the Brassey's book, *Front and Center,* a collection of articles from *Army* magazine. He and his wife, Margery, are the parents of three sons, and divide their year between residences in Northern Virginia and Lake Michigan's Little Point Sable.